A

FRIENDLY COMPANION

TO PLATO'S

GORGIAS

BY

GEORGE KIMBALL PLOCHMANN

AND

FRANKLIN E. ROBINSON

SOUTHERN ILLINOIS UNIVERSITY PRESS

CARBONDALE AND EDWARDSVILLE

Library of Congress Cataloging-in-Publication Data

Plochmann, George Kimball, 1914–
  A friendly companion to Plato's Gorgias.

  Bibliography: p.
  Includes index.
  1. Plato. Gorgias.   2. Ethics.   3. Political
science—Early works to 1700.   I. Robinson,
Franklin E. (Franklin Edward), 1940–   II. Title.
B371.P55   1988   170   87-12884
ISBN 0-8093-1404-5

To our much-loved families

Aristotle, in a dialogue now lost, tells of a farmer from Corinth who was so impressed by the *Gorgias* that he gave up farming, went to Athens, enrolled in the Academy, and put himself entirely in Plato's hands.

CONTENTS

FIGURES

PREFACE

There is no longer any reason to apologize for adding another book on some aspect of Plato's philosophy and art. Such books are coming from the presses at an accelerated pace, the expansion of the world's population being what it is, and the ratio of devoted Platonists to that population no doubt remaining fairly stable. Authors long ago ran out of *fresh* grounds for committing their ideas to paper and then to print. Even the claim of novelty of treatment is itself by now a hackneyed one, though it may not always be false.

This account of the *Gorgias* has turned out, against all our expectations, to be one of the longest of any that we know dealing with patterns and meanings rather than philological matters. Even so, we have probably thrown away more notes and sketches than are here included—many winter fires have been well kindled. The only justification for our extended treatment is the unusual sinuosity of the dialogue; its mixture of personal and structural features makes it extremely difficult to analyze smoothly and with assurance. A more concise, straightforward presentation would not, we fear, have taken care of the special intricacies.

In our chapters promising to discuss the text, we have tried to stick closely to the problems that Plato explicitly raised, having reserved more general matters for the four chapters on the dialogue as a whole. The best hint that he gives for interpreting another man's work is in the *Protagoras* (341e–347a). There Socrates illustrates the right practice by quoting *more* of a poem by Simonides, then attaching his own interpretation to what has already been discussed with the doughty sophist, who had been content to deal with a mere line or two of the poem without seeking connections, exterior or interior. For our part, we have thought it necessary to deal with a multiplicity of details as well as broad sweeps. The *Gorgias* is an illustration of the peculiar sort of philosophic exploration that Plato advocated in ever so many different ways, and it has a complicated but unifying method rather than being a collection of opinions or even arguments. The premise, moreover, that if the original structures can be uncovered, the dialogue will be found to hold together somewhat better than is often maintained—this premise seems quite sound. What emerges is not a complete theory of rhetoric—this is never Plato's aim with any topic—but an indication of what direction successful theorizing about rhetoric ought to take, given the personal impulses of the participants and their sociopolitical setting.

We are as much aware that most elements in our interpretation are by no means original as we are that despite our taking pains to eliminate them, flaws and errors of judgment have remained. Many scholars, especially in the United States, have been studying Plato in ways rather similar to ours and have applied them to a considerable list of the dialogues. The philological, historical, and critical studies are admirable preparatory exercises that must not be bypassed. If you object, as Socrates objects to Callicles, that in failing to include much notice of these we are attempting to learn pottery by making a large wine jar before trying our hand at some smaller vessel, we can only reply that we hope that our own jar will not spring such an inordinate number of leaks as to be quite useless. As a matter of fact, we have looked at so many details often left to one side that willy-nilly we have become like Shakespeare's "snapper-up of unconsid'red trifles." No one can hope to notice everything in such an intricate, inexhaustible dialogue; doubtless some of the most vital links have escaped us, or we have put upon them interpretations which other readers would deem unfruitful or unconvincing. But by paying some attention to the trifles, we think we can suggest new philosophic shadings or new artistic accents otherwise thought unworthy of consideration.

The *Gorgias* deserves not only exhaustive discussion but comment upon that very discussion, and if this results in a double focus and a long book, so be it. The heavy stress, to take one example, that we are placing upon the personal aspects of the dialogue would be unnecessary for the *Philebus*, the *Statesman*, or the *Menexenus*, which would demand a far lighter touch in this regard. Even there, however, and in the *Parmenides*, much can be learned from closer study of memory, tradition and communication, places and times, and whatever else can be found in Plato's references to different persons and their predilections.

There have been scores of excellent journal papers and several books on the *Gorgias*, and with some we have agreed wholeheartedly, with others disagreed, usually on matters of principle rather than detail, though when the principles are rearranged the details usually become topics for debate as well. The *Gorgias* is a flexible succession of structures, and has a beginning, middle, and end consisting of a dialectical situation deliberately evolving to something quite different at the close, and contrasts different levels of cognition steadily altering. Learned studies taking a few lines out of their settings and practicing exegesis upon them are, however suggestive, likely to lose some of the philosophic import and literary character of the dialogue. These essays rarely show inexpertness or lack of relevant information or goodwill; but because of their tendency to present the *Gorgias* as strung together out of separate arguments, we find them less rewarding than the studies seeking a well-knit totality. We do not gloat over Whitehead's remark, "Of all the types of men today existing, classical scholars are the most remote from the Greeks of the Periclean times," but we do take it as an admonition to try to discover this particular classic whole. This calls to mind, for instance, one of the great monuments of Platonic erudition, A. E. Taylor's prodigious *A Commentary on Plato's Timaeus*, so replete with accounts of all phases of ancient science and humane letters but unfortunately lacking much sense of a unique and seamless Platonic speculative system.

The man from whom one can learn most about Platonism, was, after all, born of good family in Athens about 427 B.C., and although we owe great debts to most of the authors cited in the Bibliography, our primary focus has always been on the *Gorgias* itself. Between us, we have accumulated something like 10,000 paper slips containing quotations from scholars and other critics of the past century and a half, but have regretfully put almost all of them aside. The reason is not that they have been unhelpful—far from it!—but because treating them fairly would add much bulk to an already thick volume.

Books and papers, some of which scarcely refer to the *Gorgias* at all but that seem especially clearheaded and convincing to us on matters of principle are writings by Richard McKeon—him most of all—and by (we list them in alphabetical order) Reginald E. Allen, John P. Anton, Allan Bloom, Robert S. Brumbaugh, Robert D. Cumming, Paul Friedländer, Robert G. Hoerber, Charles E. Kahn, Stanley Rosen, Herman L. Sinaiko, Adele Spitzer, Robert Sternfeld, Eric Voegelin, and Harold Zyskind. There is, however, no good reason to believe that all of them would agree with each other, though family resemblances might be detected in many cases, or that they would countenance what we have maintained in this book.

The quoting in a footnote of any author, even when treated favorably, is often a distortion omitting the context, statement of purpose, supporting arguments for what is being quoted, and thus depriving it of its precise meanings. To use such an author properly would require treating him or her as punctiliously as we believe Plato himself should be treated. (In the Introduction we have referred to several writers who have adopted typical positions on some general questions.) The urge to be scholarly often means a distraction from trying to assimilate oneself, if possible, to Platonic ways of philosophizing. Not only that, but the books by Dodds, Irwin, Friedländer, and certain papers contain a wealth of references to contemporary literature on specific points; hence we have repeated little of it here. But the dogmatizing and the bickering that fill many pages of the learned journals nowadays depart so far from the practice and spirit of Plato that one hesitates to enter the current debates, it being more difficult to withdraw from these, once begun. We hope that others will embark on the same sort of enterprise as this one, outdo it, and thereby help to bring Platonic studies to a closer understanding of the incredible richness of this dialogue and the others.

There is a lively temptation to incorporate references to various persons and practices better known in the twentieth century than in ancient Athens, but which would be at least indirectly pertinent to the *Gorgias* and might well have been mentioned by Plato had he known of them: salesmen, preachers and evangelists, lawyers of every sort, political propagandists, plyers of the electronic and printing media, get-rich-quick stock schemers, Nazis, advertisers—the list is almost endless. Giving in to this temptation would again lengthen this book, introducing what would amount to a whole new dimension into the exegesis.

Remote from this point, we have also avoided almost all questions of textual refurbishing, preferring to leave this to experts. Most, though by no means all, of the alterations proposed over the years seem ultimately to make no great difference to what we take to be the main effort. *Why* each line is included, and whether it contributes to the unity of the work—these are the questions we address as often as possible. We doubt that Plato wanted any small number of assertions to be taken as definitive "Platonism." It all points in the opposite direction: By composing an involuted network of statements quite obviously varied in their validity and persuasiveness, he meant to suggest an infinite number of connections to be found and made explicit between parts of his composition and also hoped to inspire readers to add further extensions and applications, made so far as possible in the Platonic manner. Plato looked for philosophical import in the writings of others, and we feel that his reader owes this much to him as well.

One of the difficulties of putting Greek into English is that the former is a relatively highly inflected language, while English is decidedly not; and even the prepositional and other phrases that communicate its relationships are not always equivalent to the Greek cases. We have usually retained the cases, numbers, word orders, and tenses of the original

Greek expressions used in our exposition, even though this frequently would make for awkwardness if these were very literally rendered into English. But it is easier this way for the reader to locate the words and phrases in the original than if we changed them to conform to single nominatives and present tenses of active voices.

A word on some of our renderings of the text into English. The general principle has been to keep, short of absurdity, a single English word for each Greek word. Here *adikaō*, for instance, is always "(I) do injustice," rather than varying that with "do wrong," "do harm," "I am unfair." *Adikeisthai* will always be "to undergo injustice," rather than "suffer" it. *Andreia* is always rendered "bravery," not varied with "courage" "manliness," or the like. *Boētheō* will be "(I) rescue," carrying the meaning of intervening at a time of stress or danger, of righting an immanent injustice rather than merely holding onto something already in good condition. *Empeiria* we have translated, after much soul-searching, as "familiarity." In other contexts "experience" fits well, for instance in the *Organon* and *Metaphysics* of Aristotle; but in the *Gorgias* Socrates is referring to the ability to accomplish something through having "learned the ropes"; "acquaintance," a frequently used word, does not imply such close contact. *Hosios* becomes "devout," since "pious" refers mainly to verbal utterances and rituals, and often connotes insincerity. Devoutness is an attitude, deepseated and genuine, the counterpart of moral justice. *Kalokagathon* would be clumsily rendered by "beautiful and good"; and "perfect gentleman," which is sometimes proposed, carries one into the country of Queen Victoria; and so we have rather arbitrarily selected "paragon," the summation of the personal and social virtues in a single person. *Kolakeia* we translate, without much misgiving, as "pandering" because "flattery" is too mild and often conveys only a positive, agreeable notion. The two minutes of hate set aside for Dr. Emmanuel Goldstein is a kind of pandering, of wanton crowd-pleasing, but certainly not flattery. *Kommotikē* becomes "embellishment," which goes beyond mere attention to the face, and Plato evidently means fancy clothing and other adornment as well. We have made *opsopoiia* into "catering," not "cookery," which fails to connote the luxuriousness and pandering that Plato implies, nor "confectionery" (suggested by Taylor), which is too limited. The Greek *rhētor* we have simply transliterated; the word *orator* will not quite do because much of the talk is about the rhetor as teacher, not merely public speaker. No translation of any word, phrase, sentence, or passage is really right, and the best one can hope for is something serviceable and understandable. The main lesson of the *Gorgias* lies not in isolated words and lines, but in what might be called the rhythm or flow of intelligible discourse exhibited from start to finish.

We have italicized all the condensed paraphrases of speeches, long or short, from the text, for easier locating. Angle brackets, ⟨ ⟩, enclosing them also include brief statements we make directly introducing the remarks paraphrased. For the most part, we have used as a base the Loeb Classical Library edition (W. R. M. Lamb, translator and editor), but altering the English version in the interests of more uniformity in rendering individual words.

First on our list of obligations are the respective chairpersons and administrators of Southern Illinois University and Murray State University who have done much to furnish us with the facilities and help necessary to completing our effort. A revolving chairmanship at Southern has placed us successively in debt to Professors James A. Diefenbeck, Matthew J. Kelly, and Elizabeth R. Eames. At Murray, the chairman of the Department of Philosophy and Religious Studies, Professor Terry H. Foreman, has been most helpful in arranging for released time to do research, the MSU Committee on Institutional Studies and Research expressed their support of our effort by approving research grants for typing the manuscript, and the Dean of the College of Humanistic Studies, Kenneth E. Harrell and the Vice-President for Academic Affairs, James L. Booth, supported the project by approval of Summer Professional Improvement Leaves and financial support for typing.

Secretaries who have typed or proofread, or both, have given a great deal of their time: Dawn Boone, Loretta Smith, Michelle Prino, Susan Hunt, and Shirley Washer. The making of this book would have been quite impossible without the aid and encouragement afforded by our two wives, who separately examined and corrected large amounts of the typescript, discussed the ethical and artistic issues of the dialogue, and put up with behavior that must have seemed obsessive from time to time. In every sense Carolyn G. Plochmann and Janet Lee Robinson were *synaitiai* of this book.

Readers whose identities are known to us and to whom we are personally extremely grateful, are Professors John P. Anton, Robert S. Brumbaugh, Joan V. O'Brien, Robert Sternfeld, Henry Teloh, and Frederick Williams, who have been most helpful in their suggestions and evaluative comments. Presumably there have been others, but a dark veil shrouds their names from us.

The Southern Illinois University Press has shown unfailing expertness, diligence, and kindness in treating all the necessary details—of which there are myriad, as an author soon comes to know—of publication. In particular we are extremely grateful to Kenney Withers, Director, Robert S. Phillips, Editorial Director, and Joyce Atwood, Chief Editor.

INTRODUCTION

Reading the *Gorgias*

The *Gorgias*, if we are not mistaken, is one of the most elusive and subtle of the writings of a most elusive and subtle thinker. Plato evidently spared few pains to complement the unusually tortuous arguments with characters who are rounded, complex men, and he must have had a different purpose from that in many of his other works whose participants, imposing as they may be for their pure dialectical acumen, are nevertheless persons quite shadowy and vague.[1] On the other hand, it would be wrong to read the *Gorgias* merely as an elaborate interplay of personages. As a philosophic disquisition, the trains of thought appear at first reading to be obscured by the repeated clashes of personalities; as a dramatic conflict of warring men it appears—again at first reading—to be retarded almost to a halt by impersonal intellectual debates virtually irrelevant to the battle of human beings ill at ease with one another. A closer scrutiny, however, proves both of these impressions onesided; the expository interpretation and the dramatic must be essayed together. When they are merged, the likeness of a Platonic dialogue to either a tragedy or a treatise begins to fade away, and the important features commence both to assert and to harmonize themselves.

These features are, taken very broadly, four in number. To us, any attempt to construe the *Gorgias* fully would have to take such issues, or ones much like them, into serious account:

First, the substantive arguments regarding the nature of rhetoric and the imperatives of the good life, together with whatever concepts Plato includes as relevant to these;

Second, the form in which this long sequence is presented, the structures of the argument and the responses at each stage, discerning where possible the method or methods used in the dialogue;

Third, the participants and their controlling—and controlled—passions. The dramatic-fictional aspects of the dialogue are concentrated here, since descriptions of town and countryside, of overt action and other visual effects, are faint in the *Gorgias*;

Fourth, the interrelations between all three, interrelations without which any attempt to state the unity of the dialogue, will prove an empty exercise.

Answers to questions raised under each of these rubrics are, we think, best found by persistently asking why Plato includes this and excludes that, why he phrases a problem one way rather than another, why a character is made to appear as he does, why the order of statements or questions is so and not otherwise, and other queries of this kind. One best finds answers not in the literary habits of other writers or even of Plato in other dialogues, but in close scrutiny of the *Gorgias* itself. There is no limit, if one steps outside the dialogue, to the likenesses and differences to be observed—to the Pythagoreans, Orphics, Empedocles, Aristotle, St. Augustine, Hobbes, Nietzsche, and many others, not to mention Hindu and Buddhist texts. But these cannot be germane to Plato's methods that he places at the disposal of Socrates and his stubborn antagonists.

The Substance of the Arguments

The overwhelming preponderance of commentary has dealt chiefly with the substance of the many statements and their supporting arguments in the *Gorgias*. If the other three aspects of the work are slighted, however, the dialectical meanings will be liable to misapprehension. Such meanings are gained by noticing the connections, causal and associative, which individual concepts and assertions have to other elements in the dialogue, connections best elicited by repeatedly going beyond the preliminary question *Whether* to the question *Why*. To treat the work as a collection of statements, interrogatives, proofs, and refutations without much else is, we think, to reduce the analysis to a learned doxography containing little philosophizing, and showing few signs of the effort to transform each reader, so far as possible, into a philosophically minded person of Plato's own sort, a participant in the dialogue yet perforce standing exterior to it and thus in a position to see the interconnections of all its parts with each other and with life itself.

Because philosophy is an activity, for Plato, as much as a collection of transformable truths, one needs to avoid the two opposite interpretive dangers of excessive liquidity of utterances and tight-frozen, static propositions. With either extreme, much of the work's substance will seem unimportant except in the sense that it is comforting, as Wood-bridge found it so, to know that educated people were talking about these matters so many centuries ago. On the one hand, to conclude that everything is hopelessly in flux in each of the dialogues is to fly in the face of some of the most heartfelt declarations in the history of philoso-phy, declarations that it is possible to find truth and moreover that cer-tain propositions are in fact true. But to see how Plato could be a se-rious philosophic and literary thinker of the highest order, setting for himself problems and finding at least partial solutions that would be of concern in the world at large in any era, demands recovery of at least phases of his thinking that will explain why certain propositions *can* be taken as true in the limited meanings and specified contexts that Plato forces upon them. On the other side, merely to like and approve what Plato said in selected locations felt to be simply consistent with each other is insufficient if he is upheld as dialectician and artist. Despite the praises showered on him by Paul Shorey, for instance, and despite that scholar's dogged rejections of criticisms prominent against Plato in the first third of this century, the "philosophy" attributed by Shorey to him strikes us as being flimsy, the "art" as a series of bits of incidental entertainment, poorly accounted for. The "philosophy" is an aggrega-tion of opinions without much method to generate and hold them to-gether, and one which could and probably should be demolished by any clearheaded thinker, including Plato himself, who would, we be-lieve, have been eager to dismantle the brittle dogmas fathered upon him. The peculiarity of Plato's manner of doing philosophy lies in something almost paradoxical: In the dialogues, in which a few pages suggest a virtual infinity of discourse with many shades of meaning, truth, and coherence, no one proposition or group of propositions can be taken as definitive unless considered in light of the whole. Just as there is no one statement summing up and exhausting "the" theory of forms, so there is none to put implicit faith in that will serve through-out the dialogues as a statement of the nature of dialectic, or justice, or rulership, or indeed any other topic. And yet there is truth.[2]

We take philosophy to comprise a system of mutual supports be-tween concepts, between methods and concepts, and between ele-ments of methods and other elements of these methods. Philosophy may at first be exhibited as a linear deduction, but at some point, or at several points, it is forced to turn back upon itself and offer some new kind of support for its original assumptions.[3] This support, however, cannot reside in the mere finding of a premise logically antecedent to what had formerly been thought to be a first principle, for that would breed infinite regress.

Plato's philosophy rests not upon any single assumption or set of assumptions from which one deduces the sequences of statements filling the dialogues, as Russell held when he undertook to derive everything that Leibniz put in his system from a small handful of premises.[4] The Platonic view that philosophy and life, thought and concrete experience, discourse and feeling are inseparable demands an integration of these opposites not by some Hegelian three-stage legerdemain but by the use of widely varied means of binding these different, usually contrary elements together. The dialogic mode of inquiry and exposition, which demands that questions, interjections, asides, assertions containing images and theories, be parceled out (though unequally) among the participants, makes the philosophic speculations become instinct with the lives of those to whom they are apportioned. In the *Gorgias* these have regard to the ethical and political life and the possibility of living it, and this happens to be true also in the other dialogues dominated by Socrates; it is rather less true where discussion is conducted or lectures are delivered by the Athenian and Eleatic Strangers, Timaeus, Critias, and Parmenides.

It is not inherently wrong to import materials from other Platonic dialogues in order to interpret the *Gorgias*. It is even permissible to introduce quotations from earlier authors to settle some questions—but by no means all—about usage. The hazard lies, however, in the many subtleties impeding anyone who tries to determine the meaning of statements in the *Gorgias* by referring to the *Phaedrus, Statesman, Republic*, or any of half a dozen other dialogues treating similar broad topics. Because there is dialectical richness in each of these works, lines quoted from them must be scrutinized in advance for *their* dialectical meanings, not only their verbal similarities, before being introduced to raise or answer questions regarding the *Gorgias*. Do a carefully established conclusion in one dialogue and an unproved flourish tossed off in another have the same weight along with the same wording? Are the meanings the same? Or has Plato forgotten what he said elsewhere, or "grown" in his conception, possibly as the result of some new friendship or illness or another trip to Syracuse?

The lesson is this: In the multiple dialectics framed through different interests, prejudices, and backgrounds of new speakers, truth-value is not a T or F baldly attached to a single proposition, with the values of compounds easily calculated from the original elements. Mr. Brown, through an honest error in judgment, commits some act such as losing a purse that works a hardship on his friend Smith. Brown says, "It was my fault," *p*, and Smith replies, "No, it was not your fault at all," *not-p*; the contradiction is plain, *p* and *not-p*. On the other hand, suppose that Smith had said, "It was your fault," *p* (despite the change in pronouns the reference in both cases is to Brown's fault, since only two men are involved), and Brown replies, "No, it was not my fault," *not-p*. Either way, there is a contradiction whose truth-profile is FFFF.[5] But the *personal* implications, perforce neglected in this scheme, are of great moment, and the kinds of opposition, both epistemically and emotionally considered, must be taken into account. Within the *Gorgias* virtually every exchange is loaded with such personal connections, the assertion and denial of a single proposition being made on different levels of understanding, and with quite different affective connotations. These varied inculpations and exculpations reflect entirely different ethical orientations. No doubt all true statements can, if kept in their contexts with their intended meanings, form a kingdom in Plato's philosophy, but not all truths are of equal weight and rank, and no one verbal statement retains the same weight throughout a single dialogue, let alone the Platonic corpus.

It comes to this, that the safest kind of importation of relevant propositions is what we would term negative or disclamatory, that is, the use of materials from other dialogues to raise questions why these same points are *not* made in the *Gorgias*. The other legitimate importation is more positive, yet is merely suggestive; one cannot confirm that a remark in the *Gorgias* actually has a given meaning merely because its expression is duplicated elsewhere. Why there are no direct references to Socrates' *daimōn*, to forms as absolute existences once seen in celestial tranquility and now recollected in a troubled life on earth, to the nature of love or friendship, to the truer art of kingship, to political classes (besides masters and slaves and a handful of professions)—examination of these and similar puzzles can improve any study of the *Gorgias* without introducing into it small foreign bodies possibly turning out to be viruses ready to destroy the living whole. The work does, however, cast at least an oblique ray of light upon many such topics prominent in other writings from the hand of Plato and furnishes insights useful for exploring all of these, yet without offering literal solutions to their problems. The *Gorgias* fits very well into Plato's open system, but its proper interpretation enables one to see why it is wrong to take any of its meanings or those of the other dialogues in relation to it prematurely for granted.

These interconnections imply that fixing the subject matter and purposes of the *Gorgias* may not be simple.[6] In the long list of aims ascribed to the dialogue (aims such as showing the superiority of dialectic over rhetoric, or of philosophy over tyrannizing the mobs, or of justice over injustice, or of Socrates as a discussant over the three rhetors he opposes), we are aware of no suggestion that the dialogue's main purpose is to show that Pericles was not the great leader he was reputed to be. Even if this was an afterthought for Plato, one may ask whether it might not have become the most pressing question in his mind. Many books on modern social policy have had their start from debates over whether Franklin Delano Roosevelt was the greatest American president of the twentieth century, with general statements piled one upon the other to prove or disprove his supremacy. Perhaps political works such as the *Gorgias* and countless studies of United States governmental policy have as their underlying aim the evaluating of individuals. Any political action is always a single event, regardless of how similar to others it may be; and the agencies bringing such events about are always persons, unless one admits tidal waves, earthquakes, and the parting of the Red Sea as causative agents. Hence if the *Gorgias* is indeed a philosophic and artistic unity, then whatever is a part of the dialogue has its function inextricably woven into the whole, thus making the unfavorable estimate of Pericles operative in determining what the unity will be.

That Pericles is Plato's target gives way before the obvious objection that the greatest emphasis, from beginning to end, falls not upon historical or personal judgments regarding individuals but rather upon general propositions extending far beyond individuals. Even the *Symposium*, with Socrates' transfiguring revelations about love—or do they really come from the great brooding prophetess?—and the earthy reminiscences and testimonials of Alcibiades, leaves one feeling that the dialogue's purpose is to point up the greatness not of Socrates but of Eros, however much Eros might be embodied in the man. The same holds true even for the *Apology* and the superiority of the examined, philosophic life.

One may thus set up a weighted scale, with general truths at the top, and ranging down through less general ones all the way to a number of observations regarding Pericles, Archelaus, Aristides, and others. Removal of one particular set of general truths—so we contend—would have the most destructive effect upon the grand design of the work, this set being contained in what we shall call the Divided Oblong (expounded most fully by Socrates in pages 463e–466a), setting out relations between various arts and their pandering imitators, among which is rhetoric. Out of this Oblong one can generate a number of subordinate statements, some of them having been adumbrated in the preceding colloquy with Gorgias, most of them to be explored and modified as need be in the subsequent conversations with Polus and Callicles. Finally, it is in terms earlier set by the Oblong that the judgment against Pericles is ultimately passed (515d–516d), a judgment which at the time when Pericles was first mentioned (455e) would have had no logical value and would have been unpersuasive in the extreme.

Methods in the Dialogue

We have already introduced the word *dialectic* rather casually, as if taking for granted that it has a place both in the original dialogue and in our own discussion. Like most words used by Plato, this one is given a large number of meanings, perhaps a subtly different one each time it appears, certainly when used in a new context. Because we ourselves are not writing a dialogue, we must depart from Plato's manner of establishing meanings, employing instead a more arbitrary approach, wherein the word has three senses, all having precedents in the dialogues: Most broadly, there is a respect in which everyone, from Socrates and the canny but anonymous Eleatic and the wide-ranging intellect Timaeus down to the most naive bystander in the *Euthydemus* and *Charmides* or even the sheeplike but bitterly resentful dicasts in the *Apology*, has a dialectic of some sort. Each person conjures up some structured relations between terms designative, descriptive, or evocative of notions of being or good, or terms related to these, together with quite distinct statements: "Justice is better than injustice," or again, "Justice is indistinguishable from injustice"; "It is advantageous to seem wise," or, "It is disadvantageous to be wise"; "Socrates is a sophist," or, " Socrates is a philosopher."[7] The dialogues thus represent struggle to support the claims of incompatible or seemingly incompatible dialectics, some of which are able to absorb or defeat others. The characters within each dialogue do not ordinarily invoke this as a primary meaning of the word *dialectic*, but their practices justify it. A little more narrowly, dialectic consists of question and answer, usually delivered in brief utterances, though sometimes the question is much longer than the answer, sometimes the reverse. The Greek, *dialegesthai*, can also be translated as "discussion," and we shall often use this word instead. The questions can be employed as establishing or refuting a doctrine put forward, and the answers can be used in the same two ways. The most specific meaning of *dialectic* lies in discussion conferring the opportunity to check what one's opponent is saying, not by countering with a speech however long or short, but by forcing an admission through questioning the implications of what the opponent has just said. Outstanding in Socratic discussion is this: The questions are sequential, dealing with closely-related topics ranged around a central issue, and requiring answers that at the outset come as close as possible to what the respondent wishes, and in later stages close to what he is forced to offer as the essential nature of the subject discussed. Dialectic is, in short, argument, substantiative or refutative; and because it requires the common concurrence of both parties, it is a way of guaranteeing at least a kind of *ut nunc* truth of the conclusion: a truth that will hold for the special meanings of the terms evolved for the passage in hand, before attempts to extend its applications have to be further examined. The fixing of meanings and the underwriting of truth of new propositions enunciated in the proof is a reciprocal affair; the new statements would more fully explicate the significations of the original terms, and the terms would, because they have been agreed to, reinforce the verity of the additional steps in the proof. The checking is of the next implications, drawn by the leader of the discussion, of what his respondent has just asserted or conceded. Socrates is so insistent upon employing this kind of discourse that it is scarcely an issue, except for brief requests (to Gorgias), admonitions (to Polus), and abuse (by Callicles).

Whether long speeches are allowed and presented, whether Polus is permitted to ask questions, whether someone refutes or is refuted, are matters relevant both to rhetorical discourse and to dialectic taken in all three of its senses.[8] To secure agreement, which is certainly a mark of dialectical procedure as practiced by Socrates (and differently by the Eleatic and Athenian Strangers and Parmenides), does not of itself convert rhetoric into dialectic, or opinion and persuasion into knowledge and truth. For example, when Gorgias remarks (448a) that no new question has been asked of him in many years, he implies that he can answer them all—which would make it appear as if he were skilled in dialectic.

Looking at the dialogues synoptically, one sees that Plato has drawn out many lines of argument in several works showing affinities in important topics. Each dialogue supplements and corrects the others, but does not wholly cancel them. An alternative to this procedure is offered by Aristotle, Thomas, and others who commence with a handful of definitions of one term, or a distinction between senses of propositions, subtly discriminating many meanings of their terms and then indicating their applications in closely argued discussion. Where Plato's distinctions and lines of argument are spread over several dialogues, Aristotle's are concentrated in a chapter or two, those of Thomas in an article or a so-called question.

Many of our readers are likely to recall one of Philo Vance's most interesting cases, whose solution hinged upon a careful listing and subsequent rearrangement of all the pertinent facts in a series of murders.[9] After first recording those facts, Vance, an intellectual aesthete if ever there was one, but a good detective nevertheless, declares: "I can see certain traceries, so to speak—certain suggestions of a pattern, but I'll admit the main design has thus far eluded me."[10] It is our feeling that Plato had a keen sense of *pattern* (which we shall now distinguish from structure and design), and that he must have subjected his concepts to a schematizing which supplied them with various kinds of contexts, each consisting of other contexts, similar or dissimilar. The unit of dialectical discourse is a simple *structure*, a single moment in the process of unfolding the dialectic, and relating a small finite number of terms or concepts. Such structures are dichotomies, that is, oppositions of several sorts, trichotomies, hierarchies, and the like; or they may be simple declarations or denials. In longer sequences there are windings and involutions of the larger patterns making for highly varied interpretations and estimates by readers.[11]

Successive structures, embodied in long speeches or discussions, make a pattern. Partial recovery of Plato's habits of thinking will, if he was indeed a responsible philosopher, reveal not only these patterns just alluded to but also his philosophic reasons for adopting them. Plato was unusually generous in leaving signposts to point where his methods have been sustained or altered. These signs are, in many instances, what are commonly called dramatic touches, and one uses them as guides, where to enforce or to drop a distinction, an evaluation, or the commitment to a hypothesis. Along with this, one must be ready to accept this continuum of carefully shaded meanings of many of the most important expressions, and the correspondent relinquishing of the habits of literal thought that are of inestimable help in coming to terms with Aristotle or William of Ockham or even Kant. But not Plato.

To be more specific, there are many ways by which one can and indeed ought to approach these patterns. One is by topical outline, dividing the succession of sentences by means of principal headings, again dividing to find subordinations, and so on. Such an outline we have written into our account with the hope that it can serve as an aid to further study, and that it can help communicate a clearer impression of beginning, middle, and end not only of the whole but of the lesser parts as well. Appended to this Introduction is an abbreviated version of a topical outline to serve as what we hope could be a helpful guide to our text.

Second, branching charts are implied over and over in the *Gorgias*, but they can scarcely be made clear by any topical outline, hence the need to pause occasionally to indicate directions of charts of this kind. Everyone reading Plato's *Sophist* is familiar with its divisions and their spatial representation by historians, but because rather similar divisions in other dialogues are not advertised as such, they often pass without notice, despite the fact that sound procedure evidently calls for them to be reconstructed from the text.

Another way of representing dual, triple, or quadruple lists dealing with analogous topics is by drawing up matrices—squares or oblongs with common topical headings and appropriate entries showing likenesses and differences in each little pigeonhole. Virtually every modern exposition of the *Republic* prints one such matrix, calling it the Divided Line, but Plato has provided many others, though without labeling them as matrix figures at all, evidently expecting his readers to detect them.[12] There are several handfuls of matrices in the *Gorgias*, and at least one of these is so significant that we have named it separately. Some branching charts can be turned into matrices with little or no alteration of content, or again, matrix oblongs and squares can be written out in dendritic style. Both can be expounded in prose, and in this form the texts have come down to our time. We suspect—though there can be no solid proof of this—that Plato filled many wax tablets with spatial renderings of his distinctions and summations.

He must have believed, however, that such diagrams merely suggested rather than ruled the concepts interpreting the nature of things. To suppose, for example, that he conceived of soul in a certain way simply because it was convenient to place the word *soul* in a particular small square of a grid would be folly. Patterned art—*technē*—alone does not answer the question, What is soul? or even, Is soul superior to body?

When Socrates asks what a cowherd does, then what a doctor does, and finally what a ruler of the state does, this is no induction in the ordinary sense of accumulating as many cases as convenient or possible and then examining negative and positive instances, weighing them by a joint method of agreement and difference. The Platonic device is directed to finding some thing or things most nearly like the subject in respect of the characteristic in question, to set up a relation carrying through all of them for the time being. In this way the respondent may come to see more quickly and clearly this relationship as manifested in the subject under inquiry. The cowherd tends, the doctor tends; very well, the ruler tends. In this regard, Plato's device is a little like certain similes in Homer, such as the closing lines of Book XX of the *Iliad*, when Achilles has virtually run amok with the passion of revenge, and his onslaught is likened for several lines to a forest fire, and for several more to the trampling of bulls on barley, the two figures nicely conveying a common effect. The fire and the bulls are not named for what they both do specifically, but only for what effect they have generally. Socrates' doctor minds no cattle, the king heals no patients, but cowherd, doctor, and ruler all have a care for their proper subjects. One might say, however, that Homer was striving to make his figures of the wrath of Achilles add excitement in a narrative, while Plato would be attempting to prove something in essential nature. He does not examine a hundred doctors; he calls upon ordinary experience to judge what is most proper to the doctor's calling that will fit the present case. On other occasions he would ask whom the doctor treats, the well or the sick, or whether he treats the patient in ways designed to give pleasure, to restore health, or to make money for himself.

On the other hand, there *are* inductions in a certain sense, as when the question is asked, Who are the happy though unjust rulers? and the example of Archelaus is given, or the question is asked, Who were the successful rhetor-rulers of an earlier day, and the answer is Miltiades, Themistocles, and their like. But is this really an induction in any recognizable meaning of the term? If an example may be dubbed a truncated induction, then the answer is a moderate affirmative. If Archelaus were merely to be named as a cut-and-dried instance, then the claims to his being used as an inductive example would be legitimate; but the truth is, he is subject to fairly searching criticism, and becomes the stimulus for an opposing theory of happiness and citizenship. All the so-called inductions in the *Gorgias* are set up as ways to discern function or value, and not the causes of limited effects that Mill and his successors have thought essential to induction.

These serial analogies are directed, as we have implied, at the essential functions of the subjects under particular scrutiny—what it means to be a king, a rhetor, a philosopher, in terms of what each one properly does. But what is considered essential derives partly from that nature of that subject, the rhetor himself, the king himself, and partly from the context—the rhetor as artist, as teacher, as just man, as a power in the city, the rhetor as the soul of a dead man unable to prevail against a just judgment. It is reasonable to expect, therefore, that the terms used in the account of the rhetor will change several times over. It is also reasonable to believe that shifts of this sort can be made either legitimately or illegitimately. Of the former kind in the *Gorgias* are those which observe the following restrictions:

1. They serve the interests of justice, that is, the rational distribution of goods and services, rewards and punishments.
2. They are dialectically based on points previously established and agreed to, and are related to them by simple agreed-upon steps in the argument.
3. They serve to expand the context in which a concept is discussed, and at the same time contract or purify the concept when considered in itself; as a sample, the legitimate comparisions of the rhetor point more and more toward his place in a society in which the interests of the general citizenry are considered and self-satisfactions are left behind.

On the other hand, the shifting of meanings becomes illegitimate in any case where there is a desire to take credit for possessing an art that includes a knowledge of justice but disclaims responsibility for teaching this knowledge in connection with other parts of the art. Again, it is illegitimate when there is an attempt to make goods of property and pleasures of the body into standards by which goods of the soul are to be judged. The final error is that of supposing that if one benefits oneself then the good or harm done to others is wholly irrelevant.[13]

The attack upon illegitimate analogies results in contradiction if the attack is successful: Two incompatible conclusions are reached, both of them with the assent of the proponent of the original illegitimate statement, and the incompatibility is duly acknowledged. The result of this in the *Gorgias* is not a stalemate (as it sometimes is in other dialogues, such as the *Lysis*, *Laches*, *Euthyphro*), but a reversal permitting Socrates to move to some new phase of his own position. Thus after Gorgias is reduced to contradiction, Socrates is able to propose the Divided Oblong; and when Polus throws in the towel, Socrates is ready to make an altogether new statement about lovers—one that carries intermittently through the rest of the dialogue, and which, with various windings and turnings, eventually becomes an aid to establishing the superiority of the philosopher over the rhetor.

The defense of any philosophical work must ultimately rest upon two considerations, the importance of the content and the consistency with which this content is developed. This consistency may take the form of logical rigor, or it may be of another sort. Rigor is at bottom the adherence to a preconceived plan for the exposition of worthwhile (i.e., novel or useful) implications drawn from a set of warranties deemed either self-evident or else arbitrarily chosen because they are independent, economical in number, and simply, clearly stated. The rigor is easily traced and justified or rebutted when the warranties are explicitly enunciated premises and the consecutants from them are theorems listed as a Spinoza or a Newton would arrange them. But what if the guiding principle, substantively, is to the effect that the kind of discourse to be employed is loose—effective but loose—and this becomes the methodic postulate describing the interchanges between the participants of the dialogue?

The *Gorgias* explores this postulate in its substance and, moreover, uses it so that the conversational exchanges are set up to conform to it.[14] An oxymoron tempts us, that the dialogue is rigorously casual. This is not false but scarcely enlightening, and the only way to justify such phrasemaking would be to invite the reader to see how the tightness and the looseness manifest themselves conjointly in details of the full exposition. Fairer than this would be the observation that Plato is attempting an extraordinarily difficult feat: to interweave disparate aspects of a person's character with each other, and whole characters with other characters, at the same time doing this almost entirely through the workingout of a number of general concepts.[15]

More than any other work by Plato, except perhaps the *Apology* and its two sequels, the *Gorgias* has a threefold rhythmic movement between a treatment of the individual person, a class of persons (such as doctors or pilots or the entire city), and the general notions attaching to any and all of these. When individuals are dealt with, they are either the four major and one minor speaking participants in the dialogue itself or are men who in some respects are held to resemble those within it. Thus Pericles is introduced not because of his generalship or his taking-on of Aspasia as a female companion, but because of his alleged rhetorical abilities, the keenness of which are never put in doubt though the judiciousness of their employment is denied. This criticism of Pericles really parallels certain points that Socrates makes against Callicles and his two guests from away—that rhetorical ability to move a crowd without thought of the ultimate good for that crowd and the city of which it is a part lacks value, indeed it does more than passing harm, even to the rhetor himself. But Socrates, of course, scores those points mainly because Callicles is the very man whose ambitions are directed toward such an exercise of rhetorical powers, much as Gorgias has exercised them in the recent past.

From the standpoint of both Plato and his protagonist Socrates, dialectic functions in any of the dialogues—and in a special way in the *Gorgias*—as a kind of intellectual impersonation. Socrates, with his intuitive intelligence, his ability to "size up" the temperaments and inclinations of his respondents together with the shapes that their arguments are likely to take, is able to forestall, agree with, or transform those arguments as need be. He approaches as closely as possible the psyches of opponents and pupils alike, not to adopt their own words, images, and arguments but to discover and weigh the meanings that *they* give to the words, the associations *they* connect with their images, and the possible cogency of the proofs as *they* conceive them.

It is no long step from this part of Socrates' activity to Plato's. He, too is an impersonator; but in addition to putting himself into the minds of Charmides, Ion, Polus, and the rest, he must impersonate Socrates as well, regardless of whether all these were historical figures. Some— and Callicles may be one of them, nobody knows—have been made up or have grown out of amalgams. Others were Plato's friends or perhaps enemies, but if he quotes them it is required of him that he make their thoughts integral with the structures and design of the whole work. To divide the dialogues into two kinds, the Socratic, which are merely reports of what the historical Socrates allegedly held, and the Platonic, in which Socrates suddenly becomes a mouthpiece for the author,[16] is to our mind a distinction that Plato would have shown needed modifying.

Another notion is that Plato had a private philosophy different in kind from any of the dialogues, which were in effect dissimulations deliberately aimed at the public. It is almost beyond belief that an author could spend perhaps half a century upon compositions showing the cooperative, impersonating character of thought (which he several times defined as the soul's silent discourse with itself),[17] yet hold in reserve a set of doctrines alien in origin and nature to his writings. True enough, he may have held back parts of what he thought as being insufficiently worked out or hard to fit into the contexts of dialogues further along in his mind or already "published"; but that he withheld an entire system whose character would falsify and whose doctrines would contravene or even countervail what he had written is to expect too much from a man who must have set great store by philosophical and personal integrity, as one surmises from his portrait of Socrates.

In the movement from personal through more general to the most general and back again, there must be some guarantee of a grounding in a principle of reason above the mere experience that can be easily gainsaid and refuted. This principle is a self-reflexive one holding on all three levels of universality, though in different ways. At the abstract level, the most general, where good, justice, rhetoric, happiness, and the like are discussed in ways intended to apply to all relevant cases, the self-reflexiveness is discursive. When participants in the dialogue or other individuals mentioned are centers of interest, self-reflexiveness takes the form of self-awareness, and sometimes self-knowledge. In the middle ground, that of general classes, there is what might be called self-justification by pragmatic fit: The entire set of statements regarding kinds of persons, of city-states and their relations can only be sanctioned because they would, if followed, help to create a satisfactory community or prevent an unsatisfactory one from coming into being or further deteriorating, and thus the statements—prescriptions—would survive within that society.

At the moment, we are interested in the kind of self-reflexiveness that is discursive, as in such dialogues as the *Sophist* and *Parmenides* when the self-awareness of persons is almost negligible. Of personal self-awareness, more later. In any treatise whose design commences with literal, finite definitions and axioms, the former are assumed to be clear and distinct, the latter so self-evident that their opposites are patently false, even nonsensical. The work most nearly resembling a literal treatise in its design, the *Timaeus*, commences with "axioms," but even they have a self-referential character. The first "axiom" is a distinction between what exists eternally and is known by reason with the aid of discourse, and becoming, which never fully is but is apprehended by opinion with the help of sensation.[18] Any principle that distinguishes the eternal known by reason from the seen-and-felt temporal leans upon itself as its own guarantee; it is a rational grasp of an eternal truth, beyond the reach of sensation, hence not subject to becoming and alteration. This kind of evidence is hidden in the *Gorgias*, and if there are axioms at all they must be of another sort.

The labeling of the premises and conclusions in the *Gorgias* as if it were a treatise, while not altogether false, is no doubt misleading. The order of questions or statements is one based in the dialogue upon (a) what a speaker holds in his mind as fundamental; (b) what he considers the step to take next; (c) what is conceded by his respondent. Occasionally the dialectical thread winds its way without a clear notion of what conclusion is to be reached (e.g., at 455a–b). On the other hand, a guiding principle of Socrates in his bout with Polus is that rhetoric is properly used for self-incrimination. From the standpoint of what he wishes Polus to understand, this is a conclusion, to be reached only after Polus has made several concessions. But from the standpoint of his own thinking, it may well have been a starting-point already adopted well before his conversation with the young rhetor began.

One finds, however, a self-reflexiveness at a lower epistemic level in the fact that the dialogue's theories of rhetoric are themselves couched in rhetorical terms, of which praise is at first the chief ingredient. Thus rhetoric is not said to be an art unless art is something honorific and unless the rhetorical art is the best of the arts, displacing as it does all the others (448c).[19] On the other side (and appearing much later in the dialogue), the superiority of the philosopher to the rhetor is established by philosophic means, or means as close to true dialectic as is possible under difficult circumstances. This never produces the rigorous self-evidence of the "axiom" in the *Timaeus*, but does bolster the case of philosophy, just as reliance of the rhetor's position on praise tends to weaken the case of rhetoric. (Were the praise to be introduced later, after sufficient analysis, it would have more precise meaning, and would be on the way to meeting dialectical standards.)

The Participants

Our interpretation of the *Gorgias* requires that we introduce what might be called depth-dialectic, partly corresponding to Wittgenstein's depth-grammar and partly quite different.[20] To his thinking, grammar penetrated to a deeper level by considering some of the psychological contexts of the meanings of words, adjusting expressions not only to their verbal syntactics but also to the circumstances of their utterance as well, that is, their use. Depth-dialectic also takes into fuller account than the ordinary the meanings of arguments in relation to the psychology of the persons upholding them.[21] It might seem that to consider so closely *these* contexts for the arguments would render the dialectic more superficial, not deeper. But to stress the reciprocal relation between dialectic and persons may enable one to reinterpret some passages whose meanings have either been much—almost too much—debated or else passed over with little or no comment. Depth-dialectic will not simplify the reading at all, indeed the reading will become more entangled than ever; but it should help to confirm and stabilize the construing of many passages. Oddly enough, greater attention to these so-called literary features of character and mood will show that the *Gorgias* is more philosophical than is sometimes believed.[22] We do not think, however, that Plato wanted his readers to care more for the kind of man each participant was than for his dialectic on some point, yet in such instances as the debate on the superiority of the philosopher over the rhetor-tyrant (506e–522e), it is important that this is argued by a philosopher with exceptional powers of analysis and exceptional stability of character; your ordinary philosopher would not suffice. But even more, Plato seems to have thought that the very act of getting philosophy to touch life, real life as it is lived, makes it deeper, more significant, less a plaything.

The *Gorgias*, more than any of the dialogues except the *Apology*, *Crito*, and *Phaedo*, depicts a personal crisis, and far more than they it affords all manner of insights into the life and mind of a sorely divided personality, Callicles. These other three dialogues focused on a well-integrated Socrates; the *Gorgias* makes another man almost equally prominent and pictures the internal conflicts of his soul.[23] If there are any discrepancies in the proofs that Socrates offers, there are certainly far more in those of Callicles; but the inconsistencies are keys to an unstable nature, not stupidity.[24]

One comes to know much about persons by knowing the grounds for their acceptance of certain beliefs and rejection of others. Are their motives those of advantage, or comfort, or revenge, or consolation; or are they merely seeking propositions that will fit together with basic premises or lead securely to desired conclusions? Does not the hope for social acceptance or preeminence guide these choices? In examining these questions of personality we have tried to avoid using modern concepts with which Plato could not possibly have been acquainted, except in terms of strained analogies. The languages of Existentialism, Psychoanalysis, General Semantics, Paretian Sociology, and a hundred other theories and methods could well be used to study the delicate checks and imbalances of Callicles' nature. But such studies, fascinating in themselves, would only divert attention from fitting the personages into the dialogue as a whole, unless one were to translate *all* of it into expressions suited to Heidegger or Freud, Korzybski or Pareto. Such a procedure carries the risk of falsifying Plato's intent as much as does the imposition of Peano-Russell symbolism. We have also tried to be bound by the indications that Plato offers for judging his participants. Such a man as Callicles might well suffer from migraine headaches or digestive upsets or perhaps psychosomatic rashes, but of this there is not a word from the author, who is generally sparing in his accounts of physical ailments, and who describes what is now called body language rather infrequently.[25]

Some relations between the participants in the *Gorgias* are explicitly set forth by Plato: Callicles is host to Gorgias and the others; Socrates and Chaerephon are at least acquaintances who have been together in the agora;[26] Polus is at least a follower, probably a pupil, of Gorgias. Every reader must take these as settled. Other relationships seem fairly evident, but are no more than hinted at, yet they do affect the discussion, and it is best to notice them.

In any of the dialogues, there are three or more points of view: those of each of the two or more participants toward the other or others; and that of Plato toward them all. The last is always the most difficult to fathom, for on occasion he appears to put such a man as Gorgias or Protagoras in a good light, and at other times casts an unfavorable reflection upon him. Even Socrates seems to be made to uphold a dishonest position, as in the *Hippias Minor*, or to be hedging, as in the first speech that he gives in the *Phaedrus* (237a–241d), or to be somewhat hedonistic and utilitarian, as in parts of the *Protagoras* and the *Gorgias* itself. It is neither easy nor candid to explain these away. As for the attitudes of the several participants toward each other, it is especially important to uncover these in the *Gorgias*.

Each participant in a Platonic dialogue is in one degree or another a contributor to its forward motion. Even those who do not speak, or who speak very little (like Chaerephon in the *Gorgias*, Cleitophon in the *Republic*, and others) are, by their very presence, contributing in a slight sense to the character of the discussion and its possible outcome. This, as we shall have occasion to show, is also true of the unnamed audience in the *Gorgias*, which in their possible giving or withholding of approval of the discussants has an effect on the persistence of the rhetors—and perhaps Socrates as well—in maintaining their respective positions.

If A says that it is raining and B replies that it is not, both persons contribute but they are not separately managing a dialectic—they imply a dialectical opposition but neither one explicitly directs it. A more sophisticated stage is reached when A proposes a definition of raining, or a pair of contraries or other opposites as having some general reference to weather, and B, in stating his own, finds that he and A either agree, modify, or clash with each other; this is a cooperative dialectic. A third and still higher stage is reached when A, having put forward a definition or statement of opposition, is answered by B, who instead of flatly stating a different one, undertakes to follow out the implications of A's remarks and offers nothing to oppose them until he has shown them to be self-contradicting in some way. We call this a managed dialectic. In several of the dialogues in which Socrates is principal, this kind obtains almost throughout, but in the *Gorgias* much of the discussion is merely cooperative. The dialogues *not* dominated by Socrates operate for the most part upon rather different principles, and are not easily made commensurate with his various modes of discussion.

Under the heading of Methods in the Dialogue we have sketched some of the ways dialectic can be self-reflexive. In some respects personal self-awareness is quite separate from the dialectical, while in others the two approach each other closely, in fact become virtually identical. For the time being, we shall expound them separately from each other.

In the *Gorgias*, this self-regarding is exhibited in assumptions about the way each participant would fare in the city in which this long conversation is taking place. By contrast, the Eleatic Stranger and Theaetetus in the *Sophist* worry not at all over whether they themselves are sophists, or try to disentangle themselves from the sophistic calling—it is sufficient to know that this breed of hunter and trader can be clearly, cleanly defined from *outside* his calling; and when at one point the sophist of noble descent comes close to being identified with the philosopher, the Stranger even then does not question whether the speakers themselves will be confused with sophists. Far different is the Stranger's method from that of Socrates, who in many dialogues besides the *Gorgias* presses the question of involvement in the kind of world each theory would envisage.[27] Although in the *Republic* little is asked about the way the parties to that superb nocturnal colloquy would prosper in the paradigm city constructed in the skies, there are many attempts to raise the issue of each participant's relation to goodness, knowledge, justice.[28] An even clearer example is the *Theaetetus*, in which the young geometer is matched not with the Eleatic but with Socrates and accordingly has a much larger, more cooperative role to play. When Socrates receives from him the proposed definition of knowledge as sensation, he accepts this long enough to establish premises assuming its truth, then gradually shows that these lead to impossible conclusions.[29] It is, in other words, and so far as this is possible given the fact that communication must be in words rather than pure sensory images, quasi sensation that is assessing sensation, and more precisely, Socrates as sensor assessing his own sensory powers and their limitations. Set off against him is Theaetetus, whose mathematical knowledge has been attested and exemplified, and who is called upon to give a consistent account of that knowledge, not by description but by definition. Because there are defects in his account, one may say that he is called upon to assess knowledge by means of quasi knowledge not yet quite firm. Gradually the two positions are brought closer so that by the end of the dialogue *both* men must admit that trying to define knowledge from below by means of true opinion is hopeless. The dialogue is replete with self-referential analysis, but it is virtually all on a cognitive level, and the few references to the character of Theaetetus are relegated to a little prologue.

In the *Gorgias*, rhetors are assessing rhetoric, persons involved or likely to be involved in the political process are estimating the worth of that process.[30] Plato is presenting the imperfect city of Athens as a backdrop, several removes—he does not say how many—from the beautiful republic laid up in the skies. One must "get along" in Athens, whereas in Callipolis speculation concerning how one would prosper could easily become a child's game unworthy of serious attention.

So much for an account of self-evaluations in connection with theories proposed in the dialogues. There are other types, less tightly linked to the dialectics and more tied to the individuals, as follows: We begin with self-evaluations. These can be the weakest of all, or the strongest of all, and examples of both are given. Self-evaluation taken as self-praise, direct or implied, and not based upon the intimate knowledge of one's relations to truth and justice, is feeble, unreliable, easily upset by simple Socratic questioning not hostile in its intent. On the other hand, when based upon examination of fundamental motives having the practice of virtue for their aim, self-evaluation can be stronger than any judgment about other individuals, since one has greater familiarity with one's own acts, aversions, desires, and passing thoughts. The personality of Socrates demonstrates that he has access to features of himself not readily accessible to his friends and acquaintances.[31] Other men lack much of this self-awareness, and fall back upon praise and blame of qualities supposed to exist in themselves, rather than analysis of underlying character traits.

Following the estimations of oneself are the many evaluations of others that often turn into poorly veiled insults or into extravagant praise, some of it ironic.[32] Perhaps the self-praise of Gorgias (449a) stems from the praise heaped upon him by Polus (448c), an encomium mercifully cut short by Socrates. Gorgias' self-satisfaction does not spring wholly from within himself, but is a response, in part (though not very reluctantly made), to the accolade of another man. Such reassurance is not given to Socrates, who derives his own self-estimate from his dialectic of the virtues and their balancing.[33]

The evaluations by individuals of other individuals shade into those accorded by the group, such as the Athenian democracy, which put a judgment, not at all favorable, upon Pericles, arresting him for embezzlement and coming within an ace of having him executed (516a). These public estimates are, we may suppose, least reliable, since agreement of one member of the crowd with some or all the others is rarely based upon clear thinking and close attention to facts in issue. This point is made indirectly by all three rhetors in the *Gorgias*, who think of the crowd as easily led by a master of persuasion. That judgment by individuals is better than any made by a group is also suggested by the fact that judgment of the dead is taken over by three dignitaries of proven capacity.[34]

The judgment of Pericles thus fits into the hierarchy of kinds of judgments. It is not stabilized, for he cannot enter the dialogue as a participant, and even if he were to be quoted on the subject of his own virtues and vices it would be secondhand judgment at best. Lacking such a foundation, such a platform from which to counter and combat other opinions, he is, so to speak, at the mercy of others, fairer if he is judged by single persons, less fair if by groups and by the city as a whole.

This grading of judgments rests upon a further principle, of course, that knowledge is best described as a process, and that self-judgment or reliable judgment of others that can rank as knowledge is no single piece of information. It is necessary for us, then, to look more closely at this knowledge, if we are to come to terms with the evaluations that begin and conclude the *Gorgias*.

One can measure the difference between the abstract nature and the individual person as a difference between purely intellectual concerns and those tinged with or governed by emotions. In the narrow sense, dialectic is concerned with the former, but more broadly it is concerned with both, it absorbs both into a single unity. Truths of the heart are not less important than truths of the intellect, neither are they more important; but the two must be carefully weighed to see how far they can be divided and when they must be joined. Truths of intellect do not become truths in the fullest sense until the sequences of their component ideas touch, move, and continually engage the one intellect that frames them. When this occurs the discursive elements expressing these abstract truths become part of the framer's experience, and in this respect are embodiments of his emotions; he stands upon what he says, partly through its having been born of his feelings and partly through the mere fact of his saying it; he has marked out a slice of territory that he must now endeavor to defend.

Unity of the Dialogue

From the outset the *Gorgias* betrays a strong tendency to go beyond the confines of the four chief participants and arrive at general matters— Who is Gorgias? soon turns into, What is rhetoric and its power?—only to turn back repeatedly to raise the issue of living in the kind of world everyone knows: of crowds, assemblies that can be swayed unduly, of docks and warships that ought or ought not to be built, of other political rhetors who may outtalk or accuse one of crimes never committed. Plato deals with the way Socrates and each of the respondents views this world and projects into it his notions of happiness, justice, disgrace, evil. Plato's intent is doubtless to show that clarifying the ethico-political matters stands as a living challenge as much as it does the structuring and patterning of concepts. Thus he makes clear a real dilemma for Callicles with his many twists of soul. One might as well invert this to say that the tangled impulses of Callicles are outgrowths of the somewhat chaotic, biased opinions that he has pieced together from earlier thinkers[35] and from his conversations with wealthy, ambitious companions, along with his interest, attributed to him by Socrates but never openly confessed, in the wishes of the common man. For Plato, the reading of corrupt poetry (even that of Homer!) and of quasi philosophies will doubtless lead not only to distorted thinking but may open floodgates of desires and aversions as well.[36]

There is a fundamental though quite understandable mistake, then, in calling the *Gorgias* a drama of ideas,[37] just as there is a mistake in calling it a drama of persons *with* ideas. Probably no single word or phrase exactly and fully expresses the unique essence of the work, unless it be—*dialogue*. We may hazard that it is an interplay of persons *because* they have opinions together with characteristic ways of arriving at them. Plato did not, in his finished writings, waste his immense gifts on the affections and hostilities of persons unless some guiding method aiming to resolve multiple problems was instinct in their interchanges. On the other hand, his genius led him to perceive the many uses of personalities in giving both clarity and far greater substance to the elaboration of certain kinds of problems, chiefly in determining the nature of the good for man.

Readers brought up on claims for universality made by Kant and Hegel, and even the implied claims of Francis Bacon and Leibniz, may object that Plato's attachment to the philosophizing we have described severely limits it, ties it to individual minds, and thus blocks every hope of creating a general philosophic system applicable far beyond the instances with which Plato was familiar. To answer this objection is not easy, for even one of the most ardent exponents of universality in science and wisdom, Aristotle, stated that tragic drama is more universal than history, but less so than science (and presumably far less so than first philosophy, metaphysics).[38] Plato's use of dozens of persons of whom we have independent information concerning their lives makes him appear as not even aspiring to the level of poetic theatre, and thus content to remain with the particulars of history, or putative history. This would, of course, make the ideas expressed by Meno, Phaedrus, Theodorus, Parmenides, and the rest, even those by the mighty Socrates, become mere adjuncts of their characters or names. The utterances would be of interest through their ascription to these men and therefore would be hedged about in space and time, no longer pieces of primary import as philosophic explorations. Another criticism, based upon the same general premises but pointed in a quite different direction, would make every refutation an argumentum ad hominem—persons attacking persons as such, even when the language is more general in expression.

The answer to this double criticism ought, we believe, to take the following shape. It is inescapable that ideas as they are generated, regardless of content or application, are products of human thinking, and their embodiment in language, whether common patois, disciplined scientific speech, or symbolic formulas, is also a product of distinctively human invention. The ideas have general content if so framed, but as framed by a speaker they are also tinged with individual sensations, memories, and experiences that betray their personal origins. The hearer in the dialogue, or the reader of its text, must correspondingly cut through his own sensory life if he is to perceive their ideas in anything like the generality intended for them.[39] Human beings are always on the thin edge between individuality and universality, even if opinions of individuals are couched in terms transcendental in scope—thing, something, true, and the like.[40] Plato evidently recognized this, and though seeking to overcome the limitations imposed, he realized that the way to truths and falsities applying to very large classes of things was through formulations shaded by the feelings, images, and prejudices of men and women. Not only that, but persons on whom he expended some of his powers of characterization are, in addition to being unique, also representative of types—Theaetetus, of the acute young men of science, as yet unable to see its topics in the more widely diffused light of the nature of knowledge; Euthyphro, of the stuffy, self-righteous young clerics; Diotima, of the seeresses, mysterious, impersonal, yet able to offer profound reflections upon humanity and its aspirations. And so for others—a constellation of many constellations of stars, and a crowd of star-crossed human beings whose natures are best revealed not by description or anecdote but in what they think and say in direct response to life situations in their own past and in the present, and as they face the uncertain future.

Despite Aristotle's remark that a tragedy is not a unity merely because its hero is a single person,[41] the simple fact is that although the oneness of Socrates cannot fully assure the oneness of a dialogue, it must contribute markedly to that unity. But it is still *not* his course of action in a particular case, as it would be in a tragedy, but rather a change of general opinions that *could* lead to decisions regarding some particular choices.[42] It comes to this: Despite random similarities between tragedy and dialogue, the hero of a drama and the leader of a discussion fulfill unlike functions. The hero thinks, then acts; Socrates has *already* acted and now he thinks on its meaning. The oneness of the leader counts in promoting unity not so much for the continuous mention of his name or quotation of his speech or description of his personality as for the fact that the reader can assume some continuity and coherency of ideas and the methods of relating them.[43] It is taken for granted, but still needs to be proven in every case, that each of Plato's six leaders of dialectic (Socrates, Parmenides, the Eleatic Stranger, Timaeus, Critias, the Athenian Stranger) has a set of principles well in hand, and that the dialogues in which they appear are explorations of ways useful in clarifying the ideas of others as well as their own. In the case of Socrates those others are either less certain than he or else much more certain but less in command of ways to apply their opinions over a sufficiently broad range of experience and thought. This could not of itself lend unity to a tragic plot, with its complication and reversal and all the rest, but it suffices for a dialogue, however much that dialogue may reflect life situations.

That reflection is found at no one point; the *Symposium* does not suddenly become lifelike at the moment when Aristophanes contracts the hiccups,[44] or in the *Phaedrus* when the eponymous young man hints that he will wrestle Socrates to keep him from leaving the riverside without giving a speech responding to that by Lysias.[45] The mystery and magic of the *Mona Lisa* lies not in the lady's smile, except incidentally. Instead it lies in the parapet, the womanly figure, her face and hair, the landscape—and of course the smile too as an image in harmony with all the rest. Through all those images together the very existence and effectiveness of the smile can be explained; otherwise that evanescent curl of the thin lips has no more artistic substance than the disembodied grin of the Cheshire Cat.

The unity of the *Mona Lisa*, however, can never quite be put into words, and neither can the unity of the *Gorgias*, but one must try to find and state that unity nevertheless, if one is to maintain that the dialogue is anything more than a seriously flawed piece of writing.[46] The difficulty in finding what holds it together is, however, a graver one than that of grasping the oneness of a painting. The dialogue is a work of two arts, not one, and in this respect it is more like a song whose words must be understood and its musical line penetrated severally and then both looked at together to see if the fabric is seamless. Plato himself proved it possible and perhaps not very difficult to write dialogue with virtually no literary touches; and in the *Menexenus* showed that argument could be rooted out in favor of rhetorical impressiveness, parts of it quite irresponsible. The question remaining, then, was whether he could also join them, as Schubert and Brahms and Hugo Wolf could join lyric and lyre.

Just as the *Gorgias* is not a tragedy in any precise sense, so it is not a comedy, although every reader has pointed out for himself a dozen comic touches. If comedy withholds ordinary human dignity and virtue from its characters, one cannot say that Plato has deliberately poured his participants into this mould.[47] It seems even less likely that a Platonic dialogue would resemble very closely any other well-recognized literary forms, whether these were in existence in his time—epic, dithyramb, ode, or the like—or those of later periods—problem dramas, novels, or, as some have proposed, instructional programs for use with computers. A dialogue, and especially the *Gorgias*, is incidentally instructive but is not a treatise or textbook or some electronic derivative from these; it is therapeutic but is not a psychiatric case study or tract; it is dramatic but not a tragedy or comedy; it is forensic but not a legal brief; it has a unity but this unity differs from that of every other kind of artistic creation.[48]

Plato defines dialectic most comprehensively as the grasping of disparate things into one and the separation of kinds according to natural divisions.[49] If so, then the unity and order of the *Gorgias* can never be discovered, even in part, unless one can resolutely pursue this joint principle in as many details as possible. A flat assertion of the unity is insufficient and in fact self-defeating. The real unity is gathered from, and found in, whatever throws light upon every part of the dialogue, whether it be a passing utterance, a major soliloquy, a solution to a problem, a question, a changing of seats or postures. The secrets of connection and separation are the focal points of the right sort of philosophical discussion to be carried on about the dialogue, if only because they are what Plato took pains to include.[50]

Poetry not harmonized with and under the stern control of dialectic Plato condemns as alien to philosophy and truth. If, on the other hand, he unites the two by a fitting proportion of their aims, then it would be missing the point to ignore the multitudes of references to persons and their families, wealth, studies, friends, and so on; metaphors and other figures of speech such as puns, hyperboles, and more; and all the other images along with allusions to the old poets and common legends that the author puts into the speakers' mouths. To use another of Wittgenstein's distinctions, the poetic devices *show*, in general, while the less figurative arguments *say*, what Plato wishes to impart. But not literally and precisely. Like the drawings and poetic verses on the pages of a William Blake manuscript, the messages and images are slightly different, yet when interpreted together they are both absorbed into a larger whole where their apparent inconsistencies are resolved. They are so aptly supplementary that in different ways they extend a common inspiration.

A frequently adopted strategem of those wishing to prove a unity in the *Gorgias* has been to contrast the statements of the three rhetors, ranging them in sequence and exhibiting what is shared and what is individual in their approaches to rhetoric and justice. This is a good start, but delusional to think that the recording of such threefold contrasts will do much by itself to prove unity.[51] One could take the twenty-fourth book of the *Iliad*, the Book of Revelations, and the Gettysburg Address and make neat little trios to show how different topics in them are set off one from another, and with a little persistence this can be done almost as convincingly as with the three rhetors of the *Gorgias* or the seven chief speakers of the *Symposium*. The listing of such contrasts, however, *would* suggest that the history of literature has some overall connectedness, and similarly the common and disparate views of the rhetors can be laid bare, showing how far they deal with the same subject matter. Again, one sees that discovering real unity lies deeper, in finding hints of what that unity might be *as stated within the* Gorgias *itself*, then showing how in a dialectical sense these hints can be made to apply to the grand design. It is like life itself, where no one chemical reaction, no one response or finite number of tests will determine the wholeness of an organism.

Some readers of the *Gorgias* have thought that to save its unity rhetoric must be its topic almost throughout, while others have held that it is the good life, with rhetoric as an incidental. To say, on the other hand, that it commences as a study of rhetoric but after a time veers over to the good of man will break up the dialogue into two parts. A more extreme view is the old judgment of Grote[53] that the three main sections, pitting Socrates against the rhetors in succession, are only connected by a loose thread. Even the wolf should be heard, so says Plato;[54] but before this wolf chews the *Gorgias* to pieces, we should see if Grote and others of his persuasion ought not to have had second thoughts. We can scarcely believe that it is a piece of youthful exuberance, with coltish disconnections and tangents, regardless of the year or years when it was being written or revised by Plato. Nor do we see it simply as a preliminary sketch for the *Republic*, despite similarities between some parts of the two works. It is instead a masterpiece standing by itself yet able to be meshed philosophically with the other dialogues; but this is not a proof that it was written late—or midway—in Plato's long career. Some artists and thinkers have been born with the mantle of maturity already lying across their shoulders—Duns Scotus, David Hume, and Thomas Mann are among them. Others take more time.[55]

Plato has a variety of philosophic-literary approaches, an aptness and a profundity, that make him a man whose shoes many influential philsophers would not be worthy to tie, whether or not one agrees with what he has said or implied. There is little question that if viewed from the standpoint of the Whitehead-Russell calculus of propositions and its successors Plato would seem to have strayed many times. But his straying, as we believe can be shown, had its good reasons. Doubtless he felt that his dialogues had an educational function as much as an expository one, and that if it was cryptic from time to time it would encourage the finding of connections and disjunctions only hinted at in the written text and thus make the reader one more anonymous participant in the dialogue. Finding these insights is fraught with all kinds of dangers because the shallows and shoals are necessarily uncharted, so that much depends upon what can only be called philosophic taste in deciding whether the analogies are strained or not, whether the differences are forced and arbitrary or clear and natural, whether the utterances are apportioned to the right speakers. When we ourselves have committed errors in matters of this kind it has been unconsciously, and yet for obvious reasons we must not try to disguise our conclusions as Plato sometimes did. For the mistakes we apologize in advance, hoping only that instead of dwelling upon the shortcomings at unprofitable length our readers will turn their attention and talents to the much more vital task of trying for a clearer statement of the underlying philosophy and art for which we have been looking. The fact is that if Plato's mission was well conceived by him, then finding this would enable his own readers to bring some fresh light into their thoughts and lives.

SUMMARY TOPICAL OUTLINE OF THE

GORGIAS

I. Colloquy between Socrates and Gorgias on the definition and power of rhetoric assumed to be an art; its effects on others (447a–461b)
   A. Prologue: the chief speakers and types of discourse: display speeches, discussion (447a–449c)
      1. The just-past and possible future displays by Gorgias (447a–c)
         a) lateness of Socrates and Chaerephon for the display just past (447a–b)
         b) whether Socrates desires to hear Gorgias display again (447b–c)
      2. Temporary interchanging of the chief speakers (447c–449c)
         a) Chaerephon replaces Socrates (447c–448a)
         b) Polus replaces the perhaps tired Gorgias (448a–c)
         c) Socrates becomes questioner, and Gorgias gradually replaces Polus in answering, regarding profession of Gorgias and kind of discourse to be conducted (448d–449c)
   B. Colloquy proper between Socrates and Gorgias on definition and power of rhetoric (449c–461b)
      1. Rhetoric itself as an art or power, defined and the definition examined (449c–456a)
         a) statement of definition as elicited from Gorgias (449c–453a)
            (1) attempts to arrive at definition (449c–452d)
            (2) definition proper, including subject matter of rhetoric—the greatest good for man (452d–e)
            (3) immediate revision of definition: rhetoric is the artificer of persuasion (452e–453a)

i) introductory: the account is true (522e–523a)
ii) account proper: place of the dead and three stages of judgment of the dead; judges; conclusions regarding punishments for evil, rewards for virtue (523a–526d)

(c) lessons of the mythic argument and the arguments preceding it; attitudes of Socrates and Callicles toward their lives; what both men should do (526d–527e)

The present summary outline omits a great deal. There are, for example, some thirty interludes altogether, a count to be exhibited only in a version of the outline carrying subdivisions much smaller than the foregoing. In the same way, most of the arguments regarding rhetoric and justice are embedded in lower ranks of an outline too lengthy to be included here.

A bald listing, long or short, of topics in ranks still does violence by its failure to notice the backward references necessary for reading every passage, except the first, to be made clear and substantial. Though ideally both the *Gorgias* and our book would be read from beginning to end, a respect for hard fact demands recognition that limited portions of *A Friendly Companion* will be consulted at any given sitting. Because of this and because of our insistence that the dialogue should be read cumulatively, with multiple backward references, we have tried to bring enough retrospective material to bear upon each passage in the text to keep the peculiarly sequential character of Plato's work in mind. For the many repetitions thus entailed we apologize, though by no means admitting the need to do so.

PART ONE

CONVERSATION WITH GORGIAS

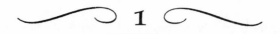

1

PROLOGUE

WHO IS GORGIAS, WHAT IS HE?

(447a–449c)

The little Prologue (447a–449c) to the *Gorgias* is no doubt the most neglected portion of the dialogue, yet it provides many hints of what is to come. Hints, but not much more, until it is looked at again after reading the remainder of the work. Such writers as Immanuel Kant throughout his first *Critique* tell the reader almost exactly what to expect, set the problem, then outline the steps to be taken in solving it in the sections to follow. Introductions to a few of Plato's dialogues—the *Sophist* is one of these—at least raise the chief question and provide the reader with part of the method to be used in answering it. In the *Gorgias* the complexities are more baffling, the method is less easy to grasp, and one must look in the Prologue not only for what is said but also for what is done (as described in what is said) to gain anything like a satisfactory notion of its relations to the work as a whole.

Let us glance at some general considerations, prompted by questions raised in the rest of the Platonic dialogues, then attaching the latter to the *Gorgias* with no attempt to answer them flatly at this juncture. We find six possible ways whereby the first two pages *might* prefigure the chief questions and many-layered method of the dialogue, these six carrying very unequal claims to being able to exhibit a unity of the dialogue.

The first is in furnishing the number and names of those who will participate in the discussion about to take place. This is minimal information but is least troublesome of the six ways; the *Gorgias* happens to name all the active participants at the outset, though recalling that there is no mention of the Slave Boy or Anytus in the *Meno* before their actual joining in (82a; 90a) could well diminish the reader's confidence that the early passages of the *Gorgias* will introduce all the speakers. We assume that, since Gorgias himself has been giving a display, there is something of an audience beyond the other four men named (Polus,

Callicles, Chaerephon, Socrates), but it is not until later that Socrates actually refers to this audience (455c) as remaining after having listened to the show of skill. We are present at a public or semipublic performance, and to an extent this is carried through to the end.

The second is in the characters of and relations between the speakers. There is far greater subtlety in depicting character required for this, of course, than there is for their mere identification or describing them as young, old, tired, refreshed; this subtlety is compounded when at least two of the personages here are found to be exceedingly complicated men, surpassing all of Plato's other creations in this respect. Still, one may conjecture a little about all five of the participants, even without being aware of the rest of the work. Indeed, this is perhaps where predictions made with no further guidance from the subsequent text are most reliable.

The third is in the manner of the speaking, whether it is to be soliloquy or a discussion with each man contributing opinions or raising questions in quick succession and inviting immediate response. Here the reader is on solider ground, for unless one or more of the men should forget the rules laid down, this reader might be assured (unreliably, it turns out) that lengthy addresses, such as those in the *Phaedrus* and *Symposium*, the *Timaeus* and *Critias*, will not be found in the *Gorgias*. This in itself does not decide an issue that depends upon, yet partly transcends, that of the style of speaking. It is frequently assumed that the *Gorgias* depicts a battle between three representatives of an art of rhetoric and a single man practicing a superior art, dialectic. This is not altogether false, but it must be tempered with the realization that the debate is so conducted that there are frequent, far-reaching adaptations on *both* sides to each other's requirements. These are such important concessions that neither rhetoric nor dialectic is presented in anything like the purity enjoyed in certain other works by Plato.[1] A sharp eye might detect hints of this double infiltration even in the Prologue.

A fourth way that this dialogue might be shaped by its Prologue is by the use of certain terms, single, paired, or grouped in other ways. These terms are by themselves not problems or propositions, but the stuff of which those are made, and their schematic relations do much to form the advent, course, and outcome of the discussion. For example, if one participant puts the concept of appearance above that of reality and his opponent reverses this or makes them equivalent, sooner or later an issue will be joined between the two men, regardless of the specific meanings accorded to each of those contraries. We may, then, list some prominent terms and sets of terms to be found in the *Gorgias*. They are in no particular order here, since it is not always easy to tell when a term is really introduced, so many are its foreshadowings.

Thus children, strength, and intelligence if introduced early (this is a hypothetical example) would foreshadow Plato's customary hierarchy, external goods, goods of the body, and goods of the soul. At any rate, the *Gorgias* makes considerable use of justice-injustice, person-city, rhetoric-discussion, knowledge-belief, question-answer, teacher-pupil, advantage-disadvantage, virtue-vice, justice-wisdom, bravery-temperance, pleasure-pain, power-weakness, appearance-reality, body-soul, life-death, accusation-defense, freedom-bondage, art-pandering, model-imitation. One should scarcely expect that in two pages Plato would be able or even wish to cram all of these in, let alone any indication of how he intends to deal with them in the more than six dozen pages remaining. Nevertheless, one may count on a few pairs to appear in the Prologue.

A fifth possibility would be in predicting the actual issues raised and the solutions offered later in the dialogue. Some aspects of the problems broached are indeed presented in the little Prologue, others are not. So evident is this that critics have from time to time asserted that the *Gorgias* remains a disunified mélange, lacking any central core.[2] The subject of later sections of the dialogue most conspicuously missing in the Prologue is power or rule and the supposed advantage attaching to it. At no point in the first two pages does Socrates or anyone else ask what gain there is in rhetoric and what one may hope for from its mastery. The display by Gorgias is presumably the least politically oriented of all types of rhetoric, and to be able to answer whatever questions are put to him (if his boast at 448a can be substantiated) is a far cry from being able to seize rule in a great city. Nor is there any casual mention of the Great King or of Pericles or the other men of power referred to later. No clear indication is given of what Socrates hopes to do with his own art of speech, which is to improve other men in the exercise of the virtues, among which justice is principal and represents his own kind of exercise of power.

Why, then, these omissions? The only sensible answer is that all three rhetors hide their real intention for some little time, and so does Socrates. It is only after Gorgias has extolled rhetoric in a general way that he begins to claim it as a bringer of freedom to the rhetor and of relative bondage to everyone else (452d). After this, it becomes easier for both Polus and Callicles to admit that the same goal, with variations, is in their minds. As for Socrates, it would be highly inappropriate for him to walk into the gathering and offer to reform these men, individually or together, by the power of his speech before having heard more than a word or two from them. His assertion that he seeks this reform and that he is one of the very few or perhaps the only one of the Athenians who can do it (521d) is made only late in the day. So much for what is said. As for what is done, the drama, if you like, it is very slight and has nothing worth putting on a stage, though as the Prologue is expounded, we shall refer to these little bits of action.

The sixth possibility would be in determining in advance who among the participants will be successful in scoring a victory, either by refuting his opponent (as in the *Ion*, *Euthyphro*, or the two dialogues named after Hippias), exhibiting a more sterling character (as in the *Apology* and the two prison dialogues), or making a more effective, comprehensive, and heartfelt speech (as in the *Symposium*). Opinions differ on the question of the winner of the battle in the *Gorgias*, just as they do on whether the arguments of Socrates are cogent or not. Some believe that Socrates defeats his opponents handily, others that he fares reasonably well, still others that he fails even though Plato would doubtless like to have his readers think Socrates victorious—and that by reasonably fair means. This question cannot possibly be decided from any hints. For instance, Socrates does not lean over to Chaerephon to say, sotto voce, Now, watch the way I'll deal with *these* three!

Despite these omissions, however, the Prologue does form a kind of paradigm for the working out of the first three of our six avenues into the *Gorgias*, however little it can furnish suggestions for the last three. The evidence should be sifted for possible philosophical significances before relegating it to the sidelines as "delightful touches" or "a setting of the stage." On the other hand, the hopes of restoring the Prologue to what we believe to be its rightful status would not persuade us to clutch at minutiae and elevate them to the rank of essential signs with independent existence. The brief pages can only lead into a great work but cannot be that work, cannot even be its most significant part.

There are, of course, two ways to read this portion; both require some care, and both have advantages and drawbacks. There is the prospective way, or what might be called the naive way, in which the first couple of Stephanus pages are read in ignorance of the rest of the dialogue, the reader trying to anticipate what takes place later. This is no doubt the more honorable way to interpret the passage, or indeed every passage in the work, but it puts an almost intolerable burden on the imagination.[3] It is a hard discipline, if one intends really to understand the text.

The second way, the retrospective, is to read the Prologue, perhaps for the seventh time, bearing in mind what the rest of the dialogue has to say and show; this gives a more sophisticated interpretation of the two little pages. We guess that most readers would, probably without hesitation, prefer to read in this fashion; and certainly it simplifies the task of showing a harmony between the first little segment and all that comes later.

For the Prologue, we intend to keep these two approaches separate so far as possible. Later, the successive portions of the work stand more nearly by themselves, and the interpretation can move forward or backward.

The Prologue Read Prospectively

The Prologue is conveniently divided into two parts: talk of the rhetorical display of Gorgias just finished and its possible repetition in the near future (447a–c), and then the temporary replacements of the chief speakers and the gradual winnowing-out of these surrogates in an effort to find out from Gorgias himself what he professes and teaches (447c–449c). The first of these parts is again divided into two, i.e. the lateness of Socrates and Chaerephon in joining the gathering (447a–b), and the question of whether Socrates would care to hear another display and Gorgias would care to present one (447b–c). This set of divisions of itself proves nothing about the orderliness of the dialogue, for even a wild dream can be broken into discrete parts and made to seem more reasonable thereby.[4] But these particular segments in the *Gorgias* do help us to anticipate certain features of later parts of the long conversation.

Some aspects of the setting and audience are too often dismissed. Of no great importance, of course, is the probability that the entire discussion takes place not in Callicles' own home but fairly close by. Socrates mentions (455c) "all the people within these walls," which indicates a fairly good-sized audience, perhaps twenty or more. The private dwellings of the time had rather small rooms corresponding to our living rooms, and they were usually dank, poorly lighted, and with insufficient furniture to make a large group comfortable for long. The display mentioned at the outset has gone on for some little time, and the discussion following would by any reasonable calculation occupy at least two and a half to three hours. Men did not often entertain or talk with even small groups of friends at home, but congregated rather in gymnasia, public porticoes, palaestras, and elsewhere. "Within these walls" is ambiguous as between the walls of a building and the walls of some roofless enclosure.

Of much greater importance for the dialogue is the actual presence of the listeners, although they utter not a word. It will account for the apparent willingness of Gorgias to continue his exhibition at the advent of Socrates (447c) and for some of his hesitations and possibly those of Polus and Callicles later on. Gorgias evidently looks upon the occasion as a way of both harvesting applause and recruiting pupils. It is conceivable that Polus, who sees himself as the alter ego of Gorgias, thinks of it in the same way. As for Socrates, he draws the discussion farther and farther away from the setting and more and more into a realm of conceptual inquiry, and consequently is little concerned with the effect he is making upon an audience.

Callicles, as host, is the first speaker, indicating to the reader something of his significance for the dialogue. ⟨You can, he says to Socrates and Chaerephon, join in a fight (*polemos*) or battle (*machēs*), but you have—here he borrows a word interjected by Socrates—arrived too late for a feast, a display by Gorgias (447a–b).⟩ Although this last reference is clear, his raising of the possibility of a battle is not. He could mean a struggle with Gorgias, but Gorgias may be a little tired by now, and surely there is no reason to believe that if his display would have been a feast for Socrates, the latter would turn against the old rhetor and quarrel with him over the quality or content of the entertainment. More likely, Callicles means that Socrates will find Polus or Callicles himself to be adversaries. But on what issues? So far as we can know at this stage, the only issue for a battle would be the feast itself, and this could well mean that Socrates would disapprove of the way Gorgias conducts himself. The tone of Callicles' early remarks is one of self-assured stability; he seems ready to face—or at least play host to—some battle scene. The argument that Polus might be the one to attract the fire of Socrates stems from the fact that followers often engage the enemy more audaciously than do their mentors. Possibly even Chaerephon is, in Callicles' mind, the man to commence a squabble with one or all of the rhetors. We find almost immediately that this little man has known in advance that Gorgias was going to perform. How could he have known this were he and Callicles not acquainted? Chaerephon, with the slenderest of speaking roles in the dialogue, is nonetheless the catalyst to bring together the others.

⟨Socrates has said that *Chaerephon is to blame for their delayed arrival* (447a–b).⟩ On another occasion he had himself to blame: he nearly missed a party because he fell to meditating raptly under a neighboring portico (*Symposium* 174d–175a), but this time Chaerephon, in spite of knowing of the display, has postponed arrival because of some chance business in the agora, both marketplace and center for political and judicial administration. (The emphasis upon these two functions varied from the time of Homer onward.)

There might be a slight irony in Socrates' expressed irritation at having missed the so-called feast. In the *Phaedrus*, he teases to have a speech by Lysias recited or read to him (227d; 228c) and says, moreover, that he is lovesick for speeches (228b). In the *Protagoras*, on the other side, he is much annoyed at the prospect of having to listen to a speech (335a–b). It might be that both impulses are in him now; he would like to have heard some small bit of what Gorgias had to say, enough to see his style of performance, but then would ask him to break off and enter into the sort of discussion more congenial to himself. In any case, one is entitled to ask why Socrates proposes to quiz Gorgias on the nature of his art and teaching before listening to any display, which he asks (447c) to have deferred. Is it a general stubbornness, or a one-track interest in something besides show? By comparing his behavior here with what is found in other places, a curious weakness, or at least a professed weakness, becomes apparent. In the *Apology*, Socrates says that in light of what his accusers have brought against him, he has forgotten what he is (17a). In the *Phaedrus*, he shows—or pretends to show—a disturbing tendency to be taken in by the mood of Lysias, and is rescued only by the mysterious daimōn (242b) who by preventing him from leaving the country scene allows him no alternative to the contradicting of his first, defamatory speech on love. The importance of Socrates' unusual gift for putting himself into the mind of his respondent must be stressed—he is already commencing to show it in the Prologue—but this talent also carries a danger. It enables him to anticipate certain lines of argument from the persons he encounters; but he risks being carried along by empathic feelings as well. Thus if he listens to one of the most successful, affecting, and honored speakers in the Greek world he may, at least for the time being, find himself unable to withhold his approval or even his enthusiasm. To Socrates this could have serious consequences.

⟨Chaerephon now says (447b) that *Gorgias is a friend of his*,⟩ which probably means that the great rhetor has been in Athens before and very likely that, if Chaerephon is telling the truth about the friendship, he has talked of him to Socrates. On the other hand, he may be adorning the truth a little. How would he know Gorgias, even if the rhetor *has* been in Athens before? Chaerephon is not a pupil, unlike Callicles he seems not to have the money to play host, he makes no mention of political connections. Yet he does know (448b) that Herodicus, a doctor, is the brother of Gorgias. If he is indeed a friend, then to some degree he forms the needed link between Gorgias and Socrates and, much more remotely, shows that there may be a link between display rhetoric and whatever sort of discourse Socrates may wish to conduct. This is not a link of equal weight, but its suggestiveness may be helpful in keeping the lines of this intricate mesh clearly in mind.[5]

⟨Chaerephon, regardless of his being a friend to Gorgias or not, evidently regards the display as a kind of speech to be turned on or off and repeated at will. *I think*, he says (447b), *that I can persuade Gorgias to give another display*,⟩ which is a trifle forward since Callicles, as host, would doubtless be the one to voice the request. Chaerephon is making a second mistake, which is to believe that successful rhetoric leaves the hearer's emotions in precisely the same condition as they were before the speechmaking began. No wonder that he was little concerned at being late! Let us loiter in the agora, Socrates, let us take our time. No matter when we arrive, Gorgias will be on hand, and everyone will wish to hear him all over again. Chaerephon understands that Gorgias is a performer, but misses the effect of the performance. Not only that, but he seems to have little conception of the manner of discourse favored by Socrates, and it may well be that he is unaware of its unique characteristics. Again, Chaerephon has evidently misconstrued Socrates' intentions. He has thought, from the latter's expressed desire to hear Gorgias' display, that this meant now, today; but that would put cart before horse, and Socrates would prefer first to be told the power of Gorgias' art and what he professes. (This might insure him against being over-persuaded, to know the underlying principle before seeing its application.) To Callicles, as to all the others, Chaerephon included, this question of Socrates' about art is just another one to be handled routinely by Gorgias, who looks upon his giving of answers as an adjunct to or even a part of his regular display. It happens, however, that a principal motive of Socrates is to break up routine, to overturn traditional patterns of thinking by asking fundamental questions, arranged systematically but each time with a new order.

There is now a shift from the late arrival and preferences of the two visitors from the agora to a new and odd interchanging of speakers. Thus Chaerephon, at Socrates' request, replaces him as questioner, and Polus, without being asked, replaces the honored rhetor from Sicily, thought to be a little tired from his display just over.

Why, then, does Socrates ask Chaerephon (447c) to commence the questioning of Gorgias? And what can be made of Chaerephon's ineptitude? One reason, and not the least prominent, is that Chaerephon has said that he is a friend of Gorgias, which Socrates himself is not. It would thus be easier for Chaerephon to elicit frank replies from Gorgias. Surely we can eliminate the suggestion that Socrates is tired.[6] But is he trying to give Chaerephon practice or test him? Certainly anyone accompanying Socrates for more than a day or two would know how to *open* a discussion of his kind. On the other hand, there is no real assurance that Socrates and Chaerephon have not met only recently[7]— perhaps in the agora whence they have just come—and have joined together upon discovering that they have an acquaintance in common, namely Callicles, and perhaps too a common interest in rhetoric. In sum, only if Chaerephon and Socrates have just recently been in contact does Socrates' request for a substitute make much sense. Timidity, respect, boredom, solicitude for Chaerephon—none of these function in Socrates here.

Chaerephon's shortcomings in debate are revealed in four ways:

1. He does not know what to ask, although Socrates has already (447c) given him his cue that it is the power and nature of Gorgias' art that is in question.
2. When he is told to ask, very simply, what Gorgias is (i.e. the name of his profession, which of course Chaerephon already knows), he fails to understand until Socrates' analogy with the shoemaker (447d) gives him the needed hint.[8]
3. But he changes tack in the next sentence, to ask twice whether Gorgias can answer any questions put to him—veering into total irrelevancy and ambivalence; it would mean quite different things to a man serious about discovering truth and a man concerned with the pleasing of audiences. To be able to answer any question does not strictly imply answering them all truly; and, moreover, the boast has to do not with inherent knowledge but with the kind of impression made on an audience.
4. When Polus preempts the role of respondent, saying it matters little whether he can answer as well as Gorgias so long as it is sufficient for Chaerephon, the latter is quick to agree wholeheartedly. This being so, Polus' responses to Chaerephon, What difference does it make? is vital.

First, Polus denies, even if without intending to, any distinction between knowledge and opinion: If you care only about opinions of which some will satisfy you, we need not concern ourselves about their epistemic strength or weakness. Second, Polus denies, again without realizing it, a distinction between reality and appearance. The reality of the true nature of Gorgias as practitioner and of his art and its power need not concern you, Chaerephon, so long as you are made aware that he is the fairest of the fair and his art is the highest. And Chaerephon very unsocratically accepts this; he is, as a New Englander would have it, a dull chisel for Socrates to lean on. But after that he seems to feel more confident, since he pretends that Gorgias has the same calling as a designated doctor and then as a painter, and allows Polus to conclude that Gorgias too would be given that title (448b–c). Not exactly brilliant, but a slight advance, though his allowing of a substitute to answer for the principal entirely misses Socrates' request not for information about Gorgias from some third party but for a full and candid statement by Gorgias himself regarding his life work and its aims. Chaerephon is, far from being Socratic in his probing, quite happy to be accepting shoddy goods.

Polus, substituting for Gorgias, is on a footing quite different from that of Chaerephon. He breaks in, univited, asks for no guidance from the man supposed to be his teacher, then abruptly, irrelevantly, pontificates on art and familiarity (*empeiria*, experience, close acquaintance).[9] But he is allowed little time for speechmaking in the Prologue, and much of what he has to say is aborted. ⟨His first attempt (448c) is designed to answer Chaerephon's prompted question, *What art does Gorgias know, as Herodicus knows medicine and Aristophon knows painting? Many arts, re-plies Polus, have been discovered through familiarity, which conducts the course of life according to art, but unfamiliarity conducts it according to chance* (kata tychēn). *The best men partake of the best arts, and Gorgias is one of the best and partakes* (metechei) *of the best art.*⟩ This is no better as a response than was that of Gorgias himself, a simple boast of his ability to answer all questions put to him. Polus is taking refuge in another irrelevancy; nor do the two sentences of his little pronouncement hang well to-gether. He seems to be claiming mastery of an art through familiarity, but leaves the very nature of the art, and what it is (knowledge?) that enables a man to attain that mastery, to one side. He is also assuming without any thought of proof that art must be the highest of human callings, or perhaps the only one worthy of the name, and that profess-ing it would of itself raise one to preeminence among all men.

Regardless of the particular content of the remarks of both men who are attempting to establish Gorgias as superior, there is a kind of inter-changeability operating between Gorgias and Polus, for they share a "professional " attitude toward the use of rhetoric.[10] No matter what they may later claim about the purpose of rhetoric as being power for the rhetor, the art *itself* and its superiority as an art is their first con-cern. Its mastery confers prestige. Gorgias couples his speaking with teaching rather than with political freedom, and Polus holds forth briefly on what one is to suppose are the epistemic grounds upon which rhetoric rests. If these two men display—and they are both doing this in their different ways—it is to display and then tout their own skill at displaying.

A pattern has been set up: (a) when Chaerephon asks the wrong question, Gorgias answers appropriately for him, but irrelevantly for Socrates; (b) when Chaerephon asks the right question, Polus answers appropriately for him, but again irrelevantly for Socrates. Both (a) and (b) fail to come to grips with the Socratic problem, for which we may twist Shakespeare a little: " Who is Gorgias, What is he, / That all his lads commend him?" The third phase (c) will, of course, be to give the appropriate answer to the right question, and that can no longer be in the hands of surrogates for either principal.

Callicles has assumed that Gorgias will display at any time he is asked;

Polus has assumed that Gorgias is tired, doubtless an excuse for Polus to intrude. The truth lies somewhere between, because of Gorgias' mental idiosyncrasies. He has in the past shown some intellectual freshness to be able to build up his "art" by himself; but years of seeking and finding rapport with his audiences have reduced his fresh understanding to a routine that has lost all novelty. He is like a popular actor, bored by repetition of matinee roles but stimulated by the applause of new audiences. Properly he should be capable, without much prompting, of answering a novel line of questions, in a novel order, with a different purpose. His eminence, however, gained from long-time familiarity with the routines of display and question fending, combined with the self-pride we have already seen—he does not reject the praise by Polus (448c)—leads one to cease hoping that he will be able to adopt new habits on the spur of the moment. The chances of sound dialogue, of a joint search for truth, will be thin.

⟨*Polus*, remarks Socrates to Gorgias (448d), *has not made good his promise to Chaerephon, despite his fine equipment; he had promised to answer sufficiently well the question asked, namely, What is Gorgias?*⟩ Gorgias has already lost the thread of the questioning, thinking perhaps that some fine phrases about art and familiarity will do nicely as identification for him. ⟨*Ask Polus*, Gorgias suggests. *No*, replies Socrates, *I shall ask you, since Polus has had more practice in rhetoric than in discussion* (dialegesthai, dialectic).⟩ "Dialectic" seems to refer here to habits of conversation that stick to the question asked, and not directly to the search for truth, much less to the grasp of eternal forms. ⟨Polus is quite unable to see how he is being rhetorical, so imbued with the benefits of rhetoric is he, and *Socrates consequently explains that he has eulogized the art of Gorgias as if someone had been censuring it* (448e)⟩, thus introducing one of the chief pairs of contraries of rhetorical theory and practice, praise and blame, into the discussion. ⟨*No one*, continues Socrates (448e–449a), *has asked what the quality of his art was* (poia tis eiē hē Gorgion technē), *but only what it was.*⟩ This is ambiguous here, for from the mouth of an ordinry man such as Chaerephon it would be asking merely to name the art—which in a left-handed way has been done already—but from a Socrates it would no doubt lead to a request for a definition. But Callicles, who has known Socrates before, would be the only man present, with the possible exception of Chaerephon, who might know that this was in Socrates' mind; and, perhaps for reasons of his own, Callicles does not wish to halt a discussion in which he foresees that Gorgias will be made to explain himself and his art.

⟨*What should we call you because of the art in which you are skilled* (449a)?⟩ This question is peculiar in several ways, for even if we assume against all likelihood that Socrates has known nothing whatever about Gorgias before arriving at the meeting, Gorgias has been introduced as just having performed a display.[11] Although rhetoric was fairly new as a profession in late fifth-century Greece, still its effects were felt all over Athens, and Socrates himself has correctly identified Polus as well practiced in the discipline (448e). Moreover, why trouble to give a name to a man's skill if one is simply to enjoy it? If Socrates is to be believed, it would be improper to praise rhetoric, but doubtless equally so to cast opprobrium upon it. The most plausible explanation is that Socrates is about to launch into the second aspect of the question, What is rhetoric? by demanding a precise accounting.

⟨My art is rhetoric, says Gorgias bluntly (449a), and I am a good rhetor⟩— this addendum being of first importance for the dialogue as a whole. Here he triply preens himself, by his self-praise, by his quoting of Homer (a mark of a cultivated man), and by his identifying himself with heroes of the Iliad who spoke this way. His adding that phrase, "I vaunt myself to be," is indeed Homeric in origin seems to carry a slight air of hope that Socrates is unacquainted with the epic source. ⟨Are you, persists Socrates, able to make others like yourself? Yes, here and elsewhere (449b).⟩ If Socrates is already aware that Polus is not only a surrogate for Gorgias but a pupil of his as well, then the present question may have an ironic twist. Gorgias, for all his conceit, may not be scattered, but Polus has already shown himself to be.

⟨If you can discuss, using question and answer, and put off using the lengthy (mēkos) style of Polus, then please keep your own promise.⟩ This gives Gorgias an opportunity to make another boast. ⟨I can speak more briefly than anyone (449b–c).⟩ Although he says that he can talk lengthily or in clipped style, he carefully avoids saying that he speaks at a length appropriate to the subject.[12] To answer as briefly as he does at first indicates his almost total inability to comprehend the real requirement for explaining a subject matter rather than merely pleasing an audience. Gorgias may also be unaware of the danger facing him if he simply answers Socrates with yes or no.

⟨On Gorgias' agreeing to speak briefly, Socrates expresses his satisfaction. Please give me a display of that very skill in brief speech (brachylogias). To which Gorgias concedes graciously—and again boastfully: You will admit that you never heard anyone else speak more briefly (449c).⟩ One may wonder why Socrates has made such a point of demanding brevity. There are the obvious reasons that he fears to drag out the discussion to inordinate length: that he is unwilling to have either party lose sight of the main issue, and that he can pin his opponent more surely with the staccato movement of a duologue. In addition, Socrates is aware that shortness and lengthiness of speech are important issues in rhetorical theory.[13] Socrates, having divined—or previously known—

the interests of the men facing him, is commencing to approach them on their own ground.

The Prologue in Retrospect

This ends the little Prologue, after which the *Gorgias* takes up the question in earnest, What is Rhetoric? together with others mated to it and into which it inevitably leads, given the Socratic predilection for finding the moral aspects of any activity.

It is possible, using some few of the materials furnished by later pages of the work, to put the Prologue in a slightly better perspective. We deal first with some insights that the Prologue affords concerning the participants, then with one or two general aspects of the argument.

A reader of this book may well wonder at our spending time on Chaerephon, scarcely more than a shadow who all but fades away after his bumbling in the Prologue. Despite this, he is made important by his having prevented Socrates from hearing Gorgias and also having abetted what he thought was Socrates' interest in rhetoric, and simultaneously having shown the pitfalls in trying without art to imitate the Socratic course of discussion. Chaerephon again (458c) will serve as a link by noting that the debate should continue between Gorgias and Socrates because the audience is applauding; a wholly extrinsic standard for judging the search for truth. He will enter the record for the last time when he says (481b) that he believes Socrates to be entirely serious in overturning the customary purposes of rhetoric. (This again does not, incidentally, imply long prior acquaintance with Socrates.) To use Leibniz' phrase regarding Descartes, Chaerephon lives in the anteroom of truth, or perhaps he is just outside the door, peering in. He is an ultimate consumer of discourse, ready to worship whichever hero steps forward and thus is a prime prospect for the rhetor's efforts, but perhaps ready to follow the Socratic life as well.

Chaerephon's remark (447b) that since Gorgias is a friend he will display again if Socrates thinks fit, or delay if he so wishes, foreshadows a leading Socratic distinction made immediately after Polus (466d) has confused "thinking fit" or willing with wishing. Tyrant-rhetors, says Socrates, may think it fitting to do some act, but this may misfire so badly that the result they end with is one they do not wish, and this gives him the chance to say that rhetors lack the real power that they believe themselves to possess. If we reflect this back to the earlier remark, does it not suggest that the display by Gorgias will, if given again, be slightly *less* effective in achieving its desired result than was hoped for? This sort of forward-and-backward reference would appear nonsense to any strict logician, but we have already spoken of the peculiar mixture of philosophical and literary arts in this dialogue.

Gorgias finds himself paired with Socrates first as a possible speaker to his listener (and presumably admirer as well), and it seems to dawn upon him very slowly that he is under attack; his offer to speak briefly is surely an expression of confidence that nothing vital to his practice of rhetoric or its underlying theory will suffer alteration. Despite the fact that he is beaten back in the presence of his star follower, of his host, and of assorted onlookers, he seems not to realize or care about the magnitude of his defeat—and certainly he does not foresee this during the Prologue. Is this lack of concern owing to magnanimity? Carelessness? Stupidity? None of these, we may suppose. More probably it betokens that in his overweening self-assurance and his firm reliance upon rhetoric, he considers the Socratic assault upon his bastions to be inconsequential and immaterial. With a trifle of help from Polus, Gorgias has tried to reveal himself to Socrates—and the reader—as a man skilled, eminent, able to teach (and therefore a master of the fundamentals of) rhetoric; and he is from out of town at least, for why otherwise would he be a guest at the home of an Athenian? He is, in other words, a celebrity among Greeks, and in his mind this in itself ensures him from the danger of refutation that would mean a dismantling of his status. Fame is the spur of this man who falls a little short of nobility.

When Polus temporarily replaces Gorgias in the Prologue, he is asked if he can give more excellent, fairer answers than his model can. When he responds to Chaerephon, What does it matter, if to *you* my answers are sufficient? this indicates that he is relieving himself of the embarrassment of saying aloud that indeed his answers *are* better than those of his elder, but it also injects a new note into the discussion, seen in light of the ensuing colloquy between Socrates and Gorgias. While Chaerephon is probably too bewildered to know exactly what he means by his own question about comparative excellence, for Polus any such question in its possible significations is beside the main point, which is to praise a calling and another man, so long as this will redound to his own advantage.

Secondly, and more important, Polus is responding to Chaerephon though he can plainly see that it was Socrates who inspired the questions about Gorgias and his profession. The satisfactoriness, if any, of his answers is judged by Polus in terms of the immediate partner in the discussion (who happens in this case to be the weaker man) and has no reference to any worth in the nature of the answers themselves. Polus is an eager but not-quite-collected practitioner of a skill that, if it were altogether an art, would render him better able to give principles and reasons and thus a fairer, more balanced account of rhetoric. He is not a fool, but his gift, such as it is, needs tuning both by the very experience that he appreciates and by the connected thinking that would turn the experience into art.

The relation of Polus to Gorgias and Socrates can be quickly dealt with. He is not referred to in the dialogue as the pupil of Gorgias, though references do come close to it: At 448d Socrates mentions to Gorgias how finely equipped Polus is for discoursing (*eis logous*); at 448d–e Socrates says, in what would imply that Gorgias is responsible, that Polus has had more practice in rhetoric than in discussion; at 462a Socrates verifies that Polus claims to know all that Gorgias knows, a boast hard to substantiate unless he had indeed been a pupil. This all comes to a certainty that Polus is intended to represent a longtime acquaintance of Gorgias, but only a high probability that he was once a pupil. The teacher-pupil relation is confirmed from sources other than Plato.

At 449b, Socrates complains about the tendency of Polus to make long speeches, despite his having so far opened his mouth for no more than a few brief lines. Does this complaint stem from Socrates' having known Polus before? Perhaps so, but more likely Socrates is reluctant to listen to him after quickly perceiving that Polus, in delivering himself of his few sentences, is heedless of objections, promptings, and legitimate questions from others. It is this more than any other feature, it would seem, that separates Polus' own style of discourse from whatever it is that Socrates practices. The rhetoric that Gorgias and Polus share is one of discharging, of giving out opinions, especially those having to do with praise and blame, and judging what effect these will have upon the hearer. Thus, in the course of a discussion, the rhetor can never develop more truthfully and worthily than his inclinations and capacities have allowed him at the outset. Teaching and learning are for him not cooperative processes.[14]

When Socrates asks Callicles whether Gorgias would be willing to discuss the power of his art, Callicles refers him to his distinguished guest, thereby momentarily putting himself at some remove from the latter and his calling. When Chaerephon asks what he believes is the same question of Gorgias, Polus breaks in at the very moment that Gorgias is saying that he is glad to be quizzed by others. From this one may assume that Polus considers himself the custodian of Gorgias' teachings, while Callicles probably does not. The differences between the two young men are not made altogether clear by this alone, but the hint should be sufficient to encourage the reader to look for further indications later on. Callicles' attitude toward rhetoric, while in general favorable, will turn out to be a mixed one. On the other hand, his attitude toward Socrates and philosophy, while seemingly cordial enough at first, shows itself in the sequel to be one of unvarnished hostility and spite. He will view Socrates not as a rhetor and teacher of rhetoric, which would be tolerable, but as an ineffectual, side-street philosopher of no set purpose who has practiced speculating long after he should have turned to more pressing matters in civic life. So the "battle" may be no more than a fencing with words, in his mind. Indeed, later on, in the midst of his dogged retreat before Socrates' attack (497b), he accuses Socrates of this very nitpicking. Although the battle may be nebulous in his mind when he first mentions it (447a), it becomes clearer and clearer in the later pages that the conflict between Socrates and Gorgias or Socrates and Polus is of little consequence as compared with the soul-searching, soul-wrenching quarrel that ensues after these two rhetors have lapsed into silence.

Trying to sum up what is common to the three rhetors appearing in the Prologue, we see that despite early emphasis upon styles of discourse, the conversations have little to do with asking and answering, with long and short speeches, or even with displaying and discussing, although these are sharply focused in supposedly settling in advance the way the machinery of the dialogue is to operate. The principal issues with Gorgias and Polus regard the possible moral worth of a skill pandering to the tastes of a public almost by definition ignorant of the rights and wrongs of the matters dealt with in a rhetorical address. More important for these issues are the substitutions taking place in the Prologue—Chaerephon, for Socrates at the latter's request; Polus for his elder in the absence of such a request from Gorgias; Gorgias for Polus at Socrates' urging;[15] again (461b) Polus, in his abrupt, skittish, yearling way, for Gorgias; then during the expounding of the crucial Divided Oblong of arts and their imitations that are panderings (463a–466a) Gorgias for Polus, followed (466a) by Polus' replacement of Gorgias and his subsequent entanglement in questions about art, power, justice, and happiness. After that (481b), when Polus is hopelessly mired, Callicles intervenes, again uninvited, and during a fairly extended passage Socrates himself takes the part of the by-then frustrated Callicles, as well as his own.

In the Prologue Socrates is something of the outsider and is outnumbered three to one, his little companion being of no particular help to him. In this gathering, however, the rhetors too are at a disadvantage, for not only will they be set against a man emerging as a mighty figure with whom two of them are unacquainted, they must also practice their common knack as best they can against a most formidable adversary, an irresistible one whose principles are bound in iron and adamant (509a), however often he may vary his tactical defense of them, mastering the little skills of his opponents either by long practice or as he goes along. The three are never really able to speak as they would to a lawcourt or assembly; they must to a considerable degree play by Socratic rules, of which hints abound almost from the very outset. This trio is, moreover, inhibited by the peculiar combination of poised immobility and driving momentum that characterizes Socrates. It is not such a wonder that in the end they are, each one separately and as forming a trio, put to a stuffy, uncomfortable silence by the interplay of their natures and of their articulated thoughts with those of Socrates. Whether they are *defeated* as well is a much more difficult question, to be treated later in our own account.

What *are* the rules that Socrates, sometimes openly, sometimes in concealment, imposes upon the discourse? They are not many, but suffice to hinder his opponents from using every one of their schemes and devices to their own advantage, however successfully they may use some of them. Short speeches are more acceptable, for the most part, than long; the best discourse consists of intimately connected questions and answers; for this purpose the short speeches are *always* better; the questions and answers themselves must not be part of a display, a routine; praise and blame are not necessarily the end of discussion, although it may seek to establish relations of better and worse; nothing should be irrelevant in the course of the discussion. Admittedly these overlap at some points, but they are all implicit in the evolution of the debate.

The second way in which Socrates is able to best his three opponents lies in the native shrewdness with which he divines their capabilities and weaknesses, their desires and aversions. Just as a therapist acutely establishes, at least in outline, a diagnosis from the first session or two with a neurotic patient and plans a method to restore him to health, Socrates has a gift of sizing up the strengths and shortcomings of his interlocutors and diagnosing their ambitions, sicknesses, fears, and intellectual prowess from the first handful of their statements, queries, evasions, courtesies. Thus Gorgias almost immediately presents himself in an image of achievement, affluence, outward success; but all these are for Socrates merely the adjuncts of excellence and are in turn faint imitations of inner worth. There is a likeness between this imitation and what is imitated, and Gorgias has never considered either the distinction or the likeness—excellence and status are all one to him. The attack upon Gorgias will first make him spell out his denial of the appropriate distinctions (knowledge and opinion, reality and appearance, truth and belief, and so forth) and then show him that his denial is out of harmony with what he offers as his underlying credo.

The tactics of Socrates is a topic suggesting that we turn to the nature of the debate and leave the debaters behind for the time being. What are the relations between question and answer, short and long speeches, and the refutations permeating the rest of the dialogue? For one thing, it is likely that questions are short, whereas answers can be short or long. One is refuted, it seems, through questions, not through answers, which simply offer oppositions not necessarily more plausible than the original statements. Yet refutative questions imply and even demand answers contradicting those statements. In both stating a thesis and substantiating it, the longer the speech the greater the cumulative effect upon the hearer (up to the point which the astute rhetor could determine). Giving a long speech allows less time for one's opponent and more difficulty in selecting the most salient or most vulnerable assertions for countering. The refutations need to be carried on in a small group, for in a large hall or open-air space it would be virtually impossible to conduct a rapid-fire sequence of questions and responses; the only opposition would be presented as another speech. Here the one proposing a thesis would have mainly to fear a more ringing voice from his opponent, or some tidier phrases, or a message which happened to be more nearly in tune with the present but temporary passions of the audience. In a smaller space, with fewer listeners, it is Socrates, not the three rhetors, who will offer the chance to refute or be refuted, and the only justification for his offer is that the audience assembled for this occasion is as small as we have supposed.

A display can, as the Prologue has made clear, consist of long or short speeches. That by Gorgias has been likened by Callicles to an elegant feast, thus hinting that it aims at pleasure, and a pleasure, furthermore, most like that of the pleasures of the body. Later, when Socrates debates with Gorgias, the other rhetors and Chaerephon take *this* to be pleasing to the audience and wish therefore to continue, thus equating the making of displays with the exercise of inquisitive and refutative discussion. The notion of battle, which may be applied subsequently to the proceedings of the day—the Prologue does not make this clear— falls a little outside the scope of the arts mentioned by Gorgias and Socrates, and indeed the only reference is a derogatory one by Socrates to the disgrace entailed in employing abuse on both sides in a conversation (457c–d). We have said that the mention of battle by Callicles is left vague and ambiguous, and in addition to the possibilities of squabbles with each of the three rhetors it may be construed as referring to the struggles internal to the souls of each of these men, or again to the struggle for recognition of supremacy of either the political life advocated by Socrates or its somewhat depraved imitation advocated by Callicles himself. If the debate were to be won by the latter, then feast and battle would amount to the same thing.

As for question and answer, there may be some desire to know on the part of the questioner, but little to impart real knowledge by the rhetors when they answer. When Socrates asks, he is recognizing the need to uncover and rectify possible inconsistencies in the statements and practices of others. Eventually, the notion of questioning takes the form of broaching three important queries (500c–d) that set the entire content and form of the last third of the dialogue. These are in some sense questions that can have one-sentence, informative answers, but the answers themselves must be ferreted out at considerable length.

*   *   *

The questions—and answers—can well be the subjects themselves of further questions or statements, or demands. In the course of the dialogue, a discussion (to use a term embracing all these pairs of contraries having to do with discourse in general) that by involution has discussion itself for a subject matter replaces discussion about display; the consideration of a just rhetoric has replaced rhetorical display as an art; and at last a question of the best life is raised, to supplant rhetoric as a just or unjust instrument. This full sequence is in a measure foreshadowed in kind though not in detail by the rapid interchange of roles in the Prologue, which warns the reader that such shifts in topics are going to take place—decisively and rationally. As in any dialogue by Plato, there is some thread or network binding the whole together.

As a result of these alterations, some abrupt, others very gradual, the participants and after them the readers are made to realize that early sections of the dialogue imply in every example, every image, every analogy, that the chief issue between Socrates and the three rhetors facing him is not the techniques of rhetoric but their moral and social effect. As a trivial but illuminating example of this, Chaerephon's acceptance of satisfying an audience as a standard (448a–b) counts him out as a true Socratic more than does the evident thickness of his wit.

There are four, and only four, possibilities as regards the unities of the Prologue and of the remainder of the Gorgias. Either (1) the Prologue is unified and the remainder is also, or (2) the Prologue is and the remainder is not; again, if the Prologue is not unified then (3) the remainder may still be, or (4) it is not. If (4) is true, there is no case to be made for any substantial artistry with which the dialogue as a whole has been composed, and if (3) is true, then at least the dialogue's worth is diminished by so much as an irrelevant preliminary passage takes away from the main course of the discussion. If (2) is to be accepted, which would be most unlikely, it might help to prove that the author was adept at coordinating a short passage, but all at sea in a large composition. At any rate, this would be little better than case (4). If, however, we wish to prove—and eventually we shall indeed so wish—that the *Gorgias* is integrated in a masterly way, both artistically and philosophically, even when departing from strictest deductive logic, we must elaborate three points: first, that the Prologue has a unity; second, that the remainder has a unity; and third, that both portions, unequal as they are in length and scope, fit together well. We have already treated the first and given it an affirmative response; for the second and third we have only been able to hint at our opinions. It is like showing how tightly bound together are the luminous fifteen notes of the horn call commencing Bruckner's *Symphony No. 4* and then assuming that all the rest holds together as wonderfully well; the task at that point is far from done. The prologues to many of the Platonic dialogues differ greatly from each other and do not, as a rule, literally anticipate or deliberately summarize all that is about to be expounded in detail. (This is not Aristotle's *Rhetorical Art*.) The *Gorgias* is no treatise and the Prologue, once its content is viewed in the multicolored light of the plural manners of its presentation, is no ordinary preamble. One can only guess from the Prologue read prospectively that the rest of a remarkable day will be filled with unnumbered windings and turnings of the discussion.

Certainly, we cannot ask the Prologue to unify singlehandedly the rest of the dialogue. If the rest does not hang together, no virtue of the Prologue can prevent the *Gorgias* from being a loose concatenation of dispersed utterances, joined by vague and implausible associations of ideas. It must consist of parts, and of parts of those parts, selected because of their affinity to common terms arranged in definite orders. The Prologue merely suggests where the reader should look in the sequel to find out where and how the parts should be joined. Then, and only then, will the Prologue have played its full role, and its own connection with the bulk of the great dialogue can be assured.

RHETORIC, JUST AND UNJUST

(449c–461b)

Foreshadowing, however faintly, not only the colloquy with Gorgias but to some degree the remainder of the dialogue as well, the Prologue might appear sufficiently independent of the first of the three major sections of the work to warrant giving it separate status altogether. It seems advisable, however, to link it more closely to the discussion with the great rhetor because it aims primarily to ask the pair of questions posed by Socrates regarding Gorgias, Who is he? and, What does he profess and teach? The conversation with Gorgias would be lost without the Prologue, while that with Polus would be less adrift though it would certainly be lost without the colloquy with Gorgias just preceding it; that with Callicles could partly be cut loose from the Prologue, less easily from the colloquy with Gorgias, but would hardly make sense without its ties to the conversation with Polus; a sliding scale of relevances.

The major portion of the colloquy with Gorgias (449c–461b) deals with rhetoric as a power and with the transmission though not transfer of this power to others. Opening with an attempt first to define rhetoric and then to delimit the definition thus gained (449c–456a), it launches after that into the question, What is involved in teaching and influencing pupils? and another, How far should one take responsibility if pupils abuse the power thus imparted to them? (456a–461b). This division reflects the two aforementioned questions that Socrates posed earlier (447b–c), in a way that the answer to one implies, loosely at any rate, the answer to the other.

Later we shall try to show how the first portion of this colloquy is a succession of dichotomies which Socrates introduces to force Gorgias to narrow the scope of his account of rhetoric and thereby discover what power is essential to it, what incidental, and what is indistinguishable in it from other arts. There is no desire to confine that power unduly, only to get rid of extraneous features that untidy thinking would include, were Gorgias not being prodded in another direction. Where these differences of opinion are not found and the subject matter can be expounded directly, one finds trichotomies.

⟨The first question (449c–d), *With what thing is rhetoric concerned*? asks not about the subject matter but about the activity and means used, *much as weaving and music are both makers, concerned with cloaks and melodies respectively. In its proper sphere, rhetoric is knowledge* (epistēmē) *concerned with speech or discourse* (peri logous).⟩ Since this is a statement unlike the ones about weaving and music, which made no claims to be knowledge but only to be art or making, and thus power, the concurrence of Gorgias that rhetoric is knowledge will show up later as a target for the Socratic elenchus (458e–459b). Meanwhile, he has fallen into the small trap. Apparently, it is one thing in Socrates' eyes to be able to make something, such as clothes or a tune, and quite another to know in any proper sense.[1] Making a melody, for example, would involve the spontaneous bubbling-up of feelings best expressible as a tuneful sequence, while knowledge of the melody might well include mathematical accounts of intervals, of harmonies implied in the melodic progressions, and other thoroughly reasoned analyses of means-and-ends relationships. This failure to see the distinction between knowledge and the power to make, to produce effects, will return later to haunt Gorgias. But meanwhile he is thinking loosely in another direction as well. The cloaks made by weaving and melodies by music are specific, separate things, put together in a determinate order calculated to be useful or pleasing. But to say that rhetoric is about speech is on a different level, for the speech, that is, syllables, nouns, clauses, and so forth, is not created but simply used by the rhetor.

⟨Socrates now pursues this idea by asking (449e–450b), *What kind of speech? Rhetoric makes men able to speak and to understand the things about which these men speak, but here there is no indication that understanding is equivalent to knowledge. Rhetoric is* not *concerned with all kinds of speech, for example, speech about health regimens.*⟩[2] There are two opposite dangers, the one stemming from the tendency of Gorgias and his wayward satellite Polus to arrogate universal powers to their art, the other to bind and cut off rhetoric from some parts of its legitimate subject matter.[3] To delimit the scope of rhetoric, first one must arrive at a definition and then in trying to show whether it is the highest art, possessing an infallible method aimed at producing nothing but the greatest goods. Gorgias, unfortunately, has leapt to the second question before tackling the first, and it is in the first that he must be specially coached by Socrates. Though Gorgias has omitted the preliminaries, obviously we cannot mean that he has never in his life realized that rhetoric is concerned with speech or, against all probability, that he has never grasped that rhetoric and some other arts differ from each other even if both use language. Instead, these statements about rhetoric must constitute a series of connected steps needed to establish it as an art of persuasive political speech. Gorgias was clearly a man concerned with order, but the order that Plato notes and parodies, in the *Symposium* (194e–197e) and in a sentence in the *Gorgias* itself (504d–e), is exhibited in balanced epithets, neat oppositions, that is, diction rather than rational content.[4]

A hint that Gorgias has scarcely ever been troubled over the *exact* nature of his art lies in the vague generalizations of which he must be cured by marking off the sort of speech helping to shape the arena in which rhetoric operates. The questions are now about subject matter; Socrates could instead have asked for a distinction between persuasive and argumentative speech, or persuasive and informative speech. But this would play into the hands of Gorgias, who would quickly trot out invidious comparisons.

⟨According to Socrates (450a–b), *medicine and gymnastics and all other arts are like rhetoric in enabling people to speak and understand what they are talking about.* To this Gorgias gives an odd answer: *Rhetoric is pursued entirely through speech, whereas the other arts are partly verbal, partly manual.*⟩ If rhetoric is really different from those others, then is it neither irrelevant nor depreciating to say that the others have something else besides, and do not depend upon speech alone? Gorgias evinces some pride in this account of rhetoric (450c).

⟨The objection—or question—raised now by Socrates (450c–d) is the obvious one, that *not all the other arts use speech combined (or alternating) with something else; mathematical arts proceed through language alone, and so does draught-playing.*⟩

⟨*The odd and even (the subjects of arithmetic), their relations (topics of logistic), and the fast and slow stars, (astronomy), are not proper topics of rhetoric which*, Gorgias says, *is about the greatest of human affairs (450e–451c).*⟩ This last sets rhetoric apart from any consideration of divine affairs, which eventually will become a chief ingredient in the judgment of the human (523a–527a). Gorgias is, of course, eager to see his art upon a pedestal, but misses this opportunity to give it that last dignity. Socrates takes the point for what it is worth, however, for he will not until the close of the dialogue, long after Gorgias has dropped out of the argument, lay down any foundation for erecting a theory of divine justice. ⟨He merely points out now (451d–452c) that *a drinking song lists several pleasures as the highest goods—health, beauty, and wealth obtained without cheating. Not only that*, he says, *but the physician, the trainer, and the moneymaker would all claim to be supplying the greatest good, for these three are the proper ends or purposes of their several arts.*⟩ These three arts are now placed on the same level; later, the moneymaker, who merely supplies external goods, will be yielding the stage to the doctor and gymnast, who furnish goods of the body. Where the goods offered by rhetoric would fit remains to be seen.

⟨Socrates cajoles Gorgias a little, and so he makes answer(452d–e) in a double statement, an effort to define rhetoric at last. *The greatest good is a cause of freedom to mankind and at the same time a cause of dominion or rule to individuals in their cities. Rhetoric is the power to persuade with speeches (a) judges in lawcourts, (b) councilors in chambers, (c) commons in the assembly, and (d) audiences at any other meetings on public affairs.*⟩ Gorgias by this time has warmed to his task, no longer giving the clipped, one-word responses that he did (on request from Socrates) at first. Because the preliminary work has been done for him by hints in the Prologue and stimulating suggestions from Socrates, he is now able to give a laudatory formula and claims more than Socrates had been intending for him to say. One suspects that his statement is the one with which Gorgias has opened countless lectures to pupils to make them aware of the power of the discipline they are proposing to learn, and of its universal, or next-to-universal, employment. The rhetor brings freedom to mankind everywhere, but status and power to himself—an almost impossible combination on the face of it, unless one can specify what enlightened courses the ruler must take to ensure the freedom for others. But even this is a contradictory notion, for the regulated state which provides freedom for all must do so by balancing the claims of everyone, and this is bound to hinder some parts of that freedom.

Oddly, the Gorgian formula leaves out the very activities that Gorgias has been carrying on before the advent of Socrates and Chaerephon at today's meeting: display speech and (presumably) the answering of questions from the audience. Gorgias has, if we may put it thus, displayed display rhetoric, but in his formula he has omitted it in favor of forensic and political speechmaking, both of them aimed at altering the actions of people rather than simply gaining their admiration. Why, then, should he engage in displays? The answer seems to lie in the very scene that forms the present setting. Gorgias is from another part of the world (though not barbarian), but has been invited to a rich man's home and will doubtless receive gifts, in addition to having the opportunity to attract students in the audience assembled by Callicles. This displaying is left out of the definition, which rests upon the conviction that rhetoric is a fine thing dealing with the greatest matters in life, and is presumably far above the currying of favors to gain an income.[5] ⟨But the truth will out in Gorgias' very next sentence, for he says that *the doctor and trainer will be the rhetor's slaves, and the moneymaker will be making money not for himself but for his rhetor* (452e).⟩

What could Gorgias mean by making doctor and trainer his slaves, and the money-getter a mere getter of money for Gorgias? It is easy enough to say that they are slaves to him if all men are, but this begs the question. If this cannot be taken for granted then are the doctor and gymnast expected to wait on Gorgias himself, or to tend to whoever is designated by Gorgias as being worthy of attention? This is not slavery in any proper sense; and it is not slavery if the moneymaker is a kind of classical investment broker. If, however, he makes money thinking it will be for himself, and Gorgias somehow persuades him to give it up, then Gorgias is admitting to Socrates that he is a cheat, a confidence man supreme. But this accords poorly with the attitude he strikes throughout his colloquy. If Gorgias snatches the money, he is at best a tyrant, a thief, or a tax collector. This is another instance of the bragging of Gorgias, rather more idle than his first group of boasts, but more difficult to object to on experiential grounds. It is easy enough to check the veracity of a statement that Gorgias can speak briefly or at length, but to look further at his relation to the three suppliers of goods and services will mean investigating his private life in a way that Socrates would be loath to undertake.

⟨To the relatively full defining statement by Gorgias, Socrates responds (452e–453a) by pruning it of those kinds of persons who are persuaded and the subjugations rhetoric brings about. *Rhetoric is simply the artificer* (dēmiourgos) *of persuasion, which is its entire business* (pragmateia) *and epitome* (kephalaion) *of its ends. It has no power outside of the souls of its hearers.*⟩ The addition of the word *souls* is instructive, implying, when taken in conjunction with doctors and trainers of the body, a distinction between soul and body that Gorgias has previously overlooked. To him, people are people, just as rhetoric is rhetoric, whether using short or long speeches, new or old questions, sound or unsound arguments.

More important, however, is that this new agreed-upon definition of rhetoric is not really the logical outcome of the divisions by which Gorgias' statement regarding rhetoric has been reached. His own definition (that it is aimed at the greatest good and is the cause of freedom, the power to persuade) resulted from the successive narrowing of the scope of rhetoric, as we have already noted. Now, however, Socrates suddenly enlarges it by dropping off the special kinds of persons addressed, retaining only the central notion that it is the power of persuasion, though Socrates does change *power* to *artificer* because *power* is still in question. The pruning is a strategy that will prove useful to him, and in fact harmonize well enough with conceptions of rhetoric entertained by his three opponents: Gorgias will again boast, this time of his ability to cajole a patient to swallow a doctor's bitter medicine or undergo the knife (456b), Polus will hint that the self-exculpatory lies of Archelaus are rhetorical in essence (471a–c), and Callicles will treat Socrates' alleged shifting from nature to convention and back again as a rhetorical device (483a–b). None of these, it goes without saying, has to do with judges or crowds.

⟨*Gorgias now* (453a) *approves Socrates' revision*, apparently taking for granted that "highest of human affairs" and "of judges, councilmen, commons and other political audiences" would be added as a matter of course.⟩

Why does Socrates not ask Gorgias about the terms that are new and hence unclear, such as *freedom, slavery, ruling, ruled?* Helping to define his conception of the power of rhetoric, they are evidently important to Gorgias. Indeed, he conceives of the rhetor as free and his listeners as slaves. He seems to believe that in every political gathering, institutional or otherwise, when men are being persuaded the persuaders use the occasion to gain their own "freedom"—whatever that is—and at the same time coerce their listeners. There is no middle ground, such as dialogue, on which both (or all) parties benefit from discourse that hampers and entangles no one.

The finding of an explicit definition being the chief aim of this part of the *Gorgias*, Socrates is unwilling to divert attention to topics on which no premises have been developed that would enable him either to accept or amend whatever definitions were offered. The purpose of a Socratic dialogue is not a glossary of useful words but the exploration of relevant parts of a subject matter wherewith to clarify its leading term or pair of contraries. In the process of defining this single term or pair, companion words such as *freedom* and *slavery* are brought forward, but if not clarified in ways other than by definition they will soon be discarded or the dialogue will end in frustration. Such ways include the putting of the terms into various kinds of oppositions, the finding of synonyms, matching terms to images, and the like.

As we said earlier, the discussion has proceeded dichotomously, to refine the notion of the special concern of rhetoric. This has turned out to be words or discourses, both speaking and understanding them, as against some unnamed counterpart, doubtless an art such as racing or dancing that uses no language. The arts of discourse work by discourse alone or else they join it with manual operations. Those using nothing but discourse deal with the greatest of human affairs, or, like the mathematical arts, they treat of numbers, rates of speed, and so forth. The art dealing with the highest human good (freedom) is divided from those of the physician, trainer, and money-maker, and persuades various political audiences and functionaries.[6] What Socrates produces at this point is a pair of objections (453a–456c) to the epistemic aspects of this claim, although the dichotomous procedure is still maintained in making them. Gorgias makes answer.

The first effort to delimit the definition (453a–455a) is to show that the implied boast, carried over from the little passage at 449d to the effect that rhetoric persuades to knowledge, overshoots the mark. Rhetoric generates belief, nothing better, so even if it deals with the greatest of human affairs it must still be subordinate to whatever could be entirely secure, as knowledge is secure, about these matters.

The delimitation commences with a brief interlude (453a–b), the first of many in the dialogue that digress into questions of the order of the conversation or else the conduct and characters of the participants. These interludes vary in length from a line or so to a couple of pages, and though they appear to interrupt the course of the argument, they are of great significance in helping the reader to determine its meaning and progress. As a rule, they take up either methodological matters or else personal themes that have already been implied in the Prologue (447a–449c), which has shown how highly charged are the emotional issues between the four main speakers. The *Gorgias* contains far more of these interspersions than does any other work from Plato's hand. We expect to take some notice of all of them, not for the sake of ritual completeness but because the dialogue lacks the certainties of a mathematical demonstration, and thus demands that any interpreter make full use of all the hints that Plato has been foresighted enough to supply.

⟨In this interlude, Socrates says (453a–b) *he discusses in order to learn what is really the case, and he persuades himself that Gorgias does likewise.*⟩ Socrates is explaining himself for more than one reason: (a) he senses that Gorgias, for all his interchanges with public and private audiences, has had little experience with Socratic debate, hence Socrates wishes to reassure the veteran rhetor that there is no reason for alarm, that he is not unfriendly; (b) he is drawing a distinction between appearance and reality that has been implicit already in the bad imitations of their respective models given by Chaerephon and Polus. This distinction will be reintroduced in various ways throughout the dialogue; (c) he is making a serious effort to show that he, too, is going to be following a persuasive line of arguing—that for once he is willing to pursue reality with a method only partly adapted to its strictest apprehension. This disclaimer must, we maintain, be taken at face value now and for the remainder of the work, for if not, then overly strong expectations of logical rigor are sure to be disappointed. Finally (d), Socrates is also twitting Gorgias about persuasion, but it is a piece of double irony since underneath it Socrates is also in earnest in a way that Gorgias could not possibly divine. ⟨In fact, Gorgias' bewilderment is reflected in his immediate response, a sort of *What then? What does all this mean?*⟩

The argument proper (453b–455a) is subdivided into the explanation of two main questions (453b–454b) and very brief replies by Gorgias to these (454b). ⟨The questions are first stated and then illustrated by Socrates: *What, in reality, is this persuasion? and again, With what things does it deal?*⟩ It is thus to be fathomed by Gorgias that although he has tried already to give answers to both queries (respectively at 450b–c and 451d), he has not succeeded in stating them clearly enough, no doubt because it was the word *rhetoric* rather than *persuasion* that was used in both cases. ⟨By way of illustration of the first question, Socrates says (453c) that *one can fairly ask what sorts of figures are painted by Zeuxis, provided other artists are figure painters as well, hence it is also reasonable to ask, since arithmetic is also an artificer of persuasion, exactly how rhetoric is unique in this respect.* The second "explanation" is nothing more than a repetition of the question: *Of what is rhetoric the ⟨persuasive⟩ art?* (454a–b)⟩ It is a little unusual to think of arithmetic (and the other mathematical sciences) as being persuasive, but of course this is just the point: One believes the results of an arithmetical proof or a rhetorical harangue, regardless of differences in subject matter. What remains to be seen, however, is whether the convictions produced by each of these are on the same solid footing. This question seems not to have entered the mind of Gorgias.

⟨As a rejoinder, he says (454b) *the persuasion is that found in lawcourts and any other crowds, and that it is persuasion about the just and the unjust.*⟩ He thus distinguishes his own calling merely by stating not its specific properties, if it has any, but by an external feature, that is, where it is performed and heard. But unless he had in mind some further notion of magniloquence or sublimity, he could not, even with the help of such an account, hope to make good his claim to having the fairest art or to being one of its finest practitioners.

To say that rhetoric is concerned with the just and the unjust is no more informative than to say that a doctor is concerned with health and disease. Yet this is precisely the issue. Gorgias comes to Athens from a far-off island, he has a new art, not one which like medicine is easily traceable back to Homer, and he is no mere novice but has achieved both eminence in speaking and effectiveness in teaching. So it will behoove Socrates to ask him, above all other men, about the nature of his art. And since he can deal with a great many kinds of topics in multifarious situations, it will be well to ask him for the very essential one that occupies him, otherwise, it might be thought that answering any chance question that came along (448a) would be his forte and his profession.[7]

Again, to say that the just and the unjust are the topics when persuading any crowds *other* than juries and councillors is to assume too much. To take an example, Pericles' speech on the war dead of Athens is only incidentally about justice and its contrary,[8] and so are countless other pieces of display and deliberative (i.e., politico-economic) oratory. Why would Gorgias simplify the discussion of rhetoric's main topics so radically, assuming that he had for years been a speaker on many kinds of occasions? The best answer seems to be compounded of three considerations: first, he was under obligation to keep his speeches short, and it was a matter of extreme pride that he could do so (449c); second, he was slightly fearful that were he to make too complicated a response he would be tripped up by his clever opponent; third, he was hopeful that justice and injustice would appeal to the present audience (and to Socrates) as indeed being of the highest rank in human affairs— nothing could be more noble than references to these, and would help in establishing his dignity. All three suggestions are the thoughts that might well pass through the head of a public speaker, a man well able to please any crowd, and they are only partially related to any real reasons why justice and injustice are central to all persuasive speech.

⟨Socrates offers (454b–c) another interlude, saying that *he suspected that this was what was meant, but it is important not to guess at one another's words; Gorgias must complete his own statement as his hypothesis allows.*⟩ In this stricture against guessing, Socrates is surreptitiously indicating that this is the very thing that Gorgias has been content to do. As a component in a display, whether of speechmaking or answering questions, it is satisfactory enough; but it falls short of being the right means to serious discussion or instruction.

⟨There is a return (454c–455a) to the point that *rhetoric creates belief, not knowledge, the latter being true only, the former being true or false indifferently. This rests upon the fact that having (already) learned is different from having (already) believed. Rhetoric,* Socrates adds, *is used in lawcourts, and the rhetor would not be able to teach, that is, generate knowledge, in the short time that is given to speechmaking.*⟩ This ends the first attempt to limit the definition of rhetoric.

We must pause to ask on what level this whole discussion is taking place, in order more clearly to identify knowledge. The scene is laid after a *successful* display by Gorgias; he is not asking, nor is Polus asking, what is the cause of some failure to impress and excite the audience, and indeed everyone seems poised to hear him again, an enthusiasm which Gorgias appears willing to encourage. He is not searching his soul in regard to whether he is in an honorable profession. If Socrates, fresh from the agora and in the company of a commonplace man, is to enter the gathering and the conversation, it must initially be on the terms of his hosts for the day, not his own. He has wrung something of a concession from Gorgias in getting the latter to promise to give short replies to his questions. But that is trifling, for Gorgias is well practiced in such replies. Socrates' late arrival, after the main event is supposedly over, means that he will have less freedom to instruct—as he would no doubt prefer—but must comport with the wishes of the others, chiefly the celebrity, so far as possible. His only requests, that displays be postponed, and that short questions and answers be the rule, do not matter to Gorgias. Almost from the outset, however, it becomes evident that Gorgias is unable to grasp the epistemic differences between dialectic of the more exalted sort and the rhetoric to which he is accustomed. Socrates must try to persuade Gorgias with what might be called bits and pieces of a reasoned discourse, but in so doing must lower its standards so that he is inducing changes of opinion, if he is lucky, by means of persuasive devices that are only moderate improvements over those of his adversary. At the very end of his colloquy with Gorgias he says that to untangle all the contradictions will take a long time; this is even after Gorgias has agreed with him at almost every turn. Agreement here is not the same as the production of knowledge.

What does Socrates mean by saying that speechmaking could not produce knowledge "in a short time"? It being impertinent to answer this with minutes and hours, we must be content to say that evidently it has to do with (a) the time of preparation of the teacher to amass and organize his subject matter in a way suited to produce such knowledge; (b) the time required to impart his lesson in a point-by-point presentation, and (if Socrates is the teacher) requesting concurrence in each step; (c) the time required for the teacher to size up his audience, be it large or small, so as to temper his presentation to those listening (again, a special Socratic trait). Agreement alone is an insufficient condition for the grasp of truth, but if there is disagreement then truth is impossible. For truth itself, the arrival at truth, and the joint grasp of truth by the participants all operate together. Put differently, one may say that truth comes to active minds disciplined by discursive interchange.

We might, then, distinguish four situations:

1. use of the best method that because of excellent respondents reaches agreement;
2. use of the best method that because of prejudiced or ill-prepared respondents fails to reach that agreement;
3. use of some second-best or other substitute method that reaches agreement;
4. use of a second-best method that fails.

If what we have been saying about Socrates' strategies and accommodations is correct, the *Gorgias* can at best prove to be an instance of the third sort. Socrates often abdicates the calling of the pure dialectician, especially in later pages, when face to face with a Callicles whose proclivities, expressed and implied, make it incumbent upon Socrates to use every means available to redirect those tendencies. On the other hand, it will be less than candid if we make this accommodation an excuse for sloppy thinking on Plato's part.[9]

⟨Socrates speaks first (455a–c): *I am, he says, unable to determine what to say about rhetoric* (455a–b).⟩ It is quite possible that this is intended to bring down his opponent's guard, but more likely that Socrates is groping for a workable strategy when so many cards are stacked against him. Besides all the problems imposed by the dramatic setting, there is a possible difficulty with the subject of rhetoric itself, which may in fact turn out to be a universal art, and would be correspondingly hard to pin down. As regards this last, Socrates is at a disadvantage if he wishes to secure agreement from Gorgias. A handful of other points remain: (a) insufficient examples of rhetorical discourse have thus far been presented, although Socrates turns out to have read Polus' text on the subject (462c) and has heard about Gorgias' displays; (b) there have been insufficient agreed-upon premises between the two antagonists; (c) there has been very little account of the other arts (except to list some of them) upon which to base a thoroughgoing critique of rhetoric, if it is indeed one among those arts. ⟨*When the city selects doctors or shipbuilders, the most skillful are to be chosen, and the rhetor does not offer advice,* says Socrates. *Similiarly, when the city decides to build walls or fight battles, the architects and generals are consulted* (455b–c).⟩ Socrates means that political decisions, which appear to be about the just and unjust, are in point of fact about the technicalities of particular states of health, military structures and operations, and the like. In another interlude (455c–d), Socrates promises to hazard a question or two in behalf of members of the audience wishing to assure themselves of the genuineness of rhetoric but who are too ashamed to ask.

⟨To the objections of Socrates, Gorgias now makes reply (455d–456a). *You yourself,* he says, *have already shown the whole power of rhetoric; the military installations of Athens were built upon the advice of Themistocles and Pericles, not the artificers—you, who say you once heard Pericles, must know that the rhetors are the ones to advise and gain consent* (455d–456a).⟩ This is an odd retort, and Socrates could if he wished counter with the historical point that both these imposing figures were not only public speakers but also able commanders of high rank.[10] True, neither man was a military architect, but the need for a fort or a dock is ordinarily first decided upon and recommended to the public by a field or naval commander who is to be the actual user of the installation and in that sense the expert. Gorgias has unwittingly played into the hands of Socrates. ⟨But the immediate response is unexpected (456a): *The power of rhetoric seems daimonic when looked at in this way!* exclaims Socrates,⟩ again a double irony, for the obvious sarcasm contains the truth that the power of the rhetor is not derived from rational deliberations but is a kind of unexplained force.[11]

Gorgias has made concessions to Socrates having to do with the confining of his art, but once again boasts about its superior capacity to make its effect felt in decisions lying within the scope of other arts and crafts. To assert this ability, however, Gorgias must prove Socrates' very point, that the rhetor moves boldly in fields where he cannot possibly claim real competence. The other point immediately follows: If the rhetor is ignorant but persuasive, then the audience must likewise be ignorant if it does not detect the speaker's shortcomings.

So much for the first half of the discourse between these two men. After having reached a stage (453a) where defining rhetoric is possible, the discourse continues by using dichotomies to establish the fact that since rhetoric is the artificer of persuasion it must be accomplished either by a teacher imparting knowledge (454e) or by a rhetor persuading to belief without the firmer foundation of knowledge (455c). Here we have, according to Socrates, the populace seeking advice from the experts, or, according to Gorgias, from the popular speakers. It is not so stated, but obviously the speakers might even contravene the advice of experts when personal motives lead them in other directions.

The second half of the discussion with Gorgias now opens; the topic is mainly the second boast of Gorgias, that he could make others, here and everywhere, to be like himself, that is, able to wield enormous power through language. What then, if those others should misuse rhetoric? Gorgias launches into what turns out to be his only extended discourse of this part of his day. It consists of some preliminary assertions regarding rhetoric per se (456a–c), then a few regarding pupils, their using and abusing of this art (456c–457c). The response from Socrates comes soon (457c–461b). ⟨Gorgias, warmed and heartened once again by Socrates' apostrophe to rhetoric as daimonic, now replies that it comprises almost all powers at *once, another claim which he thinks he can prove. A patient is better persuaded by the rhetor to undergo the harsh treatments of a doctor than he is by the doctor himself; the rhetor, not doctors, also can persuade the people at large to appoint a certain doctor to a public office; the rhetor is more persuasive, indeed, than is any of the other artificers, even in their own fields, and could well count on being appointed at any meeting* (456a–c).⟩

About the rather extravagant arrogation of Gorgias: He is silent on one significant point, for he does not say, "I went with a friend to get a patient to take what that patient *thought* was medicine prescribed and prepared by a doctor, but *I* knew all along that my companion was no doctor and that the drug was a lethal dose—perhaps some hemlock. But I still persuaded the patient, as I owed a favor to my friend, who wanted the patient out of the way." Gorgias feels, on the occasion of his visit, that the draught is really medicinal, and he would go to a patient only if accompanied by a genuine physician. Gorgias would not deliberately abuse his power in such open-and-shut cases where the variables are within his ken.[12] On the other hand, we might venture some personal reflections on Gorgias in light of his boast. It shows arrogance—"I can do it," he says in effect, "without knowledge of medicine at all, and am better at it than those having this knowledge. And after all, it is the actual *taking* of the medicine, which I can arrange, that is important." Yet his remark in the text can subordinately be taken as a humble confession—"I do not know medicine, I am an amateur, an outsider." Yet Gorgias overrides this later by insisting that one need not know medicine if one has a superior art. The rhetor is no mere appendage, in his own eyes, to the doctor or engineer, and implies that he is completing, perfecting, their several functions. They ought to be able to do what he can, though he outdoes them easily.

Let us put it otherwise. Gorgias has no special sciences and knows that he has none, but he does have something that he has taught himself to deem better, a master art or—he might just as well be saying—a master science. He has not yet admitted that he instills nothing more than belief, which must mean that for him belief is either of a piece with knowledge and blended with it or else is superior to it. The truth is, one wonders whether this would make any difference to Gorgias; when the votes are counted, it is their numbers rather than the quality of the judgments entertained by individual voters that are important. For him, all other arts would be subordinate to rhetoric, all other human goods would be subordinate to the freedom of the rhetor, and political life would have to be judged by the way this superordination and subordination worked out in practice.

Gorgias has said (456a) that rhetoric captures all the powers and keeps them under control of the rhetor; this military expression reminds us of the very opening lines with Callicles about impending battles (447a). The comparison is also kept up in the next passage.[13]

⟨The conversation surveys (456d–457a) some uses to which rhetoric is put by pupils of the master-rhetor, whom Gorgias consistently identifies with himself. *Our employment of rhetoric*, he says, *should be like that in all other contests, boxing, wrestling, and armed combat being examples; none of these should be used against everyone, friends as well as enemies. On the other hand*—and here is Gorgias' most important proviso—*merely because a boxer has struck his parents or relatives or friends is no reason to hate the trainer who taught him his art.*⟩

Those who live a quiet, secure life—if there still be any such exceptions to the rule—should remember that to Gorgias the lawcourts and especially the Assembly are places very real to him, and that he counts himself not a casual visitor to them but a combatant, more than enough reason to couple his profession with that of a boxer. The debate that he is having with Socrates is on an important matter, the very foundation on which the entire career of Gorgias has been built, yet to him it would seem at this stage considerably tamer than the rough-and-tumble of the public assemblies. Indeed, it would appear more like the displays he has put on before polite audiences. This accounts for the analogy he draws between rhetoric and martial arts, though it cannot fully explain the superficiality of his attitude. For one thing, his analogy is with the arts having to do with bodily injury or constraint, and it seems not to occur to him that it would be more appropriate to liken his own to sophistic or some other art that could improve or injure the soul. For another, he has no conception of any responsibility for the behavior of those he trains—and none for the advice that he himself would give in the Assembly or elsewhere. If he "does a good job," if the votes go his way, he is satisfied, can rub his hands—and wash them of all blame.

⟨These trainers, Gorgias continues (456d–457a) *have taught their arts assuming that they will be used justly by their pupils, that is, against enemies and unjust persons generally. The trainers are not base, and only those who use the art wrongly are base.*⟩ The question for us arises when one considers the sincerity of Gorgias' absolving the rhetor in advance. The mere fact that he admits that boxing can be used to injure just and unjust persons alike proves that he knows it to be an art dangerous at *any* time, especially when there is a bare possibility of misuse. If rhetoric is indeed like boxing, any attempt to clear the rhetor of charges of disseminating dangerous information will seem to be special pleading, and will hardly be reassuring to the little audience present, some of whose members undoubtedly will enroll for Gorgias' teaching. These members would be looking for three things: the expertness and the probity of Gorgias, and the likelihood that they will gain substantially from signing up. The paradox is that while Gorgias is seeking to guarantee his expertness and probity he is at the same time emphasizing the hazards involved in the possible gains. It could be an especially damaging admission in their eyes, for it implies that if they use rhetoric mistakenly Gorgias will no longer back them but will try to free himself of any burdens rather than coming to their aid as well-meaning but immature practitioners. The remarks by Gorgias, then, are from the standpoint of that audience quite candid, but from the standpoint of Socrates they would be a great deal less than that. Although every art carries some risk, certainly boxing, wrestling, and armed combat are among the most dangerous of all, and in fact can cause immense damage even when not abused in any way.

To summarize: Good use and evil (unjust) use are both divided (theoretically) into defeating friends and defeating enemies, making four possibilities in all. But defeating friends justly is an empty class for Gorgias, and the remainder, namely defeating enemies justly, is accompanied by no criterion for determining who is an enemy. Again, defeating enemies unjustly would appear to someone of Gorgias' temperament to be an empty heading, so what is left is defeating friends (and relatives) unjustly. As a contentious art, rhetoric is in the same case with boxing and the like, though it is not altogether clear what Gorgias would mean by defeating friends by rhetoric. It *could* signify (a) winning an election (through superior powers of speech) over a friend running for the same office; (b) gaining the vote against a friend arguing a contrary position before an assembly; (c) securing the conviction of a friend being tried on criminal charges or a judgment against one being sued or impeached; (d) gaining popular applause more enthusiastic than that accorded a friend competing in a display contest. It is hard to see how a constructive use of rhetoric, such as defending or otherwise aiding someone, could be considered unjust if it were in behalf of an enemy, unless he were also an enemy of the existing government and supporting him became an act of treason.

Because Gorgias has thus far given no explicit indication of what he takes justice to be, we must gather from his other remarks exactly what this might be. First, he has made little of virtue in general, even as a mere broad class of which justice is a narrower one, and has not mentioned any of the other personal virtues, such as wisdom and temperance, often associated in one way or another with justice. Perhaps he thinks of justice as a political matter, a conventional arrangement between men and between groups of men, not some trait in the individual soul. Thus he would exhort an audience to act justly when all this means is to make the right decisions about rivers and harbors or appointments to public office.

Second, Gorgias' account of rhetoric has been self-centered; it is an art conceived as he himself practices and teaches it, and its dignity both reflects and supports his own dignity and prestige. What else could it be but the highest art if he has made it his calling? Turn about, what else could it become in his hands but the highest of arts? Justice from this standpoint is therefore the right apportioning of power, the gaining of it by the skilled rhetor, and the proper subordination of hoi polloi who have not been privileged to share his instruction. The link between the parts of his statement is this: Socrates has asked what is the power of his art, no doubt meaning thereby to ask what it can do for the betterment of the soul; but Gorgias takes the question as relating to political preferment and views rhetoric as the speediest, surest way to this goal accordingly. To him, rhetoric that merely persuaded men to virtuous actions and did not confer advantage upon the rhetor would be no rhetoric at all.

We would not pretend to divine what is really lurking in the back of Gorgias' mind during the conversation, and perhaps Plato himself did not, but it seems clear enough that these considerations are implied by what has gone on before and that when Socrates punctures the contentions of Gorgias it is because the distinguished rhetor's conception of justice is inadequate to take care of contingencies in the teacher-pupil relations that he has brought forward of his own accord. The teacher of rhetoric, on his showing, is fully responsible for the just employment of rhetoric by his pupils everywhere and consequently to be praised, but entirely free from blame for their unjust (though not necessarily unsuccessful) employment of it anywhere.

Third and last, the teachers of rhetoric are not base (*ponēroi*—457a), who do not use it rightly. The function and status of the teacher seems of itself to prevent exhortations to be used for the wrong ends. Thus Gorgias claims a double immunity; for as rhetor he will enslave others and thus be free of their efforts to subordinate him, and as teacher he will be beyond reproach even if he has schooled a generation or two of slick-tongued scalawags.

Putting all this together with the note of aggressiveness that has pervaded the Prologue and the more recent sallies, we conclude that underneath the surface geniality of Gorgias and his pleasurable display runs a river of faint red. Rhetoric is a weapon of war, it is a way of putting down the Others, the Many, even those most skilled in the arts of medicine and architecture. To these professions Gorgias opposes himself as if he were a champion pugilist able to beat down a squad of duffers. It is little wonder that he can see, without any coaching, that rhetoric in the hands of unjust pupils would be a danger to the city in both its private and its public sectors.

Weaving all through this is a plaint familiar in modern life: I have created and transmitted a potential hazard to society. If wrongly used, society is bound to suffer. ⟨*Do not hate me, hate the man who actually causes the damage.* Gorgias expends some little ingenuity in making this point (457b–c). *The rhetor,* he says, *could speak against everyone on everything but he should at least stop short of unjustly ruining the reputation of a doctor or some other practitioner.*⟩ We have two different kinds of comments.

On the one hand, we might say that when Gorgias says (457b) that the rhetor has *no reason* to steal the reputation of the doctor, et al., this flies in the face of his earlier (452e) remark that rhetoric will make the doctor and the trainer into slaves. It would be unjust to them, not because they have done no harm but because only a part of medicine is devoted to convincing patients to take medications or embark on regimens. The rest has to do with knowledge of the body, of foods, and so forth, and of this the rhetor admittedly knows nothing.

On the other hand, we can distinguish four cases: a just use of rhetoric in speaking *for* some man or institution; a just use in speaking *against*; an unjust use in speaking for; and an unjust use in speaking against. While Gorgias never pretends that all speaking against something is unjust, still he is careful not to offend—making enemies can lead to trouble. Furthermore, in praising Themistocles and Pericles (455e) he was taking the part of civic expansiveness such as better fortifications and walls and other public works. The abuse of rhetoric that he would dread to see exercised by any identifiable pupil would be not the third but the fourth case, for then a man's reputation could be destroyed unjustly and Gorgias could only beg such a man and his community not to turn against him as the ultimate cause of this defamation.

If a new rhetor feels no restraint and goes too far, we should not hate his teacher and expel him. There is no need, at least here, to speculate on whether Plato had in mind that the person of Gorgias, either as conceived in the dialogue or as the historical figure, had ever actually been forbidden a city for this reason, much as Protagoras was driven out of Athens. Obviously, the Gorgias of the dialogue seems secure enough in that metropolis, but perhaps he is worried, knowing Polus very well or knowing Callicles rather less well, that either or both men might become the very ones whose public speaking he would like to disown. ⟨The unjust pupils, he says (457c), *are the ones to be banished and executed.*⟩

The next four pages of text (457c–461b) are Socrates' examination of this position. His habit is not to mount a direct personal attack upon a man for his actions real or presumed, but rather to look into the meaning of his premises. During this, personal aspects of the position adopted are almost invariably brought into view.

First, there are a couple of interludes (457c–458e), and then the argument is embarked upon in earnest. The first interlude (457c–458b) is in regard to the participants as they can and wish to carry forward the argument, while the second (458b–e) records the wishes of the onlookers as they would have it conducted. The first is in respect to quality of discussion, the second to its completion. ⟨Socrates opens the first interlude by saying (457c–d) that *he and Gorgias both recognize that people do not easily define what they discuss, nor do they exchange instruction.*⟩ This difficulty in defining would mean for Gorgias that it was a bother to define terms, and so long as the audience liked what was being said, this would be sufficient. For Socrates it would mean that even were some respondent to give thought to a definition, it would be necessary to examine it to make sure it fitted the real character of the thing defined. This difference between the two men toward definition is itself an instance of failure to define their terms so that instruction can take place and agreement can be secured.

⟨*There is a second aspect of this disagreement, the all-too-obvious phenomenon of irritation when the two participants, even those long familiar with arguing, define their terms differently without realizing it, and therefore lack a way to resolve the conflict. The charge by one that the other is speaking incorrectly or unclearly is coupled with annoyance and further charges of envy on both sides; the parties are now in altercation and are no longer inquiring* (457c–d).⟩ Now this degree of hostility is far away in point of intensity from the sort that Gorgias fears, where incensed dicasts order the exiling or killing of a rhetor whom they distrust. ⟨Nevertheless, it is a bar to progress in the attainment of truth, and Socrates now (457d–e) *says that it makes for a most disgraceful episode, so much so that others are annoyed with themselves even to be onlookers.*⟩ One notices here the oddly timed condemnation of such rough talk; Gorgias has not betrayed any tendencies in that direction, nor have the others.

Socrates is probably condemning obstreperous and insulting speech because, having correctly sized up his three opponents as clinging to techniques of mob appeal, he is anticipating trouble from one, two, or all three men if they are thwarted, especially in front of one another and the audience.[14] Socrates is like an orchestra conductor who at the beginning of a rehearsal of young players gives a short homily on the dangers of their possible failure to pay strict attention to his every gesture, although he has thus far made none. That Socrates is not wrong in his surmise is shown by the repeated abusive epithets thrown his way by Polus and Callicles later on; and that he is in some respect admonishing himself in advance is shown by his own hardly less inflammatory responses to the young host for the day.

⟨Socrates continues (457e–458a): *The remarks you have just made (on the impunity of the teacher) seem inharmonious with what you said at first regarding rhetoric, but I fear that you will think I am neglecting the subject and merely altercating* (ou pros to pragma philonikounta legein, *being fond of victory) if I refute you. If, on the other hand, you are like me we may continue, otherwise not.*⟩ This is the counterpart of the many boasts of Gorgias. But even so Socrates implies little regarding the rightness of his position, the superiority of his art, or the effectiveness of his appeal. Nor does he imply that he can *make* Gorgias into a person like himself.

⟨The question naturally arises, *What sort is Socrates?* and he answers this simply by remarking (458a–b) that *he is glad to refute or be refuted if anything untrue is said.*) The accent is on *refuted*, not contradicted. Properly, refutation leads to and justifies contradiction, but that is generally self-contradiction. Refutation means taking two propositions of a man's argument, be they both premises or a premise and a conclusion, and showing that they lead to incompatibility. The upshot is that an art or at least a knack of refutation is required, not mere stating of authorities to the contrary or listing of counterexamples. Socrates has not yet really refuted Gorgias at all, and now he says no more than that it appears that there is a disharmony between two parts of what the other man has asserted. The elenchus has not been at work, and the most that Socrates has done has been to call for tighter identification of rhetoric as an art, to edit the definition of rhetoric, and then to exclaim rather ironically that its power must be daimonic if Gorgias is to be believed.

⟨Socrates continues (458a–b) by saying that *the worst evil is to harbor a false belief regarding the present topic, hence the greatest benefit is to have such a belief refuted.*⟩ [15] He seems to be speaking of himself and of Gorgias impartially, though the suspicion could well be forming in the latter that Socrates scarcely had his own errors prominently in view. We stress here the distinction between fearing to err—which Socrates is now expressing—and desiring to arrive at truth—which he evinced earlier (453a–b). Fear of error arises either before or after one has uttered a substantive statement. [16] Beforehand, it is in a sense dangerous because it hampers one in stating *anything*; it becomes inhibitory, unless one has some infallible method of removing all chance to take risks, and one settles instead for the commonplace. Afterward, however, it signifies that a person stands ready to be corrected if necessary, that he has accomplished his best although this may not be good enough. This is compatible with stating the truth, when the truth is something standing poorly with one's conversational partners.

Socrates' account of discussion has again consisted of successive bifurcations: One can argue truly or falsely; if truly (reaching true opinions), there is no issue. If falsely, then there is need for refutation. Either this refutation will be accepted with equanimity or even gratitude or else it will give rise to altercation and name-calling. If the two parties are without contentiousness then the discussion can continue, otherwise not.

Now comes the second interlude (458b–e), in which not the substantive opinions of the group assembled are solicited but rather their attitudes toward continuing the discussion. ⟨Gorgias opens by claiming *to be of the same kind as Socrates, that is, ready to refute and be refuted, but*—and here the grandstand player speaks again—*we must consider whether the others are tired.*⟩ A clever tactic. Gorgias himself is the one who should be tired, for he has been doing most of the talking, both before and after the arrival of Socrates. He has, by putting the matter up to the audience, relieved himself of any possible blame for either terminating or prolonging the discussion, valid as his excuse of fatigue might be. And he has, of course, flattered the others by showing them this deference. In both ways he has blunted in advance the possible effects of an elenchus, which he can now be fairly sure is coming, for Socrates has already claimed to have detected a serious internal disharmony in the argument.

How much has Gorgias claimed in saying that he is like Socrates? Is he assuming that the two of them have the same art? the same opinions? the same temperament? We have already noted that he seems not to distinguish kinds of uses of language, except to divide rhetoric from certain other types of speech by subject matters, and have noted also that his definition of rhetoric is offered at first in terms of specific kinds of audiences. It is likely, therefore, that he can see little difference between his own uses of language and those of Socrates—except that he himself is famous, while Socrates gets no special introduction from his acquaintance Callicles. As for substantive opinions about justice and truth, Socrates has scarcely committed himself thus far, and Gorgias might well be surprised to discover, as later he must, that Socrates has given considerable thought to these topics.

The same temperament? This is more easily answered. Given Gorgias' neglect of distinctions between arts of language, we may be reasonably sure that he thinks of Socrates' questions as being little different from what are always raised by audiences everywhere and that do not embarrass and cause him to stumble in public. So Gorgias can be mindful of possible attack by Socrates and yet confident that this can be met, that it will turn out to be nothing new, nothing damaging. Hence the conclusion that Gorgias can face Socrates with the latter's same equanimity. If Gorgias is to be shown to have contradicted himself, this is not vital to his case, for he has made a good impression anyway.

⟨Chaerephon—indecisive Chaerephon—chimes in (458c) *that the others, that is, the anonymous audience, are applauding to indicate their wish to have the discussion continued. I can think of nothing*, he says, *more important than to continue the conversation.*⟩ This echoes Socrates' remark that the worst thing is to be in error on the present question, but it is prefaced by a remark about the applause, an extrinsic measure. The listeners are clapping, but here again there is ambiguity. They enjoyed Gorgias' earlier display; are they now simply enjoying the liveliness of the colloquy, or are they taking some delight in what they foretell will be the discrediting of the august rhetor? Or perhaps the downfall of Socrates?

⟨It is the turn of Callicles, whose motives hover between seeking satisfaction from a feast of words and seeking it from a battle. *No other discussion, he says (458d), has given me such pleasure, so you may keep on with it all day.*⟩ He is thus gratified, not instructed, which means that he is using a feature of rhetorical discourse as a reason for continuing. Although the motives of Callicles have not been presented as fully as they will be later, we should at least set down some possible ones, pending further disclosures: (a) Like Chaerephon, he is simply hoping to hear a good conversation and wishes to be diverted; (b) he enjoys a fight, and looks for excitement, whether he will participate in it or not; (c) he looks forward to seeing Socrates in action and hopes Socrates will eventually defeat Gorgias; (d) he is unfavorably inclined toward Socrates, but after having watched the display wishes to see *someone* defeat Gorgias.

For several reasons to be discussed later when Plato has made the complex nature of Callicles more apparent, we greatly favor the last explanation. At this point, it is much easier to see the relations between the character of Gorgias and the colloquy to which he contributes than it is of the others, including Socrates. We merely note here that Callicles is watching not only the defeat of Gorgias but also what seems to be the downfall of rhetoric, earlier alleged to be the highest of the arts.

⟨Gorgias (458d–e) has the final word in the interlude: *In view of all the urging, it would be disgraceful not to continue, after I had challenged everyone to ask whatever questions they wished.*⟩ Another accommodation to his audience, but at the same time an unconscious admission that he has not taken the full measure of his antagonist: Socrates is asking the same routine questions that I have had put to me all these years, and *what* he asks is of a piece with theirs. Probably Gorgias is not being deliberately impolite, but clearly he anticipates giving an effective demonstration— an eloquent display—before the present company, and whether or not he satisfied any strict dialectical requirements is for him quite beside the point. If he loses in one way, he will win in another.

⟨A new and last phase (458e–461b) of the colloquy begins with a brief summary by Socrates of Gorgias' position. Again Socrates prefaces this by saying, *Gorgias may be right, and I have understood him wrongly (458e),*⟩ thus seeming to flatter his respondent but in reality saying that the inconsistencies are beginning to show up so fast that it is easy to become confused.[17]

Gorgias has said three things: (a) that he can make a rhetor of anyone wishing to learn; (b) that he persuades rather than instructs: (c) that even in the questions regarding health, the rhetor will be more persuasive—to the crowd—than is the doctor. Of these, (a) and (c) are contentions that Gorgias was eager to make, while (b) involved a distinction that he had not fully considered. In all three points, Socrates' assumption, to which Gorgias accedes, is that the audience, be it a medical patient, a crowd, or a council, does *not* have the knowledge but can be moved through belief. Where Gorgias and Socrates part company is on the further point, upheld by the former, denied by the latter, that the knowledge possessed by the doctor or military engineer is of secondary importance, once the rhetor's power to persuade has been established. If the audience *did* have this knowledge, there would be no need for concern over its being misled, and presumably not even a need to speak to such listeners in the first place. A man fully aware of the value of a medication would have use of the doctor only to secure it for him; the doctor would be silent, and so would a councilman.

⟨Socrates passes on to his own assertions (459a–c): (1) *"to the crowd" is the same as "to the ignorant," for if the crowd knew, the rhetor could not be more persuasive than the doctor.*⟩ Socrates does say that the rhetor would be *less* convincing, though this need not be ruled out. But what does it mean for an audience to be ignorant? It cannot possibly be ignorance of everything, for total amentia is rarely characteristic of civic gatherings. Ignorance of the *type* of question under discussion, such as naval architecture or medical art, might be the meaning, as could ignorance of particular issues, such as the advisability of taking this medicine in this quantity at this time for this ailment, and so on. The last is attractive, but knowledge is not atomic, in the *Gorgias*. A person cannot have *knowledge* about one small item and little or none of its neighbors in a discipline; from the first moment the talk has been about entire arts, and even the person who has mastered but one rhetorical device—hyperbole, let us say—could not consider himself an accomplished rhetor. If this reading is correct, then ignorance here means ignorance of a body of relevant observations, principles, and their consecutants.

⟨*If the rhetor is more persuasive than the doctor,* Socrates remarks (459a), *then he is more persuasive than the one who knows, even though he lacks the doctor's knowledge.*⟩ But how could this come about? Gorgias has made capital of his ability to outtalk his brother, the recognized physician. Knowing little or nothing about medicine, how could he influence the patient (who by hypothesis is ignorant of the medical art as well) to accept a disagreeable treatment? Clearly it would be a matter of picking up hints from the brother, of a quick grasp of the elements of the situation such as severity of pain, family ties, and so forth, and a sizing up of the attitudes of the patient; in other words, giving voice to the patient's own beliefs and wishes in order to convince him.

⟨*He who knows no truth about medicine or any of the other arts,* Socrates continues (459b–c), *will persuade more than the one with knowledge, and will merely have some persuasive device that will make him* seem *to know.*⟩ What does it mean to know medicine or architecture, in this context? It appears (at this stage) to imply at least three things: (a) familiarity with particular effects, such as symptoms of a disease; (b) ability to trace these to a cause or causes; (c) familiarity with ways to alter the cause, or alter its relation to the usual effects. The weight of marble cylinders in a pile prevents them from spontaneously forming a column, but by lifting and carefully superposing them they can be made to form such a column, and now the weight becomes the engineer's ally.

⟨To the suggestion that the rhetor possesses only a cheap substitute for this knowledge Gorgias blandly replies (459c) *that such a device is a great labor-saver* (pollē rhastōnē), *a convenience that shortcuts the need for the artificers whom he replaces.*⟩ He is not suggesting that he has something better than the arts or can practice them as well as the experts can, but only that they can be dispensed with in certain situations usually requiring their employment. The point at which this can occur is not specified; sooner or later the doctor will have to appear on the scene with his pharmacopoeia, or the engineer with his levers and cranes. The doctor talks to patients, but he also pulverizes and dissolves the medicaments; the architect can try to convince a gathering that a doorway must be larger, but sooner or later he oversees the hoisting of the lintels. From these manipulative stages the rhetor is of course excluded (450b–d). But Gorgias would not mind; he has already swung the vote and earned the commission.

Much of this can be summarized by recurring to the Socratic division between knowledge and ignorance. To the former belong the expert artificers and the instructed (i.e., knowledgeable) pupils. If they really know that medicines are efficacious for *this* patient, then their advice to him to swallow these will necessarily be just, and if so, there is a looser sense in which the patient also knows both the right medicines and justice as it applies in his case. The other column, that headed by *ignorance*, is less inviting. The rhetor lacks this knowledge of medicine and justice, nor does his pupil possess it. The medicine may not turn out to be poison, but of that no one except the doctor can be sure. The pupil, who picks up his rhetorical devices either through instruction or through merely seeing them tried out by others, is thus persuaded and passes on what he believes to an audience that can at best believe and at bottom is quite ignorant of the truth.

This entire discussion is about cognition. Pleasures and desires are not stressed with Gorgias, but will become vital to the argument later. For the moment it suffices that the rhetor's motives are based upon considerations of prestige, popularity, and money; and although these have to do with desire, they are the extrinsic aims toward which desire points.

The last two pages (459c–461b) of the section devoted to Gorgias are

taken up with the contradictions in his statements regarding knowledge, instruction, and ignorance in relation to justice. The first part
(459c–460a) raises questions about the teacher, pupil, and justice,
while the second (460a–461b) treats the rhetor and justice.

⟨Later on, says Socrates, we might consider whether the rhetor is a match
for the other artificers, and so forth, a point on which Gorgias has insisted, or
rather, has gone past in saying that the rhetor is superior. Socrates continues
(459c–460a) that we must ask whether the rhetor is in the same relation to the
just and unjust, disgraceful and fair, good and evil, as he is to the pairs of contraries considered by the other arts. There are five possibilities that he lists,
giving Gorgias an unusual range of not altogether separated choices: (a)
the rhetor does not know what is really good or evil, fair or disgraceful, just or
unjust, but has merely learned how to apppear to the ignorant as if he did, and
better than those who really know; (b) the pupil might know about good and evil
before coming to Gorgias for lessons; (c) Gorgias, ignorant, may show the pupil
how to appear to the many to know, though he does not know; (d) or he may be
unable to teach rhetoric to one not previously knowing the truth about justice;
(e) or some other possibility.⟩ Let us take the dialectical precedents for
each of these points in turn, though they can be clustered together
without each one's excluding every other.

In (a) Gorgias has already shown that although he does not wish to
confess his ignorance, he will allow it, but claims that he is superior to
the other artificers nevertheless (459a). There is no precedent for case
(b) in the dialogue, no hint, for instance, that Polus could come to
Gorgias fully equipped on the nature of good and evil; and later on it
will be apparent that he is, with or without the lessons of Gorgias, pain-
fully ignorant in this regard. And so is Callicles. The idea expressed in
(c) follows from (a) above, but here the emphasis is on the transmission
of the belief in appearance rather than on merely possessing the appearance of knowledge by the master. There is no precedent for (d) either, unless it be on some occasion when Gorgias wishes to disown a
pupil for having abused the art. The precedent in the dialogue lies in
the hit-or-miss character of so much that Gorgias has claimed and admitted throughout; Socrates is genuinely baffled, as he shows by including (e) as a possibility.

There is a descending order of importance of the function of Gorgias
in this list. In (a) the question is raised and answered negatively whether
the rhetor knows reality or has a belief about appearance of knowledge, not of justice. In (b) regardless of what the rhetor knows, there is
no need for him to teach it or otherwise impart it. In (c) the rhetor
teaches mere appearance. In (d) the rhetor cannot teach anything about
his art to one ignorant of justice. And in (e) the assumption is that he
cannot even communicate any of these answers to someone able to
learn.

The possibilities could be put in a matrix, bearing in mind, however, that Plato does not begin to explore all the combinations. We might, then, call this a partial matrix, and there are many of these in the dialogue, especially in the section in which Callicles is the chief respondent. We can state this matrix in prose. The rhetor has a relation to reality and to appearance, he has a power either to teach reality or to impart appearances. Similarly, the pupil might learn reality (if he learns it at all) from Gorgias or from some earlier source. These are the possible headings. In case (a) above the rhetor believes in appearances; he does not know reality, nor does he teach it. Socrates does not specify what the pupil's condition is. Case (b) implies that again the rhetor does not know reality, nor does he teach it, and leaves open whether he attempts to impart appearances. Consequently the pupil cannot learn from Gorgias, but if he is to know real justice or goodness, he must have learned it beforehand. In case (c) the rhetor merely believes in appearances, does not teach reality, does impart these appearances, and the pupil, who does not come prepared with knowledge of reality, does not learn from Gorgias either. Case (d) is an imputation of failure of every kind to the rhetor, who cannot even teach rhetoric, so the presumption is that the pupil does not learn it unless he already understands justice. Again, case (e) is a signal that Gorgias not only does not know reality but cannot even impart appearances enough to apprise Socrates himself of the state of affairs that is either real or that Gorgias supposes it to be.

That this last is not a hopelessly irrelevant case is shown by the response that Gorgias now makes (460a): It looks like (a) or (c), but it is ambivalent, for he cannot bring himself to see the difference between real knowledge and pretended, real instruction and pretended. ⟨If the pupil by chance does not know justice,and so forth, beforehand, he will learn them from me, says Gorgias.⟩ Notice how he introduces this element of chance, which permits him to assume that the pupil will come to him fully equipped with the core of Gorgias' teaching already in hand—no doubt more firmly in his hand than in that of his teacher. No question of whether the pupil has already learned this lesson *rightly* seems to come into the mind of Gorgias, nor does he seem to care whether the pupil would respect him were he ignorant of justice and injustice, the central issue of all rhetoric.

⟨To examine the relations between rhetor and justice as they have been alleged by Gorgias, Socrates first shows the steps used in arriving at some his chief contradictions (460a–b). *If you make a man into a rhetor he must know justice either previously or from you. A man who has learned building is a builder, one who has learned music is a musician, one who has learned justice is a just man.*⟩ Socrates is depending heavily upon the act of learning, real learning, as being equivalent to the gaining of knowledge, not belief, and upon the corresponding equivalence between knowledge of building, music, and justice and the practice of each. He does not insist that the builder is a man who makes his life work building—building here is an art, not a career. We can set aside for the moment any question of relating justice as an ethical matter to the arts; the analogy between them has been stressed throughout this section of the dialogue, and though it may be a strained analogy it is one that both Gorgias and Socrates take for granted. But the strict relation between knowledge and practice may be open to question. There too, however, the way has been paved when we recall the analogy (amounting to an identity) between virtue and art. We build a building properly, or play a melody properly with everything in order, everything in proportion, everything serving a suitable end; and we pay back a debt, vote taxes to fund triremes, and again we find that all parts of the action are in order, in proportion, and subserving an end. It is quite true that ends, while they are frequently brought into view in this colloquy, have not been explicitly discussed except to say (451e–452d) that medicine, gymnastics, and moneymaking *have* ends that differ, and that rhetoric too has an end differing from theirs.

⟨The argument has arrived (460b) at the point where a statement of the main propositions that are to be found inconsistent is possible. It will rest upon the previously cited analogy, and has two stages (460b–c and 460c–461a). *(1) The just man does what is just,* says Socrates; (2) if this is true, the just man never wishes to act unjustly—a statement that fixes a man's wishing as a reflex of what he does habitually; *(3) the rhetor, again, will (assuming that he knows justice) be a just man and will never wish to do injustice.*⟩

There are observations upon each of these: (1) This makes justice something more than a mere inert quality like whiteness or baldness. Justice is an action, or at least characterizes an action; (2) seems to use an assumption that the doctor who knows his art wishes always to practice it as well, and will not use his knowledge of pharmacology or surgery to befuddle, harm, or kill his patient; (3) the just man *never* wishes to act unjustly, insofar as he is just, and if he does wish to act in this way then he becomes an unjust man, though Socrates would doubtless repeat that a truly just man does not fluctuate between good and evil wishing even though he is actually doing justice and refraining from unjust acts. The rhetor, then, will not only wish to do justice but because the practice and the teaching of it are firmly bound together, in Gorgias' mind, he will teach (true) justice and his pupil, having learned it from him, will also do justice as well—a charming fantasy, of course, but one that follows from the contentions of Socrates here. In the sense in which he means it, this is a notion hard to refute.[18]

⟨The second stage opens with another analogy: *Previously* (i.e., 456c–d) *you, Gorgias, said that we should not complain against the trainer if a boxer uses boxing unjustly, and then again* (457a–c), *that if the master rhetor uses rhetoric justly but his pupil uses it unjustly, we should complain not against the master but only against the pupil. But now* (460e) *we find that the rhetor is incapable of doing injustice because, like the builder knowing his structures, he knows what justice is.*⟩

This latter statement would be nonsense if we did not couple it with Socrates' use of the constructive and therapeutic arts. He would not allow that the ordinary citizen could hope to read an account of a just action, or a definition of justice regardless of how precise it was, and then come away with knowledge. Obviously, becoming a just man requires study *and* practice as onerous and prolonged as becoming a musician or naval engineer. The knowledge consequently arises from a fortunate combination of experience (or familiarity, *empeiria*) and insights (principles); and this eliminates chance. A further point, which Socrates is now resting his case upon but is not stating, is that the man who really knows rhetoric will be a rhetor, and because knowledge of rhetoric would mean knowledge of justice as an essential ingredient (454b), such a man would wish never to be ignorant of justice, nor would he wish habitually or ever to act unjustly. If, however, rhetoric is not really a subject for knowledge (as it may not be), then this gives a case without examples.

⟨There is one last compound statement of the contradictions (460c–461b). *Earlier we agreed*, says Socrates, *that rhetoric deals with the just and the unjust, and its speeches were always about justice, hence rhetoric could never be unjust; yet later you said, surprisingly enough, that the rhetor's pupil might use rhetoric unjustly. So we must agree again that the rhetor cannot use his rhetoric unjustly, nor wish to do injustice. To resolve all this will, by the Dog, god of Egypt, require no little discussion.*⟩ Thus concludes Socrates, who seems to feel that the talk should continue. In a sense it does not continue, but in another sense, as we shall see, it does most emphatically go on, even though Gorgias himself largely drops out of the conversation.

*   *   *

Where does this leave the reader? It would be pleasant and easy to think that the Philosopher has been pitted against the Rhetor, and that the former has clearly defeated his opponent. Yet philosophy is not a subject matter or a method or a way of life or set of beliefs in this first section of the dialogue. The only hint of what Socrates has been practicing lies in his plea to Gorgias to keep the answers short and to discuss rather than display (449b–c)—not a very strong clue. No one has characterized Socrates as a philosopher thus far, and general topics (other than justice and freedom) that fill the pages of philosophy books have not been dwelt upon. Socrates has merely come from the market-place, not necessarily from a gathering of students there talking about virtue or number or the soul. Callicles has given no warning that here is a man to be reckoned with in an argument. Nor is there clearcut indica-tion that Gorgias thinks himself defeated, on his own terms of what a defeat would be. Indeed, as the dialogue progresses, we shall be find-ing that the decline of Gorgias' status as rhetor is only *begun* by the efforts of Socrates in the first colloquy, and that in a very real sense it takes place gradually, after Gorgias has mostly fallen silent for a long time. There are also respects in which he is refuted by Polus and even more by Callicles as well as by Socrates; and in addition, and, not con-tradictory to this, the defeats of Polus and Callicles in their turn spell extra losses for Gorgias. The dialogue is properly named for him, he is the man typifying the *complete* rhetor, and it is his slow disillusionment with his two followers that would, we believe, make him a sadder though not an altogether wiser man.

PART TWO

CONVERSATION WITH POLUS

3

THE DIVIDED OBLONG

(461b–466a)

Let us recall the formula derivable from the remarks by Polus when he undertook (448c) to describe the vocation of Gorgias: It was the fairest of arts, he said; and this art was shortly afterward named by Gorgias himself as rhetoric (449a). Is rhetoric, then, the fairest art? and again, more searchingly, Is rhetoric an art of *any* sort? The conversation with Gorgias has examined the first of these questions. Socrates has eventually been able to show that rhetoric is not that fairest of the arts, both because of its defective grounding in the subject matters it proposes to discuss (chiefly matters of concern to other arts) and because of the cavalier attitude of Gorgias in denying his responsibility for the unjust use of rhetoric by his pupils. If every art aims at something that is good and rhetoric does not, the conclusion is obvious.

The second question is now brought forward after Socrates has seen Polus preempt the conversation (461b). It is a question raised inadvertently by Polus but very deliberately raised and then answered by Socrates. The conclusion that he reaches is again negative; yet rhetoric, if not an art, is at least *something*. Socrates has several rhetors standing before him, and they share a distinctive kind of speech that has evidently impressed an audience still at hand. What if rhetoric is *not* an art? was one question that evidently did not occur to any of the three rhetors in the Prologue, nor was it raised by Chaerephon. Because the logically prior question, What is an art? was not raised in the Prologue or in the subsequent conversation with Gorgias—though plenty of hints were dropped along the way from which an answer could be elicited—this too becomes pressing. If the problem dominating the first half or so of the dialogue is ever solved (Who is Gorgias, What is he? taken in all its bearings), then the praise of a quality must be preceded by and grounded in the definition of a nature. If one were to take the loose conceptions of Gorgias to heart, then one could be a genuine

practitioner of an art and still abuse it in applying its principles to enterprises and policies of the populace and its government.

Polus was introduced as both a partner and a kind of shadow of
Gorgias, and in the little Prologue he briefly replaced, praised, and par-
roted his elder. It is not until Gorgias is made fatally to contradict himself that Polus begins to emerge as a well-formed figure in his own
right. In the interlude (458b–e) when Gorgias, Chaerephon, and Callicles all have their say about continuing the discussion, and even the
anonymous members of the audience applaud, Polus alone has been
silent; yet a couple of pages later he contains himself no longer and
breaks in with a question and two complaints, at first against Gorgias
and then against Socrates.

This new colloquy with him (461b–481b) is almost twice as long as
that with Gorgias. It commences with an interlude (461b–462b), followed by the main body of the discussion (462b–481b), which in turn is
divided into three parts, to be more fully charted later.[1] The first of
these parts (462a–466a) resembles the Prologue in the abrupt shifting
of roles of questioner and answerer and even of the persons responding to Socrates. Polus becomes the questioner at the outset but is twice
supplanted during a passage of highest import to the dialogue.

⟨The entire colloquy starts when Polus, breathless and a little uncoor-
dinated in his utterances, interrupts to ask *whether Socrates has just expressed his real opinion of rhetoric*, without saying exactly which one of
the many hints that Socrates has supplied he, Polus, is concerned
about. He then complains that *Gorgias has through shame* (ēschunthē)
*said that the rhetor knows what is just and can teach this to all comers and then
has run into something contrary to what has been agreed upon. This, Socrates,
is boorishness* (agroikia) *on your part to lead the discussion to this* (461b–c).[2]⟩
The interruption comes not in the middle of a sentence but in a pause
during which Socrates, having shown a contradiction, evidently expects Gorgias to accede to his implied request for more time to resolve
the difficulty.

It is natural to suppose that Polus, as follower of Gorgias, is able to
answer questions as well as his master. Indeed, he will shortly claim
that he knows everything that Gorgias knows. There would have been
no irony had this claim been made before Gorgias entered into conversation with Socrates; but after Gorgias has bungled so many responses,
what he and Polus both know shines in a dimmer light. The substance
of what has been said, as well as Gorgias' manner of responding, is
no help to Polus either; it has been shown (454c–455a) that rhetoric
produces belief, not knowledge, and again (458e–459c) that rhetoric
arises from ignorance and persuades an ignorant audience. All this
gives weight to the fact that Polus at the outset stumbles into a couple of

grammatical anacolutha. Other instances of ineptitude follow, most of them stemming from his eagerness to vie with Gorgias in making an impression when none is called for. This may also signify that Gorgias' claim to be able to make each of his pupils become like himself (barring the misfortune that they decide to act unjustly) is founded on error born of pride. Polus is familiar with rhetoric in the sense of having heard its theory talked of enough for him to write something of a text-book on the subject. His actual language, however, in his subsequent conversation with Socrates shows many slight confusions, as in his mistaking affirmative and negative (466e). He seems'guided by chance rather than by art, and this according to his own lights (448c) would signify his unfamiliarity with the matters in hand. Whether he would voluntarily make a just or an unjust use of rhetoric is a different point and will be scrutinized by Socrates; but the chanciness in his nature would make him a poor political risk in either case.

⟨Socrates closes this first little section of the interlude by saying that *we keep the young alongside us to set upright* (*hoi* neōteroi epanorthōte) *our lives in deeds and words* (461c).⟩ There is a combined rigor and a flexibility in the Socratic approach that admits of the new, yet constantly seeks to purge it of error in light of certain established principles. His expression of gratitude for the young contains irony, but one must still remember that in his single-minded devotion to the way the argument is conducted, Socrates is ready to admit some worthwhile contribution as setting a new course in the debate. The seeming impossibility, indeed ludicrousness, of Socrates' remark when taken altogether straight-facedly, and the reader's consequent assumption that it must be horse-play, may blind this reader to a truth underlying the little jibe. The youthfulness of Polus sharpens the paradox implicit in his earlier assertion (448c) that from familiarity arises art, while unfamiliarity breeds chance. This observation, if it is to have weight, must be made by a more mature person, and from the mouth of Polus it seems to deny his very right to make it with any authority, or else to deny its truth.

Again, Socrates, in overtly making fun of Polus, is also allowing that the previous conversation may have gone astray partly because Gorgias has been so accustomed to responding to all questions that he has become inattentive, mechanical, and superficial when framing his answers. Once more there is a double irony: Socrates is flippantly laudatory, surreptitiously sardonic, yet underneath it all quite serious in implicating Gorgias as being responsible for the disappointing progress so far.

The second part of the interlude (461c–462b) sets conditions for proceeding with the colloquy. ⟨If *Gorgias and I stumble,* says Socrates (461c–e), *your duty is to set us right, and I shall gladly rescind whatever you think to have been wrongly admitted. On the other hand, you must answer the questions, not give lengthy speeches. Your freedom in Athens is to speak, but mine is to leave if I choose)*—two rather unequal freedoms, for Athens was specially well known for allowing free speech, while permission to leave off conversation is scarcely denied anywhere.

⟨He goes on (462a–b): *You may revoke what you please (i.e., of what Gorgias has admitted); you may by turns question and answer, and you may refute and be refuted.*⟩ Again this is lopsided. Answering comes easily to Polus—we have seen that already—but whether he can ask pertinent questions is another matter, and whether he would even *wish* to ask them is still another.[3] It is, furthermore, a privilege to be able to refute one's conversational partner without danger of reprisal, and the ability to carry out a successful refutation is not easily gained. There is, however, no privilege in being refuted as there is in asking or answering questions. In this latter regard it is because Polus claims (462a) to know all that Gorgias knows that he can either ask or answer. Another irony is lurking here, perhaps better concealed than the first. Gorgias has just made a botch of a relatively simple issue, whether through a defect of character or inattentiveness is immaterial here. So to confer upon Polus all the rights to answer questions in the manner of Gorgias is a small award indeed. True, no one says that Polus knows *only* what Gorgias knows; but Polus makes no additional claim, and though he mentions Archelaus and certain other personages and topics, these are the sorts of things one would gather from hearsay and common talk, not instruction. In a nutshell, when Socrates suggests that Polus knows what Gorgias knows and Polus eagerly confirms this, Socrates is revealing to his companions of the day (and to the reader as well) that he expects Polus to fare little better than did his mentor.

We now arrive at a central passage in the dialogue, a four-page account (462a–466a) of the nature of rhetoric and its relations to other practices. Marking a turning point, this brings into prominence many new aspects of the past conversation with Gorgias, and allows a point of departure for much that passes between Socrates and Polus, and after that between Socrates and Callicles.[4] A word in explanation of our own procedure in expounding this passage is needed. Each dialogue is from one standpoint a process, from another a design of finished structures, and anyone looking exclusively at either of these is likely to falsify the philosophical effect that Plato is trying to convey to the reader. Because many if not most expositions of the four pages in question concentrate upon the structure, we stress a little more heavily the processes whereby the structural form is built up, looking for the route traveled by Socrates in setting up the kinds of familiarities that are contrasted with kinds of arts.

The preliminary stage (462b–463d) puts rhetoric into the context that it will retain for the rest of the dialogue, with two exceptions, to be noted shortly. Polus is asking rather perfunctory questions of Socrates during this stage. There is then a little interlude (463d–e), and here Gorgias returns to the conversation, responding to Socrates throughout the culminating stage of the latter's exposition (463e–465c). Socrates attempts to clarify his meaning by contrasting certain practices with arts in this stage; after that there is another interlude (465d–466a), moderating the sharpness of the distinctions just made, putting a cap on this second exposition.

⟨Polus, to whom Socrates has so freely accorded the task of questioner, commences *(462b)* with his usual abruptness by *demanding of Socrates his account of rhetoric.*⟩ It was, of course, an assumption entertained by Gorgias and uncontested by Socrates at first, that rhetoric was an art; but the later phases of that debate threw a series of doubts upon the view that rhetoric was an art par excellence, or even one of any sort. Now the question is raised, If not an art, what can it be? It seems clear that the word *art* (*technē*) is a term connoting more than ordinarily emphatic praiseworthiness in the minds of all three major participants thus far, and that if rhetoric is shown to be anything else it will be at the expense of rhetoric itself, not of art in general. Thus it will be a blow to both Gorgias and Polus when they are told that it is no art at all but a familiarity and a routine, that is, a skill derived from repeated contact with a set of like situations coupled with a repeatable way of acting to exercise control over them: similar audiences behaving in much the same ways and "handled" by stock phrases and thoroughly drilled inflections and gestures. ⟨Socrates now (462c) *narrows the familiarity to one of producing gratification* (charitos) *and pleasure* (hēdonēs).⟩ One may presume that to Polus this securing of a well-pleased audience would be the hallmark of mastery of an art, and a fair (*kalos*) one at that. For him familiarity might be something epistemically lower than for Socrates, as when Polus said that familiarity *gives rise* to art; and because art for him is a way of pleasing, familiarity would amount to having "been around long enough" and having "tried the same old tricks." For him, then, art would have to add the notion of selecting adequate means of persuasion, of delighting a crowd. Socrates for his part will allow to familiarity the persuasive functions of an art, but whether he gives it the high moral status that the rhetors would accord it remains to be seen.[5] For him, an art seeks to discover and advance the good of what a thing is essentially and per se.

Because Polus has little conception of what knowledge is, he will be unable to account for any exactness and certainty that rhetoric may have; he merely takes it as "fair," the expression he now tries once more to inject into the argument (462c).[6] To attribute this vague excellence to rhetoric is also a mark of the self-importance of Polus, endeavoring to puff up his own calling. ⟨Socrates replies, in a brief interlude (462c–d) that *the praise should come only after it has been settled just what rhetoric is.*⟩ The contrast between examining the nature of a thing and listing its qualities, including praising and blaming them, is one that has profoundly colored the exchange between Socrates and Gorgias; the failure to perceive this occasions some of Socrates' sharpest rebukes to both Gorgias and Polus. His device is now one of finding a more simply recognized practice that can be allied to rhetoric so that they are seen as companion parts of a single whole, familiarity.

⟨*Catering* (opsopoiia, "cookery" in most translations),[7] that preparation of pleasing foods, condiments, and candies to be judged by taste and texture alone without concern for nourishment or suitability to the consumer, *is one of two parts of the same practice* (epitēdeuseos—462e), which is the most general—and neutral—expression in this passage, *along with another,* namely, *rhetoric is part of "some business"* (tinos pragmatos—463a). *What kind of business rhetoric and catering may be, Socrates hesitates to say, out of consideration, he remarks, for the feelings of Gorgias.* Nor is he even sure whether the term he is about to use will apply to what Gorgias himself practices, the reason being that *he,* Socrates, *could form no very clear idea of it from the man's own assertions.*[8]⟩ Rhetoric, then, is a familiarity or familiarizing, it is a practice and a business, something done. ⟨Socrates now adds that *it is a practice which, though not an art, yet has a shrewd, surmizing* (stochastikos) *brave soul that by nature deals cleverly* (deinēs) *with mankind: It is pandering* (kolakeia).⟩ This last means something more than flattery alone, which is merely saying pleasant things in praise of one's hearers but does not always carry with it total insincerity and willingness to betray the standards of everyone in order to curry favor and get one's own way. It is possible to pander by playing down to an audience as well as playing up. ⟨To the four characterizations of rhetoric *Socrates now adds a fifth, routine* (tribē, a practice like that of continually rubbing two sticks together to smooth them or else spark a fire). Of the whole designated in these five ways, rhetoric and catering constitute two parts, and there is *embellishment* (kommotikē, adornment, dressing in finery as well as facial cosmetics, jewelry, and the like); and fourthly *sophistry*⟩, which is a new term despite the fact that the earlier conversation has circled about the arts of language and the notion of responsibility for what is taught regarding moral behavior. Sophistry is left in an ambiguous position here and, after a little more development, will reappear only near the end of the dialogue (519e–520b), again to be left without clear designation.

⟨Socrates' next remark is in substance another very brief interlude

(463c) pertaining to the course of the discussion: *I will refrain from stating whether rhetoric is fair or disgraceful* (aischros, base).〉 This is not uncandid but merely polite, since Gorgias himself, if not a sophist, at least behaves like the sophists, moving from city to city, gravitating to the homes of the rich, receiving pay for his instruction, volunteering to take on all questioners, and promising to advance the status of his pupils.

〈The sixth expression to name the genus of rhetoric in this segment is image (*eidōlon*); *rhetoric is an image of a part of politics* (463c–d). This impels Polus to ask again *whether rhetoric is fair or not*, and now Socrates' immediate and unreassuring reply is that *rhetoric is something disgraceful, something evil* (kaka—463d).〉 These are the seventh and eighth of the expressions. Although a little earlier Socrates was reluctant even to call rhetoric pandering (462e), now he is in full sail, having allowed himself to do this because meantime he has given enough of its nature so that with a clear conscience he can state whether it is good or evil. He has at last gotten Polus to ask what kind of part (*hopoion morion*) of pandering rhetoric is (463c), even though the young man hardly knows the importance of phrasing the question this way. If the aim is to discover what rhetoric is, then it must be located in a broader field before being more narrowly defined or definitively evaluated.

A summary listing of these descriptions is given in figure 3.1. We see at once the looseness of this scheme. Socrates has ranged a number of different kinds of terms in one column; (i) and (iv) are the generic expressions that he wants to attach permanently to rhetoric so that whatever can be said about them can be said about rhetoric as well.[9] Then, (ii) and (iii) are more neutral descriptions, without pejorative import; (vii) and (viii) make up for this, however, while (vi) is in a little different position from the others, for the imitative relation has not been exploited thus far and is not offered as a near-synonym merely to reinforce familiarity and the others. That seems to be the office of (v), routine.

"Pandering" has no direct antecedents in the colloquy with Gorgias, though the distinction between speaking with knowledge and speaking with belief (454e) would easily hint at it, if belief were coupled with the notion of giving pleasure. But catering and with it pleasure are both implied in the Prologue when Callicles (447a) takes up Socrates' query about a feast and attaches it to a display just given by Gorgias. Embellishing and sophistry, having but an incidental function in the present list, are new, one reason being that throughout Socrates has been allowing Gorgias as often as possible to assume that rhetoric is allied to genuine arts of medicine, mathematics, astronomy, and the like, and has only set it off from these after showing that such an alliance rested on false premises.[10] The last of the kinds of things to which rhetoric is

---

FORMER GENERIC DESCRIPTIONS

art: asserted by Gorgias and Polus, denied by Socrates
fair thing: again asserted by Gorgias and Polus, denied by Socrates

SOCRATIC CHARACTERIZATIONS

   i   familiarity with means to produce gratification and pleasure—Socrates
  ii   practice
 iii   business
 iv   pandering
  v   routine
 vi   image of part of politics
 vii disgraceful*
viii evil*

PARTS OF THE GENUS

1a   rhetoric
1b   catering
iva embellishing
ivb sophistry
*Epithets appended to Socrates' description.

Fig. 3.1. *Preliminary description of rhetoric.*

just now joined is (vi) an image of a part of politics, although this is left vague. Images are implied, but the name is not given in the mentions of sculpture and painting early in the conversation with Gorgias. Introducing the notion here is a novelty, one to make Socrates' hearers think that rhetorical effect, as much as dialectical cogency, can be his aim.[11]

This preliminary exposition of the nature of rhetoric is suggestive, but because it is directed primarily at Polus, it has certain defects and needs revision and supplementation.

1. It places rhetoric in a broader class of things but gives little direct information regarding its special characteristics, that is, how it differs from other practices in that same class.
2. It leaves the relation between familiarity and art unclear. Is one of them generated from the other (as Polus insisted), or is there an opposition between the two?
3. It leaves relations between rhetoric and other kinds of pandering undetermined—even though they are all part of the same genus. Can we say that one is superior to the others within that grouping?
4. It gives no hint of what it means for one thing to image another.
5. It fails to specify the part of politics intended.

If Socrates is to make his case and turn the tables against the two rhetors whom he has faced, these defects must be made good so far as possible. Gorgias has failed to present a consistent view regarding justice and responsibility for pupils, and he and Polus have maintained that, regardless of the issues of knowledge and justice, rhetoric is an art and the fairest to boot. Had Gorgias sincerely affirmed that the effectiveness of rhetoric was balanced by its concern for truth and virtue the dialogue would have been over, with the participants congratulating each other and then getting ready for another pyrotechnical Gorgian display. But the old rhetor has evidently made his living by telling audiences what they wanted to hear, avoiding the distasteful and distressing admission that rhetoric is pandering. The sharp, almost embittered tone in Socrates' use of this epithet can be traced to the claim by Gorgias (452e) that rhetoric is a most powerful instrument. To Socrates, it is a dangerous one. Aiming to give nothing but temporary pleasures leads to unintended disasters.

⟨After Socrates' seemingly unmethodical exposition of what he means by rhetoric and by its place in the practices equivalent to pandering, there is another little interlude (463d–e). *I will proceed*, he says, *as if you already understand my meaning*⟩, a remark implying that Polus is so keen on praising that regardless of the shock he must be enduring when he hears his beloved rhetoric denigrated, he will at least comprehend this better than he could any demands for following a more precise and consistent account. ⟨Gorgias, now quite humbled, *admits that he does not yet follow Socrates, particulary on the matter of how rhetoric is an image of a part of politics* (463d–e). To which Socrates answers, again with some irony, that *this is likely, since what he has said is not yet clear, though the Colt is so young and so sharp* (oxus).⟩[12] All commentators feel it obligatory to notice this pun on the name of Polus, and having met this requirement we pass to the response that Gorgias now makes (463e) perhaps with a mixture of kindliness, amusement, and slight impatience: ⟨*Pay no attention to him, but tell me what you mean by saying that rhetoric is an image of a part of politics;*⟩ he is repeating his query, a way of signaling the importance of this both to him and to Plato's readers, even though it is the mildest of all of Socrates' assertions. There are two possible reasons for this repetition:

First, Gorgias is an old hand at the delivery of epithets, singly and in heaps, and so thinks that Socrates has merely employed an ancient trick of casting aspersions upon something that he does not possess. If Gorgias has heard all the questions many times over, no doubt he has rehearsed all the answers as well, and fended off dozens of attacks on rhetoric—attacks delivered with rhetorical force. Second, and perhaps contingent upon the first, Gorgias has exhibited a phenomenal degree of patience toward Socrates—a patience and courtesy that will hold throughout the dialogue—and this may just be because even with all of his own intellectual shortcomings he senses, no doubt subliminally, that Socrates commands a superior weapon. He seems willing to learn and is neither angered nor dismayed when he turns out to have moved into a position from which escape is difficult. It is not unreasonable to suppose, then, that he perceives that an "image of a part of politics" comes very close to his own formulation (452e) of the purpose of rhetoric, and it does not conflict with the formulation as radically amended by Socrates a moment later (452e–453a): Rhetoric is the artificer of persuasion. Gorgias had admitted throughout that while he knows his "art" he is ignorant of what this enables him to talk about; he knows, in other words, that there is something not totally genuine about his calling, despite its convenience (*rhastōnē*—459c), inasmuch as it replaces all those other arts that one would otherwise have to learn. What would annoy Gorgias most, it seems to us, would be the notion that rhetoric imitates a *part* of politics. To him it would deal with the whole of political life.

Polus has been questioning Socrates, but now Gorgias talks to the latter, not by asking but by answering. To be sure, Socrates' questions are at this juncture (463e–464a) so heavily loaded and (the last two) so lengthy that the only burden upon Gorgias in his total of four new responses is to give signs of agreement. But it is significant, nevertheless, that *he* is the one addressed; the account that Socrates is offering clarifies the earlier discourse with Gorgias and, it so happens, is foundation for substantial parts of the discussions to come. Polus is scarcely able, with his dubious precocity, to follow an argument, and Socrates is underlining the gravity of what he is about to say in addressing it to the older, more sober man. On both counts Plato is indicating that what is about to be said grows directly out of the previous conversation rather than being a trumped-up, ad hoc invention brought in merely to confound the young bush pilot of the discursive skies.

The culminating exposition of the Divided Oblong (463e–465d) contains six little subsections, of which the first four (463e–464a; 464a–b; 464b–c; 464c–d) set up the basic relations by establishing certain dialectical connections that can for the most part be traced. The fifth (464d–465b) discusses catering and embellishing as examples of the bogus imitation of arts; the sixth (465b–d) is an application of geometrical language to the new array, and brings the account to its conclusion. A short interlude (465d–466a) rounds out the entire section on the Oblong and introduces the next.

Although the content and details of the method of the famous Divided Line in *Republic* VI are quite different from those of the present array, there are general similarities, such as the fact that the subdivisions in both cases number four. Hence we are calling the scheme that Socrates is about to construct the Divided Oblong, mainly because one of the best ways of diagramming it is by such a figure. (The other ways are with a branching chart, most often used in scholarly expositions of the passage, and, less frequently, a series of "geometrical" proportions.) No one visual rendering, however, quite does justice to the Socratic subtleties.

⟨Socrates commences (463e) by *distinguishing in* (1), *the human being*,[13] *the soul and body* (2a, 2b). (We are giving the items in this second exposition new numbers because the order of their introduction is so different, and also because we need to keep separate the manners in which they are introduced.) Soul and body are not presented as contraries here; they are simply different, and the degree of difference is left undecided. Both are related to (vi) pandering, of course, since that is the most general heading, not as parts of a whole but as different subjects with respect to which the pandering might be carried on[14] *To each of them are assigned conditions of health* (3a), (3c), *and seeming health* (3b), (3d). *To deal with the body first,* Socrates *attaches two kinds of practitioners;* namely *doctors* (3ci) *and trainers* (3cii), *who are able to distinguish good from what are seeming but not really good bodily conditions.* The assumption is now made, though not explicitly, that neither soul nor body is self-sufficient, and each requires something to be superadded by art, either to restore or to maintain it in really good condition. *These two kinds of arts are politics* (4a) *for the soul and tendance* (therapeia) *for the body* (4b).⟩ There is, of course, a real peculiarity here: The arts of tendance are of single bodies, and by analogy the arts of politics would be of single souls; and there is no mention at all of communities, whether of bodies, souls, or human beings compounded of the two.[15] Socrates appears to be making the point that politics treats the soul, regardless of how many souls happen to be involved at one time. Whether "healthy" can be said of soul and of body in precisely the same sense is not indicated, nor whether it would be possible to treat of many souls calling them "healthy" as with a single soul. Throughout the rest of the dialogue, however, both soul and body can be healthy or unhealthy, and in the closing myth traits of both soul and body accumulated throughout one's lifetime are shown as traits of the body alone after death (fatness and scarring of the formerly living body are retained in death, while injustice of the living soul is transformed into bodily disfigurements after death [524b–c; 524e–525a]).

Art serves here to produce an end, but not any random end nor any deliberately evil one; art has already been spoken of (452b–d) as a means of achieving the best for its object. Socrates does not insist that the arts just mentioned are absolutely and uniquely necessary for the producing of health in their respective subjects. Yet the entire discussion with Gorgias and the short exchanges with Polus thus far have assumed that it is some kind of art that leads to a desired end, rather than nature or some familiarity or routine practice.

⟨Socrates completes this second segment (464a–b) of the account by *subdividing tendance of the body into medicine and gymnastic training* (5a and 5b respectively).⟩ Both of these have been said earlier (452a–b) to produce health, beautiful bodies, and strength. Again, as promoting different though entirely compatible conditions, medicine and training are themselves merely different, not contrary, and since there is no need to take them as exhausting the list of such arts of tendance, they need not to be thought of as parts that when paired form one whole.

⟨In the third little segment (464b–c), Socrates *sets up legislation* (6a) *next to gymnastics and makes justice* (6b) *the counterpart* (antistrophē) *of medicine.*⟩ This analogy at least suggests to Socrates that he should divide the art (or arts) of tendance of the real health of the soul (4a) into legislation and a companion art. These last two have been customarily set side by side in the mind of Gorgias (452e) and others, even though they might recognize that medicine aims at improvement of the body but not that politics aims at improvement of the soul—or they might even pass over the distinction between soul and body in the first place.

There is, however, the additional step, more of a gamble than the mere division of politics into two parts, namely, the placing of legislation over against gymnastics and judicature against medicine. Both analogies—or juxtapositions, or contrasts, call them what you please, for these are very unusual pairings—would be difficult to justify unless one could then show that beauty of the body is a kind of order, legislation being an art ordering the offices and arrangements of the state. In the same way, it would be desirable, indeed necessary, to show that justice is a keeping of that order and a restoring of that order when disorder threatens or supervenes in the state, and that the physician's function vis-à-vis the living body is much like this.[16] So the process whereby Socrates moves from medicine (5a) and gymnastics (5b) to legislation (6a) and justice or judicature (6b) is one of double analogy and proportion. He has been reluctant to show any disrespect to Gorgias but wishes nonetheless to make his chief point, that rhetoric is no genuine art. And so he employs the ingenious rhetorical device of personification, in the fourth of the small segments (464c–d).

⟨*Pandering*—here Socrates goes back to his preliminary exposition (463a–b) to reestablish the term—*pandering itself* (7) *only surmising, not really knowing the arts, divides into four parts corresponding to the four arts already set up. He offers the first two: catering* (formerly ib, now 7a), *which illicitly assumes the shape and works in the manner of medicine; embellishing* (formerly iva, now 7b), *which works in the manner of gymnastics, insinuating itself thereby into the likeness of the genuine arts.*⟩ Socrates expends most of his scorn upon these forms of pandering, leaving the other two aside for the moment. The scorn ought to keep Polus busy objecting for some little time.

The fifth little segment (464d–465b) takes up in more detail catering and embellishing as kinds of pandering. ⟨*Catering assumes the shape of medicine, pretending to know which foods are best for the body. If the caterer and doctor contend for honor before boys or men as foolish as boys, the doctor would starve. This is what I call pandering,* continues Socrates, *and this sort of thing* (here he is a little ambiguous, for he may be referring to catering alone or to pandering as a whole) *is a disgrace. It aims at the pleasant, it is a familiarity giving no account of the nature of the things it applies, it cannot tell the causes* (tēn aitian hekaston mē echein eipein) *of any of them.*⟩ Here the list of indictments moves from the fact that catering is no genuine art or knowledge to what it would have to furnish if it were one; in other words, in saying that catering gives no causes Socrates is himself giving a principal cause of the fact that catering is not an art. All the while he is driving home by repetition (as he does in his next remark [465a] that pandering is an evil) that it is rhetoric at which he is really taking aim. ⟨He attacks *embellishing* (465b) in much the same way as catering; it *works as if it were after the manner* (tropon) *of gymnastics, it is evildoing* (kakourgos), *deceitful* (apatēlē) *in its use of forms, colors, polish, dress, and efforts to make men take on external beauty; and it is ignoble* (agennēs) *and illiberal* (aneleutheros).⟩ Socrates is insisting that art or science provides insights into characters intrinsic to its subject, while pandering impersonates and provides only extrinsic information. This is a distinction that although important has been little used hitherto, but it will be crucial in the discussion with Callicles.

So much for catering and embellishing. ⟨Socrates, using the most formal and impersonal type of discourse possible, adopts a geometrical mode of expression (465b–c),[17] and in this sixth little segment proceeds to say that *as embellishing* (7b) *is to gymnastics* (5a), *so sophistic* (formerly ivb in the preliminary scheme, now 7c) *is to legislation* (6a), *and as catering is to medicine* (5b), *so is rhetoric* (7d) *to justice or judicature* (6b).⟩ He no longer moves from species to species within a larger class but instead moves across these classes to bind them together, again by analogy. It is plain that this last proportional relation neatly accomplishes the final merger of the two schemata, the preliminary and the culminating, which have dealt respectively with the familiarizations (or panderings) and with the arts impersonated by the panderings. If Gorgias, as presented here, were both a shrewder and a more touchy personality, he would be gravely offended; for he would see first that everything said of pandering would apply a fortiori to rhetoric even before its being re-introduced here, and second, that everything said of catering and embellishment could be attached through analogical reasoning (considering the permutable nature of proportions generally) to rhetoric as well—not in precisely the same sense, but in senses similar. The outcome of this passage is, of course, a double "proof" that rhetoric is not an art but illicitly aims at pleasure.

It comes to this: What Socrates says about images of real parts of the arts that care for the body applies as well to images of parts of the real political art. Rhetoric pretends to be justice, uses its language, but cares little or nothing for choosing the best state medical officer or the most impregnable fortifications or seaworthy warships. Rhetoric is irrational and footloose; it cannot spring from the natures of things because there is no knowledge by which to connect it with them, nor can it aim at the improvement of such natures because there is no solid intention of choosing the means for bringing this improvement about. Sophistry too is crooked, deceptive, mean, slavish in shaping and combining words, coloring them, smoothing them out, dressing them up, and persuading people by means of these instead of with words spoken in a true order reflecting how things really are, their causes, and their best purposes.

Having sought to explain the rationale for each of the steps, we present the relatively simple structure, marking successive movements of Socrates' progress in figure 3.2. The basis in the human being we have left in lower-case letters, the arts and their imitations being capitalized; it is these latter that are the crux of the argument. In our numbering, we have as much as practicable adhered to the order of first mention, which is not quite the most "logical" order.

There is a certain lack of symmetry in Socrates' labeling of some topics here, so that sophistry and embellishing are not termed seeming tendances of soul and body respectively, and indeed are given no common name at all, outside of the more general term of pandering which heads two other items (and still more activities) as well. In the same way, politics is not explicitly named the tendance of the soul, although that appears to be what is intended. One might also notice what are, in effect, two scales of excellence operating in the finished Oblong. First, embellishing is better than catering, gymnastic training than medicine, rhetoric than embellishing, and so on, remaining within a single column in each case; second, for a different reason, each of the four arts is better than its corresponding brand of pandering, so that medicine is better than catering, gymnastics than embellishing, and so for the rest. By tilting the Oblong to the right, one can show what is higher in worth (see fig. 3.3). Thus legislation is superior to judicature as giving it order,

[(1) human being]

(2a) soul
- (3a) real health — (4a) POLITICS, (6a) LEGISLATION, (6b) JUDICATURE
- (3c) seeming health — (7) PANDERING, (7c) SOPHISTIC, (7d) RHETORIC

(2b) body
- (3b) real health — (4b) TENDANCE, (5b) GYMNASTIC, (5a) MEDICINE
- (3d) seeming health — (7b) EMBELLISHING, (7a) CATERING

Fig. 3.2. *Order of construction of the Divided Oblong.*

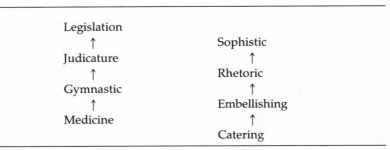

Fig. 3.3. *Tilted Divided Oblong.*

that is, determining the meanings of justice in types of actions; justice is better than gymnastics as dealing with the soul and as being all-important in the relating of human beings to each other; and gymnastics is superior to medicine in giving *greater* strength and beauty to a body already in good condition rather than simply restoring it to this condition from having previously been defective. Legislation is also superior to sophistic insofar as real good is better than seeming; and so for the other three pairs.

⟨Socrates (465d) makes an important concession, however, one applying primarily to his "geometrical" way of talking, which in a sense has taken over the culminating account though not the preliminary. *The sophists and rhetors,* he says, *are jumbled* (phurontai) *together so that it is hard to separate them, much as if we were following the lead of Anaxagoras, a lead which Polus would follow, being familiar* (empeiros) *with these things.*⟩ Socrates is evidently referring either to Anaxagoras' famous remark that in the beginning all things were together or to something similar in his writings and now lost. This reference actually reflects upon rhetors generally and not merely upon Polus, for the natural tendency of these men is to make as few distinctions as possible and then only to gain the interest of the crowd; *his* discriminations are based upon pleasures in contrast to real causes. (It should be clear, of course, that there is no reason whatever to think that Anaxagoras had rhetoric in mind in his original statement.)

It may seem that Socrates makes the concession about jumbling at the one juncture where he has used quasi-geometrical precision to establish these relations; but this is the very point where, as Whitehead would say, the exactness is a fake, and as he might have added, a fake regardless of the honesty of the man endeavoring to speak so exactly. The apparently fine-cut distinctions are not really proper to the subject matter, and it would be difficult indeed to separate rhetoric from outright sophistry, especially when sophistry has remained but a shadow in this dialogue.

Two possibilities present themselves here. It must seem to every reader that the jumbling refers to a possible confusion between sophistry and rhetoric, or even between embellishing and catering. But this may not be Socrates' whole intention. Catering caters mainly by making foods tasty, but there may be decorating as well of the meats and cakes and table-settings that doubly entices the diner. In the same way, rhetoric and catering are not altogether distinct, for a familiar vote-getting device is to fill the potential voters with popular foods. A candidate for office or a trial lawyer, furthermore, who neglects to wear the proper clothing for an occasion is far more likely to lose. The same might well apply to the sophistic teacher desiring to add knowledge to, and subtract money from, his pupils. Hence the concession does not elevate rhetoric at all, for it is not said to run together with justice but rather with catering, which pertains to the body. (*Otherwise*, Socrates hints (465d), *there would be some generalized gratification of which the body alone would be the judge*.) That Polus does indeed see all these things as one was shown by his earlier supposition that catering and rhetoric must be the same if they are parts of the same thing (462e).[18]

Doubtless Gorgias and Polus would be willing to find gratification and nothing more in food, perhaps also in embellishments, but it is quite conceivable that they would deny it as the sole end of rhetoric, for Gorgias thinks of rhetoric as aiming at persuasion, and it is by no means made clear that persuasion and gratification are one and the same, although perhaps related causally in some fashion. Thus fear implanted in an audience is certainly unpleasant but is nevertheless a means of persuading. Socrates might reply that the clever rhetor could commence a speech by exciting fear, but would gradually steer around to a resolution of the fear—a pleasant feeling—that would replace the uneasiness, and would then propose a new plan of action.

We believe that Plato had a figure much like the Divided Oblong in mind; and we assume that the two principal headings are the real arts and their imitations and that with these Socrates has strung together many kinds of dialectical relations which are in effect movements of thought and not mere dead classificatory labels. His method has been one of finding the most general headings to bind all the relevant kinds of things into a quasi unity and then by various means to distinguish new kinds having separations between them denoting their own natural integrity.[19] But that method, as employed here, is somewhat loosely applied, partly because of the problematical and changeable subject matter and partly because Socrates' present hearers are poor at making distinctions. As soon as Socrates retraces his steps, setting up stricter proportions, he apologizes by saying that the real situation is not so clear.

For the Oblong to have philosophical value instead of being a curiosity, it must not be arbitrary but must share in its construction the same kinds of transitions from concept to concept that are found in the rest of the discussion. In it the literal movements are from a concrete entity to something pertaining to it: from body to its tendance, and from soul to *its* tendance. After that the movement, still literal, is from bodily tendance to its kinds—the species gymnastics and medicine. On the other hand, the relation between something real and its imitation is an imaging relation, one lacking safeguards against inaccuracy that the whole-part or thing-appurtenance relations can possess. Parts, if they are species, must share all the general characteristics of the whole, and that which pertains can be shown to inhere in, or attach invariably (or for the most part) to, the thing to which it pertains. The image, however, must be discovered—invented, so to speak—and has characteristics that seem to be but are truly inherent neither in the real counterparts nor in what images the real, hence no causal deduction is possible, there is no essential connection between model and copy. The image itself is not a chimera except in relation to what it is imaging; rhetoric is a thing, it cannot be waived away like a mirage in the desert; but as imitative it has only a pretense of having this particular reality of its model, and in fact has a reality of a quite different sort. Since pandering imitates the real, all four parts of pandering will bear this imitative relation to the arts they image.[20] The imaging relation can at best be expressed as an analogy, and because of the weakness of such an argument when it stands by itself, the way to compensate is to produce a *series* of analogies that are brought to bear on the topic to be clarified. This the Divided Oblong seeks to do, at first casually and then in well-labeled geometrical proportions. The Oblong once expounded is a set of benchmarks that indicate the mind's wave movements from topic to topic.

Socrates has ended the exposition of the Oblong but is not done with the important applications retained throughout the dialogue though modified in significant ways to comport with further progress of the dialectic, as if it were a loose-fitting garment, not a strait jacket. Remarkably, not one of the three rhetors has any immediate comment upon it, each for reasons of his own. As for Polus, he has what may be called a single-purpose intellect, scattered as he is in his efforts to make it function; he can learn anything from Gorgias but nothing from Socrates. Gorgias retires from the present discussion at this point (his last interjection has been at 464b), and the presumption is that he accepts the dark shade just now cast upon his queenly "art"—for the duration of the dialogue but certainly not for good.

The final segment of this first section, in which Socrates, Polus, and Gorgias have exchanged roles much as roles were traded in the Prologue, is another little interlude (465d–466a), this one dealing with the length and intelligibility of the speech just given by Socrates after Gorgias has left off. ⟨It seems absurd to give a long speech when I have denied this privilege to you, Polus, but the fact is that you did not understand (ouk emanthanes) when I spoke briefly (465e).⟩ This is an important point, for Socrates may well have four different possibilities in mind here, all of which have their place:

1. Short speeches that are understood, such as those occasions when Socrates acts as questioner and easily apprehends—indeed anticipates—the responses.
2. Short speeches not understood, such as the one in which Socrates first proposed his theory of rhetoric to Polus (463c–d).
3. Long speeches not understood, such as the one made by Gorgias (456a–457c, cf. 462e–463a).
4. Long speeches that are understood; those are yet to come.

A remark or two should be in order here. Throughout the preliminary exposition of the Oblong, Polus is the sole questioner. Both his questions and the replies by Socrates are brief, and the conversation *appears* to fall into group (1). But in truth Polus understands so little, and his questions are so mechanical, that the whole performance amounts to a single long address, the questions being pro forma, merely supporting the illusory belief held by Polus that he is able to extract the answers from his respondent. The situation is little changed when Gorgias takes his turn, for he is, no matter how willing to proceed with an order in mind, frequently unable to follow the details of that arrangement. But this is still an improvement upon Polus, who has little sense of *any* order, as we shall be demonstrating later on.

One of the peculiarities of Socratic dialectic is that, in its literary dress at least, it frequently reflects either seriously or through parody, leading characteristics of the respondent. This is noticeable here, for the preliminary account is mainly a heaping-up of ephithets clustered about familiarity, a term first introduced by Polus, whereas the more authoritative exposition, setting up the Oblong, is controlled, methodical. Whether Polus grasps either style is open to some question, which he speedily puts to rest himself.

⟨After remarking that he will try to use the short answers from Polus, otherwise the long ones, Socrates challenges him to make use (chrēsthai) of his answer (465d–466a). If I cannot use, that is, first understand and then incorporate, your short answers you may make longer ones.⟩ This was a courtesy that Socrates has tossed to Polus, but an empty one, rhetorical in spirit. Socrates, we have gathered before, can perfectly well "use" the short speeches because they have been responses to his own questions. In the individual steps they are so directed and ordered in respect to common thought and experience (regardless of paradoxical conclusions often reached) that it is next to impossible to give unexpected and disconcertingly tangential answers. Polus must know by this time that he will be interrupted at the first turn if his points fit together poorly. But Socrates has proffered an invitation: Make use of the Oblong if you can. Polus will not be using it. He cannot and will not try to build his structures upon it, in whole or in part; he is, so far as Socrates lets him be, a young horse running loose in the meadow. The Oblong in Socrates' hands will be a line over which Polus should not step, though not a fence. It is not kept visible in its entirety. Only certain distinctions are held in view for the purpose of keeping Polus within proper bounds.

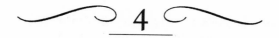

4

RHETORIC WITHOUT POWER

(466a–481b)

The colloquy in which Polus is the primary respondent (he has a little help from Gorgias) is divided into three parts, the first (461b–466a) having been devoted mainly to the Divided Oblong, the second, wherein Socrates shows that rhetoric devoid of knowledge and justice is without power, stretching for the next eight pages. This section, 466a–474b, is subdivided. With Polus alternating roles with Socrates, they attempt to estimate the worth of rhetors (466a–468e). Part of the time (468e–471d) in the second subdivision Polus continues as questioner as the conversation turns in a provisional way to the doing and undergoing of injustice and the penalties that may be assessed for committing it. The third section takes the reader from 474b to 481b.

We turn to the first subdivision of the second section, which in turn has two parts. Page 466a–467c, with Polus questioning, asks whether rhetors are worthless in their cities because they are panderers, and the single page 467c–468e examines the difference between wishing and willing, Polus now being the respondent.

⟨At 466a Polus, in response to Socrates' challenge to make use of the long answer expounding the Divided Oblong, asks, not very brightly, *whether rhetors are panderers* (466a), a question at bottom ambiguous. (Is justice virtue? can be taken as asking whether it is identical with virtue or whether it is a part of virtue.) Socrates, who has said distinctly that rhetoric is one of four parts of pandering (463a–c and 464e–465c), delivers a stinging rebuke to his errant companion: *At your age, Polus, can you not remember? What will you do later on?* Socrates, chiding him, reminds him too that *rhetoric has been termed a* part *of pandering.*⟩ This may seem a small point, but it is significant if the Oblong, which never loses its importance for Socrates although he modifies it, is apprehended and apparently agreed to by Polus and then by Callicles, though they ignore many of its details and try to circumvent it as a whole. Polus is already guilty of what Socrates conceives as an Anaxagorean muddle. Yet someone as near to befuddlement as Polus is—so Socrates thinks—will need all the help from the distinctions, including part-whole distinctions, that he can get. This would come not merely from repeating them (although your memory, Polus, is poor and needs jogging, such a tragedy at your age!) but rather by showing how they function when we consider the questions *you* want taken up.

After this little riposte, the two men settle down to the problem of the worth of rhetoric, a question far from Polus' mind at the outset of the dialogue; he took it for granted that it was the fairest art. But now he had become conscious of the taxing review that it has undergone, and also realizes that this review has taken place before the two kinds of persons whom neither he nor Gorgias would want to have in attendance: other followers, of whom Callicles is apparently one, and casual hearers, some of them likely to become pupils themselves. All of these represent the public that both Gorgias and Polus would like to persuade and dominate. If Polus knows all that Gorgias knows (462a), then presumably Polus holds the key not only to rhetoric but to power and freedom as well, for the power of the rhetor allows him to turn others into his slaves (452e). Polus will eventually add happiness to the conception of this power. Gorgias stopped short of saying that happiness is the end of the rhetor's art; to him rhetoric was the means of persuasion, but dealt with justice and freedom, or rather, if it did not use these terms directly at least it presented issues revolving around them. Thus in one sense the discussion with Polus will broaden the pattern just presented with Gorgias, and will now include the happiness that is the aim of everyone and every act in life, while in another sense it will narrow the pattern, for now the subject will not be persuasion in general but persuasion used only for the sake of obtaining power, a power which, it turns out, is that of the tyrant.

⟨Polus asks (466a–b) *whether good rhetors are worthless because they are panderers in their cities.*⟩ One notices that Polus seems dimly to have separated good rhetors from bad, though he gives not the slightest indication of a criterion; and since he has repudiated Gorgias' version of justice, it cannot be conformity to a just ideal. He is also curious about the reputation of rhetors *in their cities*. This may reflect the fact that although Gorgias and Polus have traveled much, Polus is perceiving the cut-and-run of rhetors as citizens of one city or another, much as generals or architects would be. But in the mind of both men, they themselves are quite special persons, as their practice is not only in speaking but in teaching as well, and they feel themselves distinguished by their cosmopolitan experience.

⟨To Polus, Socrates responds (466b) that *rhetors are of little account, as they have the least power of anyone, if power means something good for the rhetor himself.*⟩ This bypasses the Oblong and returns to the colloquy with Gorgias, who insisted that the doctor and engineer were slaves of the rhetor, that rhetoric was a convenience replacing all other arts (459c), and that it dealt with the highest of human concerns (451d). Socrates' present assertion is thereby in contrast to Gorgias' view, placing the rhetor not second or in the middle but at the lower end of the scale of citizens. ⟨To this Polus counters (466c) with a suggestion that he says is *in the form of a question, that rhetors are like tyrants killing, despoiling, or exiling those whom they choose.*⟩ It is clear that Polus is interested here not in the goodness of effects of power so much as in the intensity of its application, by linking it to the one kind of leader with virtually no checks upon his actions. Whether or not Socrates has suspected all along that this is what Polus had in mind, it is still a staggering revelation in view of Gorgias' earlier disavowal of responsibility for the unjust actions of his pupils and the claim that they and they alone should pay the penalty (456c–457c). Polus is implying that the rhetor, too, must in some way be not above reproach but beyond the power of other citizens to hinder him or exact retribution.[1] ⟨To the view of Gorgias (and Polus as well) expressed in the Prologue (448c; 456a–b), that *the rhetor* had an exceptional art, Polus now adds that he *has an exceptional status. He is like the tyrant in doing what he wishes, is he not?*⟩

Polus is asking this as a question, of course thinking that the affirmative answer is taken for granted. Socrates, instead of saying no, indicates that *the question is ambiguous* (466d–d): *It can mean doing what one wishes* (poiein ōn boulontai), *or else doing what one believes is best* (doxē beltiston einai).⟩ This distinction parallels but is not equivalent to the earlier one between doing what is best and doing what gives pleasure, but the language is reversed, since doing what one believes best is related to the pleasure it gives the doer, while doing what one wills brings about long-range goods by reason of its being really the best. ⟨*Doing the former,* says Socrates (466e), *is not a great power, and to this Polus should agree, for he has just said* (466b) *that great power is a good to him who possesses it. This,* Socrates replies, *is impossible to the man lacking intelligence or reason* (noun mē echōn). *You must prove, Polus, that rhetors do have this intelligence and that rhetoric is an art rather than a species of pandering* (466e–467a).⟩ One notes that the emphasis has shifted, for in the colloquy with Gorgias, discussion centered around rhetoric as connected with knowledge and being an art thereby, whereas here it is the rhetor, not his art, who is to have the intelligence. The intelligence now is of a different kind; Socrates thinks of it as knowing what is really the best, while earlier it was simply mastery of what Gorgias thought useful to his particular case in a court or assembly. To him rhetoric is beneficial to its practitioners, but it can most easily be so when the crowd's welfare or apparent welfare is considered. To Polus this is irrelevant at this point. He would, if left to himself, fuse most of the squares of the Oblong, and the ones he would keep separate would be turned upside down in their relative positions.

⟨Socrates continues (466e–467a): *If I am right, and you do not refute me, we must agree that rhetors and tyrants doing what they think fit* (dokei) *in their cities will have gained no good. You say both that power is a good and that doing what one thinks fit but without intelligence is an evil. Rhetors (and tyrants) do not do what they wish.*⟩ Here Socrates has turned the emphasis from the difficulty of bringing about the right result to the utter impossibility of bringing it about if one lacks the intelligence. Now for Polus, art *still* derives from familiarity, a condition in which knowledge is by no means a necessary ingredient, and unfamiliarity leads to chance. But since intelligence is not being considered he is, so to speak, leaving the field open to chance; one does as one wills, merely hoping for the best. The Socratic premise underlying this entire section is that art and knowledge are so closely related as to be virtually identical, and familiarity is intertwined with belief, a condition leaving room for chance, which to Polus may well be good, while to Socrates it cannot be counted on to bring about anything but evil.

⟨There is a short interlude (467b–c). *Socrates*, exclaims Polus, *gives monstrous answers.*⟩ Up to this point, he has pretty well tolerated most of what Socrates has been saying to him, partly no doubt because his understanding of it has been imperfect, but now there is a cumulative effect from the earlier responses and the present one, and Polus bursts out in frustration and disbelief. But this is also a rhetorical trick, which Socrates immediately detects, that of opposing by the use of invective. ⟨*If you cannot refute me with questions*, he says (467c), *try it with answers.* Polus gives a very strange reply: *I'm willing to answer in order to find out what you are saying.*⟩ How would this be possible in any straightforward conversation? The problem for the reader is then to decide whether Polus has the skill to refute Socrates in either way, by questioning or by answering. Can he possibly manage the dialectic?

A new little segment begins(467c–468e), with Socrates as questioner. It has two small parts: First (467c–d) the Socratic distinction between willing and wishing is clarified, and then (467d–468e) Socrates lays out (even though he frames his points as questions) a threefold list of goods, evils, and intermediates.

⟨*Doing what one wishes involves a means-ends distinction—taking bitter medicine for the sake of good health, or sailing for the sake of wealth* (got from profitable trading). *The means may be ever so unpleasant, but the end makes them worthwhile.*⟩ This example of Socrates can also relate to the sea voyages of Gorgias and Polus, and is certainly one to which Polus would agree. It can also, through an extension to the general case that Socrates himself notes (467d), refer to the arduous discussion that the two men are now having. Then (467e–468e) Socrates offers three lists as given in figure 4.1.

⟨*People*, Socrates goes on (468a–b), perform the *intermediate activities for the sake of the good, and this is true not only of walking but also of killing, banishing, or confiscating property, which are neither good nor evil in themselves, but only in reference to their ends (468c–d).*⟩

Several comments can be made regarding the threefold list presented in figure 4.2. The list extends the idea of the original distinction between ends and means. It was first assumed that all disagreeable acts are performed for the sake of an end, and the end was a good.

The three outright goods listed pertain to the soul, the body, and external property respectively, and so with the outright evils. A case could be made for walking, sitting, running, sailing, and banishing as tending toward goods (or evils) of the body, of sticks, stones and confiscating as tending toward goods (or evils) of property, and of killing, as directed at a man's soul. But this last may be too pat, and it is arguable that the list of intermediates is deliberately left in a disorganized condition simply because no values can be placed at this stage upon each item.

The unconditional goods might be chosen in the face of unfamiliarity, inexperience, lack of intelligence, but the outright evils would most certainly be avoided in every case. Thus there is a certain imbalance between the two lists.

Purposes have been considered before in the *Gorgias*, but never very carefully. Socrates has introduced them in the general sense of aiming at pleasure or at the best, but what these latter are has not been specified. As a matter of fact, the best is detailed in the present passage, but the kinds of pleasures are not made clear until after Callicles breaks into the discussion, and then only after many preliminaries have been settled. ⟨The point that is being made here is that *one wishes* (rather than wills) *to banish or kill only if there are benefits attached,* not merely other items in the intermediate column (*one does not wish to kill for the sake of walking*) or outright evils (468c). *The tyrant or rhetor thinks he is doing what is fit, even though it may be worse for him* (468d).⟩ Here we notice that Socrates is assuming that what a man does, even when in a position of power, will in the end react upon himself, not in any literal sense, of course (a tyrant killing another man may not be killed by others in return), but in the general sense of conferring some advantage or disadvantage upon him. ⟨*A man who acts without knowing as well as possible the*

GOODS	INTERMEDIATES	EVILS
wisdom	sitting	ignorance
health	walking	illness
wealth	running	poverty
etc.	sailing	etc.
	stones	
	sticks	
	etc.	

Fig. 4.1. *Kinds of goods.*

	POLUS' MAN	SOCRATES' MEN		
	1	2	3	4
Agent:				
Pitiable	—	—	more	less	more
Emulable	—	—	—	—	—
Judgments on Agent:				
Miserable	+	—	more	less	more
Not Miserable	—	+	—	—	—
Action or Passion:				
Puts to Death	+	+	+	—	—
Is Put to Death	—	—	—	+	+
Quality:				
Justly	—	+	—	—	+
Unjustly	?	—	+	+	—

Fig. 4.2. *Schematism of Socrates' reply to Polus' question.*

likely outcome of his act will run the risk of making a serious mistake and with it of incurring a misfortune. This is not power (468e).)

Two conclusions that can be drawn from this passage are that power is the receiving of benefits to oneself, or perhaps the capability to assure that such benefits will result from a chosen line of action; and that the rhetor can be mistaken regarding the ultimate results of his choices, if he lacks two kinds of knowledge: first, the probable effects of his act, for example, will executing a man stir his relatives and friends to rebellion, and, second, whether those results are in themselves good or bad. This latter is less likely to be so—more people are aware that poverty and sickness are evils than are aware of the courses of action that will lead to them, especially when these courses are indirect. Throwing one's money away directly leads to poverty, but confiscating another person's may have this effect through a circuitous chain of events.

This raises the interesting question, Where does rhetoric itself belong in this three-column list? At no point has Socrates said that rhetoric is an outright evil, nor has he agreed with Gorgias and Polus that it is the fairest of arts, an unqualified good. For them, however, even if it *is* a good, they have not looked upon it as an end in itself—it makes money for the rhetor or gets him out of trouble. Gorgias and Polus distinguish individual means from ends, but seem to have no very clear notion of a general means-ends distinction; and of intermediates they have had scarcely the foggiest conception.

But does rhetoric take its place among the intermediates, as does walking? Can it be turned toward good or evil? Here one must consult Socrates, and his answer, were he to give one, would be cautious. Art, for him, confers the power to know the good of each thing and the attendant power to choose rightly for that thing and bring about its best possible condition. If, then, rhetoric is a dissembling substitute it cannot be merely indifferent, much as any fraudulent cure for a disease is an evil, not something neutral. On the other hand, Socrates will later (480a–481b) uncover one single employment of rhetoric that is for the good, hence rhetoric cannot be totally evil. It might be safe to say that for Socrates rhetoric falls partly into the second and third columns, under the intermediate and the evil, but the balance in these two placings must at all times be observed.

We are at the end of a subdivision, and it is advisable to glance for a moment at the structure of Polus' argumentation, which is emerging more clearly. It is ill-conceived, yet not altogether uncommon. So far, he has made identifications out of pairs of terms that others have kept separate, except for his own quotation from his book, where contrary terms are explicitly established as opposites. Doubtless his inability to keep separate the paired notions of rhetoric and fair art, rhetoric and pandering, rhetor and tyrant, that allows one to assume that Polus' jumbling of things, in the manner ascribed to Anaxagoras, is not unfairly alleged. At 466a–b he starts with panderers who are either rhetors or else—but he has no opposite; then he goes on to rhetors in their own cities or—again, no opposite; rhetors in cities having most power—again, no contrast, although each of these levels could well be completed. He is building a structure consisting of a single column of terms, and because there are no subdivisions, each of the terms in that column fuses with all the others. It is into this dialectical morass that Socrates is trying to introduce some distinctions. But the reader may ask why it is that in his book Polus has indeed separated art from chance, familiarity from unfamiliarity. Perhaps the answer is that when the young colt settles down to put more fully considered ideas on wax or papyrus, he is better able to collect his thoughts and make divisions. Certainly he has received no high marks for clarity of extempore speech so far.

*   *   *

A new section (468e–474b) now commences; it mainly concerns injustice and the penalties therefore, and is divided into two subdivisions, the first dealing with the doing and undergoing of harm unjustly (468e–471d), the second (471d–474b) with the compatibility of happiness, wickedness, and punishment or paying the penalty. The functions of questioner and answerer change rapidly between the participants.

⟨Would you not accept, asks Polus (468e–469a), the liberty of doing what you think fit in your city, and emulate (zēlois) a man putting to death or confiscating property or imprisoning anyone as he thinks fit, whether justly or unjustly?⟩ The oddity in the phrasing of this question lies in the harping upon behaving in a certain way in one's own city, as if Polus believed that right and justice were entirely determinable by the customs of one's own community, every community being different. If Polus is young—and he is—and has been a pupil or companion of Gorgias for quite some time—and he has—then it would follow that Polus must feel himself a kind of migrant with no fixed domicile. Whether or not this is a reason for his continued wondering how the rhetor or tyrant fares in his own town, it betrays the fact that Polus is again thinking in terms of the immediate results of rhetorical practice rather than whether that practice is good in itself and in respect of mankind at large. His dependence upon results is again exhibited in his conscious disregard of the issue of justice versus injustice: Do we emulate the tyrant if we think it to our advantage? ⟨To this bald question Socrates makes a detailed reply, headed by the general consideration that we should not emulate those who should not be emulated, nor should we emulate the miserable (athlious) but rather pity (eleein) them (469a–b).⟩ The four major headings of the possible combinations include the agent (whether pitiable or emulable), the judgments made upon him (whether he should be thought miserable or not), action or passion (whether one puts to death or is put to death), and finally the quality of that act or passion (justly or unjustly). Exactly how many combinations could be enumerated if this partial array were completed cannot easily be determined, because

Socrates sometimes uses *more* and *less* for the condition and estimation of the agent; but he could use them for degrees of justice and injustice as well. The cases he lists constitute a rough schematism and would require much further explanation were this the main center of our attention (see fig. 4.2).

⟨Polus (469b–c) continues the questioning: *How is it that (3) the man unjustly put to death is less miserable than (2) the man killing someone unjustly or (4) the one killed justly?* Socrates' response is one leading directly back to the tyrant and his supposed power: *Doing injustice is a worse evil than undergoing it, though I wish for neither* (469c). *I would not*, he continues, *accept a tyrant's power, at least power in my sense.* Upon this, Polus repeats himself (from 466a–c), that *this power is doing as one thinks fit in one's city, putting people to death and all the rest, according to one's own opinion* (kata tēn autou doxan).⟩ We see here the shamelessness that Gorgias himself shied away from; Polus has defined a way of life, and although it is neither above nor below the law (because the law has not yet appeared in this colloquy), it is at least independent of what Polus takes to be justice. Gorgias has sought to remain within the confines of decency, along with the appearance of decency; if Polus is serious, he will move in a new and wider orbit.

⟨The response of Socrates is immediate (469c–470c), and is directed to showing that the kind of power that Polus is supposing is by no means uniquely held. *If in a crowded agora I carry a hidden dagger, boasting of a tyrant's power, that is, the ability to kill, or break a head or tear a cloak* [the soul-body-property distinction again] *as I think fit, you would have to admit that everyone shared this power.* The agora would turn into a feral jungle, with *ships and houses both public and private being put to the torch.*

But to commit this kind of destruction is certainly not to have power. To this *Polus accedes* (469e), but only because he deems that *the man exercising this sort of power will necessarily be punished* (zēmiousthai, be fined, pay a penalty).⟩ At this juncture if becomes clear what Polus has had in the back of his mind from the very first: Rhetoric is the fairest art, it is the tyrant's art, it puts the tyrant where he wishes to be; and tyranny is to be judged in terms of profit and loss, how much one can do and still go unpunished.

⟨*You have come round again*, Socrates says (470a–b), *to the point that if doing what one thinks fit is actually accompanied by advantage to the doer, then it is both a good and something of great power, otherwise not. It is better to put people to death, banish them, confiscate their property when this is done justly, and worse when unjustly* (470c). Polus hangs back from admitting all this, and instead shows his impatience once more: *A child could refute you, Socrates . . . . I should be grateful to the child*, is the reply.⟩

Although Polus should be making distinctions of some sort, he does not. He accepts the ordinary man with the dagger as being on the same level with the rhetor-tyrant, viewing the latter in terms of one criterion only—whether he will be punished. His one reason for thinking that the tyrant is in a poor predicament is that he will inevitably have to pay a penalty. Following none of the distinctions that Socrates has established, he uses what has been called a one-term dialectic, that is, a single column of terms with their contraries either not indicated or at best mere shadows implied in what might have been fuller structures.[2]

The jibe by Polus, that a child could refute Socrates, sounds a little odd, coming as it does from a young man who has shown many childish traits: sudden enthusiasm, vanity, a bumptious readiness to criticize his elders, a waywardness in his train of thought, and failure to listen closely to the direct and immediate answers given to his own questions. We cannot mean by this that the conversation is unequal to the point of unfairness on the part of Plato, for the temperament of Polus is also both tenacious and exasperating, two qualities making it possible for an immature person to *seem* to carry the day against a more judicious one when rhetoric dictates the prevailing manner of discourse, and victory before an audience is the aim. There is an involution here: A childish man is claiming that a child could refute Socrates, and this implies further that the latter's argument is so simple and so wrong that it merits no additional effort to correct it.

The answer that Socrates has given, expressing gratitude, is one of the few that would silence Polus and also be consistent with the earlier remark that he would be glad to be refuted if he had said anything untrue, that being refuted in such a case is the greatest good (458a). Here, gratitude toward the child underlines this point, for such a refutation is both most unlikely and most humiliating. In effect, even were Polus to outdo himself in concocting a brilliant confutation of Socrates' position, he would still be nothing but a child, yet would be deserving of Socrates' thanks. Another neat sally.

⟨Polus, however, is not daunted and introduces (470c–471d) a man he takes to be a "witness" (Socrates' word 471e) to the *power of tyranny, Archelaus, ruler of Macedonia.* He is *a figure of the recent past,* says Polus—*no need of ancient examples*—and although Socrates does not know him and cannot tell whether he is happy, Polus thinks him *as clear an instance of happiness as is the Great King of Persia.* To which Socrates replies (470e) that *whether Archelaus is happy or not depends upon the way he holds with culture* (paideia) *and justice. A good man* or woman (notice the addition, unusual in this dialogue!) *is happy, a base one miserable* (470e).⟩

The introduction of Archelaus could be a signal to us, as it has been to some critics, to question Plato's fairness to him, but this issue can only be decided when we see how that ruler fits into the argument. If

Plato accords a "bad press" to Archelaus, surely he accords all the unfavorable reports of his actions to an immature young man all but discredited for his other judgments and struggling to score a point in a difficult situation. Socrates, by saying he does not know Archelaus, automatically confers a freedom and a responsibility upon Polus. Other classical Greek writers, it happens, have praised this king of Macedonia, mainly for the one point that Socrates mentions, culture, which was so strong an interest that Archelaus managed to attract several artists and writers of the first rank away from Athens, at least for a time.

Polus insists upon using Archelaus as an example despite Socrates' lack of acquaintance with him, or apparently, with even his reputation.[3] Gorgias had made an attempt to use Themistocles and Pericles as examples (455e), old enough to be well known to all Athenians, one of the two having been heard firsthand by Socrates, and whose influence could be seen everywhere in the newly adorned city. ⟨Polus, for his part, selects a foreigner unknown to Socrates, and is offended by the latter's response to the point of jeering at him: *If you cannot estimate the happiness of Archelaus you cannot judge the Great King either* (470e). *Everyone knows that the man wielding that much power must be perfectly happy.*⟩ The superficiality of Polus' argument here is so apparent that it must subtract some of the credibility from his subsequent story of Archelaus' checkered career.

⟨He now launches (471a–d) into a tangled account, commencing by saying flatly that *Archelaus must be unjust* and then, as if offering some proof, saying that *he had no claim to the throne and in fact was a slave.* But this in itself shows little, and certainly does not justify the piece of sarcasm coming next, that *Archelaus was wonderfully* (thaumasiōs) *miserable because he had done an injustice by not continuing to serve the brother of his natural father.* By implication Polus is mistakenly attributing to Socrates the contention, not that injustice and misery are causally related to each other, which would be in order, but that it is impossible to be king and be happy at the same time.

After this untoward beginning, Polus embarks on a short recital of Archelaus' reported misdeeds that is lacking in a causal or even chronological relation: *Archelaus gets his uncle and cousin drunk, then murders them.* But what has this to do with his humble origins or his kingship, and at what stage did this event occur? Polus then says that *Archelaus failed to bring up his own (half) brother, but drowned him instead.* The contrast between educating a boy and drowning him is at best lopsided. And then, to cap all the crimes, *Archelaus lies to the queen, saying that the young prince tumbled into a well.* But lying is small change in comparison to murder. Polus' story ends with a repetition of the earlier sarcasm against a theory that kingship and happiness are incompatible—a the-

ory that Socrates has not entertained here.⟩ The story is so sketchy and
so garbled that instead of believing Plato to have been unfair to Archelaus, it really appears that the philosopher-artist wanted to put the
hostile reports into the mouth of a man light in weight but heavy in
pretensions. Certainly the narration has none of the ordering principles that Socrates would have employed—mention of soul, body,
property; ruler and city; wise and foolish men; or any other relations of
significance in judging political success in respect of moral good. It is
not so much that Polus makes Archelaus a thoroughly unscrupulous
man, or that he attributes, somewhat left-handedly through his sarcasm, happiness to such a scoundrel. Rather it is the fact that he has not
thought through any possible, convincing reason why Archelaus
should be so happy, nor even that he is happy. He has not quite assumed that the murdering of one's own family brings happiness, nor
has he given any indication of why kingly power brings it. He has furnished no definition of happiness or power, and has thus far left untouched the Socratic distinction between wishing and willing, though
already he has all but conceded its correctness. Even a crowd of listeners to a rhetorical address would find Polus' account badly out of
joint and almost wholly irrelevant.

⟨Another segment (471d–474b) begins, exploring the compatibility of
happiness and wickedness. Socrates does not, for the moment, raise
any of these objections to Polus' recital but counters in an interlude
(471d–472c) with the remark that *he has already spoken favorably* (448d–
449b) *of Polus' training in rhetoric but finds that he has neglected discussion*
(dialegesthai). (In truth, the compliment was at best a faint one, and
Socrates is disarming him now.) *You do not refute me in this fashion, Polus,
and I admit not one point in what you have said.* And the latter: *This is because you do not want to agree, though in fact you do* (471e).⟩[4] No doubt this
is a general assumption that Polus is making: that a man apparently disagreeing with him is underneath all his objections secretly in sympathy. Polus appears untouched by Socrates' assertion about rhetoric as
being not an art but a kind of image low in class, not even on a level
with sophistry. Just wait, Polus seems to indicate by his imperturb-
ability; if I unlimber my big guns I'll be able to crack this façade.

⟨Socrates answers by saying (471e–472a) that *Polus entertains this
thought because he is arguing on a purely rhetorical level. He is bringing repu-
table witnesses against me, as if this were a lawcourt, hoping to win because I
produce none in my own behalf; but such arguments can never get at the truth.*[5]
No matter how many you bring, I alone do not agree.⟩ This reflects a theme
increasingly prominent in the dialogue, although never explicitly argued at length: that of universal agreement. Polus, as we said, believes
so wholeheartedly in his ill-considered doctrines that he cannot con-

ceive that anyone could disagree in thought as well as in words with what he is asserting. Socrates, on the other hand, thinks of Polus as having committed himself to an error dangerous as it is serious, and that he must secure the required agreement through discussion, making Polus the witness against his former preoccupation with power at the expense of every other good. Here there is not only a difference in methods of discussion but also one regarding politics. The natural companion to Polus' view would be a bold declaration, I am the law, followed by the prediction that everyone will fall in line eventually. Socrates has not yet offered his alternative to this, and its coming will be a surprise.[6]

⟨The disquisition on contrasting manners of refutation continues: *Your kind of refuting, Polus, is worthless for arriving at truth, since a man (who is right) may be crushed by the number and good reputation of false witnesses* (472a).⟩ What Socrates is noting, of course, is the difference between interior and adventitious criteria for truth telling. It has apparently not occurred to Polus that truth is other than what wins the day in the courtroom. ⟨Socrates goes further: *Your method of bringing witnesses (true or false) will be agreed to by Nicias, Aristocrates, the house of Pericles, and nearly everyone else; but I still do not agree, alone as I am in this, for all you are doing is trying to banish me from truth* (472a–b). *When, on the other hand, it comes to* my *furnishing witnesses, I need to produce only you, much as you would need to produce me* (472b–c).⟩ The implication is that agreement here between the two disputing parties produces, or is at least a sign of, truth. Socrates is not claiming that any and all truths are generated or even signalized in this way, but only those kinds relevant to the present discussion.[7] The truth that would emerge from such an agreement would not be a single statement but rather a sequence of coherent statements, for which agreement is secure at each step as the discussion advances. Whether the first statements formulated the causes of the later or the reverse is not here in question. Socrates has little use for individual formulas without antecedents or successors. Had Polus agreed to the Divided Oblong, if only in principle, the task would have been easier.

⟨Almost as an afterthought in this little interlude, Socrates points out the importance of making a comparison (between the two modes of proof). *It is fairest to know* (eidenai) *about their differences, and most disgraceful not to, for they involve* (not only types of argument but also) *the question of knowing who is happy and who is not* (472c).⟩[8] The reader notices here, if not several pages earlier in the dialogue, that the center of interest is moving back and forth from the nature of rhetoric (and argument) to the power that is supposedly the end and purpose of rhetoric, and each time comes to rest upon the latter, in a shift of focus without a radical change of subject matter.

POLUS	SOCRATES
a. a man such as Archelaus can be happy while doing injustice	ai. this is impossible (472d)
b. an unjust man will not be happy if paying a penalty, but happy if not paying one	bi. the unjust man is miserable, and more so if paying no penalty, less so if paying it to gods and men (472e)

Fig. 4.3. *Whether happiness and wickedness are compatible.*

The interlude just past is followed by a summary (472c–473b) of the substantive argument preceding it, and this in turn is succeeded by the new argument proper, and then an interlude (473e–474b) dealing with a comparison between the punished and the unpunished man who is unjust. Whether happiness and wickedness are really compatible is the most pervasive question.

⟨The little summary mentions two points of difference between the opponents as shown in figure 4.3. Polus thinks he has refuted Socrates, to which the latter replies: *You are a friend, hence I shall try to make you maintain the view I hold.*⟩

Socrates' brief summary has bypassed the relations established in the Divided Oblong. He has not peremptorily abandoned it, but has evidently given up hope for the time being that he can secure Polus' comprehension of it, much less his agreement. Polus makes all his old mistakes when any of the distinctions arise, and Socrates evidently realizes that if he is to carry the day with Polus it must be through different lines of inquiry.

⟨So on to the argument proper (473b–474b). Polus commences by asking *whether a man unjustly plotting to make himself tyrant, but who is caught and horribly tortured, will be happier than one escaping such treatment and living out his life tyrannically ruling the city, emulated by all. Does Socrates think it impossible to refute that argument?*⟩ This is a rhetorical question, of course, for Polus thinks he knows the response; and Socrates does give an answer that in another sense is equally rhetorical, for it is about rhetoric, which is not at issue here, but only seems to be, yet is also aimed at deflating Polus by attacking him. ⟨*You are,* Socrates says, *trying to make my flesh creep with your description* (473d).⟩ It is true that Polus has used fairly graphic language, and the complaint might be that he has gone beyond what is necessary; the purely dialectical remark would have trimmed it down to the mere word "tortured," although such trimming in itself would not have assured the rightness of Polus' response. But in a sense pointing out a specific device in the opponent's argument is an ad hominem, for it puts in question his moral right to use it and implies that there is no such right. The same comment applies to Polus' use of Archelaus a couple of pages earlier, except that there his account seems so clouded and so based upon hearsay that one cannot think it material to the argument. Either kind of argument has a so-called shock value, and would be a comparatively easy way to persuade most ordinary men.

⟨Socrates, however, being anything but ordinary, detects the stratagems immediately, and passes (473d–e) to the more substantive aspects of Polus' remarks. *Neither the man on the throne nor the man on the rack can really be happier than the other, but the one who has evaded punishment is more* miserable *than the man who has not.*⟩ A hard proposition to prove, of course, both in itself and because by now the limitations in Polus are easily discerned. Socrates is removing the notions of misery and its contrary from their associations with moods, feelings, or physical pains, considering instead the value of a deed solely in itself. Neither the tortured prisoner nor the tyrant enjoying his catered viands and his fine clothes can be happy, but even that is not quite the point. The unpunished tyrant-rhetor is miserable per se, he is a wretch, even if not wretched in his bodily condition. Again, on Socrates' showing, happiness is an outcome of just action, while on the showing of Polus, happiness is the use and display of power. For Socrates, power lies in the ability to choose, or will, that end which is best for the long run, while for Polus power is a privilege lasting so long as a man is able to escape punishment for misdeeds, however gross they may be. He has given no reason to relate happiness to the exercise of power except to hint that it is the absence or erosion of penalty. The question of misery, on the other hand, is of a different sort, one having to do only with his objective placing in the world of other living beings. Socrates is merely saying that the tyrant is worse than a man at the mercy of the Eleven, much as a particular clepsydra may be a worse timekeeper than another.

Another consideration, quite separate from these, is the introduction by Socrates of the gods (472e), who have scarcely been mentioned before. There is a connection between them and the objective estimation of the worth of a man—the gods would, without reference to the success or failure of a man's search for power, judge his inherent worth and the moral quality of his actions.

⟨There is still another interlude, again dealing with methods (473e–474b). *You are laughing, Polus,* says Socrates, *and you are using another form* (eidos) *of rhetorical dodge.*⟩ The laughter is a way of showing disdain without troubling to invent sound objections, just as other rhetorical tricks short-circuit careful arguments, seeking to accomplish quickly and easily what in more responsible hands would take serious intellectual effort. ⟨Polus has indulged in it for this very reason, and responds: *You do not think you have already been refuted through your having made statements to which no one else would agree.—Ask anyone here* (473e).⟩ Again we suggest that Polus believes everyone who could be made to say what he really thinks will be found to agree with Polus himself. True to his method, he is still conceiving of his statements as true and the common possession of mankind, and the only opposites to them would be those so patently false that everyone would see them as absurd. Using the right persuasive means, one could move anyone else from the holding of propositions of the second class to those of the first. One need not start from assumptions jointly agreed upon, but by a show of superior wisdom (as in quoting from his own rather sententious writings—448c), or bringing in examples as testimonies ("witnesses"), giving hair-raising descriptions, and dissolving into gales of derisive laughter, along with countless other tricks, the unbeliever can soon be brought over to the other side. At the present juncture, Polus, in bidding Socrates to ask the company assembled whether they do not take him to be ridiculous, is counting upon a chorus of agreement, based no doubt on their common experience and conventional opinion. The "refutation" of Socrates will then be by a rude voice vote only indirectly related to the merits of the case.

The response (473e–474b) is at first sight a peculiar one. ⟨*I am not one of the politicians* (ouk eimi tōn politikōn),[9] *for only last year I was ridiculed for not understanding the voting procedure, so do not ask me to take the votes of the present company.*⟩ Viewed as a piece of rhetoric, this is merely an excellent way of taking the wind from Polus' sails: I don't care if you laugh at me, Socrates seems to be saying, I have already been through that on a much more important occasion without its having done any permanent damage to me. There may be a deeper meaning. The real issues of life cannot be decided through popular opinion, although one could be knocked out of a voting tabulation that way. It is one thing to be confused about balloting, another to err so far as to think your Archelaus an admirable and happy man. On this latter point your voting (which is merely another rhetorical device, similar to the calling of witnesses) and your jeering are of no interest to me whatever.

There is another point, less evident. The audience for this present discussion, everyone is aware, has consisted of two committed rhetors, Gorgias and probably Callicles, one waverer between Socrates and Gorgias, and a gathering of what were invited guests or chance visitors, not a very auspicious group to weigh such problems. It is not that Socrates knows that he is a doctor contending against a caterer for the verdict of children and that he would lose; rather it is his feeling that no matter how the voting goes, it will be based on reasons fundamentally prejudiced and frivolous. Were the audience to consist of Timaeus, Parmenides, the unknown visitor from Elea, not to mention Theodorus and Theaetetus, the complexion would be greatly different. Here there is division into a vivid speech, then questions and answers, Gorgian style, followed by the strangely mixed colloquies with rhetorical method always being pulled and molded into some dialectical shape by an eccentric but canny latecomer from the marketplace.[10] Socrates has employed almost as many rhetorical devices as his two opponents combined, but ultimately in the interests of truth. This distinction between truth and the generating of belief is still lost on the men facing him. If not, their votes could not possibly be the votes of men unable to separate Sicilian culinary specialties from bitter Hippocratic potions except by taste alone.

⟨Socrates goes a step farther (474a–b). *Since you, Polus, cannot devise a better kind of refutation, let me do it by producing the one witness I really require—you yourself. Simply answer my questions.*⟩ (From this point to the end of the conversation with Polus, Socrates remains the questioner, and the talk is better managed. The problem could be labeled as that of whether doing injustice is worse than undergoing it, and secondly, whether escaping a penalty for an unjust deed is worse than paying it (474b–481b). There are three portions, beginning with some preliminary remarks (474b–c), then going to a longer one, the argument proper on both topics (474c–479c), and ending with a short survey of the consequences (479c–481b).

The preliminary passage simply points up what seems here an irreconcilable difference between Socrates and Polus. The former affirms that everyone believes that doing injustice is worse than undergoing it, and that escaping (*hēgeisthai*) is worse than paying it. ⟨Polus denies all this (474b): No one *believes it*, adding (474c) that *he will answer questions, merely to hear what Socrates will say.*⟩ This remark carries with it something new. Throughout the colloquy with Gorgias it was assumed that the discussion was serious, that it involved real beliefs genuinely upheld or refuted, and that an assent in words carried with it an assent in thought. This has been largely true of the conversation so far with Polus, but now the emphasis has changed, and will remain so, at least in good part, throughout the remainder of the dialogue. Though Socrates is in earnest, his opponents are beginning to feel that his conclusions are too paradoxical for them, even though they may be forced to assent. Hence in a way we are carried back to the hour before Socrates arrived, the audience listening to the display, admiring it for its skill and address, but not forced to change their thinking on its content. For

Socrates, the issue is still the most vital to the health of his city or of any other, but he will find that regardless of *his* skill and address the victory that he might win may be hollow, not because of damage to himself in winning it but because the enemy has quietly departed the battlements that Socrates has painstakingly invested, and has retired to the comparative safety of nonchalance and amused detachment alternating with episodes of unrestrained annoyance.[11]

When Polus denies that anyone believes that doing injustice is worse and that escaping a penalty is worse than paying it, he is mistaken, for Socrates has just said that he himself believes it, and such a confession of faith can hardly be denied. But to Polus no such confession can be truthful, for does not everyone think as he thinks? From his standpoint, then, this is no mistake, but from that of Socrates it is one more in a long list.

⟨Now to the first portion (474c–d), on the undergoing of injustice, which Polus again says is more evil than the doing of it, while doing injustice is more disgraceful. Under questioning, he allows that *the fair* (kalon) *and the good are not the same, nor are evil and disgraceful.*⟩ For answer Socrates employs two devices, one of them to examine the contraries of the two evaluative expressions that Polus has used, the other to produce a chiasmic switching of these contraries, so that *fair* seems to be paired with *evil, good* with *disgraceful,* which like *fair* has many esthetic connotations. Socrates will be trying to link not only *disgraceful* but *evil* to the doing of injustice. His strategem will be to show that *fair* attaches to pleasure and to benefit, and if so, its opposite, *disgraceful,* must attach to pain and to evil.

⟨In a passage (474d–475a) that at first glance reminds one of the first rungs of the ladder of love in the *Symposium*,[12] *Socrates lists the fairness of bodies, colors, figures, sound, of laws and observances* (tous nomous kai ta epitēdeumata), *and of studies* (tōn mathēatōn) *as reaching some standards; and* (here he departs from the *Symposium*) *this is in respect of their use for an end, or of the pleasure they give.*⟩ Some readers have been more dismayed than Polus is at this account (he eagerly and punningly accepts it as fair), but the fact is that Socrates has been no apostate from the notion of goodness or fairness as something good in itself. Because it is material from the lower rungs of the ladder of love that Socrates mentions here, and then not as a scale of perfection, there is no suggestion that, for example, sounds are fair in themselves and without reference to the soul perceiving them or gaining some use from them. There are many kinds of goodness and fairness in the dialogues, and it is not inconsistent to speak of different sorts in different places. What *would* be inconsistent in the *Gorgias* would be the abrupt positing of some quintessential fairness beyond all perception or even beyond the power of a living soul to apprehend intellectually, after Socrates has labored so energetically to temper his approach to the rhetoric and theories of rhetoric of his present opponents. All the discussion in the *Gorgias* thus far—and for many pages more—is on what might be called, in several senses of the word, a pragmatic level; and it is Socrates' task to try to reform his opponents' biased and false conceptions of this pragmatism so that they might comport with a more self-supporting practical goodness. It is only after these conceptions have been thoroughly shown up for what they are (499e–500a) that he is able to consider a good life that is good in itself. Here, Socrates has only to secure agreement on a point reached by common sense, not some spiritual insight. Socrates is using pleasure as a bait, much as he would use fortune and success.

⟨Having obtained the necessary acquiescence about fairness, Socrates (475a–b) goes back to its opposite, coupling it with pain and evil, and adding a point about the comparative: *If one of two things is more fair, it surpasses the other in pleasure or benefit, or both; and the reverse holds for the more disgraceful. Hence (475b–d) it is also more painful or evil, or both.*⟩ This gives Socrates a kind of odd trilemma with which to work:

1. Doing injustice surpasses undergoing it in pain, or in evil, or in both.
2. Doing injustice does not surpass undergoing it in pain.
3. Hence it does not surpass undergoing injustice in evil *and* pain.
4. Therefore doing injustice surpasses undergoing it in evil.

⟨Socrates tacks on a little aside (475d) to Polus: *You are a patient, and should submit yourself bravely to a doctor's treatment*—a remark put to Polus when he hesitates to answer the question, *Would you rather have the evil and the disgraceful when it is more instead of less?*⟩ The answer to this would not ordinarily be a taxing one, but in the present context it is difficult for Polus to respond negatively since an admission would carry with it the implication that the tyrant-rhetor would have the undesirable life. It is like an ordinary man who would not consult a physician if an extreme exertion on one occasion caused him to become a little breathless, though an athlete might well call upon such a doctor if he found himself short of wind in every race. Polus is a contender, and his public is before him now.

⟨*All mankind agrees with you, Polus*, continues Socrates (475e–476a), *but now you agree with me that doing injustice is more evil, hence no one would choose to do it*. Socrates concludes: *I am satisfied to have you as my sole witness, whereas everyone else agrees with what you were saying.*⟩ Here, the word *everyone* could mean those present, or the Athenian citizens, or the Greeks, or perhaps some still larger group. As for Socrates' satisfaction in having Polus as his single witness, this can be taken as a rhetorical thrust: You said earlier that everyone agrees with you, and now that you have come round to agreeing with me; it is plain that everyone else must agree also, hence my concession that all the people agree with you is nullified by your fortuitous acquiescence in the truth! But from the dialectical standpoint it is also clear that if doing injustice is really an evil so extreme that it is worse than undergoing injustice, then everyone not only should but undoubtedly would avoid it. If this is the case, then Polus and indeed everyone else will construe the doing of injustice as painful and evil and will avoid it if at all possible. If you are my only witness, Polus, I need no others, for you are representative of a fundamental fact of human behavior.

⟨Balancing this argument is one on the paying and escaping of a penalty for doing injustice (476e–477d). It consists of five major steps, all of them hinging upon an equivalence between action and passion. *First, paying a just penalty and being justly punished for injustice already committed are the same thing. Second, all just things are fair, insofar as they are just.* Socrates is not saying here that justice and fairness are identical, only that just things are members of a large class of fair things. This step can be asserted from an earlier argument (474c), that all injustice is disgraceful. The *third step* used examples: *The doing of anything requires something to which this is done, for example, striking and being struck, striking hard and being struck hard, burning, cutting, and so forth.* The *fourth and longer step* applies this to penalties (476d–477a). *Paying such a penalty is undergoing something, that is, it is passive, not active, but there is someone else who exacts this penalty. If he does so rightly* (orthōs) *then he does so justly, and the man paying the penalty undergoes what is just* (which is different from spontaneously doing a just deed). *We have agreed (in step two) that what is just is fair, hence the just punisher does what is fair, and the man punished has what is fair done to him. If so, then it is also good.*⟩ This is derived from the earlier refutation (475a) of Polus after he had said (at 474c–d) that good and fair are not the same. Socrates for his part had shown that things fair are pleasurable or beneficial, and this is sufficient to consider them good, in the eyes of Polus. Again, the one justly punished is benefitted by becoming better in soul, and thus is relieved at least of the greatest evil. Socrates has assumed that if something fair and therefore good is done, then that to which or to whom it is done receives a benefit rather than receiving something pleasurable, this being the only alternative. It is a possibility presumably excluded, however, by the common experience of mankind, who receive little if any gratification from being caught and made to pay a penalty.

⟨The *fifth step*, again a longer one (477b–d), uses Socrates' three standard rubrics for kinds of goods and therefore of evils as well. *The evil of property is poverty; the evils of the body, weakness* (astheneian, *feebleness), disease, ugliness; and those of the soul, injustice, ignorance, cowardice, and the like.*) Some parts of this list are implied in the Divided Oblong (weakness would be taken care of by the gymnast, disease by the doctor, and ugliness, one could hope, by the gymnast or at least resort the embellisher); but not all parts, since the Oblong never mentioned external goods, possessions, nor did it specify vices of the soul but only the "businesses," *pragmata*, to which are accorded two arts, legislation and justice, together with the bogus panderings that seem to but do not foster the soul at all.

⟨*The most disgraceful and evil*, Socrates continues (477d), *is injustice, the very baseness of the soul itself; it is also the most painful and harmful. Being unjust, licentious, cowardly, and ignorant is more painful than being poor or sick* (477d).⟩ His right to assert these qualities (disgraceful, base, painful) of the unjust soul can be established through argument, with the notion of harmful being added as a matter of course. His list of the evils of the soul is a varied one. Injustice arises from the proof just finished, together with the Divided Oblong. Licentiousness, if it means pleasure loving without bridle or surcease,[13] is new, because even Archelaus has not been described to Socrates as drinking and wenching; his happiness has come from his having escaped penalties. Cowardice lay just beyond the accusation by Polus (461b) that Gorgias was too ashamed to admit that his pupils could abuse the power of rhetoric.[14] Ignorance has been hypothetically ascribed to both rhetors and audiences by Socrates (459a–b). There, the impression may have been given that this was merely an unfortunate circumstance, that no harm could come from bumbling counselors or confused hearers. The real importance of the ignorant mind, however, lies in the danger that it may give or act upon false counsel, to the peril of the city. One may suppose, for example, that had the stepmother of Archelaus been aware of his untrustworthiness and hence of the possibility that he had drowned her son, his rule of Macedonia would have been cut very short. But ignorance of a fact is not quite all that Socrates means here because he is speaking of a real evil in the soul. The supposition is that he is concerned with persistent, *willful* ignorance, something even the best teachers have difficulty overcoming in their pupils.

The picture that Socrates is drawing, then, pertains primarily to the individual and his shortcomings. What its political applications are will only be clarified later, when Callicles begins his account of nature and convention at work in the state. Throughout the discussion with Polus, the city-state is little more than a shadow, and even the legislature and judicature of which sophistic and rhetoric are images or imitations are not more sharply delineated.

⟨Next come two pages (477d–479c) devoted to an objection by Polus and the reply by Socrates. The objection is short, and as usual furnishes no reason: *I do not think*, says Polus—perhaps he would mutter this—*that being unjust, licentious, cowardly, and ignorant is more painful than being poor and sick* (477d).⟩ Notice that he has combined all of the evils that Socrates was merely listing, and has assumed that they belong together in one soul; his typical inability to keep distinct body and soul and all that pertains to them. The effect of this, of course, would be to hold a much more extreme position than that of Socrates, for whom being unjust *or* licentious is painful enough.

Socrates' reply is divided into two segments, the first (477d–478b) being concerned with relief from evils, the second (478b–479c) with what might be called a scale of happiness. ⟨*In case you were right*, Socrates begins (477d–e), *the harm and evil by which the soul's baseness exceeds all others must be the greatest of all evils, since you do not concede that it is* pain *that makes these evils of the soul worse than illness and poverty. Whatever*, he goes on, *confers the greatest harm must be the greatest evil.* This leaves injustice, licentiousness, and baseness of the soul as the greatest evils. In other words, remove pain as a cause of harm, and sheer evil is still there. *What, then, removes the evils? For poverty it is moneymaking, for disease medicine, and for baseness and injustice—do not speak hastily, Polus— it is just payment of penalties in the lawcourts. Those, then, who punish rightly employ justice, which is fairer than moneymaking and medicine, and thus brings about most pleasure and benefit.*⟩ This, we think, is a tricky argument. Polus has not said so exactly, but for him either poverty or disease is worse than injustice, or both of them together are worse, or else both are worse though they do not exist together. Anyway, because Socrates wishes to show that injustice is the worst, he asserts that the art relieving injustice is the best art. Justice is not treated here as a virtue in the soul itself, but as an art, one producing pleasure and benefit. Injustice is relieved by the art of justice, not by the lies necessary to keep Archelaus on his throne or the shiftiness of hired speechmakers who aid a man in overcoming a just indictment.[15] To be unrelieved is the greatest evil, to be relieved is something, at least, of a good, and since the only goods agreed to by Polus and Socrates are benefit and pleasure, it follows that these are what justice confers upon the evil man—it would go without saying that they are also conferred upon the good man.

⟨Socrates can proceed with the second segment (478b–479c), in which there are six closely-linked steps.

First, *medical treatment is not pleasant, but it produces benefit, yet the body is happier if never sick at all, rather than being sick and relieved of the sickness.*

Second, *happiness is not relief, but the freedom from having acquired the evil.* We note that this is not really a definition, but the statement of a precondition for happiness, and is the fruit of an analogy between soul and body and the respective arts putting them right when they are ailing.

Third, *the sick man receiving no treatment is more miserable than the one relieved.*

Fourth, *well then, did we not find that paying the penalty relieves baseness* (disgracefulness)? *The justice in the court is what makes us better, as if it were medicine.*

Fifth, the upshot is that *the man without evil is happiest, he who is relieved is second, and he who is unjust but paying no penalty and thus not relieved is worst.* (The man undergoing unjust treatment is dropped from the list.) *Such persons are Archelaus, other tyrants, rhetors, and dynasts.* One sees that Socrates is now accepting Polus' account of Archelaus at face value, and also the joining of tyrants with rhetors, earlier proposed by Polus (466c).

Sixth, *such men are like the sick who stay away from doctors through fear* (notice how this resembles Socrates' hint that Polus himself is staying away from the healing argument—475d). *They are afraid because ignorant, and perceive the pain and not the benefits; nor do they apprehend that a sick soul is worse than a sick body. Thus they set about to acquire money, friends, and persuasive speech in order to avoid paying any penalty* (479b–c).)

Whether or not Plato had in mind a little matrix in this argument, it is conveniently schematized in figure 4.4.

We may also summarize the argument by including body and property as well. Socrates drops part of his use of dichotomy here, as he so often does toward the end of a discussion. We may begin with the three "substrates," property, body, and soul, in which can inhere wealth, health, and justice respectively, or poverty, sickness, and injustice. For Polus, poverty or sickness or both would be worse, while for Socrates injustice is worse than either or both of the other two. Socrates examines injustice, making use of the others to clarify the argument. The practice of injustice can be divided into the undergoing of it and the doing of it. Again, for Polus undergoing is worse and more disgraceful—or rather, it was before he was forced to concede so many points to Socrates. For Socrates, doing injustice is worse and more disgraceful, and he makes no concessions. When injustice is done it either goes unpunished or it is punished, and for Polus the latter is worse, for Socrates the former, while paying the penalty is second worst, but not so glaringly evil and painful as going unpunished, because the very act of paying the penalty confers a benefit and some pleasure upon the just man. The three arts that confer benefits are thus moneymaking to gain property, medicine to heal the body's ills, and lawcourt justice to put the soul in order. The ignorant man wishes for neither of the last two, not

SOUL	RELIEF	RESULTING CONDITION
no evil	—	happiest
evil	yes	less happy
evil	yes	less miserable
evil	no	most miserable

Fig. 4.4. *Resulting conditions of the relief of evil.*

recognizing their advantages, but seeks to gain money for bribing officials, friends to spread their influence in his behalf, and persuasive speech as a talent lodged in the soul and to be used to avoid the paying of penalties, both a counterpart and a counter for justice.[16] As a convenience to the reader, figure 4.5 encapsulates the bare outline of this discussion in a summarizing matrix, part of which repeats the Divided Oblong, the rest being an extension of it.

The final two pages (479c–481b) of the colloquy with Polus treat certain consequences of the argument that has developed hitherto, and begins with a short summary of it (479c–e) before passing to the "great use," that is, the proper use of rhetoric (480a–481b), which is the most nearly final answer that Socrates can give to a man who, so to speak, bets his career upon the power of persuasion.[17]

⟨The summary by Socrates is easily disposed of, for it provokes no objection by Polus. *Injustice is the great evil, paying the penalty therefor is relief from the evil, so injustice with penalty is less evil than paying no penalty, and Archelaus and his like are most miserable, not happiest.*⟩ The only drawback to the success of Socrates' argument is that we can no longer trust the candor of Polus' responses—he merely wishes to hear what Socrates will say, and no doubt harbors the notion that underneath all the questioning Socrates will still agree with him, probably without realizing it. In his own mind, Polus has reduced Socrates from a living (and perhaps troublesome) antagonist to a display artist going through his routines.

⟨Now to the consequences. The important use of rhetoric divides into two, described in short sections (480a–d and 480e–481b), after which there is a very brief concluding word (481b). In the first use, *Socrates warns at the outset that a man must be careful not to do injustice, but if despite this he commits an unjust act he must of his own will go to a place where he can pay a penalty, as if a patient going to a doctor (480a–b). Rhetoric is no use in defending any injustice, one's own or one's parents', friends', or children's, or that of the country; but it can be used to accuse oneself or those others*—Socrates is careful not to include one's enemies or foreigners. *The punishment*

	SOUL	BODY	POSSESSIONS
KNOWLEDGE-ARTS (464b–466a)	legislation judicature or justice	gymnastics medicine	—
FAMILIARITIES OR PANDERINGS	sophistic rhetoric	gymnastics medicine	—
GOODS OF INDIVIDUALS (467e–468d)	wisdom (467e) happiness pleasure benefit	beauty health (468c)	wealth (468d)
INTERMEDIATES (468a)	—	walking banishing killing	sticks stones confiscating
EVILS OF INDIVIDUALS (477b–c)	injustice ignorance cowardice	weakness illness ugliness	poverty
EVILS OF STATE (469b–e)	doing injustice undergoing injustice	mayhem in agora	arson in city
PLEASURES OR BENEFITS (474d–475a)	studies observances	bodies	colors figures
RELIEF FROM EVILS (478b–479b)	paying the penalty is painful (479b)	undergoing medical treatments is painful (478b)	moneymaking
SCALE OF HAPPINESS (478c–e)	happiest if never unjust less if unjust but cured by paying penalty unhappiest if unjust and paying no penalty (478e)	happiest if never sick less happy if sick but cured less happy if sick and not cured (478c)	—
SCALE OF WRETCHEDNESS (479b–c)	does greatest injustice but avoids punishment because of ignorance (479b)	ill but avoids treatment through ignorance	—

Fig. 4.5. *Divided Oblong and its extension.*

may be severe, indeed it may be flogging or chains for the body, or a fine levied on one's property, or death (480b–d). Even so, this is the most legitimate use of rhetoric. The second is more paradoxical still. *If someone is an enemy or stranger who happens never to have done an injustice to us but to someone else instead, we should try to prevent his coming to trial or at any rate see to it that he receives no punishment. If he deserves to die, we should try to assure that he lives as long as possible in his business (480e–481b).*[18] The little concluding line simply confirms that if rhetoric has any uses at all, these two must be the only ones.) Such is the final squeezing of rhetoric, from its former realm (447a–449b) as the greatest and fairest of arts, into a little corner; ordinary rhetoric now rests upon the twofold ignorance of speakers and hearers, as Socrates showed Gorgias, and it is nothing but a pandering, a knack or routine with a use, for men bent upon doing injustice, which would merely stain their souls darker if Polus were to have his way, and would lift the onus of evil and disgrace from the wicked soul but would not bring it unalloyed happiness, if Socrates were to have the last word. Rhetoric, according to Socrates, can only be vindicated if turned to self-punishment and to the punishment of one's allies.[19]

The curious doctrine that the guilty enemies and foreigners should not be accused seems, in light of Socrates' purgative theory of punishment and thus of deliberate self-incrimination, to be vindictive in the extreme. Perhaps it is, for it means that the evil man, in going free and deathless, is doomed to be a disgraceful, base, pained soul. It would mean too that the criminal courts could close down most of their functions but those of meting out punishments to persons tattling on themselves or on their friends. It would mean, moreover, that unless an unjust man had had the rare opportunity of being persuaded by Socrates or someone like him to turn himself over to the authorities, or, less probably, had come to the same conclusion by himself, he would be free to go his way in his crimes. No one would accuse him because no one would wish to relieve him of the heavy burden of guilt he was carrying, unless it were a good friend or member of the family. Socrates implies (480b) that his statement of consequences follows from what was agreed to earlier. Follow it may, but it provokes Callicles into saying a few moments later that if Socrates is serious then human life is turned upside down (481c). It separates the notion of good from benefit and pleasure, which had been described a little earlier (475a) as belonging together; and it shows as stern a devotion to duty and conscience as Immanuel Kant or even the New England divines argued for in their hardiest hours.

* * *

By way of setting the dialectic of the colloquy with Gorgias against that of the colloquy with Polus, let us recall how the first narrowed the conception of rhetoric to the juncture where a definition was possible (452e–453a). Gorgias was in the habit of considering rhetoric so broadly, believing it could serve in place of all the arts, that it was virtually impossible for Socrates to disabuse him of this notion, to which Gorgias returned late in that section (459c), long after the argument had in fact shown most of the weaknesses inherent in the "art." Because Polus has used many of the same expressions, such as "fairest of the arts," and has moreover lauded Gorgias as one of rhetoric's best exponents (448c), it might be thought that he entertains the same broad—not to say loose—conception. It appears, however, to be otherwise: Polus has had so little concern for other possible arts of language, or even for arts of any sort whatever, that one may properly conclude that for him there is but a single art with a chief function of seizing power and avoiding punishment. Gorgias thought that rhetoric among other things convinced the moneymaker to turn over his earnings to the rhetor (452e) to make a patient into a docile swallower of distasteful draughts (456b); but Polus has ignored all this in favor of playing for nothing but higher stakes. The reader could expect, therefore, that the Socratic strategem would be to *broaden* rather than narrow the notion of what rhetoric really is. The peculiarity is that after having accomplished this by reintroducing questions of justice and punishment, Socrates makes the proper function of rhetoric to be very small, although its *use* is extended to far more persons. Instead of the tyrant, anyone potentially guilty of an unjust act would be free to employ persuasive means to inculpate himself. Rhetoric is for the first time the means of self-rescue, not from punishment but from enduring disgrace and pain, pain in the soul; as such it is still open to the tyrant and fratricide. The basis of this lies in the explicit introduction of the soul, which rather than the body is what endures the disgrace. So far, however, the impulses of the soul have been kept from view, and it is only after a fresh start is made, when a host of erotic impulses, bodily and psychic, are paraded, that one can begin to talk about larger issues of the right aims of the citizen in a society ready to listen to honeyed words.

The ending of this colloquy can be contrasted with the one closing the conversation with Gorgias, who had tried to give reflective answers and make thoroughly politic suggestions, but who had failed because of an inconsistency born of a timidity otherwise well concealed. There was need for further discussion to resolve the difficulty without capsizing the whole theory of rhetoric as an art, or better, an artificer, of persuasion, a theory much of it fairly unobjectionable even if superficial. Polus, for his part, has been more reckless than Gorgias by far, as if he had nothing to lose by choosing an outrageous object, the worst of tyrants, for his admiration. At the same time he has attempted to carry out the role of the aspiring young professional, wishing to enhance his reputation for common sense. He has little gift for constructing sequences, and breaks into the conversation with Gorgias no more than he breaks into his own series of questions and of answers. When Gorgias has finally been put to silence the conversation could still remain fruitful with him, but when Polus, who no longer feels that he need agree mentally when driven to concede verbally, is confronted with proven contraries to all his chief statements, the discussion with him has run dry. It will be worth looking into, whether the forthcoming debate with the enigmatic, difficult Callicles, which for its complexity makes the other two resemble school primers, will end with agreement or merely be brought to an uncomfortable halt.

PART THREE

CONVERSATION WITH CALLICLES

5

CALLICLES AND POWER

ABOVE THE LAW

(481b–492c)

The sudden incredulous, skeptical, irate query of Callicles as he abruptly reenters the conversation marks the beginning of the long and complicated section (481b–527e), more than half the dialogue, that consists of the sparring of Socrates with the imperspicuous figure serving as host for the day. Some of the complexity of the conversation may be illustrated by pointing out three ways to break it into sections that make considerable sense:

1. 481b–492c, the principal arguments of Callicles, followed by 492c–527e, the refutations and counterstatements brought against him.
2. 481b–499b, the identity of the better man, followed by 499b–527e, the nature of the better life, a part itself subdivided into three sub-sections based upon three interrelated questions.
3. 481b–492c, discussion dominated by Callicles, followed, 492c–506c, by debate between Socrates and Callicles, then 506c–509e, Socrates alone, after that 509e–520e, joint debate again, dominated this time by Socrates, then 521a–527e, Socrates alone.

We shall try to make these principles of division as clear as possible in this and the four ensuing chapters by using all of them to a greater or lesser extent, so long as they do not confuse the issue too annoyingly. This organization of Plato's, one of his more baffling, seems to be a carefully planned way of showing that one's very advocacy of a theory in (1) and (2) is a path to taking one's own place in ethical and political life, that is, as reflected in personal relations, as in (3). Or is it the other way round? Do Socrates and Callicles propound their views of how one ought to live (the question put at 492d) as a result of their being men of such and such kinds, and of having, perhaps unconsciously, chosen a manner of living? Here one may well believe that Plato favored the latter possibility because so much of the reciprocal criticism of the two men is couched in terms of how each one will turn out in the future, what fate will befall him.

So many are the perplexities hanging about the character of Callicles that it seems only fair to summarize certain traits that we find in him. He should not be reprehended as a naïve (or sophisticated) proponent of might above right, or touted as a Friedrich Nietzsche or Jean-Jacques Rousseau of the ancient world, or rejected as a puppet in the hands of Plato or a mere counterpart of Thrasymachus in the *Republic*. All of these characterizations have been alleged, some of them many times, and though there is a little truth in each of them, it is not the whole truth.

In this long portion, two men are presented whose loves, partly similar and partly dissimilar, are influential upon their own lives and thinking. Which of the two principals, runs the question, has the better life? No direct mention is made of their wealth, the number of their friends, actual chances for obtaining office, any more than of their physical strength, other intellectual interests, or the like. The task is to concentrate the two lives as much as possible in terms of their commitments to what each one considers virtue and vice.

Callicles is closely involved in what he is saying, even if much of it may be a rough mask over his underlying nature. He has arranged the entire occasion of the day—Gorgias coming as guest, Gorgias presented as featured speaker, an audience of fair size, possibly an invitation to Socrates and Chaerephon—hence he bears a special responsibility for its outcome. The colloquy with Socrates has begun with the latter's appearing to assume that Callicles is a fine citizen, probably well off; the preliminary distinction between nature and custom becomes a way of praising the man stronger than his fellow citizens who must then join together to avoid being overrun. But now the braver is the stronger, or else the wiser man must be. But the temperate is not. In the course of this exchange, Callicles is revealed as a person hoping to wield political power to assure free rein for his licentiousness. As the argument progresses, more and more of Callicles' nature is uncovered, first to Socrates, then to his two rhetor guests and the audience, which, as representatives of the deme, will one day vote for or against Callicles to rule them. It is little wonder, then, that this man, who has started out by saying (458d) that he has never enjoyed a debate as much as the one between Gorgias and Socrates—this man grows increasingly sullen as he takes his own turn. Not only are his intellectual constructions refuted but his inmost aims are laid bare, even including the growing evidence that his concern for self-rescue as a principal use of rhetoric turns out to be obsessive. For all his championing of the strong, he is something of a coward who feels pain when the enemy is about to advance.

In her adroit little poem, "Peregrine," Elinor Wylie depicts a man re-galing his listeners with accounts of his forays against society and the law, and who concludes by saying that he is a good hater but a bad lover. This may not be exactly what Callicles would say of himself, at least it is not true in the way meant by the raffish figure in the poem, but certainly the shifting of Callicles from love of a rich young man to that of the rank and file of the deme and back again, and the concurrent shifts in his opinions on which he so obviously prides himself, be-tokens a temperament whose active love is evanescent and defective. In the same way, when he moves from one object of affection or admi-ration to another, he lashes out at ideas associated with what he has just left behind. This is not a simple matter of Callicles' thinking one thing and saying another but of his letting his thoughts run in two or three directions. He then tries to hide his self-dissension by making some dogmatic pronouncement, and after that contradicting this and thereby unwillingly or even unwittingly revealing his split motives.

Several features of his character would, if taken by themselves, be ei-ther virtues or defects, but in conjunction with all the others they be-come components in a man troubled and possibly bedeviled by fear, and moreover distraught by strong—and no doubt unfocused—physi-cal desires together with self-doubts making it difficult to attain much satisfaction. It is for these reasons that Callicles seems a bad lover and a good hater, not only of the persons around him but of himself as well. Far from his being the single-voiced crier-up of strength and the rights to having more of everything, Callicles is a man whose very efforts to come to terms with the Athenian world and with himself are bound to end in demoralization.[1] But this makes him a dangerous man, one whom Socrates should by all means try to wean away from the more aggressive and self-seeking of his hopes.[2]

Callicles' soul is not always lawless and without shame, but he inter-mittently shows traits that are, and yet defends the behavior generated by them as having courage, wisdom, and natural justice. He knows at the very outset that Socrates is a lover of philosophy, and with it moder-ation and law. Thus at the arrival of Socrates he comments that his guest is too late for the feast but in time for a battle. If a soul ruled by exces-sive desire discovers in someone else *any* opinions or desires that might be shameful, such a soul sets about immediately to demolish all traces of moderation in that other. The once-rational, or largely-rational, man is seduced if he fails to exercise extreme wisdom and falls in with the habits of his seducer. But Socrates is not seduced. Whether he is able to alter the temperament of Callicles as well as refuting his arguments would have to be decided five or ten years after the dramatic date of the dialogue. If a man finds his own opinions so badly undermined, what is next for him? Callicles may move from one version of his many-sided set of opinions to another, but his commitment to each in turn is a strong one, and it is doubtful that he would ever adopt the exalted set of ideals and internal restraints that Socrates urges him to take on. Callicles is ambitious, but inhibited by his worries over carrying out his instinct for power so far that he would incur the vengeance of those he would seek tyrannically to rule. Some of his ambition is at bottom nothing but a desire to retain the status to which his good birth has accustomed him. Mixing but not balancing softness and hardness of character, he repeatedly abuses Socrates, and the latter in turn draws attention much more frequently than in any other dialogue to the personal shortcomings of his young antagonist.[3] The truth is, it requires not only certain intellectual qualifications to engage in the kind of dialectic that Socrates usually embraces but also temperamental attitudes of a rather special kind, and Callicles lacks them. It would be tempting to say that a dialectical confrontation with Socrates conducted on his terms would heal Callicles of the split between the hardness and softness alternately revealed. But the paradox is that with a man such as Callicles this dialectic is the one thing that Socrates cannot pursue as he would with a Theaetetus or even a Glaucon. Callicles is certain from his corrupted upbringing that the impassioned statement of what he takes to be principles, a statement not altogether lacking in eloquence, alternating with attacks of greater or lesser intensity against his opponent, will carry the day and be the way to power and privilege. Socrates is dealing with a man who obviously hates logic just as he hates the men (520a) who in his time were the most prominent teachers who might have instructed him in it—the sophists.

So much for an outline drawing of Callicles, a portrait whose lines will have to be filled in as the account proceeds. He is as compelling a figure as Plato ever created short of Socrates, both in his nature and in his arguments. As he is presented, these two aspects are scarcely separated, for there is little that he says about justice, government, and pleasure that does not shed light upon his strange, high-tensioned character, and in turn it must be clear that his varied pronouncements grow out of the stresses deep within him, however much some parts of his formulas must have been heard from sophists or others of the man's private circle.

*   *   *

The subsection to which we are devoting this chapter (481b–492c) commences with a statement of contrasting personalities by Socrates and Callicles (481b–488b), followed by the attempts of Socrates to elicit some definitive statement of Callicles regarding the latter's theory of the superior man (488b–492c). The earlier of these two portions has four subdivisions, the first of which is Callicles' query about the serious intentions of Socrates (481b), the second a short account by Socrates of the respective loves of the two men (481c–482c), the third a series of attacks upon Socrates as rhetor and as philosopher, together with Callicles' justification of the superior man (482c–486d), followed by a tentative, somewhat lighthearted set of responses by Socrates (486d–488b).

⟨Callicles brusquely asks a question and voices a reproach (481b–c). *Is Socrates serious?* This is asked of Chaerephon, with his incidental function in the dialogue, but who now conveys one of the most important lessons of the entire work. *Yes, Socrates is very serious. But ask him yourself.*⟩[4] This can be taken to mean that for all the personal ragging that has gone on with Polus, and with all the propositions that Socrates has either stated baldly or has reached in joint discussion—propositions on the face of them preposterous because so evidently opposed to common opinion—in spite of these, Socrates is in deep earnest. The radical paradoxes will stand; they are not ephemera like the displays of Gorgias. It is essential that this be established, even if by a minor character, a Superfluous Man, as the Russians would call him, since the suspicion is going to be thrown upon Socrates that he is wasting his time and energies upon a frivolous occupation, philosophy. Even if Chaerephon has not known Socrates well, as an onlooker here he can sense the tenor of the Socratic contentions better than do the three rhetors.

⟨Callicles' first reproach against Socrates (481c) is to the effect that *he has turned life upside down* (anatetrammenos), *and that if he is right then all of us are now doing the very opposite of what we should do.*⟩ There are three possible interpretations of this remark:[5]

First, that Socrates is saying the exact contrary of what the world thinks. It is quite true that Socrates will later point out that Callicles is only giving utterance to what everyone else (*hoî alloî*) believes but is unwilling to say (492d), though that is in reference to a different matter. Socrates, one recalls, has just succeeded in bringing Polus to admit that rhetoric should be used for incriminating oneself and asking for punishment in case one has committed an injustice (480a–c; 481a–b). To Callicles, popular opinion is evidently a source of truth, or at least a pragmatic justification for certain lines of action, and hardly anyone, he is confident, would dream of going before a judge and inculpating himself unless he thought that this would give him a lighter sentence if the evidence was overwhelmingly against him. This interpretation is strong enough, except that we really know very little about Callicles up to this point—he took a subordinate position in the Prologue and let others talk for him.

The second way of reading his query would have it that the lives are upside down to begin with, and that Socrates' disagreement with common opinion has by overturning them succeeded in righting them. But Callicles' remark is almost certainly not meant in this way, because, if it were, he would be thanking his guest. There is no word of such gratitude here, and if we are to trust what the text is telling us, rather than looking at it from the vantage point of fifty pages later, then all the reader can know is only what Socrates and the others have been saying. The ambiguities of Callicles' position, his poorly veiled and growing contempt for Socrates and the others—all this will come afterward.

Third, if we do look at the text a page or two later (483a–b), we find that Callicles' scoffing remark to Socrates about his turning of life upside down becomes quite odd in retrospect. The world, Callicles is saying, has been getting along quite well, and if Socrates reverses its conceptions of what ought to be done he will do it damage. In a few moments, however (483c–d), Callicles himself will propose a view of the superior man that will flout not only convention but all the ethical values that condition and are conditioned by it.

One may talk in fun of exalted subjects, such as rhetoric, freedom, justice, and the like, quite as often as about matters of so little moment as kinds of Sicilian cookery, fancy clothing and jewelry, and much else. The query about seriousness comes only after a long colloquy on the nature, power, and proper use of rhetoric in a society in which it is possible to act justly, but seemingly more profitable to behave with disregard for the welfare of the people or even with outrageous brutality—provided one avoids paying any penalty. The suspicion of levity is understandable partly in terms of Callicles' opinion, shown in other connections, that Socrates is really a rhetor, and that he is simply trying out his tricks to see whether they can be effective against two polished professionals.

There is, however, a personal issue, one not fully resolved until very late in the dialogue. Polus has shown himself to Callicles a capricious young fellow who pays little attention to the details of arguments, who wants to hear almost nothing except praise of rhetoric and its exponents, and who cares so little about its real nature that he makes no effort to put to rout its characterization as pandering and imitation of justice but instead leaps ahead—or perhaps sideways—to the topic of the power of the rhetor in cities (466a). Can any discussion, on any subject matter, be held seriously with such a superficial man? Callicles must be asking himself this question, but in view of all his other misapprehensions about Socrates and the strange art of dialectical proof and disproof, it is doubtful that he can assess the young man as Socrates would assess him. No doubt Callicles perceives Polus as the serious man, not Socrates, and really his standpoint must be respected until it is overthrown by use of Socratic principles. It will turn out shortly that Callicles and Socrates are no strangers to each other, hence it must be because of the immediately-preceding discussion that Callicles harbors doubts about the intentions of Socrates. His turning to Chaerephon is a gesture of annoyance, not a request for enlightenment.

The reader can assume for the moment that Socrates has won out over Gorgias and Polus, who have not tried to retrieve themselves after being interrupted just now by a third party to the discussion. But from all that can be learned in their remarks, both feel it has been an interesting conversation, with notions thrown in from time to time that neither of them had fully considered, nor thought important. Callicles has looked forward enough to a display to invite Gorgias and Polus to be his guests and to assemble an audience for the occasion; he may also enjoy the spectacle of a battle between Gorgias and Socrates, with the possibility that the former will be humbled a little, as we hope to establish later on. The whole contest has been an amusing game, a battle on the same level as a feast, an entertaining sham, in which Socrates has been toying with the overly-respectable Gorgias and the overeager Polus, paying them back in their own coin. In this situation, the difference between seriousness and play would quickly melt away for Callicles, leaving but momentary pleasure for all the participants and onlookers.

It seems to me, Chaerephon has said, *that Socrates is extremely serious* (481b). This response is perfectly correct, but doubtless made for the wrong reasons. Chaerephon has had difficulty with the most elementary aspects of Socrates' method of seeking definitions, and so he has probably gauged the seriousness of his companion in terms of the increasingly darkened mood after Polus has introduced Archelaus into the conversation. Socrates must henceforward not only prove that he is *talking* seriously, but also that the very subject talked about is one of utmost consequence, and moreover that he, Socrates, is prepared to defend his principles steadfastly. He begins the new discussion by speaking of the feelings shared by him with Callicles (481c–482c). There have been almost no personal remarks in the colloquy with Gorgias, and but few with Polus. Owing partly to his prior acquaintance with Callicles, however, Socrates is able to aver that because each of them has two loves there is a common bond. Even though the feelings are not directed toward the same object, such as the deme or Alcibiades, and certainly not toward each other, the fact that both men actually have attachments of this sort would permit, indeed force, them to meet on the basis of their real aspirations. Rarely does Socrates make a remark of this sort as prelude to serious discussion in the dialogues.[6] There is a purpose for it here.

⟨*Each man*, says Socrates (481d), *has two objects of his love, and each pair*

of objects is seemingly antithetical within itself and to the other pair. Callicles'
love of the many, the deme or common populace, is contrasted with his love for
Demus, who happens to be a young man of a well-recognized aristo-
cratic-oligarchic family. *The objects of Socrates' own affections are Alcibiades,*
whose caprices [7] *are offset by the steadfastness of philosophy, Socrates' other*
love. Socrates describes *Alcibiades as* emplēktos, *unstable, hinting that*
both *of the loves of Callicles are of that sort.* The love of Callicles is for objects changeable in themselves,[8] and, moreover, his love moves back
and forth between them. We summarize this contrast, important in
what is to come, in figure 5.1. The love that Callicles is said to feel but
which he never admits nor denies is largely onesided, resting not upon
what he can give to the beloved crowd but upon what he expects to obtain—the tacit or clearly expressed permission to rule them and then
do as he wishes. The word *love* (erōs) almost entirely drops out of the
discussion, being reintroduced only occasionally by Socrates, and its
place is taken by the oft-repeated words *desire* and *pleasure.* To Callicles,
these three would appear to be virtually synonymous. There is, incidentally, no indication whether the affections for Alcibiades, Demus,
and the deme are reciprocated or not. Whether philosophy personified
loves Socrates in return is another moot point. Even in the Divided
Oblong Socrates has not mentioned philosophy. Later it will be made to
replace rhetoric as the fairest art.[9]

Already, then, Socrates has sketched the difference between himself
and Callicles as one between a man who loves and yet does not take his
lead from a beloved human being and a man who speaks for others,
having heard what they have to say, and suffers from their frequently
holding opinions quite opposite to each other. ⟨*Callicles,* remarks *Soc-*
rates (481d–482a), *changes his mind in accordance with the moods of his two*
loves.⟩ Not only the content of the discourse of Callicles is a result of his
association with deme and Demus but his very talkativeness (in the
first third of the section) apparently stems from the same source: a
need to accommodate himself to the interests and demands of two different kinds of persons, politically speaking. ⟨There is also a split in the
nature of Callicles, for Socrates says (482b) that *Callicles must be in dishar-*
mony with himself throughout his life if he cannot refute the opinion that in-
justice of the soul and not being made to pay the penalty is the greatest evil.⟩
This is an odd condition for Socrates to be laying down, since what he
has established with Polus has no necessary hold upon Callicles, who
has up to now made no open avowal of Gorgian principles. But if Callicles accedes to the opinions voiced either by Polus or by Socrates or
agreed to by both in the earlier conversation, then Callicles will be
caught in a second case of divided loyalty.

As against Socrates' treatment of Gorgias and Polus, he is now *de-*
manding a full-fledged refutation from Callicles—he will no longer be

	CALLICLES		SOCRATES
	one (unstable)	philosophy (stable)	
inconsistent (i.e., unstable)			not inconsistent (i.e., stable)
	many (unstable)	one (unstable)*	

*The asymmetry of this diagram stems from the open question whether philosophy is one or many, symmetry demanding that it be plural. But later in the dialogue it turns out to be marked by unity.

Fig. 5.1. *Contrasts between the loves of Callicles and Socrates.*

satisfied with bald claims,[10] witnesses, counterclaims, refutations as mere exercises, and other stock devices. The implication is that if Callicles does not undertake to erase, using all the power at his command, the concessions wrung from Polus, it will show that Callicles is willing to concur with them much as he concurs with the opinions of Demus and the deme. Only this time, it will be with the Socratic point of view instead. He must, then, make a stand somewhere, and Socrates senses in Callicles' first questioning about seriousness of mood the fact that if left to himself Callicles would never hold that the worst evil is to commit injustice with impunity. Out of willingness, however, to swim with the tides, he would be ready to agree were it politic to do so. What decides him to stand and fight is his extreme dislike of Socrates, which becomes ever more apparent. He is also aware, based upon grounds that we shall soon be discussing, that Gorgias and Polus have let rhetoric down and that he has lost both of them as effective allies.

⟨*To let go the contradiction between* what Socrates seems to feel are *the opinions of Callicles and what has just been shown to Polus about injustice would, by the Dog, God of the Egyptians, leave Callicles in collision with his own nature.*⟩ It is evident either that Socrates can intuit what Callicles does think or else that he has discussed these matters on a former occasion, for hitherto Callicles has given not the slightest indication of agreement or disagreement with his guests beyond playing host to them. But Socrates' warning to his new antagonist is an echo, through the oath, of the disapproval evinced for Gorgias in the passing-off of responsibility for the abuses of rhetors insufficiently instructed in the nature of justice; or *was* this disavowed? Socrates cannot be sure of Gorgias' position (462e–463a).

⟨*It is philosophy* herself *who must be refuted* (482b), *not Socrates, not*

Demus or the deme.)[11] It is philosophy, an impersonal discipline now personified, that must be answered, because the debt to be paid is not to some individual or group who might be deceived, or whose putting of Callicles in tune with himself could be no more than a consoling gesture. This impersonality of philosophy, which always says the same (482b), implies that it is not something constructed by Socrates but is rather something toward which he is forever reaching. It acts, then, as a kind of court beyond which there can be no appeal, like the judgments of Minos in the afterworld.

It is hard to think of a similar assault mounted by Socrates before any serious discussion has begun, in the other dialogues. Even such a vociferous opponent as Thrasymachus, or such an embittered one as Anytus, receives no such critical attention before speaking his piece. Why, then, does Socrates begin with Callicles in this way? To settle an old grudge? In that case his more probable course would have been to stay away from the gathering altogether. It is conceivable though unlikely that Socrates had never connected Callicles with rhetoric and its weaknesses until this very day, and that he is now convinced both of the flaw in rhetoric and its dangerous nature in the hands of such a man as is now before him.

The stage has now been set and lighted for a rebuttal by Callicles, a fairly long one (482c–486d), vital to the development of the entire section and thus to the dialogue as a whole. The attack is on two counts, that Socrates is a demagogue who has misused the distinction between nature and convention (*nomos*, law, custom) (482c–484c), and that Socrates is a philosopher, wasting his time and abdicating his civic obligations and opportunities (484c–486d).[12] ⟨The first accusation begins with asserting that Socrates had led Gorgias and Polus astray, both of them being too modest (or ashamed) *to say what they really thought* (482c–e), proceeding to an out-and-out characterizing of *Socrates* as *a low demagogue who slips from nature to convention and back again.*⟩ Callicles then undertakes to restate the correct relations between these two terms (482e–484a). He begins (482c) with a scathing denunciation of Socrates in language not used even by the accusers at the famous trial some years later. ⟨*You appear to be a reckless demagogue, and this is because Polus put himself in the same predicament as Gorgias did; you led them both on.*⟩ His first complaint against Socrates is not that he is a philosopher but that he uses tricks that might not be tools of the philosopher at all in order to defeat the two rhetors.[13] ⟨*You, Socrates, were responsible* (482 c–d):

First, Gorgias admitted out of shame that if a man came to him without a knowledge of justice but wished to learn rhetoric, he would teach him because of a general habit of thinking others would be indignant if refused a request; but Gorgias contradicted himself.

Second, after Polus ridiculed you—rightly, I think—he conceded, as I believe he should not have, that doing wrong is more shameful than undergoing it, and he became tangled up. You, Socrates, turn the talk into vulgarity and demagoguery, while claiming to pursue the truth.)

This is a remarkable dual accusation, for its very existence shows a resentment slowly kindled into flame as Callicles has watched his two guests being refuted through their shame, as he thinks.[14] It is, of course, impossible to know the steps that pass through the mind of Callicles, but something like the following would be plausible:

1. The uglier by nature is undergoing injustice: the uglier by convention is doing injustice.
2. By nature everything uglier is more evil.
3. Truth and convention (which is popular nonsense) are opposed to each other.
4. If a man is ashamed to say what is opposed to convention, then he is forced to say what is false; the natural is the true.
5. These rhetors have been ashamed to say what is opposed to convention, hence in danger of saying what is false.
6. By getting Polus and Gorgias to agree to what is uglier by convention (i.e., doing injustice) and by following that with what is more evil by nature (undergoing injustice), you, Socrates, have entangled them when they should not have been.

Clearly this is a mélange of assertions made by Socrates as well as by Callicles himself, and is not a solid argument; but at least some of its parts emerge in his diatribe. It is apparently not Gorgias' praise of rhetoric and its efficacy that Callicles has wanted to hear, but the techniques wherewith Gorgias would lay out his case; and when he finds the old rhetor blocked at almost every turn by a simple transition in Socrates' strategy (as he conceives it), he is greatly disappointed and gives free rein to his resentment later in the dialogue (503b; 516e–517a).[15] We must ask why Callicles praises Polus for mocking at Socrates. Is it because this is an approved treatment of fellow-guests? Hardly. We believe, rather, that it is because Callicles, like Polus, cannot separate argument from invective; if anything makes the speaker seem superior to the respondent, in the opinion of the hearers, then he is doing well, doing what he needs to do. Correspondingly, if he allows himself to appear foolish, ignorant, or wicked, then he should suffer the consequences, even if the foolishness is shown by being caught in a recondite contradiction requiring great subtlety to ferret out, or the ignorance is a pardonable lack of relevant information, or the wickedness is a plain confession of wrongdoing. To Callicles, Polus started off well, then he performed badly, that is all.

The accusation that Socrates has moved between nature and convention is apparently a reprise of Socrates' own observation on the vacillating between Demus and deme (481d–e) by Callicles, who now gives no examples, only the effects on Gorgias and Polus of the alleged shifting of Socrates. If this new allegation were true, it would imply the exact contrary of Socrates' assertion that philosophy is always saying the same thing. Either he is a liar here, or else Callicles is (perhaps unconsciously) projecting his own vacillation onto Socrates and making it sound as if the latter were deliberately being tricky and unfair. This makes it all the more incumbent upon Socrates to conduct an examination both consistent and thorough of Callicles' bivalent motives and his variegated doctrines.[16]

There is a slight asymmetry in the pattern thus far: Socrates has made a kind of confession about his loves and an assertion about those of Callicles, who has paid no attention to the reference to Alcibiades. Throughout, Callicles says almost nothing about his own personal life, except to indicate the mood inspiring his perfunctory oral agreements and his intense mental disagreements with Socrates. In the absence of any explicit self-revelation, one supposes that he aims to conceal his real motives. Almost the only personal touch is contained in his claim to be "fairly friendly" toward Socrates (485e); and in light of virtually all his other remarks this can scarcely be held sincere. From Callicles' standpoint, then, it is the character of Socrates that is on view, or perhaps on trial, not his own. He constantly takes the offensive in the first half of his section (482c and 482e are early instances) and just as constantly adopts precautions that he thinks might shield him from any attack made against himself.

On the other hand, there is *some* justification for Callicles' attack. He has seen Gorgias and Polus come to near shipwreck through inconsistencies that Callicles thinks have been forced on them, and just now Socrates has accused *him* of a prevailing inconsistency generated through the two loves. It is, moreover, a general lack of coherency that Socrates is describing, rather than some small point that further discussion might resolve, as was promised (461a–b) with Gorgias. Socrates' description of Callicles, which sounds patronizing at best, would raise the hackles of a man now fast becoming his enemy rather than merely an opponent. It is an unfavorable account not less stinging because it happens to be true.

With scarcely a pause, Callicles launches into his famous distinction between nature and convention (482e–484a). His speech has been praised by readers as not only the first but the best unfolding of the strong-man theory of government, and certainly it is forceful and succinct.[17] Whether or not Callicles has ever had instruction in rhetoric, obviously he has a way with words and has thought hard if not always clearly and without prejudice about the matters in hand. Yet much of what he now expounds he could have picked up from sophists who would very likely have been attracted to his house and retinue, despite his professed abhorrence of these men (520a). The originality of his thinking, however, is never at issue; Socrates does not allude to its possible sources, and the sole question is whether the conception of government and law is an acceptable one.

⟨By nature, says Callicles, *an evil such as undergoing injustice is more disgraceful, but by convention (or customary usage) doing it is more disgraceful* (483a), and—this is important—*a man unable to rescue himelf from undergoing an injustice is a slave* (483b–c).[18] It is not immediately clear whether the slavish man has been contrasted with another individual who is stronger or with a phalanx who collectively can visit an injustice upon him. The confusion is not dispelled when Callicles says next that *the stronger man can be terrorized by the many lawmakers seeking their own advantage⟩*—in other words, the strong man becomes the slave not because he is enfeebled by poor health or advancing age but because he is placed in a dangerous predicament by others weaker than himself if taken one by one. The strength, then, is entirely relative to external comparisons, and there is no natural criterion for identifying the stronger, though Callicles apparently wants to establish it as an absolute. ⟨In spite of this, he goes on to say that *nature herself declares that it is just for the better to have more* (483d). *This*, he is certain, *shows itself both in animals and in the states and races of men.*⟩ In the first of these, Callicles tips his hand a little, patently thinking of his world as Tennyson's "nature, red in tooth and claw," and drawing an analogy between this jungle and civic society. He moves up to the city-states and the various races, and is no doubt thinking of the wars, in particular the Peloponnesian War, which regardless of any of the dates assigned to the colloquy was still either in temporary abeyance or in its debilitating progress or aftermath.

Nature and convention thus have two roles in this passage: First, they help separate the one strong man from the many weak who eventually overpower the strong; this sets the stage for determining what is just and what is unjust according to the Calliclean view. Second, they enable persons outside the original action to decide in what sense such an action as overcoming the strong is good or bad. It should be apparent in the context of the speech by Socrates prior to this that Callicles is endeavoring to distinguish justice from injustice by looking to what is palatable to the deme, yet simultaneously trying to set the strong man above all others purely for his strength and regardless of how this strength is used, for or against the public. In seeking to rule one must find out what those to be ruled really want, yet in seeking to have more of desirable goods others must have less. If we are to take Socrates' account of Callicles and his two loves seriously—and we must—then the apparently bold yet rather simplistic statement of strength and weakness, and of nature and convention, at once becomes a theory whose internal stresses will be laid bare as soon as Socrates has an opportunity to examine them (488b–491e).

We might sum up this portion of Callicles' discourse by saying that it is an attempt (whether conscious or not) to replace the Divided Oblong, first by merging legislation and justice under the single heading of convention or agreement, then by putting this below nature:

one   — superior — naturally strong
many — inferior   — strong only by agreeing to band together

Rhetoric occupies a mixed position: It is respectable if used in the service of Callicles' theory, but is impertinent demagoguery in the hands of Socrates and hence submerged in convention.

⟨The next passage (483d–484b) gives examples, applications of the principle of rule of the stronger to persons. Being evidently well-read in history and literature, which he uses to his special purposes,[19] Callicles is able (after mentioning young lions) to invoke *Xerxes and his father Darius, who were, he says, able to lead the Persians respectively against the Hellenes and the Scythians.*⟩ We might remark, however, that both of these men could be called stronger only because of their armies, organized according to law and convention—the armies that gave strength were the many, and the two kings merely set them in motion. Yet Xerxes, despite his enormous forces, was defeated at Salamis; earlier, Darius fared better against the Scythians, but he too came to grief on the plains of Marathon. ⟨Callicles is on a little safer ground when he includes *Heracles (as celebrated by Pindar)*, but offers proof of his strength and superiority by saying only that *he stole some cows (484b–c)*.[20] ⟩

In some respects, Darius and Xerxes parallel Archelaus, the hero of Polus, but there is no mention of their perhaps having acted alone to elbow their way to the throne, nor of any private misdemeanors and political crimes which had helped elevate them to a position of power.[21]

Callicles is obviously convinced that the strong man, if *really* strong, will win out against the many who by their charms and laws have tried to subdue him. Such a victory is the working-out of natural justice. The only difficulty is that none of his examples fit this outcome, except possibly Heracles, who can be dismissed as a creature of fantasy.

Were Callicles to show elsewhere a delicate sense of the way two seemingly opposite terms can coalesce when a discussion is elevated to a higher level, we could be more impressed by "law of nature," *kata nomon ge ton tēs phuseōs* (483e), when formerly he had opposed the two terms to each other. The novel expression is applied to the strong man who follows his natural bent to become a leader. But because he has already commenced to blunder in this long harangue against Socrates, we think it more likely that his new phrase—evidently new to the history of thought as well as to the dialogue—represents one of many verbal shifts that he himself might dismiss as a mere slip on his part. He neither explains nor repeats his use of it. His intention has been to keep law and nature separate so long as he can make nature appear superior to law; yet paradoxically one way to do this is to assert that nature has its own laws. If nature is indeed superior then he can appeal to the justice of giving the naturally stronger more power, more freedom, goods, and pleasures. If, however, there is a law of nature, then the stronger has a double sanction, for added to that of nature itself is a law which by the very fact that it does not arise from convention is superior to it. If Callicles has really thought out this sequence, or something like it, then his "law of nature" represents a clever move having a touch of profundity, and one to give Socrates much trouble; but if not, it is only a minor muddle on his part, and against so many commentators on this passage we would object to seeing the phrase as a deliberate way of opening new vistas, except for the historical accident that other philosophers have explored it more deliberately and more subtly.

Callicles would employ a parallel dichotomous structure throughout his argument (if we neglect the phrase just discussed), were he not impeded at almost every turn by Socrates. Two terms are set up as contraries, one of which Callicles approves because it seems to comport with his own ambitions and desires, the other being whatever he dislikes. Then, instead of introducing clear new distinctions as subdivisions under each of the primary opposites, he simply adds on new terms as falling into line with one or other of the first two. This means that if one were to accept the first division, all others would in effect be adornments upon or further characterizations of it, and then the rhetorical force of the first would rest upon this heaping-up of near-synonyms.

A partial list of these opposites clustered under two heads is given in figure 5.2. Such a division is very effective in public speaking, but against a Socrates it will not prevail, partly because the primary division is too sharp, partly because each of its two terms binds all the others in their meanings, allowing of no mixtures or exceptions.[22] Up until the culminating formulation (491c–492c) when Callicles proclaims the power of unrestricted license, he stresses the equivalences of his terms in the same column; but after this point, when forced, he takes refuge in certain inequalities, for example, that pleasure is not the same as the

NATURE	CONVENTION
strong (one)	weak (one)
one (becomes weaker)	many (become stronger)
stands alone	stand together
undergoing evil is more disgraceful	doing evil is more disgraceful
laws immediately recognized	laws must first be made
free	slavish
self-rescue possible	self-rescue not possible
terrorized	terrorizing
should have more	should have less

Fig. 5.2. *Callicles' dialectical contrasts.*

good, that one pleasure has not the same worth as some other, and so on (500d).

Neither could Socrates set a pattern of his own, similar in form but different in content, side by side with that of Callicles and simply affirm that his was the better one, nor could we as readers argue that his scheme is better simply by using a third pattern, the same in form but this time contrasting the patterns of the two men. Again, were Socrates to try to refute Callicles by introducing a different pattern, say a succession of subbranching dichotomies or trichotomies, alongside that of Callicles, this would not constitute a genuine refutation at all, imposing though it might appear to the audience. There would be no harm in Socrates' introducing a more comprehensive pattern, provided he could somehow use steps that would force the acquiescence of Callicles; and this would amount to using his own pattern to engulf rather than merely replace that of his opponent. Callicles is convinced of all that he says and unconvinced or downright disbelieving of all that the opposition says; but it would be equally unfair for a reader to be convinced by all that Socrates has to say simply because he is the chief speaker. Fortunately he does not even attempt any juxtaposition—except in his introductory remarks about love, and again in the last page or two of the dialogue when it becomes legitimate since it merely summarizes arguments that earlier established the Socratic theses.

The Socratic way here is thus to show first that the initial distinction is no real distinction at all, and subsequently that the adjunct concepts are illicitly substituted for the primary ones or else added on. The combined ingenuity, stubbornness, and shiftiness with which Callicles defends and seeks to extend his position is the reason for the great length of this colloquy, as well as the fact that although after 481b practically no explicit definitions are asked for or proffered (as they are in the *Euthyphro, Lysis, Laches, Republic,* and many other dialogues), nevertheless the discourse of Callicles teems with single words or phrases offered as equivalents to the principal terms, and the legitimacy of these must be tested.

The second half of the two-part attack upon Socrates accuses him of being a philosopher (484c–486d). Callicles deals first with what he thinks is the wrong course that Socrates has taken (484c–485a), then the course that he should take (485a–e), and finally instructs him in the correct way to use philosophy itself (485e–486d). Instead of Socrates' contrast of two kinds of objects of love, Callicles speaks of two styles of living, of two aims to pursue. It is noteworthy, however, that the manner of living Callicles advocates in this part of his impeachment is that of the man of public affairs who could remain a private citizen but fulfill his civic obligations, rather than some law-scoffing strong man who bullies or gulls the populace into submission. It is fairly clear from much of the rest of the dialogue, however, that those two ways of life which he praises are somehow merged in his mind; both are opposed to the philosophical.

The accusation, furthermore, that Socrates is useless is one having very little to do with the events of the day; Callicles has known Socrates before, has either seen him talking to pupils or been told of this or has seen other philosophers so occupying themselves, just as Socrates knows some of the more salient facts of Callicles' life. That Socrates is a demagogue could have been dredged up entirely from the present day's discussions, and may be an indication that Callicles fears that if careless he himself will be conquered by clever verbal gymnastics enhanced with suitable flourishes.

⟨Callicles lays out four complaints, closely connected with each other. *Philosophy,* he says first, *is quite proper to follow moderately in youth, but it becomes ridiculous for the older man, and eventually ruins him* (484c).⟩ The idea of the ridiculous is not much exploited earlier in the dialogue, and its meaning for Callicles is never made very clear, since here it is coupled with immoderateness, that is, pursuing philosophy long after its appropriate use has worn thin; yet excess is part and parcel of the whole of the Calliclean view of life, as seen in his notions of the superior man and (later) the right to unlimited pleasures.

⟨Second, *philosophy interferes with becoming a paragon* (kalokagathon, a man fair and good, a gentleman), *for it keeps one ignorant of the laws of the city, of terms of agreements, and of human desires and pleasures, in a word of human character* (484d).⟩ A tantalizing mixture of concerns for the natural man and the conventional, giving equal attention to both. It is, moreover, worth noting that Callicles thinks of human character as best revealed in desires and pleasures.

⟨Third, *philosophers are ridiculous in the world of business, private or public, while the politicos make themselves ridiculous in philosophic discussions* (484d–e).⟩ If taken by itself this is in essence an attack upon philosophy, but only if the politico be considered the ideal man. On the other hand, such a politico would be wasting his time in becoming competent in philosophic debate.

In these first three complaints Callicles has outlined two ways of life considered as ways of occupying one's time. In this respect it might as well be a choice between playing whist and bridge; one is simply more old-fashioned and less "free" than the other. There is, however, an interesting sidelight upon this dichotomy: an abrupt shifting back and forth between universal and individual. Callicles sees life from a very personal point of view, that is, his own self standing against potential enemies and, because of this, as a master against slaves. He would probably view the good life in terms of a contrast between one right way and all the other ways that coalesce into one wrong way. Because it is Socrates who is facing him, this wrong way can be designated as that of philosophy, a second instance of the movement from individual to universal.

⟨Fourth, *Callicles now quotes Euripides* (484e) to the effect that *each man pursues most what he excels in,* adding that *each man denigrates what he does less well* (485a). *This is a species of self-praise,* he says, *for in praising one's aims one praises oneself.*⟩ (How clearly this happens to apply to Callicles at every turn!) But the relevance of this quotation is not very clear, since Callicles has just been implying that Socrates should at all costs bestir himself and take up political life, regardless of his bumbling when he has had to attempt it. And the addendum to the quotation would be appropriate only if Callicles means that Socrates has shown his low opinion of the rhetoric of Gorgias and Polus.[23]

At this stage Callicles is implicitly making a tenuous connection between the attacks upon Socrates as demagogue and as philosopher. He has in effect improvised a tetradic division of sorts, dividing nature, which selects the one, from convention, which arises from the many; and he has begun to sketch the possible conditions of the one so that (a) this one can stand free and supreme or (b) he can be overcome by the banding together of the many. Is the deciding factor merely whether the one is outnumbered, or does he lose his boldness and knuckle under to the many? Again, the many ought to be subdivided into (c) those who choose to remain apart from the group and are thus fair game for the strong, and (d) those who, in joining together, become able to rule. Here again, Callicles has not furnished a principle of *their* strength, and allows us to think that it is adventitiously based on numbers. The first and third items of this poorly allotted fourfold group represent the Calliclean notion of the working of justice, the second and fourth of injustice. Hence both justice and injustice are determined, if that is the word, as extrinsically as are strengths and weaknesses. Now—and here Callicles attaches his two complaints together in a peculiar way— the strong and free become the young who legitimately do philosophy, as a child legitimately lisps, while the old assume the place of the many who are not banded together; they cower, they are slavish, unable to rescue themselves from legal-political enemies. The identifications are not made fully explicit, but the descriptions are held in common.[24]

There is, however, a kind of involution in this pattern. The accusation that Socrates in his use of demagoguery and tergiversation overturns both Gorgias and Polus is at bottom an imputing of strength to his defeat of them. Socrates accomplished what he set out to do alone, he asked no help from others except to get them to agree with the arguments if sound, he was (so Callicles thinks) unscrupulous in his pursuit of what he wanted.[25] But now Callicles takes back with the right hand what he has given with the left, for he puts Socrates in the camp of the weaklings. Whether or not Callicles is conscious of it, in effect he has divided strong from weak, and then within the weak subdivided stronger from weaker again. ⟨In his advocacy of the right course to take, Callicles says (485a–c) that *philosophy must be balanced in two ways, first with regard to public business and second in respect to the proper age. Lisping and little tricks become a small child but not an older man, and conversely precociously distinct speaking ill befits the child but suits the older person well. The youth should study philosophy for its liberating effects*—has Callicles himself had a turn with that discipline?—*while the older philosopher cowers in a corner, avoiding the marketplaces to which he should be going,*[26] *never saying anything free and important* (mega), *never anything fresh.*⟩ In other words, Callicles, who obviously thinks of Socrates as fairly well along in years, is now condemning him for being the weakest of the weak. In so doing he has evidently confused the nature of philosophy, which is said to liberate the young, but somehow cramps the old once they have been liberated.[27] Alternatively, it is good to be liberated, but not too much. Either interpretation has its advantages.

The next set of statements (one can scarcely call them arguments) are comprised of Callicles' admonitions to Socrates regarding the way he should live his life in the future (485e–486d). ⟨First, *Callicles* tries to persuade Socrates that he is reasonably *(epieikōs)* friendly toward *him*.⟩ Is this to disarm him, or is it an expression born of Callicles' wish to hide his own failure to entertain friendly feelings toward anyone, except possibly a few companions for an evening of dissipation? Quite probably it is both. He is often at pains to give at least the appearance of a favorable opinion of others, although sooner or later his coldness, bordering on contempt, shows through the façade. It is difficult, after the first half of his section of the dialogue is over, to believe that he has genuine warmth for anyone; he is moody, always calculating ways to show himself in the best light, elaborately impolite in a fashion that must have been born of good breeding. When his poorly suppressed hostility turns inward it becomes as strange a mixture of pride and self-pity as can be found on the Sophoclean stage.

Indeed, the claim to be friendly is odd for several reasons. First, Socrates has come to Callicles not as a petitioner but as a guest, and has better than held his own against two men who elsewhere would be formidable opponents indeed. Socrates is not licking any wounds, and is in no need of consolation from an offer of friendship. Second, although Plato has deliberately concealed any determinations of the exact ages of the participants, some of the relative ages are clear enough; and since Socrates heard Pericles addressing the Athenians on the Middle Wall (455e), which took place thirty years or so before the statesman's downfall and death, and since Callicles is just commencing a career, it is unseemly for him to be giving a much older and more experienced man such gratuitous advice. Third, there is no hint on the part of Callicles that he hopes that Socrates reciprocally feels any friendship for him. It is apparently a unilateral extending of a pretended goodwill to one he trusts will *not* return it with anything genuine.[28]

⟨As a sequel to his protestation of friendliness,[29] Callicles repeats the substance of his earlier advice, this time in the form of a *quotation or paraphrase of a speech by Zethus to his brother Amphion in Euripides'* Antiope (485e–486a). Such a quotation is interesting in itself, for it both expresses and disguises the sentiments that Callicles appears to be holding at the moment. *Zethus, the herdsman, is haranguing Amphion, his brother and a musician, on the latter's way of life: You neglect matters that you should attend to, you distort a noble soul, you give no good counsel, you will not accept any word as convncing.*⟩[30] Euripides put this into the mouth of a man who would be, to the high-born Athenian, one of the unwashed, hence to be listened to only if supported by many others like him. This is advice given to a practitioner of one of the finer arts. It may be that Callicles, forgetting this, hopes to impress Socrates and the others with this learning and cleverness. But in using these lines he fails to recognize that his very act of quoting tends to put him on the side of the musician Amphion; he is again resorting to poetry, a refinement for the cultured man whose use of it may well belie the whole practical bent that he is trying to display.[31] One more point: The use of the Zethus speech tends not to strengthen Callicles' hand but to weaken it. Surely it imparts retrospectively a mildly theatrical air to all that he has been saying before by way of criticizing Socrates, making it seem less spontaneous, less pertinent and personal, more of a set piece, more of a rehearsal for a declamation.[32]

⟨At this point (486a–b), the criticism turns into a peculiar sort of warning, peculiar because it seems a non sequitur: *It is disgraceful, is it not, that you would be unable to rescue yourself if unjustly hauled into court, no matter how depraved and petty the man accusing you.*⟩ Plainly, Socrates' earlier disposal of the unjust but unpunished man rankles with Callicles, and he is now turning over the coin; it is not the justly but the unjustly punished man who is considered, and *he* is the one who is disgraceful if he has been pursuing the philosophic life.[33] But if we consider political realities, Socrates, if the description of philosophizing that Callicles has just given has been correct, is almost the last man to be brought to trial. He is an inoffensive whisperer on the sidelines of the game of the polis, and his influence is limited to but three or four pupils. Thus it is likely that Callicles is concerned not for the welfare of Socrates at all but for his own; it is he who touts the active life, and not only the ordinary activities of law-abiding citizenry but those of the man flouting the law, contemptuous of the multitude who might come to his defense, presuming that he had successfully concealed his real motives from them.

As A. E. Taylor points out,[34] the rhetor as conceived by Callicles would be distrusted by both socioeconomic parties in late fifth-century Athens: by the well-to-do, as a spellbinder to put the guardians of their class to sleep by giving them a false sense of security, and by the many poor, for using a trick by which the hater of the people can hoodwink the ordinary citizens into thinking a rhetor the people's friend. In either case, when disillusion sets in after discovering the real aims of the rhetor, the consequences for him will be severe. On the other hand, Callicles never says outright that he will not be accepted by both socioeconomic *groups* in the city. At this point, he cannot believe that, having the power of persuasion, he will be mistreated by any sizable contingent; instead it is likely to be some chance and probably person of low class who will falsely accuse him (or Socrates) in a lawcourt. If the accused knows how to speak cleverly and boldly in his own behalf, he will not suffer the dishonoring so terrible in the eyes of the Athenians. In other words, Callicles is always counting his possible enemies, but not in the right way. He always assumes that they will have no just cause whatever for bringing charges against him, and that they are not representatives of social classes, but are spitefully acting on their own. This runs counter to his view of natural and conventional justice, for he has pointed out earlier that the many, not the single man, would have to band together to defeat the man born to excel and to rule. The single ill-favored person would be no match for the superior. Callicles can secretly dislike the masses and distrust them, but they ought not to dislike him and charge him with any of the crimes, indiscretions, and other infractions of the law that any man such as he would be bound (and allowed) to commit.

His worry over the fate of Socrates bears the same stamp of inconsistency. Any man in touch with the temper of the city would know that a philosopher *as Callicles depicts him* would scarcely be the target of a capital charge. He does not know, or at least does not take seriously, the stance of Socrates as a troublemaker or as a man claiming to know all things in heaven and earth, and the other stock charges bandied about for years, beginning with Aristophanes and his *Clouds*.[35] Were Callicles to have depicted Socrates in that guise or as a revolutionary or corrupter of the young,[36] it would be easy to imagine his adding that sooner or later a city in wartime turmoil would come to resent such a person. But philosophy makes a man retreat, not advance, and inhibits his proposing a single practical plan. Callicles can see well enough that the man who moves least in society, does the least shoving, and disapproves most of those who launch their own schemes is Socrates himself. Because he suspects, too, that such schemes are likely to misfire and bring their perpetrators into peril, he must secretly envy Socrates for his safety.

It is possible, though not highly probable, that Callicles has already had a close call or two with the public or with some chance person bringing trumped-up charges against him. More likely it is that he has had intimate friends or relatives who have come to some danger. Plato, with his many anachronisms in the *Gorgias* (and elsewhere), might well have supposed that Callicles has witnessed the fate of his beloved's father, Pyrilampes, a man of power, a member of the tyrannical group, hence liable to the disfavor of virtually everyone.

⟨Callicles continues: *There is no wisdom in an art, namely philosophy, which makes a man worse and unable to rescue himself or others from danger, leaving him dishonored, with his property confiscated* (486b–c).⟩ It is hard to know which of these troubles Callicles more, for he apparently could not tolerate life without riches any better than he could see himself without honor and status in his city—very important to the patriotic Athenians, or, for that matter, citizens of the other Greek states, most of whom in a few hours' walk could circumambulate the entire community to which they were bound.

⟨Again Callicles raises the spectre of *having one's ears boxed without the payment of any penalty* (486c),⟩ a novel juxtaposition. Heretofore he has thought of the unjust low fellow as bringing the just man who might be a philosopher (heaven help him!) into court, and the dicasts would exact a penalty on the basis of false evidence. The unjust low fellow strikes the philosopher; yet there is no action, criminal or civil, against the ruffian, no penalty levied against him. If the fine *were* to be levied, however, it would be the philosopher, the good man, who brought the charges rather than being charged. Yet not pressing a suit for ear boxing is very different from being unable to stand up against a false charge of a capital offense. Utter flaccidity of will, craven panic, or extreme stupidity might account for the latter, but all sorts of incidental and minor reasons would dissuade a man from pressing charges for a fisticuff.

One last patronizing, slighting piece of advice comes from Callicles (486c–d): ⟨*You should cease refuting people and instead emulate those of wealth and high repute and other good things*⟩—in other words, *me*.[37] One should observe how suspiciously close this is to contradicting the theory of the superior man of a few pages earlier; now the man to be emulated is one who has succeeded within the confines of present customs and laws, a man who gains (or inherits) wealth and positions of importance in the city, a man who knows his way around the lawcourts. He is the man of substance who obtains and keeps that substance by playing the political-commerical game, knowing the agreements that have been made and the desires and pleasures—in other words, the special weaknesses—of the person with whom he deals every day.[38] As a combination of "dopester" and persuasive speaker he is the perfect example of the panderer to whom Socrates referred in the prelude to the Divided Oblong (464a–465a). The natural man, the man of strength who puts himself as far as possible above the law, has suddenly become someone who knows the twists of that law, operating largely within it in order to have all that he wants, and tempering his discourse to the moods of the people he addresses.[39] This much tamer aspect of Callicles' thinking apparently reflects the first of the two loves that Socrates mentioned, that of the deme; the harsher, more independent, natural man is more nearly an expression of his plutocratic snobbery.

On the other hand, Callicles has intended that only two ways of life be contrasted, the philosopher's with that of the man of affairs. In this, the contrast is purely external, being based, as we have indicated, entirely upon the way a man spends his time, not upon his native abilities, his education, virtues, and views of his mission in life.[40] It matters little to him which of these internal marks of superiority would count for most. The picture of a philosopher idling in a corner and being hauled into court is one which, if Callicles has earlier studied philosophy himself, is deplorably superficial regardless of whether it is a favorable or unfavorable estimate of that discipline.

For Callicles the cure for philosophy is simple: Just do something different, and you yourself will be different.[41] To realign rather than totally contradict his piece of advice will require the last thirty or so pages of the dialogue. In them the contrast will be reworked into the most profound of all the contrasts which the *Gorgias* provides.

The response to Callicles is in one sense fairly brief, about two pages (486d–488b), while in another it is the remaining forty pages of the dialogue, a dozen of which are occupied with refutations, the rest with other kinds of discourse. In the two-page sector just mentioned there are three short subsections: the expressed good fortune of Socrates at having Callicles as tester of his soul (486d–487a); the soul of Callicles as tester (487a–e); and a final remark on Socrates' willingness to be improved (487e–488b).

⟨Socrates' first remark, that if *his soul were of gold it would be well to have the best stone to test it, for then he could be assured that his soul was indeed golden* (486d–e)⟩, is badinage, but its intent is serious. Despite the incongruities of the Calliclean attack upon Socrates, it would be from the latter's point of view a step in the right direction. Heretofore, the talk has dealt with evasion of reponsibilities to others, to the law, and to the virtuous ideal. Socrates tentatively (481c–482c), and then Callicles more definitely, have both tried to fix each other's natures, Socrates in respect of love, Callicles in respect of occupation. An important difference between them is that Socrates was willing to expose his own erotic tendencies at the same time that he recounted those of Callicles, while the other has virtually nothing to say of himself. The admission by Socrates, even if his tongue is thrust a little way into his cheek, draws Callicles' attention to the need for examining inner character more assiduously. Henceforth the account will be not only in reference to the outer world of results, approbation, votes, money, status, but will consider traits deeper than those. True, Callicles has used exterior marks to determine the inner worth of the Socratic way of life, and is so far forth superficial; but he has made a start, which Gorgias and Polus were disinclined or unable to do.

One may ask what relation holds between this new turn and the old, and whether the dialogue falls apart at this point. Our answer is that the entire account of art versus pandering has to do with the moral energies of the soul called forth by these two activities. This distinction as suggested in prospect animated much of the conversation with Gorgias, in portions which centered round the question, not what is rhetoric but what is a *good* rhetor. A partial answer was made explicit in the Divided Oblong and after that was applied in the conversation with Polus. Consequently, it marks no discontinuity to advert to the individual soul and the life that it chooses. The notion of rhetoric as pandering has been stated but not proven, nor has any attempt been made to refute it. Thus it is necessary to display the soul's habits, that is, its virtues and vices, as fully as possible before rhetoric can be placed definitively in one or other of the two classes to which it has been assigned, as an art by Gorgias and Polus, and as a pandering by Socrates. True, Plato seems to have chosen the long way round to make his point; but there is still economy in his method.[42]

⟨*I was fortunate*, says Socrates, *in having chanced upon you, for whenever you agree with me then I know that this must be the very truth* (486e). *Whoever tests the soul*[43] *in regard to right living should have three characteristics—*and here Socrates divides people into three groups: (1) *those who lack the necessary knowledge for testing—perhaps the audience;* (2) *those who have the knowledge and friendliness but are too ashamed to be candid, and here Gorgias and Polus are named;* (3) *those who like yourself, Callicles, have the knowledge and the goodwill (as you say you have for me) and are candid as well* (487a–b).⟩ This is not an attempt to run through all combinations, but is a simple hierarchy which places Callicles at the top; and, of course, there is a sense in which Socrates is correct. Callicles as an educated man is well *able* to know what Socrates is up to in his own philosophizing; as friendly to him, even if in a pitying way, he can be perfectly aware of the figure cut by Socrates in the city; and, with all his insolences, he is still being as honest as he can. The point about agreement, of course, recalls that made with Polus (472b), when Socrates says that no more than one witness is needed to be assured of the truth, this being Polus himself. Here, though, the securing of agreement is more serious business. Socrates has just said that Callicles possesses knowledge, goodwill, and candor—attributes that he never suggests that Polus shares. The lack of any one of them would prevent Callicles from giving his assent, unless of a casual sort. Callicles, regardless of his inner conflicts, or perhaps because of them, is a formidable opponent, and to gain his genuine approval of any point, rather than merely getting him to say yes, is a difficult task. Normal channels of philosophic debate have virtually been closed off by Callicles.

The question then arises, What if Callicles does *not* agree? Will this mean that Socrates is not speaking truly?[44] Here the response must be a compromise. As a matter of fact, there is but one place (510a–b) in the next forty pages where Callicles wholeheartedly agrees with Socrates. At any rate, the concessions made throughout the last half of the dialogue by Callicles fool no one, least of all Socrates, who goes to what might be called extreme rhetorical-dialectical pains to convince a skeptical, obdurate, yet undependable nature. He clearly means that if he can persuade *Callicles* of anything, he will know that he has struck a blow for truth indeed. And since he lays store by self-consistency (482b), then it would follow that he would expect that a victory in one sector of the war zone would imply that Callicles would be bound to accept some truths elsewhere, provided that they were dialectically connected with the first.

With Polus the context of agreement was a little different, for Socrates was raising an objection to the parade of witnesses, such as Archelaus, who would attest to the greater happiness of the successful tyrant over the one punished for his crimes. Here (487e) neither crime nor punishment is in question, only the disposition of the soul, and Callicles is cast in the role of examiner, not of a summoner of witnesses; it is no longer testimony of outsiders but of collaborating inquirers that is wanted.[45] Even so, it is more than likely that Socrates is also using another rhetorical device, pandering, if you like, which could have a very good interpretation and will be at least temporarily useful here, but in this context need signify no more than that Socrates is willing to debate seriously with this rather trying young man. What it emphatically does not mean, however, is that Socrates is willing to capitulate, but simply that he can be in accord with his opponent. This would contravene not only his treatment of Gorgias and Polus but also his conception of philosophy and its constancy.

The same light touch, reminding the reader of all three of his opponents, is evident in Socrates' next sally, which like the others seems to pass unnoticed by Callicles, now wholly engaged: ⟨*I overheard you conversing with three men and forming a partnership in wisdom,*[46] *by agreeing that one should not delve into the deeper matters of philosophy and become overly wise. I take this to be a sign of your own wisdom (487c–d).*⟩ How this could be a sign of wisdom is, of course, open to question, but one notes that in this account of the earlier meeting it must have been conceded all round that philosophy does lead to wisdom, which is far from what Callicles has been asserting just now. He has, in other words, been emphasizing what to him is the bad aspect of philosophy, though on at least one former occasion he was aware that in moderation wisdom was no fault. We can only conclude that in this suppressing of the beneficial side of philosophy he has given evidence of how deeply he has been stung by Socrates' accusation that he was capricious.

Socrates is paying back in a mock-obsequious style, the exact reverse of the slashing, arrogant attacks leveled against him by Callicles. The modern reader sees through this, and doubtless Plato's contemporaries did also; the only real issue here is whether the three respondents to Socrates, as well as the unnamed onlookers, would have noticed. Here, we may suppose, Plato's own intent was that they should merely be quieted of their anxieties or hopes that Socrates, taking grave offense at the many insults he has just now endured, would leave the gathering.[47]

⟨The third glib remark by Socrates is a plea for help. *I would be grateful to you,* he says, *to be saved from my unintentional errors in choosing a way of life. These are owing to ignorance, so I need your help to know what to pursue in later years as in earlier. I ask you not to break off halfway through your giving of advice on what end I should pursue and what means I should use. If I agree with you, but do not do what I agreed to, regard me as a fool, nothing worth* (487e–488b).⟩ Before dismissing this as rank sarcasm, one should consider that Socrates is portrayed in the dialogues as playing a number of roles in life—stonecutter, father, soldier, controversialist, gifted speaker, and man with scientific interests.[48] Although the pursuit of truth could be carried on in any of these roles, it is mainly the political life as conceived by Callicles that takes one away from philosophy. The philosophical life so disparagingly pictured by Callicles is not essential, however, to the true philosophizing—one can still think sequentially and act virtuously in other occupations. If, then, the request for suggestions is sardonic on the face of it because Callicles is such a biased judge, there is still an undercurrent of seriousness. The choice of a life is not nearly so clearcut as Callicles seems to think, and for that reason it is worth considering suggestions from anyone, even though they are recognized in advance as coming from a prejudiced source.

The short passage is, moreover, a necessary transition to the great debate to come. If Callicles has just deprecated the philosophical life, it would be crude simply to set beside that description the far more favorable one that Socrates ultimately envisages for himself both in Athens and in the afterworld—a life which in its own way combines the political with the philosophical. The life of the philosopher must be freely embraced rather than adopted because some other life (in this case that of the politico) is unsatisfactory. Socrates' remark on the advantage in having Callicles' estimation of philosophy allows himself enough room to make that choice properly and advisedly.

The next four pages (488b–492a) are devoted to Socrates' attempts to elicit a clear, consistent, definitive statement from Callicles. There is a succinct definition of natural justice (488b), followed by an examination of this (488b–489b), a modified restatement of the definition (489b–c), another short examination (489d–491a), a second modified definitory statement (491a–b), a third modified restatement (491b–d), and a final exchange between Socrates and Callicles (491d–492a). Plato, as philosopher and a man of marked literary sensibility, directs the discussion into some general speculation about the nature of man and of justice as soon as possible; but this might take one of many turns. Socrates has just faced several minutes of attack upon his imputed weaknesses, together with an unfavorable, patronizing estimate of philosophy itself, and it is conceivable that a man of his self-assurance would see fit to defend either or both of these objects of scorn before a company of

Athenians and a pair of quite distinguished outsiders. Socrates' defense, which happens to overlap in content with the *Apology* though the emphasis is different, does not take the form of a direct assault upon Callicles, which would have been quite plausible, since the two men were acquaintances and could easily dredge up antipathetic appraisals on the basis of such experience. In the end the defense becomes a two-phase effort to rehabilitate philosophy with Socrates as its embodiment, and to urge Callicles himself to join in the philosophic enterprise—a modification of Gorgias' original claim to make others, wherever they are, to be like himself (449b). If, however, our thesis that the general and the individual are unusually directly connected together in this dialogue is correct, then to root out the real meaning of Callicles' doctrine of the stronger and expose its weaknesses will in the long run discredit the young man and his present motives, and will eventually make him more of a gentleman, a paragon, as well.

From a standpoint of pattern Socrates begins an attack having two aims. First, he will show that nature and convention work together (489a), hence that the parallel dichotomies alleged by Callicles to follow from them are not true dichotomies either; and second, he will introduce threefold distinctions wherever it suits him, but these will not fit Callicles' structures. Because there are but two persons debating at the time, with their respective life-callings, *this* division is always a bipartite one between philosopher and budding politico; but the distinctions introduced to generate solutions to the many problems are chiefly in terms of threes: Not guilty of doing injustice, guilty but paying the penalty, guilty and not paying the penalty (478d) was one such trichotomy in the debate with Polus, and this is finally transformed into being rewarded with eternal blessedness, punished but eventually achieving purgation, and again, punished eternally in Tartarus (524a). There are more such trios along the way.

Tactically, the object of Socrates' examination turns out to be more complicated, for on the one hand he must find some point of focus, of unity, in the argument of Callicles if he is going to refute the main contentions; yet he cannot let this stand because his purpose is to demolish a doctrine, if he can find one, that Callicles is willing to defend rather than merely throw in as a contentious suggestion, quickly passing to other, not very harmonious versions of it. There is little to be gained if the wolf is given time in court to testify but his best efforts turn out to be random utterances.

Back to the argument itself. ⟨*Natural justice, Callicles has said* (Socrates is paraphrasing him), *comprises the right of the stronger forcibly to despoil the weaker,*[49] *the better to rule the worse, and the nobler to have more than the pettier* (488b).⟩ Again we have two parallel columns, with the terms in one seemingly being heaped up to reinforce the two headings, a fair reproduction of what Callicles had earlier maintained (483a–d). ⟨Socrates then raises three questions (488b–d):

1. *Is the same person better and stronger?—that is, Does (or must) a person having the property of being better also have that of being strong? Callicles says, Yes, he does*, but gives no examples of this, so that evidently he means to answer the question by saying rather that being stronger is identical with being better—a more extreme notion.

2. *Are the more vigorous the strong, and must the feebler listen to them, as for example when great cities attack small ones? Again the answer by Callicles is affirmative.* Socrates had identified vigor here with the ability to attack neighbors, and Callicles does not demur to this. Hostility, assault, and subjection are part and parcel of his notion of strength.

3. *Must the stronger and more vigorous be the same as the better? Or can the better be weaker and feebler, the stronger more depraved? Callicles agrees once more.*⟩

On any reading of the question this is a misstep, since by (1) better equals stronger; by (2) stronger equals more vigorous; but by (3) stronger and more vigorous may equal more depraved, not better. This is a contradiction, though its exposure does not wholly destroy Callicles' position yet. Callicles at this stage sees the stronger as the ruggedly individualistic, lonely adventurer, a man whose strength makes him immune to every ordinary attack by other individuals and with it any consideration of right and wrong is dismissed; the law of nature, the law of the jungle, decrees that the only real wrong is weakness, tempered by the fact that the many *are* weak when measured against the strong, and thus rightly subservient to him. To Callicles the strong man needs no approval of friends—of these nothing has been said thus far—nor any cooperative group organized for the advantage of all concerned. If Socrates can show, not that an outsider would denominate all this as injustice but that *within* this system of associations there is some inherent flaw, then the peril attached to being stronger will turn out to be real. The stronger and thus more isolated a man is, the more cards will eventually come to be stacked against him. Given Callicles' point that there are few strong men, there are always going to be weaker ones who can ultimately dominate the strong by agreeing among themselves to take collective action. The stronger the strong man becomes, the more numerous will be the weaker ones, with the moderately strong being shoved down the scale; equilibrium is never really established.[50]

The connection of the stronger and better man with nature breaks down because in order to maintain his superior position or even survive at all, such a man must take account of external situations, that is, possible forces of the weaklings arrayed against him, in order to determine what he can do to enhance his power or indeed *must* do to retain it.

Hence the question, How is the stronger so strong? It has been shown that the stronger is more vigorous, presumably more muscular, and better adapted for fighting and hardship; but this need not imply that strength and vigor are the same quality. Consequently, there can be room left in the concept of strength to include other attributes such as intelligence, will, ability to persuade, and so on. As a matter of fact, these too are essential for the strong to rule successfully, because only in exceptional circumstances is rule given without question to the strong man who needs to make no plans, take no steps, to consolidate his rule. The attack on Socrates has been directed against him for having just this persuasive power needed for leadership; but owing to a misdirection of his aims and a shortcircuiting of his energies, he does not use it for the only proper advantage, his own. Strength includes the ability to persuade even as Gorgias thought himself able to persuade, and as Socrates outplayed Gorgias and his satellite. Thus persuasion is a requisite for attaining power everywhere.

One more observation regarding Callicles' account of the strong man: His image is of one who is hardy, capable of standing alone, able to resist following the multitude in his thinking. When taken in their better senses these are almost precisely the qualities ascribed to or claimed by Socrates in the *Apology, Charmides, Symposium,* and elsewhere, though Callicles would certainly put a different interpretation of his words upon what he has said, and would deny vehemently that such a notion had ever occurred to him. A confirmation, however, lies in some other expressions to which Callicles turns, namely wisdom (489e) and bravery (491b), which also figure in the descriptions of Socrates by his various friends.

⟨The questioning now (488d) proceeds when *Socrates injects the many into Callicles' formulation, and the latter agrees*⟩, partly because of the logic of the situation, that the many do have to be reckoned with, and partly because after having made the strong out of the oligarchs, he must also include democratic aspects in his view of the state. He loves the deme, after all. The many are indeed stronger than the one strong man, and this, Callicles admits, is by nature; that is, a crowd of weaklings, if they act according to common agreement, are *naturally* stronger than the strongest individual, there being no limit set upon the size and hence the strength of the crowd. If so, their usages are better and fairer, not by convention only, but in their very nature. Socrates is here turning Callicles' own principle against him, that of finding the relatively dominant power in any adversarial situation and then according it the chief natural right to rule, even if, as it happens here, that right is generated through an agreement.

If the many have the last word, then their belief, that justice resides in equality of sharing, is credible. Callicles grumpily concedes (489a) at least that the many think that they, with their joint agreements, determine the character of justice; but the grumpiness portends his later resistance to this. It is probably not convention in itself that Callicles disapproves but rather several other considerations peripheral to it and which conflict in some way with his original thesis:

1. The weak who make the agreements and become the strong thereby, are still weak individually when their agreements for some reason break down.
2. The weak hamper the individual who is strong, and he should not be hampered, by a kind of self-evident right that Callicles never makes clear but which at first he obviously believes in.
3. If the agreement has been entered into by Socrates in his role as philosopher, it would be bound to be contemptible. (As we have hinted, one of Callicles' chief vacillations is between perceiving Socrates as an exceptionally formidable opponent and as a forlornly weak citizen.)
4. The agreements made by the many can well take the form of laws, and these are exceedingly hard to break or to modify, because everyone but the naturally rugged and strong will be a party to the agreement.

We may summarize by saying that there are four possibilities generated by assorting the one and many, strong and weak:

First, Callicles upholds the one ruler who is strong, along with wishing the many to have no agreements among themselves, thereby ensuring that the strong will not be overthrown.

Second, Socrates would see the ruler strong but having to consider the many weak who agree, thereby preventing themselves from being trampled; here nature and convention would work together.

Third, a possibility, not discussed, would have it that the one ruler is weak but the many would be weak also because lacking agreements; this would of course be anarchy. It is possible that Callicles sees his own deme in this light, for his contempt for the masses often shows through; hence he would think that he himself could step in and assume rule.

A fourth possibility, again not discussed, is that the one ruler is weak and the many do have agreements; this could be a democracy, and again Callicles would see this as a grand opportunity for himself.

The one point overlooked for the moment by both participants is that the many *might* select Callicles' own hero to lead them, that is, he could be both naturally stronger and conventionally acceptable as a ruler, hence the two conditions could be merged, as Socrates suggested. But for the time being he has established his point without help from this possible case, and can claim that instead of flagrantly shifting he has combined them (489a–b) by showing that Callicles' primary distinction between stronger and weaker is a false one because of his secondary distinction between nature and convention.

⟨Callicles is now furious (489b–c). *Socrates is a driveler*, he bursts out, *ready to catch me up if I miss the mark with my words. The better are the stronger. Slaves and a miscellany of fellows* (pantodapōn anthrōpōn) *who get together and say something are not making laws, though they may have more bodily vigor* (489c).⟩ First we discuss the complaint, then the substance.

This is the fourth criticism Callicles has made of Socrates, and derives partly from his picture of the philosopher cowering with his pupils, and partly from his interpretation of Socrates' present behavior before an audience. Socrates speaks insignificantly and without any let-up (*ou pausetai*). The real question is whether the man who proposes small but important changes in the wording of a formula or the man who exposes these is the driveler, and here the only likely answer would come from an examination of much of the rest of the dialogue. Thus if the last page were the only record one had of Socrates, one would be hard put whether to identify him as a serious thinker or a sophist, a carpetbagger purveying inconsequentialities. It is from this predicament, when Callicles *may* be right in his judgment of Socrates, that the latter must extricate himself. The added difficulty is that in so doing he must use more of the same tactics that have stirred Callicles to impute to him such meaningless verbal juggleries.[51]

Callicles, incidentally, has himself shifted emphasis: Now it is not the incantations of the weak using the law that he condemns but the slaves and idlers who chatter and do *not* make the laws.

⟨To explain the meanings of the words *stronger* and *better* (489d–490a), Callicles says first that *two men, even if more vigorous, are not better than one*, although a little earlier (488c–d) he had asserted that the stronger and better *were* the more vigorous. Now he goes on to say: *Your* (many) *slaves are not better than you* (individually).⟩ This ignores the possibility that slaves can be weaker one by one if it happens that they are the persons who have been defeated in battle by the very soldiers who will soon become their masters; or they may be stronger, on the other hand, if they are *not* the ones defeated but have been handed over by treaty and acquired by persons of the conquering city who themselves did little or nothing to fight for their possession.

⟨After Socrates, by now thoroughly aware of the foibles of Callicles in debate, *accuses him of playing with words* (489e), the latter is coaxed to continue (489e–490a):

The better and stronger are the wiser;[52] *the better and stronger and wiser should rule; the better and stronger and wiser ruler should have more.*⟩ By *wiser* Callicles means not wiser in mathematics or astronomy but in practical affairs, otherwise his equating of the wiser with the stronger would have little relevance here. ⟨Socrates takes him up on this by *specifying the wiser man as being a doctor* (490b), thereby reintroducing the arts which had been put to one side in this little subsection:

First, *should the wiser and more vigorous doctor have more food than others less wise and less vigorous?*

Second, *should the wiser and equally vigorous have more food than others less wise but equally vigorous?* (490c)⟩

By adding a couple of intermediates, namely "equal amounts of good" and "equally wise," one could create a neat three-by-three matrix out of the materials of these questions; it would not falsify but would unnecessarily complicate the text to do so, for Socrates considers not all possible combinations (there would be twenty-seven), but only six, arranged in pairs, which Socrates now completes by adding:

Third, *should the wiser and less vigorous have more food than the less wise and more vigorous?*⟩

Because Callicles had earlier said (488c–d) that the strong equal the more vigorous, Socrates is now breaking up this identification: stronger equals wiser equals more, equally, or less vigorous (i.e., the conclusion from the three questions).

⟨Another explosion from Callicles (490c–d): *You speak of food, drink, doctors, and such drivel. I am not speaking of these.*⟩ Callicles has unwittingly been led back to the lowest level of the Divided Oblong, and his first response shows that he has made no distinction between possible pleasuring of the body and doing what is best for it, that is, doctoring. ⟨Socrates takes him to another rung, that of clothes and shoes, which can be used as necessities or embellishments. *If the weaver wears the biggest coat, or the cobbler wears the biggest shoes, and more of them when he has no need to, certainly that is conspicuous adornment* (490d).⟩ This is the second interpretation put on "having more" by Socrates, and one might look to the gymnastic trainer acting as genuine counterpart to the fraudulent embellishers of the body. Instead, Socrates introduces the farmer who might expect to have more seeds because he is accomplished in his occupation. This peculiar twist can best be explained by repeating that Socrates is tempering his argument to the capacities of his opponents. It is clear enough that Callicles has not assimilated the lesson of the Oblong, and that he can deal only with an intermediate stage between pleasure and the best. The farmer oversees the production of a plenitude of seed, like the cook with his food, but unlike the cook the seed is not a source of pleasure in itself but serves a purpose in producing grains and fruits which *would* be pleasant to the taste, even if not tricked out in some dessert.

An interlude here (490e–491a) shows how it is possible for the two men to agree in words when their meanings are far apart. ⟨*You keep repeating the same things*, exclaims Callicles; *Yes, and about the same things*, is the rejoinder. To which Callicles adds that *Socrates never stops talking about cobblers, fullers, cooks, and doctors, as though the discussion were about them.*⟩[53] To Callicles the repetition of others is exasperating, although he himself, when talking freely in a long speech, has come close to an annoying redundancy. Socrates is falling back upon his earlier assertion (482b) that philosophy always holds the same. But Callicles has merely said that Socrates continually *talks about* cobblers, and so forth, not that his doctrines are forever the same. And it seems clear enough that this is only the first level of interpretation. The second is that there are many lessons to be learned from the simple comparisons that Socrates uses. The third is, on the other hand, that in pursuing these lessons dialectically a unity behind them all might be discerned—we do not say is necessarily discerned. But because this escapes all three rhetors, we must conclude that Socrates is matching Callicles by pretending to remain upon the first level.

⟨Callicles now offers a second and modified restatement of his theory (491a–b): *strong equals wiser in civic affairs, and brave rather than faltering by reason of softness of soul* (dia malakian tēs psychēs).⟩ It is clear that Callicles has tacitly conceded that his earlier view of the stronger leaned too heavily upon physical aspects, or at least could be mistaken for so doing. After adding *wiser* and *braver* (i.e., firmer of soul) he has withdrawn bodily vigor as one of the requisites. In so doing he is beginning to make room for the Socratic distinction between body and soul.

⟨It is the turn of Socrates to reproach *Callicles* (491b–c) for *never saying the same thing about the same subject*.⟩ This can only be a procedural complaint, because Callicles is shifting closer to the line of argument laid down by Socrates almost throughout the dialogue. On the other hand, Socrates must realize that his opponent is by no means intending to plead for scientific or philosophical intelligence as a prerequisite to ruling. Indeed, the only meaning given to *wiser* in the pages immediately preceding is "more practical," "more capable," or the like.

⟨Callicles' reply to this objection is not a defense of his own style of discourse but a new formula (491c–d), that is, a third modified restatement: *wiser and braver should be rulers of the cities; justice should be having more for rulers than for ruled.*⟩ Notice the inclusion of *should* (prosēkei, it is

fitting, seemly) in place of some part of the verb *to be*. The certainty that
by nature (which is presumably always and everywhere the same) the
strong will rule and receive extra rewards in spite of any opposition
that may arise, is now replaced with a more tentative Calliclean expression, that matters may not turn out the way he defined them, but it
would be better if they did. There is an inkling that Callicles is looking,
in a very uncertain way, to what is best here.

⟨In answer to this Socrates raises the objection that Callicles has implied that the rulers, who must rule themselves and be temperate (*sōph-
rona*) and self-mastering (*engkratē auton heautou*), should have more
than themselves. *The one who rules himself is temperate and self-mastering
over his own pleasures and desires* (491d–e).⟩ This introduces self-rule or
self-mastery, and reintroduces desires and pleasures, which like the
arts have lain fallow for a time in the conversation. Socrates is deliberately using them in a connection at variance with the animating principle of the Divided Oblong, which was that pandering seeks to promote pleasure regardless of the real good or wellbeing of that thing in
which it is promoted. In a sense, Socrates is egging Callicles on, knowing that the having more, if not of food or other commonplace tangible
goods, must signify the means to satisfy desires of other sorts—luxuries. Callicles has dismissed the making of shoes, the shrinking of
cloth, the preparation of food, and the restoring of health as acceptable
examples of activities guided by wisdom. The pandering that Socrates
has taken as the genus of rhetoric links ruling, at least in a remote way,
to speechmaking, though if we tried to torture this into syllogistic form
the best we could produce would be a fallacious Barbara in the second
figure, and the worst a three-line argument with no relation to syl-
logism at all: The ruler looks to pleasure, the rhetor looks to pleasure,
and the rhetor and the ruler are thereby connected. So far, the only
ground for using the two terms is associative, not dialectical.

⟨That pleasure and desire are not far from the very center of Callicles'
view of the ruler is shown, however, in the fact that he immediately
takes Socrates up on the idea, again exclaiming that *the temperate, those
who master themselves, are the foolish* (491e).⟩ Natural justice points elsewhere: Desires should be fostered and then satisfied, not punished.
Plainly, Callicles wants to stifle Socrates' intention to crowd all the customary virtues together in the soul of the strong ruler, for two of them,
practical wisdom and bravery, will give him much unsupervised liberty, but justice (taken as equal sharing, *to ison*, the only definition proposed thus far) and temperance (not yet defined) will inhibit the ruler's
pursuit of unlimited pleasure.[54] In the absence of justice and temperance, and with wisdom and bravery signifying what they do for
Callicles, these last two would be positive aids in collecting and exploit-

ing ways to satisfy desires. Callicles will resist any effort to establish a unity of the virtues, for reasons to emerge shortly.

It is hard to believe, but his next speech (491e–492c) is the last one in the dialogue to consist of more than a very few lines. It is the counterpoint to his first account of natural superiority (483a–484c), and is a kind of culminating statement linking the power of the ruler with the satisfaction of desires. It contains five basic contentions.

⟨First, the temperate are the foolish (ēlithious); here Socrates interrupts to say that this is not what he had in mind, but Callicles persists (491e), and the equation stands:

$$\text{temperate} = \text{foolish}$$

Second, three new equations are given (491e–492a):

natural justice = *living rightly requires letting desires be as strong as possible*
natural justice = *living rightly requires not punishing* (kolazein) *the desires*
natural justice = *living rightly requires satisfying each desire in turn through bravery and practical wisdom* (phronēsin)⟩

It seems clear that Callicles thinks of these three as not the same yet interdependent, and of the need for all of these conditions to be met in order that justice may prevail. In spite of Socrates' effort to show that natural and conventional were not distinct (489a), Callicles has reverted to his old position that they were not only different but sharply opposed to each other. Furthermore, although Callicles does not see all the virtues as belonging together, he looks upon wisdom and bravery as having to work in tandem to secure the pleasurable satisfaction of desires that he thinks rightfully belongs to the ruler.

⟨Third, *the many cannot achieve any of this, so they enslave the stronger few by praising temperance and justice because of their own lack of bravery* (492b).⟩ This remark is of doubtful courtesy because Socrates has just now said a good word for temperance. The remark repeats the concession that Callicles made earlier, when he pointed out (483b–c; 483e–484a), that the many can overcome the strong without much difficulty by their arguments and "spells," which must mean that the naturally stronger have a very slender hold upon either power or pleasure. The doctrine in itself is a peculiar one, for it puts the many in a position not only of inhibiting the strong man's attaining of political power—which is perfectly justifiable—but also of spoiling his chances for the satisfaction of private desires—which the many do not for the most part concern themselves over, unless the pleasures become too gross or interfere seriously with the satisfaction of the smaller number of desires that each member of the populace would have. Thus Callicles' point is either an irrelevancy or a damaging admission that the strong man is always at the mercy of the weak not only in regard to governing but in regard to living his own life.

⟨Fourth, *to the sons of kings or to those who obtained power through their own natural talents nothing could be more disgraceful than justice or temperance, and they would be imposing as master on themselves the law or argument or censure* (psogon) *of the many. If they did this they would be unable to give their friends more than their enemies* (492b–c).⟩ Callicles in his first point is again trying to take back with his left hand what he just gave to the people with his right; the lucky or the able ruler would be a fool not to resist any efforts of the populace to persuade him of the worth of justice and temperance. Thus we see now a continual struggle between the one and the many for the right of the one to his own pleasures. His second point is a little more complicated. This is the first time he has used the notion of friends in a general sense, though in an individual reference (485e) he has declared himself friendly toward Socrates, moved by goodwill (*eunoia*) for him (486a). But the conviction that the ruler has cronies whom he will help by loading privileges and pleasures on them is new. These friends are in a limbo, somewhere between the one strong man and the many weak, for they may or may not have natural gifts of a sort to elevate *them* to power. It is the first time that Callicles has allowed an intermediate between two opposites, and it seems to be the outcome of his growing realization that the strong man is unable to sustain his position if he stands unique and alone. The assumption is that friends will have desires comparable to those of the ruler, and will not want them confined by the will of the many.

⟨Fifth, Callicles' last contention (a double one) begins again with an equation (492c): *happiness* (eudaimonia) *and virtue* (arētē) *equal luxury* (truphē), *licentousness* (akolasia), *and freedom* (eleutheria), *if supported by force* (epikoursan). *The rest of the decorations* (kallōpismata), *namely the unnatural covenants* (para physin synthēmata), *are drivel and nothing worth* (492c).⟩ Callicles has tried to turn the tables on the Socratic exposition of the Divided Oblong, for he has described covenants and agreements as seductions and bewitchments (483e–484a), and now as adornments. *They* are the panderings.[55] He has now put two virtues, bravery and wisdom, in his column of strengths, the others in the column of weaknesses. As a last fillip, he declares the agreements of men (regarding the limitations upon pleasure) to be worthless. His ideal, were he to follow his theory to its final consequences, would be to turn every cook into a caterer for gourmets, every woman into a wine-bearing *pornē*. That his ideal is not one acceptable to the public at large is shown in his insistence that force, physical force, accompany the lux-

ury, license, and freedom. Where this would come from is not specified, and remains very indistinct in the exposition, though common
sense would tell us that it might have one of three sources: the naturally
strong man, his friends, or some sort of paid bodyguard. The idea is
not further developed.

* * *

This speech has been what might be called the high watermark of Callicles' rebellion. Thus far the whole impulse of the discussion has been
in his hands; the bold declarations are his, and when he has been asked
to explain his meaning he has merely moved sideways to equivalents,
rather than backward in retreat. He has, in effect, been aided by Socrates both in the attempt to improve the image of the stronger and also in
defining the rewards accruing to this figure in the shape of the gratification of desires, namely pleasure. He has been able to select the virtues
befitting the activities of the strong man and reject those interfering
with enjoyment of the desserts naturally due him—in his conception.
Up to this point, then, the stronger showing has been his, and Socrates
has merely asked for clarifications which although unsatisfactory could
not be put down for nonsense. On the other hand, Callicles' apparent
strength has been bought at a high dialectical price. His various efforts
to state the nature of the good, justice, and strength have suffered
amendments at his own hands almost beyond the point where Socrates
can keep up with them, as if his argument were the many-headed
hydra.[56] It appears that to such a life as Callicles advocates belongs the
self-awarded prerogative of saying whatever *seems* to fit the rhetorical
exigencies of the moment such as what one has said before, or what the
other speaker is saying, or the apparent mood of the audience, and the
like. So Callicles would say much that comes into his head when merely
allowed to give his opinion of his dialogic partners or opponent, or
tender something related to his own aspirations; and even more would
come tumbling out upon being pressed to account for discrepancies in
what he has already put forward.

The pattern of the argument, however, has been the result of a dual
effort, no doubt planned by Socrates and not fully discerned by Callicles. Had the latter realized the impending threat to the security of his
theory and his personality, he would have done more than merely
fulminate against Socrates. The truth is that without his realizing it
some fences against the wider application of his theory have been
raised, and the strong man, far from being *anyone* who happens to have
more vigor and desire, is now a rather closely specified kind of man,
with limits upon everything but his seeking of pleasure.

Callicles has begun this segment (490a) with the strong as one deserving a larger share—of what is not yet determined. Does this *stronger* mean doctors, weavers, shoemakers, farmers (490b–e)? If not, then it means men wise in public affairs (491a)—note the two-part division. These men of affairs are brave, not soft (491a–b); Callicles is adding a new characterization in the column, but the column has now become subdivided from the doctors and others.[57] To him, the practically wise and brave ought to rule cities. Socrates again subdivides by contrasting that group with those who should rule themselves, by which he means that they should rule their pleasures and desires (491d). Once more Callicles opposes this with the natural justice dictating that the desires should be made as strong as possible (491e–492a), and he stigmatizes Socrates' temperate, self-ruling people as fools and slaves (491e), the worst of them being those born to kingship but mistakenly subduing their desires when this is wholly unnecessary and against nature (492b). The best thing in life is not so much to rule, we are beginning to suspect, but the right to have more, or rather the actual taking of more. It is, in a word, Callicles' celebration of the extrinsic accompaniments of power that we are attending.

The upshot is that Socrates' efforts to divide and subdivide have resulted in Callicles' restricting of the strong ruler to one with practical sense and unhindered desires, an unlikely combination, for this man must be both wise and lacking in judgment to perceive what effects his licentious behavior would have upon the deme he rules. Nor does Callicles give any thought to the question whether the debauchery he welcomes is not at odds with the very exercise of the ordinary capacity to rule, regardless of what the populace at large may think of his libertine binges.

If Socrates is to be depicted as a bulwark of rational and republican government, then Callicles represents a mixture of democratic and oligarchic tendencies, poorly assorted. For him life is rational only up to a point, for ambition and desire ultimately dictate the course that his reason is to take. Injustice would be the accepting of any kind of restraint on lusts, so temperance really becomes the contrary of both nature and any kind of law. The ruler is a tyrant mostly without law; certainly, he gives no law to himself in order to restrain his own incessant impulses. Whether Callicles is himself a strong man, really capable of maintaining himself above the law, or a weak one who acts irrationally and then runs home for protection against the vengeance of low fellows who cannot stomach any more of his follies and ravages, it makes little difference at the moment, though the reader is beginning to have his own hunches. Plato is trying to show, we believe, what Athens will suffer either way if there is no Socrates to put Callicles on a better path.

6

PLEASURES UNLIMITED

(492d–499b)

The last half of the *Gorgias* takes on the aspect of a pummeling match, much of it conducted on a fairly high level of philosophic inquiry, much of it on a low one, regardless of the ultimate stakes involved. The reason for this oscillation is of course that although rhetoric is mentioned by name less and less as the dialogue proceeds, the entire setting is still one in which it is being practiced in every guise: long speeches, short ones, questions, answers, derisive epithets, witnesses, flattering approaches, threats, and much else. It is practiced this way on both sides.[1] The greatest and possibly the most effective device against Callicles is the concluding myth, which takes accusation, judgment, and punishment out of the realm of the temporary and fortuitous, transferring them to the eternal and inevitable.

It would be easier to follow if the battle were between two well-rehearsed noddies lacking sensitivity, each parroting old doctrines; but the fact is that both men are uncommonly perceptive, each in his own way. The sundered nature of Callicles' soul has long since begun to show itself, the most conspicuous sign being the recurrent outbreaks of anger that for the moment relax his troubled spirit.[2] He is confronted on one side with two professionals and on the other by a presumed inferior, a quarryman, who yet appears to be outmaneuvering them all, and by the latter's acquaintance Chaerephon who will surely be glad to report these proceedings well beyond the range of the audience which Callicles has assembled for the occasion. Although the host may have looked forward to a battle, his zest would last only so long as he himself was not facing an overly formidable antagonist, regardless of what had already happened to Gorgias and Polus. As we have said, to Callicles the treatment meted out to those two men by Socrates was untouched by any real concern for truth.

Like Polus, Callicles thinks in his more secure moments that everyone would like to believe as he does, and this gives him the feeling of being supported by the many and also of having gone to the right sources to ground his opinions. He has possibly discovered already that the many have diverse and often contradictory ideas, that the deme is capricious, especially in the hands of the very rhetors whom Callicles will need to emulate. The difference, however, between him and Polus is this: Polus is inexperienced and inept, while Callicles, though he cannot be much older and is undoubtedly less traveled than Polus, has absorbed more ideas through his Athenian education. The very fact that he has remained in his mother city and has sought to divine the wishes and aspirations of his own Acharnian deme makes him more confident of his notions of human history and the forces impelling it. That Polus has traveled from town to town is no guarantee of his having absorbed the complexities of business and politics in a city—any city, let alone Athens.

This very familiarity, however, enmeshes Callicles in a difficulty; for in saying what the world thinks, he must be voicing conventional morality, and as soon as he does this he has jettisoned the natural supremacy of the strong man—unless the deme actually believes in such a figure. But as soon as members of the deme do believe in him, relations of ruler to ruled begin to take on a conventional flavor. The many will support the strong man so long as he does not trample them, but this cannot last, and the superior man must set about to consolidate his position immediately. Yet Callicles does not seem to care that such consolidation involves making at least a show of fair play—he wants to rule, then grab all the bigger and more tempting portions for himself.

*   *   *

At this point (492d), then, begins the long section of refutations and counterstatements to the theory and its supporting arguments just put forward; it moves through two principal phases, and lasts to the very end of the work (527e). After a preliminary remark in which Socrates again seems to be praising Callicles for his candor, there is a subsection (492d–499b) in which the theory of unlimited rewards, mainly pleasure, is subjected to scrutiny closer than hitherto. Callicles is not utterly defeated at the end of this, and the final very long subsection (499b–527e) concerns itself with three questions regarding the better life and the worse.

The praise from Socrates turns out to be faint indeed, if one of its meanings be taken. ⟨Callicles says, because of his candor, what the world (hoi alloi, the others) only think (492d).⟩ What he would prefer to make of this is obviously that he is the only honest man who has stood up to

Socrates, present company not excepted. But Socrates may well have in mind that Callicles says what the rest of the world thinks in the sense that he is echoing ideas but presenting them as his own. It is quite true that the dichotomy between natural and conventional law seems to have been fairly new to the late fifth century, but we must always bear in mind the relative paucity of evidence regarding the entire period.[3] The likelihood, however, that Plato wants to present Callicles as a deeply reflective man is exceedingly thin. He is shown as an impetuous, moody talker, and this might lead him to think himself original; but the vacillations point the other way.

⟨Socrates continues his apparent praise: *Kindly continue, so that it can be made clear how one ought to live* (492d).⟩[4] This becomes the question of overriding importance in the dialogue. Socrates is being sly here, for he is asking his opponent to continue the discussion not so that Callicles can explain what he takes the good life to be but so the conception and the *image* of the truly good life can be manifested.

What follow are two kinds of attempts to dissuade Callicles from the stand he has taken, first by means of images (492e–494b), and then through arguments (494b–499b). To sum up the point at which Callicles has arrived, and from which Socrates will launch his attempts at dissuasion, we record this set of proportions in figure 6.1. Never stated in a single passage, but scattered through the remarks of the previous subsection, this typifies Callicles' habit of finding equivalencies (though not exact synonyms) that accumulate on the same side of a line marking off what he takes to be contraries. His proportioning is less clear than that of Socrates, but he manages in particular cases to state analogies. Although he vacillates, he does return to this multiple grouping as his main theme, and seems to continue to believe in its parts, if not all the equivalencies, right through to the end. Socrates upsets the formulation by (1) merging nature and convention; (2) by probing the essence of strength and unseating the Calliclean view of it; (3) by showing that intemperance is a life of degradation; and (4) by proving that it is self-contradictory to be guided entirely by the pursuit of pleasure and the concomitant avoidance of pain.

⟨Socrates opens the debate by condensing the Calliclean doctrine that desires must be not impeded but encouraged and satisfied as often as possible, and that this is human happiness and excellence (492d–e). *It is incorrect to say that persons wanting nothing are happy; they would be stones or corpses, says Callicles* (492e). The response of Socrates may sound strange, but it is a paradigm of the form of argument that he sometimes uses. It is a *quotation from Euripides asserting that living and dead may well be the same; and our body* (sōma) *may be our tomb* (sēma), *that part of the soul having to do with desires being over-persuadable and vacillating*

convention		weakness		the many slaves		temperance
—————————	=	——————	=	—————————————	=	————————————
nature		strength		the one strong man		desire and pleasure

Fig. 6.1. *Basic Calliclean assumptions.*

(492e–493a).⟩ The quoting of Euripides has several purposes: First, it lets the company know what they might have ignored otherwise, that Socrates will be able to hold his own if others are quoting tragic theatre; second, the very choice of Euripides is a mild thrust at Callicles, who has already used him against Socrates; third, it gives a certain authority to what Socrates is saying, much as Callicles was able to inject that note into his own pronouncements. The verse erases the rigid opposition that Callicles has been trying to establish between life and death, pleasure and it absence, just as earlier he set one up between nature and convention. Socrates does not merge all contraries wherever he finds them; he is seeking to meld only those that impede Callicles from perceiving the truth of a doctrine more subtle and comprehensive than the one he has been espousing, and one requiring a very different set of distinctions, many of them already laid out in the Oblong. Were a sharp differentiation between life and death to be upheld, incidentally, the final myth would have no currency at all.[5]

The interpretation that Socrates seems to put on the (Orphic?) identification of body and tomb is probably this: The body as seat of desires suffocates the spirit, chains it to the everyday world containing nothing but other bodies—a far remove from the opinion of Callicles, who has just said that desire and life are bound up with each other.

⟨Socrates now proposes—and this too is odd at first sight—*a number of images* that, he twice suggests, will *each cause Callicles to change his mind* (493c–d; 494a), to which Callicles peremptorily says *no*!⟩ To the modern reader, the images may be faintly amusing as efforts to persuade a dour but pleasure-engrossed young man, and one is puzzled too by the slight variations between these pictures of common objects; any reader would doubtless be far from ready to give up his wicked ways on the strength of these figures alone.

When desires, in the sense put forward by Callicles, are combined with possibilities of satisfaction and restraint, four combinations are the outcome. First, we have no desires and no satisfaction, a condition that Callicles suggests is proper to a corpse or stone. The combination of no desires with satisfying them all is either an empty class or is in a different sense identical with the first. The third is to have desires unlimited and not to satisfy them. Callicles inveighs against persons not attempting to satisfy every one of them, as being fools and slaves, lacking the requisite practical sense and bravery, while Socrates looks upon them as temperate. Finally—and here most of the discussion settles—there is the combination of desires unlimited with the effort to satisfy them all. To Callicles this is happiness and the superior ruler should pursue these by natural right, while Socrates invokes images of leaky pots, insatiable birds, catamites, and then condemns this sort of life in strongest language. In exploring these further, let us count Callicles' likening of the man without desire to a stone or corpse as the zero-image, to be followed by the three pairs offered by Socrates, these to be numbered in sequence. To keep our account brief, we have arranged these images as given in figure 6.2.

We need to ask some questions: First, Socrates generously cites wise men from Sicily or Italy as sources for the jar figures (493a), but gives none for the stone or plover. (In the same way, Callicles gives no source for *his* stone.) Why refer to the Sicilians or Italians at all? Apparently the likeness between death (or stones) and absence of desire was a commonplace of Greek thought of the time, just as it has been through the centuries; the lack of a reference to poets or other thinkers can thus be taken for granted. But the jar is more sophisticated, and there is even something timidly resembling a pun (*pithos*, jar, and *pithanos*, persuadable). Perhaps Plato wished to give credit to either Philolaus or Archytas, both Italians, as he seemed to be doing in the *Timaeus*.[6] Moreover, Gorgias and Polus are Sicilians, and Socrates, although he has pretty well disposed of their arguments, has by no means forgotten their presence and their ethical blindness and is thus attempting to keep their attention. Apart from these reasons, admittedly rather slender, there seems no excuse for the reference.

Second, why are there so many thumbnail images (a flock unusual in the rest of the dialogues), as if Plato wanted to drive home his view regardless of the cost to economical prose? The most likely answer is that a striking image is still very economical, and Socrates may think that by appealing to the eye of Callicles he can shorten the argument, knowing well from all the reproaches which the younger man has heaped upon him that Callicles is not one to be guided by intellect alone. Indeed, Callicles himself initiates the list of images by his reference to stones and corpses, and even earlier by his rather colorful description of the philosopher cowering in some corner. We have noted Callicles' reliance upon the poets in preference to the philosophers, and it is true that images are the stock-in-trade of the former more than of the latter.[7] Socrates is again appealing to Callicles on his own ground.

Third, a more difficult and important question is whether there is an order in the figures. We discern no simple hierarchy in their succes-

IMAGE	DESIRE, PLEA-SURE, PAIN	MOVEMENT AND SATISFACTION
0. stones and corpses (492e)	no desires, no thought	no movement, no satisfaction, no life
1a. leaky jar (493a–b)	overpersuadable part (desires) insatiate and thoughtless	passively filled, i.e., passive movement, no life
1b. leaky sieve (493b–c)	unbelief and forgetfulness	active, but filling is incomplete
2a. multiple jars sound and full (493d–e)	temperate	satisfaction complete; nothing to be added
2b. multiple jars, leaky, filled with difficulty (493e–494a)	licentious	almost insatiable
3a. stone and corpse* (494a)	no pleasure, no joy, no pain	not empty, no movement, no life, not completed
3b. plover (494b)	inflow and out flow are continuous	movement and life; filling and emptying are necessary to existence of bird; not complete, insatiable

*These are mentioned only in passing by Socrates, as a contrast to the bird. Obviously they return to the reference in Euripides.

Fig. 6.2. *Images used by Callicles and Socrates in examining pleasure.*

sion, but rather an interweaving—you may call it a fugal—pattern. As shown in figure 6.1, the stone (0) is repeated later (3a), the leaky jar (1a) becomes multiple jars that leak (2b), the sieve that empties as soon as it is filled (1b) turns into the plover (3b) doing much the same. But the basic outline does progress from totally lifeless through slight activity (of filling one jar) to more activity (multiple jars), and finally to a living bird. It is but one more step to the catamite, a sad little boy whose succession of patrons resembles the life of the insatiate bird, this depiction of the extreme of unshackled lust serving as counterpart to the image of unrestrained violence of the man loose with a dagger in the agora (469c–e).

Finally, we ask why Socrates twice inquires of Callicles whether he is persuaded. This is puzzling, coming after the second and third images (1a and 2a), and Socrates then continues without any reassurance that the later ones will be the slightest bit more effective. Callicles is energetic, resistant, combative—Socrates has already learned this well. Why does he even ask whether Callicles is persuaded by a couple of simple figures of speech, taken from subjects as commonplace as jars? Perhaps the answer runs something like this: Since the issue is that of desire controlled versus desire uncontrolled and encouraged to run to the limits of licentiousness, this is not a purely doctrinal matter but strikes at the heart of Callicles' moral nature, this being his real if covert aim in seeking rulership. The possible effectiveness of the figures is then a little clearer: It is a series of arguments appealing not to the intellect but rather to the eye, which is the best way to delineate raw desire and bald satisfaction in a brief discourse. Such images might well be effective with a man whose secret—for such it seems to have been up to now—has just been revealed by his outburst against temperance. Otherwise, all the images, separately or taken together, would carry little conviction.

As a further sample of the way the discussion and characters are reciprocally related in what we have called depth dialectic, we note that because the three sets of images do not convince Callicles, one may conclude that this kind of rhetoric is limited in its usefulness as a tempering device. The images have little force in persuading a man who wholeheartedly believes in throwing away all restraints, to modify this belief and undertake to improve his habits. Later (513b), Socrates will point out that Callicles' plan of living is irrational if he thinks it possible to become leader of the deme but remain unlike its members; political success rests chiefly upon delivering sentiments to the crowd that owing to antecedent conditions would appeal to that crowd. In order to play upon this, the putative leader must develop a character, or its outward appearance, like that of his supporters. The lesson of the jars and bird is temperance, through and through, and Callicles is wholly intemperate, in preference if not behavior. If he rules, he will either have to moderate his habits and become more like the deme, or else deliberately corrupt the deme, making the people more profligate, in which case it will be increasingly difficult for him as ruler to "have more." The city will turn into a carnival, the carnival into a debauch; and then will come chaos, with no possiblity that the once good populace will be brought back through any sort of persuasion to a reasonable and decent living.[8]

Socrates now (494b–499b) produces several less obviously rhetorical devices for persuading Callicles that the good life has not been well defined or described by him. They consist of three arguments, of two kinds; namely, reference to a sort of anonymous, absent witness illustrating that a certain manner of life is evil, and then two more nearly dialectical arguments that commence from the supposition that pleasure and good are identical—the hypothesis already implied with some truculence by Callicles and ultimately proven to be self-contradictory.

The first argument (494b–495a), hardly one in any proper sense, constitutes a bridge between the images just rejected by Callicles and the proofs that are to come and that demand his partial surrender. ⟨For Callicles, enjoying the happy life (chaironta eudaimonōs zē) means having desires and being able to satisfy them (494b–c). In his turn, Socrates, who commences a list of three pleasures with *eating when feeling hungry and drinking when feeling thirsty*, goes on to *scratching when there is an itch*(494c).⟩ Whether all three types of pleasure relate to the supplying of necessities for life is not in question, but the kind of eating and drinking coming to Callicles' mind would be as much born of pandering as the treatment he would expect to receive from anyone having a care for promoting health and well-being.

⟨The inclusion of scratching leads to a passage-at-arms regarding vulgar pleasures, framed by cross-admonitions, that Callicles should not be ashamed, while Socrates *should* be ashamed, to discuss such matters as scratching oneself, especially on parts of the body other than one's own head. *Such a continual activity*, says Socrates, *is no better than that of boy prostitutes* (tōn kinaidōn, *of catamites*), *which he calls dreadful, disgraceful, and wretched* (deinos kai aischros kai athlios).⟩

If the catamite-passage has ushered in a transition from imagery to reasoning, sharing some of the traits of both, then we see a nice symmetry: Socrates has tried to persuade Callicles by three sets of images in which liquids are allied to satisfactions, jars with or without leaks to the soul. Now he tries to refute him, using three nearly fullfledged proofs, of which we find the first most informal. These three are to the same effect as the images, namely that satisfaction of desire is not the good in life. The arguments are clearer than the images, leaving less room for misinterpretation, for there is a gradation of pleasures implied in scratching one's head and thence moving downward: Decent pleasures gradually shade into disgraceful ones.

In this section, the good is no transcendent reality but simply the good for each man, his good life; nor does Socrates pretend that the good is the same always. One may pursue it for oneself; it need not be doggedly pursued throughout all time.

Back to the catamite, whose body is not a stone, yet may be quite passive, with no special desires.[9] The only advantage for him would be money, not his own satisfaction. So long as money is paid, the satisfaction he provides another man's body is unlimited. It is the epitome of pleasure unlimited, in the sense in which Callicles must have meant it. He has acceded to the notion that scratching produces pleasurable life, but suddenly he is brought up sharp by the reference to the catamites. ⟨*You should feel disgrace, Socrates, to lead the talk onto such things* (494e).⟩ At 492c came the acme of Callicles' rhetorical expression of what human life should be; now he is abruptly at the point of admitting, as he is apparently doing, that satisfaction of desires is debased. If scratching is allowed, so is this dreary, onesided fornication. An audience is present, and Callicles is apparently aware that this is a fatal admission, not only in the argument with Socrates but also in the eyes of the very kinds of persons whom Callicles will have to impress in his forthcoming career.[10] What he loves most, freedom, license, luxury, leads straight to what he hates and fears most, dishonor. In his outrage he gives no genuine sign that he is above such sources of enjoyment.[11] An admission of guilt would be unthinkable, though the notion that Callicles has done a wrong both to himself and the boy has probably not dawned upon him, since he has not been publicly charged with this crime. Such a charge would be his abiding fear.

We call this a proof. Properly it narrates what Aristotle would have called an inartificial (*atechnos*) proof, a device for persuasion (along with laws, oaths, tortures, and contracts) that takes the form of bringing in witnesses to testify favorably to one's cause.[12] Socrates has already accused Polus of doing just this (471e–472b) in introducing the example of Archelaus (471a–d), remarking at various points that it would be impossible for Archelaus to be happy (472d–e), that he has led the worst life (478e–479b), and that he has been most miserable (479d–e)—expressions roughly equivalent, by the way, to those Socrates has used to describe the life of the catamite. That the catamite is a witness, too, is not acceptable from the standpoint of a strict, impersonal logic; but we are not dealing with materials meeting standards of the first four treatises of the *Organon*.[13]

⟨The conclusion (494e–495a) of this first passage in the three proofs, or quasi proofs, is put in a left-handed way by Socrates: *Is it I who am leading the argument* (logos) *this way, into scratching and catamites and other shameful topics, or is it someone who says that those enjoying themselves, regardless of the kind of pleasure, are happy, and thus does not distinguish between good and bad pleasures?*⟩ Socrates does not wait for an answer.

He turns instead to a series of equations and inequations. The second of the three arguments, and the first genuinely dialectical proof here (495a–497a), is an attempt to show that good and pleasure cannot be the same. The reason this form of discourse is again possible is that its aim is not to render a definition of pleasure, or any of the other leading terms, but to find out merely whether one or other of them is deservedly identifiable with the good. This notion of good has not been defined by either party, though its nature has been hinted at indirectly several times, differently, by each man. ⟨After Socrates, in keeping with his condemnation of the life of the catamite, states that *there must be good and evil pleasures*, and then asks *whether pleasant and good are identical*, he provokes an immediate response from Callicles (495a), which is again an equation: *pleasure = good*, prompting Socrates to rejoin that *this damages your own first arguments* (diaphtheireis . . . tous prōtous logous); *you are no longer adequate to look for truth with me if you speak against your own beliefs*.⟩ This can have one of three meanings:

At first you scolded Gorgias and Polus for having spoken against their beliefs because they were ashamed to own up to them, but now you yourself are ashamed to say what you think, namely that some pleasures are disgraceful—you almost admitted this much a moment ago when I mentioned the boy prostitute.

The strong man, you said at first, had rights to more than the weak, and thus not only more pleasures but better ones (whatever you meant by that!); but now you are saying that there is no way to discriminate any pleasures that are not equally good.

In either of these first two cases, Socrates has not only become well aware but has grown tired of the continual backing and shifting of Callicles in his effort to maintain himself in the conversation. Evidently ruled out altogether is that this is another reference to the inconsistencies of Callicles caused by his affection for both deme and Demus. It was an accusation made by Socrates (481d–e), not an admission by Callicles, that the latter was changeable because he was unable to disagree with either of his two loves.

It may be instead, or as well, that Socrates is remembering that Callicles has nowhere stated the contradictory of the equation pleasure equals good, namely, pleasure does not equal good, or even the contrary, pleasure equals evil, or again, a different but not quite opposite near-equivalent to the contradictory: good equals power, or ruling above the law.[14] The last, of course, could be what Socrates has in mind as being the statement that Callicles has just contradicted, because if Callicles' first assertions are recalled, clearly he began with a view of the good quite other than what he is now expressing. He has commenced with the sharp dichotomy between nature and convention, and then tried almost surreptitiously to introduce equivalents to each of the two terms, hoping that by ranging power along with pleasure on the side of nature he could show that power = pleasure, and that Socrates would let this slip by without an objection.[15] This is not wholly inconsistent with the statement that pleasure = good, but it makes for an even more puzzling Anaxagorean merger of goods under a single head.

The attitude of Callicles comes to this: approval of pleasure mixed with disgust with some pleasures, or at least with the admission that such pleasures can be pursued. When Socrates said earlier that scratching an itch would make a man live happily, in Callicles' view of life (494c–d), Socrates was called a demagogue without art; to specify what is to be scratched and liken this to the life of a catamite is reprehensible manners.

There is a limit, then, to the frankness of Callicles, though not necessarily to his wide-ranging pleasures. Socrates is rejecting him as a proper co-worker in the search for truth not so much because he has entangled himself in the questions of the superior man, natural law, and the rest, as because Callicles plays fast and loose with personal shame.[16]

There is another issue. The present wavering of Callicles in response to what he senses will be the reaction of the audience today or of the public tomorrow is blatantly out of step with what he has affirmed of the stronger man who does not let the weaker dictate his behavior, and with it his opinions. Callicles has once again shown the rightness of the first estimate of his nature, that regardless of his bold theories of independence, he is a man unhesitatingly ready to adapt himself to a swerving public or a capricious male lover.

⟨Socrates' conclusion (put in the form of a question, 495a) in this first loose-jointed argument is that *there must be good and evil pleasures,*⟩ a judgment that plainly compromises between the notions that all pleasures are good and that they are all evil. It is a provisional opinion, and Callicles does not immediately agree, but it will be used later against him and will introduce a host of difficulties with which he will not be able to deal.

Before taking up the further arguments against the position of Callicles, we should raise the question why pleasure is made an issue here at all. Obviously the idea of a feast, a display by Gorgias, would give pleasure and not much else to a reasonably well-educated man, because the aim of the listener is simply to enjoy the skilled exhibition. On the other hand, the talk soon turns to political and legal oratory, and there we may ask whether pleasure is the main consideration, or any consideration at all. In politics the emphasis of the rhetoric that Gorgias describes (452e) is on whether to build fortifications and docks and the like, and probably how to handle money, but no civic speaker in his right mind would say, "Build the Long Walls and you will have a great deal of fun." The same holds for forensic oratory, concerned as it is with guilt and innocence, and only by the remotest stretch could it be argued that the dicasts will have more pleasure if they imprison or execute the guilty and let the innocent go free—unless, of course, it is the *hetairai* and *pornai* who are to be allowed their freedom.

We conclude, then, that on the level of rhetoric alone and its immediate persuasive effects it is necessary to examine the nature of pleasure only as an accompaniment to or outcome of effective speaking—the delight in hearing the balanced and rolling phrases of a Gorgias. It is when Polus details the deeds of Archelaus that he says that the tyrant has *greater* pleasures than other men. This is not, however, solely owing to the use of rhetoric—indeed Gorgias would think this use of it to be scarcely rhetoric at all—but it enables Archelaus to extricate himself from the predicaments that would otherwise result were he without some persuasive powers. When Callicles enters the scene, we have the full treatment of pleasure, not as an accompaniment of good speaking but as an end of living. Rhetoric assumes a subordinate position, though it is still quite true that Callicles has a rhetoric of his own, just as everyone else must have in one degree or another, though not necessarily in the making of set speeches.[17] Instead the main task of his rhetoric lies in the balance between praise and blame—praise for the presumably freer, happier, more pleasure-filled life of the superior man, and blame for that of the philosopher, in particular Socrates, for everything he does and says.[18]

In sum, pleasure is not a new consideration in these last few pages, but appears now in a new context. Presumably there are different kinds of pleasure desired by Callicles from those of Polus.

The bald declaration that pleasure and good are the same has launched the refutative proofs (495a–499b). They will carry the discussion a step farther than the images, because in likening satisfaction to a full jar that remains full there is no clear way to show that temperance is a means of curbing the desires *before* they all get satisfied. A half-full jar is no better than one that leaks and is never full. If Callicles were to reply to Socrates' question, Yes, I am convinced! then he could still run his merry course, provided only that he could call a halt and say that he was satisfied. But temperance and the satisfaction of all one's desires are not the same.

The interchange about conflicting statements (495a–b) is a prelude to the argument proper (495b–497a), about good as unselective enjoyment (*pantōs chairein*), an argument divided into five small parts.

The first step is to assure that the good is indeed unconditional enjoyment. Socrates characterizes this as disgraceful (495b–c), and then moves on to his chief statement. It has been a double accusation of disgrace.

CALLICLES	SOCRATES
pleasant = good	pleasure ≠ knowledge
knowledge ≠ bravery	pleasure ≠ bravery
knowledge ≠ good	
bravery ≠ good	

Fig. 6.3. *Equations and inequations of Callicles and Socrates.*

The equations and inequations offered earlier are continued, but now they divide briefly into two parallel groups, those upheld by Callicles, and those by Socrates (495c–d), as shown in figure 6.3. From Callicles' statements thus far, it would follow that neither knowledge nor bravery would be pleasure, and furthermore that the good is something highly restricted in character (even though the pleasures themselves might be unlimited in number), having nothing to do with a couple of principal virtues. From Socrates' two negative statements, of course, nothing positive or negative can be concluded about knowledge and bravery, and although Socrates may later wish to hint that the virtues are some-how united, we must remember that he has not read latter-day histories of philosophy stating that Plato upheld such a doctrine. The best that he can do now is to inch toward this formulation, and the best the reader can do is to wonder what is going to be Socrates' strategy for defeating Callicles on the present question.

Because Socrates explicitly, and Callicles by implication, both say that bravery and pleasure are not the same, the discussion can proceed with that as a premise, and the two columns can eventually be merged into one.[19] Socrates, however, doubtless realizes by now that superficial concessions come cheap to Callicles, and that these maneuvers will be not much more effective than images of leaky jars.

Socrates (495e–496b) introduces six pairs of contrary terms whose individual members cannot be put off simultaneously from the subjects in which they can inhere (see fig. 6.4).[20] Speed and slowness being listed along with the five other pairs, we may assume that they refer to running, and that all twelve members in the list inhere in one way or another in living things. There is no attempt to ally human good with cosmic, though later (507e–508a) just such an alliance will be stated. The point here is that some qualities must either attach to their living subjects or else, by reason of the nature of those subjects, their op-posites will hold.[21]

The list moves from general (well off, badly off), to more particular

well off	≠	badly off (*kakos prattousin*, doing badly)
health	≠	disease
health of eyes	≠	ophthalmia
strength	≠	weakness (*astheneian*)
speed	≠	slowness
happiness	≠	evils and miseries

Fig. 6.4. *Six pairs of contrary terms introduced by Socrates.*

conditions (health and disease of eyes), and then back to the more general on which the two men are beginning to agree as being the good, namely happiness, though Socrates thinks of it as an exercise of virtue or human excellence while Callicles holds it unobtainable through the virtues that Socrates is advocating. This part of the argument is by no means a summary induction, nor would it satisfy very many inductive rules of any sort. It is a series built upon likenesses, but these are not the likenesses of images to types of behavior (as with the pots and the pleasure-bound man), for such likenesses are by and large more remote associations than one finds in common experience and discourse.[22] The likeness of each pair in the list to the other pairs stems from their all being traits, either outwardly visible or subjectively evident; they are, in other words, more nearly what we would call concepts standing for things than pictures of objects standing for other things.

⟨Fourth, there is a counterexample (496c–497a) to this present list of six parts, the fact that *hunger and thirst, which are of course painful* (as are all desires), can *be present at the same moment that the eating and drinking assuaging them and are pleasant can also exist.*⟩ If this were untrue, one would not continue to eat until all hunger was relieved, but would quit the first instant, or else the eating would be irrelevant and would not satisfy the hunger at all.

⟨Fifth, we approach the final stage of this proof (497a) as explained in figure 6.5.⟩ Socrates has not proved that these are three pairs of mutually exclusive contraries (hunger and the satisfaction derived from eating) but only that as different entities they need not succeed each other in one subject but can coexist in a single subject. This can, however, still operate as a refutation of the Calliclean proposal to regard the good as the pleasant, for if they *can* coexist, they can still be two separate natures, like sight and sound. The fact that enjoyment and feeling pain *are* contraries, and that faring well and faring ill are contraries as well, is *not* in issue, since all that Socrates is establishing here is what he

enjoyment (*chairein*)	≠	faring well
feeling pain	≠	faring ill
pleasant	≠	good

Fig. 6.5. *Counterexample to Socrates' six pairs of contrary terms.*

thinks of as the more general point of their difference. How radical is the difference between good and pleasant in some cases would be the topic of further discussion. There is, of course, no hint here that all pleasures must be evil.

⟨This second proof (which we may also call the first quasi-dialectical proof, although like the proof preceding it is not smoothly textured), is followed by an interlude (497a–c) longer than most in this dialogue, in which *Callicles commences by claiming that he does not understand these sophisms* (497a), upon which *Socrates accuses him of dissembling* (akkizē). *Go on, and you will realize how sharp* (sophos) *is your admonition of me. Do not we simultaneously cease both from thirst and from the pleasure obtained from drinking?* (497a–b). *I do not know what you are saying, is the reply.*⟩ Does this mean that Callicles pretends not to understand what is said, or that, even though understanding, he pretends not to detect any difference between the Socratic manner of discourse and the sophistical? Perhaps it means both. Callicles, never at a loss for abusive epithets if evasive answers fail him, has recently been stripped of many of his pretensions to being a highminded man; it is probable that now he will feel even readier to attack Socrates at any point at which the present company is likely to agree with his onslaughts and enjoy them. The differences between dialectic and sophistic are so subtle that twenty pages would be insufficient to uncover them. Because Callicles cannot perceive any of these at this point, it would appear that any effort to defend Socrates could well turn the attention of the group away from the discomfiture of Callicles. This would also be a hit at Gorgias, who like the sophists travels from city to city picking up pupils as he goes. ⟨It is perhaps this very message that dawns upon *Gorgias, who now* (497b) *urges Callicles to continue the argument to a conclusion, and who a moment later reminds him that it is not his honor that is at stake, so that he should permit Socrates to pursue the refutations as he wishes.*⟩ It seems unusual for Gorgias to shift the burden of lost honor onto his own art of rhetoric, which is on trial throughout. Yet his eagerness to have the discussion continued to its proper termination probably arises from a wish implied early (457b–c), that if the art taught to a pupil be misused, it should be the pupil who is punished, not the instructor, that is, not Gorgias himself. Regardless of the fact that Callicles is probably not Gorgias' pupil, Gorgias has in a sense had to take the younger man under his wing. (Anyone of Gorgias' long experience must realize that Callicles has not asked him to be a guest simply to share a few meals with him!) So Gorgias must be keenly aware that his art is on trial and will be sorely abused if left to be defended by this unusually complex host of his, unless Callicles is urged to put forth better efforts.

⟨Callicles asks that Socrates proceed with his minuscule (smikra) questions, since Gorgias wishes it. To this the reply is (497c), in what will become an ever larger issue between the two men, that Callicles is fortunate to have been initiated into the great mysteries before the lesser (smikra).[23] Socrates did not believe that this was allowed.⟩ If the questions that Socrates asks are in fact tiny ones, then Callicles may think that he himself has solved the greater ones touching this life of unlimited power and pleasures; but in truth his attention has been misdirected, away from the primary questions that Socrates has been raising about virtue and happiness. What Callicles proposes will radically alter the direction in which the entire state is actually moving in order to promote the interests of the pleasure-bound strong man, while the smaller, prior questions, relating to the improving of oneself and one's neighbors and friends, are left unattended.[24]

The third argument, or second quasi-dialectical one (497c–499b), is a trifle longer than the preceding. Much as the language appears to recall references to eternal forms, it refers to nothing directly beyond what the eye or hand or ear could perceive as good things; indeed the present passage *might* be used as evidence by persons wishing to prove that there is no standard doctrine of forms or ideas (*eidē*) at all.

This argument at which we are looking contains two main parts, first some preliminaries (497c–d) followed by a section (497d–499b) subdivided into six small portions. Forming the capstone of the series, the argument has an important place.[25] In its course, Callicles—the doughty contender, as he is thought to be, the vigorous exponent of nature above law, the patronizing young democrat-oligarch—loses most of his drive to win against Socrates. His remaining speeches are a mixture of concessions without conviction, ritual insults, and bored commonplaces. Hitherto, from the time of his full entry into the conversation onward (481b), he has dominated much of it, and has so to speak kept Socrates in his thrall, even if not on the defensive, especially before 491d, having both set the tone and outlined the structural paramaters that Socrates must dismantle. After this final Socratic elenchus (ending at 499b) the mood and direction of the colloquy are no longer in Callicles' hands.

The preliminary (497c–d) is a summary of the immediately preceding argument. Each person feels thirst and pleasure at the same time, and likewise ceases to feel them at the same time, yet does not cease to have good and evil simultaneously. The conclusion is, of course, that good things are not identical with the pleasant, nor the vile with the painful. This has disposed of one part of Callicles' attempt to lump a number of concepts in one column, placing their opposites, or what he takes to be their opposites, in another.

⟨The first stage (497d–e) of the argument proper identifies *the persons we call good; they are those in whom are present good things, as beauty is present in beautiful things.*⟩ What these good things are is not specified here, as Socrates has no affirmative premises by which to characterize and then establish them. Fools and cowards are not called good (Callicles will agree to this as a second premise of the argument in progress). What is meant by the presence of good things (*agathōn parousia*) is not quite clear at this point. It will appear later, as might be expected, that bravery is one of those good things to both Socrates and Callicles. Temperance has already been rejected by Callicles, but Socrates will include it as a virtue essential to the good life. As for pleasures, we already know how Callicles has at first ranked all of them as good, but has later conceded that some only are good, a view shared by his opponent. These virtues stand, as it were, midway between sense objects and abstract principles; one does not see them directly but can discern their presence in the visible acts of persons possessing them—a man running into a building to save a child, for instance. It would be folly on Socrates' part to talk to the rhetors opposing him in terms more attenuated and purified of physical and practical associations than this.

⟨In the second stage Socrates turns to those who enjoy and who suffer (497d–498b). *The fools and cowards can enjoy themselves, while men of reason can suffer pains, which are no respecters of degrees of intelligence and virtue. The coward may suffer more than the brave when danger threatens, but he also enjoys more when it diminishes, as in a battle when the enemy advances and then retreats.*[26]

Is there, then, equality in the degree to which the wise and the fools suffer pain or enjoy pleasure? The answer is, yes and no; *it is about equal for both kinds, but the fools and cowards enjoy and suffer a little more keenly than do the brave. Even so, the wise and brave are good, the cowards and the unthinking (aphrones) are evil, so the good and the evil feel pleasure and pain just about equally (498c).*⟩[27] This, of course, would be impossible were pleasure identical with the good.

⟨*Because there is this difference between pleasure and good, and between pain and evil, it is possible now to show that the evil person feels both good and evil in a greater measure (498d–e).*⟩ At this point one realizes that the refutation of Callicles will be per contra here, and that the summary with which the proof began is not to establish the verbal formula that the conclusion will establish, but rather that the conclusion will be opposed to Socrates' convictions and will then turn out to be patent nonsense. Callicles believes, as we have seen, that the good are good because they have pleasure, and the evil are evil through the presence of evil things, namely pains. To him it would follow that greater pains should belong to those who are already pained, greater pleasures to those who are enjoying themselves. It is the differences in degree that Socrates is insisting upon that save this argument from being a series of truisms—the pained have pains, the pleased have pleasures, and so forth.

At this point paradox ensues: ⟨The cowards have greater enjoyment (498e), for it turns out that those who are more good feel pleasure more, those less good feel pain more. The wise and the unthinking feel enjoyment about the same, as do the cowardly and the brave, but still the cowards, as was conceded earlier, feel enjoyment even more than do the brave.⟩

The final step sharpens the paradox. ⟨The good and the evil feel enjoyment similarly, but the evil person may enjoy his pleasures a little more. Then the evil man is made evil or good similarly to the good man, or even made good in a greater measure simply because he enjoys more. In other words, the evil man (i.e., the pained man) is made good more than is the good man (499a–b).⟩ Even Callicles cannot countenance this, indeed it is totally contrary to his earlier convictions, but his response is far from meek. He will attempt shortly to bluster rather than argue his way out.

Late in this argument (498e), Socrates has remarked that what is well said should be said twice or perhaps three times.[28] The consequence that he explicitly draws is that one should summarize what has already been said. It may also be that he has in mind the fact that his three refutative arguments balance in a general way the three sets of images by which he sought to convince his adversary. It requires a little ingenuity—perhaps too much, we cannot be sure—to demonstrate a more specific balance. Thus the first image is of the jar that leaks and cannot be filled, and the first argument, dealing with scratching and the catamite, points to the life of pleasure advocated by Callicles as requiring that the satisfactions be continual, never ceasing. The second image contrasts sound jars full of wine and honey with those that cannot be filled, while the second argument asks us to distinguish between contraries that can both be sloughed off at once and those which, like disease and health of the eye, cannot. Here a property, well or ill, is always attached to the eye, just as the jars are already either sound or unsound. (The significance of the jars and the filling has changed from the first image, and contraries in the first argument change in the second in their significance, too.) In the third image, there is the plover, always seeking to be filled but always excreting as well; the more and the less are achieved equally, or about equally. This matches to some degree the third argument, which pits the coward's greater feeling of pleasure at the enemy's retreat against the nearly equal, yet lesser pleasure of the brave man. As we say, these suggested analogies may be a shade too ingenious, though it must be remembered that very often Plato tries for an overall balance in other dialogues.[29] Although the parallel that we are alleging has, even if quite correctly diagnosed, no logical force, it is rhetorically effective if—but only if—Callicles is able to perceive it without a hint from Socrates. Otherwise it is merely a puzzle for the reader to decipher. But any associations that can be served up would be expected to have some persuasive or dissuasive power.[30]

Socrates' aforementioned admonition has been that one should repeat what is well said.[31] Indeed, the progress of the *Gorgias* both as a whole and in each of its three major sections, and particularly the last, is much like that of a cycloid, which like a circle comes back upon itself, but by reason of being the path of a fixed point on a rolling wheel along a track ever moves ahead when it seems to be returning to the same position.

A word on the function of the three images and proofs as contributing to the dialogue as a whole. At 492e, Callicles has likened desireless persons to the dead, and Socrates has temporarily concurred and taken the argument one stage further by saying that we may all be dead because the soul is entombed in the body, regardless of whether there be desires or not. The multiple images created by Socrates to depict what Callicles terms happiness are not built upon the premise that pleasure is always evil, or always good, but simply that the satisfaction of unlimited desires is an infinitely time-consuming task and brings no lasting satisfactions. Callicles would not balk at assuming this task, since for him anything else is a living death. The first of four defects of the images is that they assume either continuous operations or no operations at all; the later arguments will have to distinguish between simultaneity and succession in time. Second, there are three kinds of opposition which have been drawn upon but are insufficiently distinguished in the images: (1) A is not the same as (or is different from) B; (2) A is contrary to B and hence cannot be copresent with B; (3) A is contradictory to B and cannot be jointly absent, with B, from a given subject. Callicles has begun by assuming that pleasure is the same as the good, and it falls upon Socrates to show in which of the three types of opposition the relations between pleasure and good can be classified. The third defect of the images is that although they suggest equality and inequality, they cannot be used to distinguish between them with any precision. A pot can be filled a little or emptied a little, but that is not helpful in symbolizing the difference between a coward who feels pain about equally with a brave man when enemies advance—or feels pain a little more. The filling is pleasure, the emptying pain, when pots are being considered, but with the coward and the brave the problem is not the same; both the fear and the cowardice are lacks in the soul, but of very different sorts. If this could be represented by a hydraulic system at all, that system would have to give up ordinary pots, leaky or not, and would tax the ingenuity of all the engineers in Athens. Finally, and most important, the images of the jars are capable of differentiating quantities only, not qualities. A leaky pot resembles a sound one in all but the quantity of water that it retains, and so for the sieve and the rest, even including the plover, whose intake and output are evidently much the same in amount. But in the arguments, the very starting-point of Callicles (and hence of Socrates here) is that there is indeed a qualitative distinction between feeling pleasure and feeling pain—the first is good, or the good, the second evil, or the evil.

In consequence of these defects, arguments supplementing the images are needed. But why the images at all? Why not refer directly to the catamite (the reference that has dragged Callicles off his lofty perch) and the other two elenchic proofs? The answer seems to be that the images are needed to fix in the mind of Callicles the notion that repletion and depletion are important either as essentials or at least as accompaniments to pleasure and pain respectively. *This* in turn borrows from Callicles' conception of power as having more—more food, wine, whatever. It also makes use of another detail that Callicles does not quite enunciate but rather suggests: Pleasure is adventitious, for it requires something from outside to be superadded to the person.

*   *   *

As we have said, this passage sets at least a heavy half stop upon the contributions of the young Callicles to the drama and dialectical structure of the *Gorgias*. Most of the indications of his true thought and character have already been given by Plato. The many facets of his impulses are pretty well aired in his statements of preferences and animadversions, and these account for the fact that the section devoted to them is longer than the two previous sections taken together. When he changes his stance, as he does many times, it is not because he is coltish; rather it is through his effort to permit private ambition fuller scope in what he says. Polus has written a textbook of some sort, thus perhaps marking out a life for himself as a professional man. Callicles writes nothing, but sporadically thinks himself able to live life to the full, and is accordingly ready to use whatever is handy to further his ends. For Polus, words and their effective/affective uses are an end.

Callicles would not accept an effective use which is not actual, active; and words for him are only a means.

It is fairly customary to say that Gorgias and Polus are unduly weak, lacking in self-assertiveness, and that it is only when we come to the onstage boldness of Callicles that we find a man willing and fully equipped to state his honest, if shocking, opinions. Some critics have assumed that all the indications given by Plato point in one direction: that the man is bound to become a brazen tyrant if he can, or know the reason why if he cannot, and that he has desires bordering upon outrageous lusts which he intended temporarily to gratify even if never fully to slake. This interpretation would make him simple in his aggressiveness, simple in his self-will, simple in his sybaritic pursuits— and something of a monster.

We come back, however, to the old saw that when the scholars, or a substantial number of them, are pretty well agreed it is time to re-examine their premises carefully, and so we incline to think that the discrepancies in Callicles' discourse are expressive rather of serious fissures in a fundamentally sick soul—not merely wrongheaded, but sick. They show a man perhaps as tortured by conflicting emotions assailing him as he is hopeful of mollifying them through the attaining of a dictatorial status at once attractive and impossible. There is no one key to his nature, though a good place to start is with his repeated warnings to Socrates to be on guard lest the philosopher be taken prisoner and deprived of his property—and honor. But this is so confusedly put forward by him that it apparently conceals a fear for his own safety. The theme of self-rescue, self-preservation, runs through the nearly fifty pages during which he speaks, and although he repeats that he is friendly toward Socrates, wanting him to come to no harm, his friendship looks doubtful in light of his recurrent expressions of ill will and resentment. Socrates would have every right to ask for some further proof of his friendship, for Callicles has charged him with immaturity, adding that his incongruous behavior deserves a whipping. Yet by Callicles' own account philosophy makes a man inoffensive and withdrawn, certainly not obstreperous or even mildly controversial. Why, then, the whip?

The other possible explanation is somewhat bolder, more risk-laden. Socrates later remarks that Callicles is just commencing his public career (515a), true enough; yet this fact does not rule out our guessing that Callicles may already have seen a good bit of life. He has money, he has some distinguished and perhaps politically notorious friends (487c), and his favorite, Demus, is the son of an oligarch (481d). He looks down upon engineers (512c), and would not permit his daughter to marry one of them. All this leads one to believe that he could pursue and satisfy all the desires that would rumble through his body and soul, with little need to seek political preferment, especially if he had to trample upon those who accorded it to him.

The following conclusion from these points is admittedly a speculation, but then the question of Hamlet's madness, or Raskolnikov's, allows only speculative answers, and if nothing else ours will serve as a counterbalance to the usual reading of Callicles as a strenuous young man consumed by ambition but not by doubts.[32] If we go back to his repeated warnings to Socrates, together with one in return (518e–519a), could we not suppose that Callicles has *already* found himself in danger, or at least implied or imminent danger, and that he knows all too well the risks that one takes in a public life of hectic self-seeking? This would throw a new light upon his invitation to Gorgias and Polus; he calls them in, much as he would a physician if he felt ill. Callicles is never theorizing in a cloudless sky, he is a person seeking for the best protection against the very crowd that he wishes to rule and whose satisfactions he wishes to outdistance for himself. Far from being a strong man certain of both his strength and his good fortune, able when he wants to ignore hoi polloi and their weaknesses, he is a sadly divided man concealing from himself as best he can his underlying sense of perpetual jeopardy. He is a sensual man, but his anxieties keep pace with his gratifications, most of which are attempts to pacify those anxieties. Rhetoric appears to him both a remedy and a shield, much as medicine appears to a hypochondriac. In point of fact, however, it is also a barrier to his possible coming to self-awareness that would give him more confidence in justice, both as a virtue and as a relation between men in states. He resents Socrates bitterly, not only for exposing his doctrinal weaknesses before others but also for laying bare the impoverishment of his own soul and his almost total dependence upon outward circumstances including political success and plenty of flute girls for his idle time. He resents Socrates also for what he can see is greater mastery of the very art that would confer both eminence and security upon him. Lured by the image of unlimited power above the conventions that have hampered him thus far, he makes claims based upon an appeal to natural law (a law relating to the psychology of strength) which he imperfectly understands, as Socrates has little trouble in proving to him. He has a strange mixture of heroes: His Xerxes is an aggressor, but a failed conqueror, and his Heracles is no model citizen. On the other side, at least three men are his friends who even if oligarchic still manage to temper this and for the time being keep their places in civic society. He readily concedes that there are no strong men at the present time, though he could easily name a large handful were he to have a simplistic and not an alloyed respect for tyrannical figures of the age.

Although he extravagantly praises license and dispraises temperance, most of his own occupations seem moderate enough. He is a reader of the poets, offering judiciously selected quotations; he praises philosophy for its acculturative effects, even while arguing that it must not be pursued too long. But his being shocked when Socrates mentions two types of sexual pleasure seems to betoken insecurity and a touch of insincerity. His branding of talk about scratching and about young male prostitutes as vulgar is a way of exculpating himself—if anyone should *suppose* him guilty of such indulgence!—yet he is careful not to admit his practices openly. And so, regardless of some of his bolder pronouncements, one finds Callicles not an inveterate wencher and boozer who cannot refrain from his prodigies of toping and amatory exertion, but rather of an occasional and slightly two-faced indulger, a dilettante, a *Feinschmecker* who would enjoy giving the impression that his desires range beyond control when facing an approving audience, but otherwise pleading his gentlemanly origins. Were he to pursue vigorous pleasures in public, however, this could well incur the reprisals he so greatly fears unless he could recruit enough companions for safety's sake. But this would destroy the very individualistic selfhood that he has been acclaiming.

7

WHETHER THERE ARE TWO LIVES?

(499c–506c)

Because the twin aims, garbled as they may be, of Callicles are power and pleasure, it may be well to sum up some of the many relations between them before proceeding to the last portions of the dialogue.

First, if one uses rhetoric to persuade the public to grant a position of power to the speaker or to someone he supports, pleasure must itself be a component in the speeches, either in the order of the words or the sound of the voice; and it must also be one of the baits held out to the audience in promises made. This has been one of the express notions of Gorgias, and as lover of the deme Callicles would have to follow suit.

Second, pleasure is a concomitant of power in two senses: (a) as part of the mere wielding of power, even if it be intermittent enjoyment of one's ability to see things done as one wishes; and (b) as something outside of the political arena that can be more easily obtained as a result of holding that power. Polus stresses the first of these, Callicles the second.

Third, if one uses rhetoric to persuade another person to confer a pleasure (typically, this is a seduction), then the rhetoric in that limited sense has given a power to the speaker to obtain what he considers a good. Callicles gives little thought to this, evidently assuming that power of itself confers the right to whatever pleasures he chooses.

Fourth, if one enjoys pleasures in the company of another person who already possesses power, this in itself adds a certain power to the one not yet in the exalted position; joint pleasure is one of the straightest avenues to power. Callicles enthusiastically agrees later on when Socrates speaks of this possibility (510d).

Fifth, it may be said that power and pleasure would both corrupt if one or both of them were to be pursued to the exclusion of other virtues and arts. Socrates has not insisted thus far (nor will he in the remainder of the dialogue) that all power or all pleasure is evil, but only insofar as either of them would cause one to forget one's obligations to justice, temperance, wisdom, and devout respect for the gods. (Bravery, as we have said before, is not in question.) People do not ordinarily risk everything for the sake of power and pleasure unless some experiences have reminded them of these as unmixed, unrestricted ends. Earlier we suggested that Callicles might be on the road to power already, to have tried his hand in politics to satisfy his ambition; and it is much more certain that he has at least sampled the delights afforded by a large city and a full purse. Or could it be that he has been insisting on the right to unrestrained power because he has encountered some opposition already with his assaults upon the pleasure-domes, and now looks to power in order to drive back his enemies on this front? Because we think that Callicles is not a truly profligate man, despite some of his utterances, we believe this to be the less likely alternative. He has a sense of shame, or modesty, which would prevent him from attaining unmingled delight even in circumstances most propitious.

We turn to the argument. The debate with the by-now thoroughly embattled Callicles alters perceptibly at this point (499b). The two parts of his first contention, that the strong man by nature should have more and that what he should have is continual satisfaction of every desire, have been undone by various arguments and rhetorical ripostes. He does not consider himself entirely overthrown, nor is he in fact because his first speech contained both an encomium of the strong and an assault on philosophy. Except by implication, the latter issue was not raised again, so that if Socrates is to prevail over the three rhetors he must vindicate his own calling as well as show up the defects of theirs. But Callicles has at least two more strings to his bow, a bow that now has an admittedly weakened cast. One of his principal new propositions is that there are good and bad rhetors (502e–503a), and that the good are better characterized in Gorgias' way rather than as Polus described Archelaus or as Callicles himself had chosen the Persian kings and Heracles (483d–484c). He now chooses Pericles and others of the same type as his heroes—a taming indeed![1] He also falls back (511a–b) on admissions implying that it is no more the independently strong whom we should praise and emulate but the man who survives and lives long through having successfully defended himself from petty antagonists in court. After Socrates and Petrucchio have employed their ever-so-different ways of taming their partners, Callicles and Katherine could at least shake hands.

The two parts of the Callicles section dividing here are not to be taken as a joint discussion of rhetoric versus a discussion of politics, or of politics versus ethics because neither of these is a proper conceptual separation for Socrates in this dialogue[2] and because Callicles often looks upon his own career and the life of the city as being virtually identical. The section as a whole does, however, divide into an account of the superior man, the center of attention thus far, and the better life, from 499b onward. One might object that a man and his career are not separable, but for Callicles this is not true; the strong man, on his showing, is thwarted or toppled either by an agreement jointly made against him by the many or by a false charge brought against him in a trial.

It has already been concluded that there is no perfect man; certainly the philosopher amounts to little, according to all that has thus far been said, and the so-called superior man, insofar as he can be characterized with any consistency at all, has been shown up for a pleasure-ridden citizen at the mercy of his enemies. What we can look forward to now is an attempt to erect a frame around the good life, then—and only then—to fit the portrait of the philosopher into that frame, first as an outline sketch and then with the lineaments of Socrates to give the picture vitality and substance. The frame is of the better life, but not the absolutely perfect life, partly because at the very end (527d) Socrates claims no such perfection for himself, and partly because the setting, as the dialogue is constantly reminding us, is Athens, not the fair city in the skies or even the second-best city in Crete. The good man functions as well as possible, but he too may be brought up on false charges, and the likelihood is that he will be unable to rescue himself.

After some preliminaries (499b–500d), the discussion addresses the business of sorting out and answering three questions, occupying the rest of the work (500d–527e). The three are dealt with in ways differing markedly from each other, but because of their logical affinity for one another, it proves hard to disentangle their overlapping answers.

The preliminaries consist of a little interlude (499b–c), followed by several opening statements (499c–500a) by Socrates on pleasures and pains. ⟨The first remark of Callicles (499b) is still fraught with defiance, but he has already admitted in effect (497b) that Socrates by asking petty questions has actually been refuting him. Now *he jeers at his opponent for the childish pleasure afforded by extracting concessions, asserting that some of these seeming admissions were made in jest.*[3]⟩ This disavowal comports poorly with his earlier question to Chaerephon (481b), whether Socrates himself is joking, for if not he must be turning life upside down. But Callicles himself has been aiming to do just that, though in quite another way. His only hope of establishing his claim and giving his ambitions and his sexual gourmandizing proclivities free rein is to be serious and to act upon his convictions. Jesting here would be the very opposite of the candor for which Socrates has earlier praised him

(487a). Later (495b), before undertaking a step-by-step refutation, Socrates has had to reassure himself that Callicles is giving an account of what he really believes. It is apparent now that it is Callicles who is claiming not to be serious. This must mean that there are three levels in his discourse: first, his underlying views before they are challenged; second, his grouching while being refuted and his shifting of ground in order to preserve what he thinks are his chief contentions; third, his refuge in jesting.

The entire subdivision of the colloquy between Socrates and Callicles is henceforward devoted to various ways of looking at the two lives that were first dimly separated by Socrates (481d) in terms of objects of love and then more sharply by Callicles (485d–486a) in terms of assuming positions of power in the city. To commence the real task of this discussion, Socrates recapitulates (499c) an observation he made in passing (at 495a), after having excoriated continual scratching and catamiting as dreadful: There must be good and evil pleasures. This is accepted, perhaps reluctantly, by Callicles (499c), but without any argument to sustain it. The strategy of Socrates will be to build upon this admission by adding that the good pleasures are the beneficial or advantageous ones, the evil being the harmful, and that they *do* good and evil respectively. Much has been made of this by readers who would insist that here, at least, Socrates shows himself a fallen angel for having introduced a pragmatic test for goodness. In other words, Where is the pure form of good? The answer to this complaint might run that the man who chooses disadvantageous pleasures, those making him ill or otherwise miserable afterward, would not only be a fool but would actually be choosing results of his actions diametrically opposed to what he wanted to begin with.[4] The truth is, Callicles has been giving opportunists a bad name. Utilitarians ordinarily define right and wrong in terms of the useful and the harmful (not the merely useless); in so doing they presuppose that the character of the successful outcome of an action which is in question be already envisioned—the hammer is useful only when nailing, not frosting a cake. Socrates can be as utilitarian as the next man, looking up from any one point on a scale of values to the adjacent higher point; but the principle of construction of such a scale is *not* a matter of simple utility. To ask where absolutes and forms are in the present context is to ask on what Athenian street we find the gate opening out on the road to Callipolis.

At any rate, it is now (499d–e) made clear that both pleasures and pains can be worthy, producing some bodily excellence, or they can be base, producing the opposite. The reason that Socrates stops short here, not going on to include the goods of the soul in addition to those of the body, is that the discussion has wound its way down to the pleasures of the body (eating, drinking, scratching) and at the moment there are as yet no solid premises for affirming the soul's goods, let alone asserting that these might be more important than those of the body. True enough, soul and body were distinguished far back in the dialogue (463e), but Callicles seems not to have accepted this division, and it is he who is now to be persuaded.

⟨*The good is the end of all human actions, and one must do everything for its sake* (499e).[5]⟩ These are easily-identifiable goods which may or may not be pleasure-yielding. ⟨*Their value is apparent, however, though it may well require an art to judge between them* (500a).⟩ It follows from this that from an impersonal, philosophic standpoint the issue of the good life is one regarding the best principles wherewith to construct a scale of values. In terms of these principles one praises and emulates whatever or whoever is best, rejecting and even abusing what is contrary to that. From Callicles' point of view, however, the best is not in question except insofar as it can attach to degrees of power and pleasure. These are praised and all else is reviled.

⟨*Socrates now repeats some of the gist of the Divided Oblong. In this context he begs Callicles not to play but to take seriously the problem of contrasting the two lives, the rhetorico-political and the philosophical, to discover which is the best life.*⟩ He underlines the ethical aspects here; in the Divided Oblong politics was listed as an art, sophistic and rhetoric being its pandering imitators. The field was left open by Socrates at that time to discover consequences in the active life, and not all the blanks were filled in. Here, it is important to see what differences are made if one pursues the arts or pursues the imitations. It has often been said by commentators that rhetoric has been lost in the shuffle of the argument over the superior man, but this is not quite accurate. Politics is joined once again with rhetoric to show that if both are taken in the Calliclean sense no good can come of them. If Callicles is entering politics, as he is, then this will not be in the way of a true statesman but of a fraudulent impersonator.

⟨The words of Socrates are well worth quoting. *He wants to know if Callicles is seriously advocating* "doing as a man does, speaking in the assembly of the deme, practicing rhetoric, conducting politics the way you conduct it now" (ta tou andros dē tauta prattonta, legonta te en tōi dēmōi kai rhetorikēn askounta kai politeuomenon touton ton tropon) (500c). We stress this because on it hinges part of the unity of the entire dialogue.⟩

The opposition between these two lives has not been referred to since the very first speeches of Callicles and Socrates (481c–486d). It is instructive that the topic of superiority is best expressed in the form of three closely-intertwined questions, much as the problem raised by the difficulties of Book I of the *Republic* is stated by Socrates at its end

(354b–c) in rather similar form.[6] The difference lies mainly in this, that in this part of the *Gorgias* the principal search is not for more than a passable definition of good or the good life, whereas the seeking of a defining formula for *a* good is the heart and soul of the *Republic*. The reason is easily found, for it is a single concept, that of the virtue justice, which is sought in the longer dialogue, but here with Callicles two entire ways of life must be examined, replete as they may be with virtuous or vicious tendencies, with arts or their substitutes, and with social consequences which—this being a city on earth and not in the heavens—may be entirely adventitious, not to say downright hostile.

The three questions follow, stated in the form of demands:

⟨First, we must, says Socrates, distinguish between the two lives, if indeed they are two, and make certain they really are two (this is treated primarily from 500d to 506c).⟩ The reason this must be taken up is not abstract, for it has to do with the previous debate between two flesh-and-blood men. Once more, Socrates is seeking to persuade a fellow-Athenian already convinced that he, Socrates, is a sly, shifty, though somewhat monotonous rhetor interested in cultivating his own pleasures by forsaking his civic duties. Socrates, on his part, sees the issue as of extreme importance, for regardless of how he viewed his host before today, he must now deal with a Callicles who is either a strong man hoping to put himself above the law and really soliciting unlimited pleasures for himself or else a neurotic but to others a persuasive and well-connected person of considerable ambition despite his self-centered fears. Either way, as we have said, if he obtains power it will be a sad day for Athens. A man of this sort accuses his opponents of either being shifty like himself or being rustic fools. To be able to separate the philosophical from the pseudopolitical life is thus a task of great moment to the philosopher, and it is paradoxically made even greater by the fact that Callicles cannot accept it as a serious task at all. Added to the earlier difficulties that Socrates has had in correcting the misapprehensions of Callicles is the fact that he is not now asking Callicles for a simple statement of a proposition to be defended or attacked, but is rather examining two complete ways to live, ways of which *any* statement is but a partial and perhaps distorted account. Callicles' unfocused way of life and his nest of conflicts which emerge as evident discursive inconsistencies make the task of Socrates arduous almost to the point of an impossibility. It happens also that in comparison the life of Socrates is more unified, almost prosaic because his wants are simpler; when the two life-styles are set against each other there is a kind of disproportion. One is a life pointing in a half-dozen directions, the other a life pointing in but one.

We are, however, tending to speak from a Socratic point of view. Callicles would differentiate between philosopher and rhetor-politico based upon the extrinsic ground that the latter goes to Assembly meetings more often and enters into cabals with his friends, while the former sits to one side, not even willing to be a close spectator of civic life. Callicles' other premises have been shown to be wrong singly or to have been paired with others not compatible. Thus Socrates' first demand or question. It is not satisfactorily met, for two reasons. The more important one is that to ask whether something (such as the good life) is single or double, that is, whether there is one life or two, presupposes agreed-upon marks by which to make the decision. The second is that Callicles, for motives of his own, is by now so embarrassed and disgusted that he drops out of the conversation altogether (506c), hinting that he will not return. This means that although Socrates can pursue the questions uninterruptedly and thus more smoothly, they will have even less effect upon his opponent. His trump card will be the distinction between good rhetoric and bad, and he will fight Callicles using rhetorical weapons without telling him that he is employing the very weapon against which Callicles has so harshly inveighed in the past. Rhetoric can be used to improve other souls.

The second question requires that the first will have been at least tentatively answered. ⟨What *is the difference between the two lives?* (this is treated mainly between 506c and 520e).⟩ The reason for raising this problem is that merely to know that there are two lives is not also to know which one of a host of possible distinguishing marks is essential. But without facing the issue squarely one would be left in a chaos, ill-prepared to meet the third and final demand.

⟨This last question or demand, *Which life ought we to live?* (500d)⟩, is the crucial one, though to try to answer it before the other two would be to disrupt the right order of inquiry. One cannot properly choose to be a philosopher without knowing whether he is different from a figure resembling him and what his characteristics may be. Broadly, this is the question toward which most of the dialogues of Plato tend, some of them answering it carefully, in detail (though in very different terms and with unlike arguments), some of them raising the issue and then veering away from any firm solution. The *Gorgias* asks that one choose between philosopher and rhetor-tyrant; the *Protagoras* between the philosopher and sophist; the *Republic* between the philosopher and the timocrat, oligarch, democrat, and tyrant; the *Apology* and *Crito* between the philosopher and the ordinary citizen. In the *Gorgias*, this problem and its solution (found mainly in the passage 520e–527e) is confronted primarily after the differences are stated; and even then the answer must be given indirectly, through a little argument, self-confession, a myth, and then some gentle advice.

The Socratic assumption that the two men are different and the lives to which they aspire are correspondingly different, was first hinted when Socrates commenced by saying (481d) that he and Callicles have in common the fact that both are lovers (*erastai*), though with partly similar and partly dissimilar objects of their love; for the dissimilarity is enough, apparently, to bring about divergencies in their modes of thinking and living.

The divergencies, however caused, are not small. The doctrines have mostly been disposed of in the first score of pages (481b–499b), where the question has been the general one, Who is the better man? while in the remainder of the colloquy we ask, Which is the better life? To Callicles the best man, he who flouts the law, outwits or outfights his enemies, and seizes more than his fair share, is good enough, and he can let perfection go. In discussing the best life, again there is no perfect man, but one who functions as well as possible in a city far from perfect, where villains can try to injure good men, where crowds listen to demagogues, where there is some demarcation between masters and slaves, where pupils can abuse their new-found rhetorical competence, where a man with a hidden dagger can occasionally run loose in the marketplace and have his way with the groin or shoulder blades of anyone he chooses.

To discover whether Socrates is consistent one must observe not only what he says but what he is; to decide the consistency of Callicles one needs to look mainly at what he says, wondering whether it will stand by itself:[7] the man himself is full of internal stresses.

If our thesis is correct, that the relations between persons in this dialogue are of a philosophical importance approaching that of the opinions they hold, and that the relations and opinions are indeed almost indistinguishable and are certainly inseparable, then it should follow that one aim of Socrates would be to loosen the hold which settled habits of thinking have had on Callicles, putting in their place not only a new set of opinions but a confidence in Socrates as a man, despite the fact that *any* refutation is likely to alienate and breed distrust in the person refuted.[8] Callicles respects education, but in his mind it must be an education subsequently turned to personal advantage, and Socrates, even though he can quote the poets tellingly, has not moved in that direction. So far, then, as the emotional tendencies of Callicles are concerned, they do not undergo substantial alteration merely through the refuting of dogmas embodying—and hiding—them, for he is always ready to lay the refutations he suffers at the door of dishonest tactics.

He still thinks of Socrates as hovering somewhere between the world of the strong and the weak, and would relish pointing him in what he thinks is an upward direction, no doubt sensing by now that Socrates himself would look upon this as a debasing of the soul. There is a strange discrepancy here in the Calliclean thinking: He deems Socrates shifty but ineffectual, yet believes that if Socrates were to enter political life he would not thereby become less shifty, only more effective and perhaps even dangerous. The repeated abuses which Callicles levels mark his view that it is worse to be able through native gifts to rise higher politically yet not to seize the opportunity than it is to be an ordinary slavish man whom neither meager talent nor chance could ever place in a position of rule.

One thus has grounds for thinking that two types of strong men exist for Callicles, those upon whom nature shines except for their being hobbled by conventional shame and the evil of temperance and those whom Callicles would prefer to believe that he himself resembles, uninhibited and hence not to be hoodwinked and frightened by the regulations. Gorgias and Polus, as he has said, would occupy a low position for their manifest shame when confronted with propositions about justice that any strong man worth his salt would see instantly were wrong. This is no question of mastery of rhetoric but of strength of character, not the practice of rhetoric but the man practicing it. A real issue for Callicles, who is partly willing to debate it. If our premises are correct, he must now hold Socrates in somewhat greater esteem than he did formerly and than he has held his two foreign guests; Socrates, after all, was *not* ashamed to bring up the catamites and what goes with them. He entered, so to speak, into the depths of perverse human nature, while Gorgias and Polus hovered outside, content to back away by keeping to politer questions about teaching justice and using rhetoric for personal ends.

We return to the treatment of the first question, Whether the lives are really two instead of one? It is divided into a brief summary of the distinction made in the Divided Oblong between art and familiarity (500d–501c), then a one-line interlude (501c), an account of certain kinds of gratification (501d–505b), and last, a second interlude, this time with Gorgias joining in (505c–506c). The argument is carried in the first and third portions, but all four rest partly upon three agreed-upon premises which Socrates has in effect articulated, the first being a statement of existence, the second of an inequality, the third a prediction.

⟨*The good and pleasant exist* (500d).⟩ This needs inclusion here for the psychological reason that Callicles is so disgusted with the whole discussion that he is likely not only to wish himself out of it but also to declare it fruitless—a mere dispute about words.[9]

⟨*The good is not equal to the pleasant* (500d).⟩ For this, one need only go back a few pages, to 495b.

⟨*Practice and preparation are needed for judging the good and the pleasant* (500d).⟩ This last reverts to matters disputed with Gorgias, who, Socrates then contended, seriously neglected knowledge when such knowledge seemed a requisite if one were to counsel the people on the advisability of building docks or taking medicine, and so forth. It also reverts to the Divided Oblong and leaves room for concluding that there is some sort of art or science for judging the good, although it has not yet been specified. Reasons must be found, for without them what is best and what merely seems best are indiscriminable, since pleasure and pain constantly obtrude and confuse one's choices. The reasons come from an art, which is a grasp of principles unambiguously applying to similar individual cases. Gratification by itself taken as an aim is pandering to either body or soul. Do you agree, Callicles?

⟨*Yes, Callicles does agree, but only in order to reach a conclusion and to gratify Gorgias* (501c).⟩ Disregarding his seizing upon the language of Socrates as a way of slighting him with mild sarcasm, one notes that the motive for agreeing is ulterior; the conclusion which he has reason to suspect will be reached sooner or later is one he evidently now concedes will run counter to his own opinions. His view, moreover, of the obligation that he bears to Gorgias, either through common courtesy or because the venerable rhetor is especially well known, is a superficial one. He might have said that he wished to clarify some of the latter's tenets in reexamining them or persuade him to others— Socratic aims here and in other dialogues. But to say that he wishes to *gratify* Gorgias, nothing more, plays directly into Socrates' hands in another way, for a reason that Callicles is apparently not quite shrewd enough to see. Had he said that he would gratify the common audience he would have shown his readiness to pander to casual persons, men uninformed. But to gratify an expert, a gifted, trained, experienced persuader, a founding father of the whole practice of rhetoric! This shows his thinly-veiled contempt not only for the patents and exclusive purposes of dialogue but also for the ablest practitioner of the knack that Callicles apparently deems vital to his own future success. He must realize, moreover, that if Socrates overpowers him by refutation or in some other way and establishes the superiority of any other life than that of the rhetor-tyrant, it will indirectly deal a blow to Gorgias which the latter would not enjoy overhearing. This is shortsighted and mean, but such spitefulness by now comes to the reader as no surprise.

⟨This double slight is quietly put aside by Socrates, who asks *whether gratification can be wrought upon more than one soul at a time* (501d), as the opening of the five-stage discussion (501d–505b) on the gratifications aimed at in certain practices.) Chiefly, these are the fine arts or the performing arts, as we would call them, but Socrates thinks of them as kinds of pandering through their use of familiar pleasurable elements.

Flute playing is one such skill, choric recitation or singing and dithyramb another, cithara playing a third when accompanied by singing. Flute playing, for all its merits, obviates simultaneous singing for the single performer, the singing obviates the playing of any wind instrument, but a stringed instrument permits the combining of the two knacks, vocal and instrumental. Socrates is moving from simple to complex. The rhythms of instrumental playing suggest, and those of singing enforce, the imposition of rhythm upon ordered words, and this creates the medium for poetic diction. It is a step, albeit a long one, from choric dithyramb to tragedy, and it is a step which connects the effects of all these knacks as being gratifying. There is greater opportunity for influencing the thought and behavior of an audience caught up in the experiences and emotions of characters to which it may well become sympathetic because of their essential similarity to members of the audience themselves. In any plotted course of action the characters discourse one with another and in so doing propose further actions— defying the gods, defying the king, murdering an enemy or a spouse— whatever is possible or probable. In so doing they enunciate general ideas having persuasive power, and are pleasing or displeasing to the other characters and to the audience alike. Thus tragedy combines the rhythms and melody of singing and flute playing, adding to these the pleasures of words, all having a sensory and mental effect together with the enjoyment of a story. This cumulative account is one reserved for music and theatre, and is not used elsewhere in the *Gorgias*.[10] One reason for it here may be that it leads Callicles little by little beyond the concession that flute music, with all its plainness, can best make an appeal to the bodily senses and that it would be very difficult to distinguish such music that improved character from that which merely pleased the ear. Assuming this to be conceded, the rest will be easier to get him to agree to than if tragedy were to be introduced alone.

Having explained this persuasive capacity, Socrates (502d) strips it of its poetic trappings and considers rhetoric as standing by itself. The road to taking rhetoric as a knack rather than a means to political power lies through music and tragedy, and its nature is made congruent with those arts which are performed before hoi polloi on the public stage, their gratification being the chief aim. There is thus an important sense in which the present conversation reverts to interests found in the earliest parts of the discussion between Socrates and Gorgias. The famous rhetor had injected political freedom and Polus had injected political power into the debate as their major considerations. Here the pleasure afforded by the performing arts is the issue. Far from being irrelevant, as some scholars have suggested, this little listing of the arts helps bind together themes that might otherwise have remained divided: whether rhetoric is an art allied to other arts but different from them, whether rhetoric is a path to power, and whether such power is good for the individual whose ambition is to become a strong influence in the state.

There need be no issue whether good flute players exist, or cithara players, or even good tragic poets. But whether the good *rhetor* exists is a matter of concern (502e–503d), for he is more capable than the flute player of delivering what Socrates might refer to as pleasing exhortations and dehortations. The flute player might with wild rhythms drive his audience into a frenzy, but what would the audience then do? They would need a guiding hand in order to put their newly aroused energies to work in *some* direction, not simply raising a stampede. Rhetoric, on the other hand, can both arouse and orient the listeners in some line of concerted political action.[11]

⟨Callicles, again searching for bunched dichotomies, attempts (503a) to evade the trap he sees being laid by affirming a proposition he would hardly have countenanced earlier in the day: *There are bad rhetors and good ones.*⟩ Or at least the bad would formerly have been for him the fainthearted, the good would have been the bold who could say whatever they chose. Now, however, the good rhetor would be a man who, Socratic-fashion, aims at the best, whereas the others do no more than gratify, as if the audience consisted of children. These children are kin to the youngsters who talked philosophy on a side street (485d), except that for them Callicles had no more than distaste, whereas for the children he suddenly affects contempt.

⟨Who, then, who *specifically*, is a good rhetor for aiming at the best? *Callicles* continues with his twofold distinctions (503b–c) by *dividing the present-day rhetors (of whom no good ones exist,* he says, thereby dropping the strongest possible hint of what he has really come to think of Gorgias) *from those of the past: Themistocles, Cimon, Miltiades, and Pericles, who has recently died* (neōsti teteleutēkota) *and whom you, Socrates, once heard speak.*⟩[12]

The comment of Socrates (503c–d) on the four men proposed by Callicles is a trifle peremptory in tone but well-prepared for by the distinction made long ago (464a–c) between satisfaction of desires and aiming for the best. In Callicles' mind, when he speaks of good rhetors, there still lurks the notion of standards of success with the public, now perhaps modified a little by a vague notion of making a better city; but that city would doubtless turn out to be a richer and more powerful one, a *polis* capable of defeating its enemies and forming or breaking alliances at will. To this Socrates contrasts the practice of virtue. ⟨*The four men*, he says (503c–d), *would be good were virtue to consist in that very satisfaction of desires on all sides, but in fact one must give satisfaction only when this makes men better. Such nice discrimination requires an art that no one has possessed.*⟩ Later on (521d), Socrates will name one person whom he deems to have that art, though not necessarily a practical-minded rhetor skilled in dealing with assemblies.

Socrates is taking Callicles up on the political function of rhetoric, but denying that it can be fulfilled by addressing an eager populace with promises of satisfaction. In other words, he is exploring not the weakness of the rhetor as he did with Polus (466e), when the rhetor could do what he willed but not what he wished, but rather surveying his peculiar strength when the rhetor pursues the good in himself and others. The fact that Socrates would accord such a man the status of artist does not mean a turnabout on his part, for he has hitherto dealt with rhetoric as Gorgias and Polus understood it. He seizes upon Callicles' concession that there can be bad rhetors as well as good, though he interprets this differently. To Gorgias the bad rhetor might be the man who had commenced abusing the art which he, Gorgias, had taught him, though no criterion had been established at that time (456c–457c) for determining what bad tactics are and what are good. To Polus the bad rhetor, if there were any, would simply be the man unable to lie his way into a situation of advantage to himself or out of one potentially damaging. Up to this point, the Calliclean bad rhetor would be a man seemingly bold at times, but at bottom fainthearted. But Callicles, under the careful handling of Socrates, is having to change his stance.[13]

The new realization that there can be two kinds of pleasure does not of itself mean that the good pleasure is forthwith to be thought identical with a quality of the good rhetor.

What follows (503d–505b) is an effort on the part of Socrates to develop a way of separating good from bad rhetors and thus to some degree rehabilitate rhetoric. Whether the development of this criterion is itself carried out rhetorically rather than dialectically remains to be seen. The very effort of Socrates may seem to be so contrary to his every intention up to now that it is ridiculous, but one must remember that he is facing three men who see not only forms of discourse but kinds of human behavior in exclusively rhetorical terms. To them rhetoric of any sort has hitherto been taken as either the best of arts or as nothing. Correspondingly, the rhetor has been the most powerful man in the city or insignificant and slavish just as the strong man either has complete freedom or is trammeled by convention, agreement among the inferiors.

Socrates' task is now to introduce distinctions that he trusts Callicles to admit on the strength of the latter's spontaneous, if belated, willingness to recognize the difference between good and bad pleasures.

In order to fix the distinction between good and bad pleasures, he must have recourse to the notion of art, which he has been excluding for the past forty pages from the purview of rhetoric. ⟨*The good man*, he says (503d–e), *must not speak at random but rather to some end or purpose, and this, like that of the craftsmen, is to give some form* (eidos) *to whatever he is working upon.* This means that the *good rhetor is allied with the constructive craftsmen* (dēmiourgoi, *artificers*), whom Socrates now lists as *painters, builders, shipwrights, trainers, and doctors.*[14] These are set over against the troop of musicians, dithyrambists, and tragic poets seeking mainly to please.

An end, taken in Socrates' sense, is not just any purpose, for certainly crowd pleasing can be a purpose; it is rather an improvement related to the basic nature of the thing improved, whether this be nonliving or living. All of these men, from painters to doctors, bring order and system, in other words a form, into these bodies, and this is of course what it signifies to make a thing as good as possible (503d–504a).⟩

Socrates has brought back the threefold distinction he has frequently made explicitly and more often implied, between external goods or property, goods of the body, and goods of the soul. Property, being nonliving, takes pleasure in nothing, but living bodies enjoy what Callicles had said they enjoy—eating, drinking, scratching, and so forth. The soul enjoys music, tragic poetry, and also rhetoric. The list has just been augmented by the painters, builders, and shipwrights who create a form in items of property; then by the trainers and doctors who, inducing health and strength, do much the same for bodies, and finally the rhetors—the responsible ones with an art—who introduce justice and temperance into the soul (504a–d), these being instances of structure (*taxis*) and order (*kosmos*).

⟨In an odd little summary, which seems to be meant as parody of either the well-known Gorgian antithetic style or its imitation by Agathon,[15] *Socrates says that justice is engendered, injustice removed, virtue is produced, and vice expelled* (504d–e).⟩ One may believe at first that such a parody is simply an expression of good-humored verbal high jinks, but one must ask why it is placed in Socrates' mouth here and almost nowhere else in the dialogue. For a possible answer we may say that alongside the rigidity of the distinctions of each of the three rhetors, runs a predilection for conclusions, for the snap of the whip at the end of any preparatory discourse. Just such a conclusion has been reached here, but not by the upholders of undifferentiated rhetoric. Socrates has made corresponding but quite different claims for rhetoric—it is an important partner with the arts of building and healing, both of which figured earlier in Gorgias' conception of rhetoric but with not the least hint of introducing order and stability into their subjects. Hence at this juncture Socrates can introduce Gorgian flourishes, using crafts formerly listed by Gorgias as examples, but with an ethically ameliorative end that leaves Gorgias far behind.

⟨The Socratic conclusion is now (504e–505b) applied to the old distinction between healthy and sick, but extended to the soul as well as the body. *Treatment of well and sick persons must differ, for the latter cannot properly digest what the former can, and in the same way the base soul, thoughtless, licentious, unjust, and impious, must be permitted only what will improve it.*⟩ Whence the Gorgian rhetor must be forced to keep his distance. Restraining the soul is correcting it; in other words, the soul is lively, prone to run off in any direction, and thus improving it means channeling its energies and activities.

The argument has established that rhetoric can aim at gratification or at the best, and there is an extension from rhetoric to all other human enterprises as well. The next step would be to show that the philosopher and the rhetor-tyrant differ in regard to their use of rhetoric, thus making their ways of life two, not one. ⟨But Callicles, with a hint of the mock modesty that might be a parody of Socrates' own professions of ignorance (453a–b); 457e; 461c; 486d–488b), says (505c) *that he does not claim to understand what has been said;* but then he voices a totally unsocratic wish—that *someone else would take over the task of answering.*[16] To this, the present response by *Socrates* is that *his opponent cannot endure being benefited or corrected*⟩—a further instance of the interconnection between the topic of discussion and the characters of those discussing. This re-establishes, moreover, a point made earlier by Socrates (458a) that refutation is a benefit when the opinion refuted is false, and again (475d) when he suggests that Polus is like a sick patient who needs to consult a physician, that is, who needs his opinions set straight though he fears the refutative process by which this will be accomplished.

Some of these accomplishments are summarized by a matrix in figure 7.1. ⟨Thus by using the one principal concession by Callicles, Socrates has moved from the old position to a radically new one, and evidently *Callicles* senses this, for he begins to lose heart, lamely repeating (in a short interlude, 505c) his earlier assertion (501c) that *his reason for answering at all is to gratify Gorgias*—a statement meaning something rather different now that one sees that he holds Gorgias in no high esteem.⟩ But the verb *to gratify* is an indication that Callicles has still not seen all the light that he should see; and his social reason for continued participation is extrinsic to his own soul and its betterment. He has learned little of virtue. ⟨Socrates ignores his last remark, saying instead that *one*

	GRATIFICATION (501d)	FORM-GIVERS (503d)	RESULTS (504a–d)
PROPERTY	—	painters builders shipwrights	house ship, etc.
BODY	no advantage to body in pleasing if no good is done	trainers doctors	strength health
SOUL	music (three kinds) dithyramb tragedy	rhetors (e.g., Pericles, etc.)	(when good rhetoric) justice temperance virtue as a whole

Fig. 7.1. *Gratifications and forms contrasted.*

should not allow a myth, let alone an argument, to go headless (505d).[17]
In turn, Callicles ignores Socrates. He exclaims: *How you coerce!* (hōs biaios), forgetting his earlier contention (497b) that Socrates asks tiny little questions and also (489b) that he trips people up with their changing meanings. *Drop the argument, or get someone else to respond.* This alters, if it does not reverse, his previous implied promise to continue in order to please his distinguished guest. ⟨The only dialectical answer to this is for Socrates, quoting Epicharmus meanwhile (505e), to *promise to continue alone, at the same time permitting anyone else who wishes to join in the inquiry to bring it to a conclusion. This includes refuting him, lest a mistake remain. I do not speak, he says, as knowing but rather as conducting a common search* (zētō koinē meth' humōn). *If you prefer not to carry this through, we can cease now and go our separate ways* (505e–506a).⟩

We have already spoken of possible reasons for Gorgias to desire to have the discussion continued by Callicles (497b), but now (506a–b) he wants it carried forward despite Callicles' abrupt withdrawal, hence the same causes cannot quite operate here. Earlier we suggested that Gorgias wished to see an errant follower be corralled and prodded into better shape so that he himself would escape obloquy for the subsequent misuse of rhetoric by Callicles, but now it is likely that Gorgias, despite his dignity and tenacity, is in fact also bewildered by the Socratic onslaught, and wishes to see the good name of rhetoric restored since at least a variety or a part of it has been labeled good. This restoration, strangely enough, would come not from its abusing practitioner but from its severest critic, a man altogether outside the circle. For years Gorgias has gone unchallenged, there have been no new and discomfiting questions asked of him; now his whole calling, his undeniable skill, his preeminence, and his character, are being brought under scrutiny direct or indirect, and his two proponents' formulations as well as his own, are being put to near-shambles before his eyes. Gorgias, however, is no coward; he does not feel more pain when the enemy advances or take pleasure when the enemy is in flight. Throughout the colloquy in which he was the respondent, Gorgias showed himself willing to be led, if necessary, to a clearer realization of his role as speaker and teacher and the importance of justice in it. All the same, he was worried about the reactions of his audience.

⟨The remainder of this section is brief. *I should have liked to pay you, Callicles,* says Socrates (506b–c), *an Amphion's speech in return for your old one of Zethus* (echoed in the five-clause denunciation of Socrates at 485e–486a). *It is Callicles who should correct me if I am wrong, and if I am refuted I shall not be vexed but grateful to him as if to a benefactor.*⟩ The contrast between Socrates' attitude and that of Callicles toward the elenchus seems apparent, so long as we do not notice that Socrates has been martialing superior arguments against the rhetors, even if they cannot be quite convinced. Hence there may be a touch of smugness; Socrates is strutting a little, for he knows that even if his victory is not complete there is no one present at the gathering who can humiliate him.

*   *   *

Why has Callicles chosen to quit the debate? An easy answer would be that he is a poor sport, but that does not confront the question of why he falls silent here and not elsewhere. Although we have stressed the personalities in this dialogue, we cannot forever fall back on them as an excuse for the course the discussion takes. The truth appears to lie deeper. (There is also the corresponding query, Why does Callicles rejoin just three Stephanus pages later, at 509c? This will be considered in its proper place.)

Up to this point, both Socrates and Callicles have in their different ways thought of the lives they respectively advocated as possessing similarities. Socrates had pointed out (481c–d) that because each man had two loves he and Callicles must share some common feeling. Callicles had never ranged Socrates exclusively on the side of either nature or convention, and had in fact spoken disapprovingly of his sliding from one to the other (483a). He had also complained that Socrates sat on the sidelines, but not because the latter was incapable of better things; Socrates had merely hampered his career by espousing philosophy, and could not effect his own self-rescue if attacked. Yet Callicles had never explicitly said that he himself was one of the strong, naturally fitted to rule, though we may suppose that so devoted an advocate of the power and privileges of the superior man would be projecting his private self-image. He went out of his way to remark that he considered philosophy perfectly acceptable, liberating the young (484c; 485a, c), perhaps hinting thereby that he had once cultivated it himself. He repeatedly attacked Socrates for using rhetorical devices, but not for displaying any distinctively *philosophical* tricks and subtleties. He is surely perceptive enough, however, to see that if Socrates can drive a larger wedge than he has already driven between two modes of life, it will work to Callicles' own disadvantage, and that sooner or later the talk will come round to the question, Which life should be chosen? with the clear implication that it ought not to be the one he has already been charting for himself.

And so he retreats just in time, after Socrates has reintroduced the powerful distinction between art and familiarity, whose application is now (501d–502e) extended to various performing arts and then (502e–504a) the rhetoric and the rhetors whom Callicles most admires— men whose brilliant, well-authenticated accomplishments have made them heroes in the minds of nearly everyone. Their rhetoric, the gateway to this greatness and acclaim, is impugned by Socrates as leading not to injustice (Callicles would scarcely worry about that) but to depravity and sickness (504e–505a). Its *proper* use is not merely to incriminate oneself in court (480a) but also (504d–e) to generate justice and temperance in the souls of the people. Virtue is to be engendered, vice expelled, as Gorgias might say, yet as a rhetor Gorgias could not know how to implement his laudable purpose. It is for this cumulative reason that Callicles realizes that Socrates has really found a critical weakness in the way of life of the rhetor, and has thus been able, using many of Callicles' own premises, to begin a sketch of an alternative that might turn out to be superior. One must remember that a principal feature of the Socratic method is the attacking of a doctrine from within by assuming its premises and supports and finding them to be in mutual collision. Socrates has taken seriously the Calliclean view of the superior man, has attached it to his depiction of the contrast between that man and the philosopher, and has shown that because the allegedly superior man is using an inferior practice he cannot be whole and invulnerable. This will give a chance for the philosopher to be put forward, and it is precisely because Callicles himself has referred to and described the philosopher that this is the figure who can be proposed as a substitute for the strong man above the law. (Had Callicles proposed an artist as counterpoise to the rhetor-tyrant, it would have been the latter whom Socrates would have used in his turn as an alternative; but judging from the *Phaedrus, Republic,* and *Symposium,* the true artist *is* the philosopher, so the final answer would have been much the same.) If the foregoing is true, then it is not only the primacy of rhetoric as he conceives it that Callicles realizes can no longer be countenanced, but all the shibboleths entertained, habits adopted, and actions performed that he sees under attack as well. With the dual admission that there are good and bad pleasures and good and bad rhetoric must come the admission that different sorts of persons employ the preferred rhetoric and pursue the preferred pleasures, and that this distinction is in terms not of the masters and the slaves that Callicles had proposed, but something else. There *are*, then, two lives differing essentially and in terms of good and evil. Following these admissions, very little else in the Calliclean position will be safe from major assault, and we believe that Callicles, who is by no means slow-witted, is capable of perceiving this at the moment that it is established that there is a second life which he has hitherto despised but which may be upheld as better than his own life and its vindicative theories, he terminates his part in the conversation.

8

WHAT DIFFERENCES BETWEEN THE

TWO LIVES?

(506c–520e)

The three major questions regarding two lives tend to merge into one another, as we have said, although retaining some of their individuality as the discussion is carried on. The second question, "What *is* the difference?" is the most complicated issue of the whole debate between Socrates and Callicles, and on this hinges the more definitive answer to the first, "Are there really two lives?" than was originally offered (499b–506c), and also hinges the third, "Which should we live?" A sign of its importance is that this second query occupies the next fourteen pages of text, more than double that required for the first and about double the space taken up by the last. In terms of the participants, first there is a passage (506c–509c) in which Socrates conducts the discourse by himself, followed by the return of Callicles and the evaluation of his chosen life (509c–520e).

The first question has in most essentials been answered, but by an oblique path; the approach has been not through the ordinary morality of pleasure as against virtue, but rather through familiarities or knacks aiming at pleasure and arts aiming at goodness. If there is a contrast between these, then there is a contrast between the two sorts of careers in which they are practiced. The first question is, in a sense, a thin and abstract one (it is little enough to know merely that there are two ways of life); however, because the dialogue has had a cumulative effect, the question and its admittedly partial solution take their place in the total sequence. There is a peculiarity in what Callicles has been trying to do: He has insisted for his part that there *are* two ways of life, his being the better one, but the characteristics he has used to differentiate them have been superficial, born of prejudice and personal rancor. Callicles has by no means absorbed the lessons of the Divided Oblong, lessons to which Socrates has called attention in the previous four pages to show the differences between two sorts of rhetoric, one flanked by music and poetry, the other by more honest crafts, as he presents them; he has also sketched the diverging ends and motivations of the respective practitioners.

The status of the first section (506c–509c), which in part simulates a back-and-forth conversation between two participants, is a little peculiar. All the individual queries or remarks of page 506c–507a are short enough to qualify as "discussion," *dialegesthai*, with pauses at each step for assent. On the other hand, Socrates is responsible for everything said, whether by himself or putatively by Callicles.[1] This qualifies it as a speech, but it still is not the kind of rhetoric to which Socrates objected when he criticized the fumbling attempts of Polus to establish himself as both practitioner and theoretician of rhetoric. Yet we have insisted throughout that the hands of Socrates are tied, sometimes loosely and sometimes tightly, so that few of his arguments can be dialectical in any narrow sense. To sum up, we have a distinguished dialectician convinced that rhetoric must grow out of dialectic or at least be checked and guided by dialectic: he is throughout the dialogue using rhetoric but casts his statements as if in the form of a dialectical argument on a subject whose underlying topic is always the legitimate employment of rhetoric. If Plato is not subtle here—and a trifle sardonic as well—then it will be difficult to find a dialogue where he is.

In the last two-thirds (507a–509c) of the section, Socrates drops the question-and-answer pretense altogether; yet it is more nearly a two-way conversation than before. Now he addresses Callicles by name five times (507c, 507e, 508b, 508d, 509c) and, in addition, uses several pronouns and second-person-singular verbs to indicate him. He also employs the first person singular several times, another device in this setting to bring the discussion once more into a duologue form. But it is still a two-page monologue! Either way, it accomplishes its double purpose, to establish certain vital points and to tempt Callicles back into the long, strenuous colloquy.

The overriding issue in the three-page section ending at 509c is that of order, much as the overriding issue in the section attempting to answer the first major question was that of purpose or end.[2] The aim will be to establish a similarity between three things, each of which should display an order proper to itself: cosmos, soul, and speech. The section has four brief subsections: 506c–507a summarizes old statements; 507a–c offers new ones; 507c–508c gives a preliminary statement of a life to be followed; and 508c–509c examines the reproaches of Callicles.

⟨As so often happens in the *Gorgias* and other dialogues, Socrates commences the segment (506c–507a) by purporting to summarize the argument thus far. In truth, however, it is a carefully selected group of statements in a series to look like a proof, and it blends imperceptibly into a second set (507a–c) consisting of fresh formulations:

1.   *The pleasant and good are not the same* (first stated at 499b).
2.   *The pleasant is for the sake of the good* (see 500a).
3.   *The pleasant thing is that by which we are pleased* (see 498d).
4.   *The good thing (a virtue) is that by which we are good* (see 497e).
5.   *This virtue is generated by order, rightness, or art proper to each good thing* (recalling 500a).
6.   *Hence its proper order makes each thing good* (see 504a).
7.   *A soul with proper order is better than a soul without* (504b–c).
8.   *A soul having order is orderly and temperate* (504d).
9.   *Hence the temperate soul is good* (504e).⟩

One notes the rhythmic alternation between good of soul (as explored in early phases of the Callicles section) and the good of speech (in the stage just past); now Socrates takes up the soul again, this time making no pretense at talking of practical affairs in daily lives. He gives a general account of the soul, summarizing many of the conclusions reached earlier though not necessarily agreed to wholeheartedly by Callicles. He omits, however, all mention of the notions that loomed so large in Callicles' discourse, nature vs. law, strength vs. weakness, justice vs. injustice, bravery vs. cowardice, wisdom vs. ignorance, although the word *virtue*, which Socrates does use) would certainly be expected to subsume several of these expressions.

So much for the summary of what has been established, or almost established, in earlier segments. Socrates now slips in two slightly complex statements:

⟨First, *if the temperate soul is good, the unintelligent soul is evil, and this was the unthinking, licentious one* (507a).⟩ This assumes that one never calculates or reflects before plunging into a debauch. Many persons, however, who do plunge this way aver that it is for relaxation from duties they perceive as onerous, unpleasant, or merely boring. Viewed in that light, some "simple pleasures" of wine, women, and, if need be, song are not altogether senseless. Plato appears, however, to have something different in mind. Callicles has spoken of the need for continual satisfaction, and such fulfillment he calls happiness; it is this relentless pursuit that bears the opprobrium, for the calculating required to locate sources of satisfaction often takes as much time as does the actual enjoyment of the pleasures thus planned. Temperance has two sides, the cognitive and the affective; and mental control, regulation of one's thinking, is as central as is physical abstention.

⟨Second, *the intelligent man does the fitting regarding gods, which is de-*

CALLICLES	SOCRATES
weak	virtuous men
strong	gods

Fig. 8.1. *Proportions of weak and strong.*

voutness, and men, which is justice (507a–b).⟩ Up to this point the gods have figured only rarely in the *Gorgias*, and then mainly in lip service to traditional religion. Their advent here signals a substitution of the independent, immortal, and (within their proper spheres) all-powerful divinities for the strong man above the law. One might say that the natural man laid down the law to his fellow mortals until they could band together to resist him by imposing conventions of their own. To Callicles, these men were slavish. For Socrates, the virtuous man is by no means unfree, but some higher power may well be necessary to set the standards of and impulses for virtuous action.[3] Hence in figure 8.1 we set up a proportion (although the specific relation changes qualitatively from one side of the proportion to the other).

One might raise the issue whether Socrates has just now proffered a definition of devoutness (*hosiotēs*, holiness, piety) by saying that it is the doing of what is fitting with respect to the gods. An image arises of the thin, wispy spirit of Euthyphro, objecting that he himself is trying to offer an account of devoutness rather similar, but that Socrates will not listen to him.[4] A tentative answer to him is that there is no perfect form of a definition in the dialogues (such as there would be for Thomas, Ockham, or Kant), and that any word or phrase serving to guide thinking into proper channels can function as a definition, provided it can withstand the scrutinies of an able dialectician after it is offered. (Most cannot.) It is, then, both a definition and a statement that is not a definition that Socrates has given; and because he cannot examine every term in the discussion at once, he lets a workable formula hold. Its aptness is attested for now by its being coupled with a parallel definition of justice as the doing of the fitting to men.

Let us return to the argument once more:

⟨Third, *the virtuous man is also brave, for a wise one avoids or pursues the things and people or the pleasures and pains he feels that he ought to pursue, and he is steadfast in this* (507b).⟩ Bravery thus reenters the discussion, formerly a principal ingredient in the Calliclean conception of the man of strength, but now tempered by reason rather than incited by stubborn love of power and by lust.

⟨Fourth, *thus the temperate man, just, brave, and devout* (who is also prudent, or wise in practical matters [*kalōs prattein*]), *is the perfectly good one and is blessed and happy, while the base and evil man is miserable* (507c).[5] Socrates, by insisting upon wisdom as the root of virtuous action, has managed to accumulate enough premises so that he can discuss real virtue, virtue in itself, without having to separate the genuine from the sham as he did with kinds of speech. The misery of the imprudent, that is, the licentious man, has been established at 503c–d by way of the unspoken assumption that if happiness, (as Callicles suggests), is continual satisfaction of all possible desires, then failure to gain such a satisfaction would bring the very opposite of happiness.

To help determine the structures of the argument, we said earlier that if Callicles had been able to discourse by himself he would have followed a simple parallel dichotomous division almost throughout, but that his opponent kept impeding and forcing him to dredge up substitute terms (strong, wise, brave, and so forth) that would require further distinctions in the form of subbranches that could not possibly be parallel to the originals. Now that Socrates is talking alone, he can manage the strictest possible control of the shape of his own argument; but this shape is almost the reverse of that of Callicles. There is a simple division between the evil and the good, and then new terms, not exactly synonyms of the good but essential to and virtually equivalent parts of it, are rapidly introduced. Virtue is what makes someone good; and virtue is wisdom, order, rightness, art, temperance, bravery, devoutness, justice, though these are not merely favorable adjectives nor are they exact equivalents. Socrates is aiming at an account of virtue similar to that of Callicles in putting all its parts together, but differing in two other ways. Callicles did not see that wisdom and bravery and the other virtues were jointly listed and interrelated; they were made alternatives in his dogged retreat, tossed out on the path by him in an effort to block the relentless advance of Socrates. For his part, in the present passage, Socrates sees that the virtues, if not all the same, must support one another in order that each may be fully realized. An intemperate brave man, for example, will eventually abdicate the battlefield in favor of a few pints of beer—and the favors of a lissome *Biermädel*. The so-called unity of the virtues is no theoretical extreme case, for one might be brave up to a point without being entirely devout or temperate; but an essential trait of the good man is his adherence to an ideal of practicing all the virtues. Socrates has earlier taken issue with Callicles, who wished to exclude justice and temperance from his roster of good habits.

In the next segment (507c–508c), Socrates gives a preliminary account of the life to be followed, together with an extended backdrop of the controlling reasons for his choice. This further substantiates our contention that all three major questions can be phrased separately but that their answers are mainly interwoven.

⟨*To be happy we must try*, says Socrates (507c–d), *to practice temperance, avoiding the need for punishment.*⟩

This is no recapitulation of what was concluded with Polus (480a–b), though indirectly it rests upon that. There, Socrates had merely said that the best man was the one doing no injustice, the second best the man who, having done injustice, was now paying the penalty. Here, *not* doing injustice is given the more solid base of virtue, internal to the soul; otherwise, it might be owing to chance or externally applied law, or it might even be a gift of the gods.

⟨Socrates next says (507d–e) that *we should concentrate our own and our city's efforts on providing the temperance and justice needed, not living as a robber to satisfy desires. Such a brigand cannot be dear to man or god, for he communes not at all with them and forms no friendships.*⟩

By this, the community is made the first consideration of the good man, who seeks to improve it as much as his own soul. How this is to be carried out is, of course, another question, left unanswered in detail in this dialogue. Here, the community has a narrower application in friendship which, though mentioned before in the *Gorgias*, is now brought into a new light.[6] The novelty in the present passage is, of course, that friendship is mentioned in the context of virtue—the man without goodness in his soul is not one who can communicate; he is not a man to gain affection and loyal companions.

⟨In his following remark (507e–508a), Socrates greatly enlarges the background of his notion of virtue as order by projecting this order throughout the universe.[7] *Heaven, earth, gods, men—all are held together by communion, friendship, orderliness, temperance, and justice, prompting us to call the whole world "cosmos," order.*⟩ The question we pose is this: Why the abrupt extension of the context? What motivates it, and what permits it? Regarding motivation, we need only refer to the level of the discussion adopted thus far. None of the three rhetors has seriously referred to anything outside of men—and they were no better than an average lot of listeners, poorly informed on military matters, finance, and medicine. The whole conception of the "art" of these rhetors was based upon what succeeds; and this, of course, may be fickle as the wind. The distinction between body and soul (hence that between goods of the body and those of the soul) is lacking from their philosophic vocabulary. Hence they depend upon a generalized enthusiasm or distaste, as the case might be, and their intuition, no doubt abetted by advance briefings by informants and even informers, of what the crowd will want to hear. Not only is this too fragile a foundation upon which to build rhetoric as a worthwhile enterprise. Even if human beings at large are conceded to have good souls by Socrates, this is hardly enough. The soul has been presented as having neither a career in the past and future nor a wider connection in the skies that would show that the soul's order comports with and is *perhaps* generated with respect to an order superior to its own.[8] The stability of soul induced by the virtues is similar to the stability of the cosmos, but here Socrates does not quite say that it is *engendered* by it. Perhaps the virtuous soul imitates the cosmos; yet the chief use of *imitation* has been in the Divided Oblong, where political, medical, and gymnastic arts are imitated by panderings, and pandering itself imitates art. Here, *imitation* seems to imply that both virtuous soul and cosmos consist of their proper parts in some degree of likeness with each other, but without causal connection.

⟨*You miss this, Callicles,* continues Socrates (508a), *and you neglect the power of geometrical equality among gods and men; you prefer grabbing, getting more* (pleonexia), *keeping the abundance of what you think to be goods all to yourself.*⟩ Just what this means can be open to question, and we offer some possibilities:

In the first place, Callicles wants to proportion rewards to the stronger natures that he admires, that is, the men who put themselves above the law should have more of the goods. This is almost word for word what he himself said earlier (490a); but it is no longer Callicles who is speaking, and it is *his* lack of a sense of proportional equality that is an issue now.

In the second place, Callicles has been mistaken to think that all men not superior rhetors whereby they become tyrants are equal, that is, they are slaves deserving little. Callicles, with his rigid separation of weak from strong, would lump among the former the philosophers, slaves by capture or temperament, popular audiences (which in political affairs, as opposed to theatrical performances, did not, of course, include outright slaves), those who cannot cajole the courts into letting them go free, and more.

Third, Callicles has been accused (491b–c) of making statements inharmonious with each other, and one might believe that he has been deliberately violating a principle that he knew rested upon simple geometric ratios, for example, that an octave interval represents lengths of vibrating strings or columns of air in the ratio of $2:1$, a fifth $3:2$, and so forth. This reading need not be wholly wrong, assuming that Callicles had read the Pythagoreans or talked to any of them. So far from any of their notions of justice is his thinking that there is absolutely no reason to believe that he had ever read them, or that having done so he took them seriously.

Fourth, the soul has parts, and these must be in proportion to each other, with reason dominating the aggressive spirit, the latter in turn dominating the vegetative desires. This is an excellent interpretation— of Book IV of the *Republic*. No parts of the soul have as yet been explicitly distinguished in the *Gorgias*, nor is there any hint that proportionality would need to hold between reason and appetite, if indeed these were among the parts to be discriminated. All that has been said is that there is an order or rightness (*orthotēti*) or art within each of these things listed by Socrates, namely a utensil or implement (*skeuos*), body, soul, or a whole living thing (506d).

Fifth, the proportionality is obviously a measure of the more and the less, and these two have been invoked by Callicles in the rewarding of powerful man and the withholding of rewards from those lacking in power. Hence it is likely—but no more than this—that Socrates is referring to Callicles' mistaken rule for the distribution of goods. Why, then, this elaborate setting for Socrates' remark, with sun and stars and the whole firmament as backdrop? A best guess is that Callicles is a shortsighted man, educated to be sure, but formerly so taken with his images of *Machtpolitik* that he dismissed all that lies below the earth and in the skies. Hence, when he is wrong about social justice, he is wrong regarding everything significant in his own universe, such as it is. Socrates has just now insinuated that other topics (which he himself might have been pondering while cowering in a corner with pupils) do have a place in determining the tone of a proper theory of justice. Proportionate distribution in respect of virtue, not force or status, may well be the first step on a path to the best life.

⟨Socrates continues (508a–b): *We must either refute the assertion that justice and temperance are the route to happiness or, if that cannot be done, investigate its consequences.*⟩ Presenting the possibility of a refutation is, of course, a rhetorical device used earlier.[9] No such attempt at refutation is forthcoming from either party, and it is assumed, therefore, that the safest procedure will be to investigate what would follow dialectically from the original thesis. In a sense, the remainder of the dialogue is given over to just this investigation, sidetracked a little from time to time. The "overwhelming question" of the last seven pages of the work, however, What life ought we to choose? can only be settled to the ultimate satisfaction of Socrates if the thesis about virtue is adhered to and further clarified.

The final remark of Socrates (508b–c) in this short subsection has a triple basis. ⟨*Polus*, he says, *admitted that the proper use of rhetoric is self-accusation of a guilty man, admitting this not through shame* (as Callicles had averred) *but because the results are true.*⟩ Here there is no attempt to rehabilitate Polus or soothe his wounded self-pride, but rather to insist that even such a callow young man has some good sense, enough to recognize the chances for happiness of a good man are better than those of a bad one. This is in spite of the praise Polus had showered upon Archelaus. Were Socrates to be speaking directly to Polus now, he might be pressing him to admit to having tried to shock all present by extolling a patently wicked tyrant. Socrates, however, is not talking to Polus, and is merely setting out some of the "results" of the discussion, thereby lending weight to the fledgling rhetor's admission that rhetoric's use is properly that of a man who incriminates himself or his friends.

1. The results are true because doing is worse than undergoing injustice, a point that Socrates is repeating from 479c, though now on a firmer basis; the results must be in harmony with the thesis regarding virtue as the road to happiness.

2. The results also rest upon the proportion that doing injustice is worse than undergoing it by as much as it is more disgraceful—an arithmetical, not a geometrical, proportion it would seem (see fig. 8.2).

3. Lastly, the results are true because the right and proper rhetor must be just and practice justice—this also was a reason for the admission of Polus.

Again Socrates uses a rhetorical device, namely the treatment of some statement barely hinted at as if it were a premise taken for granted by all parties to the discussion. If he were conversing with Theaetetus, this would be unseemly; but he is not. Here, it is perhaps forgivable that Socrates should employ rough-and-ready devices that lie at hand for the sake of a quick result. If Callicles were practicing what he had been preaching in his first speech, thousands of Athenians would soon be dispirited, grim, insecure.

⟨We move to the fourth brief subsection (508c–509c), in which Socrates reexamines the force of some of the accusations made by Callicles from the now more secure position which Socrates has been gaining. *The failure to rescue himself or his friends from a box on the ear or confiscation of property or banishment or execution is not as disgraceful as striking, cutting, kidnapping, stealing, or housebreaking and the like (508c–e).*⟩ The striking and cutting recall the man with a dagger in the marketplace (469c–d), the kidnapping, stealing, and housebreaking being new unless we go back to Heracles (484b). This part of the little subsection obviously rests upon the three "results" already set down.

⟨*Socrates again (508e–509a) holds out to his opponent the choice between refuting his principles and abiding by them. The principles are secured most solidly, with reasons of iron and adamant.*⟩ This seems hyperbole, since the foregoing arguments are a blend of rigor and loose construction. On

doing injustice		worse		more disgraceful
undergoing injustice	=	better	=	less disgraceful

Fig. 8.2. *Proportion of doing to undergoing injustice.*

the other hand, the very fact that Socrates himself lives by them, or at any rate makes an honest attempt to live by them, makes a ponderable difference. On a purely theoretical level, this in itself would be a dubious connection, either an affirmation of the consequent or, even worse, an irrelevancy concocted to bind together two independent statements. On a practical level, however, the fact that a man propounding such principles of living actually seeks to live by them gives them a weight, hard to define in purely discursive terms, that they would not otherwise have. A similar remark holds for the doctrines of Callicles, though he is more diffuse and disjointed, less ready to sacrifice comfort and safety for the sake of largely mistaken ideals.

⟨There is a rider to this: *failure to abide by these principles, unless they are refuted beforehand, renders a man ridiculous (509a–c). If doing injustice is the greatest evil, then any self-rescue in this situation must make a man ridiculous.* In evaluating such rescue, Socrates lists many possible cases:

1. *The greatest harm is averted by the greatest rescue. Correspondingly, the most disgraceful failure of self-rescue would be inability to save oneself in this deepest crisis when the soul is besmirched through having committed unpunished injustice.*
2. *The second would be failure to "save" oneself if one were to have committed an injustice and as a consequence was being punished.*
3. *The third sort of failed rescue would be failure to save oneself if one had not committed injustice and yet were hauled into court as if one had, and then could not rescue oneself. Other and less significant kinds of self-rescue would be connected with less significant predicaments.*⟩

In all this there is an ambiguity between the interpretations put on the cases by Socrates and by Callicles. It is not fully established, only asserted, that to Socrates the greatest evil would be the unpunished corruption of the soul. In the mind of his temporarily silent antagonist, however, this evil would be punishment. Self-rescue, to Socrates, would be the saving of one's soul, while to Callicles it would be saving the life, the health and pleasures of the body, and the reputation of the man accused whether falsely or with justification.

So much by way of summary of the little soliloquy, unique but not the one crucial turning point of the debate with Callicles. Indeed, that entire debate resembles a gradual, sweeping curve, here and there more abrupt, but one eventually turning the entire discussion around, reversing the direction of Callicles' original certainties. In the section just reviewed, Socrates' chief aim has been, by using what has gone before, to establish that there are not only order of goods and evils (threefold in each case), but *proportioned* orders: the greater the evil the greater the need for the power of self-rescue and the greater the shame if one cannot bring this about.

Happiness has been said to lie in pleasure, but has been identified more recently with virtue, so that well-doing is right-doing. Again, ways to happiness and impediments to it are implied from both sides. The impediments for Callicles are the laws imposed by the many, boxing of ears, and confiscation of property fomented by the single plebeian enemy. For Socrates, the ways to happiness are being habitually virtuous and having the good fortune not to be unjustly charged, while the chief impediment is the harming of the soul. If self-rescue can then extricate such a damaged soul by applying for punishment, well and good.

At this point (509c) Callicles begins to participate again. Just as we needed to look for possible reasons for his dropping out, it now behooves us to explain the resumption of his speaking role. It would be easy to say merely that he had got hold of himself, not wishing to make a spectacle before Gorgias and the members of his own Archarnae deme, or to admit defeat to Socrates. But why choose this particular moment to reenter? Among the virtues that Socrates has named and that are, most of them, found in the cosmos as much as in man, bravery and wisdom are also paramount for Callicles though differently interpreted: Wisdom is a kind of street-smart intelligence, bravery the ability to face up to untoward situations, not to one's own defects and the means of correcting them. Socrates has also hinted at the interactive unity of the virtues, which is an improvement over Callicles' conception of their vague equivalence—as if he, too, had taken a leaf out of the book by Anaxagoras. The intemperate, disordered man is miserable, according to Socrates (507c), whereas Callicles has never quite said that the philosopher was miserable, only that philosophy was his ruin (*diaphthora*—484c–d); but the ruin merely made him ridiculous (484e), unable to care for himself in a predatory society. The highest good for Callicles would require an army of caterers, slaves, common (and passive) citizens to be lorded over, *heterai* and *pornai* and boys to suit his mood.

For his part, Socrates has pointed out (507c–508c) that we must move the city to encourage temperance and justice in the citizens, to promote community and friendship. This is a glimpse of the decent, peaceful city in which petty men would *not* bear false witness, placing even the best of men in jeopardy undeserved. While Callicles is by no means completely won over to the need for changes in his soul, this glance at a world where he could function more at ease would display itself attractively, despite the fact that it ill accorded with his own craving to have strength beyond the common run of mankind. The section from 509c to 520e is a further exploration of the characteristics of the two proposed styles of life, but with much greater emphasis upon that of Callicles, though he has been shaken loose from his original views of the naturally stronger man and has also stood ashamed in the exposure of the true nature of licentiousness. From 509c onward Callicles will no longer be given opportunity to uphold his earlier doctrine. Instead he will need to consider the choice between two paths. By the first he would have to modify his own character, making the personal sacrifices needed to live in the Socratic manner, and by the second his inclination to live by his former and now suspect ambitions and hedonistic impulses would be overcome. All along they were thought to be an ideal existence—even his best models could not show him a better way.

Although Callicles is harder to persuade to try to take up the philosophic life than Chaerephon or even Gorgias would be, there is just enough accommodation between the two worlds for Callicles to think, not that he was wholly wrong in what he had said formerly, but that the Socratic world would at least be a close second to the one he had projected for himself. Even so, Callicles is a divided spirit and remains to the end grudging, unconvinced in his heart, and therefore so abusive, though his current reasons for this behavior are now different.

He rejoins the conversation, however, not so much because he loves debate for its own sake—he is interested almost exclusively in his own ideas and lacks capacity to assimilate those of opponents unless forced to by the refutation he deplores—as that he sees a glimmer of hope that his notions of the good life may prevail. After all, Socrates has taken over his list of virtues, adding a couple (justice and temperance) that Callicles has deemed irrelevant. Socrates has accepted the fact that there *are* two lives, that there is a qualitative difference between them. As for connecting one of them with cosmic order, obviously Callicles dismisses this as so much nonsense; but here again, this would not trouble him. Above all, he would perceive that, despite Socrates' new remark, the latter would urge the city to attempt to improve its citizens; Callicles must believe that this would have little effect upon his own pursuit of power and unlimited pleasures. In his eyes, the most that Socrates could do would be to abdicate his side street and move into public places; at best, however, he would remain a passive citizen, exhorting to virtue and no longer splitting hairs, but still achieving no greater effectiveness thereby. Hence Callicles deems it safe and perhaps rather profitable to reenter the lists against Socrates.

The dialogue now changes direction a little. A more concerted effort is made to evaluate the life envisioned by Callicles as political rhetor, and eventually Callicles will be disappointed—disgruntled is a better word—that he does *not* prevail but instead finds his projected way of life riddled with even more holes than it has been. In the section 509c–520e, further difficulties are found in the life of the rhetor, answering in this way what the difference may be between the two lives. The third question, Which style of life ought we to follow? is treated from 520e to the very end of the dialogue under the guise of examining Socrates' account of his own aims.

The reentry of Callicles is not exactly furtive, but is certainly not marked by any fanfare—nor by any further statement of his views, old or fresh ones. It is initiated by another resentment-loaded concession, "in order to save the argument" (510a). Socrates, meanwhile, has laid down some of the principles required to carry forward this stage of the discussion. The first main subdivision (509c–513d) brings out several aspects of self-rescue or self-preservation hitherto merely hinted at. It is again subdivided into five little parts of which the first treats the power required to rescue oneself.

⟨A man, says Socrates (509c–d), *will be able to avoid unjust treatment* (which has been specified many times as a box on the ear or being executed when no wrong has been done, or almost any indignity or calamity in between), *not by merely wishing it but by having a power or art to avoid it.*⟩ *This revives the distinction made so long ago when* Polus boasted that the rhetor had the greatest power in the city (466b) but was countered by Socrates' insistence that wishing and willing were different and that the rhetor, in willing certain things to happen but not having the art to improve the city, will find his exhortations backfiring against his own wishes. ⟨A man, Socrates continues here (509d–510a), *never does injustice by his own wishing of it, but he needs the power to avoid it.*⟩ Socrates has reintroduced the distinction to make clear the complex situation in a lawcourt. It is simpler when an unjust man is on trial, for he is punished justly, regardless of whether he had solicited that penalty, though if he had, then such self-incrimination together with the punishment ought wholly to remove the stain from his soul. When, however, a just man is unjustly punished, what is the value, not of the punishment (we can assume that to be neutral), but of the prisoner's soul? Callicles has said that he shows weakness and foolishness, but Socrates has assumed that it is more ridiculous to be deserving of punishment. ⟨*The man who escapes the unjust punishment must have an art or power*. Surprisingly, Socrates identifies this art or power with *the art of ruling or tyrannizing or the ability to be a friend of the existing ruler*. As we might expect, Callicles voices for the first time his enthusiastic approval (510a–b).⟩

Why does Socrates apparently give himself into the hand of the enemy in this way? Why does he argue on the side of Callicles? The answer, in brief, is that he does not. The word *art* has not yet been redeemed from its application to music and theatrical poetry, the latter being rhetoric dressed up with melody, rhythm, and meter (502c), and presumably *power* has not either, because it is three times treated here as synonymous with *art*. What this signifies is that the so-called art is really no art but rather the ability to rule or tyrannize, or at least make oneself into an image pleasing enough to such a tyrant that he would accept his underling and protect him from mischance. Because Callicles' word *friendship* might rather be *cronyism*, here at last it is put to work in the political circles where Callicles wishes to conduct his affairs. Only the tyrant or his close friend is safe from unjust treatment by some chance citizen. This indicates a decline in Callicles' ambitions: Socrates perceives that Callicles is now willing to settle for being a crony of the ruler rather than the ruler himself, if only his own safety is assured. Callicles is not cowering in a corner, but neither is he strutting undisturbed and arrogant in the main square.

There is, however, a rhetorical aspect—or considering its nature, one might say angle—of this remark by Socrates. He is inducing Callicles to stay in the discussion; and, by giving the words *ruler, power, art,* and *friendship* the by-now familiar Calliclean senses, he wishes to make the conversation more attractive to his antagonist. Socrates will withdraw these meanings as soon as he lures the alienated man into making the further admissions needed. This is clearly a rhetorical trick again; but for Socrates to have continued alone much beyond 509c would be no more than an obvious tour-de-force, and he ardently wishes to replace that with some flesh-and-blood argument in order to carry stronger conviction. Consequently, the reader wishing to find fault with Socrates should pick not on his political morality but on his willingness to deal with Callicles on the latter's own ground.

⟨*Socrates continues* (510b–d) *with a suggestion of the likeness of the friend to the ruler who, if boorish, would be afraid of a man better than himself* (here Socrates is warning Callicles, a cultivated and snobbish young man) *or perhaps contemptuous of someone pettier* (one of Callicles' own epithets for Socrates). *The only friend of the tyrant would then be the man most similar to him, liking and disliking whatever the tyrant likes and dislikes, but not assert-*

ing equality, let alone superiority, to the tyrant-ruler. This crony, says Socrates, will not be harassed by people bringing charges against him, so it is politic for him to accustom himself to the same tastes as the tyrant.⟩

This is a peculiar situation. Socrates has not said what the tyrannical habits might be, whether restrained or lustful, honest or dishonest. Hence Callicles, if put in this position, will *perhaps* be able to encourage and satisfy all the desires he thought were the due of the ruler without actually ruling—and he is no longer free and independent of the law but constrained by his friendship for the tyrant and by his obsessive need to preserve his own life and property. The difficulty with all this is that such cronyism does not merely ensure the underling against false accusations; the innate injustice that is part of his toadying carries him a step farther, and his immunity encourages him to plunder and kill as does his model and supposed benefactor, the tyrant. This does the greatest possible damage to his soul, which is altered from that of a man merely keeping an eye on the main chance to one ready to commit any number of unpunished and, for the time being, unpunishable crimes. In all this, however, there is a slightly different ring from that of Callicles' former praise for the strong man above legal concerns just because superior in his conception of life and his place in it. But now we have a crony who is *not* superior to the law but merely beyond the law's reach for the present.

⟨Callicles' response (511a) to this portrait of the second-class sinner is that *Socrates twists the argument*—as indeed he does, though not in Callicles' own sense—*and that the friend will set about to kill and despoil all those who unlike himself are not imitating the tyrant. This would be a wicked man killing one virtuous and fine—a paragon* (kalokagathon), replies Socrates (511b).⟩ He has now moved to the position that the person not imitating the tyrant in his likes and dislikes is not the ordinary, indifferent citizen but the man of superior virtue. Socrates has reverted to what he has earlier tried to establish. The reason seems to be that anyone not falling into line with the tyrant's wishes and tastes will become a marked man; and the awareness of the immediate danger he is in will result in his capitulation, if he is of the ordinary run, or will distinguish him as a man of exceptional virtue if he is not. But this is circular, and such a man will be even more especially singled out as a threat to be liquidated and will thus require more and more rigorous exercise of steadfast virtue.

The dialectic has taken a new turn. Earlier, Callicles was contrasting the bold tyrant with the ineffectual philosopher. Socrates is now distinguishing the strong man (because he is virtuous), afraid of neither the tyrant nor a premature death (511b), from the survivor whose very survival bespeaks his weakness, his readiness to do another's bidding. ⟨*The art of rhetoric*, Socrates says (511c), *is one suited to such self-rescue*, hence is now transferred from the side of the independent leader to that of the subordinate.) Why, then, does Socrates suddenly call it an art? We hazard that he is setting the stage for a distinction between good arts and less good. Any art that saves the life of someone who from the standpoint of himself or of the community is better off dead is an art of dubious value. The term *art*, then, will have to be purified, rendered less ambiguous. ⟨It is to this task that Socrates now addresses himself (511c–512b), in a passage *likening the art of rhetoric to arts of swimming and piloting, both of which save lives indiscriminately, for not every passenger on a voyage is healthy. Indeed, an early death would sometimes prove an advantage. The same principle holds for engineers and generals who save persons and sometimes whole cities; incidentally, they do not put on airs as do you, Callicles.*[10] *Your contempt for the engineer*, he goes on (512c–d), *ill becomes you, for you would not permit your offspring to marry him; but if* better *and* virtue *do not mean as I mean them, you are ridiculous to censure him, or the doctor, or those others.*⟩ The arts have again been invoked in a new comparison with rhetoric, the point being to see how far each is really capable of preserving life and property, despite the questionable advisability of so doing. Long ago (462b) Socrates said rhetoric was no art at all, the arts being roughly characterized as aiming at the improvement of whatever they worked on. This is still taken for granted, in a way, because now the engineer improves the piles of rock by converting them into solid fortifications or the cartloads of timbers by making them into serviceable docks. It is a more ultimate end (happiness) which is to be brought about, however, and here piloting and engineering, and so forth, are no better than rhetoric.

The question arises why Socrates says that if the word *virtue* does *not* have the meaning he gives it, but means instead the mere power to save oneself, then Callicles is ridiculous to censure the men of the other arts. One would think him ridiculous if his opponent claimed that the meaning given to *virtue* was correct. But the epithet *ridiculous* is really the lesser of two sorts; a citizen can see at a glance that a man making such exalted claims for himself as those of Callicles is foolish for ignoring the even stronger claims of the pilots and engineers. As it is, Socrates could well go on to remark that the meaning of *virtue* he had offered is correct and that Callicles is doubly ridiculous for claiming superiority on the wrong grounds and, in addition, for being mistaken on what the grounds for any comparison of this kind ought to be.

The two sets of obsessions in the soul of Callicles have evidently been divined by Socrates: the first, his dual loves (481d), the second (486a–b), when Callicles has let it be known that any man worth his salt should be able to speak effectively against his legal opponents and detractors.

Socrates now turns to the first, Callicles' love, ambivalent as it may appear, for the deme, and his love for Demus, less ambivalent, perhaps, but which when conjoined to or even in alternation with the first love, is bound to generate disharmony in the soul of the lover.

⟨*The noble and the good differ from saving and being saved*, says Socrates (512d–513a), *and the true man, the virtuous one, would make light of any effort to live any given number of years; he should consider instead the best way to live so that he does not sacrifice all that he loves most in order to become like the Athenian people.*⟩ Neither of the loves of Callicles is tyrannical. In his love of the well-born Demus there is no need, then, to imitate him; hence Callicles would be motivated to imitate the people at large, however far beneath him he considers them to be. He cannot, without imitating, divine their preferences and aversions, cannot speak for them, cannot rule them. The same would be true in his relations with the tyrant, which Callicles has agreed (510b) should reflect the tyrant's feeling in much the same way. These three objects are not on the same footing, in the mind of Callicles. He does not deny his affection for deme and Demus, but neither does he concur when Socrates identifies them; his enthusiasm is aroused instead for the statement of propitiously cozy relations with a tyrannical ruler, and we may safely assume that, were Callicles to choose a simple avenue to political success, it would be with this last-named individual to help him.

⟨*What must Callicles do* (513a–c)? *If he thinks he can, merely by imitating the deme or Demus with the use of some art*, appear *sufficiently a friend to them, he is mistaken in the long run; he must be wholly like them in fact as well.*⟩

Socrates is not advocating here that Callicles turn his aspirations upward to true virtue but is simply exploring some implications of remaining on the lower level of common political ambitions. This helps partly to answer the second chief question, What is the difference between the two lives? and partly it prepares the way for the third question.

Friendship, then, with the deme or with Demus (who *might*, incidentally, become a tyrant himself, just as a citizen of the deme could do so, though the possibilities are left to one side) grows out of no mere trick of cajolery and pandering—the recipient will eventually see through that—but is a matter of complete assimilation to their basic likes and dislikes. If one becomes a politician, one will be a rhetor, that is, a *persuasive* speaker: merely speaking words unfitted for one's character will have no weight with an audience.[11]

⟨Callicles now answers with a trifle of humility, something not exhibited heretofore: *I share*, he says, *the feeling* (pathos) *of the many* (i.e., his deme), *hence I cannot quite believe you.*⟩ Thus he seems to be hoping, nothing *more*, that his approach will suffice to establish his position and assure his safety. ⟨*It is your love of the deme*—or is it Demus?—responds Socrates, *which resists me.*⟩

Socrates seems to be implying that he himself knows both what the many are thinking and what influence the deme or Demus (translators have taken *dēmos* both ways) has upon Callicles. Except for his having just come from the marketplace (447a), there is little hint of Socrates' contact with the many in this dialogue; indeed, he has known, or at least recognized, three men of oligarchic tendency (487c) who converse about possible excesses of wisdom, and this is almost all that we are told. Only once or twice has he called upon popular opinion to help his own case against his present opponents. Explanation of his acquaintance with Demus is also lacking.

⟨Socrates continues (513c–d) by saying that, although Callicles does not believe him, he will eventually do so if the two of them but examine the questions more than once, and better.⟩ Is this merely a recognition of a fact, quite familiar to every teacher, that repetition breeds understanding and understanding agreement? Partly, of course, it is, but it is also a sign that for the Socratic dialectic to succeed as an instrument of truth, not merely an inducer of belief in already acquiescent "persons" made of straw, the same question must be approached from more than one side. This does not necessarily mean multiple proofs for the same conclusion, such as one finds over and over in Aristotle or Saint Thomas, although such plural arguments aid in solidifying the convictions of the hearer or reader.[12] Rather, there is strength in the cross-references of proofs related to the same subject matter but not necessarily ending with the same conclusion.[13] At any rate, Socartes is aware that new belief cannot be generated in Callicles on matters which, though he is unclear about them, are repeatedly said and shown to be objects of his passionate attachment. It is as if he were the lover of a fickle woman and had mixed feelings of enchantment, disillusion, charity, and frustration, making his own behavior and speech inconstant and garbled. Yet each separate feeling was strongly, vividly held, and any unfavorable references to his lady by another man would elicit intense reactions, whatever direction they might take. So much for the little interlude.

The last four pages (509c–513d) have not tried to disprove that rhetoric of any worth exists but only to show that if it is an art and is then reduced to a knack of mouthing artificial compliments, it will be of little use in Callicles' mother city. In other words, Socrates is pointing out another inconsistency in Callicles' thinking: Even in a world of many injustices, plays for illicit power, and city hall chumminess, his cynical view of rhetoric will not really do.[14]

We may look at these four pages in another way. They have explored one half of a basic vertical distinction between good as the upper prong and evil as the lower, dealing with the latter throughout. Let us assume, Socrates could be saying, that you are right, Callicles; what then? How are you going to gain ground or even survive in life with the attitudes you are embracing? The next few pages (513d–517c) will reverse this, however, and will consider chiefly the upper prong, using the lower for contrast. They deal with public arts (513d–514e) and public rule (515a–517c).

⟨Socrates commences (513d–e) by saying that *tendance* (therapeia) *of anything can aim in one of two directions, at ignoble pleasure or at the best.*⟩ That is, the pleasures are conditions seeming to be good in the short term while the best is the long-term well-being of whatever thing is improved, its fullest realization of its own nature. ⟨*Hence, Socrates continues, we should try to make the city as good as possible; for, if we do not, no other service to it will be beneficial (513e–514a).*⟩ Socrates is apparently indicating that the city as a whole is defective, and likewise any attempt at improvement must be pointed towards the welfare of the city as a unity, not some class or group, let alone any individual.

⟨*More specifically (513a–d), we should, if put in charge of some construction, examine ourselves* (a) *to be assured that we understand the art needed and consider how able were our teachers;* (b) *to see whether we had put up buildings of our own, first private structures, later public ones;*[15] (c) *to see whether our buildings were beautiful or ugly;* (d) *to see whether our later efforts were done without guidance from our teachers. If these questions cannot be answered satisfactorily, it would be folly for us to attempt the supervision of public works.*⟩ The building art mentioned is one of the crafts, not the performing arts such as music and tragedy, and standards of beauty take their place in the account and must be met. The implication in all four questions is that unless a man has been thoroughly grounded in the art, then what he does in its name will be not by art but by some sort of fakery, its net result being shoddy goods.[16]

We might say, parenthetically, that the divisions are again dichotomous. Supervising a public construction could be done without full grasp of the art or with it, that is, already learned from some teacher; it could be done by one who had formerly erected private buildings or by one who had not. Those buildings erected could be beautiful or ugly, and of the former there might be those built with the help of teacher guides or those built independently. Now that Callicles has been partly drained of his dogmas and self-assurance and thereby of some of his resistance, it is possible for Socrates to proceed in more systematic fashion, as he did when Callicles had temporarily quit the discussion.

⟨*Questions similar to those just raised about architecture can be asked regarding state medicine (514d–e) and politics, into whose practice Callicles is just now entering* (515a).⟩ The point that Callicles is entering public life is crucial to this entire half of the *Gorgias* and perhaps to all the rest; but because we have stressed the urgency with which Socrates apprehends it, the only question we need now to raise is why Socrates first mentions it here. It is in the context of the practice of the real arts of government, as opposed to their evil imitations, that it need be made an issue, since only in the last few pages has any clear alternative to the rhetor's way of life been proposed.[17] At no stage does Socrates suggest that Callicles *not* enter political life, but he does more and more vigorously recommend a very different approach to the way such a career should be conducted. In applying the methodological sally that Callicles has been initiated into the greater mysteries before the lesser, Socrates has been urging a restraint born of attention to right order (506e). Hence he feels himself at liberty to ask a new question (515a–b): ⟨*Has Callicles ever made any single base, unjust, licentious, unthinking person wise and good before attempting to enlighten and reform the city at large*? Because Callicles most certainly has not, he takes refuge in an accusation that *Socrates is interested only in altercation* (philonikos). Socrates in turn replies that his *only wish is to know how Callicles thinks he ought to conduct himself.*⟩ To turn such men as Gorgias and Polus loose upon the city would be bad enough, but Callicles would be much worse, perhaps for his very vacillation covered by vindictiveness.

The present four pages throw new light upon a question previously broached, though not answered even tentatively: Where are there good rhetors in the city? At that time (503b–c), Callicles agreed that no good ones exist at present in Athens but suggested that Themistocles, Cimon, Miltiades, and Pericles (recently dead) were of better stamp. Now (515c) Socrates takes up his nominations. One remembers that even Callicles' first mention of these four came *after* he had been confronted with the image of unbridled lusts as the core of his manner of living and when he was prepared to admit to distinctions between good and bad pleasures (499b), good and bad rhetoric (503a), and now a hint that there may be both good and bad art. From various classical sources one may conclude that Themistocles was an able rascal, but that the other three, although high-handed from time to time, were not of the rapacious sort that Polus saw and envied in Archelaus. Had Callicles been proposing the names of successful rhetors or politicians before his principal moral crisis with Socrates over pleasures, it is doubtful that he would have chosen those men from the main stream of Athenian governmental life. Earlier, his hero had been Heracles, cited as a thief (484b–c).

Pericles is dealt with first, and receives far the most attention (515d–516d). The question is not how effective a speaker he was; this would more properly be an issue in arguing with Gorgias. It is now a matter of deciding whether he had a really beneficial effect upon Athens, and the burden of Socrates' judgment is that he did not. ⟨Socrates has heard, so he says—note the disclaimer of personal knowledge, though he did once hear Pericles speaking about the Middle Wall (455e)—*he has heard that Pericles made the Athenians lazy, cowardly, talkative, and avaricious* (argous, deilous, lalous, philargurous) *by inaugurating the system of public fees.*⟩ The adjective *cowardly* has been introduced before in connection with feeling pleasure or pain when the enemy is retreating or advancing (497e ff.). But *lazy* is new and *talkative* also,[18] except where Polus' lack of direction is mentioned; but, of course, Polus is no Athenian. Again, *avaricious*, literally "silver-loving," is a word not prominent earlier unless one thinks of Callicles' theory of natural justice, grabbing for more, as being connected with avarice.

⟨*Callicles thinks little of what Socrates has heard, which must have been*, he says (515e), *from Spartans whose ears are beaten in from boxing or from those partial to the Spartan cause.* Socrates does not contest this but insists that *it is clear knowledge that the citizens, presumably made into paragons of virtue through his rule, convicted Pericles of embezzling and nearly had him executed.*⟩ Just why this split between vague reports from hostile witnesses and what is clearly (*saphōs*) known is permitted is a little hard to fathom, except that the moral effect that a ruler has upon his people is in fact difficult to describe with any certainty. Yet it *is* puzzling that Socrates should seemingly give at least some credence to an allegation that payment for public duties should make the Athenians garrulous. Lazy and avaricious, possibly, but cowardly—probably not; the connection is too attenuated. Perhaps Socrates is setting up a sort of profile of the Athenian citizens later to contrast the effect that his kind of politics will have upon them with that of Callicles. But then it would seem more logical for him to say, Callicles, I have been living among these citizens since long before Pericles was impeached, and I have seen a change—for the worse—come over them. You may not have noticed, but I myself find them more corrupt than they were many years ago. Not only that, but I have *heard* that some of them wanted to do away with Pericles altogether on a charge, whether true or not, of embezzlement.

Of all the charges against Pericles the one that he made the Athenians more talkative is the most germane to the topic of rhetoric. Certainly the persuasive gift, whether an art or a routine, presupposes much speaking and a readiness to listen to it. Dialectic, too, when taken in any of its acceptations, presupposes considerable talking. From this standpoint, Socrates could hardly object to the Periclean influence. On the other hand, undirected talk, disorganized talk, which Polus verges on repeatedly, is hardly a commendable occupation, and moreover it frequently ends in quarrels (457d).

⟨In addition, *Socrates wonders whether a master of tame herds that turned wild would be a good one* (516a).⟩ This is an odd observation for Socrates to make since it can so easily be turned the other way: Pericles, being an excellent instructor in the virtues (let us suppose), made the Athenians so good that even he could not measure up to the standards he taught them. ⟨Callicles does not raise this elementary objection, however, and falls back one more time on the remark that *he is agreeing simply to please his opponent*.⟩ If the objection were put into words it would raise the difficulty that either Pericles is a good teacher and a less-than-good man or else that he is a good man but a less-than-good teacher; and the need would be to consider which situation would be better, which worse. But Callicles does nothing to contradict the argument and is presumably not catching sight of the dilemma. Possibly he has simply grown weary, and does not care to see his personal idol brought low, or is not really clever enough in the first place. But the reason lies deeper. Callicles has no easy way to differentiate the role of teacher (or rhetor) from the character of the man himself, so the distinction and with it the whole dilemma would collapse. If Pericles did not convince the Athenians of his innocence, to Callicles it was not only because his speaking grew ineffective for "technical" reasons but also because he lacked moral stamina to do so, regardless of whether he had taken state funds for personal use or not.

⟨*Because man is an animal* (like the cattle herds), Socrates goes on, *and since the Athenians grew more boorish and unjust after the more than thirty years of Pericles' rule, it follows that he was not a good political man* (516b–d).⟩ This condemnation is interesting because Socrates never takes into account possible mitigating circumstances—old age (Pericles was then in his middle sixties, and thus for classical times fairly well up in years), declining health, political and military stresses—not to mention the fact that the couple of obols collected for doing jury duty might be just enough to keep those in temporarily straitened circumstances from more desperate want. As a comment upon the whole career and all the policies of Pericles, the strictures of Socrates are no doubt one-sided and unjust. The query then presents itself, Why does Socrates put the matter in these terms? It would be simple to fall back on our earlier explanation, saying that because this is rhetoric Socrates feels it fair to reinterpret history for his own advantage in the debate. But that is not enough, for he has often said that he is seeking truth; and certainly it would stand him in poor stead to try to bring down a popular hero for the sake of belittling the opinions of Callicles.

The answer, if we ignore the passages in other dialogues giving a somewhat more favorable account of Pericles,[19] seems fairly clear. The Socratic strategy is to establish a single line of connected arguments, despite its apparent sidetracks. This line throughout is based upon the distinction between seeking and promoting pleasure, and again, seeking and promoting the best. If Pericles has mistakenly looked to the former as the criterion for choosing a policy, then what misfires and brings hardship or misfortune either upon the audience or upon the propounder is to be condemned.[20] Socrates is under no obligation to find or allow exceptions. The quibble would be over whether Pericles' rule as a whole should be condemned because of an unsatisfactory result from a single set of disbursements of fees. On the other hand, there is an unspoken supposition that if one should make the city as a whole morally worse, then regardless of how many acropolises had been adorned or naval battles won, these latter results would be quite secondary. Then the issue becomes one of fact. In spite of the sign that Socrates specifies, namely that the people eventually rose up against Pericles, is there any good reason to believe that they became more boorish, more corrupt than before, and that the payment of a half-day's wages for a day's public service could have ruined them? But Plato has deliberately exonerated Socrates from the charge that he makes snap judgments wide of the mark. The source of the defamatory rumors about Pericles was the Lacedemonians, the sworn enemies of all things Athenian. Then why should Socrates trust them, if in fact he does trust them, knowing that putting faith in such wartime foes is bound to be misplaced? The best answer that we can offer is that Socrates is maintaining his separateness from daily civic affairs in this dialogue: He is naïve (474a; 488a); he gets his information secondhand, perhaps from hostile outsiders. His complaint against Pericles is not easily refutable because Gorgias and Polus are also outsiders, though not unfriendly, and Callicles' information would no doubt be popular opinions shared by his associates. Socrates does not deny outright that what he has said is rumor, and rumor generated by foes. It is the *possibility* of the untoward effect that Pericles had that he is advancing, not its certainty. His argument is made stronger—and more consistent with his earlier assertions that virtuous men aim at making other men better—when he hints that the Athenians mistreated Pericles. Whether that leader had really embezzled public moneys is left open by Socrates.

Next (516d–e), Socrates indicates that the treatment of Cimon, Themistocles, and Miltiades was much the same. The mention of these men is so brief that it would be foolish to speculate either on Plato's own estimate of them or upon what Plato wishes us to think is his character Socrates' opinion.[21] The later career of Themistocles was strikingly similar to that of Alcibiades with his traitorous switching of loyalties; but of this there is no hint in the *Gorgias*, though a jibe consistent with Socrates' remark (482a) that Alcibiades is always changing his opinions could be put into the mouth of Callicles, since anachronisms so abound in the dialogue.

Pericles was likened to the herdsman whose cattle got out of control; the other three are likened (516e) to the charioteer who keeps his seat at first but later cannot. Evidently, Socrates wants his hearer to see the three military leaders as engaged in skills more risky than that of Pericles, more dependent upon personal agility than the tending of animals. The chariot driver is an agent, not an overseer of the welfare of creatures lower than himself.

⟨Socrates now (516e–517a) remarks that *Athens has had no good politicians, for neither the earlier* (named) *ones nor the more recent* (anonymous) *ones used true rhetoric.*⟩[22] Had they done so, they would not have been exiled from Athens or otherwise brought low. But Socrates follows with the very puzzling remark that they apparently did not use the pandering form of rhetoric either, a remark made even stranger when we consider that Socrates already said (455e) that he heard Pericles counseling about the Middle Wall, an address that *must* have been couched in one style of rhetoric or the other. What Socrates apparently means—and this can be no more than a guess—is that these men, both the early and the later ones, did not use either kind of rhetoric very effectively, just as a charioteer might try two different ways of keeping his place in his vehicle, neither of them successful.[23]

⟨Callicles counters (517a–b) that *none of the present crop has done any deeds such as the former leaders could do.*⟩ For the first time, it seems, he states clearly that he did not consider an art of speech of *any* king as central to the conduct of government. It is enough or almost close enough to be a man of action. The question is whether this has been his view all along or whether it is his new-found caution in the face of the Socratic onslaughts. Virtually all of Callicles' references to language and argument have been slighting. True enough, these references have been in his responses to Socrates, toward whom Callicles has felt strong antipathy on several levels; however, he has said little about better, more dignified ways of using language and gives no hint, for instance, that he thinks highly of anyone else as a speaker. Nor does he claim for himself or even for Gorgias a superior rhetorical style. We conclude that at least at this point he is convinced that actions speak louder than artful words and that one should judge leaders accordingly.

The reply by Socrates to this and other issues is a fairly long speech (517b–519d), dealing with sophistry and rhetoric in the city and trailing into another slight altercation with Callicles. The first little portion

(517b–c) is a direct response to Callicles' last remark comparing earlier with more recent public rhetors. The second (517c) is a brief interlude. This is followed by a longer segment on the paradox implied in the bad rule of a city (517c–519d). A new section (519d–520e) then begins, overlapping with the speech; it is a back-and-forth interchange dealing with rhetors, sophists, and the making of money.

The response by Socrates (517b–c) is somewhat tangential to the remark of Callicles. ⟨*The older leaders may have been more useful* (diakoni-kōteroi, *serviceable*) *to the city in getting what she desired and cleverer* (de-inoterous) *in providing ships, walls, and arsenals; but even they did not aim at the best.*⟩ Callicles has not candidly accepted the old point (463c–d) that rhetoric is a pandering that imitates the politics of justice, so it is incumbent upon Socrates now to remind him that true rhetoric must conform to the politics of true citizenship and both of them to the aim of making the worse into what is really better in deed, not in word or acceptance, though words might still be used to help secure this improvment.

The interlude (517c) is especially important despite its brevity. ⟨Says Socrates: *We have ridiculously circled round always to the same place and mis-understood one another.*⟩ This can mean one of two things: (1) We have in the past been circling and now, lately, we have reached a mutual under-standing. But the text supports this poorly, for Socrates says that this misinterpreting has been going on during all the time (*en panti gar tōi chronōi*), which includes the more recent exchanges. Hence we might decide for (2), that we still misunderstand each other and are still cir-cling back. The only difficulty with this is that the first reading seems to fit the actual progress of the dialogue better, for most of the circling comes in the first sixteen pages of the long colloquy (481b–497c). After 506c, when Callicles has temporarily withdrawn, topic after topic has been broached that although related to matters earlier discussed is nonetheless a departure; and concomitantly, Callicles has become far more passive in the discussion, not raising issues over again but mainly conceding in order to please Socrates or to hasten the argument to some conclusion—*any* conclusion.

The other little anomaly in Socrates' remark is that the *we* seems over-inclusive. Had Socrates himself misapprehended the details and gen-eral tone of Callicles' thinking, he would surely have been unable to make suitable responses in language going straight to the heart of each idea, even if he did not always use a logic unimpeachable by the stan-dards of the *Organon*'s theory of demonstration. Nor could he have achieved a summary of the discussion (506c–507a) that drew no objec-tions from any of the participants and onlookers, all of whom with the possible exception of Chaerephon were obviously more sympathetic to the Calliclean side. Consequently, the *we* seems a concession inspired by good manners, if it is the misunderstanding to which it refers. On the other hand, circling of a kind has often been done by Socrates himself, approaching the same contrast between good and evil men, pleasures, rhetoric, and rhetors many times and always from different aspects of the same position. If we accept this slight looseness of expression, then Socrates' remark seems not out of place.

The "same point" or "same place" involves reaffirming the lesson of the Divided Oblong: Socrates has insisted upon a distinction between art and familiarity, and in each case of the circling he has reapplied it. The difference between good rhetoric and bad hinges upon the fact, brought out in the debate with Gorgias, that art is knowledge, rhetoric ignorance masquerading as knowledge (455a–d; 459b,d). This is the rhetoric of Gorgias, which is the rhetoric of Polus and of Callicles as well. But if there are distinctions between good and bad generally, then there can be good rhetoric, to which the strictures of Socrates do not apply. The character of the discussion, moreover, is mirrored in the persons engaging in it, for Socrates is proceeding in a way he deems most likely to produce some fundamental improvement in Callicles' nature while the latter has, using his familiarity with common opinion and that of the wealthy autocratic class that he represents, floundered in trying to piece out a consistent doctrine which is at the same time a vivid piece of intimidation. But Socrates is not the man to be taken in by what merely seems to be real.

The two-line interlude is over, and Socrates now commences a survey of paradoxes involved in the bad ruling of a city (517c–519d). This has two parts, dealing respectively with tendance of the body (517c–518a) and tendance of the soul (518a–519d). ⟨The first is for the sake of clarifying the second, and begins with *a distinction* between *two kinds of management* (pragmateia, *system*), *that which is menial* (diakonikē) *and that which is by art. The former supplies meat and drink and such necessities to satisfy desires, while the latter, including gymnastic and medicine, has knowledge of what is healthful—that is, strength and well-being and pleasure that hides weakness and poor health—or more generally, what is worthy* (chrēston) *and what is base.*⟩ Here the providing of many ordinary necessities as well as luxuries replaces the pandering knacks formerly opposed to medicine and gymnastic. Those supplying the bodily needs, without consideration of what is best, think of themselves as ministering to the body, whereas in reality only trainers and doctors are the real ministers. Even then the contrast is different, for the putative ministers often do supply essentials, not necessarily catered luxuries, though they may well do so without genuine knowledge of the best. Hence Socrates is now distinguishing degrees of skill as well as the kinds of intent formerly stressed.

The next set of remarks (518a–519d) corresponds, though not point-for-point, with those on tendance of the body. The soul's pleasures and desires are set off from its genuine welfare, and it is assumed that only the latter should be considered. There is, however, the observation which Socrates does *not* make, that the soul need not be supplied with certain things to secure its survival, as the body needs meat and drink— which are also pleasure-givers—in order to live. The remarks on tendance of the soul are five in number:

⟨*First, you, Callicles, when asked who are fair and good citizens, offer the other kind, much as if you had named a baker or Mithaccus* (a writer on Sicilian catering) *or the like, as good trainers; and you would be angry to be told that these men do harm, not good, when they stuff the body yet cause it to lose weight* (518a–e).⟩[24] It might be mentioned that cookery rather than the persons who decorate or embellish clothes is mentioned here as imitator of trainers as well as doctors. Possibly this is because emphasis has fallen in the last couple of pages upon good rhetoric and ways to extricate it from bad; the precise lining up of embellishing with training, catering with medicine, is no longer an issue, as all of these have moved to a lower status. By "lower status" we mean relative to the best politics, the best rhetoric, the best life now being presented as something not yet really concrete but at least as an alternative to the life of the tyrant-rhetor so long in the forefront. The dialectical shifts occurring are made apparent in the very next remark.

⟨Second, *the earlier men you have been praising, Callicles, have entangled the city in harbors and arsenals and walls and tribute and such drivel, with no regard for temperance and justice; and the men now blame their ills on present-day advisors and laud Themistocles, Cimon, Pericles, who in reality caused the trouble* (518e–519a).⟩ That the Divided Oblong and its successor matrices are being treated like a stairway is shown in this, that the general heading that Socrates has given this section (at 518a) is the tendance of the soul; but now the talk is of walls and tribute, that is, property. It is, however, not property itself but persuasion *about* property that is at issue here. The distinction between soul and dockyards still holds, but the dockyards themselves have given way to their psychic connections through discourse. The dialectic no longer stresses the earlier differentiation, at one time so important. A similar blurring of the distinction between body and soul will occur later, in the myth (523e–524d).

⟨@Third, *these same citizens* (who still praise Themistocles, et al.) *may seize you, Callicles, if you are not careful, or they may seize Alcibiades when they lose what they had and have now acquired, though you are but a part-cause* (sunaitiōn) *of the evils* (tōn kakōn—519a–b).⟩ The argument is becoming a trifle more complicated. Just before this, Callicles was treated as if merely observing and commenting upon civic affairs, but now he is made an actor in city politics though his role is to undergo, not to do something. He is a politician along with Alcibiades.[25] Now all that has been said of the latter up to this point has been that he is loved by Socrates (418d) and that he is unstable (*emplēktos*, 482a), whether in his opinions or affections or both has not been made clear. Here, however, he is a man with political ambitions, presumably one who has displeased his public (true enough as historical fact, depending upon the date assigned). Both he and Callicles are putting themselves in jeopardy, for they are either causes or joint causes of the evils in the city. Just what these evils are is barely hinted at, since docks, walls, and so forth are not accounted evils and would probably be listed as intermediate between goods and evils, along with sticks and stones (468a). It is, however, not hard to believe that the two men may overextend the public budget by commissioning ships unmanned, building docks that bring in no revenue, and so forth. Or they might grab more for themselves and friends (the old boast of Callicles) and live in luxuries unshared by those with a more rightful title to them. In this warning to Callicles, Socrates is assuming him as yet insufficiently persuaded to forego doing the injustices that he has evidently planned. The mention of Alcibiades, a man precious to Socrates but teetering on the same narrow parapet as Callicles, is evidently a device to help effect this persuasion. It both leads Callicles to think that Socrates views justice and morality with eyes so clear that even his strongest personal affections cannot cloud them and also hints that Socrates would not, or could not, take steps to prevent the many indignities and pains that Alcibiades would suffer, even though Socrates might well be expected to aid him. Another reason for the reference to Alcibiades is that it could be expected to flatter Callicles to be linked to such an important (and possibly still popular) figure, an often successful general in both style and magnitude of enterprise. On the other hand, Socrates concludes, as we have noted, by saying that Callicles (and probably Alcibiades as well) would be only partly to blame for the damage to the city. The force of the warning, however, is enhanced, not diminished, by this: Even if others have had a hand in creating damage and gaining spoils, *you* will be singled out for punishment.

The next remark (519b–c) goes to the heart of Callicles' complaint against the state and his pouting, Why should anyone pick on me? ⟨*Politicians*, says Socrates, *are thoughtless when they resent the state for punishing them, saying that they have endeavored to serve it well.*⟩ He is referring to those who sought to improve Athens by increasing her income by tribute or building more docks, neglecting the real good of the people, the good of the soul. The entire view of Socrates seems a strange one, flying in the face of much historical evidence. There is always the near-catastrophe befalling Aristides, a thoroughly honorable man, at the hands of the people, as well as the execution of Socrates himself. Obviously this has not yet taken place, but it has been introduced into the conversation several times as a possibility, and Socrates himself never denies that it might happen. In other words, good men come to much grief despite their virtuous intentions. As for the others, Socrates assumes here that control of the people's thinking by the rhetor-tyrant must be complete. If such a man aims at the betterment of the public, they will necessarily become better; if they do not, it is not because of their own weaknesses or because of disruptions from outside the relation, such as bad crops or invasions. Instead it is the ruler's own shortcomings, both as man and as persuader, that are at fault.[26]

⟨Fifth, *it is the same with pretenders to statesmanship as with sophists who act absurdly* (atopon) *in claiming to be teachers of virtue yet accusing their pupils of cheating them of their fees* (519c–d).⟩ This remark is not a gratuitous slur upon the sophists but rather a deliberate attempt again to link rhetoric, as imitator of judicial politics, with sophists, imitators of the legislative. The imitators—this is the lesson of Socrates—fall short of inducing enough good in the recipient (pupil or audience) so that he will feel satisfied in his soul and not turn against the teacher or speaker as a malefactor.

What right Socrates now has to be believed divides into two questions. (1) Are modern readers in possession of enough facts so that he can be fairly convicted of onesidedness in his selection of such facts? (2) Is Callicles likely not to know them so that his silence on that score should be forgiven? (Both of these questions relate ultimately to Plato, who may or may not himself have possessed the facts to begin with.)

The answer to the first question is mixed. A large number of "pupils" of Socrates turned out badly—Meno, Alcibiades, Critias, Charmides—behaving with deviousness, irresponsibility, and cruelty, if Thucydides and Xenophon are to be credited. On these grounds, most of which Plato never mentions, one can well say that the answer by a very ordinary sophist to Socrates' charge would be that the kettle was no blacker than the pot, or perhaps not quite so black.

As for the second question, obviously Callicles cannot *know* of Socrates ultimate fate, though in an excellent position to hear rumblings of annoyance in the populace. Even without a strict chronology, very likely Plato could allow Callicles to know that some associates of Socrates had already become hungry for power, even if the Thirty had yet to form their cabal. The fact is, however, that Callicles says nothing to this effect, though the issue is of high import to him and though a tu quo-que is often one of the most effective of rebuttals. What he does is to explode once more.

We are now in a better position to summarize this argument which might have been visualized by Plato as the fleshing-out of a skeletal ma-trix of this sort (fig. 8.3).

With this in hand, it is easier to approach the question of sophistry as it enters at this critical point, the next brief segment (519d–520e) of the dialogue. ⟨It begins with a little interlude, a remark by *Socrates* (519e) who says that he *feels justified in speaking at some length* (the past couple of pages) *since Callicles is obdurately silent.*⟩ This is a trifle differ-ent from the speech made earlier (506c–509c) by Socrates, who at the time had good reason to assume that Callicles had dropped out of the discussion once and for all. He then used the occasion to reorient the dialectic in a direction of cosmic order shared by an order in the soul. Here, on the other hand, the silence of Callicles indicates not so much active withdrawal as a growing recognition that he has been outstripped and has few if any means of catching up. For his part, Socrates is en-deavoring to persuade him that the rhetor is tightly woven into a net-work of reciprocal relations with other human beings and that his suc-cess and safety are contingent not upon how much he grabs but upon his efforts to work for the inner strength and well-being of fellow citi-zens. At this point the main thrust of the little segment begins; it con-cerns the value of the sophists as members of this citizenry, and is made to play a part in Socrates' effort to determine the value of the rhetor. ⟨It is agreed, says Socrates (519e), that it is unreasonable (*alogon*) for a man A to claim to make another B good and then blame B for being base despite having been made good by A.⟩[27] This is the same argument as the earlier one regarding the rhetor; the focus has been transferred from the city, however, to the human soul.

The reply of Callicles (520a) is not altogether relevant. It is an out-burst of the sort one has grown familiar with, this time against the sophists to whom Callicles has temporarily transferred his animus, away from Socrates. ⟨*What are we to say*, he explodes, *of these people who are nothing worth?*⟩[28] The fact that Socrates has wondered how they can blame their pupils for imperfections they themselves have brought about does not signify their total lack of value in his eyes. So it is fair to ask what connection the response of Callicles must have to the dialogue as a whole, instead of being a mere passing reply, loaded with con-tempt, to the preceding remark. There are several possible explana-tions, personal in character, for Callicles' dislike of the sophists, who are evidently in some degree linked with his ambivalent feelings toward Gorgias. But there are submerged reasons, more pertinent to his whole

POLITICAL VIRTUE (VIRTUE IN THE CITY)

	REAL		SEEMING	
	PRODUCTS	PRODUCERS	PRODUCTS	PRODUCERS
SOULS	legislation justice	none yet specified none yet specified	teachings on virtue exhortation to build docks, walls, etc. false charges	sophists Themistocles Cimon, Pericles the public
BODIES	strength, beauty health	gymnast doctor	none listed loaves, dishes cookbooks, wines	none listed bakers cooks (caterers and writers) vintners

Fig. 8.3. *Summary of the Socratic argument.*

view of discourse, and, more widely, of the means and purpose of living.

Callicles has chosen not to separate the various arts of discourse unless, it has turned out, he is forced to by Socrates. He does not admire philosophical dialectic, he says the sophists are worthless, and (if we look over his past utterances) we find not one single effort to make rhetoric the finest of arts though he could easily have joined in the praises offered by Polus and Gorgias (448c,e; 456a,c; cf. 462c). Evidently Callicles has now become disillusioned with virtually *all* users of language and gives no more credit to rhetoric than to sophistic and philosophy:

1. They all purvey trivialities and are unable to cope with serious matters.
2. The moderated ideas of virtue (which Socrates has just mentioned as part of sophistic) would impede a man of vaulting ambition and unslaked desire.
3. Pursuit of these arts would remove Callicles at least temporarily from his favorite preoccupations with deme and Demus, and he too would be drawn into the debates he now fears and abhors.
4. If other men came under the influence of Socrates' talk of the better life or the sophists' teachings on justice, they would quickly identify Callicles' own behavior for what it is and incite rebellion against him or, at the very least, try to reform him as Socrates is now attempting to do. The rhetors, as the conversation with Gorgias has shown, are no better, for they too are on the side of the righteous, though without knowing what righteousness is.
5. Last and perhaps least, the mastery of words, of whatever kind it may be, seems to unfit an individual for pursuits proper to the superior man whose plan of action must not be clouded by words and dogmas.

Callicles has seen his most cherished opinions eviscerated despite his eloquent parading and stubborn defense of them, and he has been unable to refute the basic propositions upheld by Socrates. He has sought to disguise this inability by a show of apparent unwillingness, but his failure to produce effective counterarguments is glaring nevertheless. He adopts the tactic that the best defense of a doctrine is an offense, immediate, incisive, personal, repetitive. Because of his lumping of all types of reasons together, he views Socrates as a sophist as much as a philosopher and has so hinted already (497a). If we add to this the complaints against driveling (489b), catching one up on verbal slips (489b–c), demagoguery (482c, 494d), vulgarity (494e), and so forth, we see that in the mind of Callicles Socrates is an enemy not so much because he is a philosopher as because he has the stigma of sophistry attached to him. To be either one, obviously, implies asking tricky, paltry questions that a straightforward, candid man could not immediately answer, however rightminded he might be. It is at this point that Callicles must finally realize that he is surrounded by those whom he would like to have made his friends, if only for his own advantage. Because, however, they are sophists and cowards who have not dared to think as he has thought, they are not friends at all and will be of no help either in his hoped-for rise to political eminence or his much-feared call to account. They are, in short, his enemies, every one of them. Conversation with them about cooks and doctors (490b–491b) is as fruitless as conversation about virtues, arts, and the law.

The agitation of Callicles, then, has gathered its force from all the lines of argument now coming together. ⟨To him, Socrates makes reply (520a–b): *Sophist and rhetor are the same, or almost the same, with sophistic being fairer than rhetoric in the same proportion as the legislative branch of politics is fairer than the judicial*⟩ (i.e., legislation lays down the definition of right and wrong social acts, judicature merely uses these definitions, much as the rhetor makes use of the concepts that sophistry has distinguished or merged and in any event has made some shift to define). A further comparison is with the gymnasts who are superior to the doctors by reason of their taking the healthy body and making it stronger and more beautiful rather than simply restoring it to the health that it should already enjoy and which it is the function of doctors to ensure. The sophist sharpens our thinking about virtue, law, and other topics, while the rhetor simply brings these notions to the attention of the crowd and attempts therewith to sway it. ⟨Socrates puts the cap on this whole comparison (from which he conspicuously omits the philosopher) by saying that *neither of them would have the right to complain of mistreatment of themselves, inasmuch as they have taught the sort of treatment that they now receive (520b).*⟩[29]

⟨A very small new segment (520c–d) applies this observation of the paradox to the making of money by three groups of persons in the state. *The sophist, the rhetor, and finally the politico all accept fees, although they of all others could best afford to give their services for nothing.*[30] *A runner learning from a trainer could cheat him, not having learned honesty but only a speedy gait; but the sophist or rhetor who teaches justice should never fear this, for the learner from them would act justly, not otherwise. One acts unjustly through injustice, not slowness of pace (520c–d).*⟩ Evidently Socrates has several possible combinations in mind, some indirectly inherited from his conversation with Gorgias. There is (a) the slow-running and unjust pupil who cannot cheat his trainer, merely because he cannot outrun him; (b) the unjust but speedy pupil who absorbs the lesson, then takes to his heels; neither (c) the slow and just pupil nor (d) the swift and just pupil receive mention, simply because they pay their fees as promised. When Socrates has said that not slowness of pace causes one to act unjustly but injustice itself, he has been recalling a point agreed to previously (499a–b), that good things are what make people good, and he is now adding, good in one way, not in all ways, or good generally. A fast trot does not make a just man.

Throughout the first half of the dialogue, it was recognized that rhetoric, whatever its status as an art, led to more riches and that the rhetor would function as such only if he were now to receive some gain, not so much through payment of a fee (this goes unmentioned) as through some self-aggrandizement. There were also a host of comments clustered about the notion that each art or imitation of an art makes the person upon whom it is practiced better or worse. A third ingredient in the present discussion leads back to the old contention (460b–c) that one who learns an art or a virtue is a regular practitioner of it. Hence if a rhetor or sophist takes on a pupil who fails to be just, it is a sign that the teacher has been inadequate.

Socrates' interpretation of the money accruing to rhetor or sophist is in the fees, for he has disposed of other self-enrichment as an end. (Socrates continues with a rather different point that *every other service, for instance building, has a claim to compensation, but when one advises others on how to be good or manage one's household or a city, then it is a disgrace to ask for money because this service makes others desire to do the same in return* (520e).)

Socrates is considering both the teachers and the pupils and their dual responsibilities, whereas Gorgias was ready to accept all the rewards (452e) and yet unload all the responsibilities upon erring pupils (456c–457c), hoping only that they would not publicly disgrace the teacher. The conclusion Socrates has now reached is that the teachers have an enormous burden because they alone deal with justice and injustice as subjects *and* habits to be taught.[31] (Earlier—514a–c—when Socrates was describing how one ought to become a candidate for undertaking public office, he stated that there were two stages to be considered: one's work as a pupil or some professional and one's work after attaining independence from all teachers.)

The possible cases of the pupil of rhetoric-sophistic are again four: (1) The originally base pupil in whom, despite his character, justice is somehow instilled by good teaching so that he pays his teacher; Gorgias does not mention the pupil who fails to pay, and his only concern is reputation, no doubt assuming that he can ensure that the fee is paid before the pupil enters upon his own career. (2) The originally unjust pupil who because of excessive baseness or poor teaching remains unjust and cheats his instructor; this man would resemble the unregenerate rhetor-tyrant admired by Polus. (3) The pupil who was originally just but in whom injustice is instilled by corrupt teaching; here we have an approximation to Callicles' man who is originally one among the many but who becomes independent of them and of the law as well; injustice and justice merge in him, and he does as he pleases. (4) The man originally just who then remains just through instruction; it is he whom Socrates would hope for in the sons and pupils of good men.

* * *

One might say that Socrates has left a trail of devastation, for he has deprived Callicles—so far as he can make this stubborn young man follow his argument—not only of the latter's own principles but also the most respectable of the models upon whom Callicles has fallen back. Pericles and Miltiades, Themistocles and Cimon, heroes all, have been castigated for the civic damage they have wittingly or unwittingly caused, and their punishments have been shown to be on their own heads, making them little better than the luckless sophists whom Callicles despises. The difference between the Calliclean way of life and the philosophical is now as wide as it ever was in the mind of Callicles, but the characterizations have been reversed. Socrates as philosopher was condemned much earlier for being ineffectual, complacent in his retirement from the useful and bold exchanges of politics; now, that brand of politics, the best that Callicles himself can outline, has been shown to fail of its purposes and to be dangerous to its exponents even when they appear to be best. If the *Gorgias* were to end at this point it would be counted one of the most negative, skeptical, even cynical, works in the whole literature of politics.

The slightly chastened Callicles has proposed just now a career for himself, but it turns out to have at least two layers, perhaps more, so perplexing is the mixture of motives in his soul.[32] Some of these motives are related to a respect for the opinions of others that may not be altogether selfish, others to a willingness to toady to the most ordinary wish for bread and circuses, still others to his own erethic passions. Socrates has carefully explored the two principal levels, distinguishing the better from the worse and urging that the composite life which Callicles has planned be purged of its baser aspects. Were this to happen, the life-style of Callicles would begin to border upon that of the man of virtue, though its foundations would be different.[33] He would remain a lover of the deme and Demus but would no longer listen to the deme simply to discover how he might both gratify and exploit the people supporting and trusting him. Although he would like to enter the political arena, he would, instead of modeling his approach upon Pericles and those others who thought bigger harbors meant greater happiness, seek to keep material "progress" within bounds. He would not become a philosopher in any Socratic sense, would not be on the lookout to improve souls wherever he could; he would remain a man of action, a man of the people, probably still a lover of handsome men and tasty foods, a man who, though quite a reader, would still have little use for refinements of language except as they served to communicate political demands from the people to him and policies from him to the people. This much could be salvaged, though the chances are remote that Callicles will actually come to the realization that this ought to be his purpose in life. Instead, as Socrates well knows by now, Callicles is so suffused with darker passions that he will hardly view the interests of others as being of more than momentary concern to him. It is this lower level that Socrates is afraid will become dominant in Callicles and will express itself in the coming misrule of a splendid, blemished city.

9

WHICH LIFE OUGHT WE TO LIVE?

(521a–527e)

Socrates has assumed that because the Calliclean way of life has so much that is unacceptable about it, *both* he and Callicles should choose something remote from it. The difficulty is in finding a model to emulate. Callicles thought he could look to heroic Athenian leaders of wartime and peacetime; but thus far not one person, nor even a god or a *daimōn*, has been suggested and approved as exemplar for the better life. Socrates has not invoked, nor will he, the names of Parmenides (whom he evidently respected highly, judging from other dialogues)[1] or one of the finer Pythagoreans, perhaps the most likely candidates. That the real philosophic way differs from that life as it was described and excoriated by Callicles has been hinted ever since the young host gave vent to his first diatribe (484c–486d). But who or what the philosopher-model will be, a topic thus far open to question, now receives a summary and rather unexpected answer. Elsewhere, Socrates proposes other models of the wise thinker—the arcane Diotima in the *Symposium*, the philosopher-king in the *Republic*, the lover who re-collects the forms in the *Phaedrus*—but these would mean little to the arrogant patrician now before him. The life to be chosen Socrates has already embraced; so in the present conversation he is simply ratifying his old choice. It is a peculiarly self-involving case of logical necessity: He must choose this life because he *has* chosen it, and there is no other for him, not through weakness or inflexibility but through the strength of his commitment and the power of the life itself. Thus it has been both his nature and his decision, after much hard thinking, to live this career out to the end.[2] There is, however, one extrinsic aspect, namely that Socrates should choose his way precisely because no one else has done so, or at best very few have; and considering what Athens has had from her other leaders it is time that someone opt for the instilling of virtue rather than the piling on of delights, position, power, and the temporary satisfactions of a life where even the discharging of public duties is paid for by the state.

Another observation, no less obvious than the first, is that although both Callicles and Socrates seem eager for an evaluation of the same two lives, it is not really so simple. The question has been one of deciding between not two but four: the philosophic life as Callicles thinks of it at first, the political-rhetorical life as he thinks of it, and these two lives as conceived by Socrates and becoming more and more prominent in the discussion. There is, to be sure, some agreement lately reached by the two men about the nature of the political life; so, in effect, the four reduce to three, for the glow of honor and success with which Callicles earlier had adorned his ideal career has now faded. The chief disagreement remaining is between the two views of what it means to be a philosopher, and the task of Socrates, ever since his raising of the three questions (500c–d), has been to give shape and substance to the philosophic life as he conceives it, confronting a man who accepts very few of the characteristics by which Socrates wishes to have it judged. Add to this the obduracy and cynicism of Callicles, and one sees what a nearly impossible task Socrates has set for himself and why it is that he finally resorts to a myth in an effort to complete his labors of the day.[3]

The third question, Which life should be chosen? is both logically and in practice interwoven with the preceding two. In treating the second question, What is the difference between the two lives? Socrates has dealt with the life of Callicles, dragging him to a conception of it much nearer to his own view, which is that the career of the rhetor-politician has usually ended in personal disaster as well as being intrinsically reprehensible. Hence all that is left is to treat of Socrates' own life as he views it. He is certain that his *total* life-style is better than the *total* life-style of Callicles, debased as it was by a combination of slipshod reasoning about power and sleazy appetites. *What* is a thing, and what is the *best* that it can be?—this is Socrates' incessant query and self-query—whereas Callicles could at most ask, What is this thing good for, and how can I make use of it for myself? Socrates may well think that deficiencies exist in the life he is leading—he has already owned up to one of his public ineptitudes (473e–474a), and, turn about, that there are certain merits in the hopes and attitudes of Callicles, who after all has great interest in politics and the life of a cultivated man, which in this regard puts him a little above the ordinary citizen. But that is not enough to tip the balance in his favor.

The difficulty now facing Socrates is the paradox involved in any stressing of selflessness as a mission when it is one's own self that is living, or even trying to live, this life. Callicles has been consumed by egoism—Sir Willoughby Patterne, of Patterne Hall, was to have as his own epitaph, "Through very love of self himself he slew" and this could apply to the restless Greek as well. Socrates knows, as much as any man can know, that the philosophic life is best. This knowledge, however, must in turn be purified of its egocentric dross before it can have the full persuasive effect of an excellent model, so that his opponents can no longer claim that they see through what they take to be his pretensions. The solution will rest in part upon seeing how the philosophic person acts in the city inhabited by Callicles and in part upon a larger view of the career of that person's soul.

* * *

The final portion of the dialogue opens with a couple of new sallies back and forth (521a–b), ushering in a preliminary account by Socrates of his own life (521b–522e). ⟨He first admonishes Callicles to speak truly (which the latter has not done because he has not agreed with Socrates heretofore—see 486e), frankly (for which he has already received praise), well (which in a way he has already been able to do, for he has made each point forcefully even though not consistently with all the other points), and nobly (an exhortation yet to be heeded, if at all).

Callicles replies that Socrates ought to do some service.⟩ This is a trivalent suggestion meaning (a) he ought to be a schemer hiding his inner motives; (b) he should work for the practical good of the people; (c) he ought to live as he is living, but impart his own virtue to others. ⟨Socrates takes the suggestion in the first sense, no doubt the one intended, and responds that this might be pandering, to which Callicles replies that this would be as a scurrilous Mysian calls it.⟩ He is unable finally to let his own better aspects emerge and settles for letting Socrates interpret him as he will but blaming him for the worse.

Previously, Socrates has made his own goodness a conditional matter—if I am good, then someone treating me unjustly will be a wicked man. ⟨Now (521b–c), however, it is no longer hypothetical: A base man will be killing a good one. Not only that, but he will not know how justly to use the property of which he has robbed me. He will thus be ignorant, unjust, disgraceful, and evil.⟩ This is a list of epithets tailored not to the ordinary man who might confusedly bring suit, like Meletus, but rather to the very person representing what Socrates hopes that Callicles will not become. Both in content and in emphatic tone, heaping up ever harsher expressions, it shows the urgency with which Socrates is admonishing Callicles not to give himself over to a life of despoiling and plundering.

But Callicles quickly shifts ground. ⟨Such a thief, he says, is petty.⟩ In other words, I would not dream of taking your property, it is not worth enough to me, but someone else will take it, and you must be foolish indeed to think yourself safeguarded. ⟨To which Socrates replies (521c–d) that *he is not such a fool, for any citizen could undergo this. But only a base man, petty or not, would mistreat one who had done no injustice. I could even be put to death, he continues, and this would not be strange (atopon).*⟩

Looking at the ambiguities, one notes first that Callicles has said that a petty man, not some ruler, will injure Socrates, and wonders whether the speaker has at last given up the projection of himself as tyrant. Second, one sees that Callicles has dropped his old professions of friendship for Socrates (485e, 486a), no longer wishing to give the impression that he would not be the one to maltreat him, or again, that it *would* be he attempting to rescue Socrates, an old bumbler.[4] At the moment, Callicles' intent is apparently that he should be neither an attacker nor a rescuer.

Who, then, could be the attacker envisaged by him? If a tyrant (which the expression "petty fellow" would eliminate), it would be understandable, since Socrates is obviously a man least like the tyrant in tastes and character (510b) and is certainly not one to make himself popular with his deme, with his endless haranguing about virtue. Yet Callicles has also implied that he considers Socrates several notches below himself in status and grace—lower, no doubt, than the physicians and engineers who at least save lives. However, he would add, Socrates could better himself by taking an interest—what kind is not specified— in civic affairs. This is an unlikely suggestion *if* Callicles is thinking of himself either as a tyrant ready to do away with those opposing him or else as a friend hoping to protect Socrates, who would be venturing too far into unfamiliar, probably hostile, civic territory. Callicles' admonition for Socrates to enter political life and yet be able to rescue himself is so ambiguous, then, that it can only be said to amount to nothing more than an expression of mild annoyance. His complaint is, at bottom, that in his withdrawing from active society Socrates has made it less and less likely that he can help the city enlarge and enrich itself; he has taken no part in progress, so-called, and indeed if he were to participate he would do all possible to dissuade the people from building docks and walls and exact the tribute that Socrates has termed drivel but that Callicles would consider the best of all testimonies to his own civic-mindedness. What is so odd, then, is that in withdrawing, Socrates has destroyed all reasons but one for any man to bully and rob him. That single reason, of course, is that in time of stress, such as the Peloponnesian War, a group is likely to turn upon anyone not carrying his full weight, casting him out as a drone, a misfit, or a traitor. But Callicles gives no hint that he is alluding to such a possibility.

Could it be, then, that he senses instead that were Socrates to turn to political activities his ideas would be so innovative as to become immediately and fatally unpopular? Could Callicles be aware, however dimly, that Socrates underneath his apparent inaction is really a gadfly? There is unfortunately no definitive answer, for the character of Callicles and his perception of Socrates are both so exasperatingly complex.

Much has been made of this and previous passages similar to it. Can Socrates (or even Callicles) predict the philosopher's real fate? Does Plato want to foreshadow here what he considers the most unjust execution known to him? Common sense and awareness of political uncertainties on the part of the two personages is one thing, but quite another is the gift of prophecy. There is virtually nothing in the *Gorgias* to warrant assuming that Socrates could see events in the future, beyond his strong supposition that Callicles would be a threat to Athenian stability; and still less can one believe that Callicles himself could foretell such events as the death of Socrates. The celebrated *daimōn* of some other dialogues merely directs Socrates to refrain from certain courses of action that he is about to undertake; it offers hints neither of what he should do nor of what will befall him. As for Callicles' presumption that Socrates faces a violent death, he is so full of mixed motives and unreliable responses that one could scarcely be certain of his meaning if he said that he did literally foresee such an outcome. Compounded of loving and hating his emotions are, when directed outward, aimed more at Socrates than at Gorgias; and because of this, he identifies his own fate, which he positively dreads, with that of Socrates. He also looks to the way that Socrates could save himself—mainly through speech—as a way to adopt in case of peril. He has apparently abandoned Gorgias as a source of the means for self-rescue and now hardly considers his guest's opinions at all. Consequently, were Socrates to say to him, "Look, here is what I would tell them in courts if I were threatened . . . ; and you could too in a similar predicament," Callicles would no doubt take heart immediately. But the possible self-rescue of Socrates now takes an entirely different direction.

⟨If I am executed, says Socrates, in what is one of the more unusual remarks in the *Gorgias*, *it would be unjust, for I am almost the only Athenian, or perhaps the only one, who practices the true art of politics, the only one now alive who really carries on real civic business* (521d).⟩ It is one of the few places in this or any dialogue, the *Apology* being of course excepted, in which Socrates calls special attention to his own excellence.

The word *art* is here because Socrates has never denied, in fact he has insisted (464b), that politics is a double art of legislation and judicature, not of persuading a crowd concerning matters they cannot know by a speaker who does not know. *True*, however, seems to carry the argument a step higher. If Socrates has been confused, indeed ignorant, about voting procedures (474a), how could he be one of the few real politicians in Athens? It is only possible if the meaning of *politics* has undergone a change along with accompanying expressions; but this has in fact happened. Callicles has exhibited two levels in his character: that debased level in the earlier half of his colloquy with Socrates and that slightly higher one which has been emerging slowly and (because of his vacillating nature) none too securely in the last twenty pages or so. This latter is the espousing of decent politics of the marketplace and assembly, which looks to the will of the people but is administered by officers of government. It is the world of routine activity, of treading upon as few toes as possible but upon as many as necessary to get worthwhile projects done. It is the world that Socrates does not disdain but in which he confesses himself to be lost. A higher level, just now opening to view, is the one not yet described because Callicles has seen philosophy only as a false, defective sort of politics, so that Socrates has had to be content to train his guns on the Calliclean way of life, not exalt his own. It is the world where virtue, not self-centered activity, is the basis of all thinking and effort. It leaves even the best aspirations wrung from Callicles' statements far behind, and it is *truer* because genuinely and constantly devoted to seeking the best for all citizens— not that they should have more, or do more, but that they should *be* more.

Is modesty what bids Socrates to hazard that he is one of the *few* Athenian politicians rather than the only one? Perhaps; yet he does not think of himself as gaining any exclusive position and advantage.[5] Wisdom is not a commodity such as a jar of wine or a boy prostitute which if possessed by one man cannot also be owned and enjoyed by another. And yet Socrates thinks better of his little concession: He is no doubt the *only* man to be practicing his brand of politics, for he has no counterparts among the sophists and rhetors. Are there other philosophers in town? None have been mentioned, except for the young fellows who sit in corners chattering (Socrates has never disputed the description given by Callicles). Probably the best interpretation of the sentence (521d) would be this: "If there is another man in Athens besides myself both virtuous in his soul *and* able to communicate this virtue to fellow-citizens, I do not know of him." Increasingly, the notion of communicating has been transferred from that of persuading from a non-rational, pleasure-oriented base to one founded upon reason and channeled through instruction.

⟨Socrates continues (521d–522b): *Because I deal not with the elegant toys which you recommend* (Callicles had applied the expression to philosophy [486c], but Socrates is applying it to political pandering), *I will be like a doctor tried by a jury of children on a charge brought by a caterer.*⟩ The defense, both truthful and unconvincing to this juvenile jury, would be that the doctor performed his cutting and burning for the sake of their health; ultimately, he would have nothing to say. Earlier (464d–e), Socrates had used the same trio of jury, caterer, and doctor to help him differentiate between the real art of medicine and the fakery that is catering. In the prior passage the doctor would starve, while here the doctor would have nothing to say in his own defense. In the section with Polus, the effort was to make clear that rhetoric aimed at pleasures, although their kinds had not been broached; now, the distinction between rhetoric and politics has been established and the politics of pleasure clarified as well. Socrates is saying simply that, despite his trying to live the virtuous life, he can expect no favor from the populace. He is perpetually out of style, so to speak, because he was born to set right the times, themselves so likely to be further disjointed by Callicles.

⟨Socrates continues (522b): *I provide no pleasures nor do I envy those who do or those who are thus provided.*⟩ It is doubtful if Socrates means here that he never gives pleasure by any means to others; and, because the context throughout is pleasure by way of speech, his meaning seems to be that he gives no pleasure through this medium, when civic issues are at stake. Any other interpretation would make him seem a hypocrite,[6] shamelessly fishing for compliments.

⟨Socrates goes on (522b–c): *If I am said to corrupt the young by perplexing them, that is, by diverting their interests from your kinds of civic activity, Callicles, or if I am said to revile older persons, then I shall be unable to tell the truth, which is that I have behaved justly; hence anything can happen to me.*⟩ By this short speech Socrates has converted his own role from ordinary victim to heroic martyr. No longer is he merely a casual target for someone coveting his property, perhaps wanting to take revenge for an imagined slight; he is now a lone upholder of decency, a man with a kind of mission—its motivation still unspecified—and the fate he may suffer will be a calamity not so much to himself as to the city he is seeking to benefit.

Callicles cannot quite understand this. ⟨*Can anyone*, he asks, *who has adopted such a stand and is yet unable to rescue himself really cut a fine figure in civic life (522c)?*⟩ Reputation for goodness, to Callicles' equivalent to goodness itself, hinges upon one's ability to charm an audience sufficiently to undo the effects of any accusation brought against oneself. Socrates removes, or at any rate seeks to remove, the traces of this false hope by restating his own major principles (522c–e). ⟨*Keeping a good reputation has nothing to do with fine speeches, but only with avoiding the doing of injustice in word or deed to men or gods (522c–d).*⟩[7]

Our piece-by-piece comments on this passage have obscured the dichotomies made by Socrates and "edited" by Callicles, now more likely to fall in line with the Socratic arguments, though not by intention. Socrates has referred to those haled into court, and Callicles defines the accuser as a petty man, Socrates calling him a base or evil one. The issue is then whether self-rescue can be effected or not. For Callicles, failure to rescue oneself is dishonor—one would seem not to be a fine man at all—while for Socrates there are two possibilities, one of which is dishonorable, the other not. The shady use of rhetoric is the worse alternative to virtue. ⟨I would, says Socrates, be vexed if my death were brought about by my being powerless because unjust,[8] while I would accept death with equanimity were it through lack of skill in rhetoric (522d). If able to rescue myself, I would wish it to be owing to my never committing injustice; otherwise, if I cleared my name by using false argument, this would be shameful (522c–d).⟩

Before taking up the contents of the last two extended passages of the dialogue we should remark upon the relation which this listing of possibilities has to the close of the discussion with Polus, where a small hierarchy of kinds of men was set up: those without evil, those purged or relieved of evil, and worst, those who have done injustice and are not relieved (478e–479a). A second hierarchy was then made to correspond with the first: Best is a man who has done no injustice and needs not to use rhetoric to incriminate himself (this is implied rather than stated); second is someone having done injustice and then incriminating himself in order to be punished and thereby relieved of his burden; and finally, worst is the person who uses rhetoric to exculpate an unjust man who would if freed live long, burdened by his guilt (480a–d).[9] What was lacking in these earlier rankings is any positive identification of justice; it is simply the refraining from doing the sort of acts that won for Archelaus his ill-deserved crown. There has been little consideration of what it means to be brave, temperate, or wise, or of what it means to be well-prepared to carry out projects for public benefit, except for the order to be followed (514a–e). As the conclusion of the discourse with Callicles is nearing, however, there is no longer need to consider the man who has done wrong and must be punished by society, and who has banked upon the power of his own rhetoric to make his guilt clear and thus be relieved of it. Socrates is now dealing with the philosopher who does no evil rather than with the rhetor-politico likely to do a great deal. Virtue will assure one of a long life, and if it does not, well, the quality, not quantity, should be guarded; a long life may not be a good thing (511c–513a). Rhetoric thus becomes otiose, something to be discarded since the very need for it betokens the existence of injustice that with Callicles, though not with Polus, has been proved to be the lack of all virtues.

The declaration of Socrates that not rhetoric but goodness of soul is what counts, subverts all that Callicles has been envisioning for him-self, and there is no further response from him; he has but one little procedural sally left in the remainder of the dialogue (522e). His three great images of his future—that he can rule, that he can enjoy un-limited hours of delirious joy, and that he can make himself secure through superior persuasive discourse—have in effect been destroyed, at least verbally, and in the process Socrates has been enabled to set himself up as a just man, a temperate man, and (as one indifferent to the threat of premature death) a brave one.

The preliminary conclusion that Socrates now (522e) reaches forms a transition to the next argument, or myth, and its summarizing sequel. ⟨*A man who fears dying is either irrational or cowardly,* he says, referring of course to the act of dying itself. *But there is something that follows this act that he had better fear, for this is the worst of all, namely coming to the after-world with his soul full of injustice.*⟩ It is not stupidity, intemperate habits, or cowardice, but injustice, and why not one of these others is less diffi-cult to discover than why it is not all of them together. (1) It is not stu-pidity, thoughtlessness, or lack of wisdom because in many respects this cannot be helped, for if one is born without much intellect no amount of will or education can improve the situation. (2) Nor is it in-temperance, a private vice affecting others only when one's own licen-tiousness corrupts them or causes one to rob them of their due. (3) It is not cowardice alone; the two principal meanings given to the term thus far have been the feeling of pleasure or pain in face of changing for-tunes of battle and, secondly, one's foreboding of death—again, largely one's private business unless cowardice causes abdication of military duties. But why is it not all of these together, if, as many readers have assumed, the virtues are bound up in a unity? (In that case the vices which are their contraries must be similarly bound in a grim catchall.) The answer recommending itself is this: If there *is* a unity, this is not because all the virtues are the same and all the vices are also the same; rather it is a unity of organic harmony, where each virtue contributes to the welfare of the whole.[10] Justice fits with the other virtues, injustice with the other vices. There is little in all that has gone before to force us to believe that the connection is any more intimate. Injustice is the vice chosen, not so much as representative of the others as because it is the most obviously civic of the vices, and includes every kind of grabbing for more, of getting ahead at the expense of others. Everyone is likely to be affected by injustice, whereas the destructive influences of cowar-dice and the rest are much more limited.

The remainder of the dialogue, we have said, is in two parts: First there is an argument, as Socrates calls it, or a myth, as he also calls it, regarding the souls and their judgment in the afterworld (522e–526d), and then (526d–527e) a series of "lessons" to be learned from this mythic argument and from the arguments and images preceding. The first part is subdivided into a little introduction (522e–523a) and the account itself (523a–526d). One should not, however, think that because of these two-part divisions of the course of discussion the inner dialectical pattern must remain similar in kind. The passages to come contain trichotomies in rapid sequence.

There are several ways of generating lists of three, which we can summarize:

First, 1, 2, 3—all items are separate from each other to the same extent, as with the gods in the myth to follow: Zeus, Poseidon, and Pluto.

Second, 1, 2a, 2b—two items belong under one head, but are sufficiently separate that they still help to form a trio, despite being more closely akin than is either of them to the third: the reign of Kronos, the reign of Zeus (first system), the reign of Zeus (second system).

Third, 1; 2;; 2; 4—the middle mediates, that is, is a kind of qualitative mean proportional between the extremes, as in the triad Tartarus, earth, Isles of the Blest. This structure, with very different signification, was found (467e–468a) in the separation of outright good from their opposites, with walking, and so forth, capable of turning either way. There have been many isolated instances of triads before, but in the myth they reign throughout and the tale would be cut to pieces without them.

⟨The introduction commences with Socrates' request for indulgence (522e), a request he has not often made: *I should like*, he says, *to tell a fair argument that will show that what has been said before is true*.⟩ Now *kalou logou* can be rendered "beautiful discourse," or by many other phrases, but at any rate Socrates does not want it dismissed as a fairytale. Knowing how captious Callicles may be, Socrates must at least protect the lesson of the afterlife by insisting upon its connections substantively and stylistically with what has gone before. The modern reader can take it quite differently, for after all Homer is for Plato's Socrates an unlikely source for his pantheon, an unlikely arbiter of his morals, an unlikely informant on the arrangement of the three worlds. But for the only readers of whom Plato could take immediate serious account, Socrates' attaching of his story to Homer was in a measure (and despite the complaints against that poet in *Republic* II and III) a way of establishing its authority, if not authenticity. The quotations by Callicles from Euripides, Hesiod, and others are about human or at most heroic figures and do not touch the gods. Socrates may be aware from this that little hope of appealing to a religious instinct remains in Callicles, and that any attempt to relate judgment of the dead to moral issues would have to be through devices making this as close to what has been said before as possible. Callicles is a suspicious man. Just as he perceives Socrates' alleged shift between nature and convention as a cheap rhetorical trick (482c–483a), he is likely to deny the truth of this or any myth but will take it either as a literary adventure or as a way for Socrates to make a fool of him. ⟨Socrates tries to guard against this in advance (522e) by calling it *a true argument or account*, and Callicles coldly implies that *this does not matter*, merely *recommending that Socrates finish his task*.⟩

In other words, he expects more of the same moralizing from the philosopher, and the form it will take is of no consequence—a further indication of his merging of all types of speaking, except possibly his own, under the same head. It is his last utterance in the dialogue, which still continues for several pages.

Socrates offers his story—or his argument—as a true one. What, then, can this mean? Despite the fact that the Platonic Socrates frequently mentions the gods, sometimes narrates tales about them, utters several prayers, objects to their being degraded by Homer and others, it is doubtful whether he is a naïve believer in divinities in human form, though it is certain, as he himself says, that he believes in some divine thing, reasoning from the admonitory voice sounding deep within him.[11] The "geographies" offered in the dour myths of the afterworld (in the *Gorgias, Phaedrus, Republic,* and *Phaedo*) differ in many respects from each other, the gods are somewhat differently related to each other and to men, and, all in all, to treat these myths as literally true would be to destroy them by raising the specter of multiple discrepancies and clashes. To treat them even as possible events, events that might happen in the nature of things in a far-off future, would be equally risky. To interpret them as symbolic of actual relations between human beings, that is, as disguises for historical episodes, becomes wildly improbable when we consider that Socrates has already had plenty to say about *these* relations without attempting to dress them up in fantasy. Treating each god as an image for a single concept such as love, justice, and the like is doubtless as futile because these concepts could, with a little ingenuity, be as easily linked to the human participants in the dialogues. Even with that ingenuity the relations between the concepts do not, as a rule, exactly parallel either gods or men in *their* mythic relations. Yet the myths do have some relevance to what has been so carefully established in the earlier parts of the four dialogues to which they belong; and that Socrates implicitly believes in their "truth," whatever that is, can be shown by the fact that he takes issue with details of the myth that Protagoras offers, as conveying a false doctrine.[12] The relevance may be slightly different in every one of the dialogues where a myth, be it eschatological or not, appears. Hence we shall talk about the tale in the *Gorgias* and no other.

The truth of the mythic argument here seems to lie in its extension of the notions of justice and injustice and the rest into a world which, though having no more than the literary backing of Homer (and sometimes considerably less than that), is a world whose total structure makes for a clearer manifestation of the complex forces and values in issue in the common strife-ridden life of Athens. The mythic world is this real one clarified, but not fully. Ambiguities remain. The storied figures, be they gods, demigods, or men, often represent single or even plural traits buried in the welter of human characteristics where body is so often at war with soul, parent with child, friends with other people, and individuals with the broader groups of the city. Hence the difficulty of picking out exactly which trait is being specified or emphasized in the tale. But by taking the trials and satisfactions out of the clouded life of the present and the hazards of temporality and then placing them in an eternal setting, the appetites, sufferings, and resolutions of that life can, as it were, be purified a little of the conflicting, often fragmented opinions of which Socrates has been trying in other ways to rid it. At the same time he has endeavored to restore or retain what turned out to be right in the old, the fragments of truth in statements on the whole erroneous as they were uttered. Distinctions can be disputed and superseded in the day-to-day arguments; there is no call to supersede them in the transcendent world fixing their essences for eternity.

All this argues an incompleteness in the *Gorgias* up to now. To throw in a myth simply to tingle the spines of Gorgias and his cohorts or titillate the small audience hanging on may be part of the motive for including the myth. Yet it cannot be the whole.

The crucial change that Socrates has sought to introduce into the thinking of his three opponents, especially the last, is, of course, the inclusion of the soul in their shared conception of man. The three had viewed every speech and every act for its utility, its effectiveness, its success, according various degrees of importance to the utility for speaker or audience, and favoring the speaker every time. In a sense this success, bringing with it not only acclaim but also riches and the chance to indulge in pleasures inaccessible to the poor—this success is an external good. Socrates has made man a two-part entity but without attempting to introduce explicit premises from which to establish the soul's relatively greater stability and perdurance. What that would mean to Callicles in rough terms is this: "It is all very well to say that our way of doing things means debasing or even ignoring the soul, but we still have our bodies and their desires, the jugs of wine, the Daughters—and Sons—of Joy to take care of those desires. I concede, Socrates, that injustice enters the soul, not the body, and you have made me agree that it damages that soul. But you have been unable to prove that this soul is any more important, any more long-lasting, than the body. If, then, I can manage somehow to satisfy bodily appetites I can put up with the damages aforementioned, for these will come to an end when I reach old age—or when some rascal has brought capital charges against me that through my carelessness I cannot get dismissed."

Why, then, does Socrates choose a myth, or argument using images, call it what you will? The answer is that he has never tried to establish explicitly that philosophic discourse is superior to rhetoric; he has attempted to give examples in plenty of his own way of "talking through" (dialegesthai) a topic, but the intransigence of Callicles has prevented the lesson from taking hold. Callicles marches to the drumming of a different love and beloved, and all that Socrates can elicit from him is ill-concealed resentment. Consequently, the prospect of convincing any of his three opponents by a mode of speech that they either ignore or condemn is virtually nonexistent. There is no place here, then, for anything like the fourth argument on immortality in the Phaedo (96a–107a), and the best to be done to secure this vital point, the priority of the soul, is to picture its immortality and the everlasting effects of corrupting it, mainly in terms of physical reward and punishment. Obviously, the effort resembles the images of jars that Socrates invoked to try to wean Callicles away from the unlimited pleasures he had planned for himself (493a–494a).

As for exposition of the myth, it is divided into four main parts: the place where the dead are judged (523a–b); the actual judging of the dead (523b–c); the judges of the dead (523e–524a); and lastly, several conclusions to be drawn from this true account (524a–526d). We proceed, as Saint Thomas would say, to the first.

Authority for part of the story is Homer, by far the most-quoted writer in Plato's dialogues, but not always the most fully trusted, although this is not an issue here. He has said that Zeus, Poseidon, and Pluto are the three gods who divided the sovereignty of the world among themselves after taking it over from their father Kronos.[13] Whether Plato had in mind the accounts of Kronos' castration of his own father, of incest, and of the devouring of his own children (episodes succeeded by a period of comparative harmony in his son's rule of the world), is unclear. Regardless of the character of Kronos, Socrates implies that the treatment of human beings even in the time of this god has been based upon rough-and-ready distinctions between good souls and bad and between the rewards and punishments appropriate for each (523a–b).

⟨The earlier method of judging the souls of men (the gods are not judged at all, and if women are judged they are at any rate left out of the account) was instituted in the reign of Kronos and then carried over to that of

Zeus and his two brothers (523c–d). Living men, a jury of peers, judged men on their last day when the dying, clad as in life, appeared for judgment. The human judges, fallible to begin with, were easily deceived by finery.) We can imagine that bad men often slipped through and were rewarded, while the innocent were often subjected to unspeakable tortures, even after Zeus had come to take charge.

> Through tatter'd clothes small vices do appear;
> Robes and furr'd gowns hide all. Plate sin with gold,
> And the strong lance of justice hurtless breaks;
> Arm it in rags, a pigmy's straw does pierce it.[14]

The third stage, then, was to strip both judged and judges of their finery. But now there is a difficulty in the argument. Bodies and clothes of men living or dying are bodies and clothes, material and tangible. But what are they in the afterworld? The terms shift references. We suspect that the bodies now signify the habits and customs put on in the associations with other persons during a lifetime. In a manner of speaking, both clothes and customs distort, disguise, or even completely hide the natural appearances of the living person, being the work of embellishers whom long ago (465b) Socrates had stigmatized as panderers imitating genuine trainers of the body. The Calliclean jungle-world is plainly reflected in the first and second stages of the myth.

This interpretation, or one like it, seems to make sense of the requirement that the judges, too, be naked. The judgment will be made by a personage in the same condition as the soul being judged, so that he can directly grasp, though not always be persuaded by, the attitudes of new arrivals in Hades. The judges, furthermore, are hinted to have been experienced, else they would not have clothes to take off, and thus they replace the children who were to judge Socrates in an earthly lawcourt (521e) and who had to consult nothing but their own gustatory cravings.

The myth's system of judgment has changed, then, from the earlier egalitarian stage of judging the dead, a stage carried out on earth, of mortal sinners *by* mortal sinners (or at least persons subject to error), all confused by the coverings worn; now the system is much less democratic. Identity of the new judges has not been disclosed thus far, and they *may* turn out to be human like their subjects, but now at least they have the twin advantages of clearer vision and the fact that Prometheus has been told (523d–e) to strip the living person of foreknowledge of their own deaths, which enabled those about to die to set their own affairs in order, make restitution for their misdeeds if necessary, and appear before their peers with as few signs of guilty behavior as possible. One sees a certain puritanical streak here: Formerly, rhetoric could be used to inculpate oneself and secure just punishment and with it relief from the burden of injustice (480b–c); but now, the incurring of the burden implies that the burden shall remain forever. Evidently the change comes about because formerly Socrates had no way of firmly distinguishing between extrinsic behavior and intrinsic alterations in the soul; now, this lack has been overcome during his conversation with Callicles—in relation to ambition, desire, and fear. Socrates was originally developing the notion that guilt remains in life until purged by what is done to the wrongdoer; in other words, he may be punished by society if not punished already by private persons. At present, his burden is something branded into the soul, and justice is no longer conceived as an eye for an eye but rather as a working out of guilt through a fundamental change in the soul of the evildoer. Perhaps the guilt can be removed, but not through punishments meted out by other men.

The transition from the second stage (the earlier reign of Zeus) to the third (the later reign) has been made, but the judges still need to be appointed. They are no longer men but gods—gods, that is, of an order lower than the principal Olympians. ⟨Zeus, foreseeing trouble if he does not appoint judges with more than ordinary practical wisdom and *foreseeing the deaths of three of his sons who have assumed mortal bodies, ordains them to serve as the judges of the dead.* According to Socrates, *Aeacus hales—or will hale—from Europe, Minos and Rhadamanthus from Asia (Minor). There will be a roadway across a field, a lonely place of judgment offering no possibility of hiding or of putting on trappings, where the three will examine dead souls, those from Asia by Rhadamanthus, those from Europe by Aeacus, Minos waiting to decide when a case is doubtful* (523e–524a).⟩ The judgment is now, or soon to be, aristocratic in kind, not democratic, yet fairer because of the common nakedness of judges and judged and the divinity and humanity coming together in each of the judges. All souls will have left their own cities, so that no one living or dead can speak for them. Presumably they are now rid of present desires and merely bear the traces of past ones.

As a summary of the chief stages of the myth, we offer the matrix given in figure 9.1.

One may well ask why Socrates places the last system of judgment, which more nearly represents his own view of what the administration of justice should be, in a future, close by, to be sure, but as yet unrealized. All three of the judges were in point of fact traditional figures of the ancient past; none was thought to be alive in the late fifth century. It is a peculiar mixture of tenses. By means of it Socrates implies that what has not yet come to pass must necessarily do so because it has been common knowledge that the three mortals had become immortal. The

	KRONOS	ZEUS I	ZEUS II
HUMAN SOULS	judged living clothed having fore- knowledge of deaths	judged dead naked	judged dead naked, scarred, etc. no foreknowledge
JUDGES IDENTIFIED	ordinary men	Minos Rhadamanthus	Minos (Asia) Rhadamanthus (Asia) Aeacus (Europe)
JUDGES DESCRIBED	living clothed often mistaken		dead naked divine not mistaken

Fig. 9.1. *Summary of the chief stages of the myth.*

system results from a divine ordinance in a world equably ruled by three Olympians, and it is moreover bound to last forever unless Zeus introduces some new reform. (If he does, it will doubtless be to make the system even stricter, if possible.) The system has not yet been tested, just as Socrates' own efforts to improve the souls of the Athenians have not been put to the ultimate test of seeing whether the public will turn against him unjustly when it is justice that he is trying to instill in them.

⟨The conclusions from this true account now follow (524a–526d). *Death is the separation of soul from body, but both retain their natures after this separation: The body keeps its fatness or thinness* (related to training), *its scars, wounds, and all other marks* (related to medicine), *while the soul retains what it has experienced, felt, suffered. Even a Great King of Persia* (brought back for the moment from the colloquies with Polus [470e] and Callicles [483d–e]) *appears before Rhadamanthus with whatever marks and injuries he has undergone.*⟩ Where formerly, in the rule of Kronos, the body was a natural living or dead body, souls were omitted from the story, much as we would expect in the depiction of Callicles' world view. The shiftings of connections of the marks and appearances with what bear them forms a parallel with the aim of the major phases of the argument from 481c to 522e, the whole of the colloquy. One also notes that throughout that long argument the assumption has been that men are free while alive to pursue their own wishes and are neither the play-things of the gods nor the resultants of any blind march of material entities.[15] In death, however, man does the will of the gods without question or recourse, and not for a few brief years but for all time, unless it happens that his wickedness is expungeable from his soul. The adornments of the body in life are temporary and hinder the just judgment brought against it in death as they probably do in life; the dead soul is no longer embellished but scarred, and this time for always. The marks aid immeasurably in deciding the fate of the soul, its pleasures or pains. In death (the separation of soul from body, 524b), the tricking-out by the panderer disappears, and at first the body's health and natural appearance (to some extent the result of efforts by the trainer and physician, one may presume) show themselves, although this is shortly transferred to the soul and then even this must drop out of consideration.

⟨It turns out, in one of the most important conclusions of the myth, that *the soul is every bit as liable to besmirching, injuries, and crippling disfigurements as is the body (525b–d), though in the myth it is the body's hurts that symbolize the soul's.*⟩ The difference lies in the causes, which in the body would be poor food, injury, disease, or the like, but in the soul luxury, insolence, incontinence, and more of this sort. Some of these causes, such as luxury, obviously have counterparts in the rich diet that stuffs the body, but others, such as insolent pride, evidently do not.

⟨*A wicked soul is sent to be punished, either to be purged and made better as if by an art or else* (because purification is impossible, so deep are the injustices) *punished unremittingly to serve as an example (525c).*⟩ What kind of example, and how can it serve? The human beings who still have their lives to live do not see into the wretched depths of the afterworld, sequestered and hidden as it is, so its prisoners cannot affect desirable moral changes on inhabitants of this earth. Two different kinds of responses are open, the first being that the souls which have committed remediable crimes see those others and perhaps are the ones to be instructed. The other possibility is that Homer and Hesiod— or Socrates—are the ones to tell us of the eternal punishments, so that through their inspiration living persons decide to choose a better life than lusting and grabbing.

⟨*We are*, Socrates adds (525d–526b), *more likely to find the irremediably wicked in the ranks of kings, tyrants, and the powerful generally, those who have not only the will but almost unlimited opportunity to do wrong as well. Archelaus is one of these (525d). Tantalus, Sisyphus, and Tityus were singled out by Homer*[16] *as having incurred eternal physical punishment. Thersites*, who figures in the *Iliad* more than once as an evil-tongued man and here as one of limited power and therefore limited freedom, *is among the curables not yet purged of their sins. Occasionally—and no oftener—a powerful man can be found who is good, and here the example* that Socrates gives *is Aristides,* which of course takes the story far outside Homer's orbit (525e–526b).)

The meadow with its forked road stands between earth and after-world and is, in another sense, intermediate between Tartarus and the Isles of the Blest. ⟨*Those to be punished eternally bear a judge's mark different from those curable and who are therefore to be purged, then sent back to earth. The good ones, especially the philosophers who have minded their own business, are sent to the Happy Islands forever* (526b–c).⟩ This is a slightly new list of souls, for the philosopher has now been added to the group of the practical, powerful, but good men such as Aristides. Socrates has evidently hoped to persuade Callicles to visualize the philosopher as a still better alternative to the natural man who sneers at conventional justice. As in the earlier discussion, the good politician has been supplanted by the philosopher whose eye is ever fixed upon virtue. So now Aristides gives place to this man in the listing, though not yet blissfully ensconced in the Islands.

This whole mythic argument has its own fascinations—and puzzles. As a purely rhetorical exercise, one sees a number of resemblances between this tale and what has gone forward earlier in the dialogue, even in those sections featuring the other two respondents, but very quickly these considerations about rhetoric's applications turn into questions about morals.

There are, for instance, some interesting parallels between the great myth and the earlier images used by Socrates in his vain effort to persuade Callicles to give up his more seamy predilections. Death is one of the common themes: We may all be dead, now, and the body is a tomb (493a); this conception was of poetic derivation. From Homer, Socrates now borrows the notion, not that the present life is death, but that in death there is still a kind of life, even if shorn of enjoyment. If the body is already a tomb, then no future separation of soul and body is likely, but just this peculiar carrying over of the body beyond the grave (524b–c) reminds us that although in death, which *is* the sundering of soul from body, the latter remains as a telltale symbol of the condition of the soul; although the soul is separate, it cannot free itself of the signs borne by the body. In the earlier image the soul was trapped in a lusting body, preventing the soul from expressing itself most freely; in the later myth it is the soul that has succumbed to the importunings of the body and is now about to pay the heaviest of penalities for the body's seductions. Yet in this same myth, the soul is no longer imprisoned in the body or elsewhere, but only when in Tartarus and the judgment of crimes warrants retribution.

Again, Socrates has carefully included Thersites as an intermediate soul, bound for some punishment but curable—Thersites, an obsessive damner of good men. Throughout the last half of the *Gorgias*, Callicles has responded time and again to the arguments of Socrates with defamatory expressions, and one wonders if this mention of the foul-mouthed old warrior from Homer is not a politely veiled jibe against Callicles. But it is more than a tit-for-tat sally; Socrates is saying in effect that the answer to argument, even if the latter should be mistaken or inconclusive, ought never to be personal abuse.

The very use of a kind of genealogy, a pretended history, and a quasi geography as setting for the story recalls the emphasis placed (507e–508e) upon cosmic and human order, symmetry, form, but now rendered in pictorial terms. Where Socrates was formerly unable to persuade Callicles with the leaking jars (492e–494a), he is now finally extending the dimensions of his icons, giving them not only stupendous size but eternal existence as well. As a counterpart to this, judgment was formerly in the hands of dicasts, and in extreme cases even of children who could be tossed upon the wave of an enticing idea and perhaps the offer of a little pudding; but in the myth all judgment will be in the hands of honorable but pitiless kings reborn as gods.

The treatment by Socrates of Callicles resembles that described by Gorgias (456b–c) in his brief account of the doctor versus the rhetor. Socrates has used argument to try to persuade Callicles of a need to swallow the bitter draught of self-recrimination;[17] and now he is narrating more graphically what is in store for those not accepting this advice. Thus the injuries and scars on the body are the last links in a long chain of analogies between medicine as an art and the proper administration of justice.

Another point. Socrates has said (473d), You are trying, Polus, to make my flesh creep; but surely this is now the Socratic aim in limning the deformed dead and their incarceration. Here he is using his heaviest rhetorical weapon against Callicles, who despite all his crying up of strength and superiority, of disdain for law and common decency, is intermittently a tremulous man, for if he were really as strong as he pretends he would be exchanging dialectical-rhetorical fisticuffs with Socrates still. Even his attention to the wishes of his deme has something compulsive about it, born of fear that he will take an unpopular stand or be left out of their latest hopes. Added now to the terror of death, so final and so emphatically the worst thing that can befall him, is a new dread introduced with the myth, that of eternal damnation for all that Callicles has plainly been hoping to get away with; if earthly courts do not condemn him, Aeacus will, and no rhetorical stunt under heaven will lessen his penalty.

It seems to us that Socrates has earned the right to introduce the judges and their harsh decisions precisely because the nature of human justice and the superiority of the fair and temperate life over the wise (i.e., the clever) and brave life have not been established until the latter discussion (509d–520e) has been completed. In one respect, this removes Callicles' right to complain that Socrates was trying to make his flesh creep and was thus being unfair. The creeping would have been mainly the result of painting hobgoblins whose nature and appropriateness to a larger order had not been dialectically prepared. Polus had done precisely this when he threw in the tortures that a fledgling tyrant might suffer if caught (473c). Socrates would have been equally at fault had he introduced his account of the many ways of judgment at any time earlier in the dialogue.

Whether the rhetorical devices used in the myth would have much effect upon Callicles there is no way of knowing. He has let a silence fall, and the rest of Socrates' own discourse is expostulatory in its tone, indicating recognition of an apparent failure to convince him. The myth has had a marked effect, however, upon Plato's readers, which quite apart from his chief character's aims, must surely have been in Plato's mind to accomplish. The three-and-a-half pages have been singled out as one of the most powerful climaxes in a dialogue rife with climaxes, and one of the great visions of the afterworld, as conceived in ancient Greece. It tells its tale differently from Plato's other myths, though the ultimate lesson is no doubt common to all: Differences there are, real and profound, between good and bad actions; and these leave a permanent mark upon every soul and determine its abiding fate.

The special purpose of this myth is to show reward and punishment as inevitable sequels to these right and wrong actions, and to deny that a mistake will be made in individual judgments regarding them. The administration of justice under Zeus is becoming fairer and fairer, and is bound ever more tightly to the orderly nature of the universe, as divinely directed. Consisting chiefly of bundles of appetites and fervent hopes, Callicles' nature has been subjected prematurely, so to speak, to this judgment. Socrates has detected the impulses toward injustice etched into the man's bare skin and likely to remain upon it unless there can be a radical conversion. The court, which has been lurking in Callicles' mind throughout and which he fears may be the scene of his undoing, is back, this time away from his city in which he might mobilize a crowd or call upon influential friends for help. This court has been enlarged; the judges are now incorruptible, deaf to anyone pleading for undeserved mild treatment. Callicles will be a dishonored soul eternally—mere death need no longer be his fear, for it is now simply the door opening to something potentially far worse. He will count for nothing more than one minor shade in a far corner of Tartarus. At best he can hope to be released in the perhaps distant future; at worst he will be a warning to those who ought to profit by his bad example. The soul of a rhetor-tyrant is nothing worth, save as such an example to others of a career worth—exactly nothing.

The myth, then, is an echo of Socrates' earlier (503d–504a) elevation of the constructive arts by reference to an order in the world as a whole. At 507e–508a he raised moral action to a cosmic level with the idea of divine justice, introduced into a universe physically well planned. The true arts, properly practiced, are rooted in the ultimate arrangement of a cosmos beautiful in itself. The acts of human beings while alive are rewarded or punished, as the case may call for, through a process becoming so impartial and regular that no miscarriages can occur. The myth is possible only after the criteria for judgment have been clarified, and with them the nature of justice. Though that is not defined by Socrates, it is so carefully depicted that a formula, acceptable to another philosopher though not to the present company, would be but a short step away.

Another moral aspect of the myth arises from the system of justice, which even if always ordained by a god, and a supreme god at that, and universally applied (not always equably in the past), itself undergoes change. Even the king of gods and men is pragmatic enough to alter this arrangement of human destiny. The possible—though unlikely—shortcomings of his newest arrangements are an indication that the dialectic of virtue is not yet made altogether precise and rigid but may require further transforming before defining and elaborating in new talk. This is perhaps a part of what Socrates meant when he said (513c–d) that the conversation with Callicles would have to be repeated over and over and carried out even better than at present.

The last page or so of the dialogue (526d–527e) is given over to the lessons to be drawn from the myth, or better, from the entire conversation with Callicles and even with Gorgias and Polus. There is a very short section (526d–e) in which Socrates speaks of his own attitude and intentions, then a section (526e–527b) listing possible attitudes of Callicles, and finally (527b–e) one giving some general conclusions applying to both men. The first short segment is what one would expect, for Socrates could scarcely recite such a myth, so carefully integrated with all that has preceded, and then repudiate it as soon as it was over. ⟨*I am persuaded by the myth*, he says (526d–e), *and take thought how I may show my judge that my soul is in the best health; I pass by any honors and seek to be really good in life and in death; and I invite everyone else, you included, to this life.*[18]⟩ Socrates is not saying that he courts dishonor, but only that he does not look for external rewards; nor is he saying that he is ready to force others to adopt his mode of living (for it is one of the modes, contrary to what is true of the one touted by Callicles, that cannot be imposed upon anyone). Only because he finds his own way better will he recommend it to other men.[19]

⟨As for what Callicles, who remains silent, would respond, Socrates hazards some guesses, accompanied by a warning. *When you go before Aeacus, you will be dizzy, much as I am here* (in the assemblies and dicasteries). *You may, moreover, be boxed on the ear and dishonored by someone.*⟩ By whom is not specified, though doubtless it would be some other departed spirit who in life had wished ardently to wreak some vengeance upon Callicles. Plato has been criticized for taking pleasure in showing the helplessness and incompetence of the unjust as soon as they arrive in the afterworld, but we find it a little difficult to see what other direction was open to him. It is perfectly true that Callicles has accused Socrates of being unable to defend himself against the same indignities in ordinary life (486a–d); and without the setting of the myth, Socrates' turning of the tables would look like commonplace parrying. But if Socrates is playing a game, he is playing it for the highest of human stakes: the real welfare of a man of promise and the real welfare of an almost wonderful city, the greatest of his time. "I may be buffle-headed in the Assembly," he is saying, "but you, Callicles, have no conception of true goodness, the goodness of the soul, and this will have profound consequences. You have spoken of the worst effect that you think would flow directly from my own behavior—not illness, nor a faithless wife, nor ungrateful, shiftless sons, but humiliation. *I* say that this can well happen to *you*, even if you believe it the worst possible eventuality, and even if you believe that you can scrape together enough defenses so that it will not happen to you in life."

⟨*You may well despise this as an old woman's tale*, continues Socrates (527a), *and this would be quite proper were there a truer one. You and Gorgias and Polus are the wisest of the Greeks of our time, but even you three cannot prove that there is a life better than mine.*⟩ Socrates is ironic if he is taken as praising the three rhetors for the general wisdom when he himself has spent many dozens of pages—or several hours, as you will—showing them up for poorly informed, quick to make ill-considered pronouncements, and self-contradictory and vacillating to boot. If, however, the reader bears in mind that the speakers and politicians of the day, such as the unnamed successors of Pericles, have earned no better than poor marks (503b–c; 520d), we can see that Socrates is saying in effect that the three are only the best of a bad lot. In addition, *wisest* has meant all along a kind of practical sense, no clear distinction having been drawn between *phronēsis*, practical wisdom, and *sophia*, a kind of cosmic wisdom, in any part of this dialogue.[20] Finally, there is a little wryness in Socrates' remark about the wisdom of his opponents: He never praised them this way earlier in the dialogue, and it must mean that he takes them to be wise at least because they have listened to—and, he hopes, been persuaded by—Socrates himself.

⟨My life, he continues, is not only better in the sense of morally and essentially better, but it is advantageous as well (527b).⟩ This remark is one last concession to the mentalities of his respondents, for he well understands that he has not supplied premises both sound and acceptable to these men that could help him equate advantage taken by itself with externality and hence danger of wrongdoing. The advantage he is talking of here, though, is one no longer aimed at in this world of corrosive self-interest but only in the next. Oddly, the meaning has been transferred from its connection with ways to persuade, whether trustworthy or not, to a sphere in which persuasion is impossible. The dead appear with their scars and scabs to speak against them but have nothing to speak for them, hence advantage can only refer to living the kind of life that will incur no such blemishes.

The last little portion of the dialogue (527b–e) is an attempt to find a meeting of the two souls where despite heroic efforts on the part of Socrates there has been next to none. It is a resolution, the best that can be reached with a shifty but refractory opponent, and although it urges a journey to be undertaken jointly, as do the closing lines of the Republic, the tone is different. The section is subdivided into a statement of the one (compound) principle applied to morals and then to rhetoric that cannot be refuted (527b–c), along with some advice given to himself and Callicles by Socrates so that they may be happy in life and in death as well (527c–e).

We have tried to show throughout that most of the important expressions, structurally speaking, in the dialogue change their meanings in a systematic way, and this is why Socrates can come back to the same, or nearly the same, verbal formulations and still be signifying something fresh, something he had not been directly asserting before though he may have hinted at it. He is about to repeat some of the fundamental statements whose irrefutability he has sought to establish before, but they now have a new cast, partly because the myth has intervened, partly because Callicles has fallen silent. ⟨Socrates begins his final summation by saying that one statement alone cannot be confuted,⟩ and this recalls his earlier remark (509a) that his arguments are bound in iron and adamant and must either be refuted or accepted. The principle formerly so secured was that doing injustice is more disgraceful than undergoing it; this is now modified to read as follows: ⟨(1) Doing injustice is to be avoided more than undergoing it, which adds the note of urgency sounded more and more in the last fifteen or so pages. To this principle Socrates adds: (2) *A man should try not merely to seem good in private and public life, but to be so*; and again, (3) *If he becomes evil he must be corrected.*⟩ The second is not directly deducible from the first, for one might, in adhering to the first, adopt all sorts of dodges to avoid being maltreated. Similarly, the third is not deducible from the second because the second makes no allowance for the man who on impulse and for the only time in his life commits some injustice. The third is *allied* to the first which would allow that once a man has failed to avoid doing injustice the question to be asked is, What then? What does he do in order to regain the narrow path? But a strict deduction would seem to be impossible there as well.

⟨There is now (527b–c) a whole new application of this moral code to rhetoric, whose three rules correspond roughly to the preceding three moral rules: (1) *Rhetoric is good when it aids a man in paying the penalty for his acts of injustice*, that is, there are good and bad uses of rhetoric just as there are good and bad acts. (2) *Every sort of pandering must be avoided*, that is, we must not fake our discourse any more than we fake our virtues. (3) *Rhetoric, like every other activity, must be used only for pointing to what is just*, which resembles the moral principle that correction of wrongs is an absolute obligation laid upon anyone committing them.⟩ Rhetoric must never deviate from the task of persuading to truth—the concrete truth of actions judged by the clearest possible standards of virtue and vice, and according to irrefutable evidence. So conceived, rhetoric becomes an indispensable instrument of right action.

This note of urgency which has crept into Socrates' conversation and recital arises from his growing awareness that, although he has both refuted and confounded Callicles, he has not been able to turn him away from his planned course that will end in collision with the Athenian republic—to the certain disadvantage of the latter, regardless of what will devolve upon the former. What permits Socrates now to summarize this one rule, which upon inspection has turned out to be in six parts, is the fact that he has introduced the notion of indelible guilt in the living soul as well as of ineluctable wickedness and virtue that are not hidden in death and for which appropriate penalties and rewards are in store. The single exception is guilt subject to purging, but the administration of justice of dead souls is becoming ever more scrupulous and stringent.

In a sense, counseling of the stubborn Callicles is made easier by this more cosmic, if still somewhat pragmatic, conception of justice and its divine judicature, even though there is little reason to think of him as a devout man. Callicles is fearful of the consequences of his actions, though not easily frightened by any of the arguments thrust at him. Yet *any* proof, refutation, collateral reasoning, epithet, or story that will affect his future actions for the better would be more welcome than none and certainly more than the confirmations of Callicles' thinking that he might receive from the confused, irresponsible reasonings of Gorgias and Polus.

The last pieces of advice given by Socrates are exhortations to himself as well as to Callicles. They reflect the observation (497c) that Callicles has gone through the greater mysteries before the lesser, and also the account (514b–d) of the most honorable way of attempting to become a state architect or physician, ending with the admonition (514e) not to try to learn the art of pottery by commencing with a large winejar. ⟨Here Socrates says (527c–d) that *one should practice virtue alone at first, even if others condemn and treat one unjustly. If you and I, Callicles, should both practice virtue, we might turn our attention to politics at large, having gained some competence.*⟩ In this the reader sees that virtuous action is fully allied to the arts, in the sense of one's having to study its principles and attempt to practice it just as one does the arts at first— namely, at home.

⟨*Men like us should not swagger about* (recalling the stricture against viewing engineers, doctors, and generals patronizingly [512c–d]). *We especially*—here Socrates is being very generous by including himself— *never believe the same about the same things, and this gives us even less reason to think of ourselves as supremely important to the state. We are uneducated.*⟩ Socrates might add, as he surely has in mind, that your reading of Euripides and the rest, Callicles, has done little for your real education, which ought to be the correction of your base, basic impulses.

The issue between the two men is the most serious of issues: Which way of life is the better, the erotic life defined as love of wisdom, with the desires subordinated, or the erotic life defined as the pursuit of the continual satisfaction of urges of every sort? It is not simply two lives— *any* two lives, such as that of the doctor as against that of the craftsman, or even that of the rhetor versus that of the dialectician. It is devotion to goods primarily of the soul as against goods primarily of the body; and it pits two men against each other, men who are both likely to have far-reaching effects upon the welfare of the city at large. It is a continuation of a battle first joined with Polus (466b) when it took form as the issue whether the rational soul controls the bodily desires or the reverse. Based upon that issue is the distinction between the counterfeit practices or knacks of pandering, some of which serve the body directly, the others indirectly through giving their user a tighter hold upon sources of physical enjoyment. The goods served, however, are not real goods because pleasure is an unsure guide to what improves body or soul—it is not always false, but neither is it an infallible means of selecting what is ultimately advantageous, ultimately useful. It is a large question; but then, Plato was not much of a hand to argue trivial ones.

⟨Socrates ends the battle by saying that *we should take as a guide the doctrine, the* logos, *that the virtuous way of life is the best, not merely better but best of all, and that what* you *advocate is nothing worth, Callicles.*⟩

PART FOUR

UNITY OF THE DIALOGUE

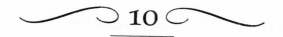

10

RHETORIC AND THE

THREE RHETORS

For us to prove the unity of the *Gorgias* requires either that we find no division between the possible philosophic and artistic unities of the work or else that we see them as separate and that the dialogue satisfies the demands of both in tandem. The fact that the peculiar literary artistry of the *Gorgias* is not also present in the three Eleatic dialogues or the *Timaeus* or even the *Laws* implies that Plato himself could separate it from the development of connected philosophic inquiries. Those, too, are masterpieces, though particulars of character and behavior are almost totally overshadowed in them by the general principles and their consecutants filling those works.

We have found it impossible to give a full interpretation of either the substantive arguments or the persons to whom they are accorded in the *Gorgias* without simultaneously taking the other into account; in depth dialectic the two are like the concavity and convexity of a curved line. Among the philosophic features we would number the arguments and their component terms, the types of reasoned oppositions and possible resolutions of them, the scope and variety of issues raised, and the cogency and correctness of the solutions, judged in light of various systematic constructions. The literary aspects, on the other hand, comprise Plato's manner of presenting the participants, the appropriateness of the spoken words and images to the persons giving voice to them, the arrangement of introductory and climactic passages, the interplay of personal asides, and above all the elusive rhythm—not only of the prose but also of the successive passages of argument taking the place of events and episodes in a drama or narrative. This rhythm cannot be judged simply by reading the work straight from beginning to end, though this is the chief way that rhythm is first found. The *Gorgias*, in making backward reference in almost every line as well as making every utterance anticipatory of what is to come, cannot be read properly

250 UNITY OF THE DIALOGUE

without looking in two directions at once. If the philosophic and the literary are in any sense one and the same, then the characters and their theories are alike expressions of some one underlying tendency within the human soul, and there is a rhythm common to both. The turning points, such as the catamite passage, are in that case not mere markers for but aspects of the raising or answering of overriding questions, and the thoughts and their embodiments in the words spoken by persons are identical.

Regardless of whether one seeks to meld the philosophical and literary aspects or treat them separately and join them later, it is still true that the greater perspicuity of the philosophic aspect and its closer connection with other dialogues is balanced by the special appropriateness of the personal touches to the particular lines of discourse in the pages under present scrutiny. Rhetoric, justice, and temperance reappear in many other dialogues, receiving definitions there as well, but Callicles never participates elsewhere in the corpus, and Gorgias and Polus receive little more than a few mentions. One should not forget, however, that despite the reappearances of the virtues and arts in the dialogues, the account furnished in the *Gorgias* is still unique. It is not a sketch for the *Republic* as much as it is a companion piece to the latter, stressing matters scarcely touched upon in that regal work, but omitting much that the *Republic* proffers so richly.

That Socrates must deal with three men, adjusting but not surrendering himself to each of their views in turn, might imply that the dialogue falls into three separate episodes, and that seeking a common thread would be a waste of time. When, however, it turns out that the subject matters of all three so-called episodes have much in common and also that the three men expounding their ideas all have partly concordant emotional concerns, the confidence of readers who would dismember the *Gorgias* should begin to fade.[1] The literary relations of the mentor-learner, host-guest, and so forth help to bind the work together. One finds connections between Gorgias and Polus, between Polus and Callicles, and between Gorgias and Callicles; these links are philosophical or literary, as the case may be, and pertain to conceptual thought, to life experience, or to some compound of the two. If the links were purely personal, one could say that the dialogue had some charm, verve, even dramatic power, and that its unity was conferred by the successive remarks or acts revealing their psychological meanings. If instead the bonds were solely philosophic, as in a treatise, then different but concordant structures of thoughts expressed as ordered terms and cohesive statements and denials, of questions and answers either appropriate or inappropriate, would give these links their ethical, political, or metaphysical meanings.

The *Gorgias* presents three men with articulated, if not always lucid, notions of what rhetoric is, but a reader might argue that in effect there is but one major conception, presumably stemming from Gorgias and adhered to by the other two rhetors: Rhetoric confers power (452e; 466b; 494c). Yet this reader may find, looking more carefully, that Gorgias thinks that rhetoric can be used or abused (456c–457c), and that Socrates manages to make Polus agree that there is a good use and a bad of rhetoric (480a–e), and moreover that Callicles believes (502d–503b) that there is a bad rhetoric in addition to the good. There are thus two conceptions of rhetoric. That there are also three is easily shown, for to the reader making slightly finer distinctions it becomes clear that the three men look upon rhetoric's relation to power quite differently. Each of these three opinions, however, is altered by the probing of Socrates, who has his own conception of persuasive speech. Hence it is justifiable to say that there are four views, and that these vie, as it were, for the adherence of the group of men gathered this day in Athens and of the readers of the *Gorgias* ever since. But even that is not quite right, for Socrates' own evaluation of rhetoric seems to divide into two parts when he converses with Polus: rhetoric is a pandering, and there is no distinction between good and bad rhetoric (436b); but later (480c), he concedes almost as an afterthought, that there is a good use of rhetoric in self-incrimination, which is scarcely pandering! Hence we now have five conceptions, not four. With a little ingenuity, the number could be further increased, and each time would require new matrices to set out the nature of rhetoric and its accompaniments. As each of the three rhetors responds to Socrates, the ideas of both parties alter a little, or at least their formulations do, and even before a new position is fully established, anticipations color the views of the discussants.[2] Hence we avoid assigning any fixed number. But to make, as we shall presently do, some kind of summary of the dialogue, bringing out a few salient points, we could not possibly fasten upon all the sets of opinions, hence must confine ourselves mainly to the views broached by the three rhetors *before* they are refuted and (in the next chapter) to some of those expressed by Socrates. Generally speaking, the opinions of two of the three rhetors are to be sought early in each of their main sections, while the more Socratic statements follow later on. With Polus the situation is different, for in confronting him Socrates immediately launches into some crucial distinctions, then Polus takes a turn, in the end giving way more and more to Socrates.

What has just been said, however, runs the risk of crowding out other concepts that although less prominent than rhetoric, power, and justice are still of great significance as their adjuncts. A more complete account of the unity of the dialogue would have to include treatments of at least the following: freedom, wisdom, bravery, pleasure, city-state, knowledge, temperance, public, teaching, exemplars, friends, nature, and more, together with whatever contraries accompany them. The full discussion would be the working out in prose of a matrix of overwhelming detail, with hundreds of boxes to be filled, and would seem ridiculous to any but the most Germanic of readers; even so, it would be closer to the true image of the *Gorgias*. Several other expressions are lightly used no more than two or three times, expressions that enjoy closer attention in other dialogues: foreigners and barbarians, cosmos, prisons, charms or talismans, dialectic, love, education, women, games, fear, sophistry, and several others.

The world of the rhetors is, despite their claim of supplanting the other arts, a rather specialized world where speaker and audience are the two poles, speech the bridge between them, and the end always popular political success. Since it is with these men that Socrates is arguing, he introduces as few new terms as he can and yet manage to broaden the scope of each general topic to connect it with the soul and its virtues and with order on many levels. Yet he also restricts all the terms by introducing distinctions to sharpen up and secure firmer applications. This, rather than merely asking random questions to find out what Gorgias, Polus, and Callicles are up to, is the burden of his line of inquiry. Their responses, both psychological and conceptual, are couched in pronouncements best grouped under the headings of their speakers, the speeches they give, and their relations to audiences.

The Speakers

Throughout, we have tried to keep to a minimum historical materials corroborating, permitting, or disputing Plato's depictions of the participants. The contexts in which other writers of the time refer to Gorgias and his companions are quite different, and some of the extant evidence is served up in associations so slight as to make it nearly impossible to interpret them safely. A random line or paragraph quoted in a later text by Aristotle or Cicero may well be as honest a report as possible, but still may not exhibit the grounds of the assertion, the emotional stance of the writer toward his topic, let alone the precise meanings of the terms. Our references, then, are to these men as the *Gorgias* presents them, but even here the men are to be taken in two ways. One resides, of course, in what they themselves say and how they say it, and the other, a little less direct, is in what other participants say or imply about them. The latter must be taken into account. One thinks of Socrates as fairly urbane and for the most part gentlemanly, but Polus speaks of him as boorish (461c). What are we to make of that? Again, one thinks of Socrates as forceful, courageous, and civic-minded, but the abuse strewn on him by Callicles would scarcely convince the reader of this view. Whether he was right or wrong, Callicles was neither light-hearted nor blinded by fanaticism. What the participants, moreover, think of their companions, as shown by their words, not actions, strongly colors the philosophic debates.[3]

Because Socrates does most of the talking, one picks up almost as many clues regarding his respondents from him as from what they themselves say, and often those clues seem more trustworthy. As a single warp thread runs through the criss-crossing woof strands, modi-fying their shape a little and in turn being modified by them, so Socra-tes traverses and penetrates the thoughts and personalities of his oppo-nents, making and being forced to make changes in his approach to them, especially in the earlier stages of each discussion. Gorgias, Polus, and Callicles occasionally react to each other, urging, berating, chiming in, or repudiating. There are the obvious personal remarks, and there are also general assertions put forward, together with re-sponses either narrowing the discourse to a mere dig at a proponent's character, or else broadening it from an expression of preference or dis-taste to a statement far wider in scope than the remark calling it forth.

Because the idea of a conflict, as opposed to a feast, is the topic first encountered in the dialogue and because these two are parceled out be-tween what turns out to be the two main contenders, it will be well to refer to the persons who might be engaged in them, in case the unity of the dialogue should somehow lie in this contrast. Callicles chides Soc-rates for being too late for a feast; and it is evident that he means a feast for everyone, that Gorgias is entertaining and enthralling *all* the guests, and that Socrates would have been among those so gratified. But for whom is meant the battle or war? Let us consider the pairs:

First, between Gorgias and the day's audience. There is no indication that the audience on hand dislikes or disapproves of what Gorgias has had to say, and the unspoken premise of the dialogue is that the audi-ence *does* like what Gorgias is displaying.

Second, between Gorgias and Polus. This becomes a possibility when Polus wants at the very outset to run away with the argument, that he thinks he can replace Gorgias and satisfy Chaerephon (and pre-sumably Socrates as well), and at the end of the first colloquy suspects that Gorgias has betrayed himself and rhetoric too through a needless concession. Yet it is hard to believe that Callicles and Socrates can antic-ipate this at 447a. Moreover, it is against Gorgias' own claim that he makes his pupils to be like himself.

Third, between Gorgias and Callicles. There is a hint of this later on, when Gorgias is losing (458d), and Callicles says he has never enjoyed a conversation so much; and still later (497b) when Gorgias urges Callicles to continue, even though it is increasingly evident that the young man is about to suffer the fate of Gorgias. There appears to be a real reluctance on the part of Gorgias to follow Callicles in his choice of a life style. Again, it is unlikely that Callicles refers to what may emerge so many pages later on, and nothing in the Prologue suggests that although Gorgias is his guest, Callicles knows his views and propensities very well. Callicles holds Gorgias in respect at the beginning.

Fourth, between Gorgias and Socrates. Here Callicles perceives a philosophic difference between the two, but *feast* is his word, *battle* that of Socrates, who at the outset appears not to know Gorgias. Callicles has, it is true, seen Socrates conversing with young boys, but he does not take philosophic talk seriously and would merely think of an argument between Socrates and Gorgias as a sham battle.

Fifth, between Polus and the audience. The young colt might disagree with the audience in his evaluation of Gorgias as the best, but there is no hint of this anywhere in the discussion, and no reason for Socrates to think that such a disagreement might turn up.

Sixth, between Polus and Callicles. If they are both pupils of Gorgias, then a rivalry is likely for his approval, and probably political rivalry is in store for them in the future. On the other hand, it would take Callicles only a short time to size up the weaknesses of Polus, a man hardly worth challenging.

Seventh, between Polus and Socrates. The mercurial nature of Polus might annoy Socrates, but except for a couple of admonitions, Socrates never lets the strife with Polus erupt into warfare; and what Callicles would consider the inadequacy of Polus as thinker against himself might be transferred to his assessment of the way Socrates would view him as well.

Eighth, between Callicles and the audience. Because the audience is without doubt representative of *hoi polloi*, the deme, surely Callicles would not wish on this occasion, when no political action is at stake, to antagonize them.

Ninth, between Socrates and the audience. This can be dismissed out of hand.

Tenth, between Socrates and Callicles. These are the only two (outside of Gorgias and Polus) who, we can be sure, have known each other reasonably well. If so, the feast still refers to the enjoyment of Gorgias' display, the battle would be one with Callicles, who has very likely shown his disapproval for Socrates' apparent withdrawal from politics, and although there are later expressions of friendliness and admiration on both sides, these have little weight, being but preludes to almost un-restrained abuse.

Probably the best answer is to construct a sliding scale. Callicles is shrewd enough to accept Socrates' word *battle* as applying to himself and Socrates; later, as matters proceed, Callicles' remark is extended, first over Polus and then over Gorgias, so that in effect they become subordinate antagonists to Socrates, and in a still lesser sense they become antagonistic to Callicles himself on the side. But neither Callicles nor Socrates could know this with any confidence in the first little inter-change in the dialogue.

Merely because the speakers converse with and about each other (as opposed to a succession of unconnected soliloquies and asides) is no ground to assume any genuine literary unity. It may suggest such a unity, but more is needed. And simply because one can summarize the three major sections of the work in a succession of triads of opinions, one cannot fully establish the unity sought for. If in a hardware store Smith bought a claw hammer, Jones a hex wrench, and Brown a floor polisher, we cannot establish any close relation between these men except to say they were all customers. If one bought a ladder, another a bucket of paint, and the third a brush, some likeness of purpose could be proven, though all three might not brighten the same building. Were Smith to purchase some white paint and the other two the same, this unanimity of choice would *help* to show that their projects were on the same house. But despite a common principle, Gorgias, Polus, and Callicles do not say the same thing, nor do their views completely harmonize; and there need be no fear of a bogus unity as if they did.

A leading principle separating Socrates from his three opponents is the distinction between art and pandering; art aims at the best, pandering at pleasure, both of these effects being lodged in persons other than the speaker, but both of them also reflecting back upon that speaker. Pandering must be judged not only for what it does to the audience, making them pleasure-bound, heedless of the best, but also for the way it affects the panderers themselves. Because it is without *logos*, a sense of connected causes, and without a sense of what is best, it renders Gorgias, for instance, scarcely able to carry on a conversation with Socrates, much less refute him. He is poorly equipped first to offer any account of his own alleged art without much prompting or to offer a consistent account, even when prompting of every kind is freely given. Hence it is Gorgias himself who stands in need of improving, just as much as his audience. Similar conclusions can be reached regarding the other two rhetors.

The principle relating them, and from which the rest of their opinions are proliferated, is that the value of rhetoric lies in its connection with power, interpreted in terms of results gained for the speakers, but this time devolving back upon the audiences. For Gorgias, his art has a power; for Polus, the master of the art has a power, and for Callicles the man of strength has a power regardless of the way he uses the art, although that is doubtless the only art of discourse worth considering. The interplay of the Socratic principle with that of the rhetors largely determines the subject matter of the conversations and the methods whereby Socrates seeks to overcome—cynics would say, overwhelm— those ranged against him. Since we have regularly discussed this opposition and interplay, we leave the bulk of the Socratic features of the discussion in temporary abeyance, even though it means falling back for the time being on the triads of opinions that we have said suggest but do not completely prove a unity.

In accord with the main rhetorical principle, the aim for Gorgias is freedom, to be gained in a political context only through counsel well received, whether really good or not. For Polus it is impunity in spite of willful wrongdoing, using every available courtroom trick. For Callicles it is first political supremacy and then its pleasurable perquisites, the way to attain both being through an uneasy and ill-specified mixture of accommodation to and molding of popular wishes.

We might add that for Gorgias there is need for rhetoric in order best to gain power; for Polus the main problem is how to employ that same rhetoric in order to gain power most quickly; with Callicles the question becomes one of the uses of power already gained with some aid from rhetoric. Gorgias thinks of rhetoric as an art, while Polus seems to care little, after his first few lines in the Prologue and in the opening page or two of his colloquy, whether it is an art or not (he does not rally to defend rhetoric against its description as a pandering); for him, rhetoric is a tool, happiness the final product. Callicles, too, looks upon rhetoric as a means to an end, but assumes that it is only one of many, education being another means, good birth still another.[4] For Gorgias pleasure is a tool, since the appeal to desires of the audience is a carrot on a stick, and a way to winning more of its members.[5] For Polus pleasure is an accompaniment to the power of a ruler, but happiness (which he conceives hazily at best) is the chief aim, not pleasure. For Callicles, early in his turn with Socrates, pleasure is an end to be cultivated as assiduously as power itself.

One may also note three chief headings under which the speaker is discussed: the rhetor in reference to himself, then the rhetor as teacher or as pupil, and finally the rhetor in relation to his opponents. The Prologue certifies that Gorgias thinks of himself as a master, not only as having discovered or learned the appropriate rules and devices but also in the sense of being a teacher to all and sundry who come to him for instruction. Gorgias never doubts his role as the practitioner of an art that regularly makes him superior to exponents of other arts. Polus agrees fully, adding that the rhetor necessarily obtains what he wills. Callicles makes no mention of his own practice—he does not, in his first and longest speech (482c–486d), explicitly contrast the rhetor-politician with the philosopher. When he says pointedly that there are no good rhetors of the present, it is not merely a sullen, gratuitous thrust at his eminent guest but his way of saying that the rhetor should be free from the sense of modesty or shame which Callicles thinks has inhibited Gorgias and Polus, and which Callicles is sure that Socrates lacks.

Two main aspects of the teacher-pupil relationship are treated in this dialogue, one being the epistemic side, having to do with the transfer of knowledge or of opinion from one man to another. Matching that is the ethico-political side. From the rhetor's standpoint the pupil is a member of an audience, a listener to be influenced, however much he will eventually become a speaker himself. In the mind of Gorgias, little difference exists between the pupil and others of this audience, for the pupil is waiting, like everyone else, to be impressed and led, although careful instruction of the Socratic sort is hardly necessary—one might say hardly desirable.[6]

There are four spheres where knowledge of what is best is applicable, and none of these four is readily open to rhetors, chiefly because they merely practice some routine based upon familiarity without being able to define their own subjects. These four are the city, discourse, the rhetors themselves, and the cosmos.

In the city, the rhetors mistake the advantages gained from past successes for real goods, and are ill-equipped to know what is best, rather than most showy, or easy, or most enhancing of their status.

In the forms of human discourse, they cannot separate out knowledge, which is necessarily true, from belief or opinion, which may be false. Hence their stock of cognitions is no stronger than its weaker parts, the beliefs, and can be reduced to such beliefs.[7] The discourse is differentiated only by rhetorical considerations of persuasive and dissuasive devices, sections of the speech, circumstances under which one speaks, and so on.

Since gratification by word or deed is the end of his discourse, the rhetor cannot reckon as a benefit the practicing of an art for the sake of painful rectification of their own ills; such an improving can be had only by serious probing, such as that which Socrates reminds Polus resembles a physician's harsh but beneficial treatment. (Polus and Callicles both become unresponsive and bored when Socrates is on the point of winning them over to the importance of self-correction.)

The cosmic order consists of proportionate values as much as it does of measures of quantity, thus geometrical language can be used to describe moral situations as well as sidereal stations and movements. The rhetors are ignorant of such mathematical discourse employed to establish relations between real natures. This is no issue with Gorgias; Polus has adopted a contrary, "Anaxagorean" view (465c–d); and Callicles thinks such speculations unworthy of a mature man (484c). Socrates tries to establish some conception of the right order, but because his opponents are unwilling to listen he finds difficulty in moving them to do the same.

Why does Plato not make the relation between Gorgias and Polus explicitly a teacher-pupil relation? Gorgias, for example, does not coach Polus in ways to combat Socrates, nor does he, except for one small occasion (463e), voice approval or disapproval of the young man's efforts, something any teacher would be expected to do under the circumstances. Nor is it clear whether Callicles is a pupil or has even known Gorgias before this visit. Possibly Plato did not wish to make Polus a real pupil in the Socratic sense, or, for that matter, to accord to Gorgias the status of real teacher. Could a man of the stamp of Gorgias set up a true pedagogic relation with *any* neophyte? There is little in his relations with Polus and Callicles answering to the subtle depiction of the lover-beloved harmony which is identical with the proper relation between teacher and pupil in the *Phaedrus* (251c–257b, especially 256a–d). Certainly there is little or nothing in the three rhetors' discourses to hint, let along assert, that their talk resembles the discourse between Socrates and Theaetetus. Perhaps Plato means to show the reader, without having anyone say it, that Polus and Callicles are both believers in and imitators of Gorgias, but not learners. There is no reason to think that they would adhere to step-by-step argument; none would have been received from Gorgias. Imitating actions or language without knowing reasons does not make a student, only a follower.

So far as ethico-political aspects of the teacher-pupil relation are concerned, we notice certain ambivalences in each of the rhetors. Gorgias eagerly takes credit for having large numbers of pupils, probably in every town he has visited, but shies away, whether in advance of or after unpleasant experiences not reported, from full responsibility for their misapplications of the skills he has imparted. Polus is glad both to be seen in the company of his distinguished elder and to flatter him, yet gives no credit for having actually learned from him. And where Gorgias is frightened that he himself will be tried and banished if his pupil misuses rhetoric, Polus consoles himself that if the rhetor *really* behaves unjustly, making irresponsible speeches and committing fratricide and the rest, he will at length place himself beyond the reach of the enemies whom this gross misconduct has made. He says nothing about the blame that would rest upon his teacher—this would no doubt be a mere trifle to the new tyrant, who would not blink at incarcerating—or worse—any former instructor scrupling at the latest course of events. Callicles, after being tamed by Socrates, appears to settle for a highly circumscribed version of a just use of rhetoric; the rhetor is a decent man against whom unjust charges may be brought, and in a lawcourt he would plead justly a defense which ought by the laws of the city to exonerate him. The fact that Gorgias repeats his disclaimer of responsibility (456e; 457b–c; 460d), that Polus cannot perceive the need to seek purgation of political error and guilt (477d), and that Callicles reiterates his own worry about the possibility that either he himself or Socrates will be brought to trial or otherwise endangered (486a–b; 486c; 509c–d; 511a; 511c; 521c), suggests that the entire dialogue is, among other things, a study in political cowardice and courage. The three rhetors praise the latter, though they may lack it themselves.

The position of Polus in this succession of moral stances is unusual, and a case may be made for each of two readings. One, the more popular, would have Polus a stepping-stone between Gorgias and Callicles, while the other would make him an extreme opposite of Gorgias, with Callicles now being a compromise between the two. As proof that he is intermediate is the fact that Gorgias, uninterested in changing the constitutional structures, works wholly within them, using the courts and tribunals in a way close to conservative.[8] Callicles initially puts his superior man above institutions and adherents of law and in this sense overturns the government. Polus, in between, would expect the rhetor to use existing ranks, working with them, but making sure that he could advance, preferably at a single leap, to the point where others would be unable to dislodge him. Again, there is the decreasing involvement in ordinary politics. For Gorgias the end is freedom, conceived as the possibility of movement between social classes; for Polus it is freedom only in the first stage, when the rhetor and would-be tyrant is trying to find the class to which he aspires; and for Callicles freedom is to rise above all social classes, in a wholly individualistic venture. For Callicles, whatever political means are used will be for an unpolitical end.

To buttress the opinion that Polus is, however, wholly opposite to Gorgias (thus forcing Callicles to be intermediary), one could show that where Gorgias looks to Pericles and Themistocles (455e) as exemplars of good rhetoric, Polus chooses a Macedonian Macbeth as illustration of the good life. Callicles at first calls upon Heracles (a man of muscle rather than of silver tongue), but soon settles upon Pericles and others of ancient renown like him, becoming almost as moderate as Gorgias in this regard.[9] One can almost hear Gorgias saying, Woe to the rhetor who breaks the law, while Polus is saying, Woe to him who does *not* break the law. Callicles, again compromising, says, Woe to the man, whether lawbreaker or not, who cannot rescue himself.[10]

Thus the position of Polus in this trio is hard to fix upon if one fails to make this distinction: In the emphasis upon rhetorical and political arts, Polus is indeed in the middle, he points up a transition; in reference to the good life, he is a high-riding maverick, whose views counter those of Gorgias, only to be tamed by Callicles.

Having spoken of the way the three see themselves as rhetors and men, and of their status as teachers or pupils, we turn to their relations to their opponents, and here this is a matter of winning or losing.

In the private gathering before us, Gorgias, Polus, and Callicles are depicted as set off against a mightier figure, and so they must practice their knack as best they can against this formidable and, in the only good sense, implacable adversary. They cannot really speak as they would in their lawcourts and assemblies or in the houses of fee-paying admirers, although to their credit they try manfully though fitfully to conform to new rules of question and answer. As it is, Gorgias cannot continue to preen himself on his talents or his art, and Polus cannot unlimber without admonitory restraint the phrases written in his chrestomathy and fixed in his otherwise spotty memory; nor can Callicles now get the ear of the rich, the powerful, and the pleasure-ridden, for it is not they who are conversing with him. Socrates is not introduced as a prospective patron, he is a ninny in practical politics (473e–474a), hence of no assistance to men wishing to get ahead in Athens, and he is a model of self-control most of the time during the long battle-argument. Not only are the orators-by-nature inhibited by his peculiar combination of poised immobility and driving momentum but they must also recognize that this man masters their own knack to better advantage than ever they can, and with an avowedly different aim.

Ultimately, Socrates provokes Callicles without any expressed intent to do so by relentless questioning about the other's scheme of living. We would say that this is Socratic dialectic, but that flourishes best where *both* parties are dedicated not to the exposition of putative truths already secured but to the joint discovery of truths as yet only dimly perceived.[11] Short of such a capacity and mood, the questionings that under better circumstances would open pathways to truth are merely stepping-stones to the enunciation of contrary doctrines having a rhetorical impact.

The question whether Socrates wins over his opponents, one, two, or all three, is thus a taxing one, and we must preface our attempt at an answer with some observations regarding the possibilities. If A were to fight B and wound him in a just cause (to set down conditions that Socrates himself might require), then A would be defeating B, no doubt, so long as A himself remained relatively unscathed. But that begs the question, unless we adopt a wholly neutral stance. Readers of the other dialogues frequently assume that Socrates is intended to be a clear winner. In the *Protagoras*, however, he ends by having drawn a tie, at least in the mind of the distinguished sophist; in the shorter dialogues, despite brilliant refutations, he is almost invariably unsuccessful in convincing his feckless respondents. In the *Parmenides* he is a young man ardently committed to a theory that he will continue to reinterpret and support in several versions throughout his life—and is roundly squelched. So if any of this were to happen in the *Gorgias*, readers would not need to show surprise. But again, defeat in the *Gorgias* could not be so clearcut either.

Winning is not always refuting, nor is losing always being refuted. If both parties agree that purely rational arguments are to be used, then the successful refuter who does not obstruct himself while bringing down his game wins. If, however, the parties are partly motivated by social, monetary, political, or psychological considerations (as they are so abundantly in the *Gorgias*), then refuting may not carry with it a clear victory.

1. If A uses valid arguments conceded point by point without reservation by B, then A wins, even if emotions obtrude, when not strong enough to overpower the logic of the arguments.
2. If A causes B to concede, using loose but emotionally effective arguments whose defects B does not notice, then A still wins, but in a different sense. To win an argument charged with emotion on either side or on both sides is very different from refuting an opponent's logic. [12]
3. If A causes B to concede, yet for some reason merely overpowers B while using arguments whose validity B can see but cannot question, then A scores a limited victory, again on personal rather than rational grounds, *except* insofar as A intended to raise the emotional intensity to the point where B could no longer oppose him, in which case his choice of weapons is completely successful.
4. If A cannot make B concede, but uses valid arguments while B does not, then A wins, but never in a personal sense.
5. If A cannot make B concede because A uses defective arguments, then B clearly wins if he is logical in his own cause.
6. If A cannot make B concede and uses weak arguments, but B, not seeing their weakness, still resists because of sheer stubbornness, then from the outsider's point of view A still wins.

7. If when A and B argue and B in his frustration injures A, then B in a sense wins the argument *if* A has been trying to convince him of the need for virtuous self-restraint, otherwise not (cf. 520c–d).

These cases are merely illustrative but by no means exhaustive, and more than one of them fits the *Gorgias*. Critics are divided between (1) and (2) as characterizing all or parts of the dialogue, though the testing by means of exercises in pure logic, whether that of Aristotle or the Stoics or any of their modern counterparts and conflators, seem to us beside the point unless used in conjunction with a psychosocial analysis of the participants and circumstances of the dialogue. Whether Socrates defeats anyone rests not solely upon whether the debate is conducted with a tight, irrefragable logic. Again, the question whether (3) applies to Socrates' encounter with Gorgias is answered by Polus and Callicles differently from the way a good many modern readers would answer it. The victory of Socrates over Callicles is at best one described in (4). Some readers would aver that (6) applies to the entire dialogue, but we deny this, believing as we do that the Socratic arguments are sufficiently strong to carry conviction, even when classical syllogistic or a modern calculus of propositions finds discrepancies here and there. Furthermore, if there are in fact such difficulties, Socrates' position need not be fundamentally wrong. Tinkering might well set all the proofs right, without significantly altering his case, and we need not accept the view of Gorgias and his copartners in the debate.

Neither Polus nor Callicles fully recognizes having been defeated, but both are well aware that Gorgias has failed to make his case, and offer what is at least verbally the same explanation, that through modesty or shame he has been unwilling to make certain admissions. It is important for Gorgias that Callicles repeats the same general charge against Polus as well. When Callicles describes Gorgias as too modest, he is apparently referring to his principles; the same accusation against Polus concerns their applications. Gorgias was not radical enough, for he should have asserted more boldly that he was not responsible for his pupil's injustices. (Would a superior man above the chattering crowd deign to assume such a responsibility?) Polus went astray, not seeing that the rhetor-tyrant was not unjust but free from all restraints of justice and injustice. Incidentally, Callicles makes this double accusation early; we doubt that he would voice it after the first twenty pages of his debate with Socrates. In the setting where it occurs, it applies doubly to Gorgias, as practitioner first and then as teacher, assuming, as Callicles may be assuming, that Polus is indeed a pupil. Has Gorgias not said that he makes his pupils *everywhere* to be like himself? His worry is that they could be unjust although he has not advocated injustice. Certainly

Callicles and perhaps Polus could be troubled that Gorgias has passed on to them his own inhibitions that seriously cramp exercise of their theories of the superiority of injustice or its irrelevance. And when Polus says (462a) that he knows all that Gorgias knows (which to him is a great deal, though to Socrates Gorgias obviously *knows* little enough), the implication is that Gorgias has in the past generously emptied his whole scattered theory of rhetoric, as well as his bag of tricks, into the lap of Polus. What Socrates must do, then, is show up the discontinuities in Polus' versions of the views of Gorgias, culminating in his praise of a monstrous Archelaus.

To understand the rhetor's estimate of the debate, one might picture the scene ten minutes after Socrates had ended. He and Chaerephon would have taken their departure, and the little audience would be breaking up, stretching, yawning after the long and patient hours. Gorgias would say, of course, that he was glad the discussion had been brought to a conclusion, though not quite the one he had expected. He might turn the tables by complaining that it was *Callicles* who in making too many needless admissions had thrown away the argument, and would derive some satisfaction from the drubbing that both Polus and Callicles had taken; he was not the only one to succumb. Polus would object that Socrates had used unfair tactics, such as myth telling, to win his argument, while he himself had used reliable history. In a moment of more than his ordinary acuteness he might say that the success of Socrates in concluding against rhetoric was itself a rhetorical success which proved the strength of rhetoric as an art—or familiarity, it did not matter. Callicles would then deny testily that Socrates had succeeded either in convincing him or in bringing the debate to a proper conclusion. His concessions to Socrates were made out of politeness and the need to hurry things along.

That, however, is not the only side. The discomfiture and defeat of Gorgias is threefold, including as it does the hard lesson learned as he watches Callicles, who is often appearing better educated and more literate and adroit than Gorgias himself but who is following out further implications of the principles laid down about rhetoric and power. Plato hints that Gorgias is never far from the center of the dialogue by having him join in again (463d) after Polus has interrupted, and by having him urge Callicles to continue the discussion to its proper conclusion (497b). Gorgias' hope for the other two to continue is again through mixed motives: (a) he realizes that they may make a poor showing, Polus after his weak beginning in the Prologue and Callicles because he is *not* a regular pupil but an unknown quantity who may yet triumph over Socrates; (b) even though he may be held partly responsible he would like to see Polus and Callicles defeated *if* they say anything outrageous, which he might well suspect they would; (c) he doubtless holds out hope, even so, that they will not be overcome by Socrates and will thus justify his own long career; (d) his curiosity regarding Socrates' tactics has been aroused, for he can surely perceive as well as Callicles can (481c) that Socrates is turning human life upside down.

The force keeping the three rhetors from admitting real defeat is the confidence that their own *empeiria*, or *tribē*, is really above refutation, above defeat in the sort of battle that Socrates can wage. It is like love or vaulting ambition; it cannot be refuted in their own eyes through enforced self-contradiction. Rhetoric, to all three men, is mainly the persuading of large audiences in lawcourts and assemblies (454b; 471e; 485a), and there would be small chance for Socrates' elaborate interrogations to get started at all in such public settings, nor much chance of humiliations. The situation at the present meeting is rather like those of larger gatherings, for there is indeed an audience for the display; but perhaps this audience does not follow all of the debating, nor thinks the rhetors come off second best. This is why Gorgias can have his contradictions exposed with *apparent* equanimity. It is also the reason why Callicles is able to concede point after sticky point, grudgingly, to be sure, and with the express reservation that he does not really believe what he says in making the concessions (495a; 501c; 510a; 513c; 514a; 516b; 516c; 522e).

There are also important respects in which the three rhetors refute each other, or, to be less sweeping, in which Polus and Callicles are the main refutative agents acting against Gorgias, with Socrates the occasion for bringing out and, as it were, underlining the damage they do. With Polus, a defect of intellect reduces, though without destroying, confidence in the opinion of Gorgias that rhetoric is the highest art and the greatest convenience. If Polus entertains favorable notions of an ungovernable tyrant-murderer and at the same time knows all that Gorgias knows (without claiming to know a great deal more besides), then clearly one must blame the doctrines of Gorgias himself. But Polus can be dismissed as an embryo academic, and it is Callicles who in his more strident moments leads one to conclude that here is defect of will as much as of intellect.

When Polus accuses Gorgias of having been ashamed to follow out his own theory this is refutation in the meager sense of flatly giving a cause for the contradiction, but it is hard to believe that Polus means that it is owing to underlying deficiencies in Gorgias' nature. Yet the latter's whole view of rhetoric's successful use hinges upon a willingness, either canny or headstrong, to rush in and persuade crowds of uninformed men regarding propositions of whose truth he is at best ignorant. Consequently, to accuse him of shame is to undercut his entire relation to his calling; it is not a technical but a moral criticism,[13] and one that Gorgias could ill afford to have leveled at him before an audience containing prospective pupils.

As we have said, then, the question of winning and losing in this dialogue is quite different from that of refuting and being refuted. The loser in three senses, but not in all, is Gorgias, but not entirely because of his inconsistency. First, he is shown up by Socrates in front of others for having insufficiently prepared himself to answer some of the most fundamental questions pertaining to his life's practice. Second, he sees his follower Polus opting for the life of an evil man at the cost of every respect for law and justice which Gorgias has never thrust aside but has simply not taken sufficiently into account. Third, he finds Callicles resorting not to plain argument but to unfriendly portraiture and insults, and claiming that justice is invented by the weak, has no place in the best life, something that Gorgias has little sought. It is his own honor, then, that hangs on the thread of this discourse. Socrates makes it clear that the man willfully misusing so powerful a weapon as rhetoric, even if he succeeds in the city, bears a heavy burden on his soul. Though Polus and Callicles are often in effect caricatures of Gorgias' position, the overturning of their claims means the overturning of his own as well. It is reasonable, therefore, for Gorgias' name and not one of theirs to serve as title of the dialogue, despite his having a speaking role half that of Polus and less than a quarter that of Callicles.

One may object that Plato has stacked the cards against the rhetors by deliberately making them ineffective antagonists to Socrates: Gorgias, too conservative and complacent, Polus, too scatterbrained in his radical position, Callicles, too divided against himself. Several answers are possible. To begin with, Plato was choosing the best of their breed, as any Athenian would be likely to have recognized. Does not Socrates say that they are the three wisest of the Greeks (527a)? But again, from a present-day vantage point one need not suppose that rhetors are necessarily superior men, free of all flaws, and indeed Plato seems to have discovered that a propensity to exploit rhetoric goes hand in hand with a superficial grasp of fundamental political matters. Another fact is that Socrates himself is presented in this dialogue (as well as in the others) as an excellent man, but certainly not perfect. Finally, Plato could also create or make use of better-equipped opponents to Socrates: Protagoras, Glaucon, Adeimantus, Simmias, Cebes, Theaetetus, and a few more. Not all but certainly most of the foils to the philosophical protagonists of dialogues by other authors are slow-witted or passive by comparison to the three rhetors of the *Gorgias*.

We might summarize by saying that the three men, presumably the best in their common interest and most dedicated in their general aspirations, give in to the Socratic elenchus, Gorgias politely if a little passively,[14] Polus reluctantly, and Callicles in a mood of angry resentment, all of them withholding full assent. Callicles is defeated verbally; but the aim of Socrates to convince and improve him is turned back because of Callicles' mixed loves (513c–d), and the reader finishes the dialogue with the uncomfortable feeling that Socrates may eventually suffer some of the evils that his opponent describes and predicts—and that this same opponent may be at least partly responsible. In the absence of a fullfledged victory such as we see in the Republic, where even Thrasymachus is made tractable (I, 354a; V, 450a), one has to fall back on a verdict of limited—decidedly limited—victory for Socrates here. He cannot establish the intellectual and emotional conditions under which his most rigorous dialectic would be used and render him the obvious conqueror, both in logic and his aims at bettering the minds and lives of his respondents. On the other hand, he uses the second string to his bow very effectively. Even if he cannot entirely overcome his antagonists but only restricts them in their rhetorical exercises, he yet establishes himself as a model whom one day they might consider worth emulating. A limited victory, then, not Pyrrhic but never clearcut—except that Plato wanted, we believe, to show that life does not always make way for coherent arguments and unswerving virtue. There is always some hope, of course, that bad human beings will turn good; and where that hope proves to be in vain, three new gods, who themselves have had a human career, will be ready to judge naked souls of all the dead.

The Speech

Because for Gorgias rhetoric is used in a fairly stable social group and is the superior art, it can replace the other arts to accomplish their same purposes. This claim is not, within the Gorgias colloquy, really refuted, for the issue turns (456c) from the apparent efficacy of rhetoric to its justification as a social practice. Socrates does counter the claim, however, as soon as Polus repeats it, first implicitly by marking rhetoric as an imitation of an art, then more openly by saying that everyone, not only the rhetor-tyrant, has the power to commit infinite mischief, like the man with a concealed dagger in the agora (469c–e). The implication, quite contrary to that of Gorgias, is that rhetoric achieves its truest, most appropriate use only when one intends to do evil. Callicles, like his two houseguests, thinks of rhetors as superior to all other men, though Socrates argues that there are plenty of craftsmen who do more for the city and are far more modest as well (511c–512d). Rhetoric is chiefly useful not for escaping its consequences of evil-doing but for rescuing oneself—so Callicles thinks—in case some inferior person should bring false charges.

The means of communication in all these interpretations of the "art" is the actual speech, and it is conducted, regardless of the speaker and of his audience, in certain obligatory ways. They might be termed technicalities, except that they are more fundamental than (for instance) introduction, exposition, defense, topics, and the like.[15] A speech *must* be either long or short (even if the length or shortness is not specified), it *must* be in the form of question or answer (or both), and it *must* either propose and substantiate a statement or argue against and refute it; in addition, it *must*, if it is to arouse an audience, contain expressions construable as praise or censure. Subsequent and subsidiary to this, the speaker can decide whether to use narrative, whether to introduce authorities and witnesses, and the like.

In the *Gorgias*, all four of these more fundamental aspects of speech-making are both treated as subject matter for comment and abundantly illustrated as well. The participants ask questions freely and also comment upon them, sometimes by asking questions about questioning, sometimes by making assertions about assertions. In speeches either short or long they talk of short and long speeches. They refute by means of questions and by means of answers.[16]

Thus there is a double focus, for much is said about speaking and speeches, and even more is illustration. When Gorgias commences by saying (449b–c) that he can speak equally well briefly or at length, the reader is allowed to judge whether this is true, for Gorgias responds to proddings by Socrates, and one wonders why he does not fare better since he considers himself an old hand at answering questions from his audience, questions naturally both rapid-fire and highly varied. Polus seems more ill at ease when required to be brief and stumbles each time he launches upon his major claims. Because he is not permitted by Socrates to speak at any length, we cannot know whether he would hit his stride if allowed to run loose. At the beginning, he falls back on his own writing, which confers smoother expression but certainly not closer relevance upon what he says. When Callicles at last intervenes, he speaks at some length (482c–486d), neither requesting permission nor justifying himself, and the issue of long and short is no longer made prominent. Indeed, there is considerable debate not over whether Callicles will talk too long but over his willingness to talk enough—that he will break off even though uninterrupted. Nor is the issue any longer that of who will ask, who will answer; it turns more to the question of whether refutation will be efficacious in bringing agreement. The style shifts farther and farther from the restraint accorded by Gorgias and Socrates to each other, to disparagement and abuse.

As for the content of the questions, this varies, and such variation is in accord with Socrates' changing purposes. Of Gorgias he asks simply who he is and what profession he follows (this is not asked of the rhetor directly). In the second main section (461b–481b), it is Polus, not Socrates, who poses the chief question: What is your account of rhetoric? (462b), and again, Do you think that good rhetors are thought to be panderers in their cities, hence worthless (466a)? When this latter has been subdivided into two other questions, pandering drops out so far as Polus is concerned. After the philippic of Callicles against philosophers, Socrates poses three new queries (488b): Should the stronger lead the weaker? Should the better rule the worse? and, Should the nobler have more than the base? Both Socrates and Callicles would, of course, answer all three in the vigorous affirmative, but differ totally on the meaning of each term. The main difference is then crystallized in the new question, How ought we to live (492d)?[17] In turn, this subdivides into three (500c): Whether there are two lives? How are they different? and, Which life should I choose? There is a steady progression of Socrates' questions from one regarding a presumed art and career of another man to a problem at the core of the philosopher's own life, not with respect to arts and their imitations but instead to virtues and their contraries.

Let us now explore a little further the matter of length of discourse, which in discussion and by example is made such a serious issue in the dialogue. The trouble with long speechmaking from the Socratic standpoint is not so much its mere length as such; throughout the dialogues there is scarcely any reference, except at the end, to the pressing shortness of time. A long speech shuts up any opposition, closes the mind of the speaker, and allows for illicit shifting of meanings before he can be called to account. (a) The hearer is honor-bound not to interrupt and raise objections to the steps and their connections; (b) the attitude of the speaker, who has insulated himself from those objections, is doubtless hardened by the very adopting of a position; (c) the speaker in a long speech is more likely to shift, intentionally or not, from one meaning of a key term to another. If to be refuted when one is entertaining and promulgating a falsehood is the benefit that Socrates avers it is (470c), then the man speaking at length would in a sense resemble the unjust man with soul unpurged or at best partly purged of the effects of his injustice.

The tendency of Polus to make speeches in place of discussing (whether questioning or answering) is doubly unappealing to Socrates, for Polus is barely interested either in Socrates' manner of life or in his ideas. Callicles, on the other hand, is at least attentive to Socrates and his way of living, however much he disapproves. When he decries the prolonged preoccupation with philosophy, a speech (482c–486d) dwarfing in duration all that Polus has attempted, Socrates does nothing to stop him, but troubles to comment upon it at length. May one suppose that the notice that Callicles pays is symptomatic of his genuine if intermittent concern for other minds and that Socrates recognizes this as at least a first requisite for fruitful discussion? The tacit admission that Callicles could speak for so long, whereas Polus and Gorgias could not, indicates some marked difference in the personal or intellectual relations, or both, between Socrates and his third opponent. This despite Callicles' highly tendentious remarks about Socrates.

Logical analysis alone has born many fruits in elucidating Plato's text; but, as we have tried to show here, it cannot altogether master this dialogue. Such analysis reduced every utterance to a kind of dead level, making it function as a premise or conclusion or corollary, or whatever. Determining the cogency of an argument then hinges upon the translating of what is said into a set of propositions each member of which must have a single value, namely T or F (usually the former) placed upon it. But this reduction is likely to carry one away from the range of participants in the *Gorgias*, where each utterance, be it a five-page speech or a five-word exclamation, is believed in part by one person, disbelieved by another, evaluated by a third, and these either faintly or strongly, plainly or with reservations, and all colored with a multitude of personal feelings. These have much to do in determining the final outcome, which means that rhetorical analysis can run separately and sometimes entirely counter to the logical. The logic of the *Organon*, marvelous as it is, rests upon quite different conceptions of simple expressions, propositions, and syllogisms, whether these last be demonstrative, dialectical, or sophistical. The logic of Descartes, which is really a method presumed to be applicable to all sciences, rests upon clear and distinct ideas and their use in long chains of reasoning. That of Spinoza (who in his coupling of method with morals is perhaps closest to Plato) makes use of adequate ideas conferring their adequacy in turn upon ideas immediately following, in a string of "geometrical" proofs. Both kinds of ideas Plato would have applauded but would have recognized that they were so perfect as to be unattainable in ordinary thinking and discourse. Plato would not have cared to break into the tight circle of Hegel's logic, leaving as it does little opportunity for deviation, short-cutting, fresh inspiration, all of which figure prominently in the dialogues. The grand discovery must remain Hegel's alone, whereas for Plato it is most often a cooperative affair though the contributors play diverse and unequal roles. The logic of Whitehead-

Russell, again, assumes at the outset that proposition p is a dummy, to be manipulated in almost endless ways in relation to itself, its negation, other propositions q and r, and a small handful of logical constants. To Plato, on the other hand, the sentence must always *say* something, hence the terms and their countless possible meanings become the focus of dialectical exploration. Wittgenstein's early resolve to look at meanings and resemblances between meanings would fit the dialogues, though his truth tables are more nearly Stoic than Platonic; but his reduction of the mind to propositions (such that when we say that the man A says the proposition p it really reduces to p's saying p)[18] would be wholly unacceptable to Plato and thus of doubtful value in explicating the dialogues. In a word, then, the proper study of Platonism is Plato, even though other logical theories are of the highest value in themselves and open up enormous tracts of exact thinking in other philosophic systems.

Without question Socrates wishes his arguments to be sound, but he also has a pressing, overriding concern to rid Athenian streets of rhetors of the baser kind. His fulfilling or neglecting to fulfill strict logical requirements would not be detected by his opponents in the present case.[19] Gorgias himself says (456b) that he is more persuasive to a patient than is the doctor. The irony is that Socrates in turn is somewhat more successful than the expert rhetor, not in cajoling the patient but in persuasive speech to the professional persuaders.

Audiences

Many kinds of audiences are mentioned in the *Gorgias*: crowds, rulers, educated Athenians, the human and divine judges of the dead, pupils, children, members of the Assembly, and so forth. Some of these persons are easy to convince by offering them pleasures, others impossible. Some are ignorant of the issues on which they are being addressed, others very knowledgeable. Some have personal attachments of various sorts, others are quite dispassionate. What they have in common is that they listen as parts of the audience and say nothing and that they are expected to take some action as a result of what they hear, usually different from what they intended beforehand. In such dialogues as the *Meno*, *Philebus*, and *Ion*, lines between speaker and audience are not nearly so clear-cut as in the *Critias*, *Symposium*, *Apology*, *Menexenus*, or even the first half of the *Phaedrus*. In the *Ion*, for example, Socrates becomes an audience of one each time Ion speaks, but in a more actively participative sense than usual; and he would become a passive, typical audience only if Ion were allowed to recite his beloved Homer at some length. The *Gorgias* sharply divides the Athenians gathered to listen from the three rhetors, Chaerephon, and Socrates, who are not at all dumbly receptive of what is being said, though each of the latter in his turn becomes a listener for a time. This is especially true when a speaker breaks away from the restriction to speak briefly (e.g., Gorgias 456a–457c; Socrates 464b–466a; Polus 471a–d; Callicles 482c–486d; Socrates 486e–488b; 506c–509c; 511c–513c; 517b–519d; 523a–527e). In one respect these are not *public* speeches at all, being primarily directed at one man at a time, but in another they are meant for the other participants and for the anonymous listeners assembled within the walls.[20]

Still another aspect of the speaker-audience relation in the *Gorgias*, but absent from the *Phaedrus* and the *Symposium*, is this: Gorgias, Polus, and Callicles all envision civic audiences beyond the one assembled for the day's feast, and the reader senses that the first of these three men is recalling, the other two are anticipating and practicing, how each could address an assembly or lawcourt. It is these larger, politically potent groups that the rhetors hope, and Socrates fears, they will get their hands on. Gorgias has done this repeatedly either directly to a political audience or group of pupils, or indirectly through a pupil to an audience. Polus, while he may later lapse into professional didacticism, now sees the rhetor-tyrant as somehow addressing the city, though chiefly in assemblies and perhaps also in lawcourts; intermediary pupils will be taken care of with his textbook. As for Callicles, his early concern is with the city as a whole, and only much later, after being forced to less and less aggressive philosophic positions, does he consider contending and appealing in the courts. For the most part there is simultaneous narrowing of the rhetor's possible arrangements and a broadening from specific audiences to the entire state as hearers.

One may look another way at the citizens. Gorgias considers roughly three classes of men with Socrates: (a) those who know and practice arts such as medicine, shoemaking, sculpture, and astronomy; (b) members of audiences at assemblies, in courts, and also chance hearers of display oratory, speeches of praise and aspersion, who then merely praise or blame the speaker afterwards for his efforts; and (c) the rhetors. For political purposes, this threefold division collapses into a two-part one: (a) men who compete for rule over others (i.e., masters who are free), and (b) those who do not, the slaves, though not in the most literal sense of wholly owned economic chattel. Thus the city's inhabitants are winners or losers. The power of rhetoric makes its possessor an infallible winner.

The audiences are therefore of many layers, these layers being the result of slicing in a number of ways. Each audience is a group, cohesive but by no means homogeneous; yet the multiple layers tend to merge as they are addressed by an effective speaker and to act as one, however different the motives animating each sector of the group may be. Indeed, there are respects in which the audiences themselves merge into one. They can be examined mainly through the eyes of the four speakers in the dialogue. For Gorgias, the wider society to which he always looks as his primary audience appears stable, though preparations for war must go forward, forts built and manned, warships commissioned. But the state is not overturned; the issues Gorgias speaks about are within the confines of government, everyone votes or shows his preferences in some public way. The craftsmen are the archetypal decent citizens, with the rhetor intruding and beating them on their own soil by means of his superior art. For Polus, society may be peaceable enough at times, but success goes to the hustler, the adventurer looking out for none but himself, the man who becomes a tyrant and can work his will upon everyone, commencing with his own family. It is an unstable world as contrasted with that of Gorgias, and the audiences will know less—much less—about the probable outcome of any line of political action. Society for Callicles is predatory through and through, for even philosophers who are exceptionally peaceable because they have abdicated their public tasks are targets for the unprincipled. In this disrupted city, every man can be subdued by the naturally stronger, yet the stronger is in turn subdued by the weaker men who band together. Even their enactment of laws is not a peaceable but a hostile act against the man having an inborn right to govern and exploit. It is small wonder, then, that Callicles, who thinks of Socrates as a driveler but still part of the Athenian crowd (has he not just come from the agora?), would treat him as abusively as he would secretly wish to treat the public for which Socrates stands as a kind of proxy.

As for economic classes in society, the situation that Gorgias discerns is confused, since we take him to be a successful friend of the rich, the man whose power of speech opens every door. On the other hand, in defining his own function, he associates himself with the craftsmen and men of science, while allowing himself to enslave the moneymaker (452e). Polus is ready to look for rich and poor but is interested in the one poor man (Archelaus is the son of a slave) who catapults himself into the seat of greatest power. Society, easily turned upside down in such a turmoil, is the setting that grants opportunity to the wily and unscrupulous and impressive. Callicles in his turn looks upon society as the hunting ground of the rich and wellborn who can convince the tyrants in an oligarchy, or the crowd in a democracy, that the aristocrats such as Callicles himself should be obeyed and pampered.

It is no surprise that the functions of rhetoric in these three versions of society should change according to this pattern. For Gorgias, rhetoric confers the greatest of benefits, bringing the advantage of a freer life—but only to the rhetor, outpacing every technician, artist, or expert by means of mesmeric speaking, with no fear of retribution unless his pupils, not he, should do some mischief. For Polus, the having of the power takes care of that possibility; the ruler merely lies some more, for his own protection. The assumption is that the audience and the city at large will enjoy, comply, and remain silent. For Callicles, rhetoric would enable the strong to realize their potentialities, as one among many evidences of ability and virtue. It is a paradox that for the man who has the least exaggeratedly glorified view of rhetoric, his own use of it would doubtless have the most damaging effect were he to pursue without pause or deviation the course which he has set himself. But there are many paradoxes in the *Gorgias*, generated mainly by the discrepancies between theory and practice when the theory is hollow, the practice unfair.

We have now made the best case that we can for the conviction that the three rhetors of themselves form a bond, a unity of sorts; but they are by no means the entire content, let alone structure, of the dialogue. What has been presented in this chapter is little more than indispensable materials employed to assert a unity; and although this examination will doubtless make our task easier, such scrutiny does not make it complete.

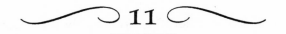

SOCRATES

One has only to glance at the many books and essays written about the character of Socrates as Plato depicts him to note the great variety of persons into whom he has been made by them. It would be a mistake, then, to try to give a simple character sketch, for each of these interpretations bears something of the truth. Part of the complexity in seeking an even-minded grasp of his nature arises from the many kinds of responses made to him by all the other participants in the two dozen or so authentic dialogues in which he is a principal figure. Accordingly, we began (in chapter 10) by dealing with the three interactions by the rhetors to this most unusual man, and now move to a consideration of what he is in himself, the demotic virtues he manifests, and finally that for which he is perhaps best known, his legendary self-knowledge.

Much to Plato's credit, he rarely presents Socrates simply as coming into a circle of disputants and asking questions few or many, resolving difficulties, putting objections to rest, and then leaving to the plaudits of the onlookers, their confusions dissipated, their mixed motives harmonized and elevated, their self-doubts wholly allayed.[1] Nor does Plato make him step into a group who at the outset totally despise him, and all philosophy as well, eventually to convince his enemies that he is the *kalokagathon* and that philosophy is eminently worthwhile. Plato treats Socrates above all as a man, in reasonably lifelike situations of mixed character both at the beginning and at the end of each dialogue; where he carries conviction to his respondents it is because of the unusual opportunity to show an extraordinary combination of cogent proof, sterling nature, and golden rhetoric, as in the *Republic* and *Symposium*. Even so, he is depicted as a man of superior intellectual curiosity, power of invention, and integrity with a most unusual gift for following an argument from start to finish. He can either discover a solution for the main problem or else show that no solution can be found, given the conditions of the inquiry. The *Gorgias* is no exception. Socrates is greeted with an empty choice between a feast and a battle, and is able after strenuous efforts only to subdue and silence his opponents, but gaining little of their concurrence, let alone hearty admiration.

To discover more about him in this dialogue one should scrutinize the partly friendly, partly hostile attitudes of those opponents, and only after that review what Socrates says of himself. Many of his co-participants look upon him as an inveterate asker of questions with few answers of his own to offer, a philosophical dialectician first and last, sometimes a hero before the crowd, a pattern of several virtues, invincible in argument, a little patronizing, to be sure, but ever a great if enigmatic personage. These attributions are not wrong, yet few of them besides inquisitiveness are offered directly and prominently in the *Gorgias*. In the arduous parade of these men, personal remarks are made, so that by the time Callicles comes to speak his piece, one has a rather clear portrait of Socrates, much of it unflattering, the small remainder at best ambiguous and grudgingly complimentary.

Socrates Himself

Plato goes to considerable length to impart freshness and unfamiliarity to the image of Socrates when he arrives at Callicles' gathering. He is made known as a philosopher only halfway into the dialogue, and then simply through Callicles' past acquaintance with and slighting opinion of him. Otherwise he is in time either for a feast or a battle, but anyone can savor the former or gird for the latter—this does not require a special custodian of truth.

Exactly what philosophy is for Socrates remains in the shadows until the last dozen pages of the *Gorgias*. In view of all the demands for definitions of rhetoric in the dialogue's first half, it would seem likely that at least one of the rhetors would demand to know either about the discussion (*dialegesthai*) that Socrates regards as different from and superior to rhetoric, or else about philosophy, whose good features must be gathered in a roundabout way, if at all, from the first forty or so pages of what seems to be bickering with Callicles.[2]

Socrates, however, is presented as a leader in the sort of discussion he proposes. With Gorgias it means that after hearing him out Socrates introduced more and more of his own distinctions, thereby controlling the dialectic. (We are taking *dialectic* now in the first of our two chief senses, that is, the way the structures of the concepts develop, whether by means of narrative, rhetorical address, or outright dialectical argument in the narrower sense. By *structure* we mean the use of terms as equivalents of other terms, or as designating superiors, inferiors, or things of similar status; we also mean terms as clarified by successive definitions or images; and we mean also the dialogical and dramatic devices that help to give these primary structures meaning. In brief, a structure relates two or more terms in some way.) It is scarcely a single step to the conclusion that *if* there is a person capable of directing, and *if* this person happens to be Socrates, then he must be the unifying personality of the *Gorgias*, binding together, in one person, the literary aspects with the philosophic structures.[3] Were he not to combine both aspects of the dialogue, it would remain an amusing excursion with a strangely talkative man settling down after missing a display he was foolish enough not to wish to hear repeated. The dialectical structures alter with each change of respondent to Socrates, who because his own approach requires that he absorb theirs so far as needed, must modify his ways of talking in order to apply his principles to the fragmented, misshapen configurations offered by the three rhetors. Socrates' gift is not only that he can see the worth of such configurations as are offered by good thinkers[4] but also that he can glean from the most unphilosophic mind something of value and assimilate it to his purposes without serious distortion.[5] Yet it must be supposed that in order to conduct a perfect dialectical session (taking the word in both of our senses), both discussants would have to be persons extraordinarily lucid of insight. (It is possible that Plato had reserved *The Philosopher* for a colloquy of this kind, with Socrates and the Eleatic Stranger the chief participants.)

Some foes of Plato think this an undeserved glorifying of Socrates, that it is artificial, and that opposing figures such as Gorgias, Callicles, Protagoras, Thrasymachus, Parmenides, not to mention Glaucon and Adeimantus, have better title than Plato accords them to dialectical supremacy. This would imply that Gorgias and Callicles, among the others, were arbitrarily flattened a trifle by Plato and made to give up prematurely and unnecessarily. But if we accept the looseness of argument as a precondition of interpreting the dialogue throughout, and accept the Socratic principle of dialectical absorption of as many traits as feasible of his opponent's methods of thinking, then Socrates does defeat these men, chiefly in terms of their own moral contentions.

It may seem to a reader of ours that we are blaming Gorgias, Polus, and Callicles for using rhetoric and then are praising Socrates for using those same devices against them. There are two answers: First, that although Socrates does not use impeccable arguments at every juncture, still they hang together better than those of the three rhetors, a number of whose aberrancies in reasoning we have pointed out along the way.

At almost every turn these men contradict themselves or leave out terms important to completing their thought. Second, the arguments of Socrates are used in the service of what we have accepted (without proof, it must be admitted) to be a better moral code than that of any of the rhetors. We believe, for instance, that his evaluation of the self-serving political man is sounder and wiser than Callicles' evaluation of the philosopher. If the reader still objects, we can only ask that he review once again the arguments—a repetition which Socrates himself thinks necessary (especially 513c–d, and elsewhere). The very difficult conditions of the debate make it incumbent upon Socrates to use the most effective kinds of reasoning in the short time available, and yet maintain the integrity of a more responsible dialectical process, eliciting the same conclusions from arguments that would not wholly convince a genuine dialectician. In other words, he must freely employ the common touch of the three rhetors, but employ it to convey the intellectual probity which he takes to be a hallmark of philosophy. These arguments of mine, says Socrates (509a), are secured by bands of iron and adamant, and will never be changed—but on the outside he uses his intellectual jiu jitsu to defeat his antagonists through their own apparent strengths. That is why agreement is his criterion for attaining truth in this dialogue. When you concur with me, he says to Polus, we will have reached the truth—I need only you as my witness (472c).[6] In the conversation with Callicles much the same point is stated, but this time with several restrictions (487d–e): both parties must be wise, candid (not bashful), friendly, when they agree. This is, of course, a moderately satisfactory test for truth only if it is known in advance that the two parties are initially at odds conceptually with one another; if Gorgias and Polus were to agree on some point, it would scarcely be enough to verify it.

At what point in the *Gorgias* the emotions of all the men, including Socrates, shade into the general conceptual structures it is very difficult to say, nor is it easy to decide when a querulous insult becomes an objection in the argument. The emotions are not bare or dumb emotions; they are all articulated, either clearly or through carefully devised signs and substitutes, and in both ways enter into the theories of the men entertaining them. Socrates himself is no disembodied Eleatic intellect coolly surveying mere mortals but a man of uncommonly well-balanced feelings and an almost abnormal sensitivity to the winds of passion wafting, or gusting, over his fellowmen.

The Socratic method is not merely one of asking shrewd questions, though there is plenty of that. Socrates is also a masterly speaker, and samples of his own best rhetoric exist in the *Gorgias*, though it is a dialogue that unlike the *Symposium, Phaedrus, Republic,* and *Phaedo* is not celebrated for his magnificent addresses. The offers he makes either to refute or to substantiate show that destructive interrogation is by no means his only interest. Insistence that his opponents restrict themselves to short speeches is roughly matched by his excuses for making long ones himself. The many compliments he dispenses fade into ironic praise, and there is also self-dispraise. His serious explorations, involuted, profound, far-reaching, are almost indistinguishable from his jesting; but the jests are again rooted in penetrating insight.

Jesting is a diversion for both speaker and hearer, but in order to choose which pleasant things are good and which not, we need an art (500a). In this connection, Socrates gives Callicles a stern warning not to make jokes with him, not to answer capriciously, in the name of the god of friendship rather than the truth (500b). With Callicles, the joke would dissemble what he actually thinks, thus leading the conversation on a false and futile path. For Socrates, however, the joke both disguises and reveals the serious thought, and when the conversation is led by a skilled discussant it need not be derailed, since Socrates is well aware of the points he is making with his own jests. The basic distinction in this part of the dialogue (499b–527e) is still between what is done for the best and what is done for its own sake. Thus we have good pleasures and bad ones. Jokes, being for the sake of pleasure, either have a good purpose more remotely or they do not; and the Socratic jest conforms to the purposes of his dialectic.[7]

When Callicles asks whether Socrates is serious (481b), he is evidently wondering whether this strange man stands ready to take the consequences of his various utterances—for example, whether *he* would walk into a lawcourt and direct attention to his own guilt, asking to be freed from the burdens thereof by being punished as fitting his misconduct. The twist is, of course, that later on (509c) Callicles comes to think of rhetoric as the only way to rescue oneself when about to be mistreated, justly or unjustly. For his part, Socrates thinks that self-rescue should rest upon nothing but inner virtue, a weak argument in the eyes of the common man.

Like the silence of the dog in Conan Doyle's story of Silver Blaze, there are significant silences in the *Gorgias*. One might have expected mention of any of four well-known traits of Socrates, famous from other dialogues, but not referred to in this one by anybody, including Socrates. They are his poverty, his homeliness, his peculiar ignorance, and the daimonic inner voice accompanying him everywhere. This is no place for a detailed discussion of the four as related to the other writings, but some attention should be paid to reasons why they are *not* accounted for in the *Gorgias*.

About the poverty. One remark that Socrates could make to any of his opponents, especially Callicles, would be: You want riches, and will use any means to gain them, for you think that they lie on the road to happiness. I am poor, as you see, but am happier than any of you.—A rhetorical device, calling himself to the stand as witness, and one easily thrown into doubt by anyone asking Socrates to *prove* that he was indeed happy. Callicles might also counter by saying that it is easy enough to seem to be happy if one neglects the struggles of civic life altogether, choosing instead the security of an idle, fruitless poverty. The chief reason for passing over the lack of property is, however, that his own is ordinarily mentioned in other dialogues as a contrast to the rewards of the sophist, not the political ruler. Though it is plain enough that Gorgias accepts money for his displays and instruction, there is no talk of it here, hence no need for Socrates to dissociate himself from this practice. When Callicles claims that Socrates could not rescue himself from any low fellow's determination to confiscate his property, there is no mention of amounts, because however much or little he had, it would all be taken.[8]

As for his stockiness, staring eyes, and general resemblance to the ugly Silenus, these traits of Socrates made famous from the *Symposium* and elsewhere are unmentioned; indeed, almost nothing is said about the bodily condition (except fatigue) of any participant in the *Gorgias*.[9] This fact is the more remarkable since voice, its strength, pitch, clarity, and the features and stance accompanying it are of great importance to a rhetor. Plato seems to take these for granted in the *Gorgias*, and it might be odd to single out Socrates for special notice just as his great hardihood, another striking feature, would be out of place here.

In the *Gorgias* Socrates, although in enemy territory, so to speak, never calls attention to or seemingly takes refuge in his famed ignorance.[10] (1) He is either a skilled rhetor already or else a phenomenally apt learner, for he uses rhetorical expedients almost constantly in his effort to defeat other rhetors: witnesses, including himself, great authors, and, of course, his present opponents; irony, abuse albeit of a moderated kind; flesh-creeping; general topics; repetition; greatly expanded statements (as at 451e–452d) where a couple of sentences are enlarged to a page); and many nearly-correct statements that his opponents appear to find acceptable. An attitude which a truly convincing speaker must strike is that he knows his subject well, hence will *not* be speaking from ignorance, to pretend which would be all but fatal to his cause. Where he does claim not to know, as at 462e, it is a reflection upon the rhetor for having been unclear. (2) There is deeper meaning to this. The dialectical method of Socrates is closely adapted to respondents, as we have said. When he asserts (in other dialogues) that he knows nothing, this often means that when he takes into account the prejudices or mistakes of these men or boys, he does not know exactly how to proceed in order to prove to them what he thinks essential; they have not furnished him with enough material from which he can directly formulate clear premises. But from one standpoint, at least, the three rhetors are easy antagonists because, paradoxically, they commence from what they consider a position of strength—they are not ignorant of rhetoric, and their main initial prejudice is only that it is an art, a high art. The problem of persuading them does not reside in starting out from their ignorance.

The ignorance, moreover, can be put into the context of Socrates' remark halfway through his debate with Callicles, that his principles are bound with iron and adamant, and that anyone failing to refute them will have to live by them or be a fool. Socrates has sketched his views of how one ought to live, and the dialogue is his effort to show, so far as possible within *their* terms, how the principles of his three opponents fail to conform to his own projected scheme. His way in the *Gorgias* is not unclear, and he is well aware of the devices with which he must cajole, bully, and in countless other ways persuade men who have an ear only for cajoling, bullying, and the rest.

The fourth feature of Socrates' unusual nature, the daimonic voice that warns him when about to embark on a second-rate course of action, appears in several dialogues, including the *Phaedrus*,[11] the composition closest to the *Gorgias* in its interest in rhetoric. There is no voice in the *Gorgias*, one reason being that Socrates only suggests, but never threatens that he might unilaterally break up the discussion as he does in the other dialogue after his derogatory speech on love as a human sickness. The nearest that he comes to an actual threat is in his remark (462a) that although Athens gives Polus the right to speak his mind, she also gives Socrates the right to cease listening if the speeches grow too long; and again (489d), that if Callicles does not become gentle in teaching Socrates, he will leave off attending. But these are both conditional, not arbitrary decisions to leave.

So much for the four "omissions" in the *Gorgias*, which have to do respectively with possible defects of the external goods, body, and (the last two) soul of Socrates. One difficulty that he mentions both in this dialogue and elsewhere,[12] is his ineptitude in political matters (473e–474a). There is no special response to his admission from Polus, but Callicles picks up the remark as a symptom of weaknesses of far longer standing. For Socrates himself, however, merely taking charge of voting procedures is by no means the best way to make the city a better one. He must carry on a unique educative process to generate truer conceptions of justice and temperance. Late in the dialogue it becomes clear that a vivid example of this has been before the reader's eyes for the past fifty pages, in his treatment of Callicles. This self-referential aspect of his discourse requires that similar encounters be conducted both by words and by the model of the speaker himself. The connection between words and deeds must be intimate for both teacher and learner, which is why Socrates says that first of all he strives to make himself good and *then* improve others (514d; 527c–d). One wonders whether the three rhetors at loggerheads with him have ever given this a passing thought.

Bravery, Temperance, Justice

We have said more than once that Socrates' primary motive in the *Gorgias* is practical and serious, far more so than is his motive in dealing with the volatile, emotion-charged Ion, whom Socrates sees as being in need merely of a trimming down, or of the spoiled dilettante Meno. There the purpose of Socrates is not simply to deflate the many puffs of hyperbolic claims inflated by his antagonists, but to dissuade them from a damaging mode of thought and behavior. Here Polus says that a child can refute Socrates, to which the reply is that in such a case the child would be his benefactor (470c). To Callicles, the child is no longer needed; I myself, he says (485e), am your benefactor. Thinking of himself as having a mission, Callicles is hoping to change another man's way of living, much as Crito wishes to alter Socrates' settled conviction to remain in prison. It makes Callicles all the more strenuous and impervious as an opponent. The complication in their polemical opposition is that Callicles hates Socrates' *defending* of his own way of life as much as he hates that way of life itself. Both appear to him exercises in aimless loquacity. To defend the philosophic way with consistency involves *defending it philosophically*, and this to Callicles amounts to a self-degrading defense of an already-degraded life-style. But there is a rub: Callicles was contemptuous of philosophers for their withdrawal to the sidelines, the refusal to enter the political frays; but now it is clear that the present defense of philosophy, carried on with the same philosophic hairsplitting he has already condemned, *is* at the same time an exercise in practical politics. Hence Callicles sees his view of philosophy both confirmed and disconfirmed at the same time.

How combat this? Socrates could turn the double involution upside down by saying that if his way of life is good, acceptable in Athens as a means of improving civic existence, then its defense is no degradation but is a natural part of the good life and hence good itself. The consistency of this is clear enough, but the premise has to be substantiated. The proof is an ad hominem argument, and must be, since what is weighted not only is styles of living but also the men who live them—this is no abstract account. The proof would lie in reviewing all relevant characteristics of each man, seen from his own standpoint and from that of his partners in the discussion, then weighed in reference to his power to pursue a single line of thought independently and act in accord with it—his bravery. If the extra self-doubts that Socrates has sown in Callicles now obtrude sufficiently to deter him from a course of tyranny, and if Socrates has not wavered in desiring truth at any cost, then the way of life he has advocated will be stronger, and he will be the more likely man to live his ideal; at the same time that ideal will be superior to the one touted by any antagonist present.

Gorgias is unwilling, or perhaps unable, to distinguish between soul and body, hence cannot talk about the soul's ruling the body so that acts and habits will be temperate. For him a man is a man, a simple unity, not a composite unity. For Polus, the soul is of little account by the side of the body, which lays down its demands for satisfaction. Because the distinction between what is healthful in satisfying these desires and what is pleasant escapes him, the inscription over the gate of the Abbey Thélème, Do As Thou Wilt, could be carved over his own door. As for Callicles, he has a slightly better conception of the soul, but deems it proper that the superior man be given more, much more, of the pleasant. It turns out, contrary to his own expectations, that the pleasures are those of the body, some of them exceptionally coarse ones at that. He had considered himself to be appearing a cultivated gentleman, and now he is shown up for patronizing male bordellos.

Here again Socrates considers the main consequences of all three positions. To enlighten Gorgias he draws for the first time the distinction between soul and body (453a), not giving, to be sure, any theological status to the soul but simply asserting its rule over the body. To Polus he maintains (in the Divided Oblong) this differentiation, attaching both arts and imitations of arts to each. Pursuit of the welfare of soul and body takes rise from knowledge, which earlier (454c–d) had been set off from belief. Against Callicles he insists that the soul is not transient and corruptible as the body is, but that the deeds done in this life leave a permanent imprint upon an enduring soul, an imprint to be erased only if slight enough to be correctible in the afterworld through prolonged suffering. One cannot attribute to Socrates as a person any degree of temperateness merely because he does not confess to or boast of private indulgences. Temperance is neither abstinence nor reticence; and the best assumption is only that his love for Alcibiades, which he does not describe at all, is not one so disturbing to him that he drops his philosophic stance for the sake of an infatuation.

We may pass on to justice, which in its fullest ramifications becomes almost the sole topic of the *Gorgias*, and whose aspects we have reviewed sufficiently in earlier chapters. In summary, the four chief speakers form a pattern. For Gorgias justice is real but unclear, therefore it is difficult to know how to teach it, though one must take for granted its being a genuine good. Meanwhile rhetoric is clearly understood in its value if not its nature; it aims at good thought of as real because there is nothing definable that is more real. Socrates' ultimate answer to this is that justice is indeed real but that it need not be confused. By the same token, the rhetoric that is without knowledge of justice does not lead to a real good. For Gorgias justice and rhetoric are things quite apart from each other, and Socrates wishes to bind them together.

Polus contends that justice may be unreal, that it may not be a good but appears at times to be good. Rhetoric is what leads to the real goods, pleasure and power, since rhetoric can and if necessary should circumvent justice. Again the Socratic response is that justice is real, ordinary rhetoric is a fake, a mere imitation of justice and the social institutions administering or promoting it. Any action done without knowledge of what is good for the thing acted upon leads to harm.

For Callicles most of what is called justice is merely conventional, with no basis in the natures of men, the superiority of some of them to the others being the final standard by which actions are to be judged. Rhetoric for its part leads to good, especially after the strong man has been put down by the many banded together to impose restrictive laws upon him and false education upon the young. Thus rhetoric is good relative to the political situation obtaining at the time. To this Socrates would answer that rhetoric is good only if combined with the total practice of virtue toward individuals first, that is, in private, though ultimately it is extended to larger groups in the polis.[13]

While justice is what Socrates aims to achieve in society, he himself must do it through one single agency, otherwise his approach to life would not be worthwhile. That agency is knowledge, which takes two forms, depending upon whether its subject matter is outside in the world or within the knower himself.

Knowledge and Self-knowledge

Of the kinds of thinking in the human soul, that which is true and necessarily so, knowledge, is what must be sought because of its reliability in a world that is a mixture of clarity and confusion. (That heavy bodies always fall toward earth is clear enough, but that conservative policies are always better is not.) Socrates never maintains that belief induced by a rhetor is *always* false. Indeed, this would spoil much of his argument against Gorgias, for if everything a man said in public were patently wrong it should be fairly easy for the general public to detect this, then find obvious alternatives. What Socrates means is that the rhetor oscillates imperceptibly between true and false many times—sometimes deliberately, sometimes not. In addition, the rhetor has little *regard* for the truth; a moral judgment against him. When he advocates dredging a harbor which, it turns out, will give enemy ships better access to the docks, this cannot be outright treason if he does not know these probable effects, but it is immoral even so for him not to have informed himself by consulting the ablest naval planners, turning his ignorance into true belief.

Under eight heads we may classify the conditions of belief, which in the *Gorgias* is a very general term covering both the true and the doubtful and often the false as well:

1. True and benefiting self and city; Socrates espouses this and would, if it were stabilized, equate it with knowledge, though he would want to interpret self-benefit more carefully.
2. False but benefiting self and city; this might in effect be accidentally useful, but could never be trusted.
3. True and not benefiting self but benefiting city; again Socrates would espouse this, perhaps more enthusiastically than class (1).
4. False and not benefiting self but benefiting city; again this would be a chance kind of benefit, hardly to be trusted.
5. True and benefiting self but not city; the three rhetors would approve this.
6. False and benefiting self but not city; this too they would approve, indifferent as they are to truth or falsity in the belief.
7. True and benefiting neither self nor city; this would be rejected out of hand by all parties aware of the effects.
8. False and benefiting neither self nor city; again this would be excluded, if detected, as it doubtless would be.

The rhetors would be glad to use classes (1), (2), (5), (6) in mixtures bewildering yet gratifying their hearers, who probably could not catch on to the deceptions. As for Socrates, he would not seek for (1) more than for (3) and would abjure (5) and (7) equally. The slipping between (1) and (3) would not constitute the kind of tergiversation practiced by the three rhetors, because to them the possibility that what was said was false would never be in question before an audience.

The fact that one can move in and out of the classes typifying true speech, (1), (3), (5), (7), shows that we are still on the level of belief, not knowledge, and that the coincidence of true belief with knowledge is just that—coincidental. What Socrates would aim at in conversation with a Theaetetus, say, is a radical distinction between the two, but with Gorgias or Meno or many other respondents he must be satisfied with true belief, true by good fortune.[14]

We pass now to knowledge of a special kind, self-knowledge. To be complete, its account would have to be no less elaborate and far-reaching than that of knowledge in general; for Plato knowledge would resemble a Cantorian infinite in which this subset is equal to the set equal to the whole. We must nevertheless indicate some of its major outlines in a narrow compass. It stands to reason that in self-knowledge knower and known somehow become identified. Because, moreover, the knower knows by means of knowledge, and because the known partly consists of knowledge and some portion of that is the same knowledge whereby the knower knows, knowledge in this case is also identified with both the knower and the known. This general observation must be true regardless of both what knowing consists in and what the self may be.

Socrates is described over and over in the standard histories as insisting that one should know oneself.[15] Both words carved upon the temple at Delphi, Know Thyself (*gnothi sauton*), are interpretable on four levels, perhaps more, and it is by no means clear on the face of it what each means in isolation from carefully erected contexts. There are, moreover, a number of combinations of the terms, although the mathematical limit, sixteen, cannot be reached and exploited here.[16]

In (1a) *to know* may signify mere acquaintance, a conjectural awareness of a passing sensation, impulse, recollection; because this act of knowing is unique like its object, it can neither be duplicated nor gainsaid. If you say you have an image of a blue wine jar I cannot deny this successfully, nor can I deny that you know that you have such an image, even though I am aware that wine jars are not glazed in that hue. I can, true enough, deny that you have an *accurate* image. But your very act of making a verbal description has already tampered with the fluent and personal character of the original perception. Your image as such is your own, and your firsthand report to me loses its essential character. Similarly, your assertion that you are thirsty or recollect having seen a ship are unimpeachable, but only so far as they go. The truth, then, of both these interior perceptions and our recognition of them as such resides in their immediacy, their ultimate particularity. They may be fragmentary, but they are in some sense real, if evanescent. When made to do service for more stable memories and experience they are seen in the end to be false. Socrates uses these images in the *Gorgias*; they appear here and there in brief references and may easily have some persuasive value, but the truth which they lack when extended beyond their proper function can only be made up by connecting them with patterns of thoughts.

In (1b) *to know* means also to have an experience, a far more closely connected whole than were the random perceptions at the first level. There are memories of like kinds of things and of contrasts. Every experience contains awareness of what belongs to it and what does not: I overheard you talking with three friends, but you were not solving a mathematical problem with them or exercising in the gymnasium. With this sense of what pertains and what does not comes the first faint stages of an ability to classify different experiences and with them the words and phrases naming them. The legitimate certitude is greater than that for the conjectures, but the subjective sense, the immediacy, may not be more intense. On the other hand, when Callicles says that Gorgias has been displaying, or when Socrates says that he cannot tell if Archelaus is happy because he does not know him,[17] these are perceptions, or at least imply perceptions in principle verifiable as having their origins in states of affairs. They are rooted in facts, the facts being discoverable in initial stages through sensation. Even a report relating to another person and his feelings can be experiential in this respect, if the grounds for so reporting are in principle repeatable events. Such are many experiences relating past to present. As helping to predict the future they are reasonably trustworthy, as all three rhetors are willing to maintain, for this is what *their* notion of familiarity consists in, despite the fact that it often slides into conjecture.

In (1c) both of the foregoing were lesser types of knowledge having their foundations in deliverances of the senses and the power of the soul to retain the impressions thus delivered. On a level of responsible intellectual exercise—and we say *responsible* because we are discussing knowledge, not belief—*to know* means to possess a method for discovering truth and for leading others to that discovery. (Its contradictory is *ignorance*, lack of understanding of how to proceed in any discursive situation.) Thus the master of a dialectic endlessly adjustable to new topics and at the same time to other intellects (all of which differ from each other because of diverse combinations of family inheritance, education, cultivation of arts and sciences, and so forth) has knowledge conceived not as fixed truth but as the coming upon truth, coming into it. Thus knowledge bears a likeness to conjecture and experience in its quality of flux, yet unlike them it comes upon conclusions tightly anchored as a result of having discursively separated out possible inconsistencies in the process. Distinction is its chief operation, its weapon, its refuge. The Socratic dialectic is one that almost invariably approaches a question or refutes an error from the inside rather than developing proofs from an external stand already determined. "From the inside" means that the stand itself, the premises, must be discovered if it is a question to be answered, or accepted if an error to be corrected; and the uses to which these premises will be put must also be worked out. In the Socratic elenchus, the chief terms and presuppositions of the first proponent must be so adopted that their implications can be worked out using a minimum of new concepts by which to alter meanings and applications. Only very gradually can the context be changed to correct or reverse the original position. It is, in a word, Socrates attacking the enemy on the latter's ground or expounding his own views in terms most nearly comprehensible to the respondent and most appealing to his present frame of mind—yet in the end reaching typical Socratic conclusions, affirmative or negative.

The third level of knowledge was a process, but the fourth (1d) represents the final outcome of a process thorough, wide-ranging, and carefully integrated, even though the terms of the dialectic may no longer be called into play. It is, then, an intuition that succeeds upon rather than remains any part of the argument, no matter how cogent and effective that might have been. In the *Phaedrus* Socrates indicates (247c–e) that this ultimate knowledge means the stripping away of all perceptions, memories, and rational steps and the predestined yet spontaneous, necessary, eternal grasp of truths which are unitary, uncompounded of separate terms, not stepped out in premises and conclusions. It is the immediate apprehension of what is essential and unchanging, and it sees existence whole because it sees what undergirds every existing thing. Like the most fleeting of perceptions, it is subjective as being incommunicable in any discourse, but there the likeness must end. Knowledge of the self, at this highest level, is not separated off from knowledge of the reality outside the self; both are perfused with the forms, most of all with the form of unity that itself unifies all the fragments donated from all three lower levels that must now drop off.[18] It seems unnecessary for us to remark that this is no issue for Socrates in the *Gorgias*, which is concerned directly with mundane, time-bound matters, putting all questions of eternity into a poetic story in which boundaries between body and soul and between living and dead are so blurred that knowledge of what is ultimately true of the soul will be reduced to mere belief, however impressive this may be as a guide to action.

It is easy to separate the self from what it means to know, provided we switch levels, trying, for instance, to join the highest kind of knowledge with the lowest level upon which the psyche or self is manifested.

But because of the general principle enunciated a short while ago, it is far more difficult to make any separation at all when both knowledge and the self are interpreted with reference to the same rank.

In (2a) *thyself* may thus signify one's momentary, subjectively entertained sensations, images, fleeting gusts of desires and aversion, even abstract terms one randomly holds and then drops, as small fractions of more complete conceptions. Hume's notion of the self (he might have said the soul) as "but a bundle or collection of different perceptions, which succeed each other with an inconceivable rapidity" [19] is never denied outright in principle by Plato, and indeed there are passages in the *Timaeus* and *Theaetetus* which confirm his having supported the view that this is at least a beginning point for investigating the soul.[20] Kant's correction of Hume, which distinguishing as it did the noumenal or transcendental self from the phenomenal or empirical self, the latter supposedly underlain by the former, left a sharp diremption that it is more than doubtful that Plato would have accepted. There are, so to speak, grades of the everyday self (a likely supposition from the fact that there are grades of knowing), and these grades merge almost imperceptibly into the higher, intellectual functions. But at the outset what I am *is* a host of sensations and images flitting, perhaps aimlessly, through my mind.

In (2b) *thyself* also signifies something manifested as experiences and those special kinds of experiences known as our own actions. These arise from more integrated functions of the soul, one's inborn capacities that make unified experience possible, one's habits controlling probable responses to various external events that move one to behave in reasonably predictable ways in accord with one's past life. Helping to determine a more fully independent self, the kinds of actions are often highly individual.[21] Socrates does not act, in the *Gorgias*, as an ordinary politician would act, and there is no way to gauge his political activity by an external standard; if there are any other politicians to whom he can be compared at present living in Athens he does not know them. The usual likenesses with craftsmen do not hold in the dialogue. Socrates likens himself not to the ordinary craftsman but rather to the doctor who cures with a disagreeable medication (e.g., 475d; 521a; 521e). It is the rhetor, not the philosopher, who is the craftsman, the artificer. As philosopher, Socrates does not make a speech or a proof as one would make a pair of shoes. There is without much doubt a wide variation from man to man in the kinds of perceptions and images in the mind (2a) and the intensity with which they impress the soul, but it would be difficult to prove this; when, however, groups of these images are transformed into clustered memories and experiences that are the root of all voluntary (and some involuntary) actions, the differences between per-

sons become accessible to the outside observer and are both more striking and more evident. This is the level that the majority of persons
would without thinking term the most nearly definitory of the self, and
it is most prominently considered by all parties to the discussion. The
Gorgias is a work in practical philosophy throughout—if that can be
separated at all from other kinds in Plato. The practical philosophy
arises from experience of one kind or another in human affairs or from
reasonable anticipation of such experience, which always relates to
doing and making. Whatever emerges later as a theory of rhetoric or of
justice receives its strength from this empirical stage.

The difficulties in making a positive identification of the self in individual cases arise from the fact that every self houses emotions impelling it to lines of action sharply conflicting with one another, and these
emotions, even before they have impelled the person to such action,
can color, seriously impede, or even cancel each other. The person who
is in some interior conflict of this kind has, therefore, an additional ob-
stacle to making a clear identification of himself as both a vessel of experience and an agent. Polus and Callicles are, in their different ways,
excellent examples of the confusion and frustration arising in this
manner.

In (2c), despite what many would deem the humble birth of the theory of practical affairs, the theory also exists in its own right. As soon
as one develops the habit of moving from one statement believed to be
true to others that may gain similar probity thereby, one begins to sense
an expansion of one's own nature; sciences (and the arts) are not ap-
pendages to the self, but become instinct with it; they are assimilated to
the memories and habits which have developed, or perhaps it would be
wiser to say that they are assimilated to processes of thinking and discoursing. At any rate, the *I think* characteristic of the self now becomes
not so much "I saw a ship yesterday," or "I tend to be liberal in my
views of foreigners and barbarians," but rather, "I know, on grounds I
can explain if you wish, that a square can be doubled in area by erecting another square upon a diagonal of the original." Regardless of the
generality of this proposition in geometry, that it applies not only to
those that one happens to have seen, and regardless of the fact that the
proposition can be held just as firmly by others of similar training,
there is still the inescapable fact that it is always something held in the
individual soul, that it is not an essence wholly unattached to a mind.
The aim of Socrates in the *Gorgias* is quite evident: to raise the interior
awareness of each of his three opponents from the second to this third
level, involving them in the very process whereby he himself has been
able to elevate his own thinking, already grounded in his experience.

It is interesting that in exploring practical philosophy in a similar way

Socrates—or anyone, for that matter—will, in extending his range of thoughts, come closer to a grasp of his own ways of thinking and therefore of himself; the best way to know one's own mind is to extend it. Just as experience was capable of unifying the multifarious perceptions in the lowest level of selfhood, so the dialectic of the third stage is capable of resolving many of the conflicts inherent in the second. The dialectic is itself *therapeia*, tendance, for it elicits increasing numbers of the stored images and the accompanying impulses, arranging them in ever clearer structures. These become connected in turn with other structures, so that a better view of oneself is gained.[22]

The knowledge won on this level has, with respect to the *Gorgias*, two principal topics: (1) One can choose a way of life by considering as many probable consequences as one is able, even though the actual consequences are by no means all apparent to the person choosing; (2) if one really *knows* what one is doing, it is impossible to say or do wrong, intentionally or otherwise, for knowledge of right and wrong is by definition true and guaranteed to be so. As for (1), not everybody makes a free choice; but given the right circumstances even the respondents in the *Gorgias* could bring themselves to such a choice—at least, Socrates hopes they could. As for (2), the knowledge, *phronēsis*, practical good sense, is partly a knowledge not of particular laws and governmental usages but of the intrinsic nature of law and its relation to the individual. Here again, the self in its process of extending becomes more insightful into its own nature, because the knowledge of law and politics is not the memorizing of statutes but the clear apprehension of their meaning for one's own character and personality—experience and emotion combined in developed, disciplined thinking.

In (2d) each of the three foregoing levels of the self has served directly as a spring for action, but the fourth does not serve directly, despite Socrates' tale of the afterworld. This fourth level refers not to the soul of everyday life, here and now, but to the soul as indestructible, immortal. Such a conception of the self is one for philosophers to ponder and is only brought into the *Gorgias* obliquely, as it were, in the form of a series of images. It is presumably above and beyond the images and experiences, except insofar as they are related to moral and immoral deeds; instead, this conception has to do with the permanent imprint of justice and injustice upon the soul, thus with the most general and abstract of moral values inhering in the self beyond any day-to-day experience or discourse. To know this self would require the most intense of experiences and the most systematic of thinking as prelude; these two levels are part of a process, but the ineffable result, which can never be proven, denied, defined literally, or described, lies beyond them all, unifying them and giving them their being.[23] Without this

form, the first two levels of self are nothing more than functions of constellations of particles whose movements are never wholly predictable
and whose purposes are never altogether clear,[24] and the third level
would be a series of discursive acts, lacking balance and unity.

It is no small task to match these two sets, of knowledge and of the
self, in any other way than to pair their members that are on the same
level, (1a)–(2a), (1b)–(2b), (1c)–(2c), (1d)–(2d); confusion arises when
the lower levels of knowing are used to explain the higher levels of the
self without making the proviso, as Socrates does in the myth in the
Gorgias, that this is a tale, an image, and that its sources are poetic legends. Without this proviso, passing images and conflicting impulses
would turn "knowledge" of the soul into nothing more than belief,
most of it no doubt false. Even experience is no sure guide to the ultimate nature of the soul; when experience is transcended, nothing in it
can definitively confirm or contradict thoughts and discourse ranging
beyond it if they are responsibly conducted.

These are the best and most obvious pairings, but there are others:
dialectic (1c) can examine not only the third level of the soul (2c) but
also the second (2b) and even the first (2a). In so doing it raises the content of (2a) and (2b) to a position where these become part and parcel of
the dialectical enterprise, and they lose their temporary and private
character. Though the perceptions (which may be false) and experiences (which are ordinarily not false) are not knowledge in any but a
secondary sense, when they become absorbed as moments in the discourse and are promoted beyond their particularity and incommunica-
bility, this does not mean that the self loses its identity, for then it extends the range of its faculties and functions.

We turn to the way these pairs relate to the Divided Oblong, the back-
bone of the *Gorgias*. It would be convenient if the two lists, each with
four ranks, could be set side by side to discover easy correspondences.
But the Divided Oblong assumes either a condition of knowledge (art)
or a condition of belief and ignorance (pandering) or both. Grades of
knowledge are otherwise omitted, and a doctor could know as truly as
a politician, a caterer as a rhetor, an embellisher as a sophist, the differences between these paired members regarding whether their proper
spheres are body or soul. The two kinds of practice, art and pandering,
are, however, allied with the third and second levels of the Oblong, as
shown in figure 11.1. The locating of pandering and art on the levels of
experience and dialectic respectively should not be taken to mean that
these are exact equivalences, but simply that they fit better there than
elsewhere. Despite Socrates' insistence late in the colloquy with Polus
that rhetoric has for its sole function the self-accusation of a man who
has committed an injustice, it is clear from the attempts of Gorgias

	KNOWLEDGE	THE KNOWN
	1d intuitive insight	2d the self as indestructible and unitary
art (knowledge) - -		
	1c dialectic	2c the self as thinking in connected structures
pandering - - - - - -		
	1b experience, memories	2b the self as experience, habits
	1a images, sensations	2a the self as random perceptions

Fig. 11.1. *Art and pandering as allied with levels of the Divided Oblong.*

(summed up by Socrates himself) to define rhetoric as the artificer of persuasion (453a) that its realm in hands other than those of the philosopher is very large. For this reason, it is likely to be troublesome to restrict to one level of knowledge or of the soul; it is based in experience, familiarity, and ordinary habit; but what if a Socrates is using it? Can it now acquire some of the rigor and disinterestedness that one attributes to dialectic?[25]

The question of personal self-knowledge (i.e., levels [2a] and [2b]) is scarcely raised in the *Gorgias* in any explicit fashion, with an exception or two: Socrates asks the question, What sort am I? (458a), that is, whether he will turn a debate and a search for truth into a personal quarrel. Again, he is grateful to Callicles for testing his soul as if it were gold, examining him for flaws (486d–488a). This latter, aside from its irony, refers to the genuine need to answer the question, Is Socrates wasting his life by everlastingly talking philosophy?

It scarcely crosses the rhetors' minds to ask questions of and about themselves. Gorgias and Polus harbor almost no self-doubts. Polus obviously dismisses self-knowledge of any sort, for he claims to know all that Gorgias knows, but since it cannot be that he has Gorgias' own interior perceptions he must be content that knowing such things as tricks with words and other pieces of exterior information exhausts the list. The situation of Callicles is different. His soul is a battlefield, and there are emotions in conflict which impel him in two—or worse, many more than two—directions at once. But his ambition is so great that he is able to put aside the asking of questions that would penetrate the defenses of any of his emotions; it is, so to speak, a shield which his feelings have erected against the powers of self-study of his very considerable intellect, an intellect which instead he uses to try to pierce the defenses of Socrates.

As for the dialectical level (1c), examination of this is indirectly made clear finally at the point when Socrates says that he is the only, or almost the only, true politician in Athens. Then the description of the philosopher, the real man of politics, and the Socratic personality and character are manifestly all one,[26] and what he says about any one of the four really applies to all of them.[27] As for dialectic in our narrower sense, Gorgias alone might be thought to be interested in pursuing it, since he is ready to have the discussion go forward; but this is a passive interest, he follows the dialectic, he does not attempt to control it. Dialectic is not integral in his character, nor in the characters of the other two.

We have already stated in what peculiar mythical sense the fourth level, (1d) and (2d), comes into play. It is never seriously discussed as it is in the *Phaedo* and *Phaedrus*.

The foregoing interpretation of self-knowledge puts us in a somewhat better position to estimate the importance of Socrates as a unifying agent of the *Gorgias*.

Socrates as Principle of Unity

Even if Socrates is the one participant active throughout the *Gorgias*, must we not still question whether it is his presence that gives the dialogue its special unity? The evidence is mixed. He is present, for example, in a couple of dozen separate works, dominates nearly all of them, yet his prominence in them does not of itself band all of *these* into one. Commentators would, for example, be quick to light upon differences between the *Lysis* and the *Theaetetus*, or the *Crito* and *Philebus*, in all of which Socrates is presented in what he can do best. By analogy we may conclude that the enduring presence of Socrates is not of itself enough to make the *Gorgias* a seamless fabric. Yet he does most to forward the discussion, beginning it, carrying it forward, and at last ending it with a claim to have proven his case. Hence we look to other aspects of his entrance into the dialogue besides his merely being on hand and apparently outfoxing his opponents, if we are to establish Plato's singleness of design. The characterization of the Eternal Questioner is insufficient, for in the *Gorgias* this role is joined with its opposite; he makes frequent pronouncements of his own, and far from his being a chilly, colorless, "objective" disputant, he has a rhetoric more eloquent than anything attempted by the other men. This is but one fact among many evident from the dialogue itself, and making the most of it is better than injecting bits of commonplace information snatched from elsewhere. When Plato is their author, bits have their uses—but chiefly where he puts them.[28]

Although the three rhetors are not mere shadows or even puppets against the backdrop of Socrates' commanding nature, it would be equally wrong to say that they are on a footing equivalent to his, and that in their interacting with him they achieve a parity. Even Callicles, so intricately cross-tensioned a human being, cannot match Socrates, the eminent cause of all the separate movements of the dialogue, who for a variety of reasons eclipses the other men:[29]

First, he divines their motives, appraises their skills, diagnoses their indecisions and disabilities, and lays bare their prejudices at the same time that they appear incapable of noticing his, two of them through lack of interest and the third, Callicles, because his very prejudices block his intellectual advance and put him at both an apparent advantage over Socrates and at a real disadvantage.

Second, his advocacy of a way of life is more independent, more self-impelled, than that of any of the others, which turn, each of them, upon finding out what the crowd wants—and wants to hear. Socrates is active, they are reactive.

Third, not only does he make a better case (though certainly not a perfect one) for the philosophic way of living than do any of his opponents for theirs, but he is more likely to live such a life—a very important consideration for this work. He must bravely fill the shoes of the philosopher in the face of slanders and harm, while Gorgias and Polus, at least, can remain smug and still stick by the majority of their convictions. All three rhetors have readied their own escape hatches, or are trying to do so.

These are the chief personal traits that render Socrates so pre-eminent. To these three more may be added, ways in which he conducts the discussion itself:

Fourth, he raises, or causes to have raised, virtually all of the most significant questions of both a general and a particular sort.

Fifth, he lays down the most stringent requirements for conducting the discussion, so that without him it would quickly deteriorate into a series of unfocused displays, with a few invidious comparisons thrown in by three men varying chiefly in the details of their attachment to rhetoric and an accompanying morality, and in the details of their jealousies and egotisms.

Sixth, he anticipates the course of the discussion from the standpoint of its content as well as its purpose and can even carry it on (506c–509c) by himself when Callicles has become seriously disgruntled. Throughout, he introduces new terms when needed; rearranges old ones in new and more stable, revealing patterns; marks the beginnings and endings of proofs; and consistently enlarges and clarifies dialectical structures.

So far, then, as one person can, short of a monologue, dominate a work of art, Socrates dominates this extraordinary text. But there is a caution to be observed, one that harks back to Aristotle's famous determination that a tragedy is not a unity simply because its hero is a single man.[30] Although the *Gorgias* is not, so we have maintained, a tragedy in any precise sense, this principle still applies pretty well to it, and consequently we feel obliged to look beyond Socrates to certain structures and finally to certain pervading doctrines enshrined in those structures before feeling confident that we have done all that is necessary to state the unity of the dialogue.

Meanwhile we must not disavow the importance of Socrates as an essential contributor to that unity. Polonius, Laertes, Rosencrantz, and that waterfly Osric may have their moments of feeling or their clever conceits; but they are schoolboys when Hamlet comes against their wits and characters, and we know them mainly as foils to his stronger nature. Gorgias and his friends are no doubt more vigorous characters and thinkers than those four Danish courtiers, but then again, they are confronted by Socrates, who in his way is mightier and more harmoniously blended than Hamlet can be. Socrates is not sicklied o'er with anything, and thought, for him, is not a pale cast but a pair of wings for flying close to the ground and for occasional soaring upward into a great empyrean.

12

ANTECEDENTS AND CONSEQUENTS

OF THE DIVIDED OBLONG

We have insisted that the Divided Oblong (464b–466a) is a kind of watershed of the *Gorgias*, and that far from being an interesting sidelight in Socrates' long pursuit of some understanding of rhetoric and some way of life better than its mere use—and misuse—it puts a sort of cap upon the first search and inaugurates the second. In brief, any account pretending to state something of the unity of the dialogue would be markedly incomplete without a reminder of the antecedent distinctions leading to it, together with all the consequent distinctions made with its help. The division between these two parts is no even division, since the Oblong occurs barely more than a quarter of the way through, just past the point when the frisky Polus has broken up the conversation with Gorgias and with that squelched any hope of settling the dilemma implied in the latter's contradiction regarding the teaching of justice and the just use of rhetoric by his pupils.

As a convenience, in figure 12.1, we insert a simplified diagram of the Divided Oblong, which in Plato's text was set down in prose.[1] Plato's striking achievement is that he could make so much of the dialogue take its lead from this very simple matrix. To clarify this, we shall be repeating some of the account given in our running chapters on the conversation's progress, but such repetition may be needed in the interests of pruning that account of what is less germane to the Oblong and its effects, in order better to represent the intellectual unity of the *Gorgias*.

The Section with Gorgias

In chapter 1 we have indicated some of the many ways in which the Prologue (447a–449c) sets a stage for the rest of the dialogue and why it should not be passed over as being perfunctory. For this reason, we

	REAL (ART)	IMITATION (PANDERING)
SOUL	legislation justice	sophistry rhetoric
BODY	gymnastic medicine	embellishment catering

Fig. 12.1. *Simplified diagram of the Divided Oblong.*

need mention only a few hints that the Prologue affords of the over-arching schematism of the Oblong. Almost immediately (447b–c), the contrast is drawn between display and discussion (see also 448d), the former being a feature of Gorgias and what is referred to here as his art. The display seems to be what the silent audience (see 455c and 458c) would enjoy more, as would Polus, Callicles, and perhaps even Chaerephon. Art is straightway allied with power (*dunamis*), though what sort of power is not asked here. Gorgias bears three relations to rhetoric: He professes or makes claims about it and about himself as rhetor; he teaches it; and he displays it (*epanelletai, didaskei, epideixetai*). As for Socrates, he mentions discussion (*dialegesthai*) but does not claim it as his calling, nor does he claim to teach it; but the whole of the *Gorgias*, it turns out, shows many traces of his peculiar kind of discussion and with it of his attempt to instruct the three rhetors.

At 448b–c Chaerephon is told to ask the pupil of Gorgias what Gorgias is. Like his brother Herodicus, a doctor, or like Aristophon, a painter, Gorgias must have *some* title. Polus replies with a sententious lifting of a statement from a textbook that he has already composed at his early age, that familiarity or experience (*empeiria*) conducts our life's course according to art, unfamiliarity according to chance or luck.[2] Men, he says, partake (*metalambanousin*) of various arts in various ways (*alloi allōn allōs*, a strained phrase, even for a pupil of Gorgias). Here we see the two words *familiarity* and *art* allied closely, though these will later be distinguished by Socrates by the expedient of making knowledge, *epistēmē*, an important ingredient of art. Gorgias, haply, has taken up the best of the arts, and no doubt for this reason is the best of men, although this point is left undecided. In this way Polus sets up what for him will serve as a scale of values, which devolves upon an individual person, Gorgias;[3] such a scale of values, Socrates evidently perceives, is far too personal, being an ad hoc adjustment of greater and lesser goods to the pursuit of particular artistic practices by one man. The Divided Oblong is one way of overcoming the weakness of

Polus' attempted hierarchy, shot through with the shiftiness of chance despite his according higher place to familiarity and art. It is Gorgias, more sober, who gives it the name (449a), though Socrates has used the word a few lines before (448d), not to identify the profession of Gorgias but to deprecate the style of Polus. Thus rhetoric already has both an excessively honorific meaning and a mildly derogatory one; the latter is reintroduced into the Oblong.

At 450a–b rhetoric is said not to deal with all kinds of speech but to be able to make men speak and understand the things about which they speak—a claim underlying almost the whole of the first principal section of the dialogue. The first rejoinder that Socrates gives to this claim is not that it is untrue, but that it cannot serve to differentiate rhetoric from medicine and gymnastic training, both of which promote just such understanding. To make this differentiation, Gorgias takes refuge (450b–c) in the fact that these are chiefly manual, not verbal arts—which would put rhetoric on the side of such patently secure types of discourse as arithmetic, logistic, and geometry. But rhetoric has a different subject matter—here the arts are pinned down this way—and while those others talk about odd and even and so forth, rhetoric deals instead, so Gorgias says, with the greatest of things (*pragmatōn*) human, and the best (450e–451d). But if so, do not health, beauty, and wealth honestly earned constitute these things (451e)? These latter prefigure, in part, goods in the sense of property, goods of the body, and goods of the soul, and here the suppliers of these, the moneymaker, the doctor, and the gymnastic trainer can all claim that it is they who confer such goods (452a–c). The doctor and trainer find their way into the Oblong as medicine and gymnastics, but the money-maker drops out.

Gorgias counters that the greatest good is the cause of freedom in mankind and of rule to single persons in their cities. This is the subject, and the audiences of the persuasive speeches given by rhetors will be judges, councillors, commons, and any chance audiences at meetings on public affairs (452d–e). Here we get a faint outline of the bodies of governmental control, later separated by Socrates in the Oblong into legislative and judicial functions, the chance audiences (such as we find assembled for Gorgias' display) being dropped from consideration.

Having said that rhetoric makes the cause of freedom its subject, Gorgias now promises that if you possess its power you can make the doctor and trainer your slaves, and the moneymaker will make money not for himself but for you (452e). Mindful no doubt of this contradiction, Socrates amends the definition of rhetoric by dropping the reference to freedom altogether: Rhetoric is the artificer of persuasion, this persuasion being its single product in the souls of the audience (452e–

453a). Socrates has made Gorgias admit that persuasion is the highest result to which rhetoric may aspire and that the claim that rhetoric produces knowledge of any sort is unprovable. This definition of rhetoric, incidentally, is allowed to stand until the Oblong, at which point it is not contradicted but a quite different kind of account is substituted. Socrates does, however, insist upon important delimitations: first, that rhetoric persuades to belief, not knowledge (454c–455a); and second, that rhetoric arises from ignorance in the soul of the speaker and is directed toward ignorance in that of the hearer (459a–c). That rhetoric is not an art (the residence of knowledge) is a vital contention in the erecting of the Oblong, and the present passage is the ground for it.

So far, the premonitory expressions that are eventually assimilated into the Oblong may seem like nothing more than mere scraps, unassorted and later thrown into a hopper which somehow gives them form. Up to this point, such an impression is largely correct. Here the doctor and trainer are on the same level, as are the audiences of lawcourts and assemblies, whereas in the Oblong there is a separation within such pairs into lower and higher. The first pair, moreover, is introduced here independently of the second, but in the Oblong both pairs find themselves in the same column of the genuine arts. The essence of the dialogue is not so much to make an unpredictable, arbitrary ordering out of what has been chaotic, but to generate coherent reasons for this eventual ordering of most of the parts, leaving for last some new insight by which a more comprehensive schematism is found.

In the course of delimiting the epistemic result of rhetoric, Gorgias volunteers (454b) that the art deals with what is (*peri toutōn ha esti*) the just and unjust, this being the first prominent use of these contraries, though they are left undefined here, indeed not even discussed. Justice becomes not the subject matter of rhetoric in the Oblong but its more authentic counterpart, which means that it should be taken there as the entire politico-judicial process of fair apportionment of goods, responsibilities, and remedies.

At 455a–b, Socrates says that it is time to see what should be said about rhetoric, and that he himself is not yet able to say this, a remark echoed in his later one (462e–463a) that he could not gather clearly Gorgias' own conception. Because of the unique feature of Socrates' dialectic, which makes use of opponents' views almost to the point of merging with them on special occasions, yet adopting a different stance from theirs as a whole—because of this feature, Socrates must initially rely upon whatever conception he can elicit from Gorgias. This is so regardless of whether that conception will later be shown to be faulty. It is this aspect of Socrates' thinking that makes the Oblong to some degree a product of the two men jointly, and even more truly of the three when we include the first utterances of Polus.

Socrates now points out (455b–d) that in selecting artificers the rhetor is not consulted if walls and harbors, and so forth, are to be built. But Gorgias is ready for him this time (455d–456a). His tacit assumption is, of course, that these structures, advocated by Themistocles and Pericles, not craftsmen, were beneficial to the people, an assumption unchallenged until very late in the conversation with Callicles (519a), when Socrates finally has amassed the dialectical strength needed to state that the walls and harbors were stuffed into the city and were in essence drivel, trash. Back at 456a, however, Socrates in content with the wry interjection that the power of rhetoric seems almost daimonic. (Since the *daimōn* is but one rank higher than mankind, to be *almost* daimonic means that the power of rhetoric is after all no more than human.)

This passage contributes to the Oblong a clearer identification of the real concerns dealt with by rhetoric. The talk is of harbors and docks, but the issue now falls under the heading of whether it is just or not to appropriate moneys for them. This identification is put in regular form, of course, in the Oblong.

The remainder of the colloquy with Gorgias (456a–461b) is occupied chiefly with the question of the responsibility at second remove for the use of rhetoric. It has hitherto been assumed all round that Gorgias, whatever his intellectual shortcomings may be, is a decent man and that his worst misdeed could only be the result of some honest mistake. Because of the peculiar nature of rhetoric, that its concern is justice, and because a man learning the art of building is a builder and the man learning the art of music is a musician, the man learning justice (under the tutelage of Gorgias or some other rhetor-instructor) is assumed to be a just man. A serious contradiction develops, however, if the rhetor teaches justice but does not know what he is teaching. The pupil then acts upon his confused impressions. Gorgias says (460a), If the pupil does not by chance know about justice and injustice, good and evil, he will learn them from me. It is the "by chance" that Socrates will seek to eliminate from the consideration of the Oblong. If justice and injustice and the alleged art dealing with them are indeed as important as Gorgias says they are, then it will pay to devise a better way of ensuring their being clearly understood and transmitted.

This passage ratifies the distinction between real and imitation, a paramount one in the Oblong. What the rhetor says cannot be trusted, not because he is an inveterate liar but because he knows so little of the essence of justice that he cannot tell the true from the false.

The Oblong Itself

Besides the terms found in the section with Gorgias and also present in the Oblong, there are two other classes, quite obviously: those important in that section, and which might well have a place in the Oblong but do not, and those in the Oblong that it would be difficult to find prepared for in the section just reviewed.

The arts of making, for example, painting, sculpture, architecture, (though prominent earlier when Socrates was hoping that Gorgias would be able to define his art) are not included, evidently giving place to arts of tendance. There is no moneymaking in the completed array, no hint of social or economic status, a point marking the great difference between the Socratic conception and that of his three opponents. Teaching is excluded from the Oblong, as are the mathematical sciences. There is a reason for this last, as there is for the others. Painting and sculpture make things unconnected directly with soul and body, but it is *these* two aspects of man that the Oblong considers. The same holds for moneymaking, though it will be important throughout the dialogue. Mathematics could well have a place (as it does in the Divided Line of the *Republic*), but here Socrates is aware that these men are concerned with action and the opinions or knowledge directing it or both, not contemplation connected to action only through practical knowledge as intermediary. But Gorgias, though he knows a little something of mathematics, has no conception of the way it could direct one to live well.

Knowledge and belief are not directly distinguished here—evidently they are merged with art and pandering-familiarity respectively. By the same token, there are not different levels of the soul, such as sense and intellect, or intuition and reason, or practical and theoretical thinking, all of them found in other dialogues. Here the sole issue is between art and familiarity, or art aiming at the best and pandering aiming at gratification. To make clear the distinction, real and seeming are introduced, a dichotomy not prominent in the earlier colloquy, though hints were given in marking the naval architect who really knows what is best for the city and the rhetor who does not. The true and false have also been used as hints for the real and the seeming (458a–b). At 459c Socrates has said that the rhetor has no need to know the truth but only a need for a device (*mechanēn*) which will make him appear to the ignorant to know when in fact he too is ignorant.

Finally, although we have had medicine, gymnastics, rhetoric, and legislation, three of their pandering counterparts, namely catering (except for a brief remark from Callicles about a feast, 447a), embellishing,[4] and sophistic, are quite new and are presented by Socrates in his commanding schematism for the first time.

Thus the Oblong is made of old and new materials. The Socratic dialectic uses here the former pronouncements and admissions, adding just enough fresh distinctions to generate a more effective scheme of relations between arts or other practices and their proper ends, as they are measured against their counterfeits. This passage, surely one of the most crucial in the dialogue, takes the form of an exchange not only with Polus, who has just now burst in, but also with Gorgias, who responds to Socrates seven times, and quite politely at that, but who must be dumfounded to hear his beloved rhetoric, to which he has devoted his life, dismissed as obsequious, unreliable, dishonorable.

The Section with Polus

The rest of the dialogue is well integrated with the Oblong, and though it serves as a sort of Continental Divide in the work as a whole, it marks a point of joining rather than sharp separation. Its chief lessons—that arts aim at the best, that what imitates these arts aims at gratification, that arts and panderings are both paired and also disjoined, that soul and body can be considered separately and require different but not wholly unlike tendances, and that analogies and part-whole relationships can be found throughout the discussion of practices—these lessons are reintroduced over and over again, in many guises.

In the colloquy between Socrates and Polus, the principal relation established by applying the lessons is that rhetoric is partly distinct from, and also inferior to, sophistic, and quite distinct from and altogether inferior to justice and its administration. But this is a Socratic lesson, and the chief bone of contention with Polus is that while this young colt puts aside any possible differentiation of rhetoric from sophistic, probably because he considers it unimportant, he thinks it vital to merge rhetoric and politics once and for all, and within politics to ignore any distinction between legislation and justice as again irrelevant; again, he denies any real distinction whatever between justice and its contrary, injustice.

The distinction most fully explored after the Oblong, follows the radical diremption between aiming at something pleasant and aiming at what is really the best, though now he no longer says "really the best" but only "what a man wishes" (466d–e). The rhetors and tyrants alike have the least power in their cities (466d), since they do little or nothing that turns out to be the best, but only what they think is best. (The word is *dokei*, a variant of *doxa*, belief.) Socrates has adopted a peculiar mode of speech, for in setting up a distinction between the good (or best) and the seeming good, his language does not ordinarily denominate the best as simply what people believe. But in the Oblong he commences with body and soul and the real condition and apparent condition of health of each. Catering and embellishing use colors and shapes to lure the onlooker, who is unspecified, to be convinced that the beautified body is the really beautiful body. In pursuing the embellishment of the body, its real beauty may well take second place to the fripperies of coiffure and cosmetics and jewels. The way, then, to make the distinction between willing and wishing would be to speak of what one would like, what one would find enjoyable, as opposed to what is really proper in regard to the best bodily condition. Consequently, there are two pairs of possibilities, not one: the distinction in terms of two types of thinking, and the distinction between things themselves and appearances that deceive one into mistaking them for the realities. The difficulty in practical life arises in trying to ascertain what is best. If the caterer were to find everyone banqueting on his food, he would think that what he willed had indeed brought about the best, which for him would be applause, good pay, and return engagements.

Polus, attempting to merge rhetoric and politics, assumes at once that the rhetor-panderer is like a tyrant in his ability to kill or maltreat anyone he wishes (466a–c). This is *after* Socrates has said that the rhetor has the smallest power within the city, unable to achieve his wished-for ends. Polus would have it that lack of power would betoken some "little man's" insignificant position in city life, power correspondingly being a freedom to do as one pleases simply because one has achieved a commanding place in city administration. Whether he behaves justly or unjustly, in this he feels responsibility to no one because his pandering will ward off potential enemies. His real feelings show themselves in his opinion that the avowed panderer will be the most respected citizen.[5]

Socrates' reply, that what one thinks best, that is, what seems best, is likely to backfire and create disadvantages for the very author of the scheme, can only be refuted, as he advises Polus, by showing that rhetoric is an art, a kind of knowledge of causes and thus interconnections, so that results of a deed can be properly evaluated and then planned for. In order to do this, one would need to separate things good from things evil and from what is intermediate between the two. The killing, banishing, or confiscating (affecting respectively soul, body, and property) are good under certain circumstances only, and are evil the rest of the time (467e–468e). Polus is as yet unwilling or unable to grasp this. Justice, in his scattered thoughts, takes second rank to rhetoric; and if rhetoric is effective, justice drops from consideration altogether. Polus has quite reversed the Socratic order. It is but a short step for him to say (470a) that paying a penalty[6] for one's misdeeds is an outright evil.

He has, then, attempted to turn the Oblong around by playing down but not denying that rhetoric is pandering or imitation, gainsaying that justice has an art whereby it is put into practice in society, and denying implicitly that rhetoric is lower than any other art or imitation of any art, such as sophistic. The lower half is not in question, and it would be impossible to say whether Polus would accept it as it stands.

To buttress his conception of a partially reversed or overturned matrix, Polus introduces two devices. First there is Archelaus (470d–471d), revealed as a tyrant full of rapine and murder, correspondingly empty of a sense of justice and injustice. Polus then asks whether, were Archelaus to be caught and horribly tortured, he would be happier than when going scot free. The two species of pandering, witness calling and telling of horror stories, are matched by a third, derision.

Pursuant to his unwillingness to separate rhetoric from politics, Polus invokes the many as a way of settling the dispute: No one would agree with Socrates if a vote were to be taken. Here the response is that the voting procedure (in which Socrates himself is a duffer—473e–474a) would be quite irrelevant. We need but one witness to the truth of the argument, not Socrates, as one might expect, but Polus, the very man who up to now has stubbornly disagreed. Socrates is hinting, it would seem, that there is a dicast not yet sufficiently delineated, the individual soul, capable of judging according to a standard and no doubt ready to be judged by the same standard, rather than hoi polloi whose politics may loosely be labeled public opinion.

Bodies, colors, figures, and the like are called fair according to a standard of either pleasure or benefit. Socrates does not deny the right of pleasure to be invoked as criterion of such bodies and colors, and he is not really contradicting what was laid out in the Oblong, where pleasure was connected to pandering. He is almost surreptitiously introducing a distinction between moral and all other kinds of judgments. Pottery, for example, should be judged according to the enjoyment it provides, and one need not ask whether it be just or unjust; but this does not hold for stealing the pottery or using a jar as a weapon. There the objective benefit—not necessarily to oneself—is the measure for determining whether the act should have been committed or not, that is, whether it is fair (475a–b). Whether pleasure *always* connects itself to pandering, and benefit similarly is allied with some real art, is left unspecified at this juncture; and it is part of the long discourse with Callicles to answer this question.

The triad property-body-soul has already been established, and although items falling under each of the three heads have been named throughout the dialogue—would it be possible *not* to speak for long of things fitting under these?—now they are used as a way of distinguishing evils and remedies (477b–478c). The defect or evil of property is poverty, that of the body disease, that of the soul injustice (with the addition of licentiousness). To rectify these ills, the arts—notice, *arts*—must be applied: moneymaking, medicine, and finally justice, which in the mind of Polus could not be far removed in character from moneymaking. The Oblong is preserved in the references to body and soul, but in effect Socrates has extended it to cover property, external goods. This is legitimate if, and perhaps only if, it becomes necessary to extend the range of subject matter to the actual conditions of daily living, from having previously dealt only with the arts and their bogus substitutes that attempt to alter those conditions. Not only that, but moneymaking, the gaining of worldly goods, left shadowy in the conversation with Gorgias, has now taken on a role as one of the chief measures of the worth of rhetoric and justice.

At 478c happiness is defined negatively, as never acquiring evil, meaning evil that one does, and in a lesser sense avoiding evil that might be done to oneself. In the addendum to the exposition of the Oblong, Socrates has said that if body and soul were not separated in such a fashion that soul dominated the body (465c–d), separation of the arts could not be accomplished. Here (479b–c) Socrates uses this priority of soul over body by saying that a sick soul is worse than a sick body just as a healthy soul is better than a healthy body. The greatest good, for Socrates, would be to achieve happiness by never taking on evil in the soul; the next would be in acquiring evil in the soul but paying a due penalty and thus having the soul's burden of evil lifted, while the worst evil would lie in a wicked soul that pays no penalty.

Applications of all the chief terms in the Polus section are narrowed successively, so that justice, which earlier had stretched over most of the blue sky, later becomes a simple matter of paying for one's misdeeds according to established laws and customs. In the same way, the trio property-body-soul now (479c) takes a narrower significance: these three determine the ways a resourceful man can avoid paying penalties justly imposed upon him, by respectively acquiring money, friends, or persuasive speech. What has happened is that a part of the changed Oblong, namely the distinction between body and soul, now determines the meaning of two other parts, justice in relation to legislation, which is the other part of politics. (The legislation is shown in the enactments relating to crimes and punishments, the justice is in their application.) This has been accomplished by making further subdivisions in the arts of tendance of the body, and thence in the arts of tendance of the soul.

The Section with Callicles

At this point the reader leaves Polus (481b), almost as abruptly as he had to attend to him when Polus stormed into the conversation. With an irritated aside to Chaerephon, Callicles enters the debate, and with the exception of a couple of interjections by Gorgias, (497b; 506a–b), no other speaker is left to face Socrates. Polus had erred chiefly in re-merging, as much as he could, the terms separated by the Oblong. Callicles, one comes to see, commits the opposite mistake of making separations where the Oblong kept the terms together, or at any rate encouraged analogies. But the response of Socrates to this is not to say: "Look, Callicles, I made it clear long ago in my account of arts and panderings that so and so, and now you had better follow my lead on these matters." The Oblong is no club for beating every chance dog; rather it is a schematism that Socrates can keep in mind, altering its application as necessary to fit new arguments and cases or else giving it a new twist when it becomes plain that the Oblong is no longer suited to the new range of problems.

When Callicles intrudes (481b–c), thus commencing the long pages that turn his opening remark regarding the battle into a self-fulfilling prophecy, he says that if Socrates is serious, human life is turned upside down. Because virtually the whole of the treatment of Polus has required applications of parts of the Oblong, this would mean that to Callicles' mind the diagram as applied to self-incrimination rotates the values and practices of human life 180 degrees. Callicles, however, distributes the blame almost equally, so that not only is it Socrates who is guilty of a kind of sophistical duplicity but also the other two men have shown their frail nerves by making needless concessions.

The gambit of Socrates is now a curious one. Where before he began by hinting that he should merely ask the simple questions of Gorgias, and began with Polus by complaining of his speechmaking, with Callicles he commences by establishing certain attachments, some of which may be of the bodily desires though others inhere in the soul. Callicles is a lover of the populace at large, not because he cares much for the individuals comprising it but because its cultivation is the shortest way to power and pleasures; and he is a lover of Demus, who is well born. Socrates is both a lover of Alcibiades, who like the two loves of Callicles is fickle, and also a lover of philosophy which is not at all fickle. Love and all related concepts such as desire and friendship were left out of the Oblong, nor did they appear with any prominence in the discourse with Polus; and so this marks either a new application of ideas headed by body or soul or an outright change in the Oblong. This swift characterization of the two participants is, incidentally, not thrown away later in the dialogue; many pages (509c–520e) are devoted not so much to Callicles' view of politics as to the way of life he wishes to adopt, and almost as many (520e–527e) are concerned with the reasons why Socrates should pursue the mode of life that *he* does. Fickleness and stability loom significantly in the contrasts between the two lives. They are two new expressions that further characterize the columns headed panderings and arts respectively.

Callicles' response to the rather neutral, matter-of-fact account of the loves is to berate Socrates in two ways, for being a demagogue (482c–484c) and then for being a philosopher (484c–486d). During the course of these two censures, he reveals the germ of his opinions regarding political strength. The fact that Callicles accuses Socrates of being a demagogue for his having extracted concessions from Gorgias and Polus rather than being a sophist shows that, among the kinds of pandering listed by Socrates, Callicles recognizes only rhetoric; this is borne out much later (520a) when he scornfully rejects the sophists as nothing worth. In other words, though rhetoric seems useful to Callicles, it is also, he thinks, an illicit weapon in the hands of others, even those toward whom he is avowedly friendly.

As a sequel to the complaint about demagogy Callicles displays his famous dichotomy between nature and convention (483a).[7] A reader might try to show ingenuity by saying that nature is on the side of the body (i.e., body ruling soul), convention ranking with mental and verbal formulation (soul ruling body); but this would be misplaced, and it is safer to treat the two terms as novelties in the dialectic. It cuts across the range of things designable as subject matters of the two political arts of the Oblong. We need not recount here the clever way Callicles separates the strong single man from the weak multitude, except to say that it leads (483b) to a theme which over and over Callicles will return to—the need to be strong enough to rescue, to extricate oneself in case of trouble. His insistence upon strength (of one kind or another, it later turns out) should not blind us to the fact that although he complains that Socrates provides no important counsels to the public, neither does he, Callicles, offer much of positive value. For self-rescue, strength is needed, as we just said, and this means that rhetoric would be at best an adjunct to native force of character or wiliness or whatever it required, as in the few prototypes of those with more strength, such as the Great King (483d); yet though this ruler of the Persian Empire is a leader of armies and taker of cities, Callicles does not say outright that he has natural gifts qualifying him for this kingship.

This, however, is not the main issue with Callicles, who resents the fact that the many take the young—the same young whom philosophers will talk to in a corner—and enchant them with discourse about justice, so moderating their urges to show their true proclivities for power (483e–484b). By an odd reversal, rhetoric is made thereby an instrument not of the naturally strong man but of the weak opposed to him. It is thus difficult to affirm that the *Gorgias* pits Socrates against three defenders of rhetoric in all its usages. If Callicles is indeed its third champion, it is only by fits and starts that he earns this title.

Callicles, who is "friendly" to Socrates, now shows his mixed feelings, ruled by distaste, for philosophy. *Philosophy* is a new term, and although *discussion* has been introduced one or twice before (447c; 462a), the two have not been coupled, and we are only left to guess that Socrates is "doing philosophy" against Gorgias, Polus, and now Callicles. The trouble with philosophy, says the latter (484d), is that it keeps one ignorant of the laws and agreements of the city, that is, of conventions which the well-informed citizen should have at his fingertips, and diverts his attention from human desires and characters that are on the level of nature (Callicles is ignoring the confession of Socrates that he is a lover of Alcibiades). Philosophers are not laughable[8] if they practice philosophy when young; but the grown man persisting in philosophizing when he should be participating in or perhaps directing civic affairs should get a whipping.

Although he does not attack the Oblong in so many words, Callicles' assault upon philosophy and philosophers requires such an overhaul of the Oblong that if his diatribe is allowed to stand unchallenged it will bring down the whole Socratic enterprise, not only in what Socrates has been trying to prove but also in what he has lived and wishes to continue to live.

First, Callicles never makes it wholly explicit, but the connection between natural strength and having more apparently leads only to having more property or experiences giving pleasure. The pleasures referred to are *alogon*, unreasoning, unreasonable, hence presumably pleasures of the body. Thus Callicles is, if this Socratic interpretation of his opponent's discourse is right, in effect turning the Divided Oblong upside down, based upon the premise of the superiority of the strong man, as shown in figure 12.2.

We include something of the original Oblong simply because Calli-

	Nature	(Free, proper rhetoric)
Conventional Distinction	Body = Soul	Arts Pandering (Illegitimate rhetoric)

Fig. 12.2. *Result of Callicles' inversion of the Divided Oblong.*

cles does not refute or even deny it. At the same time he must use most of the leading concepts that Socrates has inserted.

Second, on the other hand, from Callicles' standpoint it would be more satisfactory to add nature as a horizontal heading to art and pandering, both of which are learned and thus emerge from agreements, conventions, in his view.

Either way, Callicles has done his utmost to add one entire rank, that of nature, to the Oblong. Socrates has stopped with arts aiming at the best and pandering aiming at the satisfaction of desires (whether these are natural or not is left undertermined); but Callicles wishes to ground both of these in a conception of human nature removed from the knowledge implied in the arts but based upon the gifts with which men come into the world. The Calliclean dialectic, we might say, maintains the level of food and beautiful bodies that Socrates set up, for it will soon become clear that Callicles must satisfy those desires. Correspondingly, with the addition of nature, the arts of politics and its imitators begin to fade away in his mind, and Socrates is hard put to restore their power and autonomy. Callicles is then driven to speak of wisdom as a strength only after having conceded that some of his other candidates for desirable qualities of the naturally superior man are not as worthy as he had thought. To oppose him the upper level of the Oblong must be kept in full view, even if theoretical knowledge (e.g., mathematics) never really appears except as a dim guiding star for the practical intelligence that Socrates puts forward as essential for the good life.

After Callicles reveals one of his principal tenets (486a), almost an *idée fixe*, namely the idea of false accusation and ways to counter it, Socrates turns to eliciting from his opponent the definition of natural justice, the right to be powerful and to have more that should be enjoyed by the strong (488b–492c). This of course removes it from all personal self-control and also from art and its aims for the best. Instead, it is desire and natural strength which become literally overpowering. Socrates interposes that nature and convention are for him not antithetical. Socrates, you are a driveler, responds Callicles (489b–c), catching me up on verbal misses of the mark—another instance of the fact that he looks upon the philosopher as a cheap rhetor-panderer. But the discussion continues, and at 491b–d Callicles formulates his final and best definition of natural justice: The wiser and braver should rule cities and have more. Callicles has made this much of a concession both to conventional politics and to the Socratic arts by including the wiser. But if philosophy is the love of wisdom, and like lovers has the most intimate contact with wisdom, then is it not true that to despise philosophy will bring Callicles into as serious a contradiction as that which deflated Gorgias?

This has been Callicles' best effort, and from this time forward Socrates treats him with less respect and indeed turns into the attacker. Callicles is asked about the position of temperance (sōphrosunē) in this listing of the virtues of the ruler and says (491e–492c) that the temperate are the foolish, the thoughtless, and that justice is the having of strong desires satisfied through having bravery and wisdom. The desires (and here Callicles is required to be totally honest) are those for luxury, and to attain them one needs force. Any restraint, Callicles implies (492c), in the form of agreement is embellishment, drivel, nothing worth. It is plain from this that there are now two sorts of embellishments for Callicles, those that he or some favored person would indulge in, and those in the hands of others wishing to set limits on the first group.

In a deliberately colorful passage (492e–494b) Socrates introduces three kinds of figures relating to pots (which are items of property) and one of a bird filling and emptying itself (the living body) as images designed to convince Callicles of the wrongness of his views. He is not at all convinced, either by these figures or by an account of bodily scratching, but is disquieted by one referring to boy prostitutes. The third member of the familiar Socratic triad, the soul, is not interjected here as an image into the list, but is used very late in the dialogue in the most striking figure of all, which becomes merged with an argument-logos.

A passage (495c–496e) seeks, by means of the equating of various pairs of terms, and again negating these equations, to find the relations between knowledge, pleasure, bravery, the good, and so forth. Defects of property and of the body, it is shown, are painful but are remedied by pleasures felt at the same time; and if the defects such as eye disease are evils, then the pleasant cannot be the same as the good. These are sophisms, Callicles bursts out (497b), never stopping to think that if his own position can be demolished by petty questions it could scarcely have been impregnable to begin with. In any case, it drives home farther the point that for him philosophy, sophistry, and rhetoric are one and the same. Shortly, however, Callicles abdicates this position as well.

At 500a–b Socrates revives his distinction between the things that prepare for pleasures though ignorant of the better (and worse), which is a backward reference both to the familiarities, the experiences, of which catering is an example, and things that know good and evil, such as medicine. To follow this out, one must choose between pandering, that is, speaking to the populace (en tō dēmō), and thus doing politics (not of the original kind, the art, but the more self-seeking and unreliable sort to which Callicles has committed himself), and philosophy. Heretofore, the idea of making a choice has not been openly voiced. Two ways of life have indeed often been contrasted, but they have appeared differently in different order each time—doctor or civic architect versus rhetor, just pupil versus unjust, tyrant versus the ruled, self-excuser versus self-accuser, Callicles versus Socrates, the life of the single strong man versus the life of the weak multitude. Now, however, that the role of the natural man has been fully—and variously—expounded, it is clear that a choice can be made between that and the life of the one who will, it seems, be able to confute the overbearing presentation of a doctrine of an overbearing man. The one person who might do this is the philosopher, whom Callicles has portrayed as ineffectual, at the same time giving ground to him at every step and losing his temper into the bargain. The remainder of the dialogue is given over to the choosing between them.

Some kind of practice (meletēn tina) is needed (500d–e) for acquiring either the good or the pleasant, and in the case of the former it is something such as medicine, which fathoms the natures, causes, and reasons of the body, while for the latter catering is unconcerned with natures or causes and is nothing more than a routine or familiarization. This recalls the language of the Oblong almost word for word, like a block of ice, floating in a sea, that resembles ever so closely another block some distance away. But as our account has been trying to make clear, these blocks are not wholly disconnected, and the ice floe underneath gives them substance, however much the blocks suffer changes below and above the surface of an inland sea.

The next few pages (501d–505a) are occupied with some things (pragmateiai) which gratify, and now it is a new list aiming at the soul (the body has been disposed of with catering) and these are flute playing, cithara playing, and, rather oddly, tragedy, which Socrates here looks upon as partly mere rhetoric—that is, pandering. The rhetor himself generally looks to gratify, but here (503a–b) Socrates distinguishes between one who harangues the mob and the more noble kind who looks to the improving of citizens' souls and is hard to find at any time.

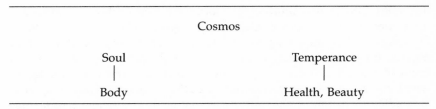

Fig. 12.3. *Socrates' expansion of the Divided Oblong.*

Candidates are sought for, and Callicles immediately proposes four, Pericles among them. The Socratic response to this is not to examine any of their careers (that will come later, 515c–516e), but to look further into the dichotomy that he has just brought back from early in his debate with Polus. Good men do not speak at random (503d–504a) but look to ends, to give form, plan, appropriateness to the external goods that they make, or, if it is the body, to set that in some order, which takes shape as health and strength (504b–d). For the soul the order is lawfulness, law, justice, and temperance (504d–e). Order and plan are thus characteristics of the arts, and if rhetoric is to attain the status of an art it will need to seek such an order. Where, though, is the model for this? In the cosmos, an entity whose very name implies such an ordering. It is this sense of proportion which Callicles has neglected, the power (508a) of geometrical equality among gods and men. He prefers *pleonexia*, having an excess, grabbing.

At 507d–e there is a peculiar back-and-forth movement in the dialectic. Socrates leads up to the point where he can talk about the cosmos through his account of temperance, which has been the most abused of the virtues by Callicles. But at 507e–508a Socrates introduces an orderly world as background for the orderliness of individual souls on earth. It is impersonal. In other words, he leads up to the cosmos through temperance, then down again to temperance from the cosmos, thereby confirming the necessity for temperance, and in a sense helping to show that temperance is living in harmony with the cosmos as a whole. Because the cosmos is by definition balanced, the temperate soul would have to be balanced. In effect Socrates has expanded the Oblong in a different direction from that of Callicles, who has by this time withdrawn his support for his own contribution. Socrates has added a new rank, as shown in figure 12.3. This passage, incidentally, is a prelude to the orderliness imposed by the gods at 523a–526d, in the myth.

Socrates now (509d–511a) develops a portrait of the Calliclean life that makes no use of the power or art required to keep us from doing injustice. To succeed, one must rule or tyrannize over the many, or at least be an associate of the existing tyrant, currying favor not by being any better or appreciably worse than he is but by having the same tastes, praising and blaming the same things. This will enable a young man to do as much injustice as he can, paying no penalty; and it will debase and maim his soul through imitation of a depraved master. (Imitation is borrowed from the Oblong, but there it meant that a kind of pandering imitates its matching art and is not directly an imitation of persons.) The imitator can kill, warns Callicles (511a), again implying that one must rescue oneself if the youthful imitator decides to pounce.

To explore the meaning of rescue, which Socrates has already (509b–c) said is ridiculous if it is simply for the sake of avoiding the paying of a just penalty, he likens it to swimming and piloting, neither of which puffs itself up, though both often save lives regardless of whether they are happy or miserable (511c–512b). We may examine this and related questions more than once (513c–d), says Socrates.

Instead of pandering, Callicles should embrace the career of tendance, but to accomplish this properly requires self-examination to be sure that he really understands the art he professes by assessing the teachers, first of architecture (property), then medicine (tendance of the body), and finally politics (i.e., goods of the soul). You, Callicles, are just beginning your life of public business in the city at large; but the question is, have you *ever* made any single evil citizen fair and good (515a–b)?

Let us talk, continues Socrates, about the four political leaders. Would an able herdsman take some tame animals and allow them to turn wild under his care (516a–b)? No rhetor either good or wicked seems able to lead the city. Well then, Callicles admits, there are no good political leaders who can match deeds with those of a bygone generation. He is obviously not thinking now of rhetoric as an art, for he has dismissed rhetoric in more than one guise and has scarcely mentioned the acquisition of an art because his natural man has no need of additional cultivation.

Socrates returns once more to the old distinction between gratifying and seeking the best (517b–c). You continually offer Sicilian cookbook writers in place of trainers (*not* doctors here), you praise the politicians who stuffed the city with docks and walls without regard to temperance and virtue. And although it was mainly the older ones who did this, it will be you yourself whom the corrupted populace will blame, though this would be only partly fair (519a–b). Yet politicians and sophists are the only persons who cannot complain if their citizens or pupils treat them badly, for they claim to expunge the very injustice that will redound to their own shabby mistreatment (519c–d). (This re-calls Gorgias' unwillingness to accept responsibility for his pupils.) Callicles spurns the sophists as nothing worth.

Socrates' response is to recall one more step in the argument regard-ing the arts and their pandering imitations: Sophistic, he says (520a–c), is fairer than rhetoric as legislation is fairer than justice and also as gymnastic training is fairer than medicine. The reason for this review is not only retrospectively to reinforce the distinctions once made but also to let it be known that a scale of perfections exists in the political careers that might be chosen.

Callicles, now feeling the ground sinking under his very feet (521a), turns angrily to Socrates: You yourself should do service, and it will be disreputable if you do not do the sort that I recommend (521b). Socra-tes' answer really amounts to a review of his reasons for choosing the philosophic life, for he knows that at bottom Callicles means that he, Socrates, can be hauled into court in this Athenian jungle and will be unable to defend himself. Only a base man, replies Socrates (521c–d), would do this, and he would not know what to do with the property he stole from me. I am almost the sole Athenian of our time to attempt the art of politics, and the only one now who practices it (521d). That, how-ever, puts me in the awkward position of being like a doctor tried by children on a charge brought by a caterer; and my defense, like that of the doctor, would provoke an outcry.

The contempt in which Callicles holds the sophists is another in-stance of our point that he makes separations, permits analogies, and tries to forbid outright mergings between items lying close together on the Divided Oblong. Sophistic and rhetoric are held by Socrates to be much alike, with sophistic superior because it resembles plan-making legislative politics, while rhetoric is an imitation of the judiciary as-pects. Sophistic, if one can accept this line of reasoning, evidently looks to the new formulations of whatever is under discussion, while rhetoric applies them in discourse before the general public. In addi-tion to the reason given above for Callicles' dislike of sophistic may be the thought that in resembling the lawmaking function it is a throwback to the many who pass laws in order to cramp the activities of the supe-rior man. The latest attempt by Callicles to revise the Oblong would now require that it be turned on its side once more, as shown in fig-ure 12.4.

Socrates now shifts his attention once and for all to the soul, which he hopes (522c–d) will be good so that inability to rescue himself from calumny could not be the result of any wrongdoing on his part and he could accordingly face death with equanimity. What is fearsome is not

SOUL	BODY
rhetoric	catering
politics	embellishing
sophistry	—
=	
philosophy	—

Fig. 12.4. *Callicles' final attempt to revise the Divided Oblong.*

dying (522e) but coming into Hades with injustice in his soul, his sins about him.

In the context of the Oblong, rationality and exact discourse are on the level of art, and art aims at the best, so it is no surprise that when Socrates offers a tale of the afterworld, he terms it a fair argument (*kalou logou*), not a myth, however much Callicles may want to take it as the latter. Death may be the separation of soul from body, but the soul takes on the aspect of the body in the afterworld. This soul-body is stripped of the living body, much as the living body is already stripped of its embellishments, but the soul-body retains its nature and the experiences it has undergone (*pathēmata*) and can appear as if unhealthy, wounded, disproportioned, ugly (524b–525a). The shift has been designed as a rhetorical device to make the ills of the soul appear as if bodily ills, which are much more obvious and more appalling to the ordinary mind unaccustomed to looking upon the soul as an entity in its own right. Socrates by this ingenious story has preserved the distinctions of the Oblong, but has also bridged the gap between soul and body by this new analogy.

The conception of punishment is now altered from what it was in the last few exchanges with Polus. There, it was not contemplated that a man could commit such injustice that he could not pay some penalty on earth sufficient to equal and thereby erase his offenses, but now it seems that misdeeds of such enormity can be done that a permanent, indelible stain is left upon the soul-body. With Polus the soul had not been in question, except for the exposition of the Oblong, and even then it was merely in relation to two kinds of temporal arts, those of justice and its twin, legislation, together with their imitations.

We gather this conception of punishment into one last schematism, as shown in figure 12.5.

This entire arrangement is bound together
by cosmos, order, the justice of Zeus

LIFE
Soul-body

arts and panderings

DEATH
Soul-body

good	—	philosophy	—	Isles of Blest
mixed	—	unnamed	—	eventual return to earth
evil	—	tyranny	—	Tartarus, etc.

Fig. 12.5. *Body and soul, reward and punishment in the Socratic view.*

There is a postlude, in which Socrates remarks upon the course that he himself might take (526d–e), then the fact that although Callicles, Polus, and Gorgias are the three wisest Greeks of their day, they cannot prove Socrates to have been wrong, and finally the course that both Socrates and Callicles should adopt in life, assuming that the latter can see the truth of what he has been told and made to admit this livelong day. Both he and Socrates should begin modestly to try to make individual souls better, then more and more of them, until finally ranging into the great city. Rhetoric must point only toward justice, and even if rightly used, the users must not swagger about. *Your* way of life is nothing worth, Callicles.

*   *   *

Our running account in this chapter is another attempt to trace certain threads that we believe help bind together the *Gorgias* through its rhythmic alternations of statements and their refutations or transformations. Among the dialectical structures are the leading versions of what we take to be the most important one in the dialogue. If this interpretation helps to uncover the unity of the work, well and good. Even this, however, does not quite satisfy the demands that we are setting up. True, it drops off almost all the artistic and personal aspects, which is not a deficiency, because the personal has been treated throughout, perhaps at indecent length. But some concerns are still bypassed, chiefly the actual principle of unity, its very meaning. Without some placing of this into the context of persons and doctrinal structures, our study will be ignoring the self-reflectiveness required for being a unified work of art and philosophy. The people participating do not give us the *ground* of unity, nor do the doctrines. To the extent to which it is granted to discourse on unity, we shall try to make a litte clearer what it is. If we can accomplish this at all, then our contention from the very outset, that the *Gorgias* does not permanently fall into two, three, or any other number of pieces, should be more nearly unassailable.

13

RHETORIC, KNOWLEDGE, REALITY

Let us recall the four levels (rather than disparate kinds or separated senses) of knowledge that we described in chapter 11, following a very familiar line in Plato's own thinking: Knowledge as
bare, unauthenticated perception, knowledge as everyday experience
of things, knowledge as thinking and rethinking of significant problems and solutions, and finally knowledge as nondiscursive insight
into the unities underlying these multifarious presentations of sense
and intellect. The first of the four comes close to being a sort of fakery;
the flow of these perceptions in driblets would offer little guide to their
own truth beyond their striking immediacy. Both the second and third
are surer indicators of the truth, the second less articulately, being based
directly upon one's sensations, memories, and habitual responses,
while the third is articulateness itself, embodied in questions, answers,
speeches long and short, substantive proofs and refutations. The fourth
is essential truth, hence is its own guide.

The three rhetors proved to be unreliable companions on the road to
truth, looking much like responsible thinkers but not really attaining
any wisdom because never genuinely loving it. Socrates in his magnanimity was the embodiment of such love, and this gave authenticity to
his utterances which helped to unify the *Gorgias* on a plane higher than
the somewhat fragmentary, divided, often evasive statements of the
men he confronted. We have never claimed that his presence could of
itself fully justify calling the dialogue an artistic and philosophic unity,
and so we turned to the structures that, mostly from his hand, were
created to show the triumph of discussion over speechmaking, of virtue over power, what is best over pleasure, knowledge over belief, reality over imitation. The only decent argument for offering a fourth chapter on unity is, then, one based upon the resemblance of our present
plan for expounding this unity to the four kinds of knowledge. Chapter
10 dealt with the shadows and hints of truth provided by the rhetors,
chapter 11 with the coming together of experience and truth as embod-

ied in a single man, chapter 12 with truth as outlined in successive transformations of arrayed concepts. It is now our task to suggest the existence of some additional unitary principle or principles emerging from the philosophy that Plato has offered in the content and design of the *Gorgias*, reapplying it in the appraisal of the dialogue as a coherent work of literature and speculation. If we do not offer a single formula it is because Plato himself offers none in the *Gorgias*, and moreover he takes pains in several other dialogues to dispose of the notion that there can be such a formula; it would be an impossible, self-defeating enterprise to define its nature.[1]

To accomplish our more limited task, however, we shall need to examine the bond between knowledge and the dialectical process by which it is attained and the dialectical form in which it is presented, and then the multiple relations between knowledge and art, purposeful action, and opinion. Having explored knowledge in its bearings with these three, we should be prepared for a final assault upon the fortress of unity in the dialogue, the first approach being to ask whether imitation is the principle whereby it is thus unified. Because it is not, the next and better approach will be to deal with the terms most nearly connected with unity, first its marks, of which there happen to be three, and second of its companions, which are the real, the true, and the good. The inquiry can take three forms, finding out first what notions of unity are explicitly provided by the text of the *Gorgias* itself, second the way these operate in what is shown by the dialogue, and third the way the most general terms can be related to each other, always bearing in mind the necessity for keeping the text meanwhile in steady view. It should be a little easier after that to suggest, so far as possible, what is meant by the undergirding unity of the *Gorgias*, if in fact such a unity can be found.

Dialectical Knowledge and Rhetoric

Knowledge is not only a leading topic for discussion but is also something actively sought by at least one participant in the *Gorgias*, despite the atmosphere of slick talking, passion, and prejudice that so often prevails. Knowledge or wisdom (*epistēmē, phronēsis*) is Socrates' ideal, and to this he would prefer to lead his three opponents, though such guidance is especially arduous. To him, the answer to the very first question, What is Gorgias? will not be an isolated piece of information, a datum picked up as a curiosity, then dropped. It is easy to say, Gorgias is a rhetor, or, Gorgias is a great man, or again, Gorgias practices a great art. Regardless of how "true" these answers might turn out to be, such talk would lead nowhere until grounded at least in an account of the nature of his so-called art. After that his relation to the art should become clearer. Such an account must be fully thought out, cohesive, running through several connected states—of the meaning of professing the art, its means and ends, its place in society, and its aiming toward good exclusively or toward good or evil indifferently. This is what Socrates wishes to extract from Gorgias especially, more than from anyone else. He succeeds in obtaining it, up to a point, though eventually his effort is frustrated by Gorgias' failure to perceive any distinction between responsibility for good and responsibility for what could be either good or evil.

The answer to the first question, What is Gorgias? is a lengthy one, and is not made satisfactorily until the final contrasts between the most just employments of rhetoric in society and the worst have been set forth, very late in the dialogue.[2] Even if one can formulate soundly a conception of justice as a balance in the soul, the question of its nature goes beyond the content of this statement by itself. It looks to what this statement has evolved from, even the most ill-considered prior utterances or the firmly held, inmost convictions of the speaker, and it looks also to what use can be made of them. The latter is in terms of deducible applications and the way they will alter the views and behavior of the person who generates this knowledge or to whom it is communicated. Eventually such knowledge, partly an intellectual exercise but more significantly an expression of the speaker's beliefs resulting from his own experience and reflection—such knowledge can be codified in the form of an array, a matrix, that will in turn lead to other matrices, subordinate, coordinate, or superordinate. The individual concept is understood, then, in the context of a statement or sentence; the sentence is grasped in the context of a sequence; this sequence is perceived clearly when schematized not by making it more "general" by giving its parts arbitrary letters but by placing the actual terms in a matrix and making them show by their "geographical positions," so to speak, what are their dialectical relationships, such as opposition, priority, equivalence, analogy, causal connectedness, and the like.

Much of the foregoing sounds, however, like the description of procedures that one finds in so many other philosophers and scientists, of whom Nicholas of Oresme is a good example. Taking a single set of principles, very straightforwardly stated, and reworking their combinations, using the initial meaning that he has given to his terms, he constructs ever more elaborate and varied theorems. (The mathematical physics of Thomas Hobbes is of the same sort.) Plato, for his part, proceeds differently. An original combination of terms is handily set up in a matrix along with coordinate expressions, and alterations can sometimes be put into other rows of that same matrix, or if not, at least entered in an adjoining one. Thus the antecedents in a dialogue are of two distinct kinds: (a) the various principles and anticipatory warranties, earlier described, and (b) the prior significations of the same terms.[3] One achieves an insight from examining the sequences (a), and insight of a quite different kind from considering the alterations in (b), where supervenience rather than deduction or induction is at work as a source of understanding.

Whether this be demonstration or inquiry (to use Aristotle's distinction) is not a simple question to answer.[4] It might even be reduced to the personal equation. The dialectical sequences ordinarily take place in question-and-answer form, and are generally conducted between two persons, one of whom is Socrates. Because he appears to have worked out in his head or in conversation elsewhere at least the main outlines of the problems and their solutions, he "knows more" or is "closer to understanding," so that he is in effect demonstrating while the less reflective respondent is merely inquiring, or being led in his inquiry. But this interpretation falls victim to certain objections. It is first of all untrue that inquiry is subordinate to the demonstration of something already known. Socrates remarks (458a–b) that his purpose is the finding of truth, through being ridded of untruth, and also gives the impression that even his most deep-seated convictions, those "bound in iron and adamant" (509a), are open to refutation, however unlikely such refutation is to be forthcoming.[5] He speaks of himself, moreover, as glad to be put to the test, to be corrected (457e–458a), even if the tester is but a child (470c), or, just as improbably, Callicles (486d–e; 506c).

It is safer to say that demonstration and inquiry are two sides of the same coin in the *Gorgias*, or rather that what seems to have been convincingly demonstrated later on turns out to have been a phase in an on-going inquiry of broader dimensions, or again that a series of questions takes its place in as settled a view as a topic such as power or justice will permit. Rhetoric can be hedged about with what might be called parametric questions—its name, its medium, its proper subject matter, its audiences, and so on. But the responses to these, even by an experienced rhetor, are at best approximations, altered as the dialogue progresses. What looked on first inspection to be a solid set of answers finally discloses itself to have been a propaedeutic, not less important for that reason, but now an incentive for further examinations of the same or closely related topics. In the *Gorgias*, at least, a principle and a tentative hypothesis are identical, viewed from two aspects.[6] From the standpoint of much medieval logic, such as that of William of Shyreswood or William of Ockham, this would be out of the question; but considering the elusiveness of rhetoric and the confusions of all three respondents to Socrates, it is doubtful that any other verdict could be rendered.

There are some riders to this account, drawn as it is from the *Gorgias* yet not fitting it exactly because of the comparative looseness of the argument in many places, even crucial places. If the knowledge were fully developed, and if the dialectical process were carried out in an unprejudiced and rational atmosphere (as in the *Philebus*), then inquiry and demonstration would be absolutely identical. But here the knowledge is so saturated with opinion, and the rational approach is often so close to being subverted by irrelevant and highly disruptive tactics, that no requirement for knowledge or dialectic is fully met. The knowledge, were it wholly integral, would involve the grasp of natures, for example those of human beings; second a grasp of their proper aims, what is truly the best for them; and finally an understanding of means to satisfy those aims. But Socrates is faced with three men, not one of whom understands what a nature is or cares in the least what is best, except for himself. When Socrates must deal with such men, he cannot erect all the structures needed for a clear mastery of the issues surrounding the character of rhetorical speech and its ability or inability to promote the real good of human life. His explicit prescriptions for the right uses of rhetoric occupy no more than a few lines in the eighty pages of the *Gorgias*.

Purposeful Action and Knowledge

Customarily, one thinks of practical issues as being applications, to some degree, of theories of knowledge and reality, though not less important for that reason. In Locke, Hume, Kant, and Schopenhauer, to take just four examples, matters of epistemology and ontology arise before any attempt is made to take up the philosophy of action, will, and choice. The reverse is true in the *Gorgias*. One is struck by the far greater proportion of references to human beings, both individuals and types, than to what are usually called abstractions. Most of the references to knowledge have mainly to do with the conduct of the discussion or else with arts to which rhetoric is being compared or contrasted. It would therefore be a convenience if one could import a collection of doctrines from other dialogues interpreting the *Gorgias* in order to state in ringing phrases a Platonic theory of insight into the eternal reality, be it forms, or the one, or the form of the one, or whatnot. Such an importation must proceed with caution, on either of the two chief views of Plato's philosophy. If, as we happen to believe, the multitudes of both apparently contradictory and apparently repetitious statements in the dialogues taken as a set can be largely explained as attacking subtly different questions with words that have shifted their meanings, the borrowings from the *Timaeus* or *Parmenides* or even from *Epistle VII* will merely recommend lines of approach to the question, Can we know the real? but will not answer it definitively. If, on the other hand, there is solid evidence within the writing of changes of mind, then the borrowing would mean even less for the *Gorgias*. On this latter showing it is fairly agreed that our dialogue is a moderately early one, a beginning of a transition to a middle period; hence if we were to make full use of the later dialogues, the result would be artificial and indeed fraudulent. (A third possibility would be to invent some theory of knowledge and pass that off as Platonism. Even this has been tried. But the Battle of Jena is not dinning in our ears, and we shall attempt no Hegelian apostrophe to reason.)

All things considered, then, we should turn up what evidence we can from the way the *Gorgias* is written, find out what this signifies for the notion of unity, and then reflexively apply that to the dialogue. If another dialogue should prove helpful, that would be only by way of suggestion.

In the *Gorgias*, purposeful changes in human life are effected chiefly through art and virtuous action. Throughout, Socrates assumes that an art is knowledge and a virtue is too, and that action based directly upon either one will be both effective and beneficial. The medical art benefits someone other than the doctor, the just decision benefits someone other than the dicast. This is held constant, and it is against this that rhetoric and other practices are measured or with which they are temporarily identified.

If art is knowledge of the best, the tugs between proper and defective consideration of what is best should influence treatment of the arts. If Polus proclaims rhetoric an art, his conception of the latter is fragmentary. Even the art of piloting is treated as having a doubtful issue, it carries a man safely to port but may still do him a disservice if he suffers from some disease, with little to live for (511c–512b). But the pilot cannot be expected to approach the passengers to ask whether they consider themselves worth preserving from the Aegean deep.

The mathematical arts (see 450d) are given little of the treatments of the *Republic, Philebus, Theaetetus, Meno*, and *Laws*. In the *Gorgias* these arts are introduced chiefly to anchor the principle of proportion,[7] a contribution of geometry to be used (reservedly) in framing the Divided Oblong (465b) and determining justice (508a). Imposition of proportion in a wide sense is the chief aim of the entire dialogue: The three rhetors have espoused doctrines which though good in part have grown out of bounds. Gorgias pits himself as an eloquent man against the populace, and so long as he is constituted their persuader, he believes that he should be awarded all the freedom, they none. How their goods and functions are divided up is no concern of his. Consequently, when he concedes that a pupil might abuse rhetoric and art unjustly, in a way this is a bad joke. Gorgias himself has *already* been unjust; rhetoric is an unjust use of what might be an art. As for Polus, he echoes Gorgias (for does he not know all that his elder knows?) but carries the argument a step farther. One might offer the equation that Polus is Gorgias plus the condoning of violence, thereby stretching the proportionality one step beyond its proper measure and virtually destroying it. Then there is Callicles, and against him the need to reestablish a principle of proportion is made fully explicit (508a). Callicles would award the superior man more—indeed infinitely more—of everything, giving as an excuse the fact that the strong are and ought to be above the law, justice, and the populace. When driven by relentless questioning to reveal what it is that the strong should have more of, he concedes that it is pleasures, which he divides into good and bad only after having been frightened by the hint that he is a paying pederast.

Socrates' complaint that Callicles is unaware of geometrical equality (proportion) is recognition of the inability of his opponent, and by extension, of the other two men as well, to grasp *any* principle of order, an order that Socrates eventually attributes not only to human dealings but to the entire universe as well. The unjust man is out of harmony (i.e., a mathematical or quasi-mathematical proportion) with an ordered universe. To have an art in such a universe means, then, to possess a method of discerning the best possible condition of the thing, not too much of it, and this in turn means seeing how it can fit into its broader context, ultimately the cosmos as a totality. Rhetoric falls short not because its practitioners lack native intelligence or skills but because their ambition is reflected in their separate and common theories of the calling as related to society. More makes less.

Third, coupled with knowledge of proportions or fitness of things is the need for enumerating ways that such fitness can be attained through mastery of causes. The man of art knows the means for producing what he has planned in his own mind. Rhetors think they know the means; they can find ways to persuade audiences, else they would not long survive as rhetors. Their aims, however, are confused (Gorgias), or mistaken (Polus), or shifting (Callicles). Otherwise rhetoric would be an art, with a dignity approaching that of dialectic, rather than sharing all the weaknesses of the other types of pandering. As pandering, rhetoric is both an abuse of the means used in the arts and a surreptitious faking of their rightful ends by unworthy ones. There can be no question of a misuse of rhetoric, for it is already the misuse of the scale of values of the political arts, a prime example being the four-rank set advocated in the Oblong. A proposition enunciated by a practitioner of the arts, qua artist, will be right; but if right, it will reflect differences between good, better, and best, or between good, bad, and intermediate. These evaluations are referred altogether to the subject matter of each art. The columns are well proportioned to the building, better than in the other building; the shoes are very comfortable and durable; the melody is excellently composed for the aulos, while the zither cannot make it sound properly. The test of the rhetor is how much he knows, not of proportions and the means to obtain them, but of generating a belief that persuades the audience to act as he wills. The artist too acts in a certain manner, he makes something, he imposes a shape or function upon the material or medium. For the rhetor the audience is his material, and if it has been persuaded it acts in the fashion advocated; if not, it remains obdurate or listless. Because responses of this sort either take place or they do not, these black-or-white results become the sole test of the efficacy of rhetoric in general and the power of some particular rhetor.

Fourth, it cannot be said that the aim of rhetoric is victory and that of dialectic is something else; discussion can aim to defeat an opponent, just as a rhetorical address can defeat. The difference is not in the intensity of belief generated by rhetoric as opposed to dialectic, for after all the dialectic of Socrates, whether carried on with others or with himself,[8] irresistibly motivates him to pursue a life quite different from the ordinary. Instead, the chief divergence is in the variety of approaches that dialectic can make to a single topic, for usually it takes rise from the combined efforts of more than one person, while rhetorical address can remain the work of a single orator over whom there is no control except in the eventual approval or disapproval of the crowd. The difference between such a limited judgment passed by the rhetor and upon him by his listeners and the multiple judgments provided in a dialectical situation in which natures, means, ends, and much more can be weighed and in which dialectic itself can become the subject of discussion from an infinite number of standpoints—this difference is striking and results in a flexibility and universality neither of which is possessed by rhetoric. The only difficulty is that the rhetor cannot see this, and the distinction remains a dialectical one in being evident only to a dialectician or to his pupil. Neither Gorgias nor Polus nor Callicles is capable of receiving such instruction.

Fifth, we thus have the great paradox of the *Gorgias*: Both Socrates' art, which is dialectic when he can practice it, and his way of life, which is the way of balanced virtues, are better than rhetoric and the struggle for power. But by the very *nature* of the superiority of the first art and manner of life and the inferiority of the second, the superiority itself cannot be taught to the three rhetors. It is a second paradox that if the superiority were to be imposed rather than taught, it would no longer be superior, for the use of the force upheld by the rhetors at once causes art to deteriorate and virtue to be corrupted, and they become no better than their imitations. Gorgias has made it clear, for instance (449b–c), that he is quite able to conduct *his* kind of question-and-answer session, and Polus is ready to accept what *he* thinks to be proof and disproof. Those happen to be dialectical devices rather more than rhetorical, so that Socrates can shift his adversaries to his own side; but the devices again become something different when dialectic is purged of its rhetorical associations as much as it can be.

One recalls that Callicles' extended recrimination (482c–486d) is against Socrates as rhetor and philosopher, not dialectician. Plato's point seems to be that the pure Socratic way is dialectic when it pertains to arts of discourse, but philosophy when it pertains to the exercise of virtue. Callicles evidently does not recognize dialectic, for he casts aspersions upon Socrates as a demagogue, and then as a philosopher who wastes his time and gives no counsel to the city. Disregarding Callicles, if dialectic and philosophy are in some sense one, then there is a like coincidence of art (or knowledge) and virtue. This is rendered a little more complicated by the fact that philosophy may also be said to exploit the rhetorical mode that makes itself available when Socrates finds himself in the unfavorable circumstances with his three opponents.

There are thus two means for philosophy, the use of discussion and the use of rhetoric. (There is but one for rhetoric itself, for question-and-answer is simply one more kind of display to titillate the audience.) Socrates, concerned not only about the moral effects of the exercise of rhetoric but also about its epistemic grounds, links the two. It is impossible to do good to others or even assure it for oneself if the motive is not based upon one firm ground: the intellectual grasp of the object for whom improvement is sought. This is a roundabout way of saying that virtue is knowledge, or at least rests wholly upon knowledge. Socrates has reached a stage, through his natural development and painstaking self-study, at which the ethical quality of his life, the epistemic certainty of his convictions, the dialectical exactness and the rhetorical plausibility of his discourse all have the same root in his soul. But this could only be fully and clearly shown either to himself or to another man like himself, and of him the *Gorgias* gives mainly the hints, the traces, and the signs through what is no more than a second-best manifestation.

Again, this is the difference between instruction that brings two souls, even if their ages and backgrounds are different, into a union.[9] Its imitative substitute is the uneasy sparring of rhetoric when that is forbidden free rein in a monologue oration and interrupted by questions.

For Gorgias, teacher and rhetor are identical. To Socrates' way of thinking, Gorgias is not a real teacher, and though he has no second sight into the souls of Polus and Callicles, Socrates is perceptive enough to identify the influence that Gorgias and his *empeiria* would have upon them. Despite all this, however, one must remember that rhetoric is designated by Gorgias as working primarily not upon individuals but upon dicasteries, assemblies, and crowds of chance hearers. None of these could be expected to acquire, like assiduous pupils, the whole art of speaking merely from having heard some display.

Because the essence of display is praise and blame, bestowed as the speaker will upon what he will, the speeches revolve around qualities rather than the essences of what is praised, the What sort? (*Poion ti?*) rather than the What? (*Ti?*). Polus, for instance, uses the *Poion ti?* in place of the essential (448e). In addition, we find the entire discussion moving from the nature of rhetoric itself, once this is tentatively broached, to its effects and qualities. The essence is stated by Gorgias and Socrates in a pair of adjoining definitions (452d–453a), and then greatly modified by Socrates in accordance with further admissions of Gorgias, in the Divided Oblong; no additional attempt is made to define rhetoric, and the question becomes one of considering whether rhetoric is good or not. Under what circumstances is the use of rhetoric *morally* permissible? Polus thinks this means, When does rhetoric bring an advantage? and assumes that the answer is, Always. Callicles takes this up by asserting that the advantage is really conferred by nature, with rhetoric now reduced to an adjunct of the strong man's innate judgment and will. Whether this will be fair to the populace now becomes the problem, and with it the further inquiry into what is universally fair and just. Thus there is a kind of relativity between the *Ti?* and *Poion ti?* questions. An inquiry into the essence of justice is in effect an inquiry into the quality of rhetoric. This does not mean that the dialogue has lost the thread of coherent argument, for even if the essence of rhetoric has been provisionally accepted it is not only possible but necessary to proceed to the question with which Polus began: Is it good, and when?

Knowledge, Opinion, Action

The history of philosophy is rife with ways to relate knowledge and opinion (*doxa*) or knowledge and belief (*pistis*). For many, belief becomes faith, and assumes a role higher than that of knowledge; for others, belief is superstition, an inadequate grasp of causes, and it cannot compete with knowledge. For certain philosophers, belief and opinion are identical, both dealing with the impermanent and uncertifiable. Or the two are different, belief being temperamental, opinion a matter of cognition. Some thinkers, again, have taken knowledge to be no higher than opinion, and have insisted that all principles are but arbitrary hypotheses. Others make opinion evolve into knowledge, given the right conditions and method. Again, the two are separated into what is found in secure, self-evident principles and what springs up in ordinary conversation and is merely proposed for examination or dispute. Of all these, probably the most common assumption has been that once knowledge is attained, one is in a quiet, safe harbor where there can be no need for further doubt, disharmony, or capitulation. Whatever (so runs this view) is known *and* known that it is known, is indubitable; anyone raising a hand in protest is making a fool of himself through failure to understand the very meanings of the terms in sentences that are self-sustaining.

What this assumption leaves out is that every bit of knowledge has an object, and not all objects are of equal rank. Had Socrates been teaching the Slave Boy the connection between political parties and revolution, he would surely have been able to exhibit, using much the same tactics as he used for instruction in doubling the square, the essentials of Athenian party politics. The boy would have stumbled and hesitated but finally been brought to understanding points about rich and poor, democrats and tyrants. But the knowledge of politics would still be about persons and institutions subject to change. This would lack what makes knowledge of mathematical objects and of the forms a knowledge more eternal, and, if anything, more eminently self-evident. Thus in the *Gorgias*, even if some positive knowledge is a goal reached, it still falls below mathematics and astronomy. Despite his remark about iron and adamant, at no point does Socrates give assurance that what is discovered to be true of rhetoric is absolutely permanent; that piece of knowledge is better than the opinions of the many or even of the three rhetors about rhetoric, but while it uses mathematical ways of talking, no one can say that it *is* mathematics, that is, talking in a mathematician's way about mathematical quantities.

Hence there is no fixed, hard-and-fast distinction in the *Gorgias* between applications of knowledge and opinion, with precise definitions of each, but only a suggestion, drawn from remarks by Socrates and from his practice throughout, that knowledge is of the true and opinion is of what may be true or may be false. What the *Gorgias* really *does* illustrate, however, is a pairing of knowledge and opinion in various ways:

First, the result of dialectical checking of every pronouncement by questioning and the requirement that what is said is at least subject to proof results not only in knowing a statement as true but also in knowing that it is known to be true. On the other hand, because knowledge pure and simple is not a topic treated directly in the *Gorgias*, knowledge of knowledge is not overtly discussed, though it is exhibited by the figure of Socrates. In him knowledge is part and parcel of the soul, and knowledge of knowledge becomes identical therefore with knowledge of the self. Again, because rhetoric is primarily either good or bad, the knowledge relating to it has action for its content, action being the main sphere of these values in the dialogue.

Second, there is also knowledge of opinion, this being Socrates' insight into the putative truths promulgated by the rhetors, either in the speeches or their conversation. As for the speeches, we have only Gorgias' admission of ignorance of their subject matters to rely on; the dialogue contains no quotations or other specific references to his public addresses, whether historical or invented by Plato. To know knowledge of opinion is not to put opinion itself upon a firmer basis but merely to show up its defects, suggest reforms. The fact that the knowledge of opinion is the possession of Socrates does not mean that he himself is wholly free of opinions and carries about with him only those cognitions above all dispute. At the outset, and for considerable stretches in the dialogue, he is tentative, and in his inquiries is unsure of the responses before they are actually given. By labeling the myth at the end an argument, he both elevates the myth and also, in a more limited sense, compromises earlier parts of the argument, making it clear that the very form of discussion and proof that he has so far carefully managed shades off into tales of what is not open to experience, not understood while one is alive.

Third, for opinion about knowledge one would look to the three rhetors and to Chaerephon. The chief—and somewhat paradoxical—feature of this sort of opinion is that it takes itself to be knowledge, that is, the opinion is that knowledge and opinion are indistinguishable, hence both can equally claim to inspire right action. The cure for this, which Socrates endeavors tirelessly to bring about, is of course to show both the shortcomings of the particular opinions held by the three rhetors and also to develop a recognizable distinction between art and pandering. Because art is knowledge of things to be done and made, one still cannot forget that there is other knowledge of the finally true and un-changing—often hinted at but never expounded in the *Gorgias*.

Fourth, the same may be said for opinion of opinion, hard to distin-guish from opinion about knowledge as it may be, because both are poorly grounded, alterable, and no doubt emotionally biased. The three rhetors hold in common an opinion about opinion, which is that an au-dience entertains opinions that are to be manipulated, intruded upon. If the speaker with his knack accomplishes this, action will be either commenced, modified, or halted, depending upon the rhetor's will.

The *Gorgias* poses the question, How ought we to live? (492d; 500c–d), and assumes a knowledge of human existence where not all discourse and all actions are as they should be. Callicles, who seems more so-phisticated intellectually than his two companions even if less traveled than they, lets the question lead in more directions, starting from con-flicts between the one strong man seeking to free himself from fetters of conventional law and the encroaching populace. Right action defies the many, and includes demands for more than one's equal share. Emerging from the long conversation with Socrates, the overall nature of philosophy figures less than the considerations joining in sound practical knowledge. Should one follow one's desires, letting pleasure guide every choice? Should one not rather develop an art to distinguish between unworthy and worthy pleasures that accord with a life deter-mined on other grounds to be good? Should one try to extend life as long as possible with the aid of pilots, doctors, and of course wily rhet-ors? Living the virtuous life requires a new way of *knowing* what is best and what must be done to obtain it without damaging other souls. This way cannot be conditioned by the morally hit-or-miss employment of rhetoric or the modes of life, forming the content of opinions advocated by any of Socrates' three opponents. Although he could easily deal with them by playing verbal tricks better than theirs or by giving more eloquent speeches to counter their own praise of tyrannical rule, it would destroy the real philosophic issue, which is, using honest philo-sophic discourse as much as will be effective in the circumstances to rescue not oneself but philosophic knowledge and with it the philo-sophic life from the hostile accusations implicit in Gorgias, crudely hinted by Polus, loudly trumpeted by Callicles.

Imitation and the Real

A strain of thinking that runs through the *Gorgias* is the use of general, speculative, systematic reflections pertinent not only to human topics but also to existence of every sort and rank. By referring to it, terms are ultimately made clear and statements are ultimately guaranteed to be true, bound securely (527b–c). To discover and make this strain evident becomes our next task. No new terms of Plato's or any others need be introduced, but the familiar ones do require separating out and juxtaposing with each other in ways we have hitherto neglected. First, we should speak of imitation, appearance, as a candidate for the sought-for principle by which the *Gorgias* is organized into a tightly knit work of philosophical and literary art.

When anything is first apprehended by opinion and is later explored by dialectic, some of its features take new places as objects of knowledge and hence as real. Yet the paradox is that their reality—when finally recognized—is *still* imitation as they are thought of and used in the context of ordinary civic experience; they remain the objects of opinion for the rhetor and for the many. Consider some of the marks of pandering: It (a) imitates the arts; (b) aims at pleasure; (c) is careless of truth and justice; (d) stealthily insinuates itself into a position to compete with or even supplant the arts. If the carelessness were studied more closely, the relations between pandering and justice would begin to emerge, for they do not occupy altogether separate realms: Not everything a rhetor says is untrue or unjust. As the possibly true connections come to the front and the false ones are exposed and discarded, what remains is that the fraction of pandering rhetoric that turns out to have a care for justice is preserved and is no longer pandering in the original sense at all.[10] Again, pandering aims exclusively at pleasure, but good pleasures have been distinguished dialectically from bad. A truce is arranged, and the rhetor-panderer is forced to attend to pleasures helping to improve what he has formerly corrupted by his own tactics. The doctrines of Callicles are gradually overcome by Socrates, even if the man himself is not wholly disabused of his errors and cured of his ambitions. Persuasion can be made compatible with the life of philosophy and virtue. Without this, however, the ground would be even more cluttered with remains of undertakings that audiences had been hoodwinked into willing only to find them contrary to their own wishes. This raises some doubt whether imitation is suitable as a rallying point if we hope to show the unity of the dialogue. We should, however, press on to test and if necessary reinforce these doubts.

The *Gorgias* acquaints the reader with reality through the pandering that remains unrecognized as such until Socrates shows it for what it is.[11] Furthermore, imitation is presented first by images of and derived from personal experience, and these images suggest a temporary measure for reality, a direction in the inquiry later to be rearranged. For most of the real things discussed in the *Gorgias* there are previously de-

REALITY	IMITATION
discussion	display
knowledge	opinion
art	pandering
medicine	catering
justice	rhetoric
real power	spurious power
Socrates' image of the philosopher	Callicles' image of the philosopher
Socrates' statesmen	Callicles' statesmen
justice under Zeus	justice under Kronos

Fig. 13.1. *Real and imitative in the dialogue.*

lineated counterparts less real but easily mistaken. The imitations are not precisely what they were pretended to be by their makers or agents, but they are still *something* [12] For this reason we have drawn up a list of real things and their imitative counterparts in the dialogue in figure 13.1. One must keep in mind that the imitations are contrasted with their correspondents and are not out-and-out negations of them.

Five remarks concerning imitation are in order:

In the first place, as corollary to the partial reality of imitation, the tyrannical life, pretending to be the one really good life, imitates the philosophic, but to someone who had suffered unwarrantedly at the hands of a tyrant it would scarcely be comforting to hear that tyranny was unreal and the suffering as well. The dialogue temporarily fixes this proportioned status of each thing under review, a status which does not change with respect to its immediate neighbors; but the neighbors are eventually shuttled about and away, and then the status does change. Apparent contradictions in the evaluations of the same things are not then difficult to interpret and remove. [13] Gorgias closely identifies himself with rhetoric, but the Oblong offers its succinct indictment of rhetoric in general. This, however, is merely the locating of rhetoric as a whole, and distinctions between exceptional kinds of ends have not yet been made, hence knowledge still identifies rhetoric wholly with pandering, branding it with the four characteristics noted earlier. Rhetoric, which began as an undifferentiated whole, is then split into two kinds, specific functions being accorded to each.

Second, reciprocity between reality and imitation does not hold. If catering imitates medicine, it does not follow that medicine imitates catering, however true it may be that both in their way supply bodily needs, one unpleasantly, the other pleasantly. It might seem that this lack of reciprocity would make it easy to distinguish caterer and doctor, rhetor and statesman, once and for all. But just as some tasty foods are healthful, so the rhetor might easily recommend some course of action both attractive and wise.

Third, in the *Gorgias* there are no imitations of imitations. Gorgias himself is imitative, surely, a bogus statesman; there is also a sense in which Polus imitates Gorgias, but not in a direct line that would make him an imitation of something already imitative, for this would raise the paradox that he could conceivably be a genuine statesman. Polus, if he does imitate Gorgias, is no more and no less a real statesman than is the older man; his imitation lies instead in his accepting and parroting what Gorgias has spent a lifetime gathering for himself. It is not the pretense of knowledge about forts and warships that Polus imitates, for he makes the very same pretext himself, but instead the knowledge, or rather sets of opinions, about rhetoric. This grasp of the knacks of rhetoric has nothing directly to do with the warships or the public, and relates to length of sentences, figures of speech, the building of climaxes, and so forth. At all events it is kept hidden from the city at large. In the same way, opinion in general has no imitation in the *Gorgias*.[14]

Fourth, using imitative means will in general lead to ends no less imitative. Though the caterer may occasionally provide healthful foods, this is coincidental to his purposes; and he would be much more disappointed if anyone found his cuisine unappetizing, though the doctor would not concern himself over that. Using rhetoric leads to what Polus thinks is power, but it is not real because so frequently it results in unforeseen reversals of fortune for the person wielding it (466b–468a). This is, of course, from the standpoint of Socrates; the rhetors, and possibly Chaerephon and the audience as well, believe ardently in the reality of what they hold most dear—and advantageous.

Finally, Socrates' main point is that real things are better than their imitations. This is his order of statement in the Divided Oblong, but only after he and the reader have been drenched in appearances, which means that in a very different way one may say that because the arts are better, that is, they proceed from knowledge, they are more real. In the Oblong itself, however, the arts come first, and the dross is left over to make a place for itself if it can. The trouble is that the three rhetors, and the peoples of the cities through which Gorgias has cut a swath, are happy to accept the dross, giving it a place of honor. Socrates would add that the honor too is mostly dross.

This does not denigrate rhetoric totally. Yet when Socrates deflates its claims to being an art (462b–c), this is met with neither cavil nor whimper from the two young men who have put their confidence in rhetoric and are staking their careers upon benefits it confers. (Evidently they care less whether rhetoric really is genuine art, as Polus had earlier claimed, 448c, than they do whether it will bring the hoped-for advantages.) Rhetoric as conceived by Gorgias and Polus can still be turned to valuable moral effect in the hands of the right speaker, though its power is not at all daimonic, as Socrates has ironically suggested (456a).

It should be clear, then, that imitation, no matter how prominently featured and exemplified, cannot be the concept of most general scope that will serve as the principle whereby the *Gorgias* is unified. Although the concept digs itself into the deepest recesses of the dialogue, its effect, if it were allowed to hold independent sway, would be divisive. However much the dialogue might be *about* imitation, if it were intended in itself to *be* no more than an imitation it would lose all claim to having the moral force that it so clearly tries to uphold. Thus the work would be split against itself, and the reader would end by thinking justifiably that Plato is a skeptic, perhaps even a deceiving cynic.

Unity and Its Three Marks

Wholeness

In our effort to find a clue to the unification of the dialogue, we must seek a principle reliable and general. This is what Socrates tries to introduce, and we shall search for it once more. We begin, then, by listing most of the hints provided by Socrates himself regarding unity, together with some comments indicating whether they are applicable to the work as a whole.

Those having to do with *argument:*

1. *One must stick to the question* (448d)—in other words, consistency of topic is essential; this is the very point we are trying to prove about the work as a whole, and we would be begging the question to invoke it as anything more than a heuristic hypothesis here.

2. *No contradictions are allowed* (461a–b; 495a)—what the *Gorgias* will show, rather, is that no contradictions are to go unresolved. But since Socrates can detect and resolve those of other men, as well as for himself, he should leave few gaps in his own argument, which happens to be the one that prevails.

3. *One should put a head on the argument* (505c–d)—in effect, the argument must be completed; this holds for the dialogue itself because the questions originally raised are answered by the time the last words are spoken. This is the conception of the whole with proper parts.

4. *The argument requires an orderly completion* (454b–c)—in other words, it must have a starting-point and progress from there to an identifiable conclusion; this notion of order is another that it is well to consider.

5. *Anaxagoras mixed things together without distinction* (465d)—taking this in the naïve sense, Socrates rejects it; simple homogeneity is not always a mark of the real.

Those relating to the *arts*:

6. *Each art has one subject matter* (450a–b)—if authorship of a philosophic dialogue is an art (and we suspect that it is!), then there should be a single subject matter, unless philosophy is an art of such different order that it is not confined to one subject. But we must remember that the scope of a subject matter has not been predetermined, and that it is quite possible that the many issues raised in the dialogue could well fall under some one head. This hints at a concept of proportionality that is further invoked elsewhere, although here it is a simple one-one ratio that is used.

7. *Rhetorical power comprises all powers* (456a–b; 466b)—although Socrates deprecates most examples of rhetoric as practiced, the dialogue itself is, qua persuasive instrument showing the weaknesses of rhetoric, itself a piece of rhetoric, and among other ways can be judged in that light.

Those relating to *justice*:

8. *The three judges of the dead issue a single decree* (524a)—divine justice is never ambiguous or inconclusive; its exercise is always unified. If this is to be applied to the *Gorgias* at all, it must mean that its lesson is one and not many.

9. *Socrates states a single lesson at the end, though it has many parts* (527b–c)—this is not inconsistent with the point immediately preceding; it offers the notion of an individual real thing that is yet compounded of different though not totally dissimilar parts.

10. *There is a single greatest good* (451d–452e)—although Gorgias, who first makes this point, thinks that the good is freedom for himself alone, it turns out that the real good to be sought is the exercise of virtue in the state despite the evils in that society; but that is still a single good. The *Gorgias* as a whole teaches this, which comports well with no. 8, above.

11. *All fair things are called fair according to a single standard* (474d)—that standard is utility and pleasure, and it applies to the *Gorgias* as a whole in evaluating it for the reader, though it cannot be taken in a sense that would originally have been immediately acceptable to Polus.

12. *Virtue is centered in the cosmos* (507e–508a)—that is, the human good would not be entirely meaningful taken by itself without a superior order in which to set it. This assertion reinforces the determination to look for the widest possible context in which the *Gorgias* itself can function as a whole.

These are made along the way, most of them being embedded in contexts where imitation looms large; but in referring to an ordered whole with discriminable proportions they envision a concept of reality resembling the one for which we are looking. The reality is compared to something less real but does not lose its reality thereby and does not exhaust the relation which, from the standpoint of imitation, is a sliding one but from the standpoint of the reality itself is clearcut and permanent. Reality defines rather than merely introduces or suggests the measure of the imitative. In the Oblong, for instance, there can be no doubt of the specified nature and worth of medicine, gymnastics, judicature, or legislation as entities; following after are the spurious counterparts whose feebler natures take rise from their models. We know what is real by intrinsic marks—its capabilities, actual functions, its ultimate purposes. These are not separable qualities, answering the question, *Poion ti*? for example, reputation, possibilities for profit, attractiveness for potential students, or the like. These latter can be had by *empeiria*, familiarity born of not-very-critical contact with the thing in question, whereas the essential is learned through arduous dialectical exploration. The inquirer by turns takes up or discards various suggestions, then formulates a statement best comprehending the marks he has accepted. A definition in the precise sense, that is, a statement in which subject and predicate are equivalent in meaning, is doubtless the best formulation, but an ordinary proposition where this identity does not hold may have to serve instead. In the *Gorgias* the latter sort far outnumber the definitory formulas, and provided they do not bury the subject with praise or blame, are satisfactory enough.

Bound up with Plato's defining or characterizing of any one kind of thing—rhetoric, justice, temperance, politics, art—is the need for justifying whatever definition or statement is being made. A bald assertion, however acutely formulated, is no better than opinion. Knowledge is revealed in such a statement only when buttressed by a self-referential account of what is involved in knowing and an account of more general aspects of existence. Thus the true and the real must underlie the processes and results of any examination of less universal topics.[15] What makes the interpretation of a Platonic dialogue especially difficult, however, is that the most fundamental, most general notions are rarely stated separately; they are slipped in, often quite casually, even humorously, and frequently they must be carefully gleaned from the conduct of the argument itself. Every dialogue refers to the self and its coming to know, but there is no dialogue exclusively concerned with the soul. Every dialogue states an important point or points about method, though none carries out a full discussion of method, and much more is shown than stated outright. Every dialogue is very careful to refer in some way to the real and its characteristics and also to contrast it with some sort of imitation; but the reader will search in vain for a final, unambiguous account of Platonic metaphysics—the *Parmenides* is not one, and neither is the *Sophist*, however much they raise the issues. Thus the *Gorgias* is not unusual in this regard, for one must search each dialogue for references, even if they are oblique, to truth and reality, such as our dozen statements relating to unity.

To establish, if we can, a principle of unity for the *Gorgias*, we concentrate upon the dozen statements in it more nearly concerned with that concept, though reality and truth are just as clearly implied in them. That these terms ought all to be linked together should be no surprise, nor should it be that one can use the twelve statements as sources for other most general terms, though the establishing of their legitimacy may be diverse. Three different issues are among the most important in considering unity and reality, the remarks quoted being illustrated by various procedures in the dialogue, with its many backings and fillings: wholes as contrasted to parts, order as against disorder, and proportion as opposed to disproportion. These form a sequence, to be shown later.

One can divide a whole apple into quarter segments, thus yielding mathematically quantitative parts, predetermined by nature. In a limited sense this division is perfect, for if the quarters are reassembled, the original whole results.

Again, one can divide an apple into seeds, core, pulp, and skin, a division physically quantitative, depending upon shape and texture of parts. Here the reassembly is more difficult, manipulatively speaking, for if anything is out of place the whole is not properly re-established. What these two divisions have in common, however, is that they are both performed with knives and tweezers.

A third division is into qualities. An apple is composed of sweetness, moistness, tartness, nutritiousness, oblate "sphericity," and so forth, and although one need not assume the existence of Whitehead's eternal objects, one may still try to synthesize these (and a multitude of other qualities we need not list) into the nature of an apple. The difficulty here is that the reassembly is so much less determinate than it is with the quantitative divisions. It is done by the mind, not the hand, and there is much uncertainty about the completeness of the result. Another serious shortcoming arises out of this taking of the qualities to be of approximately equal rank. Consideration of the more and the less essential is left out; and this, as Socrates shows but does not say early in his colloquy with Gorgias, is itself essential to orderly understanding.

The fourth kind of division is what might be called functional, and to a pomologist it would perhaps be more interesting than the others. No doubt the most prominent functions of the apple would be the specific ways in which it was nourished, grew, and reproduced itself—the chemicals that it absorbed, the characteristic rates of development, and the shapes and dimensions of the well-formed apple, and finally the preservation of the species through generations. This is no longer a physical division in the sense of being something for the scalpel to perform, but these are nevertheless the features of the most essential nature of the apple, and accordingly can be termed a division, but in a new sense.

The fifth kind of division—and here we are using that term in a much looser acceptation still—is into chronological stages, from bud to the first indications of fruit to a fully grown apple. The knife can again come into play, but it is used altogether differently in a temporal sequence and for a different reason.

There are many analogies between the wholeness and partition of an apple with that of the *Gorgias*, although at no point is the comparison perfect. At every stage what there is of the apple is present all at the same time, whereas at no point is this true of the dialogue. The quantitative division can be performed on the *Gorgias*, yielding letters, syllables, or lines, the length of the whole can be calculated from knowing how many of any of these there are, and the whole can moreover be restored easily if one has a complete text as model from which to work. Here the whole is a simple sum.

The physically quantitative division is like one into nouns and verbs, interjections, sentences phrased as questions, requests, statements, and so on. Here the parts are unlike, and are not immediately measured by length; they have functional differences, but not for a dialogue qua dialogue because the same distinctions can be made for all products of the pen whatever. Reassembly into the total collection is no great matter.

The division into qualities of the dialogue—that it is conversational, lengthy, moral in tone, tense and bordering upon the disagreeable in many places, disparaging of much of human nature and many lives, enigmatic, forceful, and so forth—this is not difficult, and again there is a democracy of qualities that fails to distinguish the essential from the adventitious. To think of the dialogue as a kind of confluence of an open set of these traits may be of some slight help to the novice reader but serves little purpose in grasping the unique structure or purpose of the work. Again we would say that if the qualities ingress into the dialogue, it is only because the work is constituted as it is prior to their multiple entry.

There are two functional divisions of the dialogue, not one, the first being to exhibit its philosophical nature, and this is into hypotheses, problems, solutions, objections, revised solutions, and more of this sort. As with the functional division of the apple, which can be combined with a partition into different sorts of tissues and the tissues into cells, this division of the dialogue may perhaps be aided if terms are to be taken as units out of which the statements, problems, and so forth, are built up. These are units of meaning, and it might in the most literal sense be possible to count these in the dialogue and total them up. *Relations* between terms, however, are infinitely more; and because this is a dialectic in which fluidity obtains, one may say that the meanings of individual terms tend to change in accordance with the other terms with which they are combined in statements, questions, and other elements. Not only is this true for the terms immediately joined in the grammatical sentences but it is also true for the terms widely separated in the dialogue, so that the notion of justice when combined with lawcourt speeches is very different from justice as meted out to the souls of the dead by three unyielding gods. Even after considering every single word of the dialogue, one could never exhaust the relations between the terms, which is why so many worthwhile interpretations at variance with one another can be made. There is, moreover, a reciprocal change of meanings in the very combinations altering the individual terms, so that divine justice would mean something different if the word *justice* were to be used twice though not in quite the same sense. This is precisely what happens between the time this notion is first introduced (454d) and in the final myth (527c).

A combination of terms, then, determines how a term shall be interpreted, and vice versa; a passage determines the interpretation of a single pair of terms, until the outer limits of the whole work are reached, the design whereby all lesser parts can be read. If one is to decide whether the work has the sought-for unity one must see how each term, statement, definition, or image contributes to the whole. When these contributions have been assessed then one must return to the parts, including the least parts. The reconstituting of the whole, the ensemble, is a matter of great difficulty because the whole is no longer a collection of printed words but an accumulation of significant utterances, dialectically rather than spatially or even grammatically linked, however much those linkages are still present. To state the philosophic wholeness or unity of the *Gorgias* on this level requires that one try to discover from the work itself whether these parts, joined together in ways advocated or indicated within the work, can be made to form a coherent succession.

What most commentators have considered an offshoot of the philosophical aspects of the dialogue is a literary division of the work into kinds of personal traits described or hinted, challenges and responses, likes and dislikes, valleys and peaks of interest, and so forth. We have maintained throughout that the *Gorgias* is primarily a philosophical work with its emphasis upon the establishing and altering of meanings of general terms, and that the literary aspects are needed to subserve this. An instance: Gorgias himself is treated as an important personage, a guest honored by the scion of a well-placed family, whose host has taken some trouble to arrange an exhibition of rhetorical skills. These are "literary touches," and if the reader's interest is entirely limited to the justification of rhetoric, for instance, or to the cogency of Socrates' refutations of his three antagonists, then such touches can be dismissed as insignificant. But if Gorgias were a minor figure with little or no influence in the cities and with no pupils or at best dismally unpromising ones, the entire ethical issue could well be omitted from the dialogue, for to include it then would be forced. The import of the prominence of Gorgias is that it makes him influential, a potentially dangerous man, either as speaker or as teacher, who must be countered; and just this is the ethico-political issue.

There is also a temporal sequence which, if removed, would ruin the dialogue as both a philosophic and literary entity at the same time. Even if there is a succession of events, it is nevertheless structural, hence different from the immediately preceding functional divisions. What is essential to the dialogue is that it begins with certain events and utterances (the events being casual meetings in the street, invitations to a gathering, or what not); and these create a probability, not a necessity, that certain lines of thought will be expounded. The first issue is not only whether rhetoric is an art but whether it is the highest art, and this requires an exhaustive search, not of all the rest of the arts, which are alluded to only cursorily, but of rhetoric itself to determine its claims. The subsequent parts of the dialogue must develop what was implicit in the opening passages so that *retrospectively* one may see that the progression was inevitable. Like a play, a novel, or a poem, a dialogue must have a beginning, a middle, and an end, though these are not, strictly speaking, divisions of any plot. For there is no overt action, except possibly in the *Apology, Crito*, and *Phaedo*, but even there it is minimal. The end is the head or conclusion, not a mere cessation but a summing-up not so much of the previously established statements as of their transforming consequences—the end caps and then changes what has gone before.

This notion of beginning and ending is not purely a question of placement in the dialogue. Like a detective story that begins in the middle, traces through a number of later episodes and finally returns to reconstruct what had occurred at the outset even before the victim was killed, a dialogue could conceivably start in the middle of a chain of reasoning and make the dialectical beginning fully explicit only by the end of the piece. (Both the *Gorgias* and the *Meno* commence with a *Poion ti?* question or assertion, and some time is spent unraveling the wrongness of that approach.) Plato does not follow this plan very often, for if he did it might well separate the reader and the participants, rather than aiding, indeed forcing, the reader to philosophize with them.

If we take the *Gorgias* to be primarily a work of philosophy rather than of literature it is because of the stronger emphasis upon general concepts and their development, with the personal aspects supporting these at every step, rather than the reverse, as in most novels. All the occasions for saying that the work is chiefly literary are occasions when the particular, the apparent, the evanescent are stressed; and these are objects of opinion, neither suggesting nor being converted into objects of knowledge until the clearer line of argument with its concepts gives the more fugitive details their rightful status in the dialogue as a whole. If human actions and passions were to dominate, then whatever philosophical content there might be should be taken as the author's way of clarifying the human condition through examples. Finding literary unity, when that is subordinate to the philosophic, requires that one make other selections of joined meanings that will later be ordered with the more general concepts. Unless this can be done, the literary aspects are at best pleasant distractions, and the author's reasons for including them may well be purely rhetorical.

In summary: The unity of a Platonic dialogue seems partly to hinge upon the feature of self-reference which is shown in two ways: first, the participants speaking of their theories are also willy-nilly committing themselves on their deepest attitudes toward their own lives; and second, a dialogue contains hints of its own unity and wholeness. We have recounted those hints and explored some possible relations they bear to the *Gorgias* as a dialogic design.

Order

As with the first concept, wholeness, order is not confined to human beings and their activities, but is allowed a wide range in the cosmos. True enough, order is most often referred to property, body, and soul, but in larger spheres there is order in the city and then in the universe, and in both we find some analogies with the threefold division in human affairs. In the city, the public structures are the property, the citizens are most like the body, while the principles animating them, including those of art and virtue, are its soul. In the cosmos the stars and their motions replace the body while again the principle of cosmic justice and rational rule by three Olympian gods resembles the soul when they assume control of the three worlds which together make one.

We could perhaps try to show how order proliferates into kinds relevant to the five senses of wholeness, but it would be an account more detailed than is warranted here. Here we have only to note that order, *taxis*, is the principle of unity that may be, but is not necessarily, embodied in a time sequence. It can be, for instance, a disposition of ruling and ruled, or superior and inferior, or cause and what is caused; everything in a good order performs its rightful function. Whether a particular ordering is good—for example, whether a man willing and wishing for the good of the citizenry is made actual ruler, or whether the rhetor proposes a course of action really prudent—is determinable by reference partly to the individual disposition, partly to the cosmos at large. The principles of justice are seen in how one man deals with another, but even more clearly by referring to the way perfect justice, administered by the gods, will operate through eternity.

What is especially interesting here is that order, like wholeness, is partly a topic of the conversations, partly a term applicable to essential relations within the conversations (such as that of speaker to audience, ruler to ruled, and so on), and partly also a term needed in the analysis of the *Gorgias* as a successful or unsuccessful work in philosophy and literature. Thus order, as we have indicated, is a chronological order and applies here to the course of the argument. It is a branch of the problem of order to trace the uses made of dichotomy and trichotomy, which we have attempted to do in the expository chapters; and it is also requisite to use this term to discover if Plato has properly set out the beginning, middle, and end of his work. Again, we feel that enough has already been said to justify our conclusion that the dialogue is ordered well.

Proportion

The third aspect of reality and unity is proportion, which specifies an order in turn specifying relations between parts and wholes, parts and other parts, or wholes and other wholes.[16] Socrates tries from the first to measure two orders, one between wholes, namely imitation and the real, the other between parts and the ordering of the real by reference to each other. Again we find a dual reference, within the dialogue as a topic of discussion or employment, and of the parts of the dialogue to its whole. Proportion is, in brief, the prototypical ordering principle of the *Gorgias*, for it sets entities in relation to each other, then gives each a measure in essential relations:

rhetoric:sophistic::judicature:legislation

These enable one to confirm significant aspects of four entities at once, though the proportion has been set up to show something of the nature of rhetoric alone. It is essential that the lesson be subordinately about the last pair because although this is not a simple predication about a single subject, those two must be at least partly understood in advance.

There are what may be called literary proportions in the *Gorgias* as well, proportions arising solely from the fact that the work is a dialogue between persons. Thus one may say that

Chaerephon:Socrates::Polus:Gorgias

for the two younger men try to replace their elders in conversation, both of them unsuccessfully. A literary proportion of another and vaguer sort is shown in this:

Gorgias:Polus::Socrates:Gorgias, Polus, and Callicles

in that the Socratic thinking comes to dominate, yet goes beyond, that of the three men, setting a standard for the kind of instruction that Gorgias should have been able to impart to Polus.

A more subtle kind of literary proportion, one much harder to express in quasi-mathematical terms, is in the ratio of outbursts of temper to inner feeling. In talking to Gorgias, Socrates encounters no overt hostility. The calling of rhetoric and its aims are, so to speak, taken for granted, the worldly success of the speaker has so long been assured. Polus makes three principal attacks against Socrates: Polus is riding on the coattails of Gorgias, and though he believes he will achieve similar success, he is young and his future is less certain. Callicles, a far more complicated personality now cast in the difficult role as host, learner, and target, is beginning his career as a politico and although ambitious sees it as hedged with serious perils. Counting his first long diatribe against philosophic life as single, there are at least fifteen exhibitions of outright bad temper against Socrates, and but one expression of enthusiastic agreement (510b). The abuse of Socrates, then, is in direct ratio to the feeling of precariousness of the speaker's future career. In a less literary way, but still attached to the parceling out of the discussion between persons, one might say that Gorgias:leading to Oblong::Polus:application of Oblong::Callicles:testing of Oblong.

So much for examples. The real, one finds, is a whole with parts and the parts become apprehended with respect to the whole; it is an ordered totality. It is proportioned, for an order always assumes not only two things which are related but at least one or, more frequently, two other things by which their relation is measured.

Proportion also measures completeness, which for a bushel of apples is easily calculated by ratios of fruit to standard baskets. The completeness of a poem is less simply decided except for the commonplace reference to a conventionally fixed form, for instance the fourteen-line sonnet. If it is not, if the verse is looser, then one must consider the relations between opposed or ambiguous concepts at the beginning, or opposed lines of action, and see whether they are clarified, resolved, and harmonized at the end, or if not whether there is some reason for their remaining unresolved. (This must also be done with the sonnet, and constitutes a second and far more important examination than merely counting lines or iambs.) If this is unexplained, then the poem remains a fragment, even if a valuable one.

* * *

So much for the general account of wholeness, order, and proportion. If now we can show how these fundamental notions run as guiding threads through the anfractuous pathways of the *Gorgias*, it may be easier to see the work as a unity. This is not mere succession of contrasting opinions about rhetoric and politics such as we rehearsed in chapter 10, a rehearsal that confessedly helped but did not finally prove the work's unity. Now we are attempting to state, using samples, some underlying principles that are drawn from the dialogue, but which we believe can be shown to ground the whole conception of rhetoric and of all the topics taken up in the discourse.

The whole, in Gorgias' conception, is of course rhetoric, and its parts are political, legal, and display, corresponding to kinds of audiences. These are not ordered to each other, but rhetoric is ordered to civic action through manipulation of audiences by affording or promising pleasure. The proportions that Gorgias sees involve the supreme freedom that he feels he enjoys, set against the comparative slavery of the citizens pliant to him. The drawback here is that the alleged proportion is really none—it is a thoroughly lopsided view of the lopsided powers of speaker and citizens. Since the Socratic theory of justice involves this very proportionality that is lacking in Gorgias, a correction is required.

This is partly accomplished by the Divided Oblong, which asserts the whole to be twofold: pandering, divided into four kinds, and art, similarly divided. Orders are found in the relations between individual arts and their imitations, between soul and body, and between the best and pleasure, the proportions being set up as stated in the matrix itself.

What is real, the arts, is the truer, the more essential. A defect, or at best an ambiguity, of the Oblong is that the body is still held to be co-equal with the soul, and though rhetoric is higher than catering, there is as yet no firm principle of rule for soul over body; supplementation is needed.

The Oblong is abstract and in some degree arbitrary, for although it has been suggested in a negative way through observing weaknesses in Gorgias' own account, the fact is that much of it is unsupported by careful argument when first the Oblong is erected. It is used, however, as a kind of hypothesis for the rest of the dialogue, to be applied and tested and, if necessary, edited into something more satisfactory and true. The application will itself constitute a first correction, because the Oblong needs connecting with actions of various sorts, all of them involving some use of rhetoric.

If Polus could overturn the entire Oblong he would of course do so, for justice, far from occupying a position of comparative honor in his thought, is subordinated to injustice, which becomes the ruling whole subdivided into kinds of acts, such as murder and lying, being the parts he excuses, even praises, before he is made to reconsider. The order is that of the rhetor-tyrant to power, but there is no binding principle of proportion, no aim of the ruler except to rule. It is scarcely better than the alleged power of a man with a hidden dagger ready for mayhem in the agora.

Improvement upon this conception is hinted in Socrates' final proofs to Polus that the proper use of rhetoric lies in self-incrimination, but they do not establish justice as a virtue in itself; justice is not brought into any clear relation with the other virtues. Even its lodgement in the soul remains difficult to specify.

It is ironic that in his attempts to extricate himself from the entangling net of Socratic elenchus, Callicles introduces one by one the virtues needed for this clarification. The whole that he envisions is the character of the superior man, stridently overrunning the law, the parts being the various aspects of character asserted to belong to him: his strength, courage, and wisdom (really cleverness), establishing the tyrant as a man who should have unlimited power and with it every pleasure desired. If Callicles lacks a sense of proportion, still he unconsciously sets up a formula relating the one to the many (citizens) analogous to that of the unrestrained strong man to the weak individuals of the crowd. There is, however, the opposed tendency in Callicles himself, to think of the superior man as unduly hindered by the many or even by some individual of low class.

To answer Callicles requires that justice be set in relation to temperance and wisdom (Courage is accorded much the same position by both parties.) Temperance especially must be rescued from his grossly derogatory estimate. A hint that justice is rooted in cosmic order and proportionality is for the time being left dangling; there is a more pressing need, not to ground this assertion or even apply it systematically, but to offer the soundest observations possible on the conduct of one's own life. Another whole is sketched in, that of the character of Socrates himself, which becomes identical with philosophic statesmanship, much as Gorgias had earlier identified himself with rhetoric.

Answering Callicles requires much time, and it is not until the final myth that he receives his most convincing counterstatements. The whole is no longer anything immediately human but is the cosmos at large whose parts are three realms. The nature of the gods implies an ordering into divine and human, rulers and ruled, and the nature of the semidivine judges implies subordination of those who are judged. The proportions are laid out to bind punishments to injustices committed, rewards to virtues. Here the body taken in the literal, earthly sense drops out, becoming a symbol or token for the soul. It is now a world where everything is eternal, every relation binding forever, everything is appropriate and therefore just, nothing is spurious and false.

Wholeness, order, and proportion are in themselves constantly in view in the dialogue, even if not named explicitly as often as their principles are employed to further the argument. If every concept in the dialogue were shuffled there would be total confusion. On the other hand, there is a subtle altering of the precise meanings of the three basic notions as the dialogue winds its way to the conclusion. For Gorgias the three terms seem to apply to an "art," but since rhetoric is identified in his mind with his own accomplishments, its divisions merely reflect different aspects of his own skills, its relations to an end being his personal aims in disguise. This individual concept undergoes a change with the Oblong, which shifts wholeness and its partner concepts to an impersonal, general level. For Polus, the shift is back again to the individual, but by now connected with ruling; the whole is not a kind of life rather than a single life.

Socrates seeks throughout to correct prejudices by showing that individual claims are refuted by considerations stemming from the very nature of art and virtue. His refutations of Polus try to reestablish a whole more nearly real, but its limits are the city. Callicles, rejecting this as his starting point, reverts once more to an individual but no longer a personal totality—a kind of superman who may or may not be Callicles himself in his dreams of hegemony. Polus' reference was fantastic: for him political power amounted to criminality. Callicles' notion is tempered by his references to some of the virtues, unfortunately for his argument not to more of them. The whole is thus a type for him, although at times it might be a type having but a single token member, at other times not.

Again, the Socratic correction is one elevating wholeness to the level of the universe itself; the whole is both general as applicable to everything and yet concrete as attaching to men in this world. The kindred notions of order and proportion undergo a like transformation, beginning in a purely human dimension, later moving to the sidereal and the divine.

From this steady development in the dialogue it seems well to assume that there was an orderly plan in Plato's mind—that this sequence could not have stemmed from chance, disconnected inspirations. The parts are not what a zoologist would call metameres, replications, but represent successive growth following a much more complex functional pattern. The plan, we presume, has not been approximated in our review of the employment of the idea of unity and its related concepts. Yet there is more to our inquiry, for even if we have found a proportioned order in the parts of the dialogue, we have still not arrived at a notion of what the final unity can be, whether it is definable at all or is merely to be suggested. If one can grasp the complex relationship between the individual utterances (themselves made up of meanings and thus subject to all the aforementioned difficulties) and the dialogue in its total organization, one will have knowledge, regardless of whether the topics in the work itself should rise no higher than the level of opinion. The result may not be knowledge of the purest sort, but at least it will be knowledge of the limitations hampering the opinions expressed in the work, together with some concrete notion of the subjects of those opinions. If the *Gorgias* is indeed mostly concerned with the level of opinion and what is defective about it, at any rate we come through it to *know* something more about rhetoric, for the knowledge acquired in exegesis will aid in winnowing out what is substantively false in opinion.

Knowledge, Unity, and the Dialogue

To say that the real is known is to say both that one has direct knowledge of reality as such and also that one can guarantee this knowledge, not through anything more real than what is already real but through both personal self-knowledge and involuted or reflexive knowledge (as we are now differentiating these last two). The processes bringing this about have been examined in chapters 11 and 12; here we need say only that the three kinds of knowledge are discursive in form, they exist in and through language, principally spoken, and in speech they ordinarily involve two or more persons beginning in opposition to one another despite their apparent agreements. Later these persons are, if possible, brought to more genuine agreement, after their disaccords have been aired. This does not mean that cognition is primarily a social affair, or that some sort of group mind, in McDougall's sense, holds sway over the heads of men and women; the dialectical interchange merely furnishes certain conditions for knowledge to be generated in the individual, much as animals and laboratory paraphernalia furnish requisites for scientific conclusions yet in no literal way form parts of those conclusions.

Self-knowledge would be needed for an expanding set of conditions about one's own motives, then those of another person, of the populace at large, and finally of the universe; without such knowledge one would be limited and biased, for to know oneself in the Socratic sense immediately implies actually correcting and reorienting oneself so far as necessary, as a musician learns to play and write tunes better, not being content merely to listen to them. All four levels of knowledge that we have detailed in chapter 11 are touched upon in the *Gorgias*, and the first two are explored with an almost grim thoroughness. Socrates' effort is to turn attention of the three rhetors away from self-conceit that reaches for but does not attain to the level of knowledge of the more genuine sort, the knowledge that sees its object through the prism of a refined self. The reason is that self-knowledge, because it can properly estimate capabilities and inadequacies of its possessor, makes no unjustified claims for either the object of direct knowledge or the validity of the cognitions themselves. Self-knowledge leads to a continuously inturned process, looking closer and closer at the root of the soul, and at the same time setting up standards for the pursuit of such knowledge. Its most nearly accurate expression lies in dialectical conversation which asks what you know, then how you know what you know, and so on. The knowing of one's own knowledge means a continuing effort to come to terms with one's whole psyche and its wider settings. Imperfections of direct, objective knowledge are especially apparent when topics such as rhetoric, sophistic, dialectic, or happiness and virtue are being considered because a *person* is always the bearer of these, and if it is another person in whom they lie, still there is a response to him in knowing him, and this too must be taken into full account. Followed out, dialectic becomes depth-dialectic.

Not only is the self-awareness generated in dialogue by argument and counterargument but it also arises in the dozens of ways persons respond to each other, even if no argument takes place—intimidation, sympathy, supplication, adoration, indifference, detestation, rebellion, and many more. In these, too, one becomes more and more conscious of one's weaknesses and strengths. Even such initially prejudiced men as the three rhetors bend a little to the arguments—and the person—of Socrates. If it is objected that this is no longer an account of rhetoric but of the interplay of men, the answer can be prompt: Rhetoric *is* in good part the interplay of persons as well as the cogency of arguments.

The third kind of knowledge is reflexive in a different sense; it is self-conscious or self-referential method. It is method prescribed, together with the reasons why the prescriptions are as they are, and with the working out of the method in context of another subject matter but with the prescriptions as part of that working out. The *Gorgias* is especially rich in these prescriptions, for they fill many of the approximately two dozen interludes (counting the procedural remarks in the entire Prologue as one). No doubt the reason is that the respondents to Socrates are especially opaque in their understanding of dialectical approaches to subject matters. If extracted from their contexts, then added together, the interludes would by no means convey a full sense of the dialectic in the *Gorgias*, let alone its manifold turns and twists in the other dialogues. Yet they do aid in ballasting a three-compartmented ship that is badly listing, and they mark out some significant boundaries for what might otherwise become desultory palaver or empty harangues.

Although self-knowledge and reflexive knowledge in these specific senses are not the same, obviously they support each other, for taken together they mark out both the standards which a person must meet in discussion and the capacities and weaknesses with which he will be able to meet them. The second result of pursuing either of them, or even both together, is not perfect objective knowledge but a kind no doubt far superior to the results of any talk directed entirely to an "objective" topic without benefit of the cautions and encouragements afforded by these vital supplements.

The *Gorgias* is a threefold search for the self. The first is in the clumsy efforts of the three rhetors to explain who they are. Since their self-knowledge is scanty, it is hardly surprising that they all "vaunt themselves to be" (in Gorgias' borrowed phrase) better than they are, the extra claim being recommended to them by their ambitions as much as by their skills. Second, there is the effort of Socrates to show them how unreliable is their kind of self-awareness; this is the destructive aspect of his managed dialectic, the elenchus that confounds them as persons through refuting the opinions that they flaunt. Third, it is the ultimate positive effect of the dialectic whereby Socrates endeavors to bring Callicles to full recognition both of what virtuous civic practice really is and of the way Callicles himself can enter into it in company with Socrates.

In a literary work one cannot look for unity in the rigorous coherence of theorems with axioms and definitions. To estimate the degree of unity in such a work as Newton's *Principia* one needs to study the deducibility of each theorem from the definitions in the General Scholium and the axioms or laws of motion. This is less taxing, however, than it is to see what Plato has been trying to do; and the interpretations of the latter are correspondingly far more varied and numerous. The beginning, middle, and end that a literary work must possess are linked by progressively manifesting the resolutions between conflicting trends in the lines of thought or of action, or of both together. The *Gorgias*, whose participants perform almost no overt actions but anticipate many, must resolve as best it can the originally diverging lines of their thinking. What appears true for the rhetors is found first to be false and then correctible, a road to virtuous action—not unlike the unjust man sentenced for a term in Tartarus, afterward to be returned to earth. Because authentic knowledge of one's self requires in the end that one practice virtue, it follows that coming to know oneself will ultimately require that one set out to be a citizen with probity, even if the pathway is a lonely one. Since the *Gorgias* reflects precisely this dialectical route, it would seem that here again it fulfills the requirements for being a piece of literature that carries through to the end a solid moral message. In this respect, then, it has, or it is, a unity. The unsatisfactoriness of the response of the three opponents to Socrates, their separate failures to accede to him, is part of the same moral lesson: Reason, in real life, must struggle against obduracy, and the path is covered with boulders. One might say that it is a paradox that the *Gorgias* is complete yet parades the uncompleted effects of the persuasiveness of Socrates, the nearly complete man.

We have, then, expounded the unity of the *Gorgias* discursively, finding this unity to lie in the patterned alterations in the embodiments of the concepts of wholeness, order, and proportion, and in the literary drive toward illustrative aptness of the characterizations reinforcing the philosophy of good deeds in a naughty world. We have, furthermore, tried to stress what seems an undeniable fact, that although the literary aspects of the dialogue appear at first glance to be side issues, mere touches to entertain and entice readers, nevertheless they have a direct bearing on the entire course of the philosophical discussion. Perhaps the most important of these is Gorgias' little boast very early, that he is not only a rhetor but a good one (449a). It is this, appearing merely to add a trifle of roundness to his personality (and which may or may not have had historical justification), that determines that the subsequent conversations will be directed not only to what rhetoric is but to what it means to be a good rhetor. This very point absolves the dialogue of falling into two separate parts. The literary, then, is intimately harmonious with the philosophical, thereby unifying, as it were, these two unities.

What puts it so in accord is the fact that the self-knowledge with its imitative substitutes—for one can pander to oneself as well as to others—is in effect a bridge between the general concepts, the philosophical aspects of the dialogue, and the personal and temporal, the literary.

What the unity is that binds together the dialogue as a whole we have not yet tried to state, and now fear that we can do little more than lead up to an intuitive awareness of it rather than baldly expounding it. We shall therefore lay down some observations on the relationships between unity and the other concepts that are even more general than are the three marks of this unity. Again, they are variously applied in the *Gorgias*, as we shall note.

1. The real is one even if there are many ones. In the *Gorgias* it is clear that art is one, philosophy is one, and the philosopher who exemplifies both is one.
2. If there are many individuals they can be grouped, and the group becomes a unity of a sort. The three rhetors, three gods, three judges are such individuals, each trio forming a unified grouping.
3. If the real is divisible in many ways, it can still be a one, which need not be single and homogeneous. Rhetoric is still one, no matter how many kinds or subdivisions it may take on at times.
4. The one is measurable by itself, though it may be introduced in a roundabout way by means of many things, even imitations. As we have pointed out, art is introduced through rhetoric and other kinds of pandering.
5. The most real is also the most true; the real can be neither imitative nor outright false. In the dialogue, art is distinct from pandering as much as possible.
6. The most true is the most unified, the most nearly one. Philosophy is most true, and its reasons are adamantine, hence it is one, it is not ambiguous, though it may enjoy subdivisions serving the whole.
7. The most true is also the most good. For Socrates art is true, for art is knowledge; art seeks the best, hence is good in itself.
8. The real is true and good, therefore, and the truth and goodness are one with the real, and hence with unity. In the work before us, philosophy is an art, a knowledge, and a practice, and all are embodied in Socrates.
9. Because the real need not be simple, it follows that neither the true nor the good need be simple; both can take on complexity. And the illustrations of this are endless.

As a rider to these, a practical standard is added, one we have already invoked: To know good is to do good; to know, in the sense of knowing one's own nature in conjunction with that of the world, involves being able effectively to practice what that nature allows and dictates. An instance of this is found in the admonition to the philosopher and his companion to do his utmost to improve the citizens but to walk modestly and never put on airs.

*   *   *

We began our study with the tentative appraisal of the *Gorgias* as a work harboring extra complexities, but confessed that we would be looking for signs of unity, thus making this a not wholly undirected, unbiased inquiry. What we have now concluded is that the complexity, when coming from the hand of a philosophic artist, is no inevitable bar to oneness. The reader should first look for hints of that unity in each detail, afterward relating every one of them to other details in light of a compelling theme. Then, in the course of examining the most general concepts in the dialogue, concepts which themselves outline an abstract unity by their own nature and meanings, the reader ought to see if they are carried through comparably with the ways they are explicitly brought into the text. The details and their compendencies have been treated earlier in this book, and now we believe that the marks of unity and the universally applicable concepts which are its brothers have been sufficiently uncovered. The measure of the unity has been erected by the work itself, so that Plato's use of the true, the good, and the real are aids, not obstacles, to finding the wholeness of his work. Such a welding is not, must not be, an abstract exercise and nothing more. Nor can it be a flat, dogmatic assertion of unity or the good. The *Gorgias* touches the truth, even if not most precisely or most exhaustively, and it nudges the reader toward that truth, toward its self-referring unity, much as Socrates nudges his three antagonists to find self-consistency within their own souls.

All the separate elements of the dialogue are arranged to enforce the lesson that to be a good rhetor is to be a philosopher, and any substitute suggested, any imitation proposed, is a falling short and in comparison nothing worth. This doctrine is an act of thought, a proposition that despite formidable impediments the discourse finally brings into clearer view, seeking to drive it home, if not to Callicles and his comrades of the day then to Plato's own readers at large. Conferred upon the images in that discourse—upon the wine jars and side-street chatter, the tyrants and tub-thumpers—is a kind of epistemic certainty gained from their conjoint effects, and from them readers can form a vision of what the truth and unity must be. The images look to be transformed into an overarching substantiation, though they never become exact proofs, of the principal lesson. As for the lesser and also the more encompassing schemata, and as for the individual arguments with their many and varied indications of generality, even if they lack the tightest cogency, they too, when collected in sequence, are able to produce the strong conviction in the second audience, long after the three alien listeners have grown bored: readers in Athens and in other times and places. The characters, three of whom misrepresent truth but in that negative way at least give intimation of its underlying tendency, and the fourth, whose approximations to truth are much more direct and pertinent, become in a broad sense images of permanent forms suggesting an ideal unity and fully-accredited being and truth. The philosopher-rhetor seeks this truth actively, and in so doing finds a unity linking his own soul with what he comes to know. This, finally, is philosophy in its completest sense, philosophy uncluttered by appearance, by fripperies and money and power, by falsehoods.

That insight, however, necessarily remains a vision admitting of no description, no subdividing, no definition; and after it is gained, readers should return to the public squares and assembly halls because reclusive fiddling with generalities remains inert, a thing apart. The vision carries over to seeing the unity of life even where divisive forces are hard at work to infiltrate the few truly cohesive impulses of the human race—the vision beyond any explicit lesson is not easily forgotten. And then there is an even higher identity that unites being and truth and the good beyond the good of living signaled in the long discourse. Plato, twofold genius, was also writing of something universal that comprehends and overrules not only the details of life but their day-to-day interrelations as well. In the three steps, from dialogue to human life to the universal grounds of its being, an active mind may discern at least one developed, well-considered, dialectically derived sense in which all things are together.

NOTES

SELECTED BIBLIOGRAPHY

INDEX

NOTES

Introduction

1. Other dialogues in which special attention must be paid to the personalities are the *Protagoras*, *Lysis*, and *Symposium*, where much must be made of the persons who teach virtue, who are friends, and who love. Slightly less is included of human traits in the *Phaedrus* and *Republic*, *Ion*, and *Meno*. The *Theaetetus*, while it commences with a sketch of the young man, proceeds with little regard for it, save for a few strokes; the *Sophist*, *Statesman*, and *Laws* manage with even less, Timaeus is described very little in the work bearing his name, and Zeno and Parmenides are introduced with a line or two. As Robert S. Brumbaugh points out in *Plato on the One: The Hypotheses in the "Parmenides"* (New Haven: Yale University Press, 1961), pp. 26–32, even in this impersonal dialogue the entrances of the speakers and onlookers are timed to indicate various philosophical relations between them; and the responses of the young Aristoteles are varied in such a way as to indicate smaller and larger breaks in the succession of proofs. A forthcoming monograph on the *Parmenides* by Robert Sternfeld and Harold Zyskind takes the same general position, but differs from Brumbaugh on details regarding the participants.

2. It would be wrong to apply as a yardstick for the *Gorgias* the description of justice in *Republic* IV or of dialectic in *Republic* VII, and even within the *Republic* the arguments in those two books cannot be read into Books I–III (or others) without dialectical adjustments. Almost the only statement of method that holds moderately well throughout the corpus is found in *Epistle VII*, 340a–345c (whose authenticity is still disputed), and here Plato specifically repudiates *any* textbook summary of his philosophy (341c–d).

3. This is true even of that most linear-minded of philosophers, Spinoza, who in the second half of part 2 of the *Ethics* furnishes the epistemic grounds to clarify and justify all definitions and axioms stated up to that point. The final propositions of part 5 show in turn how the mind can attend to the very nature of God. Without them part 1 would remain a masterly assemblage of arbitrary assumptions and their consecutant theorems.

4. Bertrand Russell, *A Critical Exposition of the Philosophy of Leibniz: With an Appendix of Leading Passages* (Cambridge: At the University Press, 1900), preface and chap. 1.

5. One might interpret this episode as a pair of alternative propositions because they are uttered by different persons, p or not-p; Either it was Brown's fault or it was not. In that case the compound is a tautology, TTTT. But the outcome is the same for our purpose, which is to show that the truth-table method neglects important features of dialogue.

6. By setting beside each other two fairly recent statements one sees how

difficult it is to decide upon the subject matter: (1) J. E. Raven, *Plato's Thought in the Making: A Study of the Development of His Metaphysics* (Cambridge: At the University Press, 1965), p. 49: "The primary purpose of the *Gorgias*, unlike that of the *Protagoras*, is immediately obvious and, so far as I know, has never been disputed. The two irreconcilable ideals of life, the Socratic and the sophistic, . . . are here brought into direct and deadly conflict." (2) Steven Rendall, "Dialogue, Philosophy, and Rhetoric: The Example of Plato's *Gorgias*," *Philosophy and Rhetoric* 10(1977):165: "The subject of the *Gorgias*, as is well known, is rhetoric."

7. *Theories* might be a good modern equivalent for *dialectics* used. Not that in this sense the plural form is ordinarily suitable.

8. All these devices receive mention as rhetorical in the *Phaedrus* (266d–267d) and are given names under which they have been enshrined in handbooks composed by the inventors of rhetoric, Gorgias and Polus among them.

9. S. S. Van Dine, *The Greene Murder Case: A Philo Vance Story* (reprint, New York: Scribner, 1956). (Van Dine was the pen name for the Vance stories of the art critic Willard Huntington Wright.)

10. Ibid. p. 328.

11. We shall be pointing out that the distinctions made by the three rhetors are virtually always twofold, such as strong-weak, one-many, good-evil, old-recent, and so forth. On the other hand, a number of the Socratic solutions, though by no means all, turn upon the introducing of three-step hierarchies, such as best-second best-worst.

12. For a book devoted in large part to this topic, see Robert S. Brumbaugh, *Plato's Mathematical Imagination: The Mathematical Passages in the Dialogues and Their Interpretation* (Bloomington: Indiana University Press, 1951).

13. These are thumbnail summaries of the mistakes made by Gorgias, Polus, and Callicles respectively, though there is some overlapping, as remarks by the last two (461b–c; 482c–e) suggest.

14. For an insightful presentation of the rigor of three pivotal arguments in the dialogue, see Charles H. Kahn, "Drama and Dialectic in Plato's *Gorgias*," *Oxford Studies in Ancient Philosophy* 1(1983):75–121. There is an interesting and somewhat different view regarding the logical rigor of the work, see Gregory Vlastos, "The Socratic Elenchus," *Oxford Studies in Ancient Philosophy* 1(1983): 27–58, and "Was Polus Refuted?" *American Journal of Philosophy* 88(1967):454–60. For a similar view see John P. Anton, "Dialectic and Health in Plato's *Gorgias*: Presuppositions and Implications," *Oxford Studies in Ancient Philosophy* 1(1980): 49–60. At every point one should consult Terence Irwin, *Plato, Gorgias* (Oxford: Clarendon Press, 1979); he closely examines the structure of the arguments and throws much light upon them, though from time to time it is from an angle very different from our own. See also Gerasimos Xenophon Santas, *Socrates: Philosophy in Plato's Early Dialogues* (London: Routledge and Kegan Paul, 1979). E. R. Dodds, ed., whose *Plato: "Gorgias": A Revised Text with Commentary* (Oxford: Clarendon Press, 1959) is, along with Irwin's, one of the small handful of important books on the subject in English, thinks that Plato's arguments are "seldom convincing and sometimes transparently fallacious," p. 30. A similar point of view is maintained in Arthur W. H. Adkins, *Merit and Responsibility: A Study in Greek Values* (Chicago: University of Chicago Press, 1975), especially chap. 13.

15. If this be true, then the proper reading of a dialogue such as the *Gorgias* is neither to take its literary aspects, those stressed by F. J. E. Woodbridge in *The*

Son Of Apollo: Themes of Plato (Boston: Houghton Mifflin, 1929) as exhausting the entire work, nor the mainly rigoristic interpretation of Vlastos, where virtually all references to characters and their interrelations are secondary if not withheld altogether in order to chart the lines of logical sequence.

16. This view has long been associated chiefly with the names of John Burnet and A. E. Taylor, despite the latter's provisos in his *Socrates* (1935; reprint, Garden City, NY: Doubleday, 1953), Introductory, especially pp. 25–31.

17. *Theaetetus* 189e; *Sophist* 263e; a rather similar point is made in the *Phaedrus*, 278a–b.

18. *Timaeus* 27d–28a.

19. At that very early stage in the dialogue, even Socrates assumes that (a) Gorgias has an art; (b) that the art has power (hence Gorgias has power); (c) that the art and its power can be specified; (d) that a display of the art is not necessary for giving an account of (a), (b), and (c), and is perhaps not even useful for it; and (e) that it is more important to know answers to (a), (b), and (c) than to hear display, even if not more obviously pleasurable, but the pleasure itself can be postponed.

20. Ludwig Wittgenstein, *Philosophical Investigations*, trans. G. E. M. Anscombe (New York: Macmillan, 1953), 1, para. 664. See also the comment on this passage in Garth Hallett, *A Companion to Wittgenstein's Philosophical Investigations* (Ithaca, NY: Cornell University Press, 1977), p. 27. Wittgenstein distinguished his *Tiefengrammatik* from ordinary grammar, *Oberflächengrammatik*, which is probably not intended as something superficial but simply sticks to the constructions found by relating nouns to verbs or adjectives, and so for the rest, which, he says, can be apprehended by the ear alone. By going deeper the philosopher comes face to face with possible uses, literal or analogical, of each of these words so classified. To us, even this is insufficient for reading the dialogues, for Plato is unconvinced that there is no thought, no speech, which floats in the sky, but is always *said*, whether it be by a person, a daimon, or a god.

21. Mention of the hints afforded by these circumstances and personalities and their importance is found in Richard McKeon, "Literary Criticism and the Concept of Imitation in Antiquity," *Modern Philology* 34(1936):35, who laments tendencies to bypass this kind of hint. An excellent attempt to relate persons and the opinions they hold is Stanley Rosen, *Plato's "Symposium"* (New Haven: Yale University Press, 1968). See also George Kimball Plochmann, "Interpreting Plato's *Symposium*," *The Modern Schoolman*, 48(1970):25–43, a discussion of Rosen's book.

22. W. K. C. Guthrie, in his *A History of Greek Philosophy*, (Cambridge: At the University Press, 1975), vol. 4, *Plato: The Man and His Dialogues: Earlier Period* pp. 284–312, is depreciative of the philosophic value of the *Gorgias*. He lists a number of topics dealt with in the dialogue and in the *Meno, Protagoras, Laches, Apology*, and *Crito* as well, concluding that "on most of these topics the *Gorgias* throws no new light" (p. 296).

23. Except for the principal dialecticians, Socrates, Parmenides, the unknown Eleatic, Timaeus, the Stranger from Athens, and Critias (assuming that Plato had written no more than half of the dialogue in which he is the narrator), more space is given to Callicles than to any other participant. Several personages are onstage for a much longer time, it is true, but they have less to say in their own right: Glaucon, Adeimantus, Theaetetus, and the Cleinias and Megillus of the *Laws* come to mind. There are more personal remarks, most of

them unflattering, passed back and forth by Socrates and Callicles than between any other pair in the dialogues, and there must be some philosophical as
well as a literary reason for this.

24. It is possible that Plato deliberately changed to Callicles the name of Critias (or of some other well-known man of tyrannical impulses) because he preferred not to have the reader prejudge the outcome of the *Gorgias*—whether
Socrates was to fail or succeed in winning Callicles to a more virtuous manner
of living. Plato covers up the fates of several other characters in his dialogues,
that of Alcibiades being the best known nor does he give much hint of what
happened to Meno or to Charmides, and says nothing about either the Peace of
the general Nicias or the latter's gross error in judgment in delaying the Sicilian
Expedition. The Athenian reader would probably have known of these fates as
well as that of Callicles-Critias. But in no case except the last is the discussion
directed at a man on issues that settled his destiny later on. For example, Socrates does not argue with Nicias (in the *Laches*) about trust in augurs or with
Meno about treason to one's city. It is only with Callicles that the debate could
be on what he actually becomes, if our suggestion of the alias is indeed correct.
(We have subsequently found that the suggestion was made more than a century ago by Jowett in his introduction to the dialogue.) For other (and we think,
more speculative) proposals, see Dodds, *Plato: "Gorgias,"* p. 12.

25. Some exceptions are the sweating and blushing of Thrasymachus (*Republic* I 350c–d), the drunken behavior of Alcibiades (*Symposium* 212d–223a),
the blushing of Hippothales (*Lysis* 204b), the change to a normal sitting posture
of Socrates (*Phaedo* 61c–d), and the shufflings of seating order and scramblings
to overhear in several dialogues. The references to the headache of Charmides
(*Charmides* 155b–157c) and the hiccups of Aristophanes (*Symposium* 185c–e,
188e–189a) are exceptions to the general point that Plato is little concerned
about bodily conditions in his participants.

26. As we shall be pointing out in chapter 1, the ineptitudes of Chaerephon
in this dialogue are easily explained if one assumes that he and Socrates have
recently met. But see our chap. 1, n. 7.

27. This is discussed from a general standpoint in George Kimball Plochmann,
"Socrates, The Stranger from Elea, and Some Others," *Classical Philology*
49(1954):223–31.

28. A chief example of this is in remarks about Socrates on the timocratic tendencies of Glaucon. See Stanley Rosen, "The Role of Eros in Plato's *Republic*,"
The Review of Metaphysics 18(1965):452–75, for shrewd observations interweaving the dramatic aspects of the dialogue with the structure of the argument and
the kinds of states envisioned.

29. *Theaetetus* 152a–186e.

30. We do not prejudge here the important issue whether rhetoric's premises
for assessing rhetoric are as reliable as the dialectician's premises. This will be
faced several times in chapters to follow.

31. This is especially true in the *Crito*, of course, where the old companion
almost completely misses the point of Socrates' devotion to philosophy. It is
also found in the *Phaedo*; in the *Symposium*. Alcibiades, though praising Socrates, betrays lack of understanding of his motives and even of his style of discourse (*Symposium* 215d; 221d–222a).

32. Socrates' disparagement of Pericles is relatively insignificant if made to
stand by itself. In the context of a theory of rhetoric and justice, however, it
gathers meaning.

33. This dialectic in turn leads to his unfavorable estimate of Pericles as statesman-rhetor and of Callicles' manner of life, which he finally describes as nothing worth.

34. It is only in the separation (*dialusis*) of a man's soul from his body, and his soul's presentation naked before the judges, that he can also see himself without trappings. Real self-understanding is no mean achievement, or mere listing of obvious traits of behavior or performance.

35. Who the thinkers are, influencing Callicles directly or indirectly, cannot, of course, be known outside of the men he refers to.

36. After complaining, for instance, of the deficiencies of the philosophical life, Callicles quotes Euripides and in the process manages to convey some added accusations which might not have occurred to him without the verses in hand (485d–486a).

37. William Chase Greene, in *Moira: Fate, Good, and Evil in Greek Thought* (Cambridge, MA: Harvard University Press, 1948), p. 255.

38. *Poetics* 9. 1451b5–11; *Metaphysics* I.1.981b8–982a2. Also *Nicomachean Ethics* VI.3–8.1139b15–1141b34.

39. Socrates would much prefer to say in the *Republic* VI (509c–511e) that one would have to ascend from stages 1 and 2 to stages 3 and 4 of the Divided Line, in a related but not identical contrast.

40. *Transcendental* is being used here in its most common medieval rather than Kantian sense.

41. *Poetics* 8. 1457a16–17.

42. Besides the *Crito*, an exception is the *Laws*, in which a resolution to secure the help of the Athenian Stranger for putting into effect the projected constitution is made on the very last page. Even in the *Crito*, where Socrates' course of action appears to hang in the balance while Crito is presenting his arguments for escape, it is implied by Plato from the outset that Socrates has not had the least intention of escaping; his counterarguments are not for the sake of strengthening his own resolve but simply to reassure his longtime companion that the latter's reputation will not be damaged if Socrates dies. So the question is not, What will Socrates do? but instead, How will he prove his point?

43. A careful defense of Plato would need to take into account such attacks as that of Charles Kauffman in his "Enactment as Argument in the *Gorgias*," *Philosophy and Rhetoric* 12(1979):128, where he says: "Socrates' contradictions are so blatant that any attempt to make him the 'victor' of the dialogue threatens Plato's credibility. . . . Socrates emerges as a tragic figure, a persona unable to recognize or escape his own inadequacies."

44. George Kimball Plochmann, "Hiccups and Hangovers in the *Symposium*," *Bucknell Review* 11(1963):1–18; reprinted as "Supporting Themes in the *Symposium*," in *Essays in Ancient Greek Philosophy*, eds. John P. Anton and George L. Kustas (Albany: State University of New York Press, 1971), pp. 328–44.

45. *Phaedrus* 236c–d.

46. Of the many works that attack Plato, perhaps the most savage and interestingly written is Warner Fite's *The Platonic Legend* (New York: Scribner, 1934). To him, Plato "was not content to live his own life. He wrote dialogues full of moral arrogance, of supercilious disdain, and of tirades of abuse aimed (but perhaps not incautiously discharged) at the victorious democracy" (p. 292). He inveighs against the *Symposium* for being poorly constructed, against the *Republic* for being tangled, and against virtually all the dialogues for having little

respect for logic and letting Socrates fall back upon "pious sophistry" instead.

47. Our remark applies primarily to Old Comedy, but by extension it could apply to later kinds, right up to those of the present day.

48. This difference is partly owing to self-reflexiveness of an especially baffling kind, as we hope to show at the proper time. Without the synoptic searches, the sense of any word, sentence, or proof in the dialogue can only be guessed at by means of analogies with other passages containing those expressions; but this will lose sight of the self-reflective character to which allusion has just been made.

49. *Phaedrus* 265d–e. In our own exposition we must employ such a joint method, even though the ideals of Plato's statement are not always maintained by the participants in the *Gorgias* itself. From the standpoint of a reader, there is dialectic in a broad structural sense in any dialogue—or in any play, poem, treatise, for that matter—even where dialectic as argument is either deliberately or inadvertently sidestepped. But the arts of writing and reading are not always the same, and the many arts, if such they can be termed, of speakers in a play or dialogue are again quite different.

50. The final myth does serve to bring together many though not all of the parts of the *Gorgias*; in this it is unlike the final *tutti* climax of Ravel's *Bolero*, merely a more emphatic repetition of the prevailing theme; unlike the triumphant theme on trumpets that shatters the emotions at the conclusion of Sibelius' *Symphony No. 2*, where a new melody suddenly shines over the full orchestra; unlike the final transformation of the brooding introductory subject in Tschaikowsky's *Symphony No. 5*, restating that subject but now in E major and on invincible brass; instead it is like the majestic passage at the end of Bruckner's *Symphony No. 8*, which contrapuntally weaves together the themes of the preceding movements. But even this climax—or the myth that Socrates narrates—does not *of itself* wholly establish the unity of all that has gone before.

51. Despite our caveat that the threefold contrasts do not ultimately prove the unity of the dialogue, we believe them to be a necessary step in that proof. Perhaps the most astute essay in this direction is by Adele Spitzer, "The Self-Reference of the *Gorgias*," *Philosophy and Rhetoric* 8(1975):1–22. The author also has many valuable suggestions for understanding the problem implied in her title.

52. Not all the dialogues are as difficult to fathom in this regard as the *Gorgias*. The *Phaedrus*, for example, can be shown to have a unity by proving that there is a steady progression running from the little myth of Boreas and the three subsequent speeches on love, then the discussion of rhetoric commencing halfway through the work, and finally seeking for a common denominator for love and rhetoric—not a very taxing assignment.

53. George Grote, *Plato and the Other Companions of Sokrates*, 3d ed., 3 vols. (London: John Murray, 1875), 2:90.

54. *Phaedrus* 272c.

55. It has become de rigueur to speak of the date of composition of the *Gorgias*. Terence Irwin sums up the matter by giving many reasons that this date is "hard to fix" (*Plato, "Gorgias,"* p. 5). With this we emphatically agree. The settling of chronology is almost invariably based by scholars, even before Lutoslawski, upon the premise that works written at the same time resemble each other in doctrine (or sometimes degree of artistry) more than do works written further apart. This is inference by what W. E. Johnson calls eduction, "from instances to instances" (*Logic* [Cambridge: At the University Press,

1924]), 3:43, and is really based upon a series of analogies, gathered under one head, from the lives and works of other writers. It is certainly a respectable conclusion for many thinkers, writers, and artists, but by no means does it hold for all. Some persons do not accomplish their creative work as others do, and the enormous complexities of Plato's thought make for problems in dating that have caused certain of the least easily discouraged of chronologists, such as Gilbert Ryle (*Plato's Progress* [Cambridge: At the University Press, 1966]), to presume a version of the dialogues that oversimplifies and exaggerates in order to support his speculations. An interesting biography is the result, but in the process the philosophical content and artistic integrity begin to disappear, and Plato becomes little more than a pamphleteer with a taste for self-advertising.

1. Prologue: Who Is Gorgias, What Is He?

1. The purest examples of rhetoric are found in the *Phaedrus* and *Symposium*. For dialectic in the sense of questions and short answers tightly arranged, the *Theaetetus* is typical; for dialectic in the sense of single speech, in which the content is carefully patterned, the long address by Timaeus in the dialogue that he dominates is outstanding. As a rule, when Socrates speaks by himself he makes use of a supposed respondent if the speech is of any considerable length—as in the *Symposium* when Diotima is called in to counsel him, or in the *Theaetetus* when Socrates puts words in the mouth of a Protagoras brought back to life. In the *Gorgias* itself (506c–509c) Socrates, arguing alone because Callicles has temporarily dropped out, still includes his antagonist in many of the steps.

2. George Grote, in *Plato and the Other Companions of Sokrates*, contends that the three sections of the dialogue are virtually independent of each other. On the other hand, he still apprehends the methodic unity of the discussion of Socrates with Gorgias more clearly than do most other commentators.

3. If, moreover, the reader happens to be familiar with the *Republic*, the *Lysis*, *Phaedrus*, and other dialogues having rather similar openings, he is unlikely to deprive himself of the benefit of insights which comparisons with those works will afford him, even before having turned the other pages of the *Gorgias*.

4. It is one thing to apprehend that a dialogue has sections and subsections— all of Plato's certainly have recognizable divisions, many of them marked off by dialogic or dramatic changes or both. It would be quite another to find that some dialogue fell into two or three separate pieces with only weak associations connecting them.

5. That Chaerephon *is* a bond between two types of discourse is partly confirmed by the fact that Socrates will shortly ask him to start the inquiry with Gorgias (447c).

6. Socrates will energetically engage three opponents, one experienced, one jejune and scatterbrained, one hostile, and all of them poorly equipped to understand him on anything like his own terms.

7. This shortness of acquaintance is made more likely in the absence of any mention here of the trip made by Chaerephon to Delphi (*Apology* 21a). Yet in that same passage Socrates claims to have had him as companion since youth, which certainly contradicts our supposition. The only counter argument is that in this group of sentences Socrates is making the strongest plea in the dialogue for trusting, tolerating, and exonerating him—he has not yet reached the defiant stage of his address. He goes a little out of his way to identify Chaerephon

as a democrat who shared in the exile, and it would be fairly natural of him, since Chaerephon cannot be called as witness, to say that he had known him for a very long time, thereby aligning himself with a good democratic man. The dramatic date of the *Gorgias* is set by Plato at about 404 B.C. at 473e and then turned topsy-turvy by making it nearer 427 B.C. at 503c, so on the second reading Socrates could have known Chaerephon for nearly thirty years in 399 B.C. and still have made his acquaintance just before the encounter with Gorgias and Callicles.

Plato has led his commentators a merry chase in their efforts to fix the dramatic dates of several if not most of the dialogues, those clustered about the day of the trial of Socrates being the chief exceptions. It is our conviction that he deliberately mixed his chronologies to suit his purposes, drawing attention to what has long been called poetic truth and its priority over history. The *Menexenus* is perhaps the prime example of such willful dodging, for in it Socrates recalls an incident taking place in 387–86 B.C., the Peace of Antalcidas (245e), in other words, about a dozen years after the historical death of Socrates. There are several other datable events in the *Gorgias* no two of which support each other as indications of a dramatic date.

In the remarks in the *Apology*, Socrates refers to Chaerephon as "vehement" (*sphodros*), and in the *Charmides* (153b) speaks of him as a "madman" (*manikos*), epithets jibing not at all with the depiction in the *Gorgias*. Here is one point in that dialogue where it can only be said that attention should be paid to it and not to the whole corpus at once. Or perhaps Chaerephon developed undesirable traits later in life.

8. Much later, one comes to realize that the analogy with a shoemaker has a little sting in it. Callicles would not let his daughter marry an engineer (512c). Would Gorgias let *his* daughter marry into the family of a shoemaker? Everything depends, in the minds of both Gorgias and Polus, upon maintaining the untouchable majesty of rhetoric, and the likening of it, in even the most superficial way, with a lowly craft would dismay and infuriate these two rhetors. Here is evidence of a small battle at the outset.

9. This statement later (462c) turns out to be a quotation or paraphrase taken from a book (a textbook?) that Polus has written.

10. The attitude of Callicles is more difficult to fathom and never emerges until much later.

11. In the *Phaedrus* (267a–c), Socrates is represented as knowing some of the contributions of both Gorgias and Polus to the theory of rhetoric. On the other hand, there is no final proof that that dialogue is meant to take place earlier or later than the *Gorgias*.

12. *Statesman* 283c, *Phaedrus* 267b.

13. In the passage from the *Phaedrus* Gorgias is credited with dividing brief talk from speech long without measure (267a–b).

14. In the *Republic* I, Thrasymachus, another rhetor, makes Socrates think of a bathman who, having poured the water, abruptly departs (344d).

15. Chaerephon has shown himself inadequate to conduct a Socratic examination; Polus is uncontradicted in his assumption that he is able to vie with Gorgias, though Socrates hints otherwise. Plato is telling his readers that Polus is in truth substituting for Gorgias, so that if there are differences between them (which there are, and important ones at that), nevertheless the links between them are strong. Polus not only says this but acts out the fact as well by his interposition. It would take another kind of egotist to assume that he could

replace Socrates, and this type is exemplified in Euthydemus and Dionyso-
dorus in the dialogue titled after the first-named of these two verbal pugilists.

2. Rhetoric, Just and Unjust

1. This becomes the germ of Socrates' claim (462c) that rhetoric is a "familiarity" (empeiria) and a knack (tribē) rather than a true art (technē) or kind of
knowledge.

2. Gorgias will contradict himself on this later on (456b–c).

3. One of these parts is justice, which in Socrates' view is inextricably combined with its practice.

4. In the Phaedrus Gorgias is listed, along with Tisias (267a–b), as having
honored probabilities above truths, made the small things seem great and the
great small, new things old and old new, and invented both conciseness and
length without measure. None of these would look promising or even pertinent
to a man concerned with arriving systematically at truth.

5. There is a slight hint that Gorgias, in giving a display, has disguised his
real character as a mover of the populace. He has apparently been giving a discourse resembling our modern Fourth-of-July oratory, quite innocuous and far
from revealing his true aims which are just beginning to emerge under the persistent questioning of Socrates. Something like this is found in Protagoras' admission that the sophists often disguise themselves as poets or prophets, and
so forth, as a screen whereby to escape malice (Protagoras 316c–e). This is the
first inkling in the Gorgias that there is an element of dissembling in the character of the rhetor, and perhaps in rhetoric itself.

6. Gorgias has unwittingly mentioned arts relating to the soul (rhetoric), the
body (physician and trainer), and exterior property (the moneymaker). He has
not, however, separated these in their types, and seems to think of them as
being on the same psychic level, differing only in their degrees of servitude.

7. This is the impression given by Hippias in both dialogues to which he
lends his name.

8. Thucydides, History 2:35–46.

9. Although Polus and Callicles both criticize Socrates for wrongheadedness
and error-ridden argument, neither of them ever gives a point-by-point disproof of what Socrates has tried to establish. If his arguments were patently
unsuited to the task he has assumed, one would expect to find their inadequacies exposed, even if by Socrates himself (see Theaetetus 197a; 210a).

10. In the Ion Socrates hints that all rhapsodes are not generals, despite Ion's
claim that he could be the best general in Greece (541b). There is no explicit
discussion of the general as rhapsode, but again the capability of addressing
troops, part of being a general, Ion says is subject to his judgment (540d). The
difference is that Ion does not claim to have a universal art, while Gorgias is
sure that the rhetor can take over the functions of every other artist. He would
say that to be a good general a man would have to be a good rhetor, with little or
nothing left over in generalship to be mastered once the other was accomplished.

11. In the same way, Socrates' own inner voice has, according to him, no
known roots in ordinary consecutive thinking. This voice, however, makes no
appearance, nor is it even mentioned, in the Gorgias—interesting in view of the
fact that Socrates hints that he might leave the discussion if his conditions are
not met (461e–462a). In the Phaedrus Socrates' will to depart is thwarted by

the *daimōn* (242b–c). There, however, love, the main power, had been put in jeopardy by both the speech of Lysias and one by Socrates himself, whereas at no point in the *Gorgias* does anything like this happen. Philosophy is disparaged by Callicles, but Socrates does not follow suit.

12. In *Republic* III, Herodicus mixes medicine and gymnastics (he is a trainer) and prolongs his life miserably by a regimen (406a–b). Were Gorgias to persuade a patient to follow suit his advice would be suspect, though his motives decent. Later in the *Gorgias* Socrates will raise new questions about the prolonging of life (511b–513a).

13. Later (466b–c) there will be further references to this aggressive aspect of rhetoric.

14. In the *Apology* the situation is a little different; Socrates is the sole speaker (except for a brief duologue with Meletus), and he is confronted by an audience many of whom have doubtless fallen victim to his elenchic treatments beforehand and thus in a mood to relish meting out punishment to him. He has had (27b) to request that they not interfere with his presentation. It is a rhetorical situation, of course, but there is little interchange verbally, and those who shout at Socrates remain unnamed and are given no thoughts to express beyond inarticulate hostility.

15. A variant of this will occur near the end of the discussion with Polus (480c–d), when Socrates indicates that the function of rhetoric must be to incriminate oneself if one has performed an injustice; the same should be done for family or friends because this rids the soul of the greatest evil.

16. The *daimōn* that accompanies Socrates in several other dialogues is a supernatural expression of this fear of error.

17. If we bury some of these inconsistencies in a footnote our readers may not be quite so convinced that we are stacking the cards against Gorgias. The following may be noted: (a) the rhetor is supposed to know justice, an abstract principle, yet by its help gives advice on warships, forts and walls, and so forth, which can hardly be said to fall under the more general heading; (b) rhetoric is the fairest of the arts yet knows little or nothing of any subject matter, hence cannot be an art; (c) the rhetor knows and imparts justice and makes his pupil to be like himself, but if the pupil acts unjustly the rhetor steps aside. This last becomes the subject of the final pages of the colloquy with Gorgias.

18. In *Republic* I, 345c–d, Socrates chides Thrasymachus for inconsistency in his use of precise or accurate meanings of words, saying that if the shepherd sells his sheep for a profit this is not in his capacity as shepherd, that is, not exercising the shepherd's art, but rather in his exercise of the art of the moneymaker. This is not quite the point in the *Gorgias*, though it is related. What Socrates is saying to Gorgias is that the just man (1) by definition acts justly and if he does not he is no longer just, and (2) the just man will, because he has the stable knowledge of justice in his soul, habitually act in the proper way. There is no suggestion here of pursuing a plurality of arts.

3. The Divided Oblong

1. The second part begins at 466a and the third at 474b.

2. In his condemnation of Socrates as a rustic, Polus is probably unconsciously reacting against the fact that the discussion has really been in the hands of Socrates, not Gorgias, despite the latter's eminence in the art of dis-

course. There never was any explicit agreement that Socrates could, or had the right to, lead the conversation, which means that his doing so came about through his superior intellectual or moral strength, not through some protocol; but this would translate itself to Polus as rudeness.

3. If we assume that Polus was the pupil of Gorgias—or even that he had traveled with him as a longtime companion—we would see that the attitude of Gorgias toward questions, that they were all cut from the same cloth, would have a numbing effect upon Polus and *his* notions of interrogatives.

4. So important is the interweaving of this passage with all that has gone before and that will come after that we shall devote chapter 12 to a separate treatment of these connections, for it would interrupt the discussion too often were we to deal with it fully here.

5. We scarcely need point out that these are not the approaches to art found in each of the other Platonic dialogues.

6. The first times were at 448c and e.

7. A. E. Taylor suggests *confectionery,* in *Plato: The Man and His Work,* new ed. (New York: Dial, 1936), p. 110.

8. This is not mere irony; if we take Socrates to be a man of great intelligence but not of superhuman perceptions, he could not possibly be certain of what was meant in Gorgias' attempts to explain his own calling and its moral worth.

9. Hans von Arnim, in *Platos Jugenddialoge und die Entstehungszeit des Phaidros,* (1914; reprint, New York: Arno, 1976), p. 186, uses a coinage that has no equivalent, unfortunately, in English. He refers to *empeiria* (and presumably with it *pandering*) as *Afterkunst,* which relates both to its spuriousness and to one's backside.

10. Gorgias admitted (459a) that he could not possibly be more convincing than was the doctor to those who had knowledge of medicine, however much he might outdo him in effectiveness (459b) when the audience is ignorant.

11. In contrast, it can be shown that practically all of the terms used in the Divided Line in the *Republic* have clear predecessors in earlier portions of that work.

12. Socrates' admission balances his asserting earlier (462e–463a) that he himself is not clear regarding what Gorgias had in mind in his conception of rhetoric.

13. Although Socrates does not explicitly refer to the human being, it would be unthinkable that he has anything else in mind. It is the starting point for his entire account, and so we have added it to help point up the unity of the discussion.

14. Some panderings, such as catering and embellishing, are for what appears to be the body's sake; presumably the body without the soul has no way of knowing how to distinguish what is good for it from what is bad, that is, what leads to good health, strength, beauty, and so forth, and what merely covers up possible defects of all these. If left to itself to estimate the value of catering and medicine, the body would leave everything confused.

15. One must bear in mind that *politics* covered, for many of the Greeks, individual ethical as well as communal matters; but that Plato did not seem to intend this here is shown by Socrates' later division of politics into legislation and judicature; and unless *these* are made analogically applicable to self-rule or sound judgment or the like in individuals, we cannot assume (as Books IV–IX of the *Republic* force one to assume) that person and state are of the same general kind.

16. In point of fact, this connection between order on a small scale and on a

large scale will be made later on, 507e–508a, although the applications are no longer quite the same.

17. In introducing the geometrical manner here, Socrates apologizes a little, saying it is to avoid excessive speech (*makrologō*). This is before a trio of men lacking a concern for mathematics. It is otherwise when Socrates commences his exposition of the Divided Line in the *Republic* VI (509d); he assumes (510c) that Glaucon knows the nature of geometrical method. In the *Timaeus* the statesman-astronomer uses proportions repeatedly and apologizes not for them but for possible inaccuracies because the actualities are not as perfect as are the models from which they are copied (29c–d; 38b; 48d; and elsewhere).

18. Polus will shortly (466a) say he thinks that Socrates has been telling him that rhetoric and pandering are identical, rather than that the former is but a part of the latter.

19. This is much the same, so far, as the method advocated by Socrates in the *Phaedrus*, 265d–e.

20. This point happens to hold true generally in the dialogues. The great difficulty in the *Timaeus*, however, is to show that there can be a provisional exception to this; in that work the imitative relation is closer, more nearly essential, and the reason seems to be that the model is a mathematical one, pure and precise, so that the near-accuracy and near-perfection of the most immediate imitations can be vouched for. When, however, the dialectic reaches imitations of imitations, the perfections begins to fall off. But at no point can the copies be considered fakeries.

4. Rhetoric Without Power

1. Notice the contrast with Gorgias, who thought of rhetoric as an art for gaining money indirectly (452e), while Polus thinks it a way of escaping the very punishment that Gorgias believed would come to the pupil or even to the teacher (457c).

2. Meyer W. Isenberg, *The Order of the Discourses in Plato's "Symposium,"* private ed. (distributed by University of Chicago Libraries, 1940), p. 12, attributes a one-term dialectic to Phaedrus and Agathon. One might say the same of Anytus in the *Meno* and Ion in the dialogue named after him. Incidentally, this is not the same as monism, though it overlaps. A monist might easily use a one-term dialectic, if he were a naïve one, but then again a very subtle use of two-term (with opposites) or three-term (including intermediates) might be employed, as with Saint Bonaventura and Hegel.

3. Other traditions have it that Socrates himself was invited to the court of Archelaus, but refused to go. Xenophon does not mention this king in the *Memorabilia* or *Symposium*, nor does Diogenes Laertius, even among his list of persons who bore the same name as Archelaus the physicist. Aristotle gives Socrates' reason for refusal (that it is disgraceful not to be able to return a favor as well as an injury) as an instance of the topic of definition (*The Rhetorical Art* II.xxiii.8).

4. This is an echo of what Socrates has said to Gorgias (461a). Throughout, there have been hints of a distinction between seeming to agree or to disagree, and really agreeing or disagreeing. This becomes a cardinal point in talking with Callicles.

5. Here we have a puzzle. Socrates will shortly (473e–474a) confess that he has been ignorant of procedures in the Council, and elsewhere (*Theaetetus*

172c–177c) he says that the philosopher is confused by lawcourts. Here, however, he appears to know a good deal about the use of witnesses. Perhaps the contradiction can be explained by saying that the intricacies of voting procedures, and so forth, are less likely to be discussed outside the chambers and courts than would be the calling of witnesses. In the *Euthyphro* Socrates seems to know so little about criminal charges that he does not recognize that Euthyphro himself has proceeded improperly against his father, nor does Socrates appear certain how he is to answer the charge brought by Meletus of the hooked nose and stringy hair. On the other hand, in looking at devoutness as described by the young priest, Socrates is well able to show the difficulties inherent in his various formulations.

6. See 521d for his self-characterization. He happens to be the only Athenian, or almost the only one, who is practicing the true political art, aiming not to favor himself but to improve the citizens.

7. Other kinds (referred to in other dialogues) would be mathematical truths and insights regarding the forms.

8. These two manners of refutation and two kinds of existence, the happy and the unhappy, give rise to two respective questions, and this anticipates very clearly the structure of two of the three questions raised with Callicles (500d) regarding two lives, the political and the philosophical. It also reaches back to the occasions when Socrates asked the single question of Gorgias (447c), what he is and professes. But there is no comparison to be made yet because Socrates has not discussed his own methods for arriving at truth, except to suggest certain procedures for conducting a debate; nor has he discussed his own calling in his conversation with Polus.

9. In his discourse with Callicles, Socrates will amend this remark (521a).

10. This pattern is roughly paralleled in the *Phaedrus*, where a myth and three speeches on eros in various forms are followed by a comparatively searching discussion of rhetoric and its relation to human life.

11. This attitude is at first belied by the vigor of Callicles' attacks upon Socrates, but he later shows that although he makes verbal concession after concession he is largely unconvinced.

12. *Symposium* 210a–211c. With a little industry, one can find almost all members of the list that appears in the *Gorgias* in the early pages of the *Meno* as well, 73c–77b, though not arranged in the hierarchic form of increasing approximation to the One, as in the *Symposium*.

13. The emphasis on unbounded pleasure foreshadows the conversation with Callicles.

14. Cowardice will emerge in the discussion with Callicles in more than one guise.

15. The notion of purging the effects of unjust action has a kind of precedent in Socrates' remark (458a) that he would be glad to be refuted were he to say anything untrue, and again (470c) that he would be grateful to the child who could rid him of trivialities (*phluarias*). What relates these associatively with the present concept of relief is Socrates' contention that knowing a subject makes one a doer of that subject or art (460a–b).

16. In the third colloquy of this dialogue, Callicles is seen as a man ready to use rhetoric in precisely this way.

17. In another way, Callicles will show himself as a man willing to bet not only his career (politics) but his very life on persuasive speech coupled with the power that Polus has been made to forswear.

18. This is altered in the concluding myth (523a–526d): Injustice puts a per-

manent scar upon the body, and this is carried over to the afterworld, so it would make little difference if a person lived briefly or long; his sins would find him out.

19. Gorgias thought (456d) the injuring of parents and friends especially blameworthy, not pausing to ask whether striking them on certain occasions could possibly do them some good. What treatment is to be measured out to enemies receives no attention at that point. True to his own habit of reducing opposites to each other, Polus blurs the distinction between friends and enemies, so Archelaus treats his own family abominably (471a–c). Socrates is restoring the distinction in the present passage, so that no longer everyone is a kind of friend (Gorgias seems to think it unfortunate if he or anyone else is mistreated) or a kind of enemy (Polus thinks it splendid to murder one's closest kin). Instead the friend receives improving treatment and only the enemy is left to suffer, but it is the consequences of his own misdeeds that he suffers, not the unjust acts of another. Here Socrates does not directly contradict the import of his question (*Republic* I, 335b), Whether a good man should harm anyone at all?

5. Power above the Law

1. In *Republic* IX (571d–572a), Socrates describes a man healthy and moderate: he awakens his rational soul and feasts it on fair arguments, feeding the desiderative part so it will be neither in want nor in surfeit and disturb the rational part with its joys and pains. He will not indulge the spirited part, allowing it to be angry. In such a condition, fulfilling these three requirements, the soul can lay hold of truth. In contrast, a soul having an unhealthy, immoderate relation to itself puts the rational part to sleep while the appetites are gorged. One knows that in such a condition the soul dares do everything as if released from all shame and prudence. This distinction, in summary, points toward that in the *Gorgias* between the soul's control of the body and the body's rule over the soul.

2. It may be supposed that Callicles has borrowed from Pyrilampes, father of the beloved Demus, some of the ambitions which marked the members of The Thirty. Earlier we have echoed the suggestion of Jowett that Callicles is a name given by Plato to Critias, another of The Thirty and whom for family reasons Plato might wish to protect from the ultimately devastating attack by Socrates, yet could not help referring to for the passions and ideas he entertained. This is speculation, nothing more; but there can be no doubt that Plato saw the storm warnings telling of the danger to his mother city and was eager to apprise his fellow citizens of the risks that they faced. By the time the *Gorgias* was written—whenever that was—all, or almost all, the members of The Thirty must have been dead, exiled, or so old that they could do no further harm; but to a follower of Socrates this was no more than a happy accident, and one could not trust that this calamity for Athens would not be repeated. It is possible, incidentally, that one reason for Plato's deliberate confusing of the chronology of events mentioned in the dialogue owes itself to his wish to say that a Callicles could certainly emerge in political life at any time.

3. For example, Socrates' treatment of Thrasymachus is more polite though certainly not altogether deferential, despite the fact that Thrasymachus is described—by Socrates himself, for he is the narrator of the *Republic*—as loud, bumptious, inept, and often rude. But there is little of personal rancor on ei-

ther side, even so, after the sophist has had his first explosive say. It is plain that unless Callicles were being flattered by Socrates (487a) as a man of knowledge, goodwill, and frankness, he would be loath to remain in the discussion at all. But *flattered* is not quite the correct word, for there is at least *some* truth in each of these ascriptions.

4. This echoes some advice given by Callicles (447c) when the newly arrived Socrates wonders whether Gorgias would be willing to discuss his calling: Ask him yourself, since he is so good at answering questions, or so he claims.

5. It may be that Callicles thinks Chaerephon is very well acquainted with Socrates, but this is no proof that Chaerephon is an old friend of the philosopher in this dialogue. Even the supposition that Callicles does believe Chaerephon to be well acquainted may be wrong; in his astonishment at the outcome of the debate with Polus, Callicles might well turn to a total stranger and exclaim, Is he serious? Can he mean what he is saying?

6. Exceptions are the *Phaedrus*, when Socrates refers to the young man's enthusiasms for Lysias (236b), and the *Charmides*, where there is talk of the fair youth as target for suitors (154b–155e), Socrates himself almost being included among them.

7. Socrates' main effort with Alcibiades was to render him more stable, as we see from the *Symposium*, in which Socrates is described as frequently talking to him in his peculiar philosophical way (215c–d; 217c), serving as an example of imperturbable bravery in an otherwise disastrous situation in combat (221a–b), and resisting the male charms of this quixotic and in some respects brilliant young man (217c–219d). These three virtues, wisdom, bravery, and temperance, are supplemented by justice in the binding together of all the features of Socrates' character in a unity. Plato does not record the great disillusionment with Alcibiades, whose early caprices hinted at in the *Gorgias* later ripened into downright treachery, first against the gods (if he was indeed guilty of profanation) and then against his city, when he twice defected. Benedict Arnold is not described as merely fickle. After leaving the tutelage of Socrates, Alcibiades could not be called fickle either. In the context of the *Gorgias*, however, it seems reasonable to believe that Alcibiades corresponds to Demus, while philosophy and the deme are paired, though dissimilar.

8. Perhaps Callicles borrows from Pyrilampes, father of Demus, some of the ambitions and opinions which made the older man join The Thirty. Demus himself seems to have been a spoiled dandy who kept a flock of peacocks. Peacocks at best make a considerable racket, are pleased to roam, and would no doubt draw unfavorable attention of the people to their wealthy owner—a not unimportant point, for it would spell divided loyalties on the part of Callicles, though the conflict would run much deeper than the troublemaking of birds.

9. It is not wisdom but *love of* wisdom that has been loved by Socrates. This seems to mean that Socrates is unwilling, despite firm iteration of his reasons for adopting the philosophic life (509c–527e), to think of the human condition as so well ordered that one can view it with the same confidence as one accepts the propositions of geometry and astronomy. The solutions to life's problems are well founded, but they are only approximate, a point he exhibits rather than proves in the *Gorgias*.

10. Socrates apparently did not think that Gorgias would even try to refute him. As for Polus, Socrates offers (462a) to let him try to do some refuting, but this is coupled with the possibility that he, Socrates, might refute Polus instead; it is also joined with the invitation to question or be questioned. Thus it is pro-

cedure that Socrates concerns himself with when talking to Polus; with Callicles it is a more fundamental struggle.

11. There is no counterpart to this; Callicles never claims that the deme cannot be refuted.

12. The distinction between nature and convention, used in the first round against Socrates, but tacitly dropped after Stephanus p. 492, is a legacy from the sophists, as is fairly well attested by historians. Whether Callicles took instruction from some of them or not, he makes good use of the distinction at first, then begins to falter when pressed for justifications, as if he had learned a little, quickly, but had not pursued the teaching far enough. Having taken over the initial premise, Callicles must improvise most of the rest of his argument. Even so, he is a much more collected thinker than Polus.

Incidentally, our own disparagement of Callicles' statement and defense of the distinction is not intended as an attack upon the theory of natural law in general; what we say about his expression "law of nature" does not carry over to other men's conceptions of it.

13. Probably Callicles disdains Gorgias by this time as much as he distrusts Socrates. He would think that anyone making as important a concession as Gorgias has made would also be in danger from the politically strong. Perhaps he also despises Gorgias as a kind of sophist, or as someone much like the sophists, it matters little which. Why, then, has Callicles invited Gorgias to his home? Either he has wished to do some lion taming to enhance his own social position, or else he has been hoping to pick up some pointers on effective public speaking. In any case his regard, if any, for Gorgias would not be altogether disinterested, and hence would be likely to fade rapidly if he sensed that Gorgias could not cope successfully with the Socratic elenchus. It is Polus, after all, not Callicles, who speaks highly of Gorgias and his art. Callicles praises only the display (447a), and this he does well before Socrates has dealt with Gorgias.

14. It is perhaps significant that the older, Homeric meaning of the word *elenchos* was "shame," not "refutation," and it may be that the two meanings are connected by Callicles here, in a kind of pun. By the time of Socrates *elenchos* had taken on the second meaning, but shortly (485d) Callicles will be quoting Homer, which must mean that he *could* have the earlier sense of the word in mind as well as the later. Educated persons, especially those with literary interests, frequently use older locutions to make a point.

15. Parallel to this, we detect a mixture of scorn and secret admiration in Callicles' repeatedly calling attention to the rhetorical (and sophistical) devices that he finds Socrates to be consciously using in the attack upon the successful but unjust man in society. Socrates should be watched, therefore, not only because he must not be allowed to win but also because he seems to know the ropes as well as Gorgias and Polus do, and his clever contrivances will be very handy to Callicles some day.

16. Since Socrates has just now, in the eyes of Callicles, beaten two supposedly skilled men at their own game, he would not shrink from using the same devices against him or in a courtroom. Despite Socrates' claim to seek out and speak the truth, Callicles obviously thinks him a fairly shrewd old party well prepared to turn the tables against an opponent. It is a mark of his complex nature, however, that he will soon vent his spleen upon Socrates by saying that the latter could not defend himself against any mean, commonplace man bringing charges against him. This is also an insult to Gorgias and Polus, to

imply that they have been defeated by a man himself unable to respond satis-factorily to ordinary calumnies. If it is simply a slip on his part, and one for which he would have to apologize, then this too is a small indication of his divided nature.

17. It is essential to remember that this account of nature and convention is introduced in the context of Callicles' disparagement of the tactics of Socrates. This does not weaken the force of the distinction, nor does it imply that Callicles never considered the matter prior to the day's discussion; one feels that the elaborateness of the statement by him bespeaks his having kept this theory bottled up for a time, and is now bringing it out for display at an opportune moment. But without its introduction as a way of rebutting Socrates it might be very difficult to argue for the unity of this part of the *Gorgias*, since the transition would otherwise be unpardonably abrupt.

18. See also the recurrent mentions of this theme, at 486b–c); 492c; 588c–d. At 522c–e and at 526a Socrates recasts the idea.

19. At 484b he quotes Pindar rather aptly; at 484e, Euripides; at 485d, Homer; and he seems well acquainted with the careers of several Athenians of the historic and recent past, 503c.

20. The examples of strength that Callicles uses constitute a motley and "unrealistic" list: animals, states, Persian kings of somewhat dubious accomplishment, and a mythical hero.

21. In point of historical fact, both Persians enjoyed a perfectly regular succession to kingship, and whatever strength they could demonstrate was incidental to the institutional power wielded by the Great King of Persia. Callicles recognizes this conventional succession when he speaks of Darius as the father of Xerxes.

22. We do not mean by this that *any* two-column division having this pattern is foredoomed to easy refutation, nor do we mean that Socrates will sooner or later take refuge in some supposedly impregnable abstract structure to resolve all philosophical difficulties. No dialectical structure is fixed at all until filled in with expressions whose meanings can be determined. Some structures, such as that of Callicles, have more obvious shortcomings than others, but all of them have their own difficulties, and their relative worth is hardly to be predetermined.

23. To those four can be added two more: Socrates treats of picayune details and verbal inaccuracies, and he repeats himself excessively. The first ones are more important and imply more thought, being first uttered before Callicles has had time to feel his growing exasperation in the face of his antagonist, and whose own reproaches in return are not on the same footing. Callicles blames Socrates for what he is; Socrates blames Callicles for the character of the reproaches themselves. This point is reinforced when Socrates says (489d) that Callicles should be more gentle in his remarks or the conversation will be broken off forthwith.

24. Although their characters and motivations are very different, there is a certain similarity between Callicles' statements and the expostulations of Crito: The latter promotes the success morality of the ordinary Athenian as much as does the former. We admire a winner, Socrates, and you have not won your trial, says Crito. You are losing altogether if you remain in jail, for your execution will confirm a total defeat. I will never be able to explain your behavior to our friends, who will not believe that you do not want to die.

25. At no point does Callicles object to the strong man's use of whatever ver-

bal tactics might be handy for subjecting the many and the weak to his control. The condemning of rhetorical devices is very onesided; it changes from legitimate to illegitimate rapidly, depending upon the person using them.

26. Callicles forgets that Socrates just arrived from the agora.

27. Apparently Callicles thinks the old have *continued* their pursuit of philosophy begun in youth; they do not come to it so late that it cannot benefit them.

28. Socrates never says in this part of the dialogue that he feels friendship for Callicles, despite complimenting him on being knowledgeable, well disposed, and candid (487a).

29. If Callicles is taken as a strong man, ruthless, single-minded, and verging on outright violence, then his protestation of friendship must be a disguise for his conscious hatred of Socrates and his intent to do him harm in the future. If, however, Callicles is a vacillator, then it seems likely that this claim to be friendly is a cloak for a plea for help, not immediately but at some future time. Socrates, as a private man, is safer than Callicles with his public career, and there must be a touch of envy in his attitude. It is a little like a homely Maude who turns on a beautiful Myrtle with the words, "You are nothing but a pretty face," hating the very thing that Maude both wants and lacks.

30. It is difficult if not impossible to reconstruct the topics of the philosophical discussions that Callicles thinks have taken place so often. No doubt they either involved such matters as cosmology and the typical presocratic subjects that Aristotle denies as an interest of Socrates (*Metaphysics* I. 3–5; 6. 987b1–2), or else they included ethico-political arguments, but so finespun and bloodless that from them no consistent planning or action could result. If Plato's dialogues are instead any clue to what occurred, the discussions must have been a mixture of general speculation and individual counsel.

31. When Socrates wanted to instill an important lesson he used a drinking song that was of a much more homely sort (451e), and not antithetical in style to the content of his lesson.

32. Our remark does not hold, of course, for most quotations in the dialogues.

33. Among all the inconsistencies of Callicles' plural accusations against Socrates should be especially noted his complaint that Socrates is a demagogue because he has defeated an outstanding rhetor, side by side with the warning that he could not rescue himself in court. But would it not be the same verbal skills that would enable Socrates to have his way in such a trial? It is apparent that the philosopher has had to think quickly and with much dexterity to win over Gorgias, and the same quick thinking should save him from any charge in a court of law.

34. *Plato, The Man and His Work*, p. 97.

35. *Apology*, 18c–d.

36. Callicles never says that Socrates has spoiled the young by his philosophizing with them. Indeed, he has liberated them, doing what is appropriate for their education at their stage in life.

37. If our interpretation is approximately correct, it is strengthened by the remark's being balanced at the very end of the dialogue when Socrates urges Callicles to follow *him*.

38. If Callicles in *this* guise is indeed the forerunner of Nietzsche, then here it must be a very different Nietzsche, who creates the *Uebermensch* on Sundays but the rest of the week earns good money as a professor, is finally married to Lou Andreas, the daughter of a general, has several promising children and as good a bank account as the professorship and a dowry would allow.

39. It is interesting that a close acquaintance with the souls of the members of the audience is made one of the requisites of the good rhetor in the *Phaedrus* (277c). The difference is in the contexts: In that dialogue, Socrates is assuming that the animating spirit behind the rhetor and the dialectician are found in the same individual. The assumptions of Callicles, needless to say, point in a quite different direction.

40. The best feature of Callicles' long list of suggestions and warnings is that he addresses himself not to the mistakes of Socrates in the past but rather to mending his ways in the future. Socrates, for all his wrongheadedness, is not beyond hope, if only he will change his habits. There is irony in the fact—one that Callicles will not recognize—that when Socrates does enter into the arena of political controversy he challenges Callicles himself and defeats him, and that moreover he does this primarily by using transformed rhetorical devices that are counterparts of the Calliclean. There is a double irony in this, that if Callicles does not mend his ways it is a sign that *he* is so corrupted that his punishment can do good only in the sense of persuading others not to follow his example.

41. After 486d, Callicles no longer impugns philosophy by name, but castigates Socrates for alleged sins against the art of discussion. But to Callicles that would still be philosophy, since he makes no firm distinction between types of discourse beyond what suits his purpose and what does not.

42. Contributions of the Divided Oblong to the unity of the dialogue will be treated in chap. 12.

43. This test is of the soul, not the body or the body and soul together. The three rhetors, as we have said, scarcely considered this distinction.

44. Socrates has not suggested that if he fails to secure Callicles' agreement he himself will not be speaking truly. It could well be that if he assures his hearers that he *is* speaking truly it will have to rest upon grounds other than the corroborating testimony of Callicles.

45. There is a family resemblance between this and one pragmatic test for truth: A true statement is one that serves as an accommodation between two minds. It is certainly not a theory that if at any time two men agree on anything this is a sign that absolute truth has been reached on whatever topic has been chosen. Its very evanescence as a guarantee for truth is reflected in Socrates' earlier remarks (481d–e) on the fickleness of Callicles. To secure his agreement might be nothing more permanent than a few moments' concurrence.

46. Tisander, Andron, and Nausicydes are rather shadowy personages in history, and whether they were all rich or oligarchically inclined, or patrons of sophists, or even sophists themselves, is not clearly known. Andron is the only one mentioned elsewhere by Plato (*Protagoras* 315c); why he is at the house of Callias and in what capacity is not evident in that dialogue.

47. He threatens to march out in the *Protagoras* after far less provocation (355b–c), and to break camp after none at all in the *Phaedrus* (242a).

48. There is also the tradition that he was a confidant and helper of Euripides in the writing of the tragedies; see Diogenes Laertius, *Lives and Opinions of Eminent Philosophers* II.5.18: *Edokei de sympoiein*—perhaps he "co-authored" some of the plays.

49. For Callicles here, the strong man never tries to help the weak, in fact is always ready to get the better of them, assuming that there is innate conflict between himself and the others. Once you can satisfy others that you are strong, you look out only for yourself. No doubt a reason Callicles later includes Pericles in his list of able rhetors of the past (503c) is that he respects the

selfish, haughty side of that leader's nature. Incidentally, Callicles is not borne out by history in his view that the laws are invariably made by the weaker. Pericles himself was responsible for many laws, and in the sixth century A.D., to take an obvious example, Justinian ordered a codification of the laws, giving the commission imperial authority. The Code Napoleon was dictated, if not in its details at least in its principles, by the strongest ruler that France ever had. Mayor Frank Hague of Jersey City—to descend in the scale considerably—declared, "I am the law." He would fit the Calliclean view of the superior man, yet he won his office through election, that is, agreement of the populace.

50. Callicles comes to realize this eventually (488d–e), that he is in fact arguing in behalf of a strong man who is bound to fail, much as the rhetor-tyrant in the Polus section is one of the weakest in the city, though the reasons there were different.

51. There is a parallel to this awkward predicament in the Apology, where the only chance that Socrates has for refuting Meletus' charge against him is in front of a large jury which will bitterly resent the tactics that Socrates must use. Members of that jury would individually remember the treatment that they had received at the philosopher's hands; but at the trial it would be even more resented because carried on in public. The tool for freeing Socrates is at the same time the one to nail shut his coffin.

52. Here one sees that wisdom is one of the virtues permitted to, or rather required of, the superior man; yet Socrates has been chastized for pursuing the love of wisdom, and has overheard Callicles agreeing with friends that any more than a moderate amount harms a man.

53. It is worth remembering that Alcibiades praises Socrates for talking in just this way (Symposium 221e–222a): His talk is of pack asses, smiths, cobblers, and tanners, and he seems always to be using the same terms for the same things . . . . You will find that they are the only discourses that have sense (noun echontas) . . . . Alcibiades admits elsewhere to being somewhat baffled by Socrates, but sees the magic in his talk.

54. Devoutness, if that were to be added, as well it might, would have a further damping effect.

55. Whether this will be found consistent with Callicles' ultimate dependence upon the lawcourts to defend him from unwarranted attack is a question not to be answered at this time.

56. This phrase is borrowed from Euthydemus 297c.

57. This marks the major revelation that Callicles will defend his position in a general way, but only at the cost of changing the precise terms of that position to conform to the demands of the Socratic elenchus. Far from remaining the unperturbed advocate of the right of the naturally strong to rule, he shows not singlemindedness but its opposite; and the section devoted to him is accordingly long and convoluted.

6. Pleasures Unlimited

1. In the section treated in the present chapter pleasures are the theme. The catamite passage (494e) is the low point in the conversation, even Callicles being, or pretending to be, disgusted. It is worthwhile to compare the tone of this with the far more dignified listing of pleasures toward the close of the Philebus: Only the pleasures unmixed with pain, and residing in the soul, can be

called goods, and they are in the fifth rank of goods at that. Socrates does not deign to list a sixth class at all (*Philebus* 66c). During the entire dialogue, no really derogatory expressions are used against each other by Socrates and his two respondents. This could be because the dialogue was written much later than the *Gorgias*, but the real reason seems to lie internally to the work. The issue in the *Philebus* is not the quality of an art (or pandering) and its effect on life private and public but rather the superiority of one kind of good divorced so far as possible from the individuals possessing it, over another kind of good.

2. One may keep in mind Thomas Mann's remark in *Buddenbrooks*, pt. 8, chap. 2, that we are most prone to become angry in our opposition to some idea when we are unsure of our own views, and are privately tempted to take the opposite side.

3. It would be like trying to reconstruct the culture of a city that may, with its outlying villages, have approached Toledo, Ohio, in size from a few of its monuments and a museum or two, a large handful of philosophical writings from two outstanding men, about four dozen plays and many fragments stretching over a considerable period, a host of bills and other rather trivial financial documents, and some first-class but admittedly inventive historians.

4. In the *Phaedrus* (258d, 259e), the question is different: How ought we to speak and write? In that dialogue, it is assumed that the audience, even a highly critical audience, will take pleasure in listening to speeches, and the problem is not to dismantle the aims of the self-seeking rhetor so much as it is the way the rhetor acquits himself in discourse. Socrates criticizes Lysias not for bad morals (although he does subsequently transform the imperfect notions of the professional speech writer in a speech of his own), but for repeating and jumbling his ideas (235a; 263a–264b).

5. If you object that Socrates could not possibly foresee that he will later on unfold this myth, we can only say that he does not invent it on the spot; he has heard it before and believed it (524a–b), and elements of it, he says, come from Homer (523a). So he may have been saving it for an auspicious occasion.

6. A. E. Taylor, *A Commentary on Plato's "Timaeus"* (Oxford: At the Clarendon Press, 1928), p. 40. For further discussion of Philolaus and Archytas and their possible identities as a source for the jar image, see Dodds, *Plato, "Gorgias,"* pp. 296–98.

7. Gorgias' story of himself and his brother and their joint visits to a patient (456b), and Polus' loosely articulated account of Archelaus (471a–d) are "arguments" closer to the utterances of poets than of philosophers. Rhetoric, even in the Socratic employment of it, leans heavily upon images and narratives. On the other hand, there are no premises now (494b) established to show that poets are generally below wise men in point of stating truths, and it may not be proper to import such premises from the *Republic*. Certainly it is not necessary to the argument.

8. It is arguable that temperance, rather than justice, is the chief virtue at issue in the Callicles section of the *Gorgias*, that all disagreements turn upon the conflicting interpretations of this notion: How much or how little is the body to receive, and of what sort? Even as late as 518e–519a Socrates criticizes the earlier rhetor-leaders as lacking regard for temperance and virtue.

9. It is tempting to range the mention of the scratching and the catamite along with the figures of the jars, and to chart them as concluding the section devoted to images. It appears, however, that a new topic has been broached, that of the quality of different pleasures, and an infinite gradation from good ones

to bad, or at least harmless ones to bad, depending upon how far down the scratching has moved.

As a general point, we note that throughout the section devoted to Callicles and his many arguments, there is a kind of blending into one another of the subsections, making it difficult and perhaps more than a little misleading to mark distinct cuts in the progress of the discussion. This is somewhat unusual in the corpus, for as a rule Plato supplies enough clues to enable one to mark boundaries in the topics or methods of approach. Where there is a dual method of outlining, as in the *Gorgias* and in part of the *Parmenides*, when it is doubtful whether nine hypotheses are intended or only eight with a kind of rider, two different considerations are at work to explain discrepancies.

10. Homosexual prostitution was forbidden by law. A citizen was allowed to dishonor another who had engaged in it. The one so dishonored was deprived of his protection against ill treatment, and this could occur without an intervening trial. It is easy to see why Callicles is dismayed.

11. One stock response in fiction and drama of a man or woman accused of infidelity or some similar departure from law or custom is, "How *dare* you accuse me of such a thing!" neither a profession of innocence nor an admission of errant behavior, though it directs suspicion to the latter.

12. Aristotle *The Rhetorical Art* i.15.1375b26–1376a32.

13. One might add, of course, that *Callicles* is being used as a witness, but this is a general observation regarding much of the dialogue.

14. One must ask whether the sharp reaction to Socrates' listing of scratching and visits to young boys bespeaks any wavering of Callicles from his expressed opinion that pleasure and good are identical, and that he would even think that pleasure is an evil. The answer is certainly no; he never admits that pleasure is anything but good, yet at the same time (499a–b) concedes that this leads to contradictory results, though berating Socrates immediately afterward for taking seriously things said in jest.

15. This statement that pleasure equals good has not thus far been refuted; and indeed Socrates will have to make use of it in modified form later on.

16. It follows from Callicles' position that pain equals disgrace or shame or evil. His fear of disapproval and of being shamed is as strong in his nature as his love of pleasure, and interferes with it at every turn.

17. We are speaking from a standpoint other than that of Gorgias and Polus. They would insist that rhetoric is an art, indeed the art of arts, no less, and would doubtless add that they are peculiarly fitted to master it. Callicles, on the other hand, is ready to seize upon any rhetorical device that carries conviction, and he uses one after another. Since he seems not to be a regular pupil of Gorgias or any other rhetor, he could scarcely be expected to care whether effective speaking was an art, so long as he could pick it up somewhere. It appears unlikely that he is among those referred to vaguely by Socrates (455c) when the latter calls attention to potential pupils for Gorgias.

18. Because the immediate response of Gorgias and Polus to Socrates' first question about rhetoric is to praise it as the fairest of arts (448c; 488e) and Gorgias as a fine practitioner of it (449a), we may assume, as Socrates seems to do (448e), that for those two men rhetoric consists in according praise and blame, which in a sense would assimilate forensic and political rhetoric to display, the sort that Gorgias has just been practicing.

19. When we talk of columns and the like, this is mainly for present-day convenience.

20. These are like contrary terms, and we have so indicated them; but as Socrates is using them, they are not quite contraries, basically terms that cannot be predicated *affirmatively* of the same subject simultaneously, though they may both be denied of it.

21. If you object that there are plenty of intermediate cases, as there would be if these terms were treated as straight contraries (e.g., hot, lukewarm, cold), we can only answer that the issue becomes one of defining terms. When do we say that a man is running slowly, indifferently, or fast?

22. The similarity of imperfect jars to men of insatiable appetites might well occur to a poet or philosopher but not to an ordinary man unless the figure of speech were for some reason caught up in common parlance. Thus many persons say "as dead as a doornail," unaware that this was sired by Charles Dickens.

23. The accusation that Callicles tackles the large questions before the small is made in various ways by Socrates at 514a–515b; 516b; 527b. Here Socrates is clearly ironic, and balances his earlier remark (486d) that he himself is delighted in having a Callicles to test him. The testing would be done, it now turns out, by someone continually putting the cart before the horse. Callicles' diatribe against the philosopher is a good example of this, being a sweeping attack upon the philosopher in general rather than a patient examination of the kinds of errors that philosophers make.

24. Could the *Republic* be written merely to install the philosopher-king as undisputed ruler without first examining the ethico-political basis upon which his right and obligation to rule the entire state must be founded?

25. It is perhaps this section that A. E. Taylor had most in mind when he spoke of the *longueurs* of the dialogue. Plato veers dangerously close to unconscious self-parody for a couple of pages. Taylor also complained that the dialogue "drags" (*Plato, The Man and His Work*, p. 102).

26. From Callicles' answer (498a), that he has taken note of the behavior of cowards and brave men in battle, one may well conclude that he has performed some military service. It would be most improbable that he had as a civilian been close enough to a battle line to distinguish different kinds of soldiers in action. We cannot determine whether Callicles himself was brave or not—either is quite possible—nor is there any use in speculating upon which battle he could have participated in.

27. This can be attached, abstract as it may seem, to the present situation of the gathering. If Socrates and Callicles are both correct in asserting that Gorgias and Polus unduly felt shame, then we may suppose that this is a form of cowardice, and that the relaxed and somewhat benign air of Gorgias after his turn is over owes itself to his relief in no longer being under direct attack. But Socrates softens his language, and in bypassing the word *shame* here he avoids insulting the other guests.

28. This apophthegm may have derived from Empedocles, though the attribution is uncertain.

29. One example of this general balancing, which is not a simple duplication, is the way the cumulative but subtly altered images of the sun, line, and cave in *Republic* VI and VII are given more practical expression by the account of education in the latter book. Another is the way in which the image of the wholly unjust man is supplemented by arguments proving his misery in the last half of Book IX. Still another is the way in which bad and good instances of rhetorical address are given critical scrutiny in the second half of the *Phaedrus*, 257b–279c.

30. If you object that Callicles could not possibly perceive this consanguinity of image and argument, we reply that he is by no means stupid, and that he is totally engaged in the discussion up to this point, only later relaxing his hold.

31. The quotation, wherever it came from, is in a way anticipatory of a more depreciative remark that Socrates will make later (517c), that the argument has come circling back to the same point; it is also a reflex of Callicles' complaint that Socrates repeats himself (490e).

32. At 519a Socrates couples the name of Callicles with that of Alcibiades, indicating that they might both get into a serious predicament. Even if history did not bear out Plato's account of Alcibiades, we would divine from the *Symposium* how complicated a man he was, in the encomium which is as much a self-portrait as it is an image of the man who wears the mask of Silenus.

7. Whether There Are Two Lives?

1. Again, these are conceptions of several men that Plato wishes to father upon Callicles, much as he did, either deliberately or through some mistake, upon Polus with his adulation of Archelaus for being a murderer when other evidence shows a different face. Here it is enough that Callicles *thinks* that the two Persians are rapacious men above the law, and similarly believes that Themistocles, one of his new heroes, is a capable and decent man, though history would attach only the first of these two adjectives to his name.

2. One might raise the issue whether such a separation between ethical and political questions is true for other dialogues, and probably the best case for such a separation could be made in regard to the *Statesman, Menexenus, Charmides, Laches,* and *Lysis,* along with the *Philebus,* though for all of these there could be plenty of debate. The *Apology, Crito, Meno, Republic,* and *Laws* make separations only temporarily, in isolated passages. There is not enough of the *Critias* for an informed judgment in this respect.

3. One finds a lopsidedness in Callicles' utterances: He frequently claims that his concessions are made lightheartedly or over-hastily, while obviously his positive statements are deadly serious. As for Socrates, there is a nearer balance between affirmative and negative, substantiating and refutative.

4. This difficulty has already been well aired by Socrates (466e−469c) in his first bout with Polus.

5. This point has been agreed to with Polus (468c).

6. In the *Sophist,* too, the question is raised at the outset (217a), where although but one question seems to be asked, it immediately breaks up into three, whose answers are interdependent. (It is the interdependence, not the number three, that we are stressing.)

7. This issue scarcely arose with Polus, against whom a few simple admonitions were sufficient to establish that he had been wayward with his arguments and that he must improve. Polus did not sketch a way of life, as does Callicles, but lists and praises certain ends of discourse, except for his one example, Archelaus. Socrates instructed Polus in the right purposes of rhetoric, and now he must advance against Callicles on the purpose of living. But in living there is still place for the art of speaking.

8. This, as we suggested, was one of the strongest motives of the 500 dicasts for the convicting of Socrates years later.

9. In the *Protagoras* (330b−c), Socrates has to reassure himself that his respon-

dent thinks of justice as a real thing (*pragma*), so that the dispute would be grounded not in mere word usage but in facts.

10. In political life, an equivalent additive method would be found in the second and third books of the *Republic*, where there is first a simple state consisting of four or five craftsmen sharing their skills, able to survive on a staple diet and with few amenities. To these few men are added the doctors, tradesmen, lawyers, and hustlers of every sort, along with all that they produce for or import into the city, which grows in size and heterogeneity. The next changes, reforming this fevered state, are of a different kind, but it is still true that the educational scheme of these and later books of the *Republic* are higher-level additions.

11. Whether this passage allows us to conclude that Plato himself had a profound distrust of all kinds of music, poetry, and drama is impossible to decide without detailed inquiry. To believe from the evidence of what Socrates is made to say here that Plato held these practices in contempt requires several assumptions. One first supposes, of course, that he either created and seconded everything he makes Socrates say in the dialogues, or else, at the opposite end, that the historical Socrates *did* say them and Plato merely echoed him. Then one must assume that to distrust any given thing from one standpoint means to distrust it from others, possibly all others, as well. Finally, one must also ignore what we have been stressing all along, namely that Socrates is fighting rhetoric with rhetoric, and that he is seizing upon the very expressions such as *gratification*, that have been used by his opponents, so that the words become means for undoing their own quite slipshod reasoning. Yet it is not a gladiatorial device; surely there *is* a respect in which even the finest of the fine arts have elements appealing to the masses.

12. We shall not labor the point that this reference to the "recent" death of Pericles places the dramatic date of the *Gorgias* once and for all in or about the year 428 B.C. The only sensible conclusion seems to be that Plato was endeavoring to introduce as many gross anachronisms as needed so that no one date could ever be definitively attributed to this partly elegant, partly convulsive colloquy. There is one possible explanation, however, which would allow the date to be moved up a decade or so despite what Callicles has just said. He has been impressed from afar by the reputation of Pericles in spite of the fact that that leader never put himself entirely beyond the law and the approval of the many. This would mean that he might not wish to emphasize that Pericles had been dead for many years. "It seems just yesterday that Franklin Roosevelt gave his Fireside Chats, and Churchill made his wonderful speech about the Royal Air Force." This is a frequently used sort of expression, and betokens neither a literal error nor absentmindedness verging on an outright defect of memory.

The other issue, regarding Plato's treatment of Pericles in the *Gorgias*, can be considered in connection with a later page, 515d–516d.

13. That there are two kinds of rhetoric here does not of itself mean that the good rhetoric is forthwith to be thought identical with the good rhetoric of the *Phaedrus* (277b–c), which turns out to be dialectic although not as dialectic (*dialegesthai*, discussion) is considered in the *Gorgias*. In the latter the criteria for good rhetoric are ethico-political, and the technical are for the most part ignored except where their use becomes especially obtrusive. In the former, the criteria have nothing directly to do with politics, and pertain to the following of a method for attaining truth. In that dialogue, technical devices are discussed at some length, and there is even a recital of authorities on the topic (266d–269c).

It may well be that some aspects of the good rhetoric turn out to be the same in both dialogues, but like so much else in the works of Plato this is a conclusion to be reached by what must itself be a dialectical inquiry, and is not to be used as a rigid assumption as soon as one's eyes light upon the two sets of distinctions.

14. The artificer, the *dēmiourgos*, revives an expression that Socrates proposed very early in his conversation with Gorgias (454a), though applied then to rhetoric itself rather than to the rhetor.

15. *Symposium* 194e–197e.

16. Rarely does Socrates, upon admitting that he does not know the subject or that he cannot follow his interlocutor, give up his own participation in the argument, unless, as at the end of the *Lysis* and *Euthyphro* and similar dialogues, the discussion has come to a standstill and the next step would be mere repetition of earlier positions and queries.

17. This recalls a little conceit (*Phaedrus* 264c), that an argument has a life of its own, and a bodily organization to boot.

8. What Difference Between the Two Lives?

1. This differs from the device, used in four other works, by which Socrates tells other persons outside the frame of the main dialogue what was said and done: The *Republic, Euthydemus, Charmides,* and most of the *Protagoras* are delivered in this manner; one must take Socrates' word that all those facing him behaved as he is now describing them. In the *Gorgias* the chief listener to whom this little monologue is addressed is present and can interrupt at any moment he wishes—a privilege denied to Polemarchus, Thrasymachus, and the two gifted brothers of Plato when Socrates is retailing their views to Timaeus and his companions the next day.

2. In Aristotelian language this would, of course, be a distinction between formal and final causes, though Plato interprets them quite differently from his pupil.

3. Commentators have long noticed that much of the discourse with Callicles is shot through with a kind of hinted prophecy that Socrates himself will be brought before a tribunal and may be unable to come to his own rescue. Because of the more recent and therefore operative accusations against him in the *Apology* (24b–c), it is interesting that in this context of the *Gorgias* Socrates should consider devoutness an essential counterpart to the one virtue to which he has been holding fast throughout the dialogue—justice. There is no hint of the introduction of new divinities in our dialogue; Minos and his two partners (523e) are mentioned in Homer and Hesiod, and while not Olympian gods in the proper sense they are at least honored beings granted eternal life.

4. At *Euthyphro* 14c–d Socrates summarizes the priest's fifth major effort to define devoutness by saying that his suggestion of sacrificing and praying can be called the science (*epistēmē*) of giving and asking. At 14e this is transformed into barter (*emporia*, merchandizing). Where Euthyphro failed was not so much in any particular formulation as in the fact that every one of his six (by our count) definitions is tied, in his own mind, to his first, namely one that devoutness is doing as he himself is doing, that is, bringing charges against his own father for murder. This self-centered account sets the tone for the real meaning of his subsequent definitions, for example, doing what is pleasing to the gods, meaning doing as he is doing to please the gods, and so on.

5. You polish off each of your two men (the unjust man who seems just and the just man who appears to be unjust) as if they were statues in a contest—this is the exclamation of Socrates himself in the *Republic* (II, 361d), interrupting a like contrast by Glaucon. But Glaucon had in mind a distinction between real and seeming as regards reputation. In the *Gorgias*, the real and and the seeming just practice different kinds of activities; at the moment, reputations are not being considered.

6. Nowhere has friendship been mentioned as a relation between the three rhetors who speak of host-guest and teacher-pupil pairings, but not of friends with each other. Callicles has spoken (486a) of goodwill (*eunoia*) toward Socrates; but, when this is joined with his recommendation that an older man still pursuing philosophy deserves a whipping (485c), one wonders just how cordial he really is.

7. Here again we see dichotomies at work in this exercise in division and subdivision. Appetites are either controlled by reason (in the temperate man) or they are not (in the intemperate). The temperate man enjoys bonds of community and friendship through communication. The intemperate, living as a robber, is dear to no man or god, hence cannot communicate, and cannot claim to have a friend.

8. Just what this order is remains unspecified in the *Gorgias*, except for the myth of the dead; it is more fully treated, though from a very different standpoint, in the *Timaeus*, chiefly 31a–40d.

9. For example, at 467c, 470c (with Polus); 482b (with Callicles).

10. Socrates is no doubt speaking out of his own experience in the construction trades and the military.

11. This point is elaborated in the *Phaedrus* (271c–272b).

12. This device of multiple proofs of the same point is one found in the last half of Book IX of the *Republic*; multiple refutations of Socrates' early version of a theory of forms are given in the first part of the *Parmenides*. This is, however, an infrequently-used device in Plato.

13. In the *Meno*, the Slave Boy has acquired a true belief, but it will require more questioning on related topics to produce knowledge in him (85c–d).

14. In the *Republic* rhetoric and pandering are scarcely mentioned, either using those words or equivalents. In an improved society where justice holds fuller sway, the Calliclean rhetoric would be altogether incapable of meeting the demands of political interchange.

15. Obviously the assumption that the private buildings will be smaller, less elaborate than the public. Socrates is hoping to cure Callicles of his grandiose tendencies which have little basis; the advice given here recalls the complaint that he had been initiated into the lesser mysteries only after the greater ones, not before (497c). The point is made again at 514e where Socrates discourages learning pottery by commencing with big wine jars.

16. This at last is the real meaning, of which its own author is unaware, of Polus' written statement that art grows out of experience (448c; 462c). The new statement can also refer back to 460b where Socrates points out a near-truism, that the man who has learned building is a builder, music a musician, doctoring a doctor.

17. Philosophy as a way of life was not mentioned with Gorgias or Polus, and certainly Callicles' sketch of what it is and its effects made it an unenviable calling.

18. There are some persons still living so prejudiced against philosophy that

they wonder what right Socrates could possibly have to complain against excessive loquacity.

19. There is a touch of satire in the reference to Pericles' association with Anaxagoras (*Phaedrus* 269e–270a); Pericles learns his own talkativeness from his teacher. In *Menexenus* 235e Pericles learns to be a (public) speaker from Aspasia, and he becomes the "best of the Hellenes." In the *Symposium* (215e), Alcibiades says he had heard Pericles and all the other great rhetors and that Socrates moves him more than they have. In the *Meno* (94a–b), Pericles is likened to Aristides: Both are unsuccessful in passing on their virtues to their sons, though Socrates does refer to Pericles as "that greatly gifted wise man." Pericles is mentioned in a few other places but not to a different effect. None of these is really inconsistent with what is said in the *Gorgias*, but to prove this would require careful explication of important parts of those other dialogues.

20. This point harks back to the distinction (466d) between doing what the ruler wishes (a mark of real power) and doing what he *thinks* is best. At the time this was first raised, Polus was apparently supposing that the autocrat would choose to do what is most advantageous to himself. At the present juncture with Callicles, on the other hand, the assumption has been that Pericles could have had the interests of the citizens at heart but that he misread their real needs, giving them a supposed benefit that in the end corrupted them. The connection between their idleness and the other less admirable traits that he promoted and their readiness to indict him for embezzlement is not made clear in what Socrates narrates.

21. It is not necessary to point up the fruitlessness of speculation regarding the *real* Socrates' view of Pericles. Even assuming that Xenophon gives a more "historical" portrait of his strange hero, one cannot clearly make out much of a consistent view of Pericles held by the philosopher. Socrates is made to say to Callias that he should woo Autolycus by finding out exactly what sort of knowledge it was that conferred on Pericles the reputation of being the wisest counsellor (Xenophon, *Symposium* VIII. 41–43). He is also made to report his hearing that Pericles put many spells or charms on Athens, making her love him (*Memorabilia* II. vi. 13). The author tries also to explain why Critias and Alcibiades ultimately left the tutelage of Socrates; they associated with the politicians, including Pericles (who gives a quite good account of the nature of law while talking to Alcibiades), and then deserted Socrates, being out of sympathy with him (ibid. I. ii. 38–48).

22. He says *true* rather than *good*, signifying that now the pandering rhetoric is not to be called rhetoric at all.

23. We doubt that the text supports this strongly, yet almost any other interpretation would make Socrates' remark seem unreasonable and out of place.

24. Socrates appears to be going out of his way to make a sally against Polus. Granted that the Sicilian traditions in cookery resembled those of France today, it is still more than coincidental that he refers to a writer of a textbook from Polus' native island (it is less likely that Socrates has Gorgias in mind because catering did not enter the account with him). But Mithaccus as an author more nearly resembles Polus in any event. That Polus has long been silent is not relevant; if our study has shown anything, it has shown how repeatedly past casual remarks and reasoned positions are put to rest, only to be resurrected much later.

25. In the *Symposium* Alcibiades praises Socrates, albeit with a touch of flippancy, for possessing the virtues of wisdom, temperance, courage, and justice,

although he illustrates rather than names them all. A man able to do this (and in his cups, too!) must have a modicum of those virtues himself. As with Pericles, however, Plato brings out widely separated facets of men's characters in different dialogues, the possible exception being that of Socrates where the explanatory gaps between stated characteristics are more nearly filled up.

26. One wonders how Socrates would have explained the fate of the arch moral improver in history, Savonarola. The objection that Florence in the late fifteenth century was not ancient Athens might hold, of course, but the weight of evidence indicates that people at large dislike and distrust those who make them really better more often than they do those who make them worse, provided only that the latter *seem* to improve the common lot while doing so.

27. The same general type of paradox is found in the old story of Protagoras and Euathlus and the latter's failure upon winning his first case, to pay the fee for instruction. I shall sue, says Protagoras, and then if you lose you must pay, and if you win you still must pay because then you have won your first case (Diogenes Laertius, IX, 56). An addition to this has Euathlus replying, If I lose, I have not won my first case, and if I win I certainly do not have to pay you. One may notice both that the victor in this is always the man who speaks last, and also that Protagoras' suit could well be Euathlus' *second* case.

28. The vehemence of this outbreak prompts one to ask whether Plato himself entertained a similar hostility toward the sophists. If it was an ill-considered prejudice, however, it was one to which Socrates gives little voice, preferring to debate with these men—in the *Protagoras*, of course, in the two dialogues with Hippias, in the *Republic* (most obviously Book I), in the *Theaetetus*, and elsewhere. In some other dialogues such as the *Symposium*, the sophists lurk in the background but are not brought onstage even when their teachings flourish in full view. Yet they are generally treated with some respect, qualified by the worry about their taking pay, but thought to be worthy of the most careful refuting, as if they were very close to the truth. Even the fun made of the versatility of Hippias (*Lesser Hippias* 368b–e; *Greater Hippias* 285b–286a) bears a stamp of mild approval though his inveterate boastfulness receives its due of derision. The *Sophist* is another matter. There are few new points made directly about this kind of teacher than have not been at least mentioned in the Socratic dialogues, that is, those dominated by Socrates; but the persistent employment of the method of fishing for the sophist, first with line and then with a network of lines, makes it seem as though he were a target of a more concerted attack. Even there he comes very close to the philosopher (230e–231a). It must be remembered, however, that the whole construction is in answer to a question by Socrates (216d–217a), how the sophist is considered vis-à-vis the statesman and the philosopher in Elea, or at most, the Italian boot. The *Sophist* is a declaration of war on these people, without doubt; but there is still no way to show that Plato thought them worthless.

29. The point that Socrates has been making throughout against rhetors and now by extension against the sophists is that they make both the exercise and rewards of justice external, whereas he himself takes them to be internal, with punishment often giving way to correction through sound education.

30. One might ask whether Plato's Socrates, who teaches virtue as persistently and openly as any sophist, is hinting here that *he* expects that out of gratitude, not contractual obligation, his pupils and hearers will give him money. The traditions of the historical Socrates' poverty and complaints by his wife that his endless talking were what kept them poor would argue against an

affirmative answer. We doubt that any definitive judgment can be coaxed from the extant sources.

31. Whether one can become virtuous by other means instead—the question of the *Meno*—is not considered in the *Gorgias*.

32. That Socrates suspects there might be a better side to Callicles is shown in his remark (495d–e) that he believes Callicles will not hold pleasant and good to be the same but will recognize that knowledge and bravery are different from each other and both are different from the good, when he has rightly looked at himself (*theasētai orthōs*). Thus the aim of the Socratic elenchus, dialectic, rhetoric—call it what you will—is to awaken the better nature of his opponent through bringing him to a clearer view of himself.

33. That this is not some wild supposition on our part is shown in the fact that at the very end of the dialogue Socrates exhorts Callicles to gain experience in the improving of souls by starting with individuals and then moving to the public, also using rhetoric for the best ends and, in a word, emulating the virtuous builder of public structures (517a–e). He is giving him rules to follow and practices to undertake rather than suggesting that he discover these for himself by becoming a philosopher. Plato is making the point, we believe, that philosophy is not the only road to right action in civic life, a notion also established, though differently, in the *Meno*.

9. Which Life Ought We to Live?

1. *Theaetetus* 183e–184a. In *Parmenides* 127b, Socrates describes the elderly philosopher as *kalon de kagathon* of appearance, fair and noble.

2. At this point we see that the old dichotomy between nature and law or agreement, which Callicles had said (482e) Socrates oscillated between and which Socrates himself said he joined together (489a), is now brought back, transformed to refer not to political compulsions but to the soul's inner motives and aspirations.

3. Our remark should not be interpreted to mean that all the myths in the dialogues, or even a considerable number of them, are to be looked at as ways of circumventing the need for further argument. Each myth is introduced in a unique setting, and each has therefore a different raison d'être.

4. This may throw light backward upon the professed friendship. On the other hand, the relation between Socrates and Callicles has, from the latter's standpoint, changed markedly since the commencement of their debate, but the opinion that Socrates evidently held from the start regarding his opponent seems only to have been confirmed. One should observe, however, that earlier (487a) Socrates had imputed knowledge, goodwill (*eunoia*), and candor to Callicles, and in the present (521a–b) he leaves out this goodwill in his urging—he knows that the false front is down.

5. It may be of interest that in the *Republic* IV (445d) Socrates suggests that the office of philosopher-king could be filled by one person or by several. And in his conversation with Callicles, Socrates has suggested (510a–d) that the tyrant might have an imitator very much like him, or pretending to be, so that some aspects of rule could presumably be shared.

6. The admiration of Phaedrus after Socrates has tendered him his great soliloquy on love and truth is profound (*Phaedrus* 257b–c); after finishing his other extraordinary speech on love, there is applause from all his hearers except Aris-

tophanes, who is a little piqued (*Symposium* 212c). Since the *Republic* is a recital by Socrates, delivered (most probably) to Timaeus, Critias, and Hermocrates, an expression of gratitude might be expected from at least one of them; and this is precisely the burden of a remark by the first-named of these men of science, historical insight, and practical sense (*Timaeus* 17a–b).

7. One recalls that injustice to the gods was called at 507a a lack of devoutness.

8. This echoes the long proof to Polus that the rhetor-tyrant is the man with least power because his injustice propels him into situations which he ordered but whose outcome he did not wish (466d–468e).

9. One may conclude that Socrates does not think Callicles has as yet committed the injustices that would make him subject to such a lifelong load of guilt. He never accuses Callicles openly of having done an outright injustice for which he ought to be punished, saying at the same time that he will avoid accusing Callicles in order to prolong his guilt in this life. Instead, he spares no pains to dissuade Callicles from embarking upon a career of injustice *in future*.

10. This is implied in the *Protagoras* (329d), in the image of a human face, in which nose and eyes, and so forth, differ yet comport with each other in appearance and function so that a oneness is achieved in both regards.

11. *Apology* 27c.

12. *Protagoras* 329b–c.

13. These three are the leaders of the Olympian gods, and are shown here dividing the rule of the world in a manner apparently satisfactory to each of them. Plato has omitted the tale of conflict between Zeus and Poseidon that Homer includes, for in the epic Zeus has just sent a message demanding that Poseidon cease and desist from all intervention in the Trojan War; the god of the sea responds haughtily and defiantly (*Iliad* XV.156–204). Shortly afterward Poseidon concedes, but with reservations. The story of the brutality of Kronos and his eating of his own children is preserved—or invented—by Hesiod, not Homer.

14. *King Lear* IV.vi.169–73.

15. In the *Laws*, there are altogether different presuppositions. The gods initiate and guide motion (X.898a–899d), and human beings are puppets in their hands (I.644d; VII.803c). The entire assumption of that dialogue, however, is that despite the practical aims of the constitution it is the work of Zeus (I.624a). Socrates, in most of the works that give him prominence, is a seeker after the gods, while the Athenian Stranger is theocratic and doctrinaire.

16. For Homer, Tityus is gnawed by ravens, Tantalus is tormented by receding waters and unpluckable fruits while he is everlastingly thirsty, and Sisyphus is unable to push huge rocks uphill. There is, however, an atmosphere of deep depression and sadness for nearly all the shades of the underworld as depicted by Odysseus (*Odyssey* XI, especially 11.576–600). Heracles, one is happy to learn, is not really punished; he dines with the gods and has a wife with beautiful ankles (11.601–4).

17. This was echoed in the conversation with Polus as well. He will not take the medicine, though he has need of it. (475d).

18. This last phrase is a reworking of Gorgias' claim (449b) that he could actually make everyone everywhere to be like himself as a rhetor.

19. Callicles, if he becomes a tyrant, will want his friends to be as like him as possible (510a–b).

20. In the *Republic*, *sophia* is gradually separated out from *phronēsis* and elevated to a position of supremacy when coupled with dialectic, or rather identi-

fied with dialectic, in Books IV–VII. That is in Callipolis. In Athens, it takes every bit of Socrates' skill to show that philosophy is not a complete waste of time, and he does this by restricting its scope to ethical matters, there being very few references to the wider cosmos, and then only to justify certain moral assumptions.

10. Rhetoric and the Three Rhetors

1. Breaks within Plato's dialogues are made in different ways, have different dramatic or philosophic intents, and are resolved by different means. In the *Phaedrus* there is an apparent line of separation about halfway through (257b), before which there has been one little mythic preamble and then three speeches on the kinds, disadvantages, and finally benefits of love, and after which there is a "sensible" discussion of rhetoric. Can the two be found to cohere? Book I of the *Republic* has often been read as if detachable from the other nine, though its arguments comport very closely with them. In the *Parmenides* there is an opening portion that some critics like to call subordinate and others prefer to term the main section, on forms (130a–135c). The *Phaedrus* and *Republic* offer literary bonds as well as philosophic, but the *Parmenides* shows little evidence that the personal and the conceptual are of anything like equal import. Most of the other dialogues have similar breaks. It is hard to believe that Plato would have been able to make each half of a dialogue cohere and been all at sea in making a single whole of them. We will not beg the question by saying that many lesser philosophers have accomplished this overall consistency because it has not yet been established here that Plato *has* created a unified *Gorgias*. But if we can make our case for this dialogue, some of the others with their alleged discontinuities and discrepancies might well be reexamined.

2. Each of the three rhetors is made to draw in his horns. Gorgias says first that he can teach rhetoric and justice as well, but later realizes that this makes him responsible for his pupils' abuses of rhetoric and decides that he can teach the speechmaking but may have to let justice go. Polus retreats from the assertion that the rhetor is the most powerful man in the city to the admission that the real use of rhetoric is to cause oneself to be punished for misdeeds. Once more, Callicles thinks the man armed with effective language will rule and have more, but afterward settles for rhetoric as a means to aid in rescuing oneself when in danger. Incidentally, Adele Spitzer's "The Self-Reference of the *Gorgias*" is one of the very few studies systematically contrasting the three rhetors (and Socrates) in their uses of rhetoric. Details of our interpretation overlap in part with hers, but we draw somewhat different conclusions from those of this interesting article.

3. There is some action besides walking in the dialogues. Examples are the clutching of Socrates' cloak in the *Republic* I, movements about the prison cell and changes of posture in the *Phaedo*, seating arrangements and some jostling in the *Symposium* and *Euthydemus*, the abrupt departure of Anytus in the *Meno*, and a handful of other overt acts. But these are hardly the stuff of drama, comic or tragic, except for the drinking of the hemlock.

4. As we have noted earlier, the first two sections of the dialogue are largely concerned with the assertion (448c) that rhetoric is the greatest of the arts. With Gorgias, the notion of the *greatest* art is brought in question, and Socrates shows how this needs strenuous recasting. Socrates immediately attacks Polus'

assumption that rhetoric is an art of *any* kind. This exhausts the opening statement, and in conversation with Callicles rhetoric as the greatest art is no longer under direct consideration.

5. The other rhetors lack Gorgias' rapport with his audience, his eagerness to display being set off against the nervousness and stumbling of Polus, and by the increasing reluctance of Callicles to continue with a discussion held in front of an audience of his own inviting.

6. No one in the *Gorgias* is described as having a son or young friend to be educated, as opposed to the *Apology* and *Crito*, where Socrates is concerned for the upbringing of his own boys, or the *Euthydemus*, in which Crito is looking for a teacher, or the *Laches*, where two men are seeking advice on a similar matter from a pair of generals, or the *Protagoras*, depicting a young man looking out for his own education, or what he hopes will be his education, or even the *Theaetetus*, with its two exceptional students evidently still enrolled in a stiff course in mathematics. In the *Gorgias*, on the other hand, Polus, though he may formerly have been a pupil of the old master, is already the author of a textbook that others have read; he is not censured as unmannerly for picking up a flaw in Gorgias' reasoning. Callicles, if he ever was a student of Gorgias, is now hoping merely to snap up a few more tricks of the rhetorical trade, enjoy hearing displays, and be the onlooker at a battle. In the narrower sense of receiving instruction, then, the education of Polus and Callicles is no longer in question, though in the broader sense of convictions about having their own life patterns called into account—patterns possibly the indirect results of the instruction received—their education is very much a thing of great moment. The corresponding point, Who will be the teacher? is also brought into prominence.

7. It is plain that Polus has little sense of the time, labor, and experience needed for a thorough mastery of an art. Perhaps this is owing to a fault in Gorgias' teaching. No matter. The point is that Polus wishes to cut short the apprentice and journeyman stages, leaping ahead to the later ones when he can command full respect for his mastery. The writing of a textbook at an early age is one indication, his ostentatious quoting from it another. Ironically, the one quotation he is allowed to offer convicts him of the very inexperience he denigrates in his text.

8. Gorgias takes some interest in what he supposes the welfare of the cities to be, both directly and through his pupils; Polus would see the city not as a traveling teacher and speaker would see it, an opportunity to gain fame and money, but rather as a community to be fathomed and exploited. Callicles is in a different situation, for Athens is his mother city, one whose demotic passions must be thoroughly grasped if he is to "have more" than anyone else.

9. The men Gorgias praises, no matter what their own propensities for limitless power might have been, were mostly restrained by electoral safeguards. Callicles makes them safe within a legal system which if left to itself would protect them very inadequately from unwarranted attacks. *All* safeguards are overthrown in Polus' account of Archelaus, represented as strong and lucky enough to get off scot free.

10. Polus emerges as the bold one, bold to the point of foolhardiness, for he speaks out in favor of a criminal. True enough, it requires less time for Socrates to defeat his view than to bring Callicles to the most damaging of his concessions, but that is precisely because for all his stumbling Polus does not vacillate as Callicles does. He may be inattentive at times, so imbued is he with his own importance and that of his art, but he wavers little. Polus is unworried over pay-

ing any penalties, of coming to grief in a lawcourt at the hands of some irresponsible citizen. He takes little or no account of philosophy—the Socratic discussion is almost as much beyond his comprehension at the end of his colloquy as it was at its commencement—whereas Callicles, for all his sporadic resentments, readily grants that to philosophize early in life is not only tolerable but desirable.

11. The *Philebus* is an excellent example of this kind of discussion. In it the argument corrects even Socrates himself on a crucial issue (20b–c), altering one whole course of the dialogue.

12. At the end of *The Sacred Fount*, Henry James' narrator says that he did not agree with the woman who had attacked his supposedly impregnable proofs regarding mutual replacements of personalities, but what he too fatally lacked was her tone.

13. There are, however, technical considerations as well. Since for Gorgias the principal use of rhetoric is to harangue an assembly on matters concerning the whole city, his primary topics are the advantages and disadvantages to be weighted in a course of action. For Polus, a knack lies in the cleverest use of contrasts between happiness and misery, and the ways of attaining the former. With Callicles the effective use of speech is in praise and blame—whether each person, and especially Socrates, is deserving of one or other of these for his speech and his way of life. Callicles is forever evaluating other persons, and bestowal of compliment or invective is his chief employment of rhetoric. One might say that if he were a soldier his entire judgment of military loss or victory would lie in whether he himself received a wound.

14. Gorgias repeatedly goes out of his way to conciliate Socrates (449b; 458d–e; 497b).

15. These are listed, not altogether respectfully, by Socrates in the *Phaedrus* (266d–e).

16. All of these, as we hinted in chapter 1, are variations on themes found in the Prologue (447a–449c).

17. Plato often buries the most important queries in the midst of paragraph-length utterances; an instance is this present question, How ought we to live? which is asked in the midst of a speech stressing two other topics.

18. *Tractatus Logico-Philosophicus* 5.541, 5.542, 5.5421.

19. To say that on other grounds the historical Gorgias was a keen logical analyst because he was the author of the little text *On Nature* is no great help here in proving that he could have noticed errors in the Socratic arguments. This text (in two slightly different versions) seeks to prove that nothing exists, that if it did it could not be known, and if known it could not be expressed. But (a) it is far from certain that the text is genuine; (b) even if it were, Plato might not have known of it or thought it worth crediting in his estimate of Gorgias; (c) it reads more like a clever parody than a logically argued text, for it is wholly self-canceling in all three of its theses; (d) even if one could set aside all these objections it would not be relevant to Gorgias' views, either the historical ones or Plato's version, regarding public speaking or his gifts in that practice.

20. The audience has a one-way relation to the speaker, and if the audience breaks in (as in the *Apology*) or is permitted to ask questions (as the description implies in the *Gorgias*, 455c), then it is assuming a different role momentarily and becomes an audience in a looser sense.

11. Socrates

1. In the *Cratylus* and *Philebus* some of this happens, though there are no onlookers and personalities hardly obtrude at all; it is not a personal victory that Socrates scores. The first of these works ends, like *Also Sprach Zarathustra* of Richard Strauss, in two keys at once, and the second reaches a solution only after Socrates has forced himself to relinquish his principal thesis that mind is the highest good.

2. This is a situation quite unlike that of the *Republic*, where philosophy (in Book V) and then dialectic (Books VI and VII) are described, illustrated, and set carefully in contexts with other arts and sciences. On the first page of that dialogue, however, Plato removes the discussion from Athens, while the first page of the *Gorgias* gives two settings within the city, a public and a semiprivate one.

3. Socrates does not always have this controlling function—for example in the *Sophist* and *Timaeus* he merely sets the stage by asking a question or offering a précis of the "social" parts of the *Republic*, this time to be completed not by an overall characterization of mathematics and dialectic but by some of the conclusions that these disciplines can reach. In both cases the solutions are offered by men foreign to Athens but distinguished in their own communities.

4. For example, the *Timaeus* (29d), also the *Republic* II (367e–368a).

5. In the *Euthydemus* he parodies his own gift (289c–290e). Cleinias, a youth of many blushes and few ideas, is suddenly endowed with the power to make a host of canny distinctions, at least according to Socrates, who is narrator.

6. This concurrence turns up again in modified and debased form as the agreement between the weak to hamper the strong, in the first version of Callicles' theory (483b–c).

7. When Socrates says of Polus (461c–d) that it is good to have young companions and sons to set straight their elders who stumble, or when he says of Callicles (486d) that it is good to have someone test his soul as if testing gold, there is irony, of course. Yet underneath is Socrates' repeated statement that truth with these men will be found when he can agree with each one. Incidentally, no similar point is made with Gorgias.

8. This is not the same point as the fine that might be assessed (*Apology* 38a–b), when Socrates again alludes to his lack of money. The fine would be an exact amount, confiscation would not.

9. Bodily condition does enter in the myth at the afterlife, but in a way difficult to interpret as connected with the participants.

10. *Charmides* 165b.

11. *Phaedrus* 242b–c.

12. *Apology* 32b; Socrates says he had held office but once. *Theaetetus* 173c–176a; the philosopher is at sea in the practical world of politicians.

13. Slightly different is the lesson of the *Crito*, of course, that it is just to obey the laws because they confer advantages upon the citizen outweighing possible injustices in their application.

14. The closing pages of the *Meno* establish class (1) as the best we can hope for in political life. True belief is a matter of divine dispensation (*theia moira*) unless we find it in a statesman who can also teach it to others (99e–100a).

15. *Charmides* 163d–165b; it happens to be a respondent, Critias, not Socrates, who refers approvingly to this inscription in the course of defining temperance as self-knowledge.

16. To justify our procedure, we remind ourselves that Polus very early had

distinguished familiarity from unfamiliarity as the grounds respectively of art and chance. It is Socrates' habit, when confronted with such a schematism, to expand it by introducing the higher terms that he deems necessary in order to give a complete (for his present purposes) display of all relevant features. To construct our schema here we have departed our custom long enough to draw upon materials from the *Phaedo, Theaetetus, Republic, Phaedrus, Meno,* and *Epistle VII,* where these distinctions are made, but have sought to confirm them by illustrations from the *Gorgias.*

17. If Socrates ever did meet Archelaus, he would doubtless have had the problem of deciding at least his mood from external signs—words, gestures, and so forth—and from them tried to fathom his motives. A single one of these signs would neither justify nor prevent applying the epithet *happy* to Archelaus, taking the word in any sense; but experience is not limited in this way, for it encompasses many memories, and this requires both a stretch of time and a variety of different perceptions and reports.

18. Cf. *Epistle VII* 340b–344d, especially 341c–d; 343b–d; 344b. Plato—for we believe it *was* Plato who wrote this remarkable passage—has a different series of steps to knowledge of the real in mind from the ones we have outlined here, but we doubt if there is a serious disharmony, as our own hierarchies stem from another famous passage in one of the dialogues, which any reader is bound to recognize.

19. *A Treatise of Human Nature,* Book I, pt. 4, sec. 6.

20. *Timaeus* 43b–c; *Theaetetus* 151e–187a, especially 157a–b; 158c–d; 159e–160a. In the latter dialogue the main question, What is knowledge? requires much space for its answering because Theaetetus almost unaccountably abdicates his obvious role as defender of mathematical science, asserting that knowledge is perception instead of some more universal and necessary kind of ratiocination. Socrates sees at once that it will be impossible to explain fully what the geometry that Theaetetus has mastered is in essence, merely by trying to interpret it from the lower standpoint. In fact, even raising the explanation to the level of belief, and later, belief with *logos*—whatever that can mean—is insufficient to give the reasons for the science that Theaetetus has already incorporated into his own soul, partly through learning from Theodorus and partly through his powers of independent discovery and teamwork with Young Socrates.

21. The ordinary conception of a habit seems to be some positive power, not a lack or incapacity. A curious situation arises when Socrates claims that as a voting citizen he is a duffer. It is hard to believe this on its face. In the *Phaedrus* he quotes special official phrases (257e–258b), giving the impression that he has carefully stored them up. In the *Republic,* though he speaks little about procedures, preferring to deal with the virtues, parts of the soul, arts, and social classes in the state, nevertheless he seems to take for granted the necessity for procedures that were matter for common mastery among free citizens of Athens. In the *Crito* he greatly respects the laws of the city and seems well informed of their underlying intent together with their weaknesses. Many scholars have found it easy to separate the speech in the *Apology* into sections paralleling traditional forms of legal address with which Socrates must have been familiar.

22. It is for this reason that Socrates is grateful to anyone who will refute and rid him of mistakes in his thinking, especially those errors which might have practical bearings (458a; 470c; 487e–488b).

23. In the *Phaedrus* Socrates uses two quite different ways of speaking about this soul. First (245c–246a) he offers a literal, uncolored proof of its immortality, and then, apologizing that it requires lengthy discourse beyond human capacity, he offers (246a–248e) the extraordinary myth of the chariot trains of gods in the heavens, followed by other souls, all gazing into the reality beyond containing the forms of beauty and justice and more. This accounts for the implantation of the apperception of these in the soul, to be recovered dimly or vividly when back in mortal form, through recollection. Neither the proof nor the myth can give the real account of the overwhelming vision—a permanent soul possessing intuitive knowledge of the forms.

24. For a description, with different emphases, of the body and its relation to sensation and intellect, see *Timaeus* 42e–47e; 61c–69a.

25. This is suggested in the *Phaedrus* where in later pages it is made clear that there is a sense in which rhetoric and dialectic are virtually ordinate and abcissa determining a single plane. The rhetoric is the address considered as a temporal—one almost would say longitudinal—sequence, the parts, that is, arranged to make for maximum effectiveness. Dialectic, on the other hand, is the vertical structures, the relations of terms to each other, whether in narration, argument, exhortation, or whatnot, and arranged to communicate the maximum of truth and clarity. In a good speech these dimensions operate together.

26. We are dividing personality from character, the former being Socrates' manner of behavior before others, his humor, good or bad, his readiness to talk, his momentary fears, hostilities, or shows of affection, while the latter is his underlying strength of habit and the wellsprings of future actions as a result of his inborn strength. In terms of our hierarchy, personality is mostly found on the second level (2b), while character is partly of the same rank and partly of the single step higher, involving as it does intellectual commitments as well.

27. This repeats, on a higher level, Gorgias' own equating of his career with that of rhetoric.

28. Our stricture may seem odd, coming as it does at the close of a section where we have cited the *Phaedrus*, *Theaetetus*, and other dialogues more often than in previous chapters. But they have not been used for simple confirmation of what is in the text of the *Gorgias* and have mostly been included for light they may throw on the exceedingly difficult question of Plato's diversified views of knowledge of the soul. Had the *Gorgias* been more explicit on this, we would have been able to stick more closely to the rule of negative importation—it is better to interpret constructively the differences than merely to quote likenesses between isolated passages in the corpus.

29. Chaerephon, the only figure without strong commitments that exclude their contraries, is so slight that he cannot act as a balance wheel in the discussion. The struggle between Socrates and the three rhetors is not one over the soul of Chaerephon, with the two sides battling to ensure that his future career will conform to one set or another of their respective views of the good life. (That kind of battle takes place between Socrates and the two eristic brothers in the *Euthydemus*, each side trying to demonstrate what sort of education would be most effective for a sensitive, unformed young man.)

30. *Poetics* viii.1451a19–20.

12. Antecedents and Consequences of the Divided Oblong

1. See chapter 3 for a fuller version with supporting interpretations of the Oblong itself.

2. Aristotle alters this quotation, *Metaphysics* I.1.981a4–6.

3. This is similar to the larval definition of piety or devoutness in the *Euthyphro* (5d), namely, doing as I am doing, which sets up the individual as the arbiter of correct and knowledgeable action.

4. Notice the difference between an early passage in the *Ion*, where Socrates says that he envies the fine dress of the rhapsodes (530b), and the opening of the *Gorgias*, where there is plenty of opportunity for a similar remark, but where there is none.

5. Adolf Hitler used to tell visitors, in the early days of his regime, that the thing distinguishing him from other leaders was that he alone knew what the German people were thinking and wanting and therefore he alone could supply their wants.

6. The Greek, *didonai dikēn*, is less removed from words for doing justice or acting justly than the English expression, paying the penalty. When we say, Justice was done, this implies an action upon the criminal rather than his own action in trying to clear his soul. The literal rendering of the original might be "giving the Just," or something of the sort.

7. Even if the dichotomy between nature and convention was borrowed from the very sophists whom Callicles despises, that has little bearing upon the way it accords with the Oblong and other structures.

8. This harks back to Socrates' objection when Polus laughs at him (473e). This is one more rhetorical device, not a genuine argument; and to say that philosophers are laughable implies that laughing will *prove* that they are ridiculous, though in truth this is no proof at all.

13. Rhetoric, Knowledge, Reality

1. To take one or two examples: In *Republic* VI (508a–509d) Socrates hints that he cannot define the form of the good, and is largely content with likening it to the sun. In *Epistle VII* he says that there will never be a writing of his which flatly states his philosophy (341c). In the *Parmenides* he shows the host of contradictions arising when unity is opposed to plurality or made somehow to stand alone. The discourse of Timaeus commences with an attempt to deduce the nature of the cosmos from a single principle of reason, but partway through breaks off and shows the work of a joint cause, necessity, which can only partly be overcome by reason. In the *Phaedrus* the ultimate forms are plural (246d–e).

2. The apparent simplicity of a question and the complexity of its proper answer is a discovery made repeatedly in the dialogues. In the *Republic*, to take an obvious example, the question put to Cephalus, What is justice? (331c) is not one to be properly answered while he is standing on one foot. No doubt Cephalus senses this and invents a sacrifice he must attend in order not to be sacrificed himself on the altar of an immense, involuted dialectic.

3. Antecedents of this second kind are found in the *Gorgias*, but mainly take the form of differing statements on the same topics by the three rhetors. In the *Republic* the successive definitions of justice illustrate the point we are making: One must consult the first, second, and third in order fully to grasp the fourth;

the same is true of the definitions of courage in the *Laches*. The leading assertions about love in the *Phaedrus* form this kind of sequence: The winged horses cannot take flight without the earlier contrasting conceptions of love to give richness to the myth of the chariots.

4. *Posterior Analytics* I.1.71a1–10; II.1.89b23–35.

5. In the *Phaedo* (100d–e) Socrates speaks of his notion of the forms as the best he can devise, which certainly does not render it immune from objection and possible refutation.

6. We are using the term *hypothesis* in a modern sense. In Aristotle, a hypothesis is one kind of principle (*Posterior Analytics* I.2.72a19–21). Plato (in the *Meno, Republic, Parmenides*, and *Phaedo*) tends often to be closer to the most popular modern usage.

7. In this connection it should be noted that the Oblong does not use the words *epistēmē, nous*, or *dianoia* in anything like the sense of mathematical or dialectical reasoning. Here, when *epistēmē* is employed, it seems to have no more exact signification than to stand for intelligence purposefully used. Although there is an important sense in which geometrical proportion is one of the leading principles creating the Oblong, still the explicit mention of it is immediately followed by an apology from Socrates, who then covers over the sharpness of geometrical distinctions with the soft wool of Anaxagorean togetherness (465d).

8. Cf. *Phaedrus* 276a, where it is implied that thinking is the interior conversation of the soul, *logon hon autē pros autēn hē psuchē* . . . . See also the *Sophist* 263e and *Theaetetus* 189e.

9. It is not only the snub noses of Socrates and Theaetetus that are alike (*Theaetetus* 143e and passim).

10. If A hands B a counterfeit coin, its deceptive character is removed for B if A says, This is a fake. Its reality for the man of false opinion, however, is as an imitation, and this is the whole substitute reality of the coin; but there is also a knowledge of counterfeits as much as ordinary numismatics exists as a knowledge of genuine mintings. It is a question of emphasis: The recognition of the fakery accords a partial reality to the coin, while to a man taken in by the counterfeit the coin may seem more real, but even this alleged reality is an imitation.

11. One strength of the *Timaeus* lies in its opposite approach: The astronomer begins with the most real, the eternal mathematical model, then moves to the imitation or copy which is the world animal, made as much like the original as possible (27d–39e). The two chief terms, however, have very different connotations and applications from those in the *Gorgias*.

12. It is scarcely necessary to point out that the *Sophist* contains an extended, highly significant treatment of relations between being, imitation, and nonbeing (232b–268d), setting up far more distinctions than we would be justified in drawing in our present account.

13. Some of these contradictions have lain in asserting that all rhetoric is pandering, then later that there are good and bad rhetorics; that rhetoric is an art, then that it is not an art, but finally that it becomes a kind of art again.

14. One more sense of imitation might be noted: In finding that no new questions had been asked of him for many years, Gorgias in giving his standard answers is imitating the former spontaneity that he must have shown when those questions were originally presented to him.

15. In what follows, we shall forsake the self and the true in favor of the more

"objective," unity and real, the former pair having been dealt with in chapters 10, 11, 12.

16. Again we dispense with the subdivision of proportion into the kinds answering to those of wholeness, but do make use of two or three kinds. Thus in the somewhat naïve instance of the man receiving more food in proportion to his capabilities as a doctor or farmer who deserves more, the Socratic complaint that Callicles has no regard for geometrical proportion (508a), means partly a quantitative relation and partly an analogy between qualities such as better and worse pleasures and better and worse lives, for this is Socrates' ultimate reference.

SELECTED BIBLIOGRAPHY

Adkins, Arthur W. H. *Merit and Responsibility: A Study in Greek Values.* Chicago: University of Chicago Press, 1975.

———. *Moral Values and Political Behaviour in Ancient Greece.* London: Chatto and Windus, 1972.

Allen, R. E. "Law and Justice in Plato's *Crito.*" *The Journal of Philosophy* 69(1972):557–67.

———. *Plato's "Euthyphro" and the Earlier Theory of Forms.* New York: Humanities Press, 1970.

Annas, Julia, ed. *Oxford Studies in Ancient Philosophy.* 2 vols. Oxford: At the Clarendon Press, 1983, 1984.

Anton, John P. "Dialectic and Health in Plato's *Gorgias:* Presuppositions and Implications," *Oxford Studies in Ancient Philosophy* 1(1980):49–60.

———. "Plato's Philosophical Use of Myth," *The Greek Orthodox Theological Review* 9(1963–64):161–80.

———, and George L. Kustas, eds. *Essays in Ancient Greek Philosophy.* Albany: State University of New York Press, 1971.

Apostle, Hippocrates G., and Lloyd P. Gerson, trans. *Aristotle: Selected Works.* Grinnell, IA: Peripatetic Press, 1982.

Aristotle. *The Nicomachean Ethics.* Translated and edited by Hippocrates G. Apostle. Dordrecht, Holland: D. Reidel, 1975.

———. *Works.* Loeb Classical Library. Various dates.

Aristotle's "Poetics," Demetrius on Style, and Selections from Aristotle's "Rhetoric," Together with Hobbes' "Digest" and Horace's "Ars Poetica." Everyman's Library. 1934.

Arnim, Hans von. *Platos Jugenddialoge, und die Entstehungszeit des Phaidros* 1914. Reprint. New York: Arno, 1976.

Astius, Fridericus (Friedrich Ast). *Lexicon Platonicum sive Vocum Platonicarum Index.* 2 vols. Reprint. Bonn: Rudolf Habelt, 1956.

Baldwin, Charles Sears. *Ancient Rhetoric and Poetic.* New York: Macmillan, 1924.

Ballard, Edward G. *Socratic Ignorance: An Essay on Platonic Self-Knowledge.* The Hague: Martinus Nijhoff, 1965.

Bambrough, Renford, ed. *New Essays on Plato and Aristotle.* London: Routledge and Kegan Paul, 1965.

Benson, Thomas W., and Michael H. Prosser, eds. *Readings in Classical Rhetoric.* Boston: Allyn and Bacon, 1969.

Bitzer, Lloyd F. "From Philosophy to Rhetoric and Back" In *Rhetoric, Philosophy, and Literature: An Exploration,* edited by Don M. Burks. West Lafayette, IN: Purdue University Press, 1978.

Bloom, Allan, trans. *The Republic of Plato.* New York: Basic Books, 1968.

Bluck, R. S., ed. *Plato's "Meno."* Cambridge: At the University Press, 1961.

Bréhier, Emile. *The Hellenic Age.* Translated by Joseph Thomas. Chicago: University of Chicago Press, 1963.

Bremer, John. *On Plato's Polity.* Houston: The Institute of Philosophy, 1984.

Brentlinger, John A. "The Divided Line and Plato's 'Theory of Intermediates.'" *Phronesis: A Journal for Ancient Philosophy* 8(1963): 146–66.

Brumbaugh, Robert S. "The Divided Line and the Direction of Inquiry." *The Philosophical Forum* 2(1970–71): 172–99.

———. *Plato for the Modern Age.* New York: Collier, 1964.

———. *Plato on the One: The Hypotheses in the "Parmenides."* New Haven: Yale University Press, 1961. Reviewed by G. K. P. in *The Modern Schoolman* 39(1962): 166–69.

———. *Plato's Mathematical Imagination: The Mathematical Passages in the Dialogues and Their Interpretation.* Bloomington: Indiana University Press, 1951.

Bryant, Donald C. "Aspects of the Rhetorical Tradition." *Quarterly Journal of Speech* 36(1950): 169–76, 326–32.

Burnet, John, ed. *Platonis Opera.* 5 vols. New York: Oxford University Press, 1903–10.

———. *Plato's "Euthyphro," "Apology of Socrates," and "Crito."* Oxford: At the Clarendon Press, 1924.

Burwick, Frederick, ed. *Selected Essays on Rhetoric by Thomas De Quincey.* Carbondale: Southern Illinois University Press, 1967.

Calhoun, George M. *Introduction to Greek Legal Science.* Oxford: At the Clarendon Press, 1944.

Campbell, George. *The Philosophy of Rhetoric.* Edited by Lloyd F. Bitzer. Carbondale: Southern Illinois University Press, 1963.

Campbell, Lewis. "Plato." *Encyclopaedia Britannica,* 11th ed.

Cary, M., et al., eds. *The Oxford Classical Dictionary.* Oxford: At the Clarendon Press, 1949.

Clay, Diskin. "Socrates' Mulishness and Heroism." *Phronesis: A Journal for Ancient Philosophy* 17(1972): 53–60.

Cooper, John M. "The Psychology of Justice in Plato." *American Philosophical Quarterly* 14(1977): 151–57.

Cornford, Francis M. *Plato's Theory of Knowledge: The "Theaetetus" and "Sophist" of Plato Translated with a Running Commentary.* London: Routledge and Kegan Paul, 1945.

Crane, Ronald S., ed. *Critics and Criticism, Ancient and Modern.* Chicago: University of Chicago Press, 1952.

Cumming, Robert D., ed. *"Euthyphro," "Apology" and "Crito" and the*

Death Scene from "Phaedo" by Plato. New York: Liberal Arts Press, 1948.

Cushman, Robert E. *Therapeia: Plato's Conception of Philosophy*. Chapel Hill: University of North Carolina Press, 1958.

Dannhauser, Werner J. *Nietzsche's View of Socrates*. Ithaca, NY: Cornell University Press, 1974.

Demos, Raphael. *The Philosophy of Plato*. New York: Scribner, 1939.

Dilman, Ilham. *Morality and the Inner Life: A Study in Plato's "Gorgias."* New York: Barnes and Noble, 1979.

Diogenes Laertius. *Lives and Opinions of Eminent Philosophers*. 2 vols. Loeb Classical Library. 1925.

Dodds, E. R. *Plato: "Gorgias:" A Revised Text with Introduction and Commentary*. Oxford: At the Clarendon Press, 1959.

———, ed. *The Greeks and the Irrational*. Berkeley: University of California Press, 1951.

Dover, K. J. *Greek Popular Morality in the Time of Plato and Aristotle*. Oxford: At the University Press, 1974.

Engnell, Richard A. "Implications for Communication of the Rhetorical Epistemology of Gorgias of Leontini." *Western Speech* 37(1973): 175–84.

Entralgo, Pedro Lain. *The Therapy of the Word in Classical Antiquity*. Edited and translated by L. J. Rather and John M. Sharp. New Haven: Yale University Press, 1970.

Field, Guy Cromwell. *Plato and His Contemporaries: A Study in Fourth-Century Life and Thought*. London: Methuen, 1930.

Findlay, J. N. "The Three Hypotheses of Platonism." *The Review of Metaphysics* 28(1975): 660–80.

Fite, Warner. *The Platonic Legend*. New York: Scribner, 1934.

Fox, Marvin. "The Trials of Socrates: An Interpretation of the First Tetralogy." *Archiv für Philosophie* 6(1953): 226–61.

Friedländer, Paul. *Plato*. Translated by Hans Meyerhoff. 3 vols. New York: Pantheon, 1958–69.

Gosling, J. C. B., ed. and trans. *Plato: "Philebus."* Oxford: At the University Press, 1975.

Green, Elvena M. "Plato's Use of Three Dramatic Elements in *Gorgias* as Means to Demonstrate His Thought." *Southern Speech Communication Journal* 33(1968): 307–15.

Greene, William Chase. *Moira: Fate, Good, and Evil in Greek Thought*. Cambridge, MA: Harvard University Press, 1944.

Grene, David. *Man in His Pride: A Study of the Political Philosophy of Thucydides and Plato*. Chicago: University of Chicago Press, 1950.

Grote, George. *Plato and the Other Companions of Sokrates*. 3d ed. 3 vols. London: John Murray, 1875.

Grube, G. M. A. *Plato's Thought*. New ed. Indianapolis: Hackett, 1980.

Gulley, Norman. "The Interpretation of 'No One Does Wrong Willingly' in Plato's Dialogues." *Phronesis: A Journal for Ancient Philosophy* 10 (1965): 82–96.

Guthrie, W. K. C. *A History of Greek Philosophy.* 5 vols. Vol. 4, *Plato: The Man and His Dialogues: Earlier Period;* vol. 5, *The Later Plato and the Academy.* Cambridge: At the University Press, 1975, 1978.

Hackforth, R. "Plato's Divided Line and Dialectic." *Classical Quarterly* 36(1942):1–9.

———. *Plato's Examination of Pleasure: A Translation of the "Philebus," with Introduction and Commentary.* Cambridge: At the University Press, 1958.

Hall, Robert William. *Plato and the Individual.* The Hague: Martinus Nijhoff, 1963.

Hamilton, W., ed. and trans. *"Gorgias": A Translation with an Introduction.* Baltimore: Penguin Books, 1960.

Harrison, E. L. "Was Gorgias a Sophist?" *Phoenix* 18(1964):183–92.

Havelock, Eric A. *The Greek Concept of Justice from Its Shadow in Homer to Its Substance in Plato.* Cambridge, MA: Harvard University Press, 1978.

———. *Preface to Plato.* Cambridge, MA: Harvard University Press, 1963.

Hillbrunner, Anthony. "Plato and Korzybski: Two Views of Truth and Rhetorical Theory." *Southern Speech Communication Journal* 24(1959):185–96.

Hoerber, Robert G. "Plato's *Lesser Hippias.*" *Phronesis: A Journal for Ancient Philosophy* 7(1962):121–31.

———. "Plato's *Lysis.*" *Phronesis: A Journal for Ancient Philosophy* 4(1959):15–28.

———. "Plato's *Meno.*" *Phronesis: A Journal for Ancient Philosophy* 5(1960):78–102.

Homer. *The Iliad.* Loeb Classical Library. 1924.

Huby, Pamela M. *"The Menexenus Reconsidered."* *Phronesis: A Journal for Ancient Philosophy* 2(1957):104–14.

Hyland, Drew. "Why Plato Wrote Dialogues." *Philosophy and Rhetoric* 1(1968):38–50.

Irwin, Terence. *Plato, "Gorgias."* Oxford: At the Clarendon Press, 1979.

———. *Plato's Moral Theory: The Early and Middle Dialogues.* Oxford: At the Clarendon Press, 1977.

Isenberg, Meyer W. "The Order of the Discourses in Plato's Symposium." Ph.D. diss. The University of Chicago, 1940.

———. "Plato's *Sophist* and the Five Stages of Knowing." *Classical Philology* 46(1951):201–11.

———. "The Unity of Plato's *Philebus.*" *Classical Philology* 35(1940):154–79.

Jowett, Benjamin, trans. *The Dialogues of Plato.* Edited by D. J. Allan and H. E. Dale. 4th ed. 4 vols. Oxford: At the Clarendon Press, 1953.

Kahn, Charles H. "Drama and Dialectic in Plato's *Gorgias.*" *Oxford Studies in Ancient Philosophy* 1(1983):75–121.

Kauffman, Charles. "Enactment as Argument in the *Gorgias.*" *Philosophy and Rhetoric* 12(1979):114–29.

Kennedy, George. *The Art of Persuasion in Greece*. Princeton: Princeton University Press, 1963.

Kerferd, G. B. "Plato's Treatment of Callicles in the *Gorgias*." *Proceedings of the Cambridge Philological Society* 20(1974):48–52.

Kierkegaard, Søren, *The Concept of Irony, with Constant Reference to Socrates*. Translated and edited by Lee M. Capel. Bloomington: Indiana University Press, 1968.

Klein, Jacob. *A Commentary on Plato's "Meno."* Chapel Hill: University of North Carolina Press, 1965.

Lanham, Richard A. *A Handlist of Rhetorical Terms: A Guide for Students of English Literature*. Berkeley: University of California Press, 1968.

Levi, Albert William. "Philosophy as Literature: The Dialogue." *Philosophy and Rhetoric* 9(1976):1–20.

Levinson, Ronald Bartlett. *In Defense of Plato*. Cambridge, MA: Harvard University Press, 1953.

Linforth, Ivan M. "Soul and Sieve in Plato's *Gorgias*." *University of California Publications in Classical Philology* 12(1944):295–314.

Lloyd, G. E. R. *Polarity and Analogy: Two Types of Argumentation in Early Greek Thought*. Cambridge: At the University Press, 1971.

Lucas, D. W. *Aristotle, "Poetics": Introduction, Commentary and Appendixes*. Oxford: At the Clarendon Press, 1968.

Lutoslawski, Wincenty. *The Origin and Growth of Plato's Logic*. London: Longmans, Green, 1897.

McCall, Marsh H., Jr. *Ancient Rhetorical Theories of Simile and Comparison*. Cambridge, MA: Harvard University Press, 1969.

MacKay, D. S. "The Problem of Individuality in Plato's Dialectic." *University of California Publications in Philosophy* 20(1937):131–54.

MacKenzie, Mary Margaret. *Plato on Punishment*. Berkeley: University of California Press, 1981.

McKeon, Richard. "Aristotle's Conceptions of Language and the Arts of Language." *Classical Philology* 41(1946):193–206; 42(1946):21–50.

———. "The Funeral Oration of Pericles." In *Great Expressions of Human Rights*, edited by R. M. McIver, pp. 29–41. New York: Harper, 1950.

———. "Literary Criticism and the Concept of Imitation in Antiquity." *Modern Philology* 34(1936):1–35.

———. "Plato and Aristotle as Historians: A Study of Method in the History of Ideas." *Ethics* 51(1940):66–101.

———. "Philosophy and Method." *Journal of Philosophy* 48(1951):653–82.

———. *Thought, Action, and Passion*. Chicago: University of Chicago Press, 1954.

Marrou, H. I. *A History of Education in Antiquity*. Translated by George Lamb. New York: Mentor, 1964.

Michelakis, Emmanuel. *Platons Lehre von der Anwendung des Gesetzes und der Begriff der Billigkeit bei Aristoteles*. Munich: Max Hueber, 1953. Reviewed by G. K. P. in *Classical Philology* 51(1956):194–95.

Miller, Joseph M., Michael H. Prosser, and Thomas W. Benson, eds. *Readings in Medieval Rhetoric.* Bloomington: Indiana University Press, 1973.

Morrow, Glenn R. "Plato and the Law of Nature." In *Essays in Political Theory: Presented to George H. Sabine,* edited by Milton R. Konvitz and Arthur E. Murphy, pp. 17–44. Port Washington, NY: Kennikat Press, 1972.

————. "Plato and the Rule of Law," *The Philosophical Review* 50(1941): 105–26.

————. "Plato's Conception of Persuasion," *The Philosophical Review* 62(1953):234–50.

————. "Plato's Cretan City, A Historical Interpretation of the Laws. Princeton: Princeton University Press, 1960.

————, ed. and trans. *Plato's Epistles.* New York: Bobbs-Merrill, 1962.

Mourelatos, A. P. D., and R. M. Rorty, eds. *Exegesis and Argument: Studies in Greek Philosophy Presented to Gregory Vlastos.* Assen, The Netherlands: Van Gorcum, 1973.

Murphy, James J. "The Metarhetorics of Plato, Augustine, and McLuhan: A Pointing Essay." *Philosophy and Rhetoric* 4(1971):201–14.

Nobles, W. Scott. "The Paradox of Plato's Attitude Toward Rhetoric." *Western Speech* 21(1957):206–10.

O'Brien, Michael J. *The Socratic Paradoxes and the Greek Mind.* Chapel Hill: University of North Carolina Press, 1967.

Olson, Elder, ed. *Aristotle's Poetics and English Literature.* Chicago: University of Chicago Press, 1965.

Owen, G. F. L. "Philosophical Invective." In *Oxford Studies in Ancient Philosophy,* edited by Julia Annas, 1:1–25. Oxford: At the Clarendon Press, 1983.

Plato. *"Apology of Socrates" and "Crito": With Extracts from the "Phaedo" and "Symposium" and from Xenophon's "Memorabilia."* Edited by Louis Dyer. Revised by Thomas Day. New York: Ginn, 1908.

————. *Euthydemus.* Translated by Rosamund Kent Sprague. Indianapolis: Bobbs-Merrill, 1965.

————. *Gorgias.* Translated with notes by Terence Irwin. Oxford: At the Clarendon Press, 1979.

————. *"Laches" and "Charmides."* Translated and edited by Rosamund Kent Sprague. Indianapolis: Bobbs-Merrill, 1973.

————. *Theaetetus.* Translated and edited by John McDowell. Oxford: At the Clarendon Press, 1973.

————. *Works.* Loeb Classical Library. 1929–45.

Platon, *Lettres.* Texte établi et traduit par Joseph Souilhé. Paris: Société d'Edition "Les Belles Lettres," 1926.

Plochmann, George Kimball. "Five Elements in Plato's Conception of Reality." *Ultimate Reality and Meaning: Interdisciplinary Studies in the Philosophy of Understanding* 4(1981):24–57.

————. "Hiccups and Hangovers in the *Symposium.*" *Bucknell Review*

11, no. 3 (May 1963):1–18. Reprinted as "Supporting Themes in the *Symposium*." In *Essays in Ancient Greek Philosophy*, edited by John P. Anton and George L. Kustas, pp. 328–44. Albany: State University of New York Press, 1971.

———. "Interpreting Plato's *Symposium*." *The Modern Schoolman* 48 (1970):25–43.

———. *Plato*. New York: Delta Books, 1973.

———. "Plato, Visual Perception, and Art." *The Journal of Aesthetics and Art Criticism* 35(1976):189–200.

———. "Plato's *Meno*: Some Questions to Be Disputed." *The Journal of Value Inquiry* 8(1974):266–82.

———. "Socrates, The Stranger from Elea, and Some Others." *Classical Philology* 49(1954):223–31.

Popper, Karl R. *The Open Society and Its Enemies*. Vol. 1. *The Spell of Plato*. New York: Harper and Row, 1963.

Quimby, Rollin W. "The Growth of Plato's Perception of Rhetoric." *Philosophy and Rhetoric* 7(1964):71–79.

Randall, John Herman, Jr. *Plato, Dramatist of the Life of Reason*. New York: Columbia University Press, 1970.

Raven, J. E. *Plato's Thought in the Making: A Study of the Development of His Metaphysics*. Cambridge: At the University Press, 1965.

Rendall, Steven. "Dialogue, Philosophy, and Rhetoric: The Example of Plato's *Gorgias*." *Philosophy and Rhetoric* 10(1977):165–79.

Ritter, Constantin. *Platon: Sein Leben, seine Schriften, seine Lehre*. 2 vols. Munich: Beck, 1910–23.

Robin, Léon, et al., eds. *Platon: Oeuvres Complètes*. Paris: Société d'Edition "Les Belles Lettres," various dates.

Robinson, Franklin E. "Plato's *Gorgias*: Socrates' Argument in the Socrates-Polus Colloquy." *Midwestern Journal of Philosophy* 5(1977):43–49.

Robinson, Richard. *Plato's Earlier Dialectic*. 2d ed. New York: Oxford University Press, 1953.

Romilly, J. de. *Magic and Rhetoric in Ancient Greece*. Cambridge, MA: Harvard University Press, 1975.

Rosen, Stanley. "The Role of Eros in Plato's *Republic*." *The Review of Metaphysics* 18(1965):452–75.

———. *Plato's Symposium*. New Haven: Yale University Press, 1968.

Ross, W. D. *Plato's Theory of Ideas*. Oxford: At the University Press, 1951.

Russell, Bertrand. *A Critical Exposition of the Philosophy of Leibniz: With an Appendix of Leading Passages*. Cambridge: At the University Press, 1900.

Ryle, Gilbert. *Plato's Progress*. Cambridge: At the University Press, 1966.

Santas, Garasimos Xenophon. *Socrates: Philosophy in Plato's Early Dialogues*. London: Routledge and Kegan Paul, 1979.

Sayre, Kenneth M. *Plato's Analytic Method*. Chicago: University of Chicago Press, 1969.

Schmalzriedt, Egidius. *Platon: Der Schriftsteller und die Wahrheit*. Munich: R. Piper, 1969.

Shorey, Paul. *The Unity of Plato's Thought*. Decennial Publications of the University of Chicago, 1st ser., vol. 6. Chicago: University of Chicago Press, 1924.

———. *What Plato Said*. Chicago: University of Chicago Press, 1933.

Simon, Bennett, M. D. *Mind and Madness in Ancient Greece: The Classical Roots of Modern Psychiatry*. Ithaca, NY: Cornell University Press, 1978.

Sinaiko, Herman L. *Love, Knowledge, and Discourse in Plato: Dialogue and Dialectic in "Phaedrus," "Republic," "Parmenides."* Chicago: University of Chicago Press, 1965.

Sinclair, T. A. *A History of Greek Political Thought*. Reprint. Cleveland: Meridian, 1968.

Skemp, J. B., trans. *Plato's "Statesman."* New Haven: Yale University Press, 1952.

Smith, Bromley. "*Gorgias:* A Study of Oratorical Style." *Quarterly Journal of Speech Education* 7(1921):355–59.

———. "Some Rhetorical Figures Rhetorically Considered." *Quarterly Journal of Speech* 20(1934):16–29.

Spiegelberg, Herbert, ed. *The Socratic Enigma: A Collection of Testimonies Through Twenty-four Centuries*. New York: Bobbs-Merrill, 1964.

Spitzer, Adele. "The Self-Reference of the *Gorgias.*" *Philosophy and Rhetoric* 8(1975):1–22.

Sprague, Rosamund Kent. "Logic and Literary Form in Plato." *The Personalist* 48(1967):560–72.

Stack, George J. "On the Notion of Dialectics." *Philosophy Today* 15 (1971):276–88.

Stallknecht, Newton P., and Robert S. Brumbaugh. *The Compass of Philosophy*. New York: Longmans, Green, 1954.

Stannard, Jerry. "Socratic Eros and Platonic Dialectic." *Phronesis: A Journal for Ancient Philosophy* 4(1959):120–31.

Stenzel, Julius. *Plato's Method of Dialectic*. Translated by D. J. Allan. Reprint. New York: Russell and Russell, 1964.

Sternfield, Robert, and Harold Zyskind. *Plato's "Meno": A Philosophy of Man as Acquisitive*. Carbondale: Southern Illinois University Press, 1978.

Stewart, J. A. *The Myths of Plato*. Edited and newly introduced by G. R. Levy. Carbondale: Southern Illinois University Press, 1960.

Strauss, Leo. *The Argument and the Action of Plato's "Laws."* Chicago: University of Chicago Press, 1975.

Taylor, A. E. *A Commentary on Plato's "Timaeus."* Oxford: At the Clarendon Press, 1928.

———. *Plato, the Man and His Work*. New ed. New York: Dial, 1936.

———. *Socrates*. 1935. Reprint. Garden City, NY: Doubleday, 1953.

Tejera, Victorino. "Irony and Allegory in the *Phaedrus.*" *Philosophy and Rhetoric* 8(1975):71–87.

Telford, Kenneth A. *Aristotle's Poetics: Translation and Analysis*. Chicago: Henry Regnery, 1961.

Thompson, W. H. *The "Gorgias" of Plato: With English Notes, Introduction, and Appendix*. Reprint. New York: Arno, 1973.

Thompson, Wayne N. "The *Symposium*: A Neglected Source for Plato's Ideas on Rhetoric." *Southern Speech Communication Journal* 37(1972): 219–32.

Tracy, Theodore James, S. J. *Physiological Theory and the Doctrine of the Mean in Plato and Aristotle*. Chicago: Loyola University Press, 1969.

Trevaskis, J. R. "Division and Its Relation to Dialectic and Ontology in Plato." *Phronesis: A Journal for Ancient Philosophy* 12(1967):118–29.

Versenyi, Laszlo. *Socratic Humanism*. New Haven: Yale University Press, 1963. Comments by G. K. P. in *Philosophy Forum* 11(1971):114–119.

Vlastos, Gregory. Introduction in *Plato's "Protagoras."* Translated by M. Ostwald. Edited by Gregory Vlastos, pp. vii–lvi. New York: Bobbs-Merrill, 1956.

————. "Was Polus Refuted?" *American Journal of Philosophy* 88(1967): 454–60.

————, ed. *The Philosophy of Socrates: A Collection of Critical Essays*. Garden City, NY: Doubleday Anchor, 1971.

————, ed. *Plato: A Collection of Critical Essays*. Vol. 1, *Metaphysics and Epistemology*; vol. 2, *Ethics, Politics, and Philosophy of Art and Religion*. Garden City, NY: Doubleday, 1971.

————. *Platonic Studies*. Princeton: Princeton University Press, 1981.

————. "The Socratic Elenchus." *Oxford Studies in Ancient Philosophy* 1(1983):27–58.

Voegelin, Eric. *Plato*. Baton Rouge: Louisiana State University Press, 1966.

Weaver, Richard M. *The Ethics of Rhetoric*. Chicago: Henry Regnery, 1965.

Weingartner, Rudolph H. *The Unity of the Platonic Dialogue: The "Cratylus," the "Protagoras," the "Parmenides."* Indianapolis: Bobbs-Merrill, 1973.

West, Thomas G. *Plato's "Apology of Socrates": An Interpretation with a New Translation*. Ithaca, NY: Cornell University Press, 1979.

White, Nicholas P. *A Companion to Plato's "Republic."* Indianapolis: Hackett, 1979.

Wilamowitz-Moellendorff, Ulrich von. *Platon: Sein Leben und seine Werke*. Edited by Bruno Snell. Reprint of 5th ed. Berlin: Weidmannsche Verlagsbuchhandlung, 1959.

Wild, John. *Plato's Modern Enemies and the Theory of Natural Law*. Chicago: University of Chicago Press, 1953.

————. *Plato's Theory of Man: An Introduction to the Realistic Philosophy of Culture*. Cambridge, MA: Harvard University Press, 1946.

Winspear, Alban D. *The Genesis of Plato's Thought*. New York: Dryden, 1940.

Wittgenstein, Ludwig. *Philosophical Investigations*. Translated by G. E. M. Anscombe. New York: Macmillan, 1953.

Woodbridge, F. J. E. *The Son of Apollo: Themes of Plato*. Boston: Houghton Mifflin, 1929.

Wycherley, R. E. *How the Greeks Built Cities*. 2d ed. Garden City, NY: Doubleday, 1969.

Xenophon, *Memorabilia and Oeconomicus*. Loeb Classical Library. 1918.

———. *"Symposium" and "Apology."* Loeb Classical Library. 1918.

Zaslavsky, Robert. *Platonic Myth and Platonic Writing*. Washington, D.C.: University Press of America, 1981.

Zeller, Eduard. *Plato and the Older Academy*. Translated by Sarah F. Alleyne and Alfred Goodwin. London: Longmans, 1888.

Zimmern, Alfred E. *The Greek Commonwealth: Politics and Economics in Fifth-Century Athens*. 3d ed., rev. Oxford: At the Clarendon Press, 1922.

INDEX

GEORGE KIMBALL PLOCHMAN, Emeritus Professor of Philosophy, Southern Illinois University, is editor of the Philosophical Explorations series published by Southern Illinois University Press, and author of a number of books, including *Terms in Their Propositional Contexts in Wittgenstein's Tractatus: An Index* and *Plato*.

FRANKLIN EDWARD ROBINSON is Associate Professor of Philosophy at Murray State University. He is a past Associate Editor of the *Midwestern Journal of Philosophy*.